Competing for THIRD EDITION
ADVANTAGE

ROBERT E. HOSKISSON
Rice University

MICHAEL A. HITT
Texas A&M University

R. DUANE IRELAND
Texas A&M University

JEFFREY S. HARRISON
University of Richmond

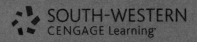
SOUTH-WESTERN
CENGAGE Learning·

Australia • Brazil • Japan • Korea • Mexico • Singapore • Spain • United Kingdom • United States

SOUTH-WESTERN
CENGAGE Learning·

Competing for Advantage, Third Edition, International Edition
Robert E. Hoskisson,
Michael A. Hitt,
R. Duane Ireland, and
Jeffrey S. Harrison

Senior Vice President,
LRS/Acquisitions & Solutions
Planning: Jack W. Calhoun

Editorial Director, Business &
Economics: Erin Joyner

Acquisitions Editor:
Michele Rhoades

Editorial Assistant:
Tamara Grega

Marketing Manager:
Jonathan Monahan

Senior Marketing
Communications Manager:
Jim Overly

Marketing Coordinator:
Courtney Doyle Chambers

Art and Cover Direction,
Production Management, and
Composition: PreMediaGlobal

Media Editor: Kristen Meere

Rights Acquisition Director:
Audrey Pettengill

Rights Acquisition Specialist,
Text/Image: John Hill

Manufacturing Planner:
Ron Montgomery

Cover Image (B/W):
JoLin/iStockphoto

Cover Image (Color):
Shutterstock Images/
ARTSILENSEcom

Internal Image:
© Lennart Loft/Getty Images

Library of Congress Control Number: 2012939203

International Edition:

ISBN-13: 978-0-538-47562-4

ISBN-10: 0-538-47562-5

Cengage Learning International Offices

Asia
www.cengageasia.com
tel: (65) 6410 1200

Australia/New Zealand
www.cengage.com.au
tel: (61) 3 9685 4111

Brazil
www.cengage.com.br
tel: (55) 11 3665 9900

India
www.cengage.co.in
tel: (91) 11 4364 1111

Latin America
www.cengage.com.mx
tel: (52) 55 1500 6000

UK/Europe/Middle East/Africa
www.cengage.co.uk
tel: (44) 0 1264 332 424

Represented in Canada by Nelson Education, Ltd.
www.nelson.com
tel: (416) 752 9100/(800) 668 0671

Cengage Learning is a leading provider of customized learning solutions with office locations around the globe, including Singapore, the United Kingdom, Australia, Mexico, Brazil, and Japan. Locate your local office at: **www.cengage.com/global**

For product information and free companion resources:
www.cengage.com/international
Visit your local office: **www.cengage.com/global**
Visit our corporate website: **www.cengage.com**

Printed in the United States of America
1 2 3 4 5 6 7 16 15 14 13 12

To my mother, Carol R. Hoskisson, a loving mother and one who cared deeply for and served those around her.
ROBERT E. HOSKISSON

To my mother, ElRey, and my brother, Don. We lost both of you before your time. Your wit, grace, and caring meant much to me as it did to so many others.
MIKE

To my son, Scott. We've traveled many roads and many miles together as "concert buddies." I deeply cherish every one of these trips and will steadfastly know that each of us is always "standing on the top of that hill with all we've got," keeping our good eye to the sun while doing so.
DAD (R. DUANE IRELAND)

To Marie for her pure heart and her willingness to give me a place in it.
JEFFREY S. HARRISON

ABOUT THE AUTHORS

ROBERT E. HOSKISSON

Robert E. Hoskisson is the George R. Brown Chair of Strategic Management at the Jesse H. Jones Graduate School of Business, Rice University. He received his Ph.D. from the University of California-Irvine. Professor Hoskisson's research topics focus on corporate governance, acquisitions and divestitures, corporate and international diversification, corporate entrepreneurship, privatization, and cooperative strategy. He teaches courses in corporate and international strategic management, cooperative strategy, and strategy consulting, among others. Professor Hoskisson's research has appeared in over 120 publications, including articles in the *Academy of Management Journal, Academy of Management Review, Strategic Management Journal, Organization Science, Journal of Management, Journal of International Business Studies, Journal of Management Studies, Organization Research Methods, Journal of Business Venturing, Entrepreneurship Theory and Practice, Academy of Management Perspectives, Academy of Management Executive, Journal of World Business, California Management Review*, and 26 co-authored books. He is currently an associate editor of the *Strategic Management Journal*, as well as serving on the Editorial Review Board of the *Academy of Management Journal*. Professor Hoskisson has served on several editorial boards for such publications as the *Academy of Management Journal* (including consulting editor and guest editor of a special issue), *Journal of Management* (including associate editor), *Organization Science, Journal of International Business Studies* (consulting editor), *Journal of Management Studies* (guest editor of a special issue), and *Entrepreneurship Theory and Practice*. He has co-authored several books including *Strategic Management: Competitiveness and Globalization*, 10th edition (South-Western Cengage Learning, 2013), *Understanding Business Strategy*, 3rd edition (South-Western Cengage Learning, 2012), *New Frontiers in Entrepreneurship* (Springer, 2010), and *Downscoping: How to Tame the Diversified Firm* (Oxford University Press, 1994).

He has an appointment as a Special Professor at the University of Nottingham and as an Honorary Professor at Xi'an Jiao Tong University. He is a Fellow of the Academy of Management and a charter member of the Academy of Management Journals Hall of Fame. He is also a Fellow of the Strategic Management Society. In 1998, he received an award for Outstanding Academic Contributions to Competitiveness, American Society for Competitiveness. He also received the William G. Dyer Distinguished Alumni Award given at the Marriott School of Management, Brigham Young University. He completed three years of service as a representative at large on the Board of Governors of the Academy of Management and currently is president-elect of the Strategic Management Society.

MICHAEL A. HITT

Michael A. Hitt is a University Distinguished Professor and holds the Joe B. Foster Chair in Business Leadership at Texas A&M University. He received his Ph.D. from the University of Colorado. He has authored or co-authored several books and book chapters. His co-authored and coedited books include *Strategic Management: Competitiveness and Globalization* (South-Western-Cengage, 2013), *Understanding Business Strategy* (South-Western), *Mergers and Acquisitions: Creating Value for Stakeholders* (Oxford University Press, 2001), *Handbook of Strategic Management* (Blackwell Publishing, 2001), *Strategic Entrepreneurship: Creating a New Mindset* (Blackwell Publishing, 2002), and *Great Minds in Management: The Process of Theory Development* (Oxford University Press, 2005).

His numerous journal articles have appeared in such publications as the *Academy of Management Journal, Academy of Management Review, Strategic Management Journal, Journal of Applied Psychology, Organization Science, Journal of Management Studies,* and *Journal of Management,* among others. He has also served on the editorial review boards of several journals, including *Academy of Management Journal, Academy of Management Review, Academy of Management Executive, Journal of Applied Psychology, Journal of World Business,* and *Journal of Applied Behavioral Sciences.* Furthermore, Professor Hitt served as consulting editor (1988–1990) and editor (1991–1993) of *Academy of Management Journal.* He has been a coeditor for special issues of *Strategic Management Journal, Academy of Management Review, Journal of Engineering and Technology Management,* and *Academy of Management Executive.* He also co-founded the *Strategic Entrepreneurship Journal* and served as one of its first coeditors.

Professor Hitt is a past president of the Academy of Management and the Strategic Management Society. He received the 1996 Award for Outstanding Academic Contributions to Competitiveness and the 1999 Award for Outstanding Intellectual Contributions to Competitiveness Research, both awarded by the American Society for Competitiveness. He is a member of the Academy of Management Journals Hall of Fame and a Fellow of the Academy of Management and of the Strategic Management Society. He received an honorary doctorate (Doctor Honoris Causa) from the Universidad Carlos III de Madrid for his contributions to the field.

R. DUANE IRELAND

R. Duane Ireland is a University Distinguished Professor and holds the Conn Chair in New Ventures Leadership in the Mays Business School at Texas A&M University, where he previously served as head of the management department. Prior to joining Texas A&M University, he held positions at University of Richmond, Baylor University, and Oklahoma State University.

He is interested in research questions related to both the entrepreneurship and strategic management disciplines. He is co-author of multiple books, including *Strategic Management: Competitiveness and Globalization,* (South-Western Cengage Learning, 2013), 10th edition, *Entrepreneurship: Successfully Launching New Ventures,* (Prentice Hall, 2013), 4th edition, and *Understanding Business Strategy,*

(South-Western Cengage Learning, 2012), 3rd edition. His work has been published in a range of journals, including *Academy of Management Review, Academy of Management Journal, Administrative Science Quarterly, Strategic Management Journal, Academy of Management Executive, Journal of Management, Journal of Management Studies, Decision Sciences, Human Relations, Strategic Entrepreneurship Journal, British Journal of Management, Journal of Business Venturing,* and *Entrepreneurship: Theory & Practice.* Working with colleagues, he has served as a guest editor for special issues of *Academy of Management Review, Academy of Management Executive, Strategic Management Journal, Journal of Business Venturing, Organizational Research Methods,* and *Journal of Engineering and Technology Management.* He has also served in various editorial capacities including terms as a member of the editorial review boards for *Academy of Management Review, Academy of Management Journal, Academy of Management Executive, Journal of Management, Journal of Business Venturing,* and *Entrepreneurship: Theory & Practice.* He recently completed a term as editor of the *Academy of Management Journal.* Currently, he is the vice president of the Academy of Management.

He received the 1999 award for Outstanding Intellectual Contribution to Competitiveness Research from the American Society for Competitiveness. He is a Fellow of the Academy of Management and a Fellow of the Strategic Management Society. Two of his papers received Best Paper awards from *Academy of Management Journal* (2000) and *Academy of Management Executive* (1999).

JEFFREY S. HARRISON

Jeffrey S. Harrison is the W. David Robbins Chair of Strategic Management in the Robins School of Business at the University of Richmond. Prior to his current appointment, he served as the Fred G. Peelen Professor of Global Hospitality Strategy at Cornell University. He now serves or has served on the editorial review boards of *Strategic Management Journal, Academy of Management Journal,* and *Academy of Management Executive.*

Dr. Harrison's research interests include strategic management and business ethics, with particular expertise in the areas of mergers and acquisitions, diversification, strategic alliances, and stakeholder management. Much of his work has been published in prestigious academic journals such as *Academy of Management Journal, Strategic Management Journal,* and *Journal of Business Ethics.* He has authored or co-authored numerous books, including *Foundations of Strategic Management,* (South-Western Cengage Learning, 2014) 6th edition, *Strategic Management of Organizations and Stakeholders,* (Wiley, 2003), *Stakeholder Theory: The State of the Art,* (Cambridge University Press, 2010), and *Mergers and Acquisitions: A Guide to Creating Value for Stakeholders,* (Oxford University Press, 2001).

Dr. Harrison helped organize the Stakeholder Strategy Interest Group at the Strategic Management Society and has served in a variety of leadership roles in that group. He has also provided consulting and executive training services to many companies on a wide range of strategic, entrepreneurial, and other business issues.

BRIEF CONTENTS

PART 1 STRATEGIC THINKING   **1**

1 Introduction to Strategic Management 2

2 Strategic Leadership 34

PART 2 STRATEGIC ANALYSIS   **71**

3 The External Environment: Opportunities, Threats, Industry
       Competition, and Competitor Analysis 72

4 The Internal Organization: Resources, Capabilities, and
       Core Competencies 106

PART 3 CREATING COMPETITIVE ADVANTAGE   **141**

5 Business-Level Strategy 142

6 Competitive Rivalry and Competitive Dynamics 172

7 Cooperative Strategy 200

8 Corporate-Level Strategy 225

9 Acquisition and Restructuring Strategies 257

10 International Strategy 284

**PART 4 MONITORING AND CREATING
         ENTREPRENEURIAL OPPORTUNITIES**   **319**

11 Corporate Governance 320

12 Strategic Entrepreneurship 351

13 Strategic Flexibility and Real Options Analysis 372

Glossary 405
Name Index 413
Company Index 440
Subject Index 443

CONTENTS

Preface   xvii

Part 1: Strategic Thinking   1

CHAPTER 1: INTRODUCTION TO STRATEGIC MANAGEMENT   2

The Competitive Landscape   3
   Globalization of Markets and Industries   4
   Economic Volatility   5
   Technological Advances   6
   Coping with Hypercompetitive Influences   7
The Emergence of Strategic Management as a Business Discipline   8
   Early Influences on the Strategy Concept   9
   Modern Strategic Management   10
Three Perspectives on Value Creation   11
   The I/O Model of Above-Average Returns   11
   The Resource-Based Model of Above-Average Returns   14
   The Stakeholder Model of Responsible Firm Behavior and Firm Performance   17
Strategic Thinking and the Strategic Management Process   20
   Strategic Thinking   21
   The Strategic Management Process   22
Summary   24
Ethics Questions   25

CHAPTER 2: STRATEGIC LEADERSHIP   34

Strategic Leaders as a Key Resource through Their Influences on
Strategic Decisions   35
   Strategic Leadership Style   36
   Managerial Discretion and Decision Biases   37
Top Management Teams   40
   Top Management Team Heterogeneity   40
   The CEO and Top Management Team Power   42
   Executive Succession Processes   44
Key Strategic Leadership Responsibilities and Actions   46
   Ensure that the Firm Is Well Positioned Economically   48
   Acquire, Develop, and Manage Key Resources   50
   Develop and Manage Relationships with External Stakeholders   53

Determine and Communicate Strategic Direction   54
Oversee Formulation and Implementation of Specific Strategies   57
Establish Balanced Controls   58
Summary   60
Ethics Questions   62

Part 2: Strategic Analysis   71

CHAPTER 3: THE EXTERNAL ENVIRONMENT: OPPORTUNITIES, THREATS, INDUSTRY COMPETITION, AND COMPETITOR ANALYSIS   72

The General, Industry, and Competitor Environments   73
External Environmental Analysis   74
Scanning   76
Monitoring   77
Forecasting   77
Assessing   77
Segments of the General Environment   78
The Demographic Segment   78
The Economic Segment   80
The Political/Legal Segment   81
The Sociocultural Segment   82
The Technological Segment   83
The Global Segment   84
The Physical Environment Segment   86
Industry Environment Analysis   86
Threat of New Entrants   88
Bargaining Power of Suppliers   91
Bargaining Power of Buyers   92
Threat of Substitute Products   92
Intensity of Rivalry among Competitors   93
Complementors   95
Interpreting Industry Analyses   95
Analysis of Direct Competitors   96
Strategic Groups   96
Understanding Competitors and Their Intentions   97
Summary   99
Ethics Questions   100

CHAPTER 4: THE INTERNAL ORGANIZATION: RESOURCES, CAPABILITIES, AND CORE COMPETENCIES   106

Internal Analysis and Value Creation   108
Conditions Influencing Internal Analysis   108
Creating Value   110

Resources, Capabilities, and Core Competencies   112
   Resources   112
   Capabilities   115
   Core Competencies   116
Building Core Competencies   118
   Four Criteria of Sustainable Competitive Advantage   118
   Value Chain Analysis   121
   Outsourcing   125
   When Core Competencies Lose Their Value   126
Firm Performance   126
   Stakeholder Objectives and Power   127
   Measures of Firm Performance   128
   Balancing Stakeholder Performance   131
   Sustainable Development   131
Summary   133
Ethics Questions   134

Part 3: Creating Competitive Advantage 141

CHAPTER 5: BUSINESS-LEVEL STRATEGY 142

Economic Logic and Business-Level Strategy   143
   Types of Business-Level Strategy   144
   Serving Customers   145
   Strategy and Structure   148
Cost Leadership Strategy   149
   Successful Execution of the Cost Leadership Strategy   149
   Using the Functional Structure to Implement the Cost Leadership Strategy   152
   Competitive Risks of the Cost Leadership Strategy   154
Differentiation Strategy   154
   Successful Execution of the Differentiation Strategy   155
   Using the Functional Structure to Implement the Differentiation Strategy   157
   Competitive Risks of the Differentiation Strategy   159
Focus Strategies   159
   Focused Cost Leadership Strategy   160
   Focused Differentiation Strategy   160
   Using the Simple or Functional Structures to Implement Focus Strategies   161
   Competitive Risks of Focus Strategies   161
Integrated Cost Leadership/Differentiation Strategy   162
   Successful Execution of the Integrated Cost Leadership/Differentiation Strategy   162
   Using a Flexible Structure to Implement the Integrated Cost Leadership/Differentiation Strategy   163
   Competitive Risks of the Integrated Cost Leadership/Differentiation Strategy   165

Summary   166
Ethics Questions   168

CHAPTER 6: COMPETITIVE RIVALRY AND COMPETITIVE DYNAMICS 172

A Model of Competitive Rivalry   175
Competitor Analysis   176
  Market Commonality   176
  Resource Similarity   177
Drivers of Competitive Actions and Responses   179
Competitive Rivalry   180
  Strategic and Tactical Actions   181
Likelihood of Attack   181
  First-Mover Incentives   182
  Organizational Size   183
  Quality   184
Likelihood of Response   185
  Type of Competitive Action   186
  Actor's Reputation   186
  Dependence on the Market   187
Competitive Dynamics   188
  Slow-Cycle Markets   188
  Fast-Cycle Markets   190
  Standard-Cycle Markets   192
Summary   193
Ethics Questions   195

CHAPTER 7: COOPERATIVE STRATEGY 200

The Importance of Cooperative Strategy   201
  Strategic Alliances in Slow-Cycle Markets   203
  Strategic Alliances in Fast-Cycle Markets   203
  Strategic Alliances in Standard-Cycle Markets   204
  Types of Alliances and Other Cooperative Strategies   204
Cooperative Strategies that Enhance Differentiation or Reduce Costs   205
  Complementary Strategic Alliances   206
  Network Cooperative Strategies   207
Cooperative Strategies that Address Forces in the External Environment   209
  Competitive Response Alliances   209
  Uncertainty-Reducing Alliances   209
  Competition-Reducing Cooperative Strategies   209
  Associations and Consortia   210
Cooperative Strategies that Promote Growth and/or Diversification   211
  Diversifying Strategic Alliances   212
  Franchising   212
  International Cooperative Strategies   212

Competitive Risks of Cooperative Strategies   214

Implementing and Managing Cooperative Strategies   216

Summary   218

Ethics Questions   219

CHAPTER 8: CORPORATE-LEVEL STRATEGY   **225**

Levels of Diversification   226
   Low Levels of Diversification   226
   Moderate and High Levels of Diversification   227
Reasons for Diversification   229
Diversification and the Multidivisional Structure   231
Related Diversification   232
   Operational Relatedness: Sharing Activities   233
   *Using the Cooperative Form of the Multidivisional Structure to Implement the Related
   Constrained Strategy   233*
   Corporate Relatedness: Transferring of Core Competencies   235
   *Using the Strategic Business-Unit Form of the Multidivisional Structure to Implement the
   Related Linked Strategy   235*
   Market Power through Multipoint Competition and Vertical Integration   237
   Simultaneous Operational Relatedness and Corporate Relatedness   238
Unrelated Diversification   239
   Efficient Internal Capital Market Allocation   240
   Restructuring   241
   *Using the Competitive Form of the Multidivisional Structure to Implement the Unrelated
   Diversification Strategy   242*
Value-Neutral Diversification: Incentives and Resources   243
   Incentives to Diversify   243
   Resources and Diversification   246
Value-Reducing Diversification: Managerial Motives to Diversify   246
Summary   248
Ethics Questions   250

CHAPTER 9: ACQUISITION AND RESTRUCTURING STRATEGIES   **257**

The Popularity of Merger and Acquisition Strategies   258
   Mergers, Acquisitions, and Takeovers: What Are the Differences?   259
Reasons for Acquisitions   260
   Increase Market Power   260
   Overcome Entry Barriers   262
   Reduce Costs and Risks Associated with New Product Development   262
   Increase Speed to Market   263
   Increase Diversification and Reshape the Firm's Competitive Scope   263
   Learn and Develop New Capabilities   264

Problems in Achieving Acquisition Success   265
   Integration Difficulties and an Inability to Achieve Synergy   266
   Inadequate Evaluation of Target   267
   Large or Extraordinary Debt   267
   Too Much Diversification   268
   Managers Too Focused on Acquisitions   269
   Firm Becomes Too Large   269
Effective Acquisitions   270
Restructuring   272
   Downsizing   272
   Downscoping   273
   Leveraged Buyouts   274
   Outcomes from Restructuring   275
Summary   276
Ethics Questions   277

CHAPTER 10: INTERNATIONAL STRATEGY   284

Incentives for Using an International Strategy   286
   Increased Market Size   286
   Return on Investment   287
   Economies of Scale, Scope, and Learning   287
   Obtain Resources and Achieve Other Location Advantages   288
International Corporate-Level Strategy   289
   International Scope: Worldwide Presence or Regionalization   289
   Multidomestic Strategy   292
   Global Strategy   293
   Transnational Strategy   295
International Business-Level Strategy   296
Choice of International Entry Mode   299
   Exporting   299
   Licensing   301
   Strategic Alliances   302
   Acquisitions   303
   New Wholly-Owned Subsidiary   303
   Dynamics of Mode of Entry   304
Strategic Competitiveness Outcomes   305
   International Diversification and Returns   305
   International Diversification and Innovation   306
   Risks in an International Environment   307
   Complexity of Managing Multinational Firms   309
Summary   310
Ethics Questions   312

Part 4: Monitoring and Creating Entrepreneurial Opportunities 319

CHAPTER 11: CORPORATE GOVERNANCE 320

Separation of Ownership and Managerial Control   323
  Agency Relationships   324
  Product Diversification as an Example of an Agency Problem   325
  Agency Costs and Governance Mechanisms   326
Ownership Concentration   328
  Influence of Institutional Owners   329
Board of Directors   330
  Board Effectiveness   332
Executive Compensation   333
  The Effectiveness of Executive Compensation   334
Market for Corporate Control   335
  Managerial Defense Tactics   337
International Corporate Governance   338
  Corporate Governance in Germany   339
  Corporate Governance in Japan   340
  Global Corporate Governance   341
Governance Mechanisms, Stakeholder Management, and Ethical Behavior   341
Summary   342
Ethics Questions   344

CHAPTER 12: STRATEGIC ENTREPRENEURSHIP 351

Strategic Entrepreneurship and Innovation   352
  Innovation   353
  Entrepreneurs   354
  International Entrepreneurship   355
Internal Innovation   357
  Incremental Innovations   357
  Radical Innovations   357
Implementing Internal Innovation   359
  Cross-Functional Product Development Teams   360
  Facilitating Integration and Implementation   361
  Creating Value from Internal Innovation   361
Innovation through Cooperative Strategies   362
Innovation through Acquisitions   363
Creating Value through Strategic Entrepreneurship   364
Summary   365
Ethics Questions   366

CHAPTER 13: STRATEGIC FLEXIBILITY AND REAL OPTIONS ANALYSIS   372

Real Options Analysis   374
    Types of Real Options   375
    Purpose and Importance of Real Options Analysis   377
    Value Drivers for Real Options   383
Valuation of Real Options   386
Implementation Requirements of Real Options   386
Summary   387
Ethics Questions   389
Appendix: Detailed Valuation Guidelines   389

Glossary   405
Name Index   413
Company Index   440
Subject Index   443

PREFACE

UPDATES AND HIGHLIGHTS FOUND IN THE THIRD EDITION

Our goal in developing the Third Edition of *Competing for Advantage* was to present an up-to-date explanation of the strategic management process. In doing so, we maintained the highest standards of intellectual integrity while simultaneously providing thoughtful practical examples of the conceptual points we sought to illustrate. We also sought to present our material in a readable style. To accomplish these objectives, we read the most recent academic research to insure that our content is highly current and relevant to the organizations that are relevant to our MBA and EMBA student audiences. Furthermore, we continuously read articles in the best practitioner publications (e.g., *Wall Street Journal, Bloomberg BusinessWeek, Fortune, Financial Times, Forbes*, and many others). After identifying interesting examples that effectively illustrated the conceptual ideas on which we focused, we related them to particular concepts so that students can see how they are applied in practice. Although the examples are usually brief, students have found them useful, not only to illustrate the conceptual application but also to facilitate efforts to identify and solve organizational problems.

So, both the concepts and the examples included in this third edition are current. We updated all the examples from the second edition and inserted many new examples, including a focus on services, healthcare, technology and innovation, crisis management, corporate social responsibility, and green strategies. For instance, in Chapter 1, there are several examples of crisis management: one concerning the Japanese earthquake and its supply change implications and one dealing with the recession and the firm crises associated with it. We use, for instance, Caterpillar's successful anticipation and planning for the volatility associated with the recession. Chapter 2 focuses on strategic leadership; herein, we provide new examples of strategic change by Steve Ballmer as Microsoft's CEO and the recent selection of a female CEO at IBM, Virginia Rometty. We also discuss the Internet hacking scandal associated with the tabloid newspaper in Rupert Murdoch's media empire, News Corp. In Chapter 3, focused on external environmental analysis, we added a new section on the physical environment, discussing the importance of climate change issues and the use of green strategies to deal with these issues. In Chapter 4, on internal analysis, we introduce situations surrounding Kodak's bankruptcy, Nike's core competencies, and how Twitter, as a new competitor, offers another way to create value in media firms. We also explain that many firms are using sustainability as part of their strategies and are establishing sustainability as an organizational competency. Example firms include McDonald's, Burger King, Chipotle Mexican Grill, and Walmart.

In Chapter 5, on business-level strategy, we added content on the use of outsourcing for the reduction of costs in the discussion of the cost leadership strategy.

We also added a number of current examples in this chapter such as Amazon.com's introduction of the Kindle Fire to lead the market in e-book readers and to compete with Apple's iPad. We discuss the success of Ryanair's cost leadership strategy exemplified by its 10 percent increase in passengers to 72 million during the economic recession in 2010. And we also used examples of major Asian companies such as the Li Ning Company, the largest sporting goods manufacturer in China. Chapter 6, focused on competitive dynamics, was updated with a number of examples. For instance, the chapter discusses how FedEx and UPS compete across several product markets, including package delivery by both land and air and the increasing e-commerce segment. Johnson & Johnson's recent competitive problems associated with product quality are discussed. Innovation is an important tool for remaining competitive; Cooper Tire is highly dependent on the replacement tire market, and the chapter discusses how it relies on continuous innovation to remain competitive.

A number of global examples are included in this edition as well. For instance, Chapter 7, on cooperative strategy, contains an interesting new example of Ericson, a global network management company with more than two hundred and fifty million customers worldwide. This chapter also describes instances of firms joining associations and consortia to deal with the green movement and sustainability issues. Chapter 8 deals with corporate strategy. In this chapter, we add a number of service industry examples along with the traditional manufacturing industry cases. There are examples from Medifast and Catholic Health Initiatives as well as the hospitality and real estate brokerages as diversified service firms. This chapter also presents an example in the solar industry, which represents a continuing focus on green strategies and sustainability. In Chapter 9, on acquisition strategy, we added examples such as one dealing with Google's acquisition of Motorola Mobility. In addition, we include instances of large emerging economy firms pursuing developed economy acquisitions such as JBS, a Brazilian meat producer, making a number of acquisitions in the United States. We also discuss Bristol-Myers Squibb's acquisition of hepatitis C drug producer Inhibitex.

Chapter 10, focused on international strategy, contains many new examples and a significant updating of the literature. There are important discussions of firms in many different countries including China, Mexico, India, and Russia. One section includes an interesting discussion on an annual corruption index suggesting the institutional risks companies face when entering foreign countries.

Chapter 11's consideration of corporate governance introduces a number of updates including information on recent regulations regarding proxy voting "say on pay," where large institutional investors have a vote on executive compensation packages and can nominate board members for a proxy vote who support their positions. We also provide updates on the Dodd-Frank regulation of the financial industry which pertains to corporate governance. Ethical issues in corporate governance are examined, including the scandal associated with News Corp. mentioned earlier, and how the executive leaders can improve organizational culture by the way they govern the firm.

In Chapter 12 on strategic entrepreneurship, we include a discussion on Tim Cook, Apple's new CEO, and how he intends to maintain the strong culture committed to innovation that Steve Jobs created. Finally, in Chapter 13, we have updated the real options literature and provided associated examples that apply this important decision-making tool.

We think that students will find the updates very useful conceptually. In addition, the many application-oriented examples appearing throughout this third edition of *Competing for Advantage* should prove instructive.

PURPOSE AND ORGANIZATION OF THE BOOK

The purpose of this book is to provide a comprehensive yet concise description of the core concepts of strategic management that firms need to use to meet the challenge of competing in the current fast-paced and globally competitive environment. Written to meet the educational needs of full-time and part-time MBA students as well as those pursuing an Executive MBA degree, this book will also serve the practicing manager, consultant, or corporate trainer whose firms or clients are faced with global economic challenges in achieving competitive advantage over their rivals. CEOs, line managers, and especially executives charged with developing and implementing strategic initiatives will find much to challenge their thinking and put to prescriptive use while reading and studying this book.

Our examination of strategic management is distinctive in several important ways. The book contains a detailed treatment of multiple perspectives, including traditional industrial organization economics, the resource-based view, and the stakeholder perspective. These three perspectives form the foundation upon which other important ideas and tools for developing and effectively implementing strategies are built. The net effect is an integrated approach that demonstrates how firms can be ethical and efficient simultaneously, socially responsible and profitable, responsive to multiple stakeholders, and capable of sustaining high financial performance over the long term.

Another distinguishing feature of this book is that strategies and methods for implementing them are treated within the same chapters. For example, the organizational structures required for implementing each of the business-level strategies are discussed in Chapter 5 on business strategies. This is also done for chapters on cooperative strategies (Chapter 7), corporate-level strategies (Chapter 9), and international strategies (Chapter 10). This approach provides students with a more complete understanding of the organizational implications of selecting a particular strategy. We also describe patterns of competitive rivalry and competitive dynamics, because these phenomena occur as firms implement business strategies to compete in their chosen markets. The chapter in which these important topics are considered discusses concisely yet thoroughly the competitive dynamics in slow-cycle, fast-cycle, and standard-cycle markets.

To ensure that our descriptions of the core concepts of strategic management are accurate and up-to-date, we draw extensively from both current and classic academic research, using as guides the literature in economics, finance, marketing, business ethics, entrepreneurship, and social psychology in addition to strategic management. Also, to fulfill our purpose of providing contemporary insights and analysis, we use numerous current examples from the business press to illustrate how companies use the concepts presented here to achieve multiple goals and especially to improve firm performance. We tackle the critical issues of the day: strategic leadership, corporate governance, business ethics, competitive rivalry and competitive dynamics, strategic entrepreneurship, and real options. In fact, this is the only leading MBA-level strategic management text with separate chapters on corporate governance, strategic entrepreneurship, and real options analysis.

This book also fully incorporates concepts of globalization and technological change. Increasing globalization and rapid technological change make the strategic management process highly challenging for managers. These trends create a high level of complexity and turbulence during the strategy development process and also increase the need for speed in making strategic decisions. We integrate issues associated with globalization and technological change in the chapters throughout the book. To emphasize their importance, we also discuss globalization and technological change in a separate chapter on international strategy.

Additionally, because the strategic management process is most effective when grounded in ethical practices, ethics questions are presented at the end of each chapter. These questions challenge readers to place chapter-specific strategic management practices within an ethical context.

PARTS OF THE STRATEGIC MANAGEMENT PROCESS

Strategic Thinking is the foundation for the effective use of strategic management; as such, it is the first of this book's themes. Then in Part 2, we focus on the principles and techniques of **Strategic Analysis**. In Part 3, we examine the topic of **Creating Competitive Advantage**. This discussion shows how firms create competitive advantage by developing and implementing effective business-level, cooperative, corporate-level, and international strategies. In Part 4, **Monitoring and Creating Entrepreneurial Opportunities**, we emphasize the important trend toward increased corporate governance that emerged in the post-Enron era. Because more intensive corporate governance tends to make firms more conservative, we integrate a discussion of strategic entrepreneurship into this section. We end with a chapter on real options—a technique that flows naturally from strategic entrepreneurship. Integrating these topics allows us to show how increased governance can in turn create a need for firms to actively identify and exploit entrepreneurial opportunities.

Part 1—Strategic Thinking

Strategic thinking and the strategic leadership resulting from it are critical inputs to an effective strategic management process. In Chapter 1, we discuss strategic thinking and its link with effective strategic management. This relationship is more critical in the current competitive environment, which is characterized by globalization and increased technological change. Chapter 1 also examines the emergence of strategic management as a discipline. Some of the important early work in the field is reviewed, as are prominent contemporary ideas in the field.

Three major perspectives that influence strategic thinking are introduced in Chapter 1. The industrial organization (I/O) model of value creation, which is based in industrial organization economics, focuses on how competitive forces in the firm's external environment shape the firm's strategy. The resource-based model of value creation focuses on how strategy is shaped by the firm's idiosyncratic and valuable resources, capabilities, and core competencies. The stakeholder model of responsible firm behavior and firm performance envisions the firm at the center of a network of stakeholders. According to this model, firms that recognize the needs of stakeholders and that effectively manage relationships with a broad group of stakeholders are more likely to achieve high performance over the long term. The first chapter closes with a discussion of the key elements of strategic thinking and how it can be effectively integrated into the strategic management process. This process is described in detail, and the strategic management model described in Chapter 1 serves as an outline for the rest of the book.

Because of the important role of managers in the strategic management process, Chapter 2 uses a comprehensive model to describe how managers, as strategic leaders, foster better strategic thinking throughout the organization. This chapter opens with a discussion of individual strategic leaders, their decision-making styles, and factors that influence their strategic decisions. The chapter then broadens to a discussion of top management teams, including the influence of team heterogeneity, team power, and executive succession processes. The rest of the chapter explains key strategic leadership responsibilities and actions, which include ensuring that the firm is well positioned economically, managing strategic resources, managing relationships with external stakeholders, determining strategic direction, overseeing formulation and implementation of specific strategies, and establishing balanced controls.

Part 2—Strategic Analysis

In Part 2 of the book, we focus on how firms analyze their external environment and internal organization. After managers are oriented toward strategic thinking and understand principles of effective strategic leadership, the results of these analyses provide the information and knowledge needed to achieve competitive advantages by selecting and using particular strategies.

Chapter 3 examines the different tools the firm uses to analyze the three parts of its external environment (the general environment, the industry environment, and competitors). By studying its general environment, the firm identifies opportunities and threats. The I/O model provides the foundation that firms use to study industries. The primary purpose of examining this part of the external environment is to determine the profitability potential of an industry or an industry segment. Competitor analysis, the third part of the firm's external environment, yields information that allows the firm to know more about its competitors and about the actions and responses each competitor might take while competing in different markets.

The emphasis in Chapter 4 is on internal analysis, and the purpose is to identify the resources, capabilities, and core competencies that can help a firm to achieve competitive advantages. Whereas Chapter 3 focused on what a firm *might do* as suggested by the external environment, this chapter focuses on what a firm *can do* as suggested by its resources, capabilities, and core competencies.

The resource-based view of the firm is the underlying theoretical framework for Chapter 4's discussions. Four criteria that firms use to identify core competencies— value, rarity, imperfect imitability, and nonsubstitutability—are described. In addition, we examine the value chain in terms of value chain activities and support functions to show how firms determine those activities with which they can or cannot create value. This analysis also provides information suggesting when a firm should outsource an activity in the value chain to a supplier. Finally, firms are cautioned to remain flexible so that core competencies do not become core rigidities. An understanding derived from strategic analysis is the foundation needed to focus on the strategies firms can use to create competitive advantages.

Chapter 4 concludes with a detailed examination of firm performance from multiple perspectives. The demands and needs of multiple stakeholders, as well as their power to influence the firm, are described. Multiple measures of firm performance are introduced, including both financial and nonfinancial measures. The chapter closes with a discussion of sustainable performance.

Part 3—Creating Competitive Advantage

In chapters of Part 3, we simultaneously discuss formulation and implementation, components of the strategic management process that are examined separately in other books. Our joint treatment of formulation and implementation actions is comprehensive and integrated. For example, our study of business-level strategies in Chapter 5 includes analyses of cost leadership, differentiation, focused cost leadership, focused differentiation, and integrated cost leadership/differentiation strategies. After explaining the characteristics of each strategy, we describe the unique organizational structure that firms match to each type of business-level strategy. In this manner, we link formulation (i.e., the selection of a business-level strategy) with implementation (i.e., the appropriate organizational structure matched with individual business-level strategies). This important and unique pattern of linking strategy with structure is followed in the remaining chapters of Part 3.

Chapter 6 also focuses on business-level strategy in describing patterns of competitive rivalry between individual firms as well as patterns of competitive dynamics among all firms that compete within an industry. An important reason for the firm to understand competitive rivalry and competitive dynamics is to learn how to predict the actions that competitors might take against it as well as how the competitor might respond in retaliation against the focal firm's competitive action. The chapter examines factors that are important to competitive rivalry (e.g., awareness, motivation, and ability as drivers of a firm's competitive behavior). The chapter also analyzes dimensions of competitive dynamics (e.g., the effects of varying rates of competitive speed in different markets). Thus, in total, the chapter's analysis of rivalry and dynamics highlights their influences on firms' competitive actions and competitive responses.

We focus on cooperative strategies in Chapter 7. Cooperative strategies such as strategic alliances, joint ventures, and network strategies have become increasingly important to firms. A key reason for this importance is that few, if any, firms have the resources necessary to either internally develop or acquire from external sources all of the resources needed to create value. Cooperative strategy is another path that firms follow when gaining access to and developing new resources and capabilities as well as exploiting current ones. This chapter examines strategies that have evolved in response to the challenges and opportunities created by increasing globalization and technological change. The chapter also explains the risks associated with cooperative strategies, including inadequate contracts, opportunism, and misrepresentation of competencies by partners. Dominant approaches for managing strategic alliances are also explored to explain how risk is managed when the firm cooperates with others to create value.

Chapter 8 begins our discussion of corporate-level strategy. Concerned with the businesses in which the diversified firm intends to compete—and with how it will manage its portfolio of businesses—the chapter discusses four major corporate-level strategies. These strategies range from one with relatively little diversification (single business) to one with substantial diversification (unrelated diversification). In addition, the unique organizational structures required to successfully implement each corporate-level strategy are described.

The analysis of corporate-level strategy and diversification is extended in Chapter 9, where we discuss mergers and acquisitions. Mergers and acquisitions have been popular for many decades, and recent trends suggest that their popularity is unlikely to decline much in the next few years. Although many mergers and acquisitions fail, some succeed. Chapter 9 presents reasons that account for failure as well as those that contribute to merger and acquisition success. The dominant approaches to restructuring (downsizing, downscoping, and leveraged buyouts) are also discussed in this chapter. Successful firms restructure their portfolio of businesses as necessary. Restructuring can be initiated to deal with merger and acquisition failures or to adjust the firm's portfolio of businesses in response to emerging opportunities in its external environment.

Chapter 10 explores both corporate-level and business-level international strategies. As in the previous chapters in Part 3, we describe the organizational structures necessary to implement each of the corporate-level strategies. We also discuss some of the implications of implementing international business-level strategies in a particular country. After selecting an international strategy, a firm must decide which mode of entry to pursue when implementing the chosen strategy. Exporting, licensing, strategic alliances, acquisitions, and establishing a new wholly-owned subsidiary are entry modes that firms consider when entering markets. We also discuss outcomes of international diversification and the attendant political and economic risks.

Part 4—Monitoring and Creating Entrepreneurial Opportunities

Corporate governance, strategic entrepreneurship, and real options analysis are examined in Part 4, the book's final section. Corporate governance, given the implementation of Sarbanes-Oxley and Dodd-Frank as well as global reach, creates a challenging context for governing firms appropriately and thus represents a critically important topic warranting a separate chapter. Therefore, Chapter 11 describes major corporate governance mechanisms and how they can be effectively used to ensure that the actions of the firm's agents (key decision makers) are aligned with the principals' (owners') best interests. The chapter examines large institutional investors, boards of directors, and executive compensation as dominant governance mechanisms and indicates how they can be effectively used in the current business environment. In addition, we discuss trends in international corporate governance along with the need for continuous displays of ethical behavior by top-level managers and members of the firm's board of directors.

Combining Chapter 11's examination of effective corporate governance mechanisms with Chapter 2's study of successful strategic leadership practices yields a comprehensive treatment of how the strategic management process can be used to ethically achieve a competitive advantage. In addition to grounding the analysis of effective corporate governance and strategic leadership in current research, we provide several company-specific examples to enhance understanding of how these principles can be successfully applied in today's business organizations.

Although corporate governance is important, increasingly stringent governance can create a more conservative strategic management process, particularly when selecting and implementing the firm's strategies. A highly conservative approach to the strategic management process increases the need for firms to pursue aggressively the identification and exploitation of entrepreneurial opportunities. Accordingly, Chapter 12 emphasizes actions that firms can take to create entrepreneurial opportunities and to manage them strategically in order to gain and sustain a competitive advantage. Entrepreneurship is commonly practiced in existing firms to renew current competitive advantages while simultaneously enhancing the firm's ability to create new competitive advantages for future success. Furthermore, we examine how cooperative strategies and merger and acquisition strategies can be used in a more entrepreneurial manner to create competitive advantages.

The final chapter focuses on how to manage entrepreneurial opportunities in an uncertain environment using real options tools. This chapter is of significant value for readers interested in understanding all aspects of the strategic management process. Originally contributed by Jeff Reuer and updated by the authors, this chapter provides up-to-date methods for planning and calculating the value of potential entrepreneurial projects. Successful use of these methods increases the firm's flexibility when making decisions within the context of uncertain technological, product, and market environments.

SUMMARY

This book offers comprehensive yet concise coverage of the core concepts in strategic management as well as an explanation of the strategic management process that professional managers and those pursuing an MBA or EMBA degree will find useful. The book is comprehensive in that it examines traditional strategic management topics (e.g., industry analysis) along with other important topics (e.g., corporate governance, strategic leadership, competitive rivalry and competitive dynamics, strategic entrepreneurship, and real options) to help prepare students for a successful managerial career. The book's four themes—strategic thinking, strategic analysis, creating competitive advantage, and monitoring and creating entrepreneurial opportunities—are the foundation for providing readers with an integrated traditional and contemporary analysis of an effective strategic management process. We hope that all readers—instructors, students, and managers—will find the book helpful in understanding and successfully using strategic management concepts. We wish you well with your careers and with your use of the strategic management process.

TOOLS FOR TEACHING AND LEARNING

Instructor's Resource CD-ROM

(ISBN 978-0-538-48175-5) Key ancillaries—**Instructor's Manual, Test Bank**, and **PowerPoint**®—are provided on CD-ROM for easy customization in files formatted for Microsoft Office's core word processor, Microsoft Word, and its core presentation graphics program, PowerPoint. The Instructor's Manual contains outlines, sample syllabi, and discussion prompts. Test questions are provided in several formats: true/false, multiple-choice, essay, and case scenarios (problem-solving application questions). PowerPoint slides for each chapter of the text provide a complete chapter overview combined with figures and tables from the text.

Competing for Advantage Website

(www.cengagebrain.com) Broad online support is provided on the text's dedicated Website, including a map to relevant Harvard Business School cases.

Accessing CengageBrain

1. Use your browser to go to www.CengageBrain.com.
2. The first time you go to the site, you will need to register. It's free. Click on "Sign Up" in the top right corner of the page and fill out the registration information. (After you have signed in once, whenever you return to CengageBrain, you will enter the user name and password you have chosen and you will be taken to the companion site for your book.)
3. Once you have registered and logged in for the first time, go to the "Search for Books or Materials" bar and enter the author or ISBN for your textbook. When the title of your text appears, click on it and you will be taken to the companion site. There you can chose among the various folders provided on the Student side of the site. NOTE: If you are currently using more than one Cengage textbook, the same user name and password will give you access to all the companion sites for your Cengage titles. After you have entered the information for each title, they will all appear listed in the pull-down menu in the "Search for Books or Materials" bar. Whenever you return to CengageBrain, you can click on the title of the site you wish to visit and go directly there.

Write Experience 2.0 Writing Tool for Strategic Management

Cengage Learning's Write Experience is a new technology that is the first in higher education to offer students the opportunity to improve their writing and analytical skills without adding to your workload. Offered through an exclusive agreement with Vantage Learning, creator of the software used for GMAT essay grading, Write Experience evaluates students' answers to a select set of assignments for writing for voice, style, format, and originality. For more information about this unique course solution, contact your local sales representative or visit www.cengage.com/writeexperience. Better Writing. Better Outcomes. Write Experience.

Business Insights Global

Put a complete business library at your student's fingertips! This premier online business research tool allows you and your students to search thousands of periodicals, journals, references, financial data, industry charts and more. This powerful research tool saves time for students—whether they are preparing for a presentation, conducting research for a case analysis, or analyzing company data. You can use Business Insights Global to quickly and easily assign readings or research projects. Please contact your Cengage Learning representative for additional information about this research tool.

Coursemate

This dynamic interactive learning tool includes study tools such as online, quizzing, PowerPoint slides, and videos helping to insure that your students come to class and are prepared to succeed in your course.

Micromatic Strategic Management Simulation

The Micromatic Business Simulation Game allows students to decide their company's mission, goals, policies, and strategies. Students as individuals or teams make their decisions on a quarterly basis, determining price, sales, and promotion budgets, operations decisions, and financing requirements. Each decision round requires students to make approximately 100 decisions. Micromatic is classified as a medium to complex business simulation game which helps students to understand how functional areas of a business fit together without being bogged down in needless detail. This simulation provides students with an excellent capstone experience in decision making. Please contact your Cengage Learning representative for additional information about this simulation.

Custom Case Selection

Cengage Learning is dedicated to making the educational experience unique for all learners by creating custom materials that best suit your course needs. Please contact your Cengage Learning representative to discuss how you can easily add a unique set of cases for your course from case providers such as Harvard Business School Publishing, Darden, Stanford, and Ivey.

ACKNOWLEDGMENTS

We are grateful to the team at Cengage for working diligently on this project and to our students and colleagues (including many reviewers) who have provided valuable insights, thereby helping us to improve the overall quality of the book. We are especially appreciative of our families for giving us support and encouragement and to our academic institutions for allowing us to pursue this and other book projects. We would be remiss if we did not also thank the many hundreds of authors we have cited in this volume for adding so much to the field through their thoughtful observations and rigorous research. In particular, we are grateful to Jeffrey Reuer for his insights on real options. This book reflects the work of numerous scholars with a common purpose of discovering and disseminating valuable research findings that help foster understanding and improve the strategic management process. We sincerely hope that we have presented the material in a way that is useful to graduate business students and others who are interested in learning how to help a firm "Compete for Advantage."

Robert E. Hoskisson
Michael A. Hitt
R. Duane Ireland
Jeffrey S. Harrison

PART 1

STRATEGIC THINKING

CHAPTER 1   Introduction to Strategic Management   2
CHAPTER 2   Strategic Leadership   34

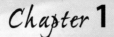

Chapter **1**

INTRODUCTION TO STRATEGIC MANAGEMENT

KNOWLEDGE OBJECTIVES

Studying this chapter should provide you with the strategic management knowledge needed to:

1. Describe the 21st-century competitive landscape and explain how globalization, economic volatility, and technological changes shape it.

2. Use the industrial organization (I/O) model to explain how firms can earn above-average returns.

3. Use the resource-based model to explain how firms can earn above-average returns.

4. Explain the stakeholder perspective and how effective management of stakeholders can lead to high firm performance and responsible firm behavior.

5. Define strategic thinking and explain how it is used to guide decision making during the strategic management process.

6. Describe the strategic management process.

Business executives face a world that is increasingly complex and ever changing. Rapidly advancing technologies in areas such as communications and transportation have led to unprecedented levels of global trade and awareness. These trends, combined with dramatic economic, social, and political changes have created a globally interconnected marketplace characterized by intense competition.[1] Strategic management is a discipline that has emerged in response to the need for mental models and strategic planning tools that can help executives guide their firms in this challenging global business environment. Strategic management primarily involves the actions organizations take to achieve competitive advantage and create value for the organization and its stakeholders.

Competitive advantage comes from successful formulation and execution of strategies that are different from and create more value than the strategies of competitors.[2] When a firm is able to achieve a competitive advantage, that advantage normally can be sustained only for a limited period.[3] A **sustainable competitive advantage** (hereafter called *competitive advantage*) is possible only after competitors' efforts to duplicate the value-creating strategy have ceased or failed. The speed with which competitors are able to acquire the skills needed to duplicate the benefits of a firm's value-creating strategy determines how long the competitive advantage will last.[4] Firms must understand how to exploit a competitive advantage if they intend to create more value than competitors, which can then lead to higher returns for those who have invested money and other resources in the firm.[5] When a firm earns returns that are higher than those of competitors, it is an indication that the strategies the firm is pursuing are leading to competitive advantage.

The **strategic management process** (as illustrated later in the chapter by Figure 1.6) is the full set of commitments, decisions, and actions required for a firm to create value and earn returns that are higher than those of competitors.[6] In its simplest form, the process involves analyzing the firm and its environment, and then using the information to formulate and implement strategies that lead to competitive advantage. Strategic leaders guide the strategy-creation process, help the organization acquire and develop needed resources, manage relationships with key organizational stakeholders, and develop adequate organizational controls to ensure that the process is successful in leading to desired firm outcomes. The responsibilities of effective strategic leaders are discussed in Chapter 2.

This chapter introduces several topics. First, we examine some of the major characteristics of the 21st-century competitive landscape that form the context in which strategies are created and executed. We then relate a brief history of the major events and central ideas that played a prominent role in the creation of the field now called strategic management. The early ideas lay the groundwork for a discussion of three prominent models in strategic management. The first model (industrial organization) suggests that the external environment is the primary determinant of a firm's strategies. The key to this model is identifying and competing successfully in an attractive (i.e., profitable) industry.[7] The second model (resource based) proposes that a firm's unique resources and capabilities are the critical link to value creation.[8] The third model (stakeholder) suggests that long-term competitive advantage is a function of the strength of a firm's relationships with stakeholders and how those relationships are managed.[9] Comprehensive explanations in this and the next three chapters show that through the combined use of these models firms obtain the strategic inputs they need to successfully formulate and implement strategies.

The final section of this chapter begins with an examination of the characteristics of strategic thinking and how strategic leaders can encourage this sort of thinking within their firms. *Strategic thinking* describes the more creative aspects of strategic management.[10] The strategic management process, as it will be examined in this book, is then described in detail. Effective strategic actions taken in the context of carefully integrated strategy formulation and implementation plans result in high firm performance.[11]

THE COMPETITIVE LANDSCAPE

The sports car manufacturer Saab, photographic products icon Kodak, consumer electronics retailer Circuit City, book retailer Borders, and Twinkie-maker Hostess have more than just well-known brand names in common. Each of them enjoyed a rather lengthy period of success in their industries followed by a period of decline and ultimately bankruptcy, either for the purpose of restructuring or for complete liquidation.[12] Frequently businesses become uncompetitive because they are unable to make the changes necessary for continued success.

The airline industry is very competitive, with many players. The de-regulation of the U.S. airlines in 1978 led to price wars among the "legacy carriers" like United, American, and Delta, and the entrance of new competitors. Especially effective have been low-cost, limited route carriers such as Southwest Airlines in the U.S. and RyanAir in Europe. Terrorist attacks such as those on September 11, 2001 have led to significant changes in technology, especially with regard to security. Volatile economic conditions have also presented a tremendous challenge, as changes in oil prices and demand shifts have made it difficult to compete. In an effort to enhance performance in this very difficult competitive environment, most of the major carriers have formed global alliances. For instance, the Star Alliance includes many carriers, such as Spanair, Singapore Airlines, United, Ethiopian Airlines, Egyptair, Lufthansa, and Air China.[13] These types of alliances provide code sharing, which means that each partner in the alliance can sell flights on other airlines and customers typically will have to check their bags only once even if they change airlines during their trip. The industry has also been marked with a high level of consolidation as many airlines have acquired other carriers to gain economies of scale and increase efficiency.[14] All these efforts have had mixed results, as many airlines have had to seek protection from creditors just to stay solvent.[15] American Airlines was the last of the "legacy" airlines to file for Chapter 11 bankruptcy protection.[16]

Changes in the airline industry are, in part, a result of globalization, economic volatility, and rapid changes in technology, particularly in the area of security. The large U.S. carriers, in particular, have been unable to sustain their competitiveness in light of these changes. They have been slow to adopt a global mind-set, and they have been unable to make remain competitive while making all of the technological changes needed. We will now examine these trends toward globalization, economic volatility, and rapid technological change.

Globalization of Markets and Industries

The fundamental nature of competition in many of the world's industries is changing.[17] One of the most important of these changes is the continuous increase in the globalization of the world's markets. **Globalization** can be defined as increasing economic interdependence among countries as reflected in the flow of goods and services, financial capital, and knowledge across country borders.[18] Relatively unfettered by artificial constraints, such as high tariffs, the global economy significantly expands and complicates a firm's competitive environment.[19] In global markets and industries, financial capital might be obtained in one national market and used to buy raw materials in another. Manufacturing equipment bought from a third national market can then be used to produce products that are sold in numerous markets. Thus, globalization increases the range of opportunities for companies competing in the 21st century and is a fundamental driver of the business economies in today's competitive landscape.[20]

Globalization has contributed to **hypercompetition**, or extremely intense rivalry among firms.[21] The term often is used to capture the realities of the 21st-century competitive landscape. As shown in Figure 1.1, hypercompetition results from the dynamics

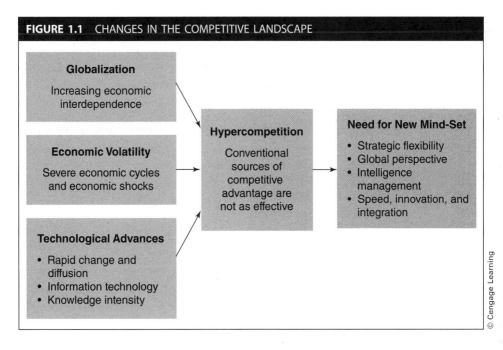

FIGURE 1.1 CHANGES IN THE COMPETITIVE LANDSCAPE

© Cengage Learning

of strategic maneuvering among global and innovative combatants in a volatile economy. It is a condition of rapidly escalating competition based on price-quality positioning, competition to create new know-how and establish first-mover advantage, and competition to protect or invade established product or geographic markets.[22] In a hypercompetitive market, firms often aggressively challenge their competitors in the hopes of improving their competitive position and ultimately their performance.[23]

Partly because of globalization and hypercompetition, the leaders of many multinational companies are now finding less relevance in traditional industry or national boundaries. Instead, multinational enterprises are now thinking in terms of building global enterprises consisting of a set of highly integrated businesses that build on and utilize an international resource base of workers, technologies, and marketplaces to create value.[24] For example, the consumer food and products giant Unilever, with over 400 brands, coordinates an international network of manufacturing and distribution facilities and develops new products in association with numerous business partners, governments, and non-government scientific organizations, as well as through research centers in India, the United Kingdom, China, North America, and the Netherlands.[25] Remarkably, more than half of Unilever's business is in emerging markets.[26]

Economic Volatility

Because globalization has led to such high levels of market and industry interconnectedness, business cycles and other broad economic influences have a huge impact on firms around the globe.[27] This point is evident in the early years of the 21st century, with two global economic downturns, including the "Great Recession" that began in 2007.[28] Fundamental economic factors make continued economic volatility likely. Among these factors is the amount of debt countries have accumulated.

As of 2011, Japan was the most indebted nation (relative to national production), with its national debt equal to 234 percent of its GDP (gross domestic product). Greece was in second place, followed by Italy, Iceland, Belgium, Ireland, and the Unites States.[29] Uncertainty regarding the ability of governments to pay their debts can destabilize financial markets because those debts represent investments for investors and financial institutions in the home countries as well as other countries.[30] Instability in financial markets is linked to economic malaise, and actions taken by governments to reduce their debts may also have a detrimental impact because frequently they involve cutting back on expenditures that are linked to employment (i.e., government employees) as well as products and services (i.e., national defense spending, infrastructure).[31] Other fundamental economic factors associated with economic volatility, such as exchange rates and trade balances, will be discussed in Chapter 3.

Sudden disruptive shocks or crises can also lead to economic turbulence.[32] Wars, terrorism, assassinations and revolts, and even natural disasters can influence economic conditions.[33] For instance, a huge earthquake in Japan on March 11, 2011 rattled through the Japanese economy, including its industry-leading automobile sector. Shortly after the quake, Toyota faced a shortage of 500 components from its severely crippled suppliers. Two months after the quake, automobile factories at Toyota, Nissan, and Honda were running at about half capacity, hoping to return to full capacity in the fall.[34] Also affected were companies in other countries that buy parts from Japan.[35] These companies, faced with shortages, had to look elsewhere for supplies, and some of them have now made permanent changes to their supply acquisition strategies.[36] The quake also had a significant impact on the nuclear energy industry because of subsequent problems at the Fukushima Dai-ichi nuclear power plant.[37] Not only did the shutdown of the plant cause power shortages that closed factories in the region, but it also led citizens and leaders around the world to question (again) whether nuclear energy is really safe.

Economic volatility is not the same as economic stagnation. Business cycles exist, which means that there will be upturns and downturns in the economy.[38] However, because of global economic interconnectedness, strategic managers should be prepared for shocks and should do what they can to acquire resources, including a strong strategy that will help them weather stormy economic conditions.[39] Caterpillar is an example of a company that has been able to prosper in difficult times. According to CFO Ed Rapp, the recession actually forced Caterpillar out of complacency: "You really find out who you are, what your capabilities are, in tough times. It forces you to reflect on what really differentiates you in the eyes of your customers."[40] In good times, Caterpillar puts its managers through training programs that require them to plan for major economic downturns, essentially using booms to help plan for the bust.[41]

Technological Advances

In addition to globalization and economic volatility, rapid technological change is also associated with hypercompetition.[42] Three categories of technological trends are significantly altering the nature of competition. The first is the increasing rate of technological change and diffusion. Both the rate of change of technology and the speed at which new technologies become available have increased substantially over the past 20 to 25 years.[43] Short product life cycles resulting from rapid diffusions of new technologies place a competitive premium on a firm's being able to quickly introduce new goods and services into the marketplace.[44] Sometimes disruptive technologies, also known as breakthrough or radical innovations, destroy the value of existing technology and create new markets.[45] Some have referred to this concept as Schumpeterian innovation, from the work of the famous economist Joseph A. Schumpeter. He suggested that such innovations emerge from a process of creative destruction in which existing technologies are replaced by new ones.[46] Digital imaging, which has practically eliminated demand for photographic film, is an example of a disruptive technology.[47]

A second category of technological trends that are influencing competition is the dramatic changes in information technology that have occurred in recent years. Smart phones, artificial intelligence, virtual reality, and cloud computing are examples of how information is used differently as a result of technological developments. An important outcome of these changes is that the ability to effectively and efficiently access and use information has become a significant source of competitive advantage within many industries.[48] The Internet provides an infrastructure that allows the delivery of information to computers in any location, and now cloud computing means that the bulk of information processing and storage may not even occur within the firm that is using it.[49] Access to significant quantities of relatively inexpensive information yields strategic opportunities for a range of industries and companies.

Finally, increasing knowledge intensity is dramatically influencing the competitive environment. Knowledge (information, intelligence, and expertise) is the basis of technology and its application. In the 21st-century competitive landscape, knowledge is a critical organizational resource and is increasingly a valuable source of competitive advantage.[50] As a result, many companies now strive to transmute the accumulated knowledge of individual employees into a corporate asset. The probability of a firm achieving value creation in today's business environment is enhanced for the firms that are aware that their survival depends on the ability to capture intelligence, transform it into usable knowledge, and diffuse it rapidly throughout the company.[51] Firms accepting this challenge shift their focus from merely obtaining information to exploiting that information to gain a competitive advantage over rival firms.[52] We discuss the trend toward increased rivalry more fully in Chapter 6.

Coping with Hypercompetitive Influences

Many implications are associated with the hypercompetitive environment resulting from globalization, economic volatility, and technological advances. A survey of over 1,500 CEOs by IBM indicated that close to 80 percent of them believed that their competitive environment would become more demanding in the future, but fewer than half of them felt their companies were well prepared for it.[53] Traditional ways of looking at competitiveness are unlikely to lead to competitive advantage. Conventional sources of competitive advantage, such as economies of scale and huge advertising budgets, are not as effective as they once were.[54] Managers must adopt a new mind-set that values speed, innovation, and integration along with the challenges that evolve from constantly changing conditions.[55] Global competition has increased performance standards in many dimensions, including quality, cost, productivity, product introduction time, and operational efficiency.[56] Moreover, these standards are not static; they are exacting, requiring continuous improvement from a firm and its employees. As they accept the challenges posed by these increasing standards, companies improve their capabilities and individual workers sharpen their skills. Thus, in the 21st-century competitive landscape, only firms capable of meeting, if not exceeding, global standards typically develop competitive advantage.[57]

Also, to achieve high performance, firms must be able to adapt quickly to changes in the competitive landscape. Such adaptation requires that firms develop strategic flexibility.[58] **Strategic flexibility** is a set of capabilities used to respond to various demands and opportunities existing in a dynamic and uncertain competitive environment (managing strategic flexibility is addressed more fully in Chapter 13). Thus, strategically flexible firms know how to cope with uncertainty and its accompanying risks.[59] Continuous learning provides the firm with new and up-to-date sets of skills, which allow it to adapt to its environment as it encounters changes.[60] Strategic thinking, described later in this chapter, can help a firm remain strategically flexible. Effective strategic leadership, the topic of Chapter 2, is essential to both strategic thinking and flexibility.

The changes described in this section did not occur all at once. The strategic landscape of today emerged from several decades of dramatic economic, social, technological, and political changes. The field of strategic management was born of the need for managers to effectively deal with such changes. A brief history of the intellectual emergence of the field is presented in the next section. This history will serve as a conceptual foundation for the development of strategic management concepts found in this and other chapters.

THE EMERGENCE OF STRATEGIC MANAGEMENT AS A BUSINESS DISCIPLINE

Many of the competitive trends and influences that were described in the last section began to take shape right after World War II. Specifically, the era brought with it management challenges associated with dramatic advances in technology, especially in communications and transportation, as well as increasing national and global competition. Rapid economic, social, technological, and political changes created a turbulent business environment. In addition, the sheer size and complexity of business firms made them difficult to manage. Scholars and consulting firms recognized that organizational success depended on the organization successfully navigating an increasingly difficult external environment.[61]

By the middle of the last century, many business schools were offering a course called "business policy," a capstone course that was intended to help students examine complicated, high-level business problems through integration of knowledge obtained from the various functional disciplines of business.[62] Eventually, the American Assembly of Collegiate Schools of Business (now called the Association to Advance Collegiate Schools of Business) made the business policy course a requirement for accreditation. Also, the major academic management society, the Academy of Management, formed a Business Policy and Planning Division to support academic research and teaching on the subject. The business policy course, as it was typically taught, used business cases to challenge students to develop policies that would solve business problems through an integrated, multifunctional approach.[63] However, business policy was considered as a course more than a field of study.[64] Outside the academic arena, consulting firms such as the Boston Consulting Group were developing tools to help top managers guide their firms.

Early Influences on the Strategy Concept

In 1962 Alfred Chandler, a business historian, published a book that was among the most influential in guiding early business policy scholarship. Chandler defined strategy as the "determination of the basic long-term goals and objectives of an enterprise, and the adoption of courses of action and the allocation of resources necessary for carrying out these goals."[65] His definition embraced the notion that a firm should establish goals, strategies to achieve them, and an implementation (allocation) plan, but it did not address the essential role strategy plays in linking the firm to its environment. Shortly thereafter, Igor Ansoff discussed strategy in terms of product-market scope, growth vector, competitive advantage, and synergy.[66] Ansoff's definition, with its treatment of market factors, is oriented more toward the external environment. He also advanced the idea that the objectives of the firm should attempt to balance the conflicting claims of various internal and external stakeholders, including stockholders, managers, employees, suppliers, and vendors. He divided objectives into two categories, economic and social, with the social objectives acting as constraints on the economic objectives.

About the same time (1965), Edmund Learned, C. Ronald Christensen, Kenneth Andrews, and William Guth published what would become a classic book on the strategic management process. They defined strategy as "the pattern of objectives, purposes, or goals and major policies and plans for achieving these goals, stated in such a way as to define what business the company is in or is to be in and the kind of company it is or is to be."[67] They identified the four components of strategy development as "(1) market opportunity, (2) corporate competences and resources, (3) personal values and aspirations, and (4) acknowledged obligations to segments of society other than stockholders."[68] This treatment of the strategy concept foreshadowed the importance of an economic approach to strategy formulation (market opportunity), as well as the importance of resources and capabilities and an acknowledgement of firm obligations to broad groups of stakeholders.[69] As we will discuss later in this chapter, industrial organization (I/O) economics, the resource-based view, and the stakeholder perspective serve as theoretical foundations for this book.

Several other concepts were also important to the development of the foundational literature of modern strategic management. One of the most important is recognition that organizations are systems that depend on their external environments for survival.[70] Dependence comes from the need for transactions with external stakeholders in order for resources such as raw materials, supplies, machinery, sales dollars, and long-term capital to be obtained. As Ian MacMillan writes, "Thus, all organizations are dependent upon the environment for the provision of certain inputs; which the organization then transforms into outputs; which it, in turn, uses to get more inputs."[71] Jeffrey Pfeffer and Gerald Salancik observed that firm dependence on external stakeholders also gives those stakeholders a certain amount of control over the firm.[72] Associated with the systems perspective and resource dependence is recognition that strategy formulation contains both rational-deductive and political processes.[73] Consequently, in addition to economically based strategies, firms should develop political strategies to deal with stakeholders—such as shareholders, employee groups and unions, competitors, and suppliers—that can facilitate achievement of firm goals.[74]

The ideas of Henry Mintzberg also significantly affected the business policy field.[75] Defining strategy as "a pattern in a stream of decisions," he challenged the underlying assumption that strategies are always a reflection of deliberate plans conceived in advance of particular organizational decisions.[76] Instead, he argued that organizations learn from a process of trial and error. This perspective is consistent with the view that firms can and should learn from their external stakeholders. The importance of organizational learning processes to strategic success has been widely acknowledged.[77]

In another important work, Michael Jensen and William Meckling contributed to the perspective that managers serve as agents for the owners or shareholders.[78] **Agency theory** argues that agency problems exist when managers take actions that are in their own best interests rather than those of the shareholders. The popularity of agency theory influenced strategic management scholars and business executives to keep their focus on shareholder returns as a primary criterion for firm success.[79]

Another major advance came from Oliver Williamson, who examined the efficiency of economic activity within and between markets and organizational hierarchies.[80] **Transaction cost economics** suggests that firms are better off purchasing required resources through a market transaction unless particular conditions exist that make creating them internally more efficient.[81] For example, if there are many potential suppliers of a resource needed by a firm, then a market mechanism can be used. But when there are only a small number of suppliers, there is a much larger risk that they will try to take maximum advantage of their situation. This situation can lead to a firm foregoing a market transaction in favor of internalizing the supplier organization through vertical integration.[82]

Modern Strategic Management

The early work in the field of business policy was fragmented. By the late 1970s, interest in the topic was growing, and the term *strategic management* began to replace *business policy*. The new title was broader in scope and implied that a focus on simply establishing business policies to integrate functional strategies was not a sufficient solution to the strategic challenges executives were facing.[83] In May of 1977, scholars and practitioners who were experts on the topic gathered at the University of Pittsburgh to share ideas. At that meeting, Dan Schendel and Charles Hofer, the conference organizers, presented a model of the fundamental activities in the strategic management process.[84] It included organizational goal formulation, environmental analysis, strategy formulation, strategy evaluation, strategy implementation, and strategic control. The general premise underlying their model was that the most effective firm strategies were those that best "fit" the environmental situation. This **deterministic perspective** of strategy formulation argues that firms should adapt to their environments because characteristics of the environment determine which strategies will succeed.[85]

Environmental determinism was challenged by Jay Bourgeois, who stated that "the strategy of a firm cannot be predicted, nor is it predestined; the strategic decisions made by managers cannot be assumed to be the product of deterministic forces in their environments ... On the contrary, the very nature of the concept of strategy assumes a human agent who is able to take actions that attempt to distinguish one's firm from the competitors."[86] The principle of **enactment** means that firms do not have to entirely submit to environmental forces because they can, in part, create their own environments through strategic actions.[87] These actions might include forming alliances and joint ventures with stakeholders, investing in leading technologies, advertising, or political lobbying.[88] The truth is that adaptation and enactment are both important to strategy formulation. A firm should attempt to predict and adapt to trends and influences over which it has no control or that would be too expensive to influence.[89] On the other hand, firms can also influence their environments in ways that make them better suited to organizational success.

The early advances in strategic management are all incorporated into this book. Our model of the strategic management process is comprehensive, in that it includes all of the activities that were identified as important in the significant early work, such as goal setting, external orientation, development and management of internal resources, formulation and implementation of specific strategies, political strategies, transaction costs, agency theory, the importance and role of external stakeholders, and organizational learning. In addition, state-of-the-art thinking is included on other very important topics such as international strategy, cooperative strategy, technology and innovation, strategic leadership, corporate governance, corporate entrepreneurship, and real options theory.

THREE PERSPECTIVES ON VALUE CREATION

Beginning in the 1980s, as the field of strategic management began to grow and develop, three perspectives gained momentum as comprehensive ways to organize the central ideas and activities associated with strategic management. They are industrial organization (I/O) economics, the resource-based view, and the stakeholder approach. These three perspectives serve as a foundation for much of what is found in this book.

The I/O Model of Above-Average Returns

The strategic management process is dynamic, as ever-changing markets and competitive structures must be coordinated with a firm's continuously evolving strategic inputs.[90] From the 1960s through the 1980s, the external environment was thought to be the primary determinant of strategies that firms selected to be successful.[91] Consistent with this deterministic view, the (I/O) model of above-average returns explains the dominant influence of the external environment on a firm's strategic actions. The model specifies that the industry in which a firm chooses to compete has a stronger influence on the firm's performance than do the choices managers make inside their organizations.[92] The firm's performance is believed to be determined primarily by a range of industry properties, including economies of scale, barriers to market entry, product differentiation, and the degree of concentration of firms in the industry.[93] We examine these industry characteristics in Chapter 3 more fully.

The pharmaceuticals industry is an excellent example of how industry characteristics can influence firm performance. The pharmaceuticals industry has features that make it hard for new companies to enter, including patents, economies of scale, the length of time it takes to bring a drug to market, the cost of the research and development process, and well-developed and sometimes even exclusive relationships with customers and suppliers. Many patients who use a drug absolutely need it to be healthy, so if the drug is new and still protected by a patent, the company has a captive customer and can charge a high price for the drug.[94] As a result of these factors, the big pharmaceuticals companies tend to enjoy returns that are superior to firms in other industries.[95]

Grounded in economics, the I/O model has four underlying assumptions. First, the external environment is assumed to impose pressures and constraints that determine the strategies that result in above-average returns. Second, most firms competing within a particular industry or industry segment are assumed to control similar strategically relevant resources and to pursue similar strategies in light of those resources. Third, resources used to implement strategies are assumed to be highly mobile across firms. Because of resource mobility, any resource differences that might develop between firms will be short lived. Fourth, organizational decision makers are assumed to be rational and committed to acting in the firm's best interests, as shown by their profit-maximizing behaviors.[96] The I/O model challenges firms to locate the most attractive industry in which to compete.[97] Because most firms are assumed to have similar strategically relevant resources that are mobile across companies, competitiveness generally can be increased only when firms find the industry with the highest profit potential and learn how to use their resources to implement the strategy required by the industry's structural characteristics.[98]

In the 1980s, the work of Michael Porter captured a lot of attention from strategic management scholars and practitioners.[99] Porter's work reinforced the importance of the economic theory upon which much of the field of strategic management was already based.[100] The early stage of development of strategic management is reflected in one of his early books, *Competitive Strategy:* "Competitive strategy is an area of primary concern to managers, depending on a subtle understanding of industries and competitors. Yet the strategy field has offered few analytical techniques for gaining this understanding, and those that have emerged lack breadth and comprehensiveness."[101]

Porter's books and articles helped to fill the theoretical void. He provided a description of the forces that determine the nature and level of competition in an industry, as well as suggestions for how to use this information to develop competitive advantage. The five forces model (explained in Chapter 3) explains that an industry's profitability (i.e., its rate of return on invested capital relative to its cost of capital) is a function of interactions among suppliers, buyers, competitive rivalry among firms currently in the industry, product substitutes, and potential entrants to the industry.[102] The model suggests that firms typically can earn above-average returns by manufacturing standardized products or producing standardized services

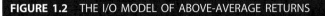

FIGURE 1.2 THE I/O MODEL OF ABOVE-AVERAGE RETURNS

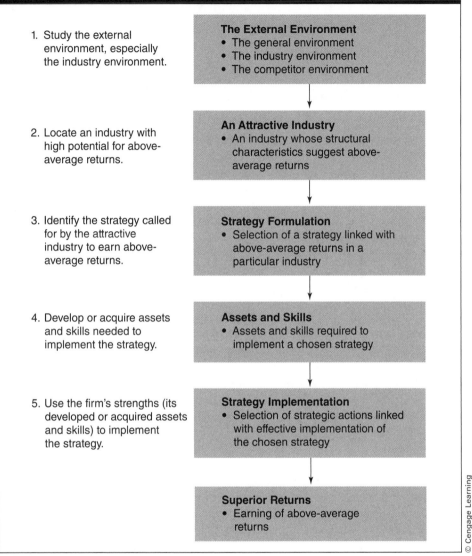

at costs below those of competitors (a cost-leadership strategy) or by manufacturing differentiated products for which customers are willing to pay a premium price (a differentiation strategy, described in depth in Chapter 5).

As shown in Figure 1.2, the I/O model proposes that above-average returns are earned when firms implement the strategy dictated by the characteristics of the general, industry, and competitor environments. Companies that develop or acquire the internal skills needed to implement strategies required by the external environment are likely to succeed, while those that do not are likely to fail. Hence, this model suggests that external characteristics rather than the firm's unique internal resources and capabilities primarily determine financial returns.

Research findings support the I/O model in the sense that they demonstrate that much of a firm's profitability is determined by the industry or industries in which it chooses to operate. However, they do not support the idea that industry characteristics are the *primary* determinant of firm profitability. Individual firm characteristics such as the strategies and the resources they possess explain more of the variance than industry structure.[103] Successful competition mandates that a firm build a unique set of resources and capabilities within the industry or industries in which the firm competes.

The Resource-Based Model of Above-Average Returns

In a general sense, the central question of strategic management is why some firms outperform other firms. Before the I/O model and other economic approaches became the favored answers to this question, as noted above, much of the early effort focused on firm competencies.[104] Distinctive competencies are firm attributes that allow it to pursue a strategy better than other firms.[105] One of the first competencies identified as a source of persistent performance was general management capability.[106] Because of their influence on the decisions of the firm, general managers tend to have a large impact on firm performance.[107] Much of the early work was devoted to determining how to define a high-quality manager.

Around the same time, Edith Penrose published a book in which she argued that firms could be understood both as an administrative framework that links and coordinates the activities of numerous groups and individuals *and* as a collection of resources.[108] Her discussion of the administrative framework foreshadowed the importance of the stakeholder perspective that will be discussed in the next section. Her second perspective, that firms can be viewed from a resource-based perspective, has become very significant in the strategic management field.[109] It is closely linked to the distinctive competencies approach because resources serve as the foundation for the establishment of competencies.[110] Another early contribution to this literature envisioned resources as important because of their ability to facilitate implementation of a product market strategy, which ties the resource-based view to the I/O perspective.[111]

The resource-based model assumes that an individual firm's unique collection of resources and capabilities, rather than the structural characteristics of the industry in which it competes, is the primary influence on the selection and use of its strategy or strategies.[112] Capabilities evolve and must be managed dynamically in pursuit of value creation.[113] The model also assumes that across time, firms acquire different resources and develop unique capabilities. Therefore, not all firms competing within a particular industry possess the same resources and capabilities.[114] Additionally, *the model assumes that resources may not be easily transferable across firms* and that the differences in resources are the basis of competitive advantage.[115]

Resources—such as capital equipment, the skills of individual employees, patents, finances, and talented managers—are inputs into a firm's production process. In general, a firm's resources fall into three categories: physical, human, and organizational capital. Described fully in Chapter 4, resources may be either tangible or intangible. Individual resources alone may not yield a competitive advantage. Competitive advantages tend to be formed through the combination and integration of sets of resources.[116] A **capability** comes from resources that allow a firm to perform a task or an activity in an integrative manner. For example, Discovery Communications has used its capability in education to help it develop programming not only for elementary and secondary schools in the United States, but also educationally oriented television programming in 38 languages that is broadcast in Europe, the Asia-Pacific region, Latin America, the Middle East, and Africa.[117] Capabilities evolve over time and must be managed dynamically in pursuit of higher firm performance.[118] Through the firm's continued use, capabilities become stronger and more difficult for competitors to understand and imitate.

Figure 1.3 shows the resource-based model of superior returns. Instead of focusing on the accumulation of resources necessary to successfully use the strategy

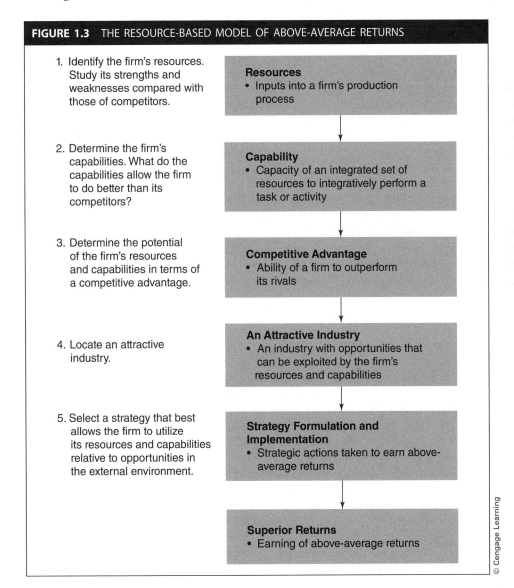

FIGURE 1.3   THE RESOURCE-BASED MODEL OF ABOVE-AVERAGE RETURNS

1. Identify the firm's resources. Study its strengths and weaknesses compared with those of competitors.

Resources
- Inputs into a firm's production process

2. Determine the firm's capabilities. What do the capabilities allow the firm to do better than its competitors?

Capability
- Capacity of an integrated set of resources to integratively perform a task or activity

3. Determine the potential of the firm's resources and capabilities in terms of a competitive advantage.

Competitive Advantage
- Ability of a firm to outperform its rivals

4. Locate an attractive industry.

An Attractive Industry
- An industry with opportunities that can be exploited by the firm's resources and capabilities

5. Select a strategy that best allows the firm to utilize its resources and capabilities relative to opportunities in the external environment.

Strategy Formulation and Implementation
- Strategic actions taken to earn above-average returns

Superior Returns
- Earning of above-average returns

© Cengage Learning

dictated by conditions and constraints in the external environment (I/O model), the resource-based view suggests that a firm's unique resources and capabilities provide the basis for a strategy. The strategy chosen should allow the firm to effectively use its competitive advantages to exploit opportunities in its external environment.

Not all of a firm's resources and capabilities have the potential to be a source of competitive advantage. This potential is realized when resources and capabilities are valuable, rare, costly to imitate, and nonsubstitutable.[119] Resources are *valuable* when they allow a firm to take advantage of opportunities or neutralize threats in its external environment. They are *rare* when possessed by few, if any, current and potential competitors. Resources are *costly to imitate* when other firms either cannot obtain them or are at a cost disadvantage in obtaining them compared with the firm that already possesses them. And, they are *nonsubstitutable* when they have no structural equivalents. In other words, there are no other products or services that can be used to fill the same need.

When these four criteria are met, resources and capabilities become core competencies. **Core competencies** are resources and capabilities that serve as a source of competitive advantage for a firm over its rivals.[120] Often related to a firm's skills in terms of organizational functions (e.g., Walmart's distribution skills are superior to those of its competitors), core competencies, when developed, nurtured, and applied throughout a firm, contribute to the earning of above-average returns.[121] For example, one set of important competencies is product related, such as a firm's capability to develop innovative new products and to reengineer existing products to satisfy changing consumer tastes.[122] Managerial competencies are also important.[123] Such competencies may include the capability to effectively organize and govern complex and diverse operations and the capability to create and communicate a strategic vision.[124]

In an interview, Daniel Wolterman, recently named one of the 100 Most Powerful People in Healthcare by *Modern Healthcare* magazine, explained his approach to managing the Houston-based Memorial Hermann Healthcare System: "I love complexity, so this job is a lot of fun. I follow a relatively simple approach to management. First, I surround myself with carefully selected, talented leaders and establish a culture that supports the organization's mission and my personal philosophies. Second, we undergo a series of processes to determine a shared vision for the organization. Third, we develop strategies to achieve our vision."[125] Wolterman has made huge investments in training to develop superior human resources and has also invested heavily in information technology with the objective of building core competencies in quality and patient safety. These efforts have paid off, as Memorial Hermann has received national awards in both areas.[126]

Firms must also continuously develop their competencies to keep them up to date.[127] This development requires a systematic program for updating old skills and introducing new ones. Such programs are especially important in rapidly changing environments, such as those that exist in high-technology industries.[128] As noted previously, research shows that both the industry environment and a firm's internal resources affect a firm's performance over time.[129] While the I/O model focuses on external forces and a firm's relationship relative to external stakeholders such as customers, suppliers, and competitors, the resource-based model emphasizes internal strengths and weaknesses, many of which reside in internal stakeholders such as employees and managers. A third model, the stakeholder perspective, provides a framework for understanding how firms can simultaneously manage relationships with internal and external stakeholders to create and sustain competitive advantage. It is well suited to the morally turbulent times in which we live because it is based on a moral as well as an economic foundation.

The Stakeholder Model of Responsible Firm Behavior and Firm Performance

In 1984, Edward Freeman advanced a process for strategic management that addressed many of the concerns that scholars had identified as important at the time. Called the stakeholder approach, it embraced external analysis as a way to help firms deal with an increasingly turbulent environment. According to Freeman, "The business environment of the 1980s and beyond is complex, to say the least. If the corporation is to successfully meet the challenges posed by this environment, it must begin to adapt integrative strategic management processes which focus the attention of management externally as a matter of routine."[130]

From a stakeholder perspective, the firm can be envisioned as a nexus of formal and social contracts with its stakeholders.[131] **Stakeholders** are the individuals and groups who can affect, and are affected by, the strategic outcomes a firm achieves and who have enforceable claims on a firm's performance.[132] Claims on a firm's performance are enforced through the stakeholders' ability to withhold participation essential to the organization's survival, competitiveness, and profitability.[133] As illustrated in Figure 1.4, stakeholders of primary interest to the firm can be separated into at least three groups: capital market stakeholders (shareholders and the major suppliers of a firm's capital), product market stakeholders (the firm's primary customers, suppliers, host communities, and unions representing the workforce), and organizational stakeholders (all of a firm's employees, including both non-managerial and managerial personnel). Secondary stakeholders, such as activists, government, or non-governmental organizations, should not be ignored, but typically should not be given significant attention during the strategic planning process.[134]

Stakeholder theory suggests that firms that take particularly good care of their primary stakeholders will function more effectively and thus create more value.[135] The additional value the firm creates can be reinvested in the firm and distributed back to the stakeholders who helped to create it.[136] For example, a firm might distribute additional value to customers by increasing the quality, safety, or service of its products while keeping prices reasonable. Or a firm could distribute value back to employees in the form of increased wages, benefits, profit sharing, or in-house programs such as recreational facilities or day care. Similarly, a firm could allocate more value to shareholders in the form of higher dividends. Research suggests that stakeholders will reciprocate as a result of this type of behavior with higher levels of motivation and loyalty.[137] They are also more likely to share valuable information with the firm that can lead to innovation.[138] The principle of fairness suggests that more value should be distributed to the stakeholders most responsible for creating it.[139]

Beyond simply allocating resources fairly, stakeholder theory also suggests that firms should consider the needs of their primary stakeholders when making

FIGURE 1.4 THE THREE STAKEHOLDER GROUPS

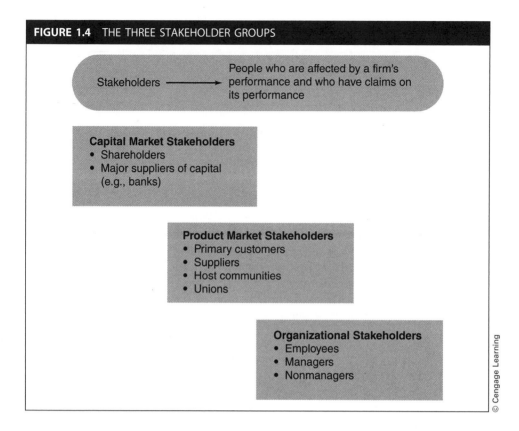

Stakeholders ⟶ People who are affected by a firm's performance and who have claims on its performance

Capital Market Stakeholders
- Shareholders
- Major suppliers of capital (e.g., banks)

Product Market Stakeholders
- Primary customers
- Suppliers
- Host communities
- Unions

Organizational Stakeholders
- Employees
- Managers
- Nonmanagers

© Cengage Learning

decisions and that they should treat them with respect and integrity.[140] Consequently, this approach addresses a critical problem that management is facing today, manifested by the "Occupy Wall Street" movement in the U.S. and similar protests elsewhere early in this decade—a general lack of trust of big businesses and their managers.[141] Corporate scandals have reduced trust among stakeholders and in society in general and have simultaneously led to increased government legislation and regulation such as the Dodd-Frank Wall Street Reform and Consumer Protection Act in the United States.[142] Societies throughout the world are demanding better ethical performance, and the stakeholder perspective's moral component may provide at least part of the answer.[143] Although the stakeholder perspective is more about effective management than about social responsibility, firms that practice stakeholder management also tend to score high on corporate social responsibility (CSR) because their primary stakeholders care about things like the natural environment, diversity, fair labor practices, and other societal interests.[144]

Whole Foods Market is a good example of a company that genuinely seems to care about (and for) its stakeholders. For many years, a generous stock-purchase program, health benefits for part-time employees, town-hall type employee participation in the selection of regional presidents, and perks such as massage therapy and language classes, have placed Whole Foods on the list of *Fortune's* Best Companies to Work For.[145] Management listens to employees and frequently uses their suggestions. Customers are delighted by a large variety of high-quality, healthy products, and excellent customer service at prices that are higher than local supermarkets but typically lower than smaller health food stores. In an effort to alleviate poverty in the countries from which they source products, the Whole Planet Foundation provides microcredit to create or expand home-based businesses. A part of Whole Foods' stakeholder philosophy states: "Our goal is to balance the needs and desires of our customers, Team Members, shareholders, suppliers, communities and the environment while creating value for all."[146]

There are additional costs associated with treating stakeholders in the manner suggested by stakeholder theory, which means that *managers should exercise prudence when determining how much time, attention, and other resources should be allocated to any particular stakeholder.*[147] Allocating too much value to stakeholders amounts to "giving away the store." Nevertheless, in spite of the additional costs, research supports the idea that firms that practice stakeholder management principles tend to outperform those that do not.[148] This research implies that stakeholder relationships can be managed in such a way as to create competitive advantage (see Figure 1.5). Competitive advantage may come from a variety of sources.[149] As mentioned previously, a firm that has excellent stakeholder relationships based on trust and mutual satisfaction of goals is more likely to obtain knowledge from them that can be used to make better strategic decisions.[150] **Strategic intelligence,** the information firms collect from their network of stakeholders, can be used to help a firm deal with diverse competitive situations and can also stimulate innovation.[151]

In addition to the knowledge-based advantages of a stakeholder-based approach, firms with trustworthy reputations draw customers, suppliers, and business partners to them. This can lead to firm growth through the gain of superior resources and increased business opportunities.[152] In addition, the transaction costs associated with making and enforcing agreements are reduced because there is less need for elaborate contractual safeguards and contingencies.[153] Of course, excellent stakeholder relationships also can enhance implementation of strategies, because people are more committed to a course of action when they believe they have had some influence on the decision to pursue it, even if it is not exactly what they wanted the firm to do.[154] In addition, responsible behavior can lead to intangible assets that buffer and protect a firm from negative actions such as adverse regulation, legal suits and penalties, consumer retaliation, strikes, walkouts, and bad press.[155] As a result, a stakeholder management approach can reduce firm risk.[156]

In a comprehensive sense, a firm can be viewed as a bundle of market activities, a bundle of resources, or a network of relationships.[157] The three perspectives we have examined in this section have reflected each of these different approaches. Market activities are understood through the application of the I/O model. The development and effective use of a firm's resources, capabilities, and competencies are understood through the application of the resource-based model. Effective management of relationships is reflected by the stakeholder model. The most successful organizations learn how to appropriately integrate the information and knowledge gained from each of these perspectives. In turn, appropriate integration of the outcomes that result in using each model is the foundation for determining the firm's strategic direction and for selecting and implementing its strategies. The next

FIGURE 1.5 THE STAKEHOLDER MODEL OF RESPONSIBLE FIRM BEHAVIOR AND FIRM PERFORMANCE

1. Examine the firm's environment, especially groups and individuals with influence on firm outcomes.

Environmental Analysis
- The general environment
- The industry environment
- The internal environment

2. Determine which external stakeholders should be given primary consideration during strategic planning.

Key Stakeholders
- Powerful or otherwise important to the firm

3. Collect detailed information about primary stakeholders inside and outside the firm.

Strategic Intelligence
- Information about the needs and desires of stakeholders
- Information about opportunities to create value

4. Use information collected in combination with information about internal stakeholders to create strategies and implementation plans.

Balanced Strategies
- Value creating strategies that consider the interests of a broad group of stakeholders

5. Manage relationships with internal and external stakeholders to optimize value creation.

Excellent Stakeholder Relationships
- Trust and cooperation
- Knowledge sharing
- Fewer negative responses

Performance Outcomes
- More value created
- High returns
- Responsible firm behavior

© Cengage Learning

section will examine strategic thinking and outline the strategic management process that forms the foundation for this book.

STRATEGIC THINKING AND THE STRATEGIC MANAGEMENT PROCESS

Strategic management incorporates both a process and a way of thinking about the firm and its environment. In this book, the term "strategic thinking" is associated with the more creative aspects of strategic management that result in new strategies and organizational changes.[158] Strategic thinking is discussed first, followed by a description of the strategic management process.

Strategic Thinking

One of the most essential characteristics of firms that have sustained high levels of performance is their ability to innovate and make timely changes to their structures, systems, technologies, and products and services so that they continue to stay ahead of their competitors.[159] For example, during the difficult first decade of the new century, CEO Sam Palmisano led his management team in revitalizing IBM through a focus on international growth and innovation in fast growing business areas such as supercomputing and analytics as well as high margin businesses like systems integration and services.[160] Strategic managers in these types of firms have developed a **strategic thinking competency**, which is defined as "the knowledge skills, and abilities needed to detect market opportunities, formulate a vision to capitalize on these opportunities, and engineer feasible strategies to realize organizational and stakeholder value."[161]

Strategic thinking is intent focused, comprehensive, and opportunistic; considers multiple time horizons; and is hypothesis driven.[162] Strategic intent is the term used to describe a dream that challenges and energizes a company, a vision used by managers to elicit the help of others in creating a firm's competitive advantage.[163] It exists when employees at all levels of a firm are committed to the pursuit of a specific (and significant) goal. Strategic thinking is also comprehensive in that it envisions the firm as a system that is part of a larger system, with a recognition of the interdependencies of the firm's parts and how they interface with parts of their external environment.[164] Opportunism, as it relates to strategic thinking, means that a firm learns to take advantage of unanticipated opportunities as they arise.[165]

When people consider strategic thinking, they frequently think about the long term, and strategic intent is clearly a long-term proposition. However, strategic thinking also involves learning from the past and considering what the firm should do now to exploit its current competitive advantages.[166] In short, it addresses past, present, and future. Finally, strategic thinking is hypothesis testing in that after creative ideas are generated and carefully evaluated, they are implemented. In other words, strategic thinking means that managers are willing to take risks.[167]

Firms can encourage strategic thinking in a number of ways. First, top managers need to be champions of change rather than protectors of the status quo.[168] Innovations frequently bubble up from the operating sectors of an organization rather than from an "innovation" department.[169] Consequently, the second way a firm can encourage strategic thinking is to have systems and processes in place that capture new ideas when they occur. Firms may also train their managers and employees in methods and processes associated with strategic thinking.[170] Sometimes they use retreats or consultant interventions and training to accomplish this purpose. In addition, it is important for strategic leaders to foster a climate that allows or even encourages risk taking.[171] All of these ideas are associated with strategic leadership and fostering an innovative culture, which is the topic of Chapter 2. Firms must also provide enough flexibility in their strategic management process to allow incorporation of new ideas with high potential as they are introduced.[172] Chapter 12 on strategic entrepreneurship discusses ways of capturing new ideas.

The Strategic Management Process

The strategic management process is a logical approach for helping a firm effectively respond to the challenges of the 21st-century competitive landscape. Figure 1.6, which outlines the process, also provides a road map for the topics examined in this book. Strategic thinking, as discussed, is the decision-making medium through which the firm uses the strategic management process to shape its present and influence its future while pursuing value creation and high financial returns.[173]

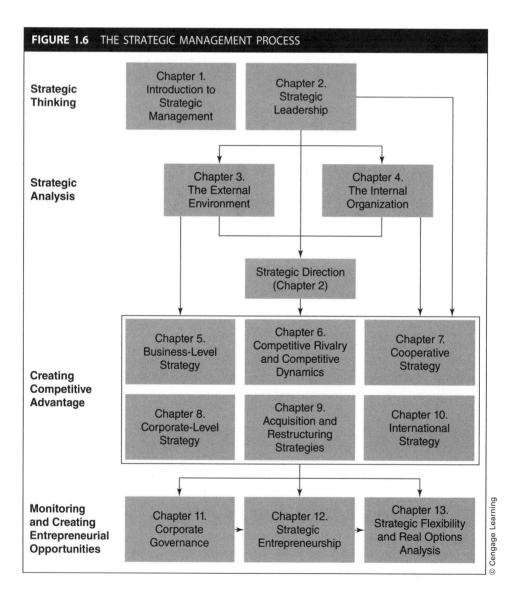

FIGURE 1.6 THE STRATEGIC MANAGEMENT PROCESS

© Cengage Learning

As strategic thinkers, strategic leaders are responsible for establishing and using an effective strategic management process in their firms.[174] Because strategic leaders are the engines driving the development and subsequent use of the strategic management process and because strategic direction is so closely associated with strategic leadership, Chapter 2 examines strategic leadership. Strategic direction is reflected in the firm's vision, mission, purpose, and long-term goals. The discussions in the first two chapters provide the foundation for a detailed treatment of the strategic management process—a treatment that begins with Part 2 of the book.

The two key sources of information-based inputs to the strategic management process are discussed in Part 2. As shown in Figure 1.6, these inputs are derived from an analysis of the firm's external environment (Chapter 3) and its internal organization (Chapter 4). These analyses identify the external environment's opportunities and threats and the resources, capabilities, and core competencies that collectively form or constitute the firm's internal organization. With knowledge about opportunities and threats and competitive advantages, the firm is prepared to develop its strategic direction, as well as the specific strategies it will use to create competitive advantage (see Figure 1.6).

The different strategies firms use to create competitive advantage are discussed in Part 3. First, we examine business-level strategies (Chapter 5). The central focus of business-level strategy is determining the competitive advantages the firm will use to effectively compete in specific product markets. A diversified firm competing in multiple product markets and businesses has a business-level strategy for each distinct product market area. A company competing in a single product market has only one business-level strategy. In all instances, a business-level strategy describes a firm's actions that are designed to exploit its competitive advantage over rivals. In the course of competition, competitors respond to each other's actions and reactions. Indeed, competitors respond to and try to anticipate each other's actions. Thus, the dynamics of competition are an important input when a firm selects and uses strategies.[175] Competitive rivalry and competitive dynamics are discussed in Chapter 6. Cooperative strategies, examined in Chapter 7, are also important to competitive dynamics. The trend toward cooperation reflects the increasing importance of forming partnerships to both share and develop competitive resources.[176]

Used in diversified organizations, corporate-level strategy (Chapter 8) is concerned with determining the businesses in which the company intends to compete as well as how resources are to be allocated among those businesses. Merger and acquisition strategies (Chapter 9) are the primary means diversified firms use to create corporate-level competitive advantages. International strategies (Chapter 10) also are used as a source of value creation and above-average returns. The various organizational structures required to support the use of the strategies examined in Chapters 5 through 10 are included in the respective chapters. Thus, individual organizational structures that should be used to effectively support the use of each unique business-level strategy are presented in Chapter 5. Chapters 6 through 10 present the same type of analysis of strategy-structure matches that firms use to create competitive advantage when using cooperative, corporate-level, merger and acquisition, and international strategies.

As with all organizational actions, strategies must be monitored to assess their success. Corporate governance (Chapter 11) is concerned with making certain that effective and appropriate strategic decisions and actions are occurring in the firm. Governance reflects the firm's values and is used to ensure that the company's actions are aligned with stakeholders' (especially stockholders') interests. With stakeholders voicing demands for improved corporate governance, organizations are challenged to satisfy stakeholders' interests while trying to accomplish the strategic outcomes of value creation and above-average returns.[177]

Although very important, governance of the firm may result in cautious, even risk-avoiding strategic decisions. Because strict governance may constrain efforts to find entrepreneurial opportunities, a natural tension exists between the firm's need for order (as represented by governance) and some chaos (which commonly results from pursuing entrepreneurial opportunities). Chapter 12 examines the need for the firm to continuously seek entrepreneurial opportunities—those that the firm can pursue in its efforts to be successful while competing in its chosen markets. Chapter 13 contains a tool that is useful in evaluating new ventures as well as maintaining strategic flexibility. Real options analysis examines the real choices firms are given subsequent to making the decision to pursue a particular investment.[178] Firms have the right but not the obligation to pursue the option, which increases strategic flexibility in the future while reducing perceived risks.[179]

Primarily because they are related to how a firm interacts with its stakeholders, almost all strategic decisions have ethical dimensions.[180] Especially in the turbulent and often ambiguous 21st-century competitive landscape, those making strategic decisions are challenged to recognize how their decisions affect capital market, product market, and organizational stakeholders. Consequently, each of the chapters provides "Ethics Questions" to stimulate discussion of ethical issues. Most of the questions have no clear answers, but they should facilitate examination of the ethical dimensions of strategic topics.

SUMMARY

▶ Strategic management has emerged in response to the need for mental models and planning tools that help executives guide their firms in this challenging global business environment. It is concerned primarily with the actions organizations take to achieve competitive advantage and create value for the organization and its stakeholders.

▶ The competitive environment is characterized by globalization, economic volatility, and rapid changes in technology. Globalization can be defined as the increasing economic interdependence among countries as reflected in the flow of goods and services, financial capital, and knowledge across country borders. Economic volatility is a result of natural business cycles as well as disasters and crises. The three categories of technological trends that are altering the nature of competition are increases in the rate of technological change and diffusion, changes in information technology, and increases in knowledge intensity.

▶ The (I/O) model of above-average returns explains the dominant influence of the external environment on a firm's strategic actions. The model specifies that the industry in which a firm chooses to compete has a stronger influence on the firm's performance than do the choices managers make inside their organizations.

- The resource-based model assumes that an individual firm's unique collection of resources and capabilities is the primary influence on the selection and use of its strategy or strategies. Resources are inputs into a firm's production process, such as capital equipment, the skills of individual employees, patents, finances, and talented managers. Resources and capabilities realize their competitive potential when they are valuable, rare, costly to imitate, and nonsubstitutable.
- From a stakeholder perspective, the firm can be envisioned as a nexus of formal and social contracts with its stakeholders. Stakeholders are the individuals and groups who can affect, and are affected by, the strategic outcomes a firm achieves and who have enforceable claims on a firm's performance. The stakeholder perspective posits that stakeholder relationships can be managed in such a way as to create competitive advantage.
- Strategic thinking is associated with the more creative aspects of strategic management. It is intent focused, comprehensive, and opportunistic; considers multiple time horizons; and is hypothesis driven. Strategic thinking is the decision-making medium through which the firm uses the strategic management process to shape its present and influence its future while pursuing value creation and high financial returns.
- The strategic management process is the full set of commitments, decisions, and actions required for a firm to create value and earn returns that are higher than those of competitors. In its simplest form, it involves analyzing the firm and its environment and then using the information to formulate and implement strategies that lead to competitive advantage. Thus, the strategic management process is used to match the conditions of an ever-changing market and competitive structure with a firm's continuously evolving resources, capabilities, and competencies.

ETHICS QUESTIONS

1. How should ethical considerations be included in analyses of the firm's external environment and its internal organization?
2. To what extent does a firm have an ethical responsibility to provide information to its stakeholders that they will not find agreeable? How does the amount and type of information shared vary from one stakeholder to another (i.e., employees, shareholders, financial intermediaries, customers, and communities in which the firm operates)?
3. Do firms face ethical challenges, perhaps even ethical dilemmas, when trying to satisfy both the short-term and long-term expectations of capital market stakeholders?
4. What types of ethical issues and challenges do firms encounter when competing internationally?
5. What ethical responsibilities does the firm have when it earns above-average returns? Who should make decisions regarding this issue, and why?
6. What should top-level managers do to ensure that a firm's strategic management process leads to outcomes that are consistent with the firm's values?

NOTES

[1] M. A. Hitt, K. T. Haynes, & R. Serpa, 2010, Strategic leadership for the 21st century, *Business Horizons*, 53: 437–444.

[2] D. Rodlophe & E. Vaara, 2009, Causation, counterfactuals, and competitive advantage, *Strategic Management Journal*, 30: 1245–1264; D. G. Sirmon, M. A. Hitt, & R. D. Ireland, 2007, Managing firm resources in dynamic environments to create value: Looking inside the black box, *Academy of Management Review*, 32: 273–292.

[3] R. A. D'Aveni, 2010, The age of temporary advantage, *Strategic Management Journal*, 31: 1371–1385; D. Lei & J. W. Slocum, 2005, Strategic and organizational requirements for competitive advantage. *Academy of Management Executive*, 19(1): 31–45; T. J. Douglas & J. A. Ryman, 2003, Understanding competitive advantage in the general hospital industry: Evaluating strategic competencies, *Strategic Management Journal*, 24: 333–347.

[4] A. D. Henderson, M. E. Raynor & M. Ahmed, 2012, How long must a firm be great to rule out chance? Benchmarking sustained superior performance without being fooled by randomness, *Strategic Management Journal*, in press; K. Shimizu & M. A. Hitt, 2004, Strategic flexibility: Organizational preparedness to reverse ineffective strategic decisions, *Academy of Management Executive*, 18(4): 44–59; D. J. Teece, G. Pisano, & A. Shuen, 1997, Dynamic capabilities and strategic management, *Strategic Management Journal*, 18: 509–533.

[5] D. G. Sirmon, M. A. Hitt, J.-L. Arregle, & J. T. Campbell, 2010, The dynamic interplay of capability strengths and weaknesses: Investigating the bases of temporary competitive advantage, *Strategic Management Journal*, 31: 1386–1409; A. M. McGahan & M. E. Porter, 2003, The emergence and sustainability of abnormal profits, *Strategic Organization*, 1: 79–108.

[6] R. P. Rumelt, D. E. Schendel, & D. J. Teece (eds.), 1994, *Fundamental Issues in Strategy*, Boston, MA: Harvard Business School Press, 527–530.

[7] M. E. Porter, 2008, The five competitive forces that shape strategy, *Harvard Business Review*, January: 79–92; M. Song, R. J. Calantone, & C. Anthony, 2002, Competitive forces and strategic choice decisions: An experimental investigation in the United States and Japan, *Strategic Management Journal*, 23: 969–978; A. Nair & S. Kotha, 2001, Does group membership matter? Evidence from the Japanese steel industry, *Strategic Management Journal*, 22: 221–235; A. M. McGahan & M. E. Porter, 1997, How much does industry matter, really? *Strategic Management Journal*, 18 (summer special issue): 15–30.

[8] J. Kraaijenbrink, J.-C. Spender, & A. J. Groen, 2010, The resource-based view: A review and assessment of its critiques, *Journal of Management*, 36: 349–372; D. G. Sirmon & M. A. Hitt, 2003, Managing resources: Linking unique resources, management and wealth creation in family firms, *Entrepreneurship Theory and Practice*, 27(4): 339–358; J. B. Barney, 2002, Strategic management: From informed conversation to academic discipline, *Academy of Management Executive*, 16(2): 53–57; J. B. Barney, 2001, Is the resource based "view" a useful perspective for strategic management research? Yes, *Academy of Management Review*, 26: 41–56.

[9] R. A. Phillips & R. E. Freeman (eds.), 2010, *Stakeholders*, Cheltenham, UK: Edward Elgar Publishing; J. P. Walsh, 2005, Taking stock of stakeholder management, *Academy of Management Review*, 30: 426–438; R. E. Freeman & J. McVea, 2001, A stakeholder approach to strategic management, in M. A. Hitt, R. E. Freeman, & J. R. Harrison (eds.), *Handbook of Strategic Management*, Oxford, UK: Blackwell Publishers, 189–207; J. E. Post, L. E. Preston, & S. Sachs, 2002, *Redefining the Corporation: Stakeholder Management and Organizational Wealth*, Stanford, CA: Stanford University Press.

[10] L. Dragoni, I.-S. Oh, P. Vankatwyk, & P. E. Tesluk, 2011, Developing executive leaders: The relative contribution of cognitive ability, personality, and the accumulation of work experience in predicting strategic thinking competency, *Personnel Psychology*, 64: 829–864; J. M. Liedtka, 2001, Strategy formulation: The roles of conversation and design, in M. A. Hitt, R. E. Freeman, & J. R. Harrison (eds.), *Handbook of Strategic Management*, Oxford, UK: Blackwell Publishers, 70–94.

[11] M. C. Mankins & R. Steele, 2005, Turning great strategy into great performance, *Harvard Business Review*, 83(7): 64–72; M. J. Epstein & R. A. Westbrook, 2001, Linking actions to profits in strategic decision making, *Sloan Management Review*, 42(3): 39–49.

[12] J. Palank, M. Spector, & J. Jargon, 2012, Twinkies maker Hostess files for Chapter 11 protection, *Wall Street Journal Online*, January 13; D. Fitzgerald & M. Jarzemsky, 2012, Kodak sues Fujifilm over patents. *Wall Street Journal Online*, January 13; C. Zander, A. Molin, V. Fuhrmans, & S. Terlep, 2011, Saab automobile, 1950–2011, *Wall Street Journal*, December 20: B1–B2; J. Milliot, 2011, Borders bankruptcy to ripple through industry, *Publishers Weekly*, February 21: 6.

[13] S. Mills, 2011, Airline alliance survey, *Airline Business*, September: 32–47.

[14] C. R. Bateman & A. D. Westphal, 2011, Investigating the presence of transfer pricing and its impact in U.S. airline mergers, *Academy of Marketing Studies Journal*, 15: 45–60; J. Smisek, 2011, The biggest airline merger in history yields big changes, *Forbes*, October 24: 103.

[15] R. K. Jayanti & S. V. Jayanti, 2011, Effects of airline bankruptcies: An event study, *Journal of Services Marketing*, 25: 399–409.

[16] D. Brady, 2011, American Airlines' last-mover disadvantage, *Bloomberg Business Week*, December 5: 25–26.

[17] M. T. Dacin, 2011, Assembling the global enterprise, *Global Strategy Journal*, 1: 50–53; R. Belderbos & L. Sleuwaegen, 2005, Competitive drivers and international plant configuration strategies: A product-level test, *Strategic Management Journal*, 26: 577–593.

[18] C. Costea, A. Varga, F. Cinatti, & U. Kishinev, 2011, How transnational companies are affected by globalization, *International Journal of Management Cases*, 13: 286–290; V. Govindarajan & A. K. Gupta, 2001, *The Quest for Global Dominance*, San Francisco, CA: Jossey-Bass.

[19] T. M. Devinney, 2011, Social responsibility, global strategy, and the multinational enterprise: Global monitory democracy and the meaning of place and

space, *Global Strategy Journal*, 1: 329–344; S. J. Chang & S. Park, 2005, Types of firms generating network externalities and MNCs' co-location decisions. *Strategic Management Journal*, 26: 595–615; S. C. Voelpel, M. Dous, & T. H. Davenport, 2005, Five steps to creating global knowledge-sharing systems: Siemens' ShareNet, *Academy of Management Executive*, 19(2): 9–23.

20 M. P. Koza, S. Tallman, & A. Altaay, 2011, The strategic assembly of global firms: A microstructural analysis of local learning and global adaptation, *Global Strategy Journal*, 1: 27–46; T. Khanna, K. G. Palepu, & J. Sinha, 2005, Strategies that fit emerging markets, *Harvard Business Review*, 83(6): 63–76; R. J. Trent & R. M. Monczka, 2002, Pursuing competitive advantage through integrated global sourcing, *Academy of Management Executive*, 16(2): 66–80.

21 C.-H. Lee, N. Venkatraman, H. Tanriverdi, & B. Iyer, 2010, Complementarity-based hypercompetition in the software industry: Theory and empirical test, 1990–2002, *Strategic Management Journal*, 31: 1431–1456.

22 F. D. Hermelo & R. Vassolo, 2010, Institutional development and hypercompetition in emerging economies, *Strategic Management Journal*, 31: 1457–1473; G. McNamara, P. M. Vaaler, & C. Devers, 2003, Same as it ever was: The search for evidence of increasing hypercompetition, *Strategic Management Journal*, 24: 261–278; R. A. D'Aveni, 1995, Coping with hypercompetition: Utilizing the new 7S's framework, *Academy of Management Executive*, 9(3): 46.

23 M.-J. Chen, H.-C. Lin, & J. G. Michel, 2010, Navigating in a hypercompetitive environment: The roles of action aggressiveness and TMT integration, *Strategic Management Journal*, 31: 1410–1430; J. Ferrier, 2001, Navigating the competitive landscape: The drivers and consequences of competitive aggressiveness, *Academy of Management Journal*, 44: 858–877.

24 A. Ariño, 2011, Building the global enterprise: Strategic assembly, *Global Strategy Journal*, 1: 47–49.

25 Introduction to Unilever, 2012, http://www.unilever.com/aboutus/introductiontounilever/, accessed January 16, 2012.

26 Our footprint, *Unilever Annual Report 2011*, 8.

27 S. Nadkarni, P. Herrmann, & P. D. Perez, 2011, Domestic mindsets and early international performance: The moderating effect of global industry conditions, *Strategic Management Journal*, 32: 510–531.

28 N. Rapp & K. Benner, 2011, Anatomy of a soft economy, *Fortune*, September 5: 63; J. Srodes, 2010, The great recession of 2011–2012, *American Spectator*, 43(1): 14–21.

29 B. Dumaine, 2011, Who's most in debt? *The Economist*, August 15: 22.

30 The road to Rome, *The Economist*, 2011, July 16: 73.

31 S. Tully, 2011, Will Europe come tumbling down? *Fortune*, September 5: 65–67; Muddle, fuddle, toil and trouble, *The Economist*, 2011, March 19: 81; *The Economist*, If Greece goes ... June 25: 13.

32 D. E. Westney, 2011, Global strategy and global business environment: Changing models of the global business environment, *Global Strategy Journal*, 1: 377–381.

33 C. H. Oh & J. Oetzel, 2011, Multinationals' response to major disasters: How does subsidiary investment vary in response to the type of disaster and the quality of country governance, *Strategic Management Journal*, 32: 658–681.

34 Japanese carmakers are shaken, *The Economist*, 2011, May 21: 71.

35 K. Nozawa, 2011, Parts squeeze spurs hunt for non-Japan suppliers, *Nikkei Report*, April 5: 1.

36 C. Dawson, 2011, Quake still rattles suppliers, *Wall Street Journal*, September 29: B12.

37 Living with radiation, *The Economist*, 2011, April 9: 48.

38 L. Lamey, B. Deleersnyder, E. M. Jan-Benedict, & M. G. Dekimpe, 2012, The effect of business-cycle fluctuations on private-label share: What has marketing conduct got to do with it? *Journal of Marketing*, 1: 1–19; R. Onwumere, R. Stewart, & S. Yu, 2011, A review of business cycle theory and forecast of the current business cycle, *Journal of Business and Economics Research*, 9(2): 49–59.

39 G. W. S. Dowell, M. B. Shackell, & N. V. Stuart, 2011, Boards, CEOs, and surviving a financial crisis: Evidence from the internet shakeout, *Strategic Management Journal*, 32: 1025–1045; J. Collins & M. T. Hansen, 2011, Collins on chaos, *Fortune*, October 17: 157–170; W. P. Wan & D. W. Yiu, 2009, From crisis to opportunity: Environmental jolts, corporate acquisitions and firm performance, *Strategic Management Journal*, 30: 791–801; S.-H. Lee & M. Makhija, 2009, Flexibility in internationalization: Is it valuable during an economic crisis? *Strategic Management Journal*, 30: 537–555.

40 G. Colvin, 2011, Caterpillar is absolutely crushing it, *Fortune*, May 23: 139.

41 Ibid., 141.

42 Hitt, et al., Strategic leadership; R. A. D'Aveni, 2004, Corporate spheres of influence, *MIT Sloan Management Review*, 45(4): 38–46; Ferrier, Navigating the competitive landscape; M. A. Hitt, B. W. Keats, & S. M. DeMarie, 1998, Navigating in the new competitive landscape: Building competitive advantage and strategic flexibility in the 21st century, *Academy of Management Executive*, 12(4): 22–42; R. A. Bettis & M. A. Hitt, 1995, The new competitive landscape, *Strategic Management Journal*, 16(special summer issue): 7–19.

43 R. A. D'Aveni, 2010, The age of temporary advantage, *Strategic Management Journal*, 31: 1371–1385

44 J. Grahovac & D. J. Miller, 2009, Competitive advantage and performance: The impact of value creation and costliness of imitation, *Strategic Management Journal*, 30: 1192–1212.

45 V. Govindarajan, P. Kopalle, & E. Danneels, 2011, The effect of mainstream and emerging customer orientations on radical and disruptive innovations, *Journal of Product Innovation Management*, 54: 797–810; C. M. Christensen, M. W. Johnson, & D. K. Rigby, 2002, Foundations for growth: How to identify and build disruptive new businesses, *MIT Sloan Management Review*, 43(3): 22–31; C. M. Christensen, 1997, *The Innovator's Dilemma*, Boston, MA: Harvard Business School Press.

46 J. Schumpeter, 1934, *The Theory of Economic Development*, Cambridge, MA: Harvard University Press.

47 C. Sandstrom, 2011, High-end disruptive technologies with an inferior performance, *International Journal of Technology Management*, 56: 109–122.

48 Y. Lu & K. Ramamurthy, 2011, Understanding the link between information technology capability and organizational agility: An empirical examination, *MIS Quarterly*, 35: 931–954; G. Ferguson, S. Mathur, & B. Shah, 2005, Evolving from information to insight, *MIT Sloan Management Review*, 46(2): 51–58.

49 I. Brandic & R. Buyya, 2012, Recent advances in utility and cloud computing, *Future Generation Computer Systems*, 28(1): 36–38.

50 H. Yang, C. Phelps, & H. K. Steensma, 2010, Learning from what others have learned from you: The effects of knowledge spillovers on originating firms, *Academy of Management Journal*, 53: 371–389; A. C. Inkpen & E. W. K. Tsang, 2005, Social capital, networks, and knowledge transfer, *Academy of Management Review*, 30: 146–165; A. S. DeNisi, M. A. Hitt, & S. E. Jackson, 2003, The knowledge-based approach to sustainable competitive advantage, in S. E. Jackson, M. A. Hitt, & A. S. DeNisi (eds.), *Managing Knowledge for Sustained Competitive Advantage*, San Francisco, CA: Jossey-Bass, 3–33.

51 S. Chaudhuri, U. Dayal, & V. Naraasayya, 2011, An overview of business intelligence technology, *Communications of the ACM*, 54: 88–98; S. K. Ethiraj, P. Kale, M. S. Krishnan, & J. V. Singh, 2005, Where do capabilities come from and how do they matter? *Strategic Management Journal*, 26: 25–45; V. Anand, W. H. Glick, & C. C. Manz, 2002, Thriving on the knowledge of outsiders: Tapping organizational social capital, *Academy of Management Executive*, 16(1): 87–101; L. Rosenkopf & A. Nerkar, 2001, Beyond local search: Boundary-spanning, exploration, and impact on the optical disk industry, *Strategic Management Journal*, 22: 287–306.

52 D. F. Kuratko, R. D. Ireland, & J. S. Hornsby, 2001, Improving firm performance through entrepreneurial actions: Insights from Acordia Inc.'s corporate entrepreneurship strategy, *Academy of Management Executive*, 15(4): 60–71; T. K. Kayworth & R. D. Ireland, 1998, The use of corporate IT standards as a means of implementing the cost leadership strategy, *Journal of Information Technology Management*, IX(4): 13–42.

53 A. McAfee, 2011, What every CEO needs to know about the cloud, *Harvard Business Review*, November, 125–132.

54 J. L. Stimpert & J. A. Laux, 2011, Does size matter? Economies of scale in the banking industry, *Journal of Business & Economics Research*, 9: 47–55; J. D. Wolpert, 2002, Breaking out of the innovation box, *Harvard Business Review*, 80(8): 77–83.

55 J. L. Boyd & R. K. F. Bresser, 2008, Performance implications of delayed competitive responses: Evidence from the U.S. retail industry, *Strategic Management Journal*, 29: 1077–1096; L. Yu, 2005, Does knowledge sharing payoff? *MIT Sloan Management Review*, 46(3): 5; L. Valikangas & M. Gibbert, 2005, Boundary-setting strategies for escaping innovation traps, *MIT Sloan Management Review*, 46(3): 58–65.

56 K. Das, 2011, A quality integrated strategic level global supply chain model, *International Journal of Production Research*, 49: 5–31; J. Santos, Y. Doz, & P. Williamson, 2004, Is your innovation process global? *MIT Sloan Management Review*, 45(4): 31–37.

57 W. Scott-Jackson, S. Druck, T. Mortimer, & J. Viney, 2011, HR's 9a impact: Building strategic differentiating capabilities, *Strategic HR Review*, 10: 33–39; J. A. Robins, S. Tallman, & K. Fladmoe-Lindquist, 2002, Autonomy and dependence of international cooperative ventures: An exploration of the strategic performance of U.S. ventures in Mexico, *Strategic Management Journal*, 23: 881–901; M. Subramaniam & N. Venkatraman, 2001, Determinants of transnational new product development capability: Testing the influence of transferring and deploying tacit overseas knowledge, *Strategic Management Journal*, 22: 359–378.

58 P. Ussahawanitchakit & P. Sriboonlue, 2011, Transformational leadership, strategic flexibility, learning capability, continuous improvement, and firm performance: Evidence from Thailand, *International Journal of Business Strategy*, 11: 162–172.

59 V. Arnold, T. Benford, J. Canada, & S. G. Sutton, 2011, The role of strategic enterprise risk management and organizational flexibility in easing new regulatory compliance, *International Journal of Accounting Information Systems*, 12(3): 171–188; K. R. Harrigan, 2001, Strategic flexibility in old and new economies, in M. A. Hitt, R. E. Freeman, & J. R. Harrison (eds.), *Handbook of Strategic Management*, Oxford, UK: Blackwell Publishers, 97–123.

60 A. Parmigini & W. Mitchell, 2009, Complementarity, capabilities, and the boundaries of the firm: The impact of within-firm and interfirm expertise on the concurrent sourcing of complementary components, *Strategic Management Journal*, 30: 1065–1091; K. Uhlenbruck, K. E. Meyer, & M. A. Hitt, 2003, Organizational transformation in transition economies: Resource-based and organizational learning perspectives, *Journal of Management Studies*, 40: 257–282.

61 D. E. Schendel & C. W. Hofer, 1979, *Strategic Management: A New View of Business Policy and Planning*, Boston, MA: Little, Brown and Company.

62 R. A. Gordon & J. E. Howell, 1959, *Higher Education for Business*, New York: Columbia University Press, 206.

63 M. A. Hitt, 2005, Spotlight on strategic management, *Business Horizons*, 48: 371–377.

64 R. E. Hoskisson, M. A. Hitt, W. P. Wan, & D. Yiu, 1999, Swings of a pendulum: Theory and research in strategic management, *Journal of Management*, 25: 417–456.

65 A. D. Chandler, 1962, *Strategy and Structure: Chapters in the History of the American Industrial Enterprise*, Cambridge, MA: MIT Press, 16.

66 H. I. Ansoff, 1965, *Corporate Strategy: An Analytic Approach to Business for Growth and Expansion*, New York: McGraw-Hill.

67 E. P. Learned, C. R. Christensen, K. R. Andrews, & W. D. Guth, 1965, *Business Policy: Text and Cases*, Homewood, IL: Irwin, 17.

68 Ibid., 21.

69 J. S. Harrison, 2011, Stakeholder theory in strategic management: A retrospective, in R. A. Phillips (ed.), *Stakeholder Theory: Impact and Prospects*, Cheltenham, UK: Edward Elgar, 99–110; Hitt, Spotlight on strategic management.

70 R. Ackoff, 1974, *Redesigning the Future*, New York: Wiley; J. March & H. Simon, 1958, *Organizations*, New York: Wiley; C. I. Barnard, 1938, *Functions of the Executive*, Cambridge, MA: Harvard University Press.

71 I. C. MacMillan, 1978, *Strategy Formulation: Political Concepts*, St. Paul, MN: West Publishing Co., 66.

72 J. Pfeffer & G. R. Salancik, 1978, *The External Control of Organizations: A Resource Dependence Perspective*, New York: Harper & Row.

73 Ibid.; D. Katz & R. L. Kahn, 1978, *The Social Psychology of Organizations*, 2nd ed., New York: Wiley; J. D. Thompson, 1967, *Organizations in Action*, New York: McGraw-Hill.

74 MacMillan, *Strategy Formulation*, 110.

75 H. Mintzberg, 1978, Managerial work: Analysis from observation, *Management Science*, 18: B97–B110;

H. Mintzberg, 1971, Patterns in strategy formation, *Management Science*, 24: 934–948.

76 Mintzberg, *Managerial work*, B110.

77 C. B. Bingham & K. M. Eisenhardt, 2011, Rational heuristics: The 'simple rules' that strategists learn from process experience, *Strategic Management Journal*, 32: 1437–1464; C. Zook & J. Allen, 2011, The great repeatable business model, *Harvard Business Review*, 89(11): 106–114.

78 M. Jensen & W. Meckling, 1976, Theory of the firm: Managerial behavior, agency costs and capital structure, *Journal of Financial Economics*, 3: 305–360.

79 R. B. Adams, A. N. Licht, & L. Sagiv, 2011, Shareholders and stakeholders: How do directors decide? *Strategic Management Journal*, 32: 1331–1355; Harrison, Stakeholder theory in strategic management; J. McClellan, 2011, Stakeholders vs. shareholders, *Public Relations Strategist*, 17(1): 32–33; J. Argenti, 1997, Stakeholders: The case against, *Long Range Planning*, 30: 446–449.

80 O. E. Williamson, 1975, *Markets and Hierarchies: Analysis and Antitrust Implications*, New York: The Free Press.

81 S.-F. S. Chen, 2010, Transaction cost implication of private branding and empirical evidence, *Strategic Management Journal*, 31: 371–389; E. W. K. Tsang, 2006, Behavioral assumptions and theory development: The case of transaction cost economics, *Strategic Management Journal*, 27: 999–1011.

82 M. H. Safizadeh, J. M. Field, & L. P. Ritzman, 2008, Sourcing practices and boundaries of the firm in the financial services industry, *Strategic Management Journal*, 29: 79–91, Williamson, *Markets and Hierarchies*.

83 Schendel & Hofer, *Strategic Management*.

84 Ibid.; C. W. Hofer & D. E. Schendel, 1978, *Strategy Formulation: Analytical Concepts*, St. Paul, MN: West Publishing Co.

85 L. G. Hrebiniak & W. F. Joyce, 1985, Organizational adaptation: Strategic choice and environmental determinism, *Administrative Science Quarterly*, 30: 336–349.

86 L. J. Bourgeois III, 1984, Strategic management and determinism, *Academy of Management Review*, 9: 589.

87 L. Smirchich & C. Stubbart, 1985, Strategic management in an enacted world, *Academy of Management Review*, 10: 724–736.

88 A. Kaul, 2012, Technology and corporate scope: Firm and rival innovation as antecedents of corporate transactions, *Strategic Management Journal*, forthcoming; J. S. Harrison & C. H. St. John, 1996, Managing and partnering with external stakeholders, *Academy of Management Executive*, 10(2): 46–60.

89 J. S. Harrison & C. H. St. John, 2010, *Foundations of Strategic Management*, 5th Ed. Mason, OH: South-Western Cengage Learning.

90 E. L. Chen, R. Katila, R. McDonald, & K. M. Eisenhardt, 2010, Life in the fast lane: Origins of competitive interaction in new vs. established markets, *Strategic Management Journal*, 31: 1527–1547; R. D. Ireland & C. C. Miller, 2004, Decision-making and firm success, *Academy of Management Executive*, 18(4): 8–12.

91 N. Argyres & A. M. McGahan, 2002, An interview with Michael Porter, *Academy of Management Executive*, 16(2): 43–52; Hoskisson, Hitt, Wan, & Yiu, Swings of a pendulum.

92 M. E. Porter, 2008, The five competitive forces that shape strategy, *Harvard Business Review*, January:

79–93; E. H. Bowman & C. E. Helfat, 2001, Does corporate strategy matter? *Strategic Management Journal*, 22: 1–23.

93 H. Shi, 2012, Economies of scale in the Australian tourism industry, *Applied Economics*, 44: 4355–4367; Y. M. Bendeck & E. R. Waller, 2011, Consolidation, concentration, and valuation in the banking industry, *Journal of Business & Economics Research*, 9: 41–48; A. Seth & H. Thomas, 1994, Theories of the firm: Implications for strategy research, *Journal of Management Studies*, 31: 165–191; J. S. Bain, 1956, *Barriers to New Competition*, Cambridge, MA: Harvard University Press.

94 K. Eban, 2011, Painful medicine, *Fortune*, November 21: 143–152; G. Colvin, 2011, Disease hunter. *Fortune*, May 23: 80–86.

95 Ranked within industries, *Fortune*, 2011, May 23: F34.

96 Shamsie, The context of dominance.

97 J. W. Backmann, 2002, Competitive strategy: It's O.K. to be different, *Academy of Management Executive*, 16(2): 61–65; B. Wernerfelt & C. A. Montgomery, 1986, What is an attractive industry? *Management Science*, 32: 1223–1230.

98 L. F. Feldman, C. G. Brush, & T. Manolova, 2005, Co-alignment in the resource-performance relationship: Strategy as mediator, *Journal of Business Venturing*, 20: 359–383.

99 M. E. Porter, 1985, *Competitive Advantage*, New York: The Free Press; M. E. Porter, 1981, The contributions of industrial organization to strategic management, *Academy of Management Review*, 6: 609–620.

100 Schendel & Hofer, *Strategic Management;* Christensen, Berg, Bower, Hamermesh, & Porter, *Business Policy*.

101 M. E. Porter, 1980, *Competitive Strategy*, New York: The Free Press, ix.

102 Porter, The five competitive forces that shape strategy; Porter, *Competitive Advantage*.

103 C. Yi-Min & L. Feng-Jyh, 2010, The persistence of superior performance at industry and firm levels: Evidence from the IT industry in Taiwan, *Industry & Innovation*, 17: 469–486; J. C. Short, D. J. Ketchen, Jr., T. B. Palmer, & G. T. M. Hult, Firm, strategic group, and industry influences on performance, *Strategic Management Journal*, 28: 147–167; A. M. McGahan, 1999, Competition, strategy and business performance, *California Management Review*, 41(3): 74–101; McGahan & Porter, How much does industry matter, really? 15–30.

104 J. B. Barney & A. M. Arikan, 2001, The resource-based view: Origins and implications, in M. A. Hitt, R. E. Freeman, & J. S. Harrison (eds.), *Handbook of Strategic Management*, Oxford, UK: Blackwell Publishers, 124–188.

105 M. T. Bolivar-Ramos, V. J. Garcia-Morales, & A. Mihi-Ramirez, 2011, Influence of technological distinctive competencies and organizational learning on organizational innovation to improve organizational performance, *Economic & Management*, 16: 670–675; M. A. Hitt & R. D. Ireland, 1985, Corporate distinctive competence, strategy, industry and performance, *Strategic Management Journal*, 6: 273–293.

106 T. R. Holcomb, R. M. Holmes, Jr., & B. L. Connelly, 2009, Making the most of what you have: Managerial ability as a source of resource value creation, *Strategic Management Journal*, 30: 457–485; R. A. Gordon & J. E. Howell, 1959, *Higher Education for Business*, New York: Columbia University Press.

107 M. F. Wiersema & Y. Zhang, 2011, CEO dismissal: The role of investment analysts, *Strategic Management Journal*, 11: 1161–1182; S. Nadkarni & P. Herrmann, 2010, CEO personality, strategic flexibility, and firm performance: The case of the Indian business process outsourcing industry, *Academy of Management Journal*, 53: 1050–1073; A. Mackey, 2008, The effect of CEOs on firm performance, *Strategic Management Journal*, 29: 1357–1367.

108 E. T. Penrose, 1959, *The Theory of the Growth of the Firm*, New York: Wiley.

109 J. B. Barney, D. J. Ketchen, & M. Wright, 2011, The future of resource-based theory: Revitalization or decline? *Journal of Management*, 37: 1299–1315; W. P. Wan, R. E. Hoskisson, J. C. Short, & D. W. Yiu, Resource-based theory and corporate diversification: Accomplishments and opportunities, *Journal of Management*, 37: 1335–1368; F. J. Acedo, C. Barroso, & J. L. Galan, 2006, The resource-based theory: Dissemination and main trends, *Strategic Management Journal*, 27: 621–636; Barney & Arikan, The resource-based view.

110 D. G. Sirmon & M. A. Hitt, 2009, Contingencies within dynamic managerial capabilities: Interdependent effects of resource investment and deployment on firm performance, *Strategic Management Journal*, 30: 1375–1394.

111 B. Wernerfelt, 1984, A resource-based view of the firm, *Strategic Management Journal*, 5: 171–180.

112 M. H. Kunc & J. D. W. Morecroft, 2010, Managerial decision making and firm performance under a resource-based paradigm, *Strategic Management Journal*, 31: 1164–1182; B.-S. Teng & J. L. Cummings, 2002, Trade-offs in managing resources and capabilities, *Academy of Management Executive*, 16(2): 81–91.

113 R. W. Coff, 2010, The coevolution of rent appropriation and capability development, *Strategic Management Journal*, 31: 711–733; C. Lee, K. Lee, & J. M. Pennings, 2001, Internal capabilities, external networks, and performance: A study on technology-based ventures, *Strategic Management Journal*, 22 (special issue): 615–640; C. C. Markides, 1999, A dynamic view of strategy, *Sloan Management Review*, 40(3): 55–72.

114 P. L. Drnevich & A. P. Kriauciunas, 2011, Clarifying the conditions and limits of the contributions of ordinary and dynamic capabilities to relative firm performance, *Strategic Management Journal*, 32: 254–279.

115 D. G. Sirmon, M. A. Hitt, J.-L. Arregle, & J. T. Campbell, 2010, The dynamic interplay of capability strengths and weaknesses: Investigating the bases of temporary competitive advantage, *Strategic Management Journal*, 31: 1386–1409; P. Bansal, 2005, Evolving sustainability: A longitudinal study of corporate sustainable development, *Strategic Management Journal*, 26: 197–218.

116 D. G. Sirmon, M. A. Hitt, R. D. Ireland, & B. A. Gilbert, 2011, Resource orchestration to create competitive advantage: Breadth, depth and life cycle effects, *Journal of Management*, 37: 1390–1412; M. A. Hitt, 2011, Relevance of strategic management theory and research for supply chain management, *Journal of Supply Chain Management*, 47: 9–13.

117 J. Birger, 2011, Surprising bargain stocks, *Fortune*, September 6: 115–118.

118 E. Danneels, 2011, Trying to become a different type of company: Dynamic capability at Smith Corona, *Strategic Management Journal*, 32: 1–31; S. Winter, 2003, Understanding dynamic capabilities, *Strategic Management Journal*, 10: 991–995; M. Blyler & R. W. Coff, 2003, Dynamic capabilities, social capital, and rent appropriation: Ties that split pies, *Strategic Management Journal*, 24: 677–686.

119 M. J. Leiblein, 2011, What do resource- and capability-based theories propose? *Journal of Management*, 37: 909–932; A. A. Lado, N. G. Boyd, P. Wright, & M. Kroll, 2006, Paradox and theorizing within the resource-based view, *Academy of Management Review*, 31: 115–131; D. M. De Carolis, 2003, Competencies and imitability in the pharmaceutical industry: An analysis of their relationship with firm performance, *Journal of Management*, 29: 27–50; Barney, Is the resource-based "view" a useful perspective?; J. B. Barney, 1995, Looking inside for competitive advantage, *Academy of Management Executive*, 9(4): 56.

120 W. B. Edgar & C. A. Lockwood, 2011, Understanding, finding, and applying core competencies: A framework, guide, and description for corporate managers and research professionals, *Academy of Strategic Management Journal*, 10(2): 61–82; F. S. Nobre & D. S. Walker, 2011, An ability-based view of the organization: Strategic-resource and contingency domains, *Learning Organization*, 18: 333–345.

121 A. Bakay, A. Elkassabgi, & M. Moqbel, 2011, Resource allocation, level of international diversification and firm performance, *International Journal of Business & Management*, 6(12): 87–93; T. Ravinchandran and C. Lertwongsatien, Effect of information systems resources and capabilities on firm performance: A resource-based perspective, *Journal of Management Information Systems*, 21: 237–276.

122 E. Fang, R. W. Palmatier, & R. Grewal, 2011, Effects of customer and innovation asset configuration strategies on firm performance, *Journal of Marketing Research*, 48: 587–602; S. Aydin, A. T. Cetin, & G. Ozer, 2007, The relationship between marketing and product development process and their effects on firm performance, *Academy of Marketing Studies Journal*, 11: 53–68.

123 V. Wickramasinghe & N. De Zoyza, 2011, Managerial competency requirements than enhance organizational competences: A study of a Sri Lankan telecom organization, *International Journal of Human Resource Management*, 22: 2981–3000; R. D. Ireland, M. A. Hitt, & D. Vaidyanath, 2002, Alliance management as a source of competitive advantage, *Journal of Management*, 28: 413–446.

124 P. Kaipa & M. Kriger, 2010, Empowerment, vision and positive leadership, *Journal of Management Inquiry*, 19: 110–115; A. Fanelli, V. F. Misangyi, & H. L. Tosi, 2009, In charisma we trust: The effects of CEO charismatic visions on securities analysts, *Organization Science*, 20: 1101–1033.

125 D. J. Wolterman, 2010, Interview with Daniel J. Wolterman, FACHE, President and Chief Executive Officer, Memorial Hermann Healthcare System, *Journal of Healthcare Management*, 55: 73.

126 Interview with Daniel J. Wolterman, 74.

127 D. Palacios-Marqués, D. Ribeiro-Soriano, & I. Gil-Pechuán, 2011, The effect of learning-based distinctive competencies on firm performance: A study of Spanish hospitality firms, *Cornell Hospitality Quarterly*, 52(2): 102–110.

128 B. Arslan & M. Ozturan, 2011, The path to information technology business value: The case of Turkey, *Technology & Investment*, 2: 52–63; Y. Wang,

H.-P. Lo, & Y. Yang, 2004, The constituents of core competencies and firm performance: Evidence from high-technology firms in China, *Journal of Engineering & Technology Management*, 21: 249–280.

129 Yi-Min & Feng-Jyh, The persistence of superior performance; Short, et al., Firm, strategic group, and industry influences on performance; T. R. Crook, D. J. Ketchen, Jr., J. G. Coombs, & S. Y. Todd, 2008, Strategic resources and performance: A meta-analysis, *Strategic Management Journal*, 29: 1141–1154; G. Hawawini, V. Subramanian, & P. Verdin, 2003, Is performance driven by industry- or firm-specific factors? A new look at the evidence, *Strategic Management Journal*, 24: 1–16.

130 R. E. Freeman, 1984, *Strategic Management: A Stakeholder Approach*, Boston, MA: Pitman Publishing, 249.

131 M. C. Jensen & W. H. Meckling, 1976, Theory of the firm: Managerial behavior, agency costs and ownership structure, *Journal of Financial Economics*, 3: 305–360.

132 T. M. Jones & A. C. Wicks, 1999, Convergent stakeholder theory, *Academy of Management Review*, 24: 206–221; Freeman, *Strategic Management*, 53–54.

133 S. Sharma & I. Henriques, 2005, Stakeholder influences on sustainability practices in the Canadian Forest products industry, *Strategic Management Journal*, 26: 159–180; G. Donaldson & J. W. Lorsch, 1983, *Decision Making at the Top: The Shaping of Strategic Direction*, New York: Basic Books, 37–40.

134 F. Ackermann & C. Eden, 2011, Strategic management of stakeholders: Theory and practice, *Long Range Planning*, 44: 179–196; Walsh, Taking stock of stakeholder management; C. Eesley & M. J. Lenox, 2006, Firm responses to secondary stakeholder action, *Strategic Management Journal*, 27: 765–781.

135 R. A. Phillips & R. E. Freeman (eds.), 2010, *Stakeholders*, Cheltenham, UK: Edward Elgar Publishing; R. E. Freeman, J. S. Harrison, & A. C. Wicks, 2007, *Managing for Stakeholders: Survival, Reputation and Success*, New Haven, CT: Yale University Press; Freeman, *Strategic Management*.

136 J. S. Harrison, D. A. Bosse, & R. A. Phillips, 2010, Managing for stakeholders, stakeholder utility functions and competitive advantage, *Strategic Management Journal*, 31: 58–74.

137 D. A. Bosse, R. A. Phillips, & J. S. Harrison, 2009, Stakeholders, reciprocity and firm performance, *Strategic Management Journal*, 30: 447–456; T. W. Dunfee, 2006, A critical perspective of integrative social contracts theory: Recurring criticisms and next generation research topics, *Journal of Business Ethics*, 68: 303; E. Fehr & S. Gachter, 2000, Fairness and retaliation: The economics of reciprocity, *Journal of Economic Perspectives*, 14(3): 159–181.

138 Harrison, et al., Managing for stakeholders.

139 R. A. Phillips, 2003, *Stakeholder Theory and Organizational Ethics*, San Francisco, CA: Berrett-Koehler Publishers.

140 Harrison, et al. Managing for stakeholders.

141 G. Colvin, 2011, What really has the 99% up in arms? *Fortune*, November 7: 87; S. A. Waddock, C. Bodwell, & S. B. Graves, 2002, Responsibility: The new business imperative, *Academy of Management Executive*, 16(2): 132–148.

142 G. Colvin, 2011, What's next for Wall Street? *Fortune*, December 26: 156–158.

143 R. E. Freeman, J. S. Harrison, A. C. Wicks, B. Parmar, & S. de Colle, 2010, *Stakeholder Theory: The State of the Art*, Cambridge, MA: Cambridge University Press; R. Phillips, R. E. Freeman, & A. C. Wicks, 2003, What stakeholder theory is not, *Business Ethics Quarterly*, 13: 481; C. W. L. Hill & T. M. Jones, 1992, Stakeholder-agency theory, *Journal of Management Studies*, 29: 131–154.

144 Freeman, et al., *Stakeholder Theory*; Walsh, Taking stock of stakeholder management.

145 2011, Whole Foods Market, *Fortune*, May 23: 30.

146 *Whole Foods Market 2010 Annual Report*, 2.

147 Harrison, et al., Managing for stakeholders.

148 J. Choi & H. Wang, 2009, Stakeholder relations and the persistence of corporate financial performance, *Strategic Management Journal*, 30: 895–907; A. Kacperczyk, 2009, With greater power comes greater responsibility? Takeover protection and corporate attention to stakeholders, *Strategic Management Journal*, 30: 261–285; R. Sisodia, D. B. Wolfe, & J. Sheth, 2007, *Firms of Endearment: How World-Class Companies Profit from Passion and Purpose*, Upper Saddle River, NJ: Wharton School Publishing; A. J. Hillman & G. D. Keim, 2001, Shareholder value, stakeholder management, and social issues: What's the bottom line? *Strategic Management Journal*, 22: 125–139; S. L. Berman, A. C. Wicks, S. Kotha, & T. M. Jones, 1999, Does stakeholder orientation matter? The relationship between stakeholder management models and firm financial performance, *Academy of Management Journal*, 42(5): 488–506; L. E. Preston & H. J. Sapienza, 1990, Stakeholder management and corporate performance, *Journal of Behavioral Economics*, 19: 361–375.

149 B. L. Parmar, R. E. Freeman, J. S. Harrison, A. C. Wicks, L. Purnell, & S. de Colle, 2010, Stakeholder theory: The state of the art, *Academy of Management Annals*, 3: 403–445; T. M. Jones, 1995, Instrumental stakeholder theory: A synthesis of ethics and economics, *Academy of Management Review*, 20: 404–437; T. Donaldson & L. E. Preston, 1995, The stakeholder theory of the corporation: Concepts, evidence, and implications, *Academy of Management Review*, 20: 65–91.

150 Harrison, et al., Managing for stakeholders; P. A. Argenti, R. A. Howell, & K. A. Beck, 2005, The strategic communication imperative. *MIT Sloan Management Review*, 46(3): 83–89; S. L. Hart & S. Sharma, 2004, Engaging fringe stakeholders for competitive imagination, *Academy of Management Executive*, 18(1): 7–18.

151 M. Maccoby & T. Scudder, 2011, Strategic intelligence: A conceptual system of leadership for change, *Performance Improvement*, 50: 32–40; J. Johannesson & I. Palona, 2010, Environmental turbulence and the success of a firm's intelligence strategy: Development of research instruments, *International Journal of Management*, 27: 448–458; P. Nutt, 2004, Expanding the search for alternatives during strategic decision-making, *Academy of Management Executive*, 18(4): 13–28; M. Maccoby, 2001, Successful leaders employ strategic intelligence, *Research Technology Management*, 44(3): 58–60.

152 Harrison, et al., Managing for stakeholders; V. P. Rindova, I. O. Williamson, A. P. Petkova, & J. M. Sever, 2005, Being good or being known: An empirical examination of the dimensions, antecedents, and consequences of organizational reputation, *Academy of Management Journal*, 48: 1033–1049; B. R. Barringer & J. S. Harrison, 2000, Walking a tightrope: Creating value through interorgnizational relationships, *Journal of Management*, 26: 367–403.

153 M. H. Hansen, R. E. Hoskisson, & J. B. Barney, 2008, Competitive advantage in alliance governance: Resolving the opportunism minimization-gain maximization paradox, *Managerial and Decision Economics*, 29: 191–208; Williamson, *Markets and Hierarchies*.

154 F. Stinglhamber, D. De Cremer, & L. F. Mercken, 2006, Support as a mediator of the relationship between justice and trust, *Group and Organization Management*, 31: 442–468; K. A. Hegtvedt, 2005, Doing justice to the group: Examining the roles of the group in justice research, *Annual Review of Sociology*, 31: 25–45; C. C. Chen, Y.-R. Chen, & K. Xin, 2004, Guanxi practices and trust in management: A procedural justice perspective, *Organization Science*, 15: 200–209.

155 Freeman, et al., *Stakeholder Theory*; N. A. Gardberg, 2006, Corporate citizenship: Creating intangible assets across institutional environments, *Academy of Management Review*, 31: 329–346; Harrison & St. John, Managing and partnering with external stakeholders; B. Cornell & A. C. Shapiro, 1987, Corporate stakeholders and corporate finance, *Financial Management*, 15: 5–14.

156 A. Mackey, T. B. Mackey, & J. B. Barney, 2007, Corporate social responsibility and firm performance: Investor preferences and corporate strategies, *Academy of Management Review*, 32: 817–835; P. Bromiley, K. D. Miller, & D. Rau, 2001, Risk in strategic management research, in M. A. Hitt, R. E. Freeman, & J. S. Harrison (eds.), *Handbook of Strategic Management*, Oxford, UK: Blackwell Publishers, 259–288; S. B. Graves & S. A. Waddock, 1994, Institutional owners and corporate social performance, *Academy of Management Journal*, 37: 1035–1046.

157 J. Shaner & M. Maznevski, 2011, The relationship between networks, institutional development, and performance in foreign investments, *Strategic Management Journal*, 32: 556–568; D. Lavie, 2006, The competitive advantage of interconnected firms: An extension of the resource-based view, *Academy of Management Review*, 31: 638–658.

158 E. F. Goldman & A. Casey, 2010, Building a culture that encourages strategic thinking, *Journal of Leadership & Organizational Studies*, 17(2): 119–128; S. French, 2009, Re-framing strategic thinking: The research aims and outcomes, *Journal of Management Development*, 28: 205–224.

159 D. W. Cravens, N. F. Piercy, & A. Baldauf, 2009, Management framework guiding strategic thinking in rapidly changing markets, *Journal of Marketing Management*, 25: 31–49.

160 J. Hempel, 2011, IBM's super second act, *Fortune*, March 21: 115–124.

161 L. Dragoni, I.-S. Oh, P. Vankatwyk, & P. E. Tesluk, 2011, Developing executive leaders: The relative contribution of cognitive ability, personality, and the accumulation of work experience in predicting strategic thinking competency, *Personnel Psychology*, 64: 829–864.

162 J. M. Leidtka, 2001, Strategy formulation: The roles of conversation and design, in M. A. Hitt, R. E. Freeman, & J. S. Harrison (eds.), *Handbook of Strategic Management*, Oxford, UK: Blackwell Publishers, 70–93.

163 G. Hamel & C. K. Prahalad, 2005, Strategic intent, *Harvard Business Review*, 83(7/8): 148–161; G. Hamel & C. K. Prahalad, 1994, *Competing for the Future*, Boston, MA: Harvard Business School Press.

164 H. R. Greve, 2009, Bigger and safer: The diffusion of competitive advantage, *Strategic Management Journal*, 30: 1–23; Ackoff, *Redesigning the Future*.

165 P. P. Tallon & A. Pinsonneault, 2011, Competing perspectives on the link between strategic information technology alignment and organizational agility: Insights from a mediation model, *MIS Quarterly*, 35: 463–486.

166 J. D. Campbell, 2009, Learning from the past, *Advisor Today*, 104(8): 58; R. Neustadt & E. May, 1986, *Thinking in Time: The Uses of History for Decision Makers*, New York: The Free Press, 251.

167 S. Hu, D. Blettner, & R. A. Bettis, 2011, Adaptive aspirations: Performance consequences of risk preferences at extremes and alternative reference groups, *Strategic Management Journal*, 32: 1426–1436.

168 Y. Ling, Z. Simsek, M. H. Lubatkin, & J. F. Veiga, 2008, Transformational leadership's role in promoting corporate entrepreneurship: Examining the CEO-TMT interface, *Academy of Management Journal*, 51: 557–576; G. Lundquist, 2004, The missing ingredients in corporate innovation, *Research Technology Management*, 47(5): 11–12.

169 M. Terziovski, 2010, Innovation practice and its performance implications in small and medium enterprises in the manufacturing sector: A resource-base view, *Strategic Management Journal*, 31: 892–902; G. Hamel, 2000, *Leading the Revolution*, Boston, MA: Harvard Business School Press.

170 G. Spreitzer & C. Porath, 2012, Creating sustainable performance, *Harvard Business Review*, January–February: 93–99; Lundquist, The missing ingredients.

171 J. Gibb & J. M. Haar, 2010, Risk taking, innovativeness and competitive rivalry: A three way interaction towards firm performance, *International Journal of Innovation Management*, 14: 871–891; F. Stone, 2006, How to encourage risk taking in your organization, *Employment Relations Today*, 32(4): 7–13.

172 J. Chen, Z. Zhou, & W. Anquan, 2005, A system model for corporate entrepreneurship, *International Journal of Manpower*, 26: 529–536.

173 I. Bonn, 2005, Improving strategic thinking: A multi-level approach, *Leadership and Organizational Development Journal*, 26: 336–354.

174 T. Hutzschenreuter & I. Kleindienst, 2006, Strategy-process research: What have we learned and what is still to be explored, *Journal of Management*, 32: 673–721; M. A. Hitt & R. D. Ireland, 2002, The essence of strategic leadership: Managing human and social capital, *Journal of Leadership and Organization Studies*, 9(1): 3–14.

175 E. L. Chen, R. Katila, R. McDonald, & K. M. Eisenhardt, 2010, Life in the fast lane: Origins of competitive interaction in new vs. established markets, *Strategic Management Journal*, 31: 1527–1547; D. J. Ketchen, C. C. Snow, & V. L. Street, 2004, Improving firm performance by matching strategic decision-making processes to competitive dynamics, *Academy of Management Executive*, 18(4): 29–43.

176 C. Haeussler, H. Patzelt, & S. A. Zahra, 2012, Strategic alliances and product development in high technology new firms: The moderating effect of technological capabilities, *Journal of Business Venturing*, 27(2): 217–233; P. Evans & B. Wolf, 2005, Collaboration rules, *Harvard Business Review*, 83(7): 96–104.

177 M. H. Shah & F. M. Shaikh, 2011, Globalization and recent trends in corporate governance and strategic management, *Journal of Business Strategies*, 5(1): 32–38.

[178] C. Krychowski & B. V. Quélin, Real options and strategic investment decisions: Can they be of use to scholars? *Academy of Management Perspectives*, 24(2): 65–78; L. Trigeorgis, 1997, *Real Options*, Cambridge, MA: MIT Press.

[179] J. J. Reuer & M. J. Leiblein, 2000, Downside risk implications of multinationality and international joint ventures, *Academy of Management Journal*, 43: 203–214.

[180] J. D. Harris & R. E. Freeman, 2008, The impossibility of the separation thesis, *Business Ethics Quarterly*, 18: 541–548; J. R. Ehrenfeld, 2005, The roots of sustainability. *MIT Sloan Management Review*, 46(2): 23–25; L. K. Trevino & G. R. Weaver, 2003, *Managing Ethics in Business Organizations*, Stanford, CA: Stanford University Press.

Chapter 2

STRATEGIC LEADERSHIP

KNOWLEDGE OBJECTIVES

Studying this chapter should provide you with the strategic management knowledge needed to:

1. Define strategic leadership and describe the importance of top-level managers as resources.

2. Discuss the characteristics of effective strategic leaders and the factors that influence their ability to make effective strategic decisions, including managerial discretion and decision biases.

3. Define top management teams and explain their effects on firm performance.

4. Describe the factors that influence the ability of top managers to be effective strategic leaders.

5. Describe the processes associated with ensuring that a firm is well-positioned economically and identify the characteristics of a well-defined strategy.

6. Explain how strategic leaders acquire, develop, and manage firm resources to create one or more competitive advantages.

7. Describe how strategic leaders manage relationships with external stakeholders in order to reduce uncertainty and enhance value creation.

8. Discuss the roles of strategic leadership in determining and communicating the firm's strategic direction.

9. Discuss the importance and use of organizational controls.

Strategic leaders can profoundly influence firm performance.[1] Legendary business chief executive officers (CEOs) such as Jack Welch at General Electric, Sam Walton at Walmart, and Akio Morita at Sony led their organizations to greater success than any of their many formidable competitors, yet they were very different in their approaches. Jack Welch was notorious for creating difficult targets for his subordinates and penalizing them when they did not perform. He drove managers to high levels of success or facilitated their departure from the firm, figuring that he was doing them a favor by helping them find some other situation in which they could excel.[2] Sam Walton took a positive and caring approach to the retailing business, treating customers as royalty and calling employees "associates." He also took an unconventional approach to the market by placing huge stores in rural areas and stocking them from warehouses that were centrally located near groups of stores. Although we now consider these features business-as-usual, they were anything but normal in the early days of Walmart.[3] Akio Morita pushed hard on innovation and adopted a forward-looking, global perspective. He is heralded as a diplomat whose broad vision of Japan's role in the world economy helped Sony and other Japanese companies achieve high levels of success in international markets.[4]

Despite these different approaches, all of these leaders were visionaries, or transformational leaders: they established a clear view of what they wanted to accomplish. They were also agents of change, leading others to make their vision a reality. Effective strategic leadership is a requirement for successful strategic management. **Strategic leadership** is the ability to anticipate, envision, maintain flexibility, and empower others to create strategic change as necessary. Multifunctional in nature, strategic leadership involves managing through others, managing an entire enterprise rather than a functional subunit, and coping with change. Because of the complex and often global orientation of the job, strategic leaders must learn how to effectively influence human behavior in an uncertain environment. By word and/or by personal example, and through their ability to envision the future, effective strategic leaders meaningfully influence the behaviors, thoughts, and feelings of those with whom they work.[5] Transformational leadership entails motivating followers to do more than is expected, to continuously enrich their capabilities, and to place the organization's interests above their own.[6]

This chapter begins by focusing on individual strategic leaders as a key resource for the firm—the personal characteristics that make them effective and the influences on their abilities to make effective strategic decisions. Then we examine top management teams and their influence on organizations, as well as factors associated with executive succession. The rest of the chapter discusses six key components of effective strategic leadership: ensuring that the firm is well-positioned economically, managing key resources, developing and maintaining effective relationships with key stakeholders, determining a strategic direction, overseeing the formulation and implementation of specific strategies, and establishing balanced organizational control systems. These activities influence the amount of value a firm creates and its economic performance.

STRATEGIC LEADERS AS A KEY RESOURCE THROUGH THEIR INFLUENCES ON STRATEGIC DECISIONS

Not all managers have the capacity to become effective strategic leaders. Furthermore, it may be that strategic leadership skills can be analyzed as a hierarchy in which managers must master lower-level skills before they fine-tune higher-level skills, as illustrated in the following levels from the book *Good to Great* by Jim Collins.[7]

- ▶ *Level 1: Highly Capable Individual.* The most basic skills for becoming a capable individual are developing skills and a strong work ethic.
- ▶ *Level 2: Contributing Team Member.* Next, a person must be able to work effectively in teams and make useful contributions to the achievement of team goals.

- *Level 3: Competent Manager.* Once the two lower-level skills are mastered, competent management comes from the ability to organize people and resources so as to achieve organizational objectives.
- *Level 4: Effective Leader.* Not all competent managers are effective leaders. Leadership entails the ability to articulate a clear strategic intent and motivate followers to high levels of performance.
- *Level 5: Level 5 Executive.* These are people with unwavering resolve to lead their companies to greatness. Frequently they are humble, attributing success to the team they have assembled rather than focusing on their own personal achievements. A Level 5 leader might also be called a transformational leader.

Although the book *Good to Great* has been criticized, the concept of a skills hierarchy is a useful idea and to a degree has been verified by academic research.[8] People will not be able to contribute well to a team until they have attained a certain level of personal competence. Also, the skills at Levels 1 and 2 (more basic skills) seem essential to becoming an excellent manager or leader. Furthermore, since competent management is defined as an ability to organize people and resources to achieve objectives, it seems reasonable that effective leaders also need these skills. The book suggests that many have lower level skills, whereas very few have higher level skills (Level 5), suggesting that those with appropriate skills are a key resource for an organization. Steve Jobs, deceased CEO of Apple, is one who exemplified a transformational leader and was definitely a key source of Apple's tremendous success by ushering in an era focused on personal technology through iTunes, iPods, iPhones and iPads. He did this by "his ability to inspire loyalty in customers, his controlling leadership style, and his devotion to simple and elegant product design."[9]

However, besides general skills that any organization might be able to utilize, one must also understand the strategic situation of a particular company in order to make appropriate strategic decisions. Although the ability to establish a strategic vision and create passion and energy among a firm's employees to realize the vision and achieve outstanding performance are essential, research has shown that human and social capital are necessary for understanding the business and are also indicators of future success.[10]

Strategic Leadership Style

Strategic leaders direct the strategic management process in different ways. The CEO sets the tone for the amount of management participation in strategic decisions and the way the decisions are implemented.[11] Some CEOs apply a very traditional "commander" approach, using meetings with top management team members to collect information but then individually deciding on strategies and directing subordinates to carry them out. A more collaborative style entails jointly arriving at strategies and implementation plans with members of the top management team. In other organizations, the CEO may delegate most strategy-making responsibilities to subordinates, allocating resources to them and giving them responsibility for effective utilization.[12] The appropriateness of various decision-making styles tends to vary depending on the competitive situation. In situations in which rapid decisions are required, such as emergencies or unexpected shifts in the business environment, a more directive approach may be more appropriate. However, in general, a more participative style will lead to better decisions because managers share and consider a greater amount of relevant information.[13] Also, implementation may be easier and more successful because managers feel that they are a part of the decisions they are working to implement.[14]

The cultural and functional backgrounds of top managers may also influence the way strategic decisions are made.[15] An ongoing debate exists regarding whether it is appropriate to try to match the backgrounds of managers with the competitive situation in which they will lead. For instance, it may be appropriate for managers with production-operations backgrounds to run businesses that try to achieve low cost positions because of the internal focus on efficiency and engineering.[16] Alternatively, businesses that are seeking to differentiate their products may need someone with training in marketing or research and development (R&D) because of the need for innovation and market awareness. Growth strategies, in general, may call for a person with a strong marketing background, a willingness to take risks, and a high tolerance for ambiguity.[17] Nevertheless, these same characteristics may be inappropriate in turnaround situations. Some evidence also exists that strategic change and innovation are more likely when a manager is younger and has less time in the organization but is well-educated.[18] There is no absolute formula for matching a strategic leader to a competitive situation. The point to understand is that the effectiveness of strategic leadership may depend, in part, on how well the background and skills of a particular leader fit with the challenges the firm is facing.

Managerial Discretion and Decision Biases

Managerial discretion and decision biases can also influence the effectiveness of strategic decisions. Because strategic decisions are intended to help a firm develop one or more competitive advantages, how managers exercise discretion (latitude for action) is critical to the firm's success.[19] Managers often use their discretion when making strategic decisions, including those associated with implementation of strategies.[20] Top executives must be action oriented; thus, the decisions that they make should spur the company to action. However, they are constrained by a number of factors that influence the level of discretion they have when making decisions. Some of these factors are associated with the external environment, such as the industry structure, the rate of market growth in the firm's primary industry, and the degree to which products can be differentiated. Consider, for example, that managers in a firm that produces a basic commodity are fairly limited in determining how they might alter their product to make it more appealing to the market. Characteristics of the organization, including its size, age, resources, and culture, can also influence discretion. For instance, strong organizational cultures can have a significant effect on the decisions that are made. Finally, discretion is influenced by individual characteristics of the manager, including commitment to the firm and its strategic outcomes, tolerance for ambiguity, skills in working with different people, and aspiration levels (see Figure 2.1).

In addition to managerial discretion, decision-making biases can have a significant effect on strategic decisions.[21] Strategic managers tend to rely on a limited set of heuristics, or "rules of thumb," when they make strategic decisions.[22] These

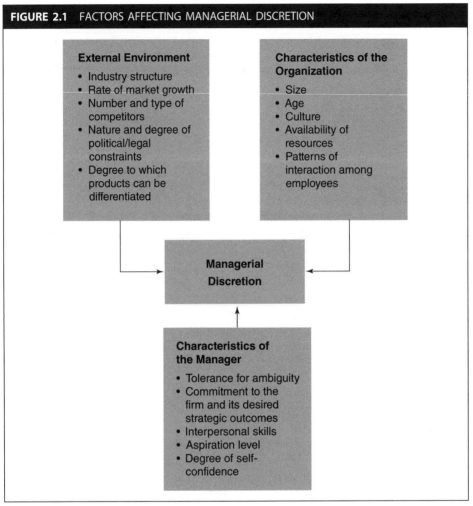

FIGURE 2.1 FACTORS AFFECTING MANAGERIAL DISCRETION

External Environment
- Industry structure
- Rate of market growth
- Number and type of competitors
- Nature and degree of political/legal constraints
- Degree to which products can be differentiated

Characteristics of the Organization
- Size
- Age
- Culture
- Availability of resources
- Patterns of interaction among employees

Managerial Discretion

Characteristics of the Manager
- Tolerance for ambiguity
- Commitment to the firm and its desired strategic outcomes
- Interpersonal skills
- Aspiration level
- Degree of self-confidence

SOURCE: Adapted from S. Finkelstein & D. C. Hambrick, 1996, *Strategic Leadership: Top Executives and Their Effects on Organizations*, St. Paul, MN: West Publishing Company.

heuristics help managers simplify what might otherwise be an overwhelmingly complicated and uncertain decision environment. However, heuristics also can lead to suboptimal decisions.[23] Although dozens of potential decision-making biases have been described in the research literature,[24] five seem to have the most potential for influencing strategic decisions:[25]

▶ *Reliance on Previously Formed Beliefs.* Executives bring a number of preconceived ideas into any decision process. Some of them are a function of the executives' past experiences, whereas others are based on things they may have read or heard about, regardless of whether they have any actual empirical validity. Especially important to strategic decisions are beliefs about causality—that is, how the salient decision variables fit together. For instance, executives may believe that particular strategic actions will bring particular firm results.

Clearly, experience is a valuable executive resource; however, preconceived ideas may cause decision makers to overlook information that could lead to different conclusions.[26] Stereotypes also fit into this category—that is, when executives hold preconceived notions about the abilities or potential behavior of individuals based on variables such as gender, nationality, religion, or race. Holding a stereotype can result in an executive ignoring the individual skills, background, and performance of a person who is being considered for a strategic position and thereby potentially choosing an individual who will not lead as effectively.

▶ *Focus on Limited Objectives.* Executives also tend to focus on a limited number of firm targets instead of thinking broadly about other worthwhile objectives.[27] For instance, a primary focus on budgetary controls may lead managers to focus on selected critical performance targets.[28] Too much focus on financial objectives, such as shareholder returns or return-on-equity, can lead to short-sighted decisions, where the firm takes actions with immediate financial benefits while damaging its longer-term performance.[29] It can also lead to neglect of and less favorable relationships with stakeholders that are important to firm competitiveness, such as customers, suppliers, the communities in which firms operate, or even employees.[30]

▶ *Exposure to Limited Decision Alternatives.* In an effort to simplify decision processes, executives tend to limit the number of alternatives for achieving a particular goal.[31] Instead, they rely on intuition to supplement rationality.[32] The problem is that in an effort to speed up decision processes, they may overlook viable or even potentially more successful alternatives.

▶ *Insensitivity to Outcome Probabilities.* Frequently, decision makers do not understand, trust, or use outcome probabilities to guide decision processes; that is, they tend to be more influenced by the magnitude of potential decision outcomes rather than the probability that they will occur.[33] They may also consider decision situations as unique and therefore discount information that might otherwise help them assess the probability of success.[34] The obvious danger associated with this bias is that, on the basis of the high potential returns that might accrue, strategic leaders will guide their firms into situations that are unlikely to be successful.

▶ *Illusion of Control.* As decision makers approach a particular decision situation, they may believe that they have more control over the outcomes from that decision than they actually have.[35] This bias manifests itself in executives assessing lower probabilities of failure, which is related to the previous bias. However, it also results in a feeling among decision makers that they can use their professional skills to fix problems that occur as a decision is implemented.[36] This problem is linked to overconfidence or overoptimism.[37] Consequently, this bias can lead to poor decisions at the outset and inadequate planning for implementation of those decisions.

Hubris, which can be defined as excessive pride, leading to a feeling of invincibility, can magnify the effects of each of these potential biases.[38] CEOs tend to garner media attention, and they may win awards and gain other types of public recognition.[39] Research has shown that when CEOs begin to believe the glowing press accounts and to feel that they are unlikely to make errors, they are more likely to make poor strategic decisions.[40] Top executives need to have self-confidence, but they must also guard against allowing it to reach the point of hubris. Perhaps that is why some of the greatest business leaders of our day exhibit an unusual degree of humility.[41]

Awareness of decision-making biases can help strategic leaders at least partially overcome them. For instance, leaders can provide an open decision-making environment that invites new perspectives and challenges existing assumptions and strategies. Also, problems associated with the neglect of prior probabilities can be addressed through real options analysis (see Chapter 13). In addition, strategic leaders can address problems associated with decision biases by surrounding themselves with a top management team composed of individuals who have divergent views and varying backgrounds. It is important also to evaluate the decision processes used. "A recent McKinsey study of more than 1,000 business investments, for instance, showed that when companies worked to reduce the effects of bias, they raised their returns on investment by seven percentage points."[42]

TOP MANAGEMENT TEAMS

In most firms, complex organizational challenges and the need for substantial information, knowledge, and skills to address these challenges result in a need for teams of executives to provide strategic leadership. The quality of strategic thinking and subsequent strategic decisions made by a top management team affect the firm's ability to innovate and engage in effective strategic change.[43] Top-level managers are an important resource for firms seeking to successfully use the strategic management process.[44]

A **top management team** is composed of the CEO and other key managers who are responsible for setting the direction of the firm and formulating and implementing its strategies. For instance, a team may include a chief operating officer (COO) and an assortment of other high-ranking officials typically representing the major businesses and/or functional areas of the firm, as well as members of the board of directors. The decisions resulting from strategic thinking that top-level managers engage in influence how the firm is designed, the nature of its strategies, and whether it will achieve its goals. Thus, a critical element of organizational success is having a top management team with superior managerial and decision-making skills.[45]

Several factors influence the ability of top management teams to exercise effective strategic leadership, including team heterogeneity, team power, and executive succession processes.

Top Management Team Heterogeneity

The job of top-level executives is complex and requires a broad knowledge of the firm's operations, as well as the three key parts of the firm's external environment—the general, industry, and competitor environments. (Chapter 3 explores these environments in depth.) The overwhelming complexity and strength of environmental forces, as well as the need to manage a wide variety of stakeholder relationships, require formation of a fairly diverse top management team with a wide variety of strengths, capabilities, and knowledge.[46] This normally requires a **heterogeneous top management team** composed of individuals with different functional backgrounds, experience, and education. The more heterogeneous a top management team is—the more varied the expertise and knowledge within the team—the more capacity it has to provide effective strategic leadership in formulating strategy.[47]

Steve Ballmer has been Microsoft's chief executive officer since 2000, but Bill Gates only recently (2008) retired from day-to-day operating decisions as chairman of the board. Since that time, Ballmer has replaced almost every major division head at Microsoft and has overseen "a dramatic shift away from the company's PC-first heritage."[48] The Windows Vista operating system was a distinct setback for Microsoft; it was poorly implemented and Windows 7 was mostly a fix of Windows Vista. The upcoming launch of Windows 8, under the leadership of Steven Sinofsky, portends to be much more successful and is based on lessons learned from Vista's failure. Ballmer also hired Qi Lu from Yahoo! to revamp Microsoft search business. This has paid off in Bing (Microsoft's search offering) improving its market share. Microsoft's acquisition of Skype also brought in a new player, Tony Bates, whom he has put in charge to help move this acquisition to the next level of excellence. Ballmer has focused on improving the vision for new products, a function he took over from Gates' former leadership. One former board member, James I. Cash, indicated, "He's learned to manage through people and made a commitment to interdisciplinary work. I think he will come off looking like a real unique and special leader."[49] Although his success with these changes remains to be seen, he has to deal with a large and diverse top management team.

Members of a heterogeneous top management team benefit from discussing the different perspectives that team members advance. In many cases, these discussions increase the quality of the team's decisions, especially when a synthesis emerges from the diverse perspectives that are superior to any one individual's perspective.[50] Having members with substantive expertise in the firm's core functions and businesses is also important to a top management team's effectiveness. In a high-technology industry, it may be critical for a firm's top management team to have R&D expertise, particularly when growth strategies are being implemented.[51] Heterogeneous top management teams have sometimes demonstrated a propensity to take stronger competitive actions and reactions than more homogeneous teams.[52]

More heterogeneity in top management teams is also positively associated with innovation and strategic change.[53] Team heterogeneity may encourage members to "think outside the box" and thus be more creative in making decisions. In essence, thinking outside the box means "thinking beyond the common mental models that shape the way people see the world."[54] Therefore, firms that need to change their strategies are more likely to do so if they have top management teams with diverse backgrounds and expertise. A team with various areas of expertise is more likely to identify environmental changes (opportunities and threats) or changes within the firms that require a different strategic direction.[55] Research also shows that more heterogeneity among top management team members promotes debate, which often leads to better strategic decisions. In turn, better strategic decisions produce higher firm performance.[56]

Once a decision is made, the next challenge is to create a level of cohesion among team members that will facilitate effective implementation of the change.

One of the great challenges facing strategic leaders is integrating the diverse opinions and behavior of a heterogeneous team into a common way of thinking and behaving.[57] In general, the more heterogeneous and larger the top management team is, the more difficult it is for the team to effectively implement strategies.[58] Comprehensive and long-term strategic plans can be inhibited by communication difficulties among top executives who have different backgrounds and different cognitive skills.[59] As a result, a group of top executives with diverse backgrounds may inhibit the process of decision making if it is not effectively managed. In these cases, top management teams may fail to comprehensively examine threats and opportunities, leading to suboptimal strategic decisions.

Virginia Rometty was promoted to CEO of IBM in late 2011. IBM, a top technology firm, is continually changing and has a global strategy. Rometty has played a key part in recent moves, including the acquisition of a consulting arm of PricewaterhouseCoopers as well as helping to establish delivery centers for IT services in China and India. She helped both manage the integration process of the PricewaterhouseCoopers acquisition and formulate the IT service strategies in these large, emerging economies.[60] She obviously has to meet the challenges managing a diverse team among IBM's various businesses, both across services and products as well as across a diverse set of geographic markets. One IBM customer echoed her abilities to facilitate this diversity. Under her direction, IBM staffers engaged in "collaborative problem solving, which I think the future of IT is all about." It will be interesting to see how IBM thrives under Rometty's leadership as she continues to work with Samuel Palmisano, the former CEO, who will remain as chairman of IBM's board.[61]

The CEO and Top Management Team Power

Chapter 11 discusses the board of directors as a governance mechanism for monitoring a firm's strategic direction and for representing stakeholders' interests, especially those of shareholders. Here, we focus on the characteristics that give the CEO and top management team power relative to the board and the influence these characteristics can have on the amount of strategic leadership the board provides.[62] An underlying premise is that higher performance normally is achieved when the board of directors is more directly involved in shaping a firm's strategic direction.[63] However, directors may find it difficult to direct the strategic actions of powerful CEOs and top management teams.[64] Their relative power is at least partially a function of social or business ties with directors and their tenure as members of the team.

It is not uncommon for a powerful CEO to appoint a number of sympathetic outside board members such as friends, family members, or principals in companies with which the firm conducts business. CEOs may also appoint board members who are on the top management team and report directly to the CEO.[65] In either case, the CEO may have significant control over the board's actions. Westphal and Zajac have asked the "central question" of "whether boards are an effective management control mechanism … or whether they are a 'management tool,' … a rubber stamp for management initiatives … and often surrender to management their major domain of decision-making authority, which includes the right to hire, fire, and compensate top management."[66]

Pfizer is an example of a giant pharmaceutical firm which stumbled, at least in part, because of an ineffective board. Jeffrey Kindler, CEO of Pfizer, the world's largest pharmaceutical company, stepped down in December 2010. Pfizer had built an extraordinarily successful company, realizing $68 billion annual sales on blockbuster drugs such as Lipitor and Viagra. However, under Kindler, its stock price had sagged from a high of $49 down to $17 as its pipeline of drugs dried up. Kindler evidently had difficulties trusting his colleagues and, at times, appeared to undermine many of his potential successors. He sought outside ideas from those who may not have had the necessary knowledge. He was also known for micromanaging his executive teams' endeavors. *Fortune Magazine* summed it up this way: "The story of Jeff Kindler's tenure at Pfizer is a saga of ambition, intrigue, backstabbing, and betrayal–all exacerbated by a board that allowed the problems to fester for years."[67] This suggests that if a board stays too distant from the strategic decision-making processes, political problems can get in the way of the rational process of making decisions, which can confuse the decisions necessary to create a stable financial future. Ian Read has been appointed as the new Pfizer CEO and Chairman of the board; Read has been a longtime inside manager of the major drug producer.

Despite the highly visible examples of poor governance in low-performing firms, close ties between board members and CEOs do not always lead to less board member involvement in strategic decisions. In fact, research shows that social ties between the CEO and board members may actually increase board members' involvement in strategic decisions. Thus, strong relationships between the CEO and the board of directors may result in positive or negative outcomes for firms, depending on how those relationships are managed.[68] The important point is to recognize and safeguard against the risks.

Another way for a CEO to achieve power relative to the board is to serve as chair of the board.[69] This practice, called **CEO duality**, has become more common in the United States. Although it varies across industries, duality occurs most often in the largest firms, as exemplified in Ian Read's appointment to both positions in the previously mentioned Pfizer illustration. Increased shareholder activism, however, has brought CEO duality under scrutiny and attack in both U.S. and European firms. Duality has been criticized for causing poor performance and slow response to change in a number of firms, although the research does not provide clear direction.[70]

Historically, an **independent board leadership structure**, in which different people held the positions of CEO and board chair, was believed to enhance a board's ability to monitor top-level managers' decisions and actions, particularly in terms of the firm's financial performance (see Chapter 11).[71] Consistent with this view, the two jobs are always separate in Britain. However, the British model can also lead to problems, particularly to power struggles and confusion regarding firm leadership.[72] Also, **stewardship theory** suggests that top managers want to do the right thing for the firm's shareholders and that reducing the amount of interference with their actions will increase the profit potential of the firm.[73] From this perspective, CEO duality would be expected to facilitate effective decisions and actions. In these instances, the increased effectiveness gained through CEO duality accrues from the individual who wants to perform effectively and be the best possible steward of the firm's assets.[74] Because of this person's positive orientation and actions, extra governance and the coordination costs resulting from an independent board leadership structure would be unnecessary. These arguments demonstrate that there is no clear answer regarding the influence of CEO duality on strategic decision making.

An additional influence on the power of the CEO and other top management team members is their tenure in the organization. CEOs with long tenure—on the team and in the organization—have a greater influence on board decisions.[75] And it follows that CEOs with greater influence may take actions in their own best interests, the outcomes of which increase their compensation from the company.[76] Long tenure is known to restrict the breadth of an executive's knowledge base. With the limited perspectives associated with a restricted knowledge base, long-tenured top executives typically develop fewer alternatives to evaluate in making strategic decisions.[77] However, long-tenured managers also may be able to exercise more effective strategic control, thereby obviating the need for board members' involvement because effective strategic control generally produces higher performance.[78]

To strengthen the firm, boards of directors should develop an effective relationship with the firm's top management team that makes sense in a particular competitive situation.[79] Specifically, the relative degree of power held by the board and top management team members should be examined in light of the situation. The abundance of resources in a firm's external environment and the volatility of that environment may affect the ideal balance of power between boards and top management teams.[80] For instance, a volatile and uncertain environment may create a situation in which a powerful CEO is needed to move quickly, and a diverse top management team could create less cohesion among team members and prevent or stall a necessary strategic move.[81] By developing effective working relationships, boards, CEOs, and other top management team members are able to serve the best interests of the firm's stakeholders.[82]

Executive Succession Processes

The choice of top executives, especially CEOs, is a critical organizational decision with important implications for the firm's performance.[83] Many companies use leadership screening systems to identify individuals with managerial and strategic leadership potential. The most effective of these systems assess people within the firm and gain valuable information about the capabilities of other companies' managers, particularly their strategic leaders.[84] Based on the results of these assessments, training and development programs are provided for current managers in an attempt to preselect and shape the skills of people who may become tomorrow's leaders. The "ten-step talent" management development program at General Electric, for example, is considered one of the most effective in the world.[85]

Organizations select strategic leaders from two types of managerial labor markets: internal and external.[86] An *internal managerial labor market* consists of the opportunities for managerial positions within a firm, and an *external managerial labor market* consists of career opportunities for managers in organizations other than the one for which they work currently.

In the past, companies have strongly preferred that insiders fill top management positions because of a desire for continuity and a continuing commitment to the firm's current vision, mission, and chosen strategies.[87] Research shows that insider CEOs are more effective and provide more successful change programs after three years.[88] Several benefits are thought to accrue to firms when insiders are selected as new CEOs. Because of their experience with the firm and the industry environment in which they compete, insiders are familiar with company products, markets, technologies, and operating procedures. Also, internal hiring produces lower turnover among existing personnel, many of whom possess valuable firm-specific knowledge such as unique routines, processes, documentation, or trade secrets.

Thus, when the firm is performing well, internal succession is favored because it is assumed that hiring from inside keeps within the firm the important knowledge necessary to sustain the high performance. For an inside move to the top to occur successfully, however, firms must develop and implement effective succession management programs, which help develop managers so that one will eventually be prepared to ascend to the top.[89]

Given the impressive success of General Electric over the past 20-plus years and its highly effective management development program, an insider, Jeffrey Immelt, was chosen to succeed Jack Welch.[90] Similarly, at IBM, Virginia Rometty, also an insider, was selected to replace Samuel Palmisano. However, because of changing competitive landscapes and varying levels of performance, an increasing number of boards of directors have been turning to outsiders to succeed CEOs.[91] Firms often hire an executive recruitment firm, or "headhunter," to help identify and recruit strong candidates. Although valid reasons often exist for selecting an outsider, often this is done because boards have not established well-developed, internal succession places. However, if strategic change is needed often an outsider is selected. For example, research suggests that executives who have spent their entire careers with a particular firm may become "stale in the saddle."[92] Long tenure with a firm seems to reduce the number of innovative ideas top executives are able to develop to cope with conditions their firms face. Given the importance of innovation for a firm's success in today's competitive landscape, an inability to innovate or to create conditions that stimulate innovation throughout a firm is a liability in a strategic leader. The diverse knowledge base and social networks they have developed while working for other organizations is another reason to hire from the external managerial labor market.[93] Unique combinations of diverse knowledge sets might create synergy as the foundation for developing new competitive advantages.

Figure 2.2 shows how the composition of the top management team and CEO succession (managerial labor market) may interact to affect strategy. For example, when the top management team is homogeneous (its members have similar functional experiences and educational backgrounds) and a new CEO is selected from inside the firm, the firm's current strategy is unlikely to change. On the other hand, when a new CEO is selected from outside the firm and the top management team is heterogeneous, there is a high probability that strategy will change. When the new CEO is from inside the firm and a heterogeneous top management team is in place, the strategy may not change, but innovation is likely to continue. An external CEO succession with a homogeneous team creates a more ambiguous situation.

Given the need for diverse managerial perspectives in an increasingly competitive marketplace, it is unfortunate that some firms are still reluctant to fill their top jobs with individuals who might bring a different view to the table.[94] In particular, minority groups and especially women are underrepresented in the top positions of major for-profit organizations.[95] From a resource-based perspective, this is

FIGURE 2.2 EFFECT OF CEO SUCCESSION AND TOP MANAGEMENT TEAM
COMPOSITION ON STRATEGY

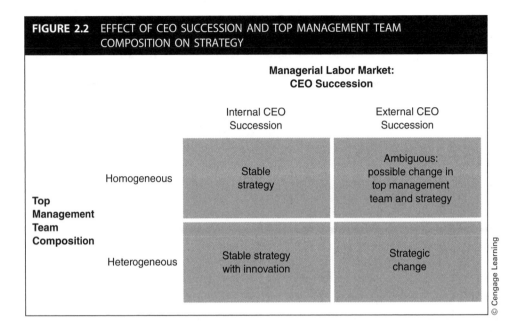

unfortunate because it signals that some firms are not taking full advantage of the resources they possess.[96] The stakeholder view also would suggest that a firm that creates a "glass ceiling" for some of its members with regard to their promotion potential is missing opportunities to foster relationships with diverse segments of society.

Nevertheless, women are making slow but steady progress in receiving more appointments in upper-level positions in for-profit firms, particularly in certain industries.[97] For example, Xerox CEO Ursala Burns (took over the helm from Anne Mulcahy and was the first female to female successor CEO among Fortune 500 firms), IBM CEO Virginia Rometty, and Hewlett Packard CEO Meg Whitman (also former CEO of eBay) are examples of women who have broken through the gender barrier. Additionally, organizations are beginning to utilize women's potential managerial talents through memberships on corporate boards of directors. In the top 100 firms in New York, 17 percent of board members are women.[98] These additional appointments suggest that women's ability to represent stakeholders' and especially shareholders' best interests in for-profit companies at the level of the board of directors is being more broadly recognized.

KEY STRATEGIC LEADERSHIP RESPONSIBILITIES AND ACTIONS

The primary responsibility for strategic thinking, and the effective strategic leadership that can result from it, rests with the top management team and, in particular, with the CEO. Strategic leadership is an extremely complex, but critical, form of leadership. Strategies cannot be formulated and implemented to achieve above-average returns unless strategic leaders successfully fulfill several important responsibilities.

As described in Chapter 1, the I/O economic, resource-based, and stakeholder perspectives envision the strategic management process from different points of view. The three perspectives also provide different views regarding the primary responsibilities of strategic leaders. From an economic perspective, top managers have the primary responsibility for ensuring that firm strategies will lead to above-average economic performance by monitoring the external environment and positioning the firm optimally in terms of its strategic direction, strategies, and implementation plans.[99] According to the resource-based view, top managers are primarily responsible for making sure their organizations acquire, develop, and utilize resources that lead to achieving competitive advantage.[100] Finally, the stakeholder perspective gives top managers primary responsibility for managing relationships with important constituencies to facilitate the creation of value.[101]

These three perspectives reflect the varied responsibilities and tasks associated with strategic leadership. They emphasize different aspects of a strategic leader's job, but in reality top managers have all of the responsibilities outlined by each of the perspectives, although they may give them a different priority. As illustrated in Figure 2.3, the responsibilities of strategic leaders are translated into specific tasks associated with the strategic management process. These tasks include determining and communicating strategic direction, facilitating and overseeing the formulation and implementation of specific strategies, and establishing balanced controls to ensure that the firm is accomplishing what it should to move in the desired direction. When executed properly, these actions result in the establishment of competitive advantage, creation of greater value for the firm and its stakeholders, and, ultimately, above-average financial performance.

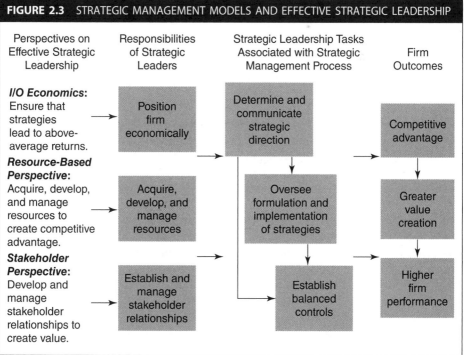

FIGURE 2.3 STRATEGIC MANAGEMENT MODELS AND EFFECTIVE STRATEGIC LEADERSHIP

Perspectives on Effective Strategic Leadership	Responsibilities of Strategic Leaders	Strategic Leadership Tasks Associated with Strategic Management Process	Firm Outcomes
I/O Economics: Ensure that strategies lead to above-average returns.	Position firm economically	Determine and communicate strategic direction	Competitive advantage
Resource-Based Perspective: Acquire, develop, and manage resources to create competitive advantage.	Acquire, develop, and manage resources	Oversee formulation and implementation of strategies	Greater value creation
Stakeholder Perspective: Develop and manage stakeholder relationships to create value.	Establish and manage stakeholder relationships	Establish balanced controls	Higher firm performance

© Cengage Learning

Strategic leaders have substantial decision-making responsibilities that cannot be delegated.[102] The rest of this chapter discusses some of the most important of these, using the responsibilities and tasks found in Figure 2.3 as an outline.

Ensure that the Firm Is Well Positioned Economically

The I/O economic model is based on the idea that economic performance is determined by a firm's general, industry, and competitor environments and by how well the firm implements the strategy dictated by those environments (see Chapter 1). Consequently, strategic leadership involves selecting industries and industry segments in which to compete and responding to changes that occur in those environments. Effective strategic leaders engage in strategic thinking that leads to the firm and its environment being continuously aligned. Individual judgment plays an important part in learning about and analyzing the firm's external conditions. As Dan DiMicco, CEO of the steel giant Nucor, put it, "What I get paid for is not looking at yesterday, but looking at the future."[103]

Another way to envision the positioning responsibility of strategic leaders is to say that they should clearly define a firm's strategy, which is a manifestation of strategic intent. Strategic intent was defined in the first chapter as the way a firm leverages its resources, capabilities, and core competencies to accomplish its goals in the competitive environment.[104] Unfortunately, the term "strategy" has taken on so many meanings that it can be used to mean almost anything. For instance, some firms may define their strategy in terms of how they treat people, whereas others may talk about particular markets or products. Hambrick and Fredrickson suggest that strategy is "the central, integrated, externally oriented concept of how we will achieve our objectives."[105] Their view is consistent with our definition in Chapter 1 that strategy is an integrated and coordinated set of commitments and actions designed to exploit core competencies and gain a competitive advantage. A firm's fundamental purposes, reflected in its mission and goals, are treated separately from a firm's strategy. Instead, the strategy becomes a vehicle to achieve the firm's purposes. Organizational arrangements such as structures, processes, rewards systems, and functional policies also support but do not define strategy. Strategic leaders use the tools of strategic analysis, including analysis of industries, markets, competitors, and internal strengths and weaknesses, to help them determine firm strategy.[106]

Five important elements that identify a firm's strategy are arenas, growth vehicles, differentiators, staging, and the economic logic that ties all the elements together (see Figure 2.4). *Arenas* involve a firm's **scope**, which is the breadth of a firm's activities across products, markets, geographic regions, core technologies, and value creation stages. Defining the business is a critical starting point for all strategic planning and management.[107] Firms like Siemens AG, Sony, and General Electric have broad scope because of their involvement in a wide range of industries throughout the world. On the other hand, Frontier Airlines focuses its efforts exclusively on airline transportation in the western United States. McDonald's has wide geographic scope, but most of its revenues come from a particular technology—fast food preparation and delivery.

Growth vehicles also are important to understanding a firm's strategy. Some of the commonly used vehicles are internal development, joint ventures, licensing,

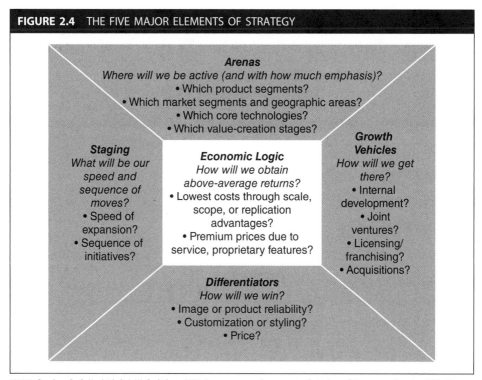

FIGURE 2.4 THE FIVE MAJOR ELEMENTS OF STRATEGY

Arenas
Where will we be active (and with how much emphasis)?
• Which product segments?
• Which market segments and geographic areas?
• Which core technologies?
• Which value-creation stages?

Staging
What will be our speed and sequence of moves?
• Speed of expansion?
• Sequence of initiatives?

Economic Logic
How will we obtain above-average returns?
• Lowest costs through scale, scope, or replication advantages?
• Premium prices due to service, proprietary features?

Growth Vehicles
How will we get there?
• Internal development?
• Joint ventures?
• Licensing/ franchising?
• Acquisitions?

Differentiators
How will we win?
• Image or product reliability?
• Customization or styling?
• Price?

SOURCE: Based on D. C. Hambrick & J. W. Fredrickson, 2005, Are you sure you have a strategy? *Academy of Management Executive*, 19(4): 54, reprinted from 15(4).

franchising, and acquisitions. General Electric has historically engaged in frequent acquisitions to increase the scope of its businesses, as well as many joint ventures to enter new markets (such as China). Choice Hotels used franchising to become one of the fastest growing hotel operators in the country using middle market brands such as the Comfort Inn, Comfort Suites, Cambria Suites, Sleep Inn, Mainstay Suites, Quality Inn, Clarion, EconoLodge, Rodeway Inn, and Suburban Extended Stay throughout the United States and more than 40 countries and territories.[108] On the other hand, hotel and restaurant chains such as Marriott and Starbucks, respectively, have grown rapidly primarily through internal development rather than franchising.

Differentiators help a firm determine how it is expected to win customers in the marketplace. Southwest Airlines attracts customers through rock-bottom prices and by staying on schedule. McDonald's draws people in by offering them dependable quality and convenient locations. A company like General Electric has a more difficult problem in defining a consistent differentiator for its multitude of businesses. In fact, in diversified firms it is probably a better idea to allow the top management team of each distinct business to determine how it will win customers. However, even firms as highly diversified as General Electric may try to establish core competencies that differentiate several businesses in similar ways. For instance, General Electric stresses finding innovative ways to satisfy customer needs. According to CEO Jeffrey Immelt: "For GE, imagination at work is more than a slogan or tagline. It is a reason for being."[109]

Staging has to do with the timing of strategy and the sequence of moves the firm will take to carry it out. It is especially important because of the speed with which the competitive environment is changing.[110] For instance, Microsoft has been criticized because it is sometimes slow to respond to changes in its markets such as the move to mobile computing.[111] However, being fast to market is not a guarantee of success either. Consider that Yahoo! Inc. was an early entrant in the search market, but through a series of missteps, the company now struggles to survive in this market.[112] Strategic leaders must make sure that everything is in place as they execute a strategy. As an example, Boeing had to work out problems with its unions before building its 787 Dreamliner, which required major changes to the firm's manufacturing processes.[113]

The *economic logic* of a strategy pulls together the other four elements. From an economic perspective, a strategy is unsuccessful unless its elements lead to above-average returns. When everything comes together, the results can be outstanding. The Boeing case, however, also illustrates one of the major themes of this book—the need for constant reassessment of strategy in an ever-changing external environment. For example, as consumers demanded cutting-edge products and better service, Dell lost its number one slot to rival Hewlett-Packard, but as the move to mobile and cloud computing illustrates, Apple has become the leader through the iPad tablet and other mobile devices.[114]

Acquire, Develop, and Manage Key Resources

The resource-based perspective focuses attention on the value of organizational resources in achieving competitive advantage. Strategic leaders are primarily responsible for ensuring that their firms acquire and develop the resources they need to achieve competitive success. Briefly mentioned in Chapter 1, *core competencies* are resources and capabilities that serve as a source of competitive advantage for a firm over its rivals. Firms develop and exploit core competencies in many different functional areas. Strategic leaders must verify that the firm's competencies are emphasized in strategy implementation efforts.

Much of Chapter 4 deals with organizational resources and their potential as sources of competitive advantage. However, two resources—human capital and organizational culture—are so closely related to strategic leadership that we discuss them briefly here.

Manage Human Capital. The ability to manage human capital, or the knowledge and skills of a firm's entire workforce, may be the most critical of the strategic leader's skills.[115] Intellectual capital, including the ability to manage knowledge and create and commercialize innovation, affects a strategic leader's success.[116] Competent strategic leaders also establish the context through which stakeholders (such as employees, customers, and suppliers) can perform at peak efficiency.[117] The crux of strategic leadership is the ability to manage the firm's operations and employees effectively in order to sustain high performance over time.

From the perspective of human capital, employees are viewed as a capital resource that requires investment.[118] These investments are productive, in that much of the development of U.S. industry can be attributed to the effectiveness of its human capital, leading to the conviction in many business firms today that "as the dynamics of competition accelerate, people are perhaps the only truly sustainable source of competitive advantage."[119] Human capital's increasing importance suggests a significant role for the firm's human resource management activities.[120] As a support activity (see Chapter 4), human resource management practices facilitate people's efforts to successfully select and especially to use the firm's strategies.[121]

Finding the human capital necessary to run an organization effectively is a challenge that many firms attempt to solve by using temporary employees. Other firms try to improve their recruiting and selection techniques. Solving the problem, however, requires more than hiring temporary employees; it requires building effective commitments to organizational goals as well. Hiring star players is also insufficient; rather, a strategic leader needs to build an effective organizational team committed to achieving the company's strategic intent.[122]

Increasingly, international experience has become essential to the development necessary for strategic leaders.[123] Because nearly every industry is targeting fast-growing foreign markets, more companies are requiring "global competency" among their top managers. Thus, companies trying to learn how to compete successfully in the global economy should find opportunities for their future strategic leaders to work in locations outside of their home nation. When multinational corporations invest in emerging economies, they are also wise to invest in human capital in foreign subsidiaries.[124] Furthermore, because international management capabilities are becoming important, managing "inpatriation" (the process of transferring host-country or third-country national managers into the domestic market of multinational firms) has become an important means of building global core competencies.[125]

Effective training and development programs increase the probability that a manager will be a successful strategic leader. These programs have grown progressively important as knowledge has become more integral to gaining and sustaining a competitive advantage.[126] Additionally, such programs build knowledge and skills, inculcate a common set of core values, and offer a systematic view of the organization, thus promoting the firm's strategic vision and organizational cohesion. The programs also contribute to the development of core competencies. Furthermore, they help strategic leaders improve skills that are critical to completing other tasks associated with effective strategic leadership, such as determining the firm's strategic direction, exploiting and maintaining the firm's core competencies, and developing an organizational culture that supports ethical practices. Thus, building human capital is vital to the effective execution of strategic leadership.

Strategic leaders must acquire the skills necessary to help develop human capital in their areas of responsibility. This challenge is important, given that most strategic leaders need to enhance their human resource management and collaborative abilities.[127] For example, firms that value human resources and have effective reward plans for employees have obtained higher returns on their initial public offerings.[128] When human capital investments are successful, the result is a workforce capable of learning continuously. Continuous learning and leveraging the firm's expanding knowledge base are linked with strategic success.[129]

Programs that achieve outstanding results in the training of future strategic leaders become a competitive advantage for a firm. General Electric's system of training and development of future strategic leaders is comprehensive and thought to be among the best.[130] Accordingly, it may be a source of competitive advantage for the firm.

Ensure an Effective Organizational Culture. An **organizational culture** consists of a complex set of ideologies, symbols, and core values that is shared throughout the firm and influences the way business is conducted. Evidence suggests that a firm can develop core competencies in terms of both the capabilities it possesses and the way the capabilities are used to produce strategic actions. In other words, because the organizational culture influences how the firm conducts its business and helps regulate and control employees' behavior, it can be a source of competitive advantage.[131] Thus, shaping the context within which the firm formulates and implements its strategies—that is, shaping the organizational culture—is a central task of strategic leaders.[132]

An organizational culture often encourages (or discourages) the pursuit of entrepreneurial opportunities, especially in large firms.[133] Entrepreneurial opportunities are an important source of growth and innovation; therefore, a key role of strategic leaders is to encourage and promote innovation by pursuing entrepreneurial opportunities.[134] One way to do this is to invest in opportunities as real options— that is, opportunities that provide options to make additional worthwhile investments in the future, if the situation calls for it. For example, a firm may purchase property now because it wants the option to build on it in the future. Chapter 12 describes how large firms use strategic entrepreneurship to pursue entrepreneurial opportunities and to gain first-mover advantages. Chapter 13 covers the real options approach. Medium and small firms also rely on strategic entrepreneurship when trying to develop innovations as the foundation for earning above-average returns. In firms of all sizes, strategic entrepreneurship is more likely to be successful when employees have an entrepreneurial orientation. Five dimensions characterize a firm's entrepreneurial orientation: autonomy, innovativeness, risk taking, proactiveness, and competitive aggressiveness.[135] In combination, these dimensions influence the actions a firm takes in efforts to be innovative and launch new ventures.

Autonomy allows employees to take actions that are free of organizational constraints and permits individuals and groups to be self-directed. *Innovativeness* "reflects a firm's tendency to engage in and support new ideas, novelty, experimentation, and creative processes that may result in new products, services, or technological processes."[136] Cultures with a tendency toward innovativeness encourage employees to think beyond existing knowledge, technologies, and parameters in efforts to find creative ways to add value. *Risk taking* reflects a willingness by employees and their firm to accept risks when pursuing entrepreneurial opportunities. These risks can include assuming significant levels of debt and allocating substantial other resources (e.g., people) to projects that may not be completed. *Proactiveness* describes a firm's ability to be a market leader rather than a follower. Proactive organizational cultures constantly use processes to anticipate future market needs and to satisfy them before competitors learn how to do so. Finally, *competitive aggressiveness* is a firm's propensity to take actions that allow it to consistently and substantially outperform its rivals.[137]

Changing a firm's organizational culture is more difficult than maintaining it, but effective strategic leaders recognize when change is needed. Incremental changes to the firm's culture typically are used to implement strategies. More significant and sometimes even radical changes to organizational culture are used to support the selection of strategies that differ from those the firm has implemented historically. Regardless of the reasons for change, shaping and reinforcing a new culture require effective communication and problem solving, along with the selection of the right people (those who have the values desired for the organization), effective performance appraisals (establishing goals and measuring individual performance toward goals that fit in with the new core values), and appropriate reward systems (rewarding the desired behaviors that reflect the new core values).[138]

Evidence suggests that cultural changes succeed only when the firm's CEO, other key top management team members, and middle-level managers actively support them.[139] Ronald Johnson was recently hired by J.C. Penney to become its CEO. Johnson was formerly the marketing director for Apple Computer Stores. Johnson's new vision suggests that it will be a "seismic shift cutting across all aspects of the company's pricing, promotion, presentation and products."[140] Such a dramatic change will require all employees, and especially the middle-level and top executives, to implement this new strategy. However, J.C. Penney might experience some customer and supplier pushback regarding its new schemes as they seek to adjust to the "new J.C. Penney." In the store, the floor will convert from the current open seas of racks to 100 individual shop concepts for private and national brands, including Izod, Arizona, and Liz Claiborne. Each month, J.C. Penney's will stage sales and promotions tied to holidays and special events such as Valentine's Day or the Super Bowl.[141] In this example we see the importance of successfully changing an organization's culture linked to efforts to develop human capital and manage stakeholders to develop competitive advantage.

Develop and Manage Relationships with External Stakeholders

Many of the benefits associated with effective stakeholder management (as outlined in Chapter 1) depend on the actions and attitudes of the top management team, and especially the CEO. A CEO who fosters excellent relationships with key stakeholders can help the organization acquire timely and more accurate information about the external environment, which can enhance planning and decision making.[142] Furthermore, firms that have better reputations because of excellent stakeholder relationships may have the advantage of attracting customers and business partners, giving them more and better strategic options from which to select.[143] Also, a relationship of trust between top managers and external stakeholders can help to facilitate acquisition of valuable resources and reduce transaction costs associated with elaborate contractual safeguards and contingencies that might otherwise be necessary.[144] As the business world continues to increase in complexity and businesses become more interdependent, the leadership role of managing external stakeholders takes on even more strategic importance.[145]

This section emphasizes the responsibilities of top managers in creating and managing relationships with external stakeholders. The last section, derived from the resource-based view, emphasizes the strategic role top managers play in acquiring, developing, and managing internal resources, especially human capital and organizational culture. Although discussed separately, these two perspectives overlap, as do the roles strategic leaders play. For instance, from a resource-based perspective, stakeholder relationships *are* strategic resources that can help a firm acquire additional resources and thereby maintain competitive advantage.[146] Also, the stakeholder perspective includes management of both external *and* internal stakeholders.

Economic positioning also is conceptually linked to the other two perspectives. For instance, external stakeholder management is closely associated with the monitoring that occurs as strategic leaders position their firms in their industries. Also, possession of particular resources and skills positions a firm relative to its competitors. Responsibilities associated with all three of the perspectives result in strategic direction and formulation and implementation of specific strategies (see Figure 2.3).

Determine and Communicate Strategic Direction

The **strategic direction** of a firm defines its image and character over time, framed within the context of the conditions in which it operates. Like a firm's strategy, it grows out of strategic intent and is a function of the resources and capabilities a firm possesses or wishes to possess, as well as what the firm wants to do for its stakeholders. The CEO is the chief architect of strategic direction, although most top executives obtain input from many people inside and outside the organization.[147] Research has shown that having an effective strategic direction and properly reinforcing it can positively affect performance as measured by growth in sales, profits, employment, and net worth.[148]

Strategic direction is reflected in the firm's mission, vision, purpose, long-term goals, and values, which tend to be interconnected. In fact, sometimes a mission statement includes many of these things, such as Novartis' mission statement found in Table 2.1. Novartis has five divisions representing pharmaceuticals, Alcon (eye care products), Sandoz (generic drugs), vaccines and diagnostics, and consumer health.

A carefully constructed strategic mission should help the firm define the scope of its operations as well as its unique purposes.[149] With regard to scope, Novartis

---

TABLE 2.1 MISSION OF NOVARTIS

Purpose

We want to discover, develop and successfully market innovative products to prevent and cure diseases, to ease suffering, and to enhance the quality of life. We also want to provide a shareholder return that reflects outstanding performance and to adequately reward those who invest ideas and work in our company.

People

We strive to provide our associates with the safest possible workplace and to promote their health and well-being. We are an integral part of the communities that host our operations. We pay living wages worldwide, contributing to the stability and prosperity of these communities.

With more than 120,000 associates in 140 countries worldwide, Novartis associates share a vision of **a better today and tomorrow for patients**—a vision that drives our growth and success. The greatest job satisfaction for our associates is the knowledge that they improve the quality of life for patients with increasing precision and efficiency through breakthrough science and innovation.

Our performance-oriented culture and responsible approach attract top experts in all areas—research and development, marketing and sales, finance and administration. Our talented associates have made us a global leader in healthcare. Novartis is committed to rewarding the people who invest ideas and work in our company.

SOURCE: Adapted from the following Website: http://www.novartis.com/about-novartis/our-mission/index.shtml, visited on February 21, 2012.

has defined its businesses in terms of customer functions. Specifically, the company's products and services prevent and cure diseases, ease suffering, and enhance the quality of life. Typically, purposes are defined in terms of what a firm intends to do for particular stakeholders. For instance, a firm may want to achieve high returns for shareholders or provide a motivating environment for employees. In the Novartis example, in addition to what the company intends to do for its customers, it aspires to help employees realize professional ambitions and to contribute to society and the environment. The company values of openness, innovation, and financial success are also found in the mission statement.

Some firms also include the concept of sustainability in their mission statement. **Sustainable development,** the concept that a firm can and should operate without adversely influencing its environment, has been gaining strategic importance in recent years.[150] The ideal long-term vision has two parts: a core ideology and an envisioned future. The core ideology motivates employees through the company's heritage, and the envisioned future encourages employees to stretch beyond their comfort zones.[151] "Stretch goals" promote higher levels of personal and organizational performance.[152] The vision of Novartis is reflected by a desire to be recognized for having a positive effect on the lives of customers, employees, the environment, and society. This vision is built on a long history of success in the health sciences. Novartis also wants to remain in the top quartile of its industry based on growth in earnings. Achieving this goal over the long term will require a very high level of motivation among managers and employees. The company will have to continue to innovate and change in order to remain competitive in its volatile and highly competitive industry.

Although the Novartis example is particularly comprehensive, it is not unusual to find many of the components of strategic direction in a strategic mission statement. On the other hand, sometimes strategic direction is not found in a written statement, or it is divided into an assortment of statements with different names and purposes. Also, labels are used in a variety of different ways. What is most important is that the firm has a well-defined strategic direction and that it communicates the direction to internal and, to some extent, external stakeholders. Annual reports, speeches, press releases, training sessions, meetings, interpersonal communication, and comments from executives are all vehicles for communicating strategic direction.[153]

Internal stakeholders, including executives, managers, and employees, need to know the strategic direction so that it can guide them in their decision making. The firm can also communicate certain elements of its strategic direction to external stakeholders to help them know what to expect from the organization. Obviously, investors use such information to help them predict the firm's future performance. However, customers, communities, suppliers, venture partners, special interest groups, and regulators can benefit from understanding what the firm values and how it conducts business. In the wake of recent corporate scandals, this element of strategic direction has been receiving significantly more attention.

Establish Values and Ethical Practices. Mission statements often refer to values associated with ethical practices. In addition, codes of ethics frequently are created to reinforce those values. For instance, United Technologies has a twenty page code of ethics based on the values of trust, respect, and integrity.[154] Nevertheless, values statements and codes of ethics are not a guarantee that managers and employees will act ethically.[155] The infamous sixty-four-page "Code of Ethics" allegedly published by Enron Corporation begins with a statement from CEO Kenneth Lay: "As officers and employees of Enron Corp., its subsidiaries, and its affiliated companies, we are responsible for conducting the business affairs of the companies in accordance with all applicable laws and in a moral and honest manner."[156] Managerial opportunism may explain the behavior and decisions of key executives at Enron, where stockholders lost almost all the value in their Enron stock during the firm's bankruptcy proceeding. The bankruptcy was precipitated by off-balance-sheet partnerships formed by Enron managers.[157] The reputation of Arthur Andersen, Enron's auditor, was also damaged beyond repair, resulting ultimately in the company surrendering its license to practice as certified public accountants.[158]

There were a number of recent departures of CEOs based on ethical lapses and associated corporate scandals. Jon Corzine, former CEO of MF Global, left the organization because it defaulted on its loans and lost control of investors' funds and was forced into bankruptcy. Interestingly, Corzine was a former U.S. senator, former Democratic governor of New Jersey, and ex-CEO of Goldman Sachs, a famous investment bank. In addition, CEO Michael Woodford was forced to resign from Japanese camera maker Olympus after he questioned billions of dollars in takeover costs that had been put in its books by former executives of the company. Although the company used the excuse that Woodford's style was "too independent and not respectful enough of Japanese culture," company representatives have since admitted that it had falsified the books in regard to the costs questioned by Woodford.[159]

Ethical companies encourage and enable people at all organizational levels to act ethically when doing what is necessary to implement the firm's strategies. In turn, ethical practices and the judgment on which they are based create "social capital" in the organization in that "goodwill available to individuals and groups" in the organization increases.[160] Thus, leadership is essential in providing examples upon which to model the ethics values, and the approach that leaders provide influences the values that employees adopt in the interaction with stakeholders.[161] Alternately, when unethical practices evolve in an organization, they become like a contagious disease.[162] Firms that have been reported to have poor ethical behavior, such as practicing fraud or having to restate financial results, see their overall corporate value in the stock market drop precipitously.[163]

News Corp. chairman Rupert Murdoch supervises a global media empire that covers newspapers, cable news companies, as well as newspaper organizations. The *News of the World* tabloid owned by Murdoch but amounting to only 3 percent of the News Corp. assets, participated in phone hacking that caused a scandal that called into question the integrity of the whole media empire. The scandal caused News Corp. stock to drop by $5 billion worth of equity. In the process, those politicians who associated with the CEO of *News of the World*, Rebekah Brooks, a former newspaper executive at News Corp., had their credibility questioned. Andrew Coulson, one of the former executives at News Corp., was indicted and had to be fired by the British Prime Minister, David Cameron, because he had hired Coulson as his press secretary. Much of the scandal could have been avoided had Murdoch and his executives apologized and performed an open investigation into the dealings of *News of the World*. Instead, News Corp. uses this ethic of responding: "If you are attacked from the outside, you defend." They never admitted wrongdoing or sought to get to the bottom of the issue, and created instead a lax focus on ethics. Apparently the newspaper ethic at the *News of the World* tabloid focused on "scoop-obsessed ... cut throat competition in which the ends—a good story—always justifies the frequently unedifying means."[164] This is an example where the informal ethics of the company leaders caused havoc not only to the individual tabloid (the tabloid was shut down), but also cast doubt on all the media outlets of the News Corp. empire and even impacted the political credibility of the U.K. Prime Minister, David Cameron.[165]

To properly influence employees' judgment and behavior, ethical practices must shape the firm's decision-making process and be an integral part of an organization's culture. In fact, research has found that a value-based culture is the most effective means of ensuring that employees comply with the firm's ethical requirements.[166] Evidence also suggests that managers' values are critical in shaping a firm's cultural values.[167] Consequently, firms should employ ethical strategic leaders—leaders who include ethical practices as part of their long-term vision for the firm, who desire to do the right thing, and for whom honesty, trust, and integrity are important. Strategic leaders who consistently display these qualities inspire employees as they work with others to develop and support an organizational culture in which ethical practices are the expected behavioral norms. In addition to being good examples, top managers may also institute formal programs to manage ethics. Operating much like control systems, these programs help inculcate values throughout the organization.[168]

Additional actions strategic leaders can take to develop an ethical organizational culture include (1) establishing and communicating specific goals to describe the firm's ethical standards (e.g., developing and disseminating a code of conduct); (2) continuously revising and updating the code of conduct on the basis of input from people throughout the firm and from other stakeholders (e.g., customers and suppliers); (3) disseminating the code of conduct to all stakeholders to inform them of the firm's ethical standards and practices; (4) developing and implementing methods and procedures to use in achieving the firm's ethical standards (e.g., using internal auditing practices that are consistent with the standards); (5) creating and using explicit reward systems that recognize acts of courage (e.g., rewarding those who use proper channels and procedures to report observed wrongdoing); and (6) creating a work environment in which all people are treated with dignity.[169] The effectiveness of these actions increases when they are taken simultaneously, thereby making them mutually supportive.

Oversee Formulation and Implementation of Specific Strategies

Strategic leaders are responsible for ensuring that appropriate strategies are both formulated and successfully implemented. Earlier in this chapter we outlined the responsibilities of strategic leaders from three perspectives. Each of these perspectives results in a slightly different but interrelated view of strategy formulation and implementation. I/O economics suggests that strategy is based on evaluation of the external environment and positioning the firm optimally in that environment. Implementation involves developing structures, systems, and programs to reinforce the position.[170] The resource-based view focuses on the acquisition and development of uniquely valuable resources and capabilities that are hard for competitors to imitate, thus leading to competitive advantage. Implementation plans involve making optimal use of and supporting those resources and capabilities.[171] The stakeholder perspective leads to strategies that attempt to make optimal use of relationships with stakeholders to create value. Implementation involves activities such as collecting information from stakeholders, assessing their needs and desires, integrating this knowledge into strategic decisions, effectively managing internal stakeholders, and forming interorganizational relationships with external stakeholders.[172] Chapters 5 through 10 discuss the specific nature of these strategies and how they are implemented.

Strategic direction also influences a firm's specific strategies. For instance, a firm's mission defines its basic approach to corporate-level strategy and may contain clues regarding the resources and skills that form the base for its business-level strategies. In addition, strategic direction serves as a guide to many aspects of a firm's strategy implementation process, including motivation, leadership, employee empowerment, and organizational design. In the case of Novartis, the company is supporting its mission by transforming its headquarters in Basel, Switzerland, into an ultramodern, high-performance workplace that facilitates research and fosters communication and collaboration.[173]

Once strategic leaders have guided the establishment of the firm's strategic direction, strategies, and implementation plans, their final responsibility is to establish organizational control systems to ensure that the plans are actually executed and to measure their success and provide feedback.

Establish Balanced Controls

Organizational controls have long been viewed as an important part of strategy implementation processes. Controls are necessary to help ensure that firms achieve their desired outcomes.[174] Defined as the "formal, information-based … procedures used by managers to maintain or alter patterns in organizational activities," controls help strategic leaders build credibility, demonstrate the value of strategies to the firm's stakeholders, and promote and support strategic change.[175] Most critically, controls provide the parameters within which strategies are to be implemented, as well as corrective actions to be taken when implementation-related adjustments are required.

We examine control structures associated with each strategy type (Business-level in Chapter 5, Cooperative Strategy in Chapter 7, Corporate-level in Chapter 8, and International Strategy in Chapter 10). Chapter 11 on corporate governance discusses top executive controls in greater detail, but here we look briefly at financial and strategic controls because strategic leaders are responsible for their development and effective use. Financial control focuses on short-term financial outcomes. In contrast, *strategic control* focuses on the content of strategic actions, rather than their outcomes. Some strategic actions can be correct, but poor financial outcomes may still result because of external conditions, such as a recession in the economy, unexpected domestic or foreign government actions, or natural disasters.[176] Therefore, an emphasis on financial control often produces more short-term and risk-averse managerial decisions because financial outcomes may be caused by events beyond managers' direct control. Alternatively, strategic control encourages lower-level managers to make decisions that incorporate moderate and acceptable levels of risk because outcomes are shared between the business-level executives making strategic proposals and the corporate-level executives evaluating them.

The Balanced Scorecard. The **balanced scorecard** is a framework that strategic leaders can use to verify that they have established both financial controls and strategic controls to assess their firm's performance.[177] This technique is most appropriate when dealing with business-level strategies but can also apply to corporate-level strategies.

The underlying premise of the balanced scorecard is that firms jeopardize their future performance possibilities when financial controls are emphasized at the expense of strategic controls,[178] in that financial controls provide feedback about outcomes achieved from past actions but do not communicate the drivers of the firm's future performance.[179] Thus, an overemphasis on financial controls could promote organizational behavior that has a net effect of sacrificing the firm's long-term, value-creating potential for short-term performance gains.[180] An appropriate balance of financial controls and strategic controls, rather than an overemphasis on either, allows firms to effectively monitor their performance.

Four perspectives are integrated to form the balanced scorecard framework (see Figure 2.5): *financial* (concerned with growth, profitability, and risk from the shareholders' perspective), *customer* (concerned with the amount of value that customers perceive was created by the firm's products), *internal business processes* (with a focus on the priorities for various business processes that create customer and shareholder satisfaction), and *learning and growth* (concerned with the firm's effort to create a climate that supports change, innovation, and growth). Thus, using the balanced scorecard's framework allows the firm to understand how it looks to shareholders (financial perspective), how customers view it (customer perspective), the processes it must emphasize to successfully use its competitive advantage (internal perspective), and what it can do to improve its performance in order to grow (learning and growth perspective). Porsche used a balanced-scorecard approach to promote learning and continuous improvement while maintaining a market-leading position among sports car manufacturers.[181]

Firms use different criteria to measure their standing relative to the scorecard's four perspectives (see Figure 2.5). These criteria should be established on the basis of what the firm is trying to accomplish and its strategic direction. The firm should select the number of criteria that will allow it to have both a strategic understanding and a financial understanding of its performance without becoming immersed in too many details.[182] Several performance criteria, such as those associated with financial and customer as well as purely internal perspectives, will be discussed in Chapter 4. Of course, the criteria frequently are interrelated.

Strategic leaders play an important role in determining a proper balance between strategic controls and financial controls for their firm. This is true in single-business firms as well as in diversified corporations. In fact, most corporate restructuring is designed to refocus the firm on its core businesses, thereby allowing

FIGURE 2.5 STRATEGIC CONTROLS AND FINANCIAL CONTROLS IN A BALANCED SCORECARD FRAMEWORK

Perspectives	Criteria
Financial	• Cash flow • Return on equity • Return on assets
Customer	• Assessment of ability to anticipate customers' needs • Effectiveness of customer service practices • Percentage of repeat business • Quality of communications with customers
Internal Business Processes	• Asset utilization improvements • Improvements in employee morale • Changes in turnover rates
Learning and Growth	• Improvements in innovation ability • Number of new products compared to competitors' • Increases in employees' skills

© Cengage Learning

top executives to reestablish strategic control of their separate business units.[183] Thus, both strategic controls and financial controls support effective use of the firm's corporate-level strategy.

SUMMARY

▶ Effective strategic leadership is a prerequisite to successful use of the strategic management process. Strategic leadership entails the ability to anticipate events, envision possibilities, maintain flexibility, and empower others to create strategic change.

▶ Strategic leadership skills fall into a hierarchy, where managers must master lower-level skills before they fine-tune higher-level skills. Level 5 Executives have mastered all the skills.

▶ Strategic leaders differ in the way they direct the strategic management process. A traditional "commander" approach limits manager participation in strategic decisions, whereas a more collaborative style entails jointly arriving at strategies and implementation plans with members of the top management team. The appropriate style depends on the nature of the competitive situation.

- Top managers are constrained by a number of factors that influence the level of discretion they have when making decisions. Some of these factors are associated with the external environment, such as the industry structure, the rate of market growth in the firm's primary industry, and the degree to which products can be differentiated.

- Strategic managers sometimes rely on heuristics, or "rules of thumb," when they make strategic decisions. These heuristics help managers simplify what might otherwise be an overwhelmingly complicated and uncertain decision environment, but they also can lead to suboptimal decisions. Awareness of decision-making biases, use of real options analysis, and formation of a heterogeneous top management team can help strategic decision makers reduce the ill effects of decision biases.

- A top management team is composed of the chief executive officer and other key managers who are responsible for setting the direction of the firm and formulating and implementing its strategies. The quality of strategic thinking and subsequent strategic decisions made by a top management team affect the firm's ability to innovate and engage in effective strategic change.

- The overwhelming complexity and strength of environmental forces, as well as the need to manage a wide variety of stakeholder relationships, require formation of a heterogeneous top management team composed of individuals with different functional backgrounds, experience, and education. The more heterogeneous a top management team is, with varied expertise and knowledge, the more capacity it has to provide effective strategic leadership in formulating strategy.

- Higher firm performance normally is achieved when the board of directors is more directly involved in shaping a firm's strategic direction. However, directors may find it difficult to direct the strategic actions of powerful CEOs and top management teams. The relative power of top managers is at least partially a function of social or business ties with directors, their tenure as members of the top management team, and whether the CEO also serves as chair of the board.

- Organizations select strategic leaders from two types of managerial labor markets—internal and external. Use of the internal or external market depends, in part, on the need for change in the organization.

- Six key components of effective strategic leadership include ensuring that the firm is well-positioned economically, managing key resources, developing and maintaining effective relationships with key stakeholders, determining a strategic direction (which includes establishing values and ethical practices), overseeing the formulation and implementation of specific strategies, and establishing balanced organizational control systems.

- Strategic direction is reflected in the firm's mission, vision, purpose, long-term goals, and values, which tend to be interconnected. There are several vehicles, such as annual reports, speeches, and press releases, for communicating strategic direction.

- An effective balance between strategic and financial controls allows for the flexible use of core competencies, but within the parameters indicated by the firm's financial position. The balanced scorecard is a tool that strategic leaders use to develop an appropriate balance between the firm's strategic and financial controls.

ETHICS QUESTIONS

1. What are the ethical issues influencing managerial discretion? Has the current business environment changed the influence of ethics on managerial discretion? If so, how?

2. How have ethical lapses influenced regulatory changes and how has the current stakeholders' view changed the expectations for strategic leaders in formulating and implementing contemporary strategies?

3. What should a newly appointed CEO from the external managerial labor market do to understand a firm's ethical climate? How important are the CEO's efforts to understand this climate?

4. Are ethical strategic leaders more effective than unethical strategic leaders? If so, why? If not, why not?

5. Assume that you are working in an organization that you believe has an unethical culture. What actions could you take to change that culture to make it more ethical?

6. Is corporate downsizing ethical? If not, why not? If corporate downsizing is ethical, what can strategic leaders do to mitigate the negative effects associated with reducing the size of their firm's labor force?

NOTES

1. A. G. Lafley & N. M. Tichy, 2011, The art and science of finding the right CEO, *Harvard Business Review*, 89(10): 66–74.

2. 2006, Leadership styles at GE and Canon, *Strategic Direction*, 22(1): 15–20; R. Barnes, 2004, Executives who didn't survive Jack Welch's GE are now running 3M, Home Depot, *Knight Ridder Tribune Business News*, April 24, 1.

3. B. Moreton, 2009, *To Serve God and Wal-Mart: The Making of Christian Free Enterprise*, Cambridge, MA: Harvard University Press; C. H. Tong & L.-I. Tong, 2006, Exploring the cornerstones of Wal-Mart's success and competitiveness, *Competitiveness Review*, 16(2): 143–149.

4. J. Greco, 1999, Akio Morita: A founder of Japan, Inc., *The Journal of Business Strategy*, 20(5): 38–39.

5. A. J. Kinicki, K. J. L. Jacobson, B. M. Galvin, & G. E. Prussia, 2011, A multilevel systems model of leadership, *Journal of Leadership & Organization Studies*, 18(2): 133–149.

6. Z. Zhen & S. J. Peterson, 2011, Advice networks in teams: The role of transformational leadership and members' core self-evaluations, *Journal of Applied Psychology*, 96(5): 1004–1017.

7. J. Collins, 2001, *Good to Great: Why Some Companies Make the Leap ... and Others Don't*, New York: Harper Business.

8. R. W. Evans & F. C. Butler, 2011, An upper echelons view of 'Good to Great': Principles for behavioral integration in the top management team, *Journal of Leadership Studies*, 5(2): 89–97.

9. 2011, The magician, *Economist*, October 8, 15.

10. J. Tian, J. Haleblian, & N. Rajagopalan, 2011, The effects of board human and social capital on investor reactions to new CEO selection, *Strategic Management Journal*, 32(7): 731–747.

11. E. Ng & G. Sears, 2012, CEO leadership styles and the implementation of organizational diversity practices: Moderating effects of social values and age, *Journal of Business Ethics*, 105(1): 41–52.

12. M. Carpenter & J. Fredrickson, 2001, Top management teams, global strategic posture, and the moderating role of uncertainty, *Academy of Management Journal*, 44: 533–545; S. F. Slater, 1989, The influence of style on business unit performance, *Journal of Management*, 15: 441–455.

13. L. Markóczy, 2001, Consensus formation during strategic change, *Strategic Management Journal*, 22: 1013–1031; D. Knight, C. L. Pearce, K. G. Smith, J. D. Olian, H. P. Sims, K. A. Smith, & P. Flood, 1999, Top management team diversity, group process, and strategic consensus, *Strategic Management Journal*, 20: 446–465.

14. H. Wang, A. S. Tsui, & K. R. Xin, 2011, CEO leadership behaviors, organizational performance, and employees' attitudes, *Leadership Quarterly*, 22(1): 92–105; M. de Luque, N. T. Washburn, D. A. Waldman, & R. J. House, 2008, Unrequited profit: How stakeholder and economic values relate to subordinates' perceptions of leadership and firm performance, *Administrative Science Quarterly*, 53(4): 626–654.

15. G. Sadri, T. J. Weber, & W. A. Gentry, 2011, Empathetic emotion and leadership performance: An empirical analysis across 38 countries, *Leadership Quarterly*, 22(5): 818–830; M. A. Hitt, M. T. Dacin, B. B. Tyler, & D. Park, 1997, Understanding the differences in Korean and U.S. executives' strategic orientations, *Strategic Management Journal*, 18: 159–167; Slater, The influence of style on business unit performance; A. S. Thomas, R. J. Litschert, & K. Ramaswamy, 1991, The performance impact of

strategy–manager co-alignment: An empirical examination, *Strategic Management Journal*, 12: 509–522.

16 V. Govindarajan, 1989, Implementing competitive strategies at the business unit level: Implications of matching managers to strategies, *Strategic Management Journal*, 10: 251–269.

17 A. K. Gupta & V. Govindarajan, 1984, Business unit strategy, managerial characteristics, and business unit effectiveness at strategy implementation, *Academy of Management Journal*, 27: 25–41.

18 M. F. Wiersema & K. A. Bantel, 1992, Top management team demography and corporate strategic change, *Academy of Management Journal*, 35: 91–121; K. A. Bantel & S. E. Jackson, 1989, Top management and innovations in banking: Does the composition of the top team make a difference? *Strategic Management Journal*, 10: 107–124.

19 C. Crossland & D. C. Hambrick, 2011, Differences in managerial discretion across countries: How nation–level institutions affect the degree to which CEOs matter, *Strategic Management Journal*, 32(8): 797–819; D. C. Hambrick & E. Abrahamson, 1995, Assessing managerial discretion across industries: A multi-method approach, *Academy of Management Journal*, 38: 1427–1441; D. C. Hambrick & S. Finkelstein, 1987, Managerial discretion: A bridge between polar views of organizational outcomes, in B. Staw & L. L. Cummings (eds.), *Research in Organizational Behavior*, Greenwich, CT: JAI Press, 369–406.

20 D. G. Sirmon, M. A. Hitt, R. D. Ireland, & B. Gilbert, 2011, Resource orchestration to create competitive advantage: Breadth, depth, and life cycle effects, *Journal of Management*, 37(5): 1390–1412; R. Whittington, 2003, The work of strategizing and organizing: For a practice perspective, *Strategic Organization*, 1: 117–125.

21 M. Workman, 2012, Bias in strategic initiative continuance decisions: Framing interactions and HRD practices, *Management Decision*, 50(1): 21–42; T. K. Das & B.-S. Teng, 1999, Cognitive biases and strategic decision processes: An integrative perspective, *Journal of Management Studies*, 36: 757–778; C. R. Schwenk, 1995, Strategic decision making, *Journal of Management*, 21: 471–493.

22 D. Kahneman, P. Slovic, & A. Tversky (eds.), 1982, *Judgment under Uncertainty: Heuristics and Biases*, New York: Cambridge University Press; A. Tversky & D. Kahneman, 1974, Judgment under uncertainty: Heuristics and biases, *Science*, 185: 1124–1131.

23 M. S. Gary & R. E. Wood, 2011, Mental models, decision rules and performance heterogeneity, *Strategic Management Journal*, 32: 569–594; Kahneman, Slovic, & Tversky, *Judgment under Uncertainty*.

24 M. H. Bazerman, 1994. *Judgment in Managerial Decision Making*, 3rd ed., New York: Wiley; R. M. Hogarth, 1980, *Judgment and Choice: The Psychology of Decision*, Chichester, UK: Wiley.

25 Das & Teng, Cognitive biases and strategic decision processes; J. G. March & Z. Shapira, 1987, Managerial perspectives on risk and risk taking, *Management Science*, 33: 1404–1418.

26 C. R. Schwenk, 1984, Cognitive simplification processes in strategic decision-making, *Strategic Management Journal*, 5: 111–128.

27 March & Shapira, Managerial perspectives.

28 R. E. Hoskisson, M. A. Hitt, & C. W. L. Hill, 1991, Managerial risk taking in diversified firms: An evolutionary perspective, *Organization Science*, 2: 296–314.

29 J. Devan, K. Millan, & P. Shirke, 2005, Balancing short- and long-term performance, *McKinsey Quarterly*, 1: 31–33.

30 J. P. Walsh & W. R. Nord, 2005, Taking stock of stakeholder management, *Academy of Management Review*, 30: 426–438; J. E. Post, L. E. Preston, & S. Sauter-Sachs, 2002, *Redefining the Corporation: Stakeholder Management and Organizational Wealth*, Stanford, CA: Stanford University Press.

31 March & Shapira, Managerial perspectives; J. W. Fredrickson, 1984, The comprehensiveness of strategic decision processes: Extension, observations, future directions, *Academy of Management Journal*, 27: 445–466.

32 J. W. Fredrickson, 1986, An exploratory approach to measuring perceptions of strategic decision constructs, *Strategic Management Journal*, 7: 473–483.

33 Z. Shapira, 1995, *Risk Taking: A Managerial Perspective*, New York: Russell Sage Foundation.

34 D. Kahneman & D. Lovallo, 1993, Timid choices and bold forecasts: A cognitive perspective on risk taking, *Management Science*, 39: 17–31.

35 R. Durand, 2003, Predicting a firm's forecasting ability: The roles of organizational illusion of control and organizational attention, *Strategic Management Journal*, 9: 821–838; E. J. Langer, 1975, Illusion of control, *Journal of Personality and Social Psychology*, 32: 311–328.

36 Shapira, *Risk Taking*; C. Vlek & P. J. Stallen, 1980, Rational and personal aspects of risk, *Acta Psychologica*, 45: 273–300.

37 D. García, F. Sangiorgi, & B. Urošević, 2007, Overconfidence and market efficiency with heterogeneous assets, *Economic Theory*, 30: 313–336; R. A. Lowe & A. Arvids, 2006, Overoptimism and the performance of entrepreneurial firms, *Management Science*, 52: 173–186.

38 N. J. Fast, N. Sivanathan, N. D. Mayer, & A. D. Galinsky, 2012, Power and overconfident decision-making, *Organizational Behavior & Human Decision Processes*, 117(2): 249–260; N. J. Hiller & D. C. Hambrick, 2005, Conceptualizing executive hubris: The role of (hyper-) core self-evaluations in strategic decision making, *Strategic Management Journal*, 26: 297–319.

39 J. B. Wade, J. F. Porac, T. G. Pollock, & S. D. Graffin, 2006, The burden of celebrity: The impact of CEO certification contests on CEO pay and performance, *Academy of Management Journal*, 49: 643–660.

40 S. Park, J. D. Westphal, & I. Stern, 2011, Set up for a fall: The insidious effects of flattery and opinion conformity toward corporate leaders, *Administrative Science Quarterly*, 56(2): 257–302; M. L. A. Hayward, V. P. Rindova, & T. G. Pollock, 2004, Believing one's own press: The causes and consequences of CEO celebrity, *Strategic Management Journal*, 25: 637–653.

41 Collins, *Good to Great*.

42 D. Kahneman, D. Lovallo, & O. Sibony, 2011, Before you make that big decision, *Harvard Business Review*, 89(6): 50–60.

43 A. Carmeli, A. Tishler, & A. C. Edmondson, 2012, CEO relational leadership and strategic decision quality in top management teams: The role of team trust and learning from failure, *Strategic Organization*, 10(1): 31–54; A. L. Iaquito & J. W. Fredrickson, 1997, Top management team agreement about the strategic decision process: A test of some of its

determinants and consequences, *Strategic Management Journal*, 18: 63–75.

[44] J. P. Gander, 2010, The managerial limit to the growth of firms revisited, *Managerial & Decision Economics*, 31(8): 549–555; R. Castanias & C. Helfat, 2001, The managerial rents model: Theory and empirical analysis, *Journal of Management*, 27: 661–678.

[45] B. Frisch, 2011, Who really makes the big decisions in your company? *Harvard Business Review*, 89(12): 104–111; M. Beer & R. Eisenstat, 2000, The silent killers of strategy implementation and learning, *Sloan Management Review*, 41(4): 29–40; C. M. Christensen, 1997, Making strategy: Learning by doing, *Harvard Business Review*, 75(6): 141–156.

[46] K. Talke, S. Salomo, & A. Kock, 2011, Top management team diversity and strategic innovation orientation: The relationship and consequences for innovativeness and performance. *Journal of Product Innovation Management*, 28(6): 819–832; C. Pegels, Y. Song, & B. Yang, 2000, Management heterogeneity, competitive interaction groups, and firm performance, *Strategic Management Journal*, 21: 911–923.

[47] S. T. Bell, A. J. Villado, M. A. Lukasik, L. Belau, & A. L. Briggs, 2011, Getting specific about demographic diversity variable and team performance relationships: A meta-analysis, *Journal of Management*, 37(3): 709–743.

[48] A. Vance, 2012, c:\\Ballmer [Reboots], *Bloomberg Business Week*, January 16, 46–52.

[49] Ibid., 49.

[50] K. Talke, S. Salomo, & K. Rost, 2010, How top management team diversity affects innovativeness and performance via the strategic choice to focus on innovation fields, *Research Policy*, 39(7): 907–918; D. Knight, C. L. Pearce, K. G. Smith, J. D. Olian, H. P. Sims, K. A. Smith, & P. Flood, 1999, Top management team diversity, group process, and strategic consensus, *Strategic Management Journal*, 20: 446–465.

[51] A. S. Alexiev, J. P. Jansen, F. J. Van den Bosch, & H. W. Volberda, 2010, Top management team advice seeking and exploratory innovation: The moderating role of TMT heterogeneity, *Journal of Management Studies*, 47(7): 1343–1364; J. Bunderson, 2003, Team member functional background and involvement in management teams: Direct effects and the moderating role of power and centralization, *Academy of Management Journal*, 46: 458–474.

[52] K. Bongjin, M. L. Burns, & J. E. Prescott, 2009, The strategic role of the board: The impact of board structure on top management team strategic action capability, *Corporate Governance: An International Review*, 17(6): 728–743; D. C. Hambrick, T. S. Cho, & M. J. Chen, 1996, The influence of top management team heterogeneity on firms' competitive moves, *Administrative Science Quarterly*, 41: 659–684.

[53] W. Yong, W. Zelong, & L. Qiaozhuan, 2011, Top management team diversity and strategic change: The moderating effects of pay imparity and organization slack, *Journal of Organizational Change Management*, 24(3): 267–281; S. Wally & M. Becerra, 2001, Top management team characteristics and strategic changes in international diversification: The case of U.S. multinationals in the European community, *Group & Organization Management*, 26: 165–188; W. Boeker, 1997, Strategic change: The influence of managerial characteristics and organizational growth, *Academy of Management Journal*, 40: 152–170.

[54] J. Magretta, 2002, The behavior behind the buzzwords, *MIT Sloan Management Review*, 43(4): 90.

[55] Wiersema & Bantel, Top management team demography and corporate strategic change; Bantel & Jackson, Top management and innovations in banking.

[56] J. J. Distefano & M. L. Maznevski, 2000, Creating value with diverse teams in global management, *Organizational Dynamics*, 29(1): 45–63; T. Simons, L. H. Pelled, & K. A. Smith, 1999, Making use of difference, diversity, debate, and decision comprehensiveness in top management teams, *Academy of Management Journal*, 42: 662–673.

[57] A. Carmeli, J. Schaubroeck, & A. Tishler, 2011, How CEO empowering leadership shapes top management team processes: Implications for firm performance, *Leadership Quarterly*, 22(2): 399–411; Z. Simsek, J. F. Veiga, M. H. Lubatkin, & R. H. Dino, 2005, Modeling the multilevel determinants of top management team behavioral integration, *Academy of Management Journal*, 48: 69–84.

[58] E. M. Wong, M. E. Ormiston, & P. E. Tetlock, 2011, The effects of top management team integrative complexity and decentralized decision making on corporate social performance, *Academy of Management Journal*, 54(6): 1207–1228; S. Finkelstein & D. C. Hambrick, 1996, *Strategic Leadership: Top Executives and Their Effects on Organizations*, New York: West Publishing, 148.

[59] L. Xin, H. Ndofor, R. L. Priem, & J. C. Picken, 2010, Top management team communication networks, environmental uncertainty, and organizational performance: A contingency view, *Journal of Managerial Issues*, 22(4): 436–455; C. C. Miller, L. M. Burke, & W. H. Glick, 1998, Cognitive diversity among upper-echelon executives: Implications for strategic decision processes, *Strategic Management Journal*, 19: 39–58.

[60] 2011, Steady as she goes, *Economist*, October 29, 79.

[61] S. E. Ante & J. S. Lublin, 2011, IBM picks sales chief as next CEO, *Wall Street Journal*, October 26, B1.

[62] T. Buyl, C. Boone, W. Hendricks, & P. Matthyssens, 2011, Top management team functional diversity and firm performance: The moderating role of CEO characteristics, *Journal of Management Studies*, 48: 151–177.

[63] S. Machold, M. Huse, A. Minichilli, & M. Nordqvist, 2011, Board leadership and strategy involvement in small firms: A team production approach, *Corporate Governance: An International Review*, 19(4): 368–383; L. Tihanyi, R. A. Johnson, R. E. Hoskisson, & M. A. Hitt, 2003, Institutional ownership and international diversification: The effects of boards of directors and technological opportunity, *Academy of Management Journal*, 46: 195–211; W. Q. Judge, Jr. & C. P. Zeithaml, 1992, Institutional and strategic choice perspectives on board involvement in the strategic decision process, *Academy of Management Journal*, 35: 766–794.

[64] C. Fracassi & G. Tate, 2012, External networking and internal firm governance, *Journal of Finance*, 67(1): 153–194; G. Kassinis & N. Vafeas, 2002, Corporate boards and outside stakeholders as determinants of environmental litigation, *Strategic Management Journal*, 23: 399–415; B. R. Golden & E. J. Zajac, 2001, When will boards influence strategy? Inclination times power equals strategic change, *Strategic Management Journal*, 22: 1087–1111.

[65] M. Carpenter & J. Westphal, 2001, Strategic context of external network ties: Examining the impact of

director appointments on board involvement in strategic decision making, *Academy of Management Journal*, 44: 639–660.

[66] J. D. Westphal & E. J. Zajac, 1995, Who shall govern? CEO/board power, demographic similarity, and new director selection, *Administrative Science Quarterly*, 40: 60.

[67] P. Elkind, J. Reingold, & D. Burke, 2011, Inside Pfizer's palace coup, *Fortune*, August 15, 76–91.

[68] M. A. Abebe, A. Angriawan, & Y. Lui, 2011, CEO power and organizational turnaround in declining firms: Does environment play a role? *Journal of Leadership and Organizational Studies*, 18: 260–273; J. D. Westphal, 1999, Collaboration in the boardroom: Behavioral and performance consequences of CEO-board social ties, *Academy of Management Journal*, 42: 7–24.

[69] A. Dey, E. Engel, & X. Liu, 2011, CEO and board chair roles: To split or not to split? *Journal of Corporate Finance*, 17(5): 1595–1618; J. Roberts & P. Stiles, 1999, The relationship between chairmen and chief executives: Competitive or complementary roles? *Long Range Planning*, 32(1): 36–48.

[70] Y. Deutsch, T. Keil, & T. Laamanen, 2011, A dual agency view of board compensation: The joint effects of outside director and CEO stock options on firm risk, *Strategic Management Journal*, 32: 212–227; I. Filatotchev & M. Wright, 2011, Agency perspectives on corporate governance of multinational enterprises, *Journal of Management Studies*, 48(2): 471–486; J. Coles & W. Hesterly, 2000, Independence of the chairman and board composition: Firm choices and shareholder value, *Journal of Management*, 26: 195–214; B. K. Boyd, 1995, CEO duality and firm performance: A contingency model, *Strategic Management Journal*, 16: 301.

[71] J. Tang, M. Crossan, & W. G. Rowe, 2011, Dominant CEO, deviant strategy, and extreme performance: The moderating role of a powerful board, *Journal of Management Studies*, 48(7): 1479–1503; C. M. Daily & D. R. Dalton, 1995, CEO and director turnover in failing firms: An illusion of change? *Strategic Management Journal*, 16: 393–400.

[72] Dey, Engel, & Liu, CEO and board chair roles: To split or not to split; J. W. Lorsch & A. Zelleke, 2005, Should the CEO be the chairman? *Sloan Management Review*, 46(2): 71–81.

[73] R. Albanese, M. T. Dacin, & I. C. Harris, 1997, Agents as stewards, *Academy of Management Review*, 22: 609–611; J. H. Davis, F. D. Schoorman, & L. Donaldson, 1997, Toward a stewardship theory of management, *Academy of Management Review*, 22: 20–47.

[74] C. S. Tuggle, D. G. Sirmon, C. R. Reutzel, & L. Bierman, 2010, Commanding board of director attention: Investigating how organizational performance and CEO duality affect board members' attention to monitoring, *Strategic Management Journal*, 31(9): 946–968.

[75] M. A. Carpenter, 2002, The implications of strategy and social context for the relationship between top management team heterogeneity and firm performance, *Strategic Management Journal*, 23: 275–284; J. D. Westphal & E. J. Zajac, 1997, Defections from the inner circle: Social exchange, reciprocity and diffusion of board independence in U.S. corporations, *Administrative Science Quarterly*, 42(1): 161–183.

[76] J. G. Combs & M. S. Skill, 2003, Managerialist and human capital explanations for key executive pay premiums: A contingency perspective, *Academy of Management Journal*, 46: 63–73.

[77] D. Souder, Z. Simsek, & S. G. Johnson, 2012, The differing effects of agent and founder CEOs on the firm's market expansion, *Strategic Management Journal*, 33(1): 23–41.

[78] R. A. Johnson, R. E. Hoskisson, & M. A. Hitt, 1993, Board involvement in restructuring: The effect of board versus managerial controls and characteristics, *Strategic Management Journal*, 14 (summer special issue): 33–50.

[79] E. E. Lawler III, D. Finegold, G. Benson, & J. Conger, 2002, Adding value in the boardroom, *MIT Sloan Management Review*, 43(2): 92–93.

[80] Boyd, CEO duality and firm performance.

[81] M. Carpenter & J. Fredrickson, 2001, Top management teams, global strategic posture, and the moderating role of uncertainty, *Academy of Management Journal*, 44: 533–545.

[82] A. P. Kakabadse, N. K. Kakabadse, & R. Knyght, 2010, The chemistry factor in the Chairman/CEO relationship, *European Management Journal*, 28(4): 285–296; M. Schneider, 2002, A stakeholder model of organizational leadership, *Organization Science*, 13: 209–220.

[83] Lafley & Tichy, The art and science of finding the right CEO; M. Sorcher & J. Brant, 2002, Are you picking the right leaders? *Harvard Business Review*, 80(2): 78–85; D. A. Waldman, G. G. Ramirez, R. J. House, & P. Puranam, 2001, Does leadership matter? CEO leadership attributes and profitability under conditions of perceived environmental uncertainty, *Academy of Management Journal*, 44: 134–143.

[84] J. M. Citrin, 2012, When naming a CEO, ignore the market reaction, *Harvard Business Review*, 90(1/2): 30; A. Kakabadse & N. Kakabadse, 2001, Dynamics of executive succession, *Corporate Governance*, 1(3): 9–14.

[85] B. Kowitt, 2011, The man powering up GE, *Fortune*, December 26, 58–65; R. Charan, 2000, GE's ten-step talent plan, *Fortune*, April 17, 232.

[86] R. E. Hoskisson, D. Yiu, & H. Kim, 2010, Capital and labor market congruence and corporate governance: Effects on corporate innovation and global competitiveness, in D. B. Audretsch, G. B. Dagnini, R. Faraci, & R. E. Hoskisson (eds.), *New Frontiers in Entrepreneurship: Recognizing, Seizing, and Executing Opportunities*, New York: Springer 67–93.

[87] W. Shen & A. A. Cannella, 2003, Will succession planning increase shareholder wealth? Evidence from investor reactions to relay CEO successions, *Strategic Management Journal*, 24: 191–198.

[88] Y. Zhang & N. Rajagopalan, 2010, Once an outsider, always an outsider? CEO origin, strategic change, and firm performance, *Strategic Management Journal*, 31(3): 334–346.

[89] Y. Zhang & N. Rajagopalan, 2010, CEO succession planning: Finally at the center stage of the boardroom, *Business Horizons*, 53(5): 455–462; D. C. Carey & D. Ogden, 2000, *CEO Succession: A Window on How Boards Can Get It Right When Choosing a New Chief Executive*, New York: Oxford University Press.

[90] S. B. Shepard, 2002, A Talk with Jeff Immelt: Jack Welch's successor charts a course for GE in the 21st century, *Business Week*, January 28, 102–104.

[91] L. Greiner, T. Cummings, & A. Bhambri, 2002, When new CEOs succeed and fail: 4-D theory of strategic transformation, *Organizational Dynamics*, 32: 1–16.

92 D. Miller, 1991, Stale in the saddle: CEO tenure and the match between organization and environment, *Management Science*, 37: 34–52.

93 V. Anand, W. H. Glick, & C. C. Manz, 2002, Thriving on the knowledge of outsiders: Tapping organizational social capital, *Academy of Management Executive*, 16(1): 87–101.

94 J. M. Barron, D. V. Chulkov, & G. R. Waddell, 2011, Top management team turnover, CEO succession type, and strategic change, *Journal of Business Research*, 64(8): 904–910; N. A. Ashkanasy, C. E. J. Hartel, & C. S. Daus, 2002, Diversity and emotion: The new frontiers in organizational behavior research, *Journal of Management*, 28: 307–338.

95 G. N. Powell, D. A. Butterfield, & J. D. Parent, 2002, Gender and managerial stereotypes: Have the times changed? *Journal of Management*, 28: 177–193.

96 B. Srinidhi, F. A. Gul, & J. Tsui, 2011, Female directors and earnings quality, *Contemporary Accounting Research*, 28(5): 1610–1644; K. Campbell & A. M. Vera, 2010, Female board appointments and firm valuation: Short and long-term effects, *Journal of Management & Governance*, 14(1): 37–59.

97 2011, Growth of women on boards, in C-suites a 'trot', *Financial Executive*, 27(10): 10; C. E. Helfat, D. Harris, & P. J. Wolfson, 2006, The pipeline to the top: Women and men in the top executive ranks of U.S. corporations, *Academy of Management Perspectives*, 20(4): 42–64.

98 Growth of women on boards, in C-suites a 'trot'.

99 O. Chatain, 2011, Value creation, competition, and performance in buyer-supplier relationships, *Strategic Management Journal*, 32: 76–102; R. D. Ireland & M. A. Hitt, 2005, Achieving and maintaining strategic competitiveness in the 21st century: The role of strategic leadership, *Academy of Management Executive*, 19(4): 63–77, originally published in 12(1): 43–57; A. Cannella, Jr., A. Pettigrew, & D. Hambrick, 2001, Upper echelons: Donald Hambrick on executives and strategy, *Academy of Management Executive*, 15(3): 36–52; D. Lei, M. A. Hitt, & R. Bettis, 1996, Dynamic core competencies through meta-learning and strategic context, *Journal of Management*, 22: 547–567.

100 D. G. Sirmon, M. A. Hitt, R. D. Ireland, & B. Gilbert, 2011, Resource orchestration to create competitive advantage: Breadth, depth, and life cycle effects, *Journal of Management*, 37(5): 1390–1412.

101 J. S. Harrison, D. A. Bosse, & R. A. Phillips, 2010, Managing for stakeholders, stakeholder utility functions and competitive advantage, *Strategic Management Journal*, 31: 58–74; J. S. Harrison, 2003, *Strategic Management of Resources and Relationships*, New York: Wiley; R. E. Freeman, 1984, *Strategic Management: A Stakeholder Approach*, Boston: Pitman.

102 Finkelstein & Hambrick, *Strategic Leadership*, 2.

103 S. Berfield, 2006, Most inspiring steel boss, *Business Week*, December 18, 61.

104 G. Hamel & C. K. Prahalad, 1989, Strategic intent, *Harvard Business Review*, 67(3): 63–76.

105 D. C. Hambrick & J. W. Fredrickson, 2005, Are you sure you have a strategy? *Academy of Management Executive*, 19(4): 51–62, reprinted from 15(4).

106 H. A. Ndofor, D. G. Sirmon, & X. He, 2011, Firm resources, competitive actions and performance: Investigating a mediated model with evidence from the in-vitro diagnostics industry, *Strategic Management Journal*, 32: 640–657.

107 D. F. Abell, 1980, *Defining the Business: The Starting Point of Strategic Planning*, Englewood Cliffs, NJ: Prentice Hall.

108 2012, Choice Hotels International, http://www.wikinvest.com, February 20.

109 2012, General Electric, http://www.ge.com/company/advertising, February 20.

110 S. Mohammed & S. Nadkarni, 2011, Temporal diversity and team performance: The moderating role of team temporal leadership, *Academy of Management Journal*, 54(3): 489–508; K. M. Eisenhardt & S. L. Brown, 1998, Time pacing: Competing in markets that won't stand still, *Harvard Business Review*, March–April: 59–69.

111 A. Vance, 2012, c:\\Ballmer [Reboots], Bloomberg Business Week, January 16, 49.

112 A. Efrati, A. Das, V. Monga, & J. S. Lublin, 2012, Yahoo CEO faces big new problems, *Wall Street Journal*, February 15, B3.

113 D. Kesmodel & D. Michaels, 2011, For Boeing, it's been a long, strange trip—after three-year delay, plane maker readies 787 Dreamliner production, *Wall Street Journal*, September 21, B1.

114 2012, IT leaders continue to juggle multiple priorities in 2012, *CIO*, January 19, 2.

115 R. E. Ployhart, C. H. Van Idderkinge, & W. J. MacKenzie, 2011, Acquiring and developing human capital in service contexts: The interconnectedness of human capital resources, *Academy of Management Journal*, 54: 353–368; J. A. Oxman, 2002, The hidden leverage of human capital, *MIT Sloan Management Review*, 43(4): 79–83.

116 N. Argyres, 2011, Using organizational economics to study organizational capability development and strategy, *Organization Science*, 22: 1138–1143; D. J. Teece, 2000, *Managing Intellectual Capital: Organizational, Strategic and Policy Dimensions*, Oxford, UK: Oxford University Press.

117 C. Fernandez-Araoz, B. Groysberg, & N. Nohria, 2011, How to hang on to your high potentials, *Harvard Business Review*, 89(10): 76–83.

118 J. Pfeffer, 2010, Building sustainable organizations: The human factor, *Academy of Management Perspectives*, 24(1): 34–45; C. A. Lengnick-Hall & J. A. Wolff, 1999, Similarities and contradictions in the core logic of three strategy research streams, *Strategic Management Journal*, 20: 1109–1132.

119 S. A. Snell & M. A. Youndt, 1995, Human resource management and firm performance: Testing a contingency model of executive controls, *Journal of Management*, 21: 711–737.

120 F. DiBemardino, 2011, The missing link: Measuring and managing financial performance of the human capital investment, *People & Strategy*, 34(2): 44–49; W. Watson, W. H. Stewart, & A. Barnir, 2003, The effects of human capital, organizational demography, and interpersonal processes on venture partner perceptions of firm profit and growth, *Journal of Business Venturing*, 18: 145–164; D. Ulrich, 1998, A new mandate for human resources, *Harvard Business Review*, 76(1): 124–134.

121 P. M. Wright & G. C. McMahan, 2011, Exploring human capital: Putting 'human' back into strategic human resource management, *Human Resource Management Journal*, 21: 93–104; J. Pfeffer, 1994, *Competitive Advantage through People*, Cambridge, MA: Harvard Business School Press, 4.

122 Carmeli, Tishler, & Edmondson, CEO relational leadership and strategic decision quality in top

management teams; L. Gratton, 2001, *Living Strategy: Putting People at the Heart of Corporate Purpose*, London: Financial Times/Prentice Hall.

[123] J. S. Sidhu & H. W. Volberda, 2011, Coordination of globally distributed teams: A co-evolution perspective on offshoring, *International Business Review*, 20: 278–290; A. Yan, G. Zhu, & D. T. Hall, 2002, International assignments for career building: A model of agency relationships and psychological contracts, *Academy of Management Review*, 27: 373–391.

[124] C. Keen & Y. Wu, 2011, An ambidextrous learning model for the internationalization of firms from emerging economies, *Journal of International Entrepreneurship*, 9(4): 316–339.

[125] M. Harvey, T. Kiessling, & M. Moeller, 2011, Globalization and the inward flow of immigrants: Issues associated with the inpatriation of global managers. *Human Resource Development Quarterly*, 22(2): 177–194; M. G. Harvey & M. R. Buckley, 1997, Managing inpatriates: Building a global core competency, *Journal of World Business*, 32(1): 35–52.

[126] C. Gaimon, G. F. Ozkan, & K. Napoleon, 2011, Dynamic resource capabilities: Managing workforce knowledge with a technology upgrade, *Organization Science*, 22(6): 1560–1578; C. A. Bartlett & S. Ghoshal, 2002, Building competitive advantage through people, *MIT Sloan Management Review*, 43(2): 34–41; D. M. De Carolis & D. L. Deeds, 1999, The impact of stocks and flows of organizational knowledge on firm performance: An empirical investigation of the biotechnology industry, *Strategic Management Journal*, 20: 953–968.

[127] J. Abele, 2011, Bringing minds together, *Harvard Business Review*, 89(7/8): 86–93; R. Cross & L. Prusak, 2002, The people who make organizations go—or stop, *Harvard Business Review*, 80(6): 105–112.

[128] S. B. Bach, W. Q. Judge, & T. J. Dean, 2008, A knowledge-based view of IPO success: Superior knowledge, isolating mechanisms, and the creation of market value, *Journal of Managerial Issues*, 20(4): 507–525; T. M. Welbourne & L. A. Cyr, 1999, The human resource executive effect in initial public offering firms, *Academy of Management Journal*, 42: 616–629.

[129] Gaimon, Ozkan, & Napoleon, Dynamic resource capabilities: Managing workforce knowledge with a technology upgrade; Bartlett & Ghoshal, Building competitive advantage through people.

[130] H. Collingwood & D. L. Coutu, 2002, Jack on Jack, *Harvard Business Review*, 80(2): 88–94.

[131] A. Klein, 2011, Corporate culture: Its value as a resource for competitive advantage, *Journal of Business Strategy*, 32(2): 21–28; A. K. Gupta & V. Govindarajan, 2000, Knowledge management's social dimension: Lessons from Nucor steel, *Sloan Management Review*, 42(1): 71–80; C. M. Fiol, 1991, Managing culture as a competitive resource: An identity-based view of sustainable competitive advantage, *Journal of Management*, 17: 191–211; J. B. Barney, 1986, Organizational culture: Can it be a source of sustained competitive advantage? *Academy of Management Review*, 11: 656–665.

[132] A. J. Bock, T. Opsahl, G. George, & D. M. Gann, 2012, The effects of culture and structure on strategic flexibility during business model innovation, *Journal of Management Studies*, 49: 279–305; J. Kotter, 2011, Corporate culture: Whose job is it? *Forbes*, http://blog.forbes.com/johnkotter, February 17.

[133] H. Lin & E. F. McDonough III, 2011, Investigating the role of leadership and organizational culture in fostering innovation ambidexterity, *IEEE Transactions on Engineering Management*, 58(3): 497–509.

[134] M. A. Hitt, R. D. Ireland, D. G. Sirmon, & C. A. Trahms, 2011, Strategic entrepreneurship: Creating value for individuals, organizations and society, *Academy of Management Perspectives*, 25(2): 57–75; D. S. Elenkov, W. Judge, & P. Wright, 2005, Strategic leadership and executive innovation influence: An international multi-cluster comparative study, *Strategic Management Journal*, 26: 665–682.

[135] B. A. George, 2011, Entrepreneurial orientation: A theoretical and empirical examination of the consequences of differing construct representations, *Journal of Management Studies*, 48(6): 1291–1313; G. T. Lumpkin & G. G. Dess, 1996, Clarifying the entrepreneurial orientation construct and linking it to performance, *Academy of Management Review*, 21: 135–172.

[136] Lumpkin & Dess, Clarifying the entrepreneurial orientation construct and linking it to performance, 142.

[137] Ibid., 137.

[138] D. Park, R. Chinta, M. Lee, J. Turner, & L. Kilbourne, 2011. Macro-fit versus micro-fit of the organization with its environment: Implications for strategic leadership. *International Journal of Management*, 28(2): 488–492; R. A. Burgelman & Y. L. Doz, 2001, The power of strategic integration, *Sloan Management Review*, 42(3): 28–38; P. H. Fuchs, K. E. Mifflin, D. Miller, & J. O. Whitney, 2000, Strategic integration: Competing in the age of capabilities, *California Management Review*, 42(3): 118–147.

[139] A. M. L. Raes, M. G. Heijltes, U. Glunk, & R. A. Roe, 2011, The interface of the top management team and middle managers: A process model, *Academy of Management Review*, 36: 102–126; H. N. Nguyen & S. Mohamed, 2011, Leadership behaviors, organizational culture and knowledge management practices: An empirical investigation, *Journal of Management Development*, 30(2): 206–221; J. E. Dutton, S. J. Ashford, R. M. O'Neill, E. Hayes, & E. E. Wierba, 1997, Reading the wind: How middle managers assess the context for selling issues to top managers, *Strategic Management Journal*, 18: 407–425.

[140] N. Zmuda, 2012, JCP reinvention is bold bet, but hardly fail-safe, *Advertising Age*, January 30, 1–22.

[141] K. Talley, 2012, Penney CEO says profit won't suffer, *Wall Street Journal*, January 27, B6.

[142] J. Peloza & J. Shang, 2011, How can corporate social responsibility activities create value for stakeholders? A systematic review, *Journal of the Academy of Marketing Science*, 39: 117–135; R. E. Freeman & W. M. Evan, 1990, Corporate governance: A stakeholder interpretation, *Journal of Behavioral Economics*, 19: 337–359.

[143] S. Helm, 2011, Employees' awareness of their impact on corporate reputation, *Journal of Business Research*, 64(7): 657–663; C. J. Fombrun, 2001, Corporate reputations as economic assets, in M. A. Hitt, R. E. Freeman, & J. S. Harrison, *Handbook of Strategic Management*, Oxford, UK: Blackwell Publishers, 289–312.

[144] M. Pirson & D. Malhotra, 2011, Foundations of organizational trust: What matters to different stakeholders? *Organization Science*, 22(4): 1087–1104.

[145] M. A. Hitt, K. T. Haynes, & R. Serpa, 2010, Strategic leadership for the 21st century, *Business Horizons*, 53: 437–444.

146 B. Neville, S. Bell, & G. Whitwell, 2011, Stakeholder salience revisited: Refining, redefining, and refueling an underdeveloped conceptual tool, *Journal of Business Ethics*, 102(3): 357–378; D. Lavie, 2006, The competitive advantage of interconnected firms: An extension of the resource-based view, *Academy of Management Review*, 31: 638–658.

147 J. E. Rogers, 2011, The CEO of Duke Energy on learning to work with green activists, *Harvard Business Review*, 89(5): 51–54; R. C. Ford, 2002, Darden restaurants CEO Joe Lee on the importance of core values: Integrity and fairness, *Academy of Management Executive*, 16(1): 31–36; P. W. Beamish, 1999, Sony's Yoshihide Nakamura on structure and decision making, *Academy of Management Executive*, 13(4): 12–16.

148 J. R. Baum, E. A. Locke, & S. A. Kirkpatrick, 1998, A longitudinal study of the relation of vision and vision communication to venture growth in entrepreneurial firms, *Journal of Applied Psychology*, 83: 43–54.

149 M. Wasden, 2011, Why you need an identity crisis, *Finweek*, December 15, 38; R. D. Ireland & M. A. Hitt, 1992, Mission statements: Importance, challenge, and recommendations for development, *Business Horizons*, 35(3): 34–42.

150 D. Kiron, N. Kruschwitz, K. Haanaes, & I. von Streng Velken, 2012, Sustainability nears a tipping point, *MIT Sloan Management Review*, 53(2): 69–74; G. Kassinis & N. Vafeas, 2006, Stakeholder pressures and environmental performance, *Academy of Management Review*, 49: 145–159.

151 I. M. Levin, 2000, Vision revisited, *Journal of Applied Behavioral Science*, 36: 91–107; J. C. Collins & J. I. Porras, 1996, Building your company's vision, *Harvard Business Review*, 74(5): 65–77.

152 S. B. Sitkin, K. E. See, C. Miller, M. W. Lawless, & A. M. Carton, 2011, The paradox of stretch goals: Organizations in pursuit of the seemingly impossible, *Academy of Management Review*, 36(3): 544–566; S. Kerr & S. Landauer, 2004, Using stretch goals to promote organizational effectiveness and personal growth, *Academy of Management Executive*, 18(4): 134–138; K. R. Thompson, W. A. Hochwarter, & N. J. Mathys, 1997, Stretch targets: What makes them effective? *Academy of Management Executive*, 11(3): 48–59.

153 R. Goffee & G. Jones, 2006, Getting personal on the topic of leadership: Authentic self-expression works for those at the top, *Human Resource Management International Digest*, 14(4): 32–40.

154 2012, *Code of Ethics*, Hartford, CT: United Technologies, http://utc.com/Governance/Ethics/Code+of+Ethics, accessed on February 21.

155 K. M. Gilley, C. J. Robertson, & T. C. Mazur, 2010, The bottom-line benefits of ethics code commitment, *Business Horizons*, 53(1): 31–37; J. M. Stevens, H. K. Steensma, D. A. Harrison, & P. L. Cochran, 2005, Symbolic or substantive document? Influence of ethics codes on financial executives' decisions, *Strategic Management Journal*, 26: 181–195.

156 2006, *Enron Code of Ethics July 2000*, The Smoking Gun, http://www.thesmokinggun.com/graphics/packageart/enron/enron.pdf, December 15.

157 S. Forest, W. Zellner & H. Timmons, 2001, The Enron debacle, *Business Week*, November 12, 106–110.

158 E. Feldman, 2006, A basic quantification of the competitive implications of the demise of Arthur Andersen, *Review of Industrial Organization*, 29: 193–212.

159 S. Adams, 2011, Steve Jobs, Jon Corzine among 2011's biggest CEO departures, *Forbes*, December 8, 30.

160 R. Rumelt, 2011, *Good strategy/bad strategy*, New York: Crowne Business; P. S. Adler & S.-W. Kwon, 2002, Social capital: Prospects for a new concept, *Academy of Management Review*, 27: 17–40.

161 E. Wallace, L. Chernatony, & I. Buil, 2011, How leadership and commitment influence bank employees' adoption of their bank's values, *Journal of Business Ethics*, 101(3): 397–414; T. A. Stewart, 2001, Right now the only capital that matters is social capital, *Business 2.0*, December, 128–130.

162 V. Anand, B. E. Ashforth, & M. Joshi, 2005, Business as usual: The acceptance and perpetuation of corruption in organizations, *Academy of Management Executive*, 19(4): 9–23; D. J. Brass, K. D. Butterfield, & B. C. Skaggs, 1998, Relationships and unethical behavior: A social network perspective, *Academy of Management Review*, 23: 14–31.

163 W. Wallace, 2000, The value relevance of accounting: The rest of the story, *European Management Journal*, 18(6): 675–682.

164 L. Grove, M. Giglio, D. Ephron, & W. Underhill, 2011, Rupert's red menace, *Newsweek*, July 25, 40–44.

165 P. M. Barrett, F. Gillette, R. Farzad, J. Browning, L. Fortado, & T. Penny, 2011, Ink-stained wretchedness, *Bloomberg Businessweek*, July 18, 4–6; S. Forbes, 2011, Why Rupert Murdoch will survive and thrive again, 2011, *Forbes*, July 18, 30.

166 C. C. Maurer, P. Bansal, & M. M. Crossan, 2011, Creating economic value through social venues: Introducing a culturally informed resource-based view, *Organization Science*, 22: 432–448; L. K. Trevino, G. R. Weaver, D. G. Toffler, & B. Ley, 1999, Managing ethics and legal compliance: What works and what hurts, *California Management Review*, 41(2): 131–151.

167 T. Yaffe & R. Kark, 2011, Leading by example: The case of leader OCB, *Journal of Applied Psychology*, 96(4): 806–826; J. A. Petrick & J. F. Quinn, 2001, The challenge of leadership accountability for integrity capacity as a strategic asset, *Journal of Business Ethics*, 34: 331–343; R. C. Mayer, J. H. Davis, & F. D. Schoorman, 1995, An integrative model of organizational trust, *Academy of Management Review*, 20: 709–734.

168 J. R. Cohen, L. W. Pant, & D. J. Sharp, 2001, An examination of differences in ethical decision-making between Canadian business students and accounting professionals, *Journal of Business Ethics*, 30: 319–336; G. R. Weaver, L. K. Trevino, & P. L. Cochran, 1999, Corporate ethics programs as control systems: Influences of executive commitment and environmental factors, *Academy of Management Journal*, 42: 41–57.

169 R. T. Mowday, 2011, Elevating the dialogue on professional ethics to the next level: Reflections on the experience of the Academy of Management, *Management & Organization Review*, 7(3): 505–509; N. N. Leila Trapp, 2011, Staff attitudes to talking openly about ethical dilemmas: The role of business ethics conceptions and trust, *Journal of Business Ethics*, 103(4): 543–552; P. E. Murphy, 1995, Corporate ethics statements: Current status and future prospects, *Journal of Business Ethics*, 14: 727–740.

170. P. Fuda & R. Badham, 2011, Fire, snowball, mask, movie: How leaders spark and sustain change, *Harvard Business Review*, 89(11): 145–148; L. G. Hrebiniak & W. F. Joyce, 2001, Implementing strategy: An appraisal and agenda for future research, in M. A. Hitt, R. E. Freeman, & J. S. Harrison (eds.), *Handbook of Strategic Management*, Oxford, UK: Blackwell Publishers, 433–463.

171. J. A. Martin, 2011, Dynamic managerial capabilities and the multibusiness team: The role of episodic teams in executive leadership groups, *Organization Science*, 22(1): 118–140; J. B. Barney, 1995, Looking inside for competitive advantage, *Academy of Management Executive*, November, 49–61.

172. R. Kanter, 2011, How great companies think differently, *Harvard Business Review*, 89(11): 66–78; B. R. Barringer & J. S. Harrison, 2000, Walking a tightrope: Creating value through interorganizational relationships, *Journal of Management*, 26: 367–404.

173. 2012, Basel Headquarters, Novartis, http://www.novartis.com/about-novartis/locations/basel-headquarters.shtml, accessed on February 23.

174. M. Z. Elbashir, P. A. Collier, & S. G. Sutton, 2011, The role of organizational absorptive capacity in strategic use of business intelligence to support integrated management control systems, *Accounting Review*, 86(1): 155–184; J. H. Gittell, 2000, Paradox of coordination and control, *California Management Review*, 42(3): 101–117; L. J. Kirsch, 1996, The management of complex tasks in organizations: Controlling the systems development process, *Organization Science*, 7: 1–21.

175. M. D. Shields, F. J. Deng, & Y. Kato, 2000, The design and effects of control systems: Tests of direct- and indirect-effects models, *Accounting, Organizations and Society*, 25: 185–202; R. Simons, 1994, How new top managers use control systems as levers of strategic renewal, *Strategic Management Journal*, 15: 170–171.

176. R. E. White, R. E. Hoskisson, D. W. Yiu, & G. D. Bruton, 2008, Employment and market innovation in Chinese business group affiliated firms: The role of group control systems, *Management & Organization Review*, 4(2): 225–256; K. J. Laverty, 1996, Economic "short-termism": The debate, the unresolved issues, and the implications for management practice and research, *Academy of Management Review*, 21: 825–860.

177. E. E. Tapinos, R. G. Dyson, & M. M. Meadows, 2011, Does the balanced scorecard make a difference to the strategy development process? *Journal of the Operational Research Society*, 62(5): 888–899; R. S. Kaplan & D. P. Norton, 2000, *The Strategy-Focused Organization: How Balanced Scorecard Companies Thrive in the New Business Environment*, Boston: Harvard Business School Press.

178. N. Jarrar & M. Smith, 2011, Product diversification: The need for innovation and the role of a balanced scorecard, *Journal of Applied Management Accounting Research*, 9(2): 43–60; B. E. Becker, M. A. Huselid, & D. Ulrich, 2001, *The HR Scorecard: Linking People, Strategy, and Performance*, Boston: Harvard Business School Press, 21.

179. Kaplan & Norton, *The Strategy-Focused Organization*.

180. L. Yuan, L. Xiyao, L. Yi, & R. R. Barnes, 2011, Knowledge communication, exploitation and endogenous innovation: The moderating effects of internal controls in SMEs, *R&D Management*, 41(2): 156–172; R. S. Kaplan & D. P. Norton, 2001, Transforming the balanced scorecard from performance measurement to strategic management: Part I, *Accounting Horizons*, 15(1): 87–104.

181. J. D. Gunkel & G. Probst, 2003, Implementation of the balanced scorecard as a means of corporate learning: The Porsche case, Cranfield, UK: European Case Clearing House.

182. R. S. Kaplan & D. P. Norton, 2008, Mastering the management system, *Harvard Business Review*, 86(1): 62–77; M. A. Mische, 2001, *Strategic Renewal: Becoming a High-Performance Organization*, Upper Saddle River, NJ: Prentice Hall, 181.

183. K. P. Coyne & S. T. Coyne, 2010, When you've got to cut costs now, *Harvard Business Review*, 88(5): 74–82; R. E. Hoskisson, R. A. Johnson, L. Tihanyi, & R. E. White, 2005, Diversified business groups and corporate refocusing in emerging economies, *Journal of Management*, 31: 941–965; R. E. Hoskisson & M. A. Hitt, 1994, *Downscoping: How to Tame the Diversified Firm*, New York: Oxford University Press.

PART 2

STRATEGIC ANALYSIS

CHAPTER 3 The External Environment: Opportunities, Threats, Industry Competition, and Competitor Analysis 72

CHAPTER 4 The Internal Organization: Resources, Capabilities, and Core Competencies 106

Chapter **3**

THE EXTERNAL ENVIRONMENT: OPPORTUNITIES, THREATS, INDUSTRY COMPETITION, AND COMPETITOR ANALYSIS

KNOWLEDGE OBJECTIVES

Studying this chapter should provide you with the strategic management knowledge needed to:

1. Explain the importance of analyzing and understanding the firm's external environment.

2. Define and describe the general environment and the industry environment.

3. Discuss the four activities of the external environmental analysis process.

4. Name and describe the general environment's seven segments.

5. Identify the five competitive forces and explain how they determine an industry's profit potential.

6. Define strategic groups and describe their influence on the firm.

7. Describe what firms need to know about their competitors and different methods used to collect intelligence about them.

The *external environment* of a firm profoundly influences the firm's growth and profitability.[1] Major events such as a war, economic cycles, and the emergence of new technologies are a few conditions in the external environment that affect firms in the United States and other countries throughout the world. External environmental conditions such as these create threats to and opportunities for firms that, in turn, have major effects on firms' strategic actions.[2]

This chapter focuses on how firms analyze and understand the external environment. The external environment influences the firms' strategic options, as well as the decisions made in light of them. The firms' understanding of the external environment is integrated with knowledge about its internal organization (discussed in Chapter 4) to form its strategic direction, and to take strategic actions that result in value creation and above-average returns.

As noted in Chapter 1, the environmental conditions in the current global economy differ from those that firms previously faced. Technological changes and the continuing growth of information gathering and processing capabilities demand more timely and effective competitive actions and responses.[3] The rapid sociological changes occurring in many countries affect labor practices and the nature of products demanded by increasingly diverse consumers. Governmental policies and laws also affect where and how firms choose to compete.[4] De-regulation and changes in local government, such as those in the global electric utilities industry, affect not only the general competitive environment, but also the strategic decisions made by companies competing globally. To achieve value creation, firms must be aware of and understand the various dimensions of the external environment.[5]

Firms learn about the external environment by acquiring information on competitors, customers, and other stakeholders to build their own base of knowledge and capabilities.[6] Firms may use this base to imitate the capabilities of their strongest competitors (and even may imitate successful firms in other industries), and they may use it to build new knowledge and capabilities to achieve a competitive advantage.[7] On the basis of the new information, knowledge, and capabilities, firms can take actions to buffer themselves against environmental effects or to build relationships with stakeholders in their environment. To build their knowledge and capabilities and to take actions that buffer or build bridges to external stakeholders, organizations must effectively analyze the external environment.

THE GENERAL, INDUSTRY, AND COMPETITOR ENVIRONMENTS

An integrated understanding of the external and internal environments is essential for firms to comprehend the present and predict the future.[8] A firm's external environment includes the general environment and industry and competitor environments.

The **general environment** is composed of dimensions in the broader society that influence an industry and the firms within it.[9] We group these dimensions into seven environmental *segments*: demographic, economic, political/legal, sociocultural, technological, global, and physical (see Figure 3.1). Table 3.1 includes examples of *elements* analyzed in each of these segments. Firms cannot directly control the general environment's segments and elements. The recent bankruptcy filings by American Airlines and Kodak highlight this fact. In fact, during the most recent severe economic recession, companies around the globe were challenged to understand the effects of the economy's decline on their current and future strategies. Similarly, the wars in Iraq and Afghanistan have had numerous economic, political, and social repercussions throughout the world. Accordingly, successful companies gather the information they need to understand each segment and its implications for selecting and implementing appropriate strategies.

The **industry environment** is the set of factors that directly influences a firm and its competitive actions and competitive responses: the threat of new entrants, the power of suppliers, the power of buyers, the threat of product substitutes, and the intensity or rivalry among competitors (see Figure 3.1). The interactions among these five factors determine an industry's profit potential. The challenge is to locate a position within an industry where a firm can favorably influence those factors or where it can successfully defend against their influence. The greater a firm's capacity to favorably influence its industry environment, the greater is the likelihood that the firm will earn above-average returns. How companies gather and interpret information about their competitors is called *competitor analysis*. Understanding the firm's **competitor environment** complements the insights provided by studying the general and industry environments.

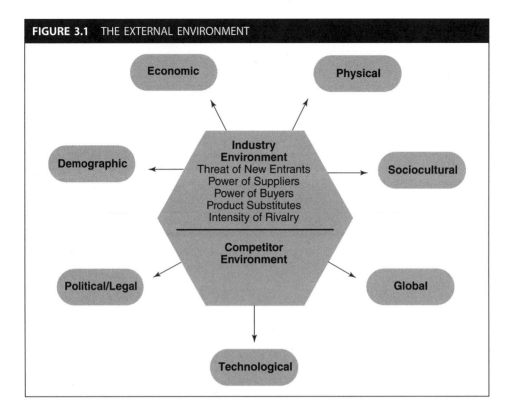

FIGURE 3.1 THE EXTERNAL ENVIRONMENT

Economic

Physical

Demographic

Industry Environment
Threat of New Entrants
Power of Suppliers
Power of Buyers
Product Substitutes
Intensity of Rivalry

Competitor Environment

Sociocultural

Political/Legal

Global

Technological

Analysis of the general environment is focused on the future; analysis of the industry environment is focused on the factors and conditions influencing a firm's profitability within its industry; and analysis of the competitor environment is focused on predicting the dynamic of competitors' actions, responses, and intentions. In combination, the results of the three analyses of the firm's external environment influence its strategic intent and strategic actions. Although we discuss each analysis separately, performance improves when the firm integrates the insights provided by all three analyses.

EXTERNAL ENVIRONMENTAL ANALYSIS

Most firms face external environments that are highly turbulent, complex, and global—conditions that make interpreting them increasingly difficult.[10] To cope with what are often ambiguous and incomplete environmental data and to increase their understanding of the general environment, firms engage in a process called *external environmental analysis*. The continuous process includes four activities: scanning, monitoring, forecasting, and assessing (see Table 3.2). Completing this analysis is a difficult, yet significant, activity.

An important objective of studying the external environment is identifying opportunities and threats. An **opportunity** is a condition in the external environment that, if exploited, helps a company achieve value creation. For instance, Walmart sees an excellent opportunity for the continuing growth of its stores in

TABLE 3.1 THE GENERAL ENVIRONMENT: SEGMENTS AND ELEMENTS

Demographic Segment	▶ Population size ▶ Age structure ▶ Geographic distribution	▶ Ethnic mix ▶ Income distribution
Economic Segment	▶ Inflation rates ▶ Interest rates ▶ Trade deficits or surpluses ▶ Budget deficits or surpluses	▶ Personal savings rate ▶ Business savings rates ▶ Gross domestic product
Political/Legal Segment	▶ Antitrust laws ▶ Taxation laws ▶ De-regulation philosophies	▶ Labor training laws ▶ Educational philosophies and policies
Sociocultural Segment	▶ Women in the workforce ▶ Workforce diversity ▶ Attitudes about the quality of work life	▶ Shifts in work and career preferences ▶ Shifts in preferences regarding product and service characteristics
Technological Segment	▶ Product innovations ▶ Applications of knowledge	▶ Focus of private and government-supported R&D expenditures ▶ New communication technologies
Global Segment	▶ Important political events ▶ Critical global markets	▶ Newly industrialized countries ▶ Different cultural and institutional attributes
Physical environment segment	▶ Energy consumption ▶ Practices used to develop energy sources ▶ Renewable energy efforts ▶ Minimizing a firm's environmental footprint	▶ Availability of water as a resource ▶ Producing environmentally friendly products ▶ Reacting to natural or man-made disasters

TABLE 3.2 COMPONENTS OF THE EXTERNAL ENVIRONMENTAL ANALYSIS

Scanning	▶	Identifying early signals of environmental changes and trends
Monitoring	▶	Detecting meaning through ongoing observations of environmental changes and trends
Forecasting	▶	Developing projections of anticipated outcomes based on monitored changes and trends
Assessing	▶	Determining the timing and importance of environmental changes and trends for firms' strategies and their management

China. China's economy as reflected by its gross domestic product has grown rapidly over the last few decades. And, due to this increase, disposable income of the Chinese consumer has also grown.[11] Likewise, many foreign multinational firms have established major R&D centers in China, partly to take advantage of the extensive Chinese market but also to gain access to valuable technological capabilities. For example, approximately 12 percent of Alcatel-Lucent's 2400 patents in 2010 came from China. Interestingly, China had $153.7 billion investment in R&D in 2010, second only to that in the United States.[12]

A **threat** is a condition in the general environment that may hinder a company's efforts to achieve value creation.[13] The once revered firm Polaroid can attest to the seriousness of external threats. At one time, Polaroid was a leader in its industry and considered one of the top 50 firms in the United States. However, the company failed to respond quickly enough to the threat from digital photography, and eventually the company had to file for bankruptcy protection. Technology companies face competitive threats as well. For example, Apple's iPhone poses a significant threat to Research In Motion's Blackberry phones. And, Apple's iPad poses a major threat to laptop PCs causing potential problems for Dell, HP and Lenova, among others. As these examples indicate, opportunities suggest competitive possibilities, whereas threats are potential constraints.

Several sources can be used to analyze the general environment, including a variety of printed materials: trade publications, newspapers, and business publications; the results of academic research and public polls; publications produced by trade shows, suppliers, customers, and employees of public-sector organizations. External network contacts can be particularly rich sources of information on the environment.[14] Much information can be obtained by people in the firm's "boundary-spanning" positions. Salespeople, purchasing managers, public relations directors, and customer service representatives, each of whom interacts with external constituents, are examples of individuals in boundary-spanning positions.[15]

Scanning

Scanning entails the study of all segments in the general environment. Through scanning, firms identify early signals of potential changes in the general environment and detect changes that are already under way.[16] When scanning, the firm often deals with ambiguous, incomplete, or unconnected data and information. Environmental scanning is critically important for firms competing in highly volatile environments. In addition, scanning activities must be aligned with the organizational context; a scanning system designed for a volatile environment is inappropriate for a firm in a stable environment.[17]

Some analysts expect the pressure brought to bear by the trend toward early retirement on countries such as the United States, France, Germany, and Japan to be significant and challenging. Governments in these countries appear to be offering state-funded pensions to their future elderly populations—but the costs of those pensions cannot be met with the present taxes and social security contribution rates.[18] Firms selling financial planning services and options should analyze this trend to determine whether it represents an opportunity for them to help governments find a way to meet their responsibilities.

Many firms use specialized software to help them identify events that are taking place in the environment and announced in public sources. For example, news event detection procedures use information-based systems to categorize text and reduce the trade-off between an important event that is missed and false alarms.[19] The Internet provides multiple opportunities for scanning. For example, Amazon.com records significant information about individuals visiting its Website, particularly if a purchase is made. Amazon then welcomes those visitors by name when they return to the Website. The firm even sends messages to them about specials and new products similar to those purchased in previous visits.

Additionally, many Websites and advertisers on the Internet obtain information from those who visit their sites using files called "cookies." These files are saved to the visitors' hard drives, allowing customers to connect more quickly to the Website, but also allowing the firm to solicit a variety of information about them. Because cookies are often placed without customers' knowledge, their use can be considered questionable practice. Because of this, the European Union (EU) passed legislation in 2011 regulating the use of software cookies.[20]

Monitoring

In **monitoring**, analysts observe environmental changes to identify important emerging trends from among those spotted by scanning.[21] Critical to successful monitoring is the firm's ability to detect meaning in different environmental events and trends. For example, the number of Hispanic Americans continues to grow in the United States and currently represents the largest ethnic minority in the country. This group of citizens has increased political and economic power and, as a growing percentage of the market, provides good target markets for companies.[22] Companies in the retail sector could monitor this change in the economic segment to determine the degree to which competitively important trends and business opportunities are emerging. By monitoring trends, firms can be better prepared to introduce new goods and services at the appropriate time to take advantage of the opportunities these trends provide.[23]

Effective monitoring requires the firm to identify important stakeholders. Because the importance of different stakeholders can vary over a firm's life cycle, careful attention must be given to the firm's needs and its stakeholder groups over time.[24] Scanning and monitoring are particularly important when a firm competes in an industry with high technological uncertainty. Scanning and monitoring not only can provide the firm with information but can also serve as a means of importing new knowledge about markets and about how to successfully commercialize new technologies that the firm has developed.[25]

Forecasting

Scanning and monitoring are concerned with events and trends in the general environment at a point in time. When **forecasting**, analysts develop feasible projections of potential events, and how quickly they may occur, as a result of the changes and trends detected through scanning and monitoring.[26] For example, analysts might forecast the time that will be required for a new technology to reach the marketplace, the length of time before different corporate training procedures are required to deal with anticipated changes in the composition of the workforce, or how much time will elapse before changes in governmental taxation policies affect consumers' purchasing patterns.

Forecasting events and outcomes accurately is a significant challenge. For instance, a number of consumer product producers such as Procter & Gamble and Unilever felt pressure from their markets to reduce their prices during the economic downturn in the later part of the first decade of the 21st century. However, demand began to increase for their name brand products as the economy improved.[27]

Assessing

The objective of **assessing** is to determine the timing and significance of the effects of environmental changes and trends on the strategic management of the firm.[28] Through scanning, monitoring, and forecasting, analysts are able to understand the general environment. Going a step further, the intent of assessing is to specify the implications of that understanding for the organization. Without assessment, the firm is left with data that may be interesting but are of unknown competitive relevance.

The accuracy of assessing environmental trends may be even more important for strategy than the analysis of competitors. This is because accurately assessing the environmental trends can allow the opportunity to move ahead of competitors by providing a product that best satisfies consumer needs when they initially change. As such, the firm gains first mover advantages (discussed further in Chapter 6). Alternatively, new threats must also be identified in the trends. This allows the firm to prepare for the threats by avoiding them or building their capabilities to meet the threats.

SEGMENTS OF THE GENERAL ENVIRONMENT

The general environment is composed of segments (and their individual elements) that are external to the firm (see Table 3.1). Although the degree of impact varies, these environmental segments affect each industry and its firms. The challenge to the firm is to scan, monitor, forecast, and assess those elements in each segment that are of the greatest importance. Resulting from these efforts should be a recognition of environmental changes, trends, opportunities, and threats. Opportunities are then matched with a firm's core competencies (the matching process is discussed further in Chapter 4).

The Demographic Segment

The **demographic segment** involves a population's size, age structure, geographic distribution, ethnic mix, and income distribution.[29] Demographic segments are analyzed on a global basis because of their potential effects across countries' borders and because many firms compete in global markets.

Population Size. Only a little more than one-sixth of the world's population lives in developed countries, while the rest of the world's population lives in developing nations. India is projected to be the largest nation with more than 1.8 billion inhabitants with China, the United States, Indonesia, and Pakistan as the next four most populous countries by 2050.[30]

Observing demographic changes in populations highlights the importance of this environmental segment. The world is projected to have almost 9.3 billion people by 2050 but the growth is imbalanced across countries. For example, some advanced nations have a negative population growth, after discounting the effects of immigration. In some countries, including the United States and several European nations, couples are averaging fewer than two children. This birthrate will reduce populations in some countries over time, although immigration is still producing an increase in population in the United States, which now has more than 312 million residents. International immigrants compose about 20 percent of the new inhabitants in the United States each year with births representing the other 80 percent.[31] These projections suggest major 21st-century challenges and business opportunities in this country.

Age Structure. In some countries, the population's average age is increasing. In the United States, for example, the age-65-and-older population increased by a smaller percentage than the under-65 population in the 1990s. However, in the period 2010–2030, the population aged 65 and older is projected to grow by 77.6 percent.[32] As with the U.S. Labor force, other countries also are witnessing a trend toward an older workforce. Contributing to this growth are increasing life expectancies.

The aging trend suggests numerous opportunities for firms to develop goods and services to meet the needs of an increasingly older population. For example, the elderly use a lot of prescription drugs, so Walmart began a program to sell hundreds of generic drugs for only four dollars. In so doing, the firm is able to increase its sales and provide an important service to a population that might not be able to afford the drugs otherwise. Meanwhile, some observers expect the action to have a ripple effect on the entire healthcare industry.[33]

It has been projected that up to one-half of the females and one-third of the males born at the end of the 1990s in developed countries could live to be 100 years old, with some of them possibly living to be 200 or more.[34] If these life spans become a reality, a host of interesting business opportunities and societal issues will emerge. For example, the effect on individuals' pension plans will be significant and will create potential opportunities for financial institutions, as well as possible threats to government-sponsored retirement and health plans. There are also ramifications regarding the workforce. Because a labor force can be critical to competitive success, firms across the globe must learn to work effectively with older labor forces. Also, countries with increasing life expectancies need to ensure that there are enough workers to support the entire population and promote economic growth. In Japan, the government is providing incentives to encourage people to work longer.[35]

Geographic Distribution. For decades, the U.S. population has been shifting from the north and east to the west and south and that trend continued in the first decade of the 21st century.[36] Similarly, the trend of relocating from metropolitan to nonmetropolitan areas continues. These trends are changing local and state governments' tax bases. In turn, business firms' decisions regarding location are influenced by the degree of support that different taxing agencies offer.

The geographic distribution of populations throughout the world varies by country. For example, 60 percent of the population in China lives in rural areas but metropolitan areas have experienced substantial growth in the last decade. In fact, Shanghai has a population of more than 18 million and Beijing's population is more than 15 million.[37] Information about the income distribution of major population centers can help firms to decide where to locate their operations to reach the largest potential markets for their goods and services.

Ethnic Mix. The ethnic mix of populations continues to change. Within the United States, the ethnicity of states and their cities varies significantly. Firms are challenged to be sensitive to these changes. Through careful study, companies can develop and market products that satisfy the unique needs of different ethnic groups. Hispanics are the largest ethnic minority in the United States, and the U.S. Hispanic market is the third largest Latin American economy in the world (behind only Brazil and Mexico).[38] Changes in ethnic mix also affect a workforce's composition. In the

United States, for example, the population and labor force will continue to diversify, as immigration accounts for a sizable part of growth, as noted earlier. As projected, Hispanics and Asians accounted for more than 20 percent of the U.S. population in 2010.[39] Effective management of a culturally diverse workforce can produce a competitive advantage. For example, heterogeneous work teams have been shown to produce more effective strategic analyses, more creativity and innovation, and higher-quality decisions than homogenous work teams.[40] However, evidence also suggests that diverse work teams are difficult to manage to achieve these outcomes.[41]

Income Distribution. Understanding how income is distributed within and across populations informs firms of the purchasing power and discretionary income of different groups. Studies of income distributions suggest that although living standards have improved over time, variations exist within and between nations.[42] Of interest to firms are the average incomes of households and individuals. For instance, the increase in dual-career couples has had a notable effect on average incomes in the United States. Although real income has been declining in general, the income of dual-career couples has increased. These figures yield strategically relevant information for firms.

Another example of a change in income distributions is occurring in China. Rapid economic growth, especially in the coastal region, has created a rising generation of young and wealthy Chinese. These trend-conscious individuals buy coffee at Starbucks and shop online at Tiffany & Co. And, those in the larger metropolitan areas (e.g., Shanghai, Beijing) have more economic opportunities and higher incomes on average.[43]

The Economic Segment

The health of a nation's economy affects individual firms and industries. Because of this, companies study the economic environment to identify changes, trends, and their strategic implications.

The **economic environment** refers to the nature and direction of the economy in which a firm competes or may compete.[44] Aspects of the economy that deserve ongoing attention include growth in gross national product (GNP), interest rates, inflation, foreign exchange rates, and trade balances. Growth in GNP, often reported per capita or adjusted for inflation, is a general indication of the strength of the economy. GNP growth influences and is influenced by the other factors.

Interest rates and inflation are interconnected. Low interest rates encourage new investment, which leads to higher GNP.[45] However, the increased production increases the demand for supplies, which can increase inflationary pressures. The U.S. Federal Reserve sets the interest rate at which banks borrow money from the U.S. government, which then influences other interest rates. Consequentially, when the Federal Reserve is concerned about inflation, it raises interest rates, and when the economy is slowing down (i.e., slower growth in GNP), it lowers interest rates. Thus, the government attempts to manage the economy so that in positive cycles, inflation does not become too high and that a decline cycle is short and not too steep. Of course, firms must adjust their strategies to adapt to these economic cycles. Depending on how well they adjust to the economic changes, some are more likely to survive than others.[46]

Because nations are interconnected as a result of the global economy, firms must scan, monitor, forecast, and assess the health of economics outside their host nations. For example, many nations throughout the world are affected by the U.S. economy, which is the largest consumer of oil, automobiles, and many other goods. To keep up with consumer demand, the United States imports more goods than it exports.[47] This imbalance means that foreign countries have substantial surplus dollars to invest in the United States. Foreign investment has grown tremendously in recent years, with many foreign firms building factories or buying companies.[48] This trend extends beyond the United States. For example, both Chinese and Indian companies are extending their reach well beyond their national borders. And, many foreign firms have made investments in China and to a lesser degree, India.

Both inflation and trade surpluses are among the influences on foreign exchange rates.[49] Foreign exchange rates affect whether firms that make investments in other countries are able to withdraw the earnings on those investments successfully. For instance, if a foreign country has very high inflation and exchange rates have changed dramatically since an investment was made, a firm might actually lose money if it tries to convert its earnings from that investment back into its home currency.

Although this discussion of economic forces is simplified, it illustrates the importance to firms of staying abreast of economic trends as they formulate and implement strategies, including international strategies.

The Political/Legal Segment

Economic issues are intertwined with the realities of the external environment's political/legal segment. The **political/legal segment** is the arena in which organizations and interest groups compete for attention, resources, and a voice in overseeing the body of laws and regulations guiding the interactions among nations.[50] Essentially, this segment represents how organizations try to influence government and how governments influence them.[51] Constantly changing, these influences affect the nature of competition through laws, regulations, and policies (see Table 3.1). Sometimes the penalties for inadequately responding to these forces can be harsh. For instance, the EU fined Microsoft €280.5 million for defying antitrust orders.[52]

Firms must carefully analyze a new political administration's business-related policies and philosophies. Antitrust laws, taxation laws, industries chosen for deregulation or additional regulation, labor training laws, and the degree of commitment to educational institutions are areas in which an administration's policies can affect the operations and profitability of industries and individual firms. Often, firms develop a political strategy to influence governmental policies and actions that might affect them. The effects of global governmental policies on a firm's competitive position increase the importance of forming an effective political strategy.[53]

Business firms across the globe must confront an interesting array of political/legal questions and issues. For example, the debate continues over trade policies. Some believe that a nation should erect trade barriers to protect products manufactured by its companies. Others argue that free trade across nations serves the best interests of individual countries and their citizens. The International Monetary Fund (IMF) classifies trade barriers as restrictive when tariffs total at least 25 percent of a product's price. At the other extreme, the IMF stipulates that a nation has open trade when its tariffs are between 0 and 9 percent.[54] Although controversial, a number of countries (including the United States, nations in the EU, Japan, Australia, Canada, Chile, Singapore, and Mexico) are cooperating in an effort to reduce or eventually eliminate trade barriers. The North American Free Trade Agreement (NAFTA) is one example of this trend. The treaty has significantly affected trade, with total U.S. exports of $411.5 billion in 2010 up 23.4 percent over 2009, and up 109 percent over 1993. U.S. exports to NAFTA countries accounted for more than 32 percent of all U.S. exports in 2010.[55]

There are also political risks with which businesses must contend.[56] These risks are most prominent in developing countries but also in countries with unstable leadership and where economic crises are dominant. For example, the changes in government in the Middle Eastern countries (e.g., Egypt, Libya, and Tunisia) present uncertainties for foreign and domestic businesses operating there. The unrest also affects companies globally because of the potential influence on oil prices.[57] Additionally, the EU economic crises have created significant problems for businesses operating in several of those countries (e.g., Greece, Italy).[58] A major economic crisis in a particular part of the world can create economic shocks in other global regions sometimes resulting in substantial negative influences on business operations (e.g., significant increases in the price of energy, major increases in interest rates, rapid declines in stock prices).[59] Finally, some political and institutional environments are more conducive to business economic activities and to specific strategies that they employ than are others.[60]

The Sociocultural Segment

The **sociocultural segment** is concerned with a society's attitudes and cultural values. Because attitudes and values form the cornerstone of a society, they often drive demographic, economic, political/legal, and technological conditions and changes.[61]

Sociocultural segments differ across countries. For example, the United States spends a higher percentage of its GDP on healthcare than any other Organisation for Economic Co-operation and Development (OECD) country. Interestingly, the U.S. rate of citizens' access to healthcare is below that of OECD members and other countries, even though all federal, state, and local government spending on healthcare is greater than any other category of spending such as education, defense, retirement, etc.[62]

Retirement planning also reflects a society's values. A study in 15 countries indicated that retirement planning in the United States starts earlier than in other countries: "Americans are involved in retirement issues to a greater extent than other countries, particularly in Western Europe where the Social Security and pensions systems provide a much higher percentage of income in retirement."[63] U.S. residents start planning for retirement in their 30s, whereas people in Portugal, Spain, Italy, and Japan start in their 40s and 50s. Attitudes regarding saving for retirement affect a nation's economic and political/legal segments.

As already mentioned, a significant trend in many countries is increased workforce diversity. This diversity includes female workers, who are a valuable source of highly productive employees. Women now account for about half the workforce in the United States and Sweden, with many other countries close behind.[64] An increasing number of women are also starting and managing their own businesses. Using data from the U.S. Census Bureau, the Center for Women's Business Research estimates that about half (47.7 percent) of the privately owned firms in the United States are majority owned by women. The number of new businesses started by women also continues to increase, and currently about 38 percent of all start-ups in the United States are by women.[65] Because of equal pay and equal opportunity legislation in many countries, relative pay for women is increasing. However, pay differentials between men and women still exist. The growing gender, ethnic, and cultural diversity in the workforce creates challenges and opportunities,[66] including those related to combining the best of both men's and women's traditional leadership styles. This combination can benefit a firm by identifying ways to facilitate all employees' contributions. Some companies provide training to nurture the leadership potential of women and members of ethnic minorities. Although cultural diversity can present challenges in organizations, it can also produce benefits such as learning and knowledge transfer if managed properly.[67] Changes in organizational structure and management practices often are required to eliminate subtle barriers that may exist. Learning to manage diversity in the domestic workforce can increase a firm's effectiveness in managing a globally diverse workforce, as the firm acquires more international operations.

Another manifestation of changing attitudes toward work is the continuing growth of contingency workers (part-time, temporary, and contract employees) throughout the global economy. This trend is significant in several parts of the world, including Canada, Japan, Latin America, Western Europe, and the United States. The fastest growing group of contingency workers is in the technical and professional area. Contributing to this growth are corporate restructurings and a breakdown of lifetime employment practices. In conjunction with the growing emphasis on temporary employment, careers are growing shorter and more flexible. In fact, there are predictions that the average career in a particular field may be as short as four years in the not-too-distant future. This trend is linked to the volatility in industries and the steady development of new industries.[68]

The continued growth of suburban communities in the United States and abroad is another sociocultural trend. The increasing number of people living in the suburbs has a number of effects. For example, because of the resulting often-longer commute times to urban businesses, there is pressure for better transportation and superhighway systems (e.g., outer beltways to serve the suburban communities). On the other hand, some businesses are locating in the suburbs closer to their employees. Suburban growth also affects the number of electronic telecommuters, which is increasing rapidly in the 21st century.[69] This work-style option is feasible because of changes in the technological segment. Also, beyond the suburbs, "micropolitan" areas are increasing in importance. These are classified by the U.S. Census Bureau as communities that are often 100 miles or more from a large city and have 10,000 to 49,999 residents. These areas offer big-city amenities such as strip malls and major chain restaurants, but living costs are much lower.[70]

The Technological Segment

Pervasive and diversified in scope, technological changes affect many societal sectors. These effects occur primarily through new products, processes, and materials. The **technological segment** includes the institutions and activities involved with creating new knowledge and translating that knowledge into new outputs, products, processes, and materials.

Given the rapid pace of technological change, it is vital for firms to thoroughly study the technological segment.[71] The importance of these efforts is suggested by the finding that firms that adopt new technology early often achieve higher market shares and earn higher returns. Thus, executives must verify that their firm is continuously scanning the external environment to identify potential substitutes for technologies that are in current use, as well as to discover newly emerging technologies from which their firm could derive competitive advantage.[72] Chapter 1 outlined three categories of technological trends that are altering the nature of competition: the increasing rate of technological change and diffusion, changes in information technology, and increasing knowledge intensity. The Internet is at the heart of all of these trends.

Among its other valuable uses, the Internet is an excellent source of data and information that can help a firm to understand its external environment. Access to experts on topics from chemical engineering to semiconductor manufacturing, to the Library of Congress, and even to satellite photographs is available through the Internet. Other information available through this technology includes Securities and Exchange Commission (SEC) filings, Commerce Department data, Bureau of the Census information, new patent filings, and stock market updates. Internet technology is also facilitating business transactions between companies, as well as between a company and its customers. Thus, a competitive advantage may accrue to the company that derives full value from the Internet in terms of both e-commerce activities and transactions taken to process the firm's work flow.

Wireless communication technologies, including handheld wireless devices, represent another important technological opportunity. The use of handheld computers with wireless network connectivity, Web-enabled mobile phones, and other emerging platforms (e.g., iPads) are becoming the dominant form of communication and commerce.[73] Wireless local area networks, known as Wi-Fi ("wireless fidelity"), are already available in many restaurants, hotels, office buildings, schools, and other venues.

Clearly, the Internet and wireless forms of communication are important technological developments for many reasons. One reason is that they facilitate the diffusion of other technology and knowledge critical for achieving and maintaining a competitive advantage.[74] Technological knowledge is particularly important. Certainly on a global scale, the technological opportunities and threats in the general environment affect whether firms obtain new technology from external sources (such as licensing and acquisition) or develop it internally.[75]

The Global Segment

The **global segment** includes relevant new global markets, existing markets that are changing, important international political events, and critical cultural and institutional characteristics of global markets.[76] Globalization was defined in Chapter 1 as the increasing economic interdependence among countries as reflected in the flow of goods and services, financial capital, and knowledge across country borders. Globalization of business markets creates opportunities for firms;[77] for example, they can identify and enter valuable global markets.[78] Economically maturing countries such as China and India may be particularly advantageous targets as a result of an increase in developing country funds, reduced trade barriers, and substantial macro-economic reforms in those countries.[79] China's admission to the World Trade Organization in 2001 was a significant milestone in facilitating trade and investment in that country. India produces more people with technical degrees than any other country except the United States. As a result, many multinational companies are dramatically increasing their investments there. Cisco Systems, Intel, and Microsoft have each committed more than $1 billion to their Indian operations for research and the hiring of thousands of workers.

Moving into international markets extends a firm's reach and potential. The larger total market increases the probability that a firm will earn a return on its innovations. Toyota receives about half of its total sales revenue from outside Japan, its home country. Well over half of the sales revenues of McDonald's and almost all of those of Nokia are from outside their home countries.[80] Certainly, firms entering new markets can diffuse the knowledge they have created and learn from the new markets as well.[81] Global markets also offer firms more opportunities to obtain the resources needed for success.

Nevertheless, globalization of business markets creates challenges as well as opportunities for firms.[82] The low cost of Chinese products threatened many global firms in industries such as textiles, where average wage rates make Chinese garments so inexpensive that companies in other countries found it hard to compete. In recent years, Chinese manufacturing has had to cope with rising costs and decreasing demand (partly because of the global recession). Yet, it is still a major competitor for outsourced manufacturing for Western firms.[83] Also, the large number of technically trained workers in India does not mean that non-Indian multinationals have a monopoly on hiring Indian employees. In fact, rapidly developing Indian firms are hiring more of their own citizens and even expanding their operations outside India into regions that have traditionally been dominated by Western firms. For example, Tata Consultancy Services Ltd. and Infosys Technologies Ltd., two IT consulting firms, have been expanding their presence in European and United States' markets.

Of course, investment risks abound in less economically mature countries. For instance, a few years ago Argentina's market was full of promise, but in 2001 Argentina experienced a financial crisis that placed it on the brink of bankruptcy.[84] By 2005 Argentina was still struggling to complete its debt restructuring. In addition, although economic growth has increased since the 2002 Argentine recession, Argentina has experienced difficulties raising needed investment capital because of its tarnished reputation from failing to pay its debts.[85]

As firms expand into global markets, they need to recognize their differing sociocultural and institutional attributes. Companies competing in South Korea, for example, must understand the value placed in that country on hierarchical order, formality, and self-control, as well as on duty rather than rights. Furthermore, the ideology of Korea and many other Asian countries is based on communitarianism, a belief that stresses the connection between the community and the individual. Korea's approach differs from those of Japan and China, however, in that it focuses on *inhwa*, or harmony. Inhwa is based on a respect of hierarchical relationships and obedience to authority. Alternatively, the approach in China stresses *guanxi*—personal relationships or good connections—while in Japan, the focus is on *wa*, or group harmony and social cohesion.[86]

From an institutional perspective, China can be characterized by a major emphasis on centralized government planning,[87] in contrast to the United States and many other Western countries. These types of differences create the necessity to have a top management team with the experience, knowledge, and sensitivity necessary to effectively analyze this segment of the environment. In addition U.S. managers must become comfortable with and effective in building relationships with key stakeholders when they enter these countries.[88] Building good relational capabilities is especially important for firms that develop global supply chains.[89]

The Physical Environment Segment

The **physical environment segment** involves the changes to the physical environment and business practices to respond to and sometimes to prevent those changes.[90] Firms engaging in these practices are concerned with sustaining the physical environment with particular focus on ecological, social, and economic systems.[91] Some refer to this activity as sustainability. And, many firms are now developing sustainability strategies and integrating them with their corporate strategies.[92]

Major issues in the physical environment segment include global warming (which appears to be effecting major changes in weather patterns and energy consumption conservation). Other issues involve actions a firm can implement as a greening strategy to ensure a positive effect on the natural environment or at least minimize the negative effects. The U.S. Energy Policy Act of 2005 provides incentives to businesses to implement efficient energy strategies (e.g., by providing tax deductions for energy improvements).[93]

Also companies have developed and market "green" or environmentally friendly products. For example, Siemens AG obtains approximately $38 billion annually from sales of wind power, solar energy, and energy conservation electricity grids. And, Siemens refers to about 25 percent of its 400,000 employees as "green-collar employees."[94] Another company, PepsiCo, is pursuing a strategy of linking green activities in each of its businesses to financial results. In so doing, it hopes to develop technologies that conserve energy, are environmentally friendly, and are used across all of their businesses. PepsiCo is hoping that these strategies have not only a positive influence on the natural environment but also reduce the firm's costs. For example, actions to implement a fleet of all-electric delivery trucks in Frito-Lay, one of PepsiCo's major businesses, are estimated to save 500,000 gallons of diesel annually and reduce their greenhouse emissions by 75 percent over their traditional fleet of trucks.[95]

A key objective of analyzing the general environment is identifying anticipated changes and trends among external elements. With a focus on the future, the analysis of the general environment allows firms to identify opportunities and threats. Also critical to a firm's future operations is an understanding of its industry environment and its competitors.

INDUSTRY ENVIRONMENT ANALYSIS

An **industry** is a group of firms producing products that are close substitutes. In the course of competition, these firms influence one another. Typically, industries include a rich mix of competitive strategies that companies use to pursue value creation and above-average returns. In part, these strategies are chosen because of the influence of an industry's characteristics.[96] For example, some industries are more dynamic (i.e., they experience a significant amount of change) and other industries have more resources. Both the degree of change and the quantity of resources available influence the strategies firms can employ to be successful.[97] In fact, specific norms of behavior (practices) develop over time to which firms must adhere in order to be successful.[98] And, each industry often has unique sets of resources. For example, because of specific skills needed, some of the human resources may be unique to an industry such as petroleum engineers in the oil industry and accountants in professional accounting firms. Thus, firms in the industry must not only recruit people with the skills needed, but they must try to recruit among the best in order to gain a competitive advantage.[99] Compared with the general environment, the industry environment more directly affects the firm's value creation and above-average returns.[100] For example, the biotechnology industry has more than 700 publicly-listed firms across North America, Europe, and Asia and the industry has achieved double-digit growth for a number of years. Thus, firms in this industry have strong potential to create value for their stakeholders.[101]

The intensity of industry competition and an industry's profit potential (as measured by the long-run return on invested capital) are functions of five forces of competition: the threats posed by new entrants, the power of suppliers, the power of buyers, product substitutes, and the intensity of rivalry among competitors (see Figure 3.2).

The five forces model of competition expands the arena for competitive analysis. Historically, when studying the competitive environment, firms concentrated on

FIGURE 3.2 THE FIVE FORCES OF COMPETITION MODEL

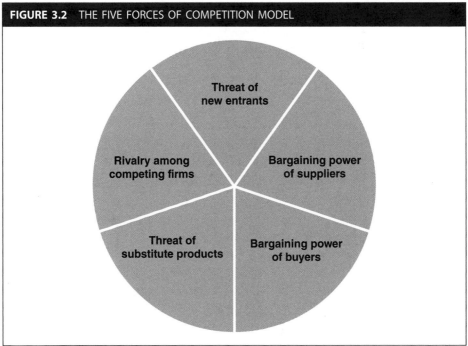

© Cengage Learning

companies with which they competed directly. However, firms must search more broadly to identify current and potential competitors by identifying potential customers as well as the firms serving them. Competing for the same customers and thus being influenced by how customers value location and firm capabilities in their decisions is referred to as the *market microstructure*.[102] Understanding this area is particularly important because in recent years industry boundaries have become blurred. For example, in the electrical utilities industry, cogenerators (firms that also produce power) are competing with regional utility companies. Moreover, telecommunications companies now compete with broadcasters, software manufacturers provide personal financial services, airlines sell mutual funds, and automakers sell insurance and provide financing.[103] In addition to focusing on customers rather than specific industry boundaries to define markets, geographic boundaries must also be considered. Research suggests that different geographic markets for the same product can have considerably different competitive conditions.[104]

The five forces model acknowledges that suppliers can become a firm's competitors (by integrating forward), as can buyers (by integrating backward). Several firms have integrated forward in the pharmaceutical industry by acquiring distributors or wholesalers. In addition, firms choosing to enter a new market and those producing products that are adequate substitutes for existing products can become the competition of a company.

Threat of New Entrants

Identifying new entrants is important because they can threaten the market share of existing competitors. One reason new entrants pose such a threat is that they bring additional production capacity. Unless the demand for a good or service is increasing, additional capacity holds consumers' costs down, resulting in less revenue and lower returns for competing firms. Often, new entrants have a keen interest in gaining a large market share. As a result, new competitors sometimes force existing firms to be more effective and efficient and to learn how to compete in new ways (for example, using an Internet-based distribution channel).

The likelihood that firms will enter an industry is a function of several factors, two of which are *barriers to entry* and the *retaliation* expected from current industry participants. Entry barriers make it difficult for new firms to enter an industry and often place them at a competitive disadvantage even when they are able to enter. As such, high entry barriers increase the returns for existing firms in the industry and may allow some firms to dominate the industry.[105]

Barriers to Entry. Existing competitors try to develop barriers to entry. In contrast, potential entrants seek markets in which the entry barriers are relatively insignificant. The absence of entry barriers increases the probability that a new entrant can operate profitably. There are several kinds of potentially significant entry barriers, including economies of scale, product differentiation, capital requirements, switching costs, access to distribution channels, cost advantages independent of scale, and government policy.[106] When firms enter an industry with significant entry barriers, they must have superior capabilities in order to survive.[107] Yet, there are special cases when the entry of new rivals benefits incumbents in the industry. For example, new rivals might attract new customers or suppliers to the industry.[108]

Economies of Scale. *Economies of scale* are "the marginal improvements in efficiency that a firm experiences as it incrementally increases its size."[109] Therefore, as the quantity of a product produced during a given period increases, the cost of manufacturing each unit declines. Economies of scale can be developed in most business functions, such as marketing, manufacturing, R&D, and purchasing. Increasing economies of scale enhances a firm's flexibility. For example, a firm may choose to reduce its price and capture a greater share of the market. Alternatively, it may keep its price constant to increase profits.

New entrants face a dilemma when confronting current competitors' scale economies. Small-scale entry places them at a cost disadvantage. Alternatively, large-scale entry, in which the new entrant manufactures large volumes of a product to gain economies of scale, risks strong competitive retaliation.

Also important for the firm to understand are instances of current competitive realities that reduce the ability of economies of scale to create an entry barrier. Many companies now customize their products for large numbers of small customer groups. Customized products are not manufactured in volumes necessary to achieve economies of scale. Customization is made possible by new flexible manufacturing systems. In fact, the new manufacturing technology facilitated by advanced computerization has allowed the development of mass customization in some industries. Mass customized products can be individualized to the customer in a very short time, often within a day. Mass customization has become common in manufacturing products.[110] Companies manufacturing customized products learn how to respond quickly to customers' desires rather than developing scale economies. In fact, there is a new product on the market that provides a vision of the future in customization. The product is MakerBot 3-D printer which can manufacture small plastic replacement products in a consumer's home (e.g., a new paper towel holder). Thus, customers may develop their own customized products instead of ordering them from businesses.[111]

Product Differentiation. Over time, customers may come to believe that a firm's product is unique. This belief can result from the firm's service to the customer, effective advertising campaigns, or being the first to market a good or service. Companies such as Coca-Cola, PepsiCo, and the world's automobile manufacturers spend a great deal of money on advertising to convince potential customers of their products' distinctiveness. Customers valuing a product's uniqueness tend to become loyal to both the product and the company producing it. Typically, new entrants must allocate substantial resources to overcome existing customer loyalties. To combat the perception of uniqueness, new entrants frequently offer products at lower prices. This decision, however, may result in lower profits or even losses.

Capital Requirements. Competing in a new industry requires the firm to meet certain *capital requirements*. In addition to physical facilities, capital is needed for inventories, marketing activities, and other critical business functions. Even when competing in a new industry is attractive, the capital required for successful market entry may not be available for a firm to pursue an apparent market opportunity.

For example, entering the steel and defense industries would be very difficult because of the substantial resource investments required to be competitive. One way a firm could enter the steel industry, however, is with a highly efficient mini-mill. A firm might enter the defense industry through the acquisition of an existing firm because of the knowledge requirements.

Switching Costs. *Switching costs* are the one-time costs customers incur when they buy from a different supplier. The costs of buying new ancillary equipment and of retraining employees, and even the psychological costs of ending a relationship, may be incurred in switching to a new supplier. In some cases, switching costs are low, such as when a consumer switches to a different soft drink. Switching costs can vary as a function of time. For example, in terms of hours toward graduation, the cost to a student of transferring from one university to another as a freshman is much lower than when that student transfers as a senior. Occasionally, a manufacturer's decision to produce a new, innovative product creates high switching costs for the final consumer. Customer loyalty programs, such as airlines awarding frequent flier miles, are intended to increase the customer's switching costs.

If switching costs are high, a new entrant must offer either a substantially lower price or a much better product to attract buyers. Usually, the more established the relationship between parties, the greater is the cost incurred to switch to an alternative offering. This is because of trust that is developed between the parties and the willingness of one party to help the other when a special request is needed (e.g., quick response to a special order).[112]

Access to Distribution Channels. Over time, industry participants typically develop effective means of distributing products. Once a relationship with its distributors has been developed, a firm will nurture it to create switching costs for the distributors. *Access to distribution channels* can be a strong barrier to entry, particularly in consumer nondurable goods industries (for example, in grocery stores where shelf space is limited) and in international markets. Thus, new entrants have to persuade distributors to carry their products, either in addition to or in place of those currently distributed. Price breaks and cooperative advertising allowances may be used for this purpose; however, such practices reduce the new entrant's profit potential.

Cost Advantages Independent of Scale. Sometimes, established competitors have cost advantages—such as proprietary product technology, favorable access to raw materials, desirable locations, and government subsidies—that new entrants cannot duplicate. Successful competition requires new entrants to reduce the strategic relevance of these factors. Delivering purchases directly to the buyer can counter the advantage of a desirable location; new food establishments in an undesirable location often follow this practice. Similarly, automobile dealerships located in unattractive areas can provide superior service (such as picking up a car to be serviced and then delivering it to the customer) to overcome a competitor's location advantage.

Government Policy. Through licensing and permit requirements, *government policy* can also control entry into an industry. Liquor retailing, banking, and trucking are examples of industries in which government decisions and actions affect entry possibilities. Also, governments often restrict entry into some industries because of the need to provide quality service or to protect jobs. Alternatively, de-regulation of industries, such as airlines or utilities in the United States, can increase competition as more firms are permitted to enter.[113] Some of the most widely publicized government actions are those involving antitrust cases. For instance, both the U.S. and European governments pursued an antitrust case against Microsoft. The final settlement in the United States involved a relatively small penalty for the company; however, the EU judgments were more severe.[114]

Expected Retaliation. Firms seeking to enter an industry also anticipate the reactions of firms in the industry. An expectation of swift and vigorous competitive responses reduces the likelihood of entry. Vigorous retaliation can be expected when the existing firm has a major stake in the industry (for example, it has fixed assets with few, if any, alternative uses), when it has substantial resources, and when industry growth is slow or constrained. For example, any firms that attempt to enter the steel or information technology industries at the current time can expect significant retaliation from existing competitors.

Locating market niches not served by incumbents allows the new entrant to avoid entry barriers. Small entrepreneurial firms are generally best suited for identifying and serving neglected market segments. When Honda first entered the U.S. market, it concentrated on small-engine motorcycles, a market that firms such as Harley-Davidson ignored. By targeting this neglected niche, Honda avoided competition. After consolidating its position, Honda used its strength to attack rivals by introducing larger motorcycles and competing in the broader market. (Competitive actions and competitive responses between firms such as Honda and Harley-Davidson are discussed briefly at the end of this chapter and fully in Chapter 6.)

Bargaining Power of Suppliers

Supplier firms can use tactics such as increasing their prices and reducing the quality or availability of their products to exert power over firms competing within an industry. If a particular firm is unable to recover cost increases by its suppliers through its pricing structure, its profitability is reduced by its suppliers' actions. A supplier group is powerful when

- It is dominated by a few large companies and is more concentrated than the industry to which it sells.
- Satisfactory substitute products are not available to industry firms.
- Industry firms are not a significant customer for the supplier group.
- Suppliers' goods are critical to buyers' marketplace success.
- The effectiveness of suppliers' products has created high switching costs for industry firms.
- It poses a credible threat to integrate forward into the buyers' industry. Credibility is enhanced when suppliers have substantial resources and provide a highly differentiated product.

The automobile manufacturing industry is an example of an industry in which suppliers' bargaining power is relatively low. For example, Nissan and Toyota place significant pressure on their suppliers to provide parts at reduced prices.[115] Because they sell their products to a small number of large firms and because they are not credible threats to integrate forward, auto parts suppliers have little power relative to automobile manufacturers such as Toyota and Nissan.

Dependence on suppliers can have some positive benefits if the buyer and supplier develop a positive and trusting relationship over time.[116] However there are risks to the dependence that go beyond a supplier exercising its power in disadvantageous ways. For example, major disruptions in global supply chains due to significant political events (e.g., military strikes, terrorist acts) or natural disasters (e.g., the tsunami that hit Japan in 2010) can have severe consequences to a buyer that has no alternative suppliers.[117]

Bargaining Power of Buyers

Firms seek to maximize their return on invested capital. Alternatively, buyers (customers of an industry or firm) want to buy products at the lowest possible price—the point at which the industry earns the lowest acceptable rate of return on its invested capital. To reduce their costs, buyers bargain for higher quality, greater levels of service, and lower prices. These outcomes are often achieved by encouraging competitive battles among the industry's firms. Customers (buyer groups) are powerful when

- They purchase a large portion of an industry's total output.
- The sales of the product being purchased account for a significant portion of the seller's annual revenues.
- They could switch to another product at little, if any, cost.
- The industry's products are undifferentiated or standardized, and the buyers would pose a credible threat if they were to integrate backward into the sellers' industry.

Armed with greater amounts of information about the manufacturer's costs and the power of the Internet as a shopping and distribution alternative, consumers have increased their bargaining power in many industries. However, consumers also develop relationships with and loyalties to suppliers, especially because they are responsive to satisfying their needs through their products and/or follow up service. Thus, suppliers can overcome buyer power by taking actions that build strong relationships with the consumers and thereby gain their loyalty.[118]

Threat of Substitute Products

Substitute products are goods or services from outside an industry that perform similar or the same functions as a product that the industry produces. For example, NutraSweet and sugar perform the same function, but with different characteristics; as a sugar substitute, NutraSweet places an upper limit on sugar manufacturers' prices. Other product substitutes include e-mail instead of fax machines, plastic containers rather than glass jars, tea instead of coffee, and satellite services in the place of digital cable services. Newspaper circulation has declined in recent years because of many substitute news outlets, including cable television, the Internet, e-mail, and cell phones. For example, although the changing formats make comparisons difficult, the data suggest that the Chicago Tribune's circulation declined by about 3.3 percent on the weekday editions and 1.7 percent on the Sunday edition in 2010.[119]

In general, product substitutes present a strong threat to a firm when customers have few, if any, switching costs and when the substitute product's price is lower or its quality and performance capabilities are equal to or greater than those of the competing product. Differentiating a product on dimensions that customers value (such as price, quality, service after the sale, and location) reduces a substitute's attractiveness.

Intensity of Rivalry among Competitors

Because an industry's firms are mutually dependent, actions taken by one company usually invite competitive responses. *Competitive rivalry* intensifies when a firm is challenged by a competitor's actions or when an opportunity to improve its market position is recognized.

Firms within industries are rarely homogeneous; they differ in resources and capabilities and seek to differentiate themselves from competitors.[120] Typically, firms seek to differentiate their products from competitors' offerings in ways that customers value and in which the firms have a competitive advantage. Visible dimensions on which rivalry is based include price, quality, and innovation. Various factors influence the intensity of rivalry between or among competitors.

Numerous or Equally Balanced Competitors. Intense rivalries are common in industries with many companies. With multiple competitors, it is common for a few firms to believe that they can act without eliciting a response. However, evidence suggests that other firms generally are aware of competitors' actions, often choosing to respond to them. At the other extreme, industries with only a few firms of equivalent size and power also tend to have strong rivalries. The large and often similar-sized resource bases of these firms permit vigorous actions and responses. The competitive battles between Airbus and Boeing in aircraft manufacturing exemplify intense rivalries between pairs of relatively equivalent competitors.

Slow Industry Growth. When a market is growing, firms try to effectively use resources to serve an expanding customer base. Growing markets reduce the pressure to take customers from competitors. However, rivalry in no-growth or slow-growth markets becomes more intense as firms battle to increase their market shares by attracting competitors' customers.

Typically, battles to protect market shares are fierce. The instability in the market that results from these competitive engagements reduces profitability for firms throughout the industry, as is demonstrated by the commercial aircraft industry. To expand market share, Boeing and Airbus compete aggressively by introducing new products and differentiating products and services. Both firms are likely to win some battles and lose others.

High Fixed Costs or High Storage Costs. When fixed costs account for a large part of total costs, companies try to maximize the use of their productive capacity. Doing so allows the firm to spread costs across a larger volume of output. However, when many firms attempt to maximize their productive capacity, excess capacity is created throughout the industry. To then reduce inventories, individual companies typically cut the price of their products and offer rebates and other special discounts to customers. These practices often intensify competition. The pattern of excess capacity at the industry level followed by intense rivalry at the firm level is observed frequently in industries with high storage costs. Perishable products, for example, lose their value rapidly. As their inventories grow, producers of perishable goods often use pricing strategies to sell products quickly.

Lack of Differentiation or Low Switching Costs. When buyers find a differentiated product that satisfies their needs, they frequently purchase the product loyally over time. Industries with many companies that have successfully differentiated their products have less rivalry, resulting in lower competition for individual firms.[121] However, when buyers view products as commodities (as products with few differentiated features of capabilities), rivalry intensifies. In these instances, buyers' purchasing decisions are based primarily on price and, to a lesser degree, service.

The effect of switching costs is identical to that described for differentiated products. The lower the buyers' switching costs, the easier it is for competitors to attract buyers through pricing and service offerings. High switching costs, however, at least partially insulate the firm from rivals' efforts to attract customers. Interestingly, the switching costs—such as pilot and mechanic training—are high in aircraft purchases, yet the rivalry between Boeing and Airbus remains intense because the stakes for both are extremely high.

High Strategic Stakes. Competitive rivalry is likely to be high when it is important for several of the competitors to perform well in the market. For example, although Samsung is diversified and is a market leader in other businesses, it has targeted market leadership in the consumer electronics market. This market is quite important to Sony and other major competitors such as Hitachi, Matsushita, NEC, and Mitsubishi. Thus substantial rivalry is common in this market.

High strategic stakes can also exist in terms of geographic location. For example, Japanese automobile manufacturers are committed to a significant presence in the U.S. marketplace. A key reason for this is that the United States is one of the world's single largest markets for auto manufacturers' products. The Chinese auto market is growing and becoming quite large (and competitive) as well. Because of the stakes involved for Japanese and U.S. manufacturers, rivalry among firms in the United States and the global automobile industry is intense. It should be noted that while close proximity tends to promote greater rivalry, physically proximate competition has potentially positive benefits as well.[122] For example, when competitors are located near each other, it is easier for suppliers to serve them and they can develop economies of scale that lead to lower production costs. Additionally, communications with key industry stakeholders such as suppliers are facilitated and more efficient when they are located close to the firm.[123]

High Exit Barriers. Sometimes companies continue competing in an industry even though the returns on their invested capital are low or negative. Firms making this choice likely face high exit barriers, which include economic, strategic, and emotional factors causing companies to remain in an industry when the profitability of doing so is questionable. Common exit barriers are

▶ Specialized assets (assets with values linked to a particular business or location)
▶ Fixed costs of exit (such as labor agreements)
▶ Strategic interrelationships (relationships of mutual dependence, such as those between one business and other parts of a company's operations, including shared facilities and access to financial markets)
▶ Emotional barriers (aversion to economically justified business decisions because of fear for one's own career, loyalty to employees, and so forth)[124]
▶ Government and social restrictions (more common outside the United States, these restrictions often are based on government concerns for job losses and regional economic effects).

Complementors

A five forces analysis is a powerful way to examine competitive forces in an industry. However, complementors, sometimes labeled a sixth force, can also powerfully influence competition.[125] **Complementors** are the companies that sell complementary goods or services that are compatible with the focal firm's own products or services. They could also include suppliers and buyers who have a strong "network" relationship with the focal firm. A strong network of complementors can solidify a competitive advantage. For instance, Google's position as an Internet search engine is solidified because of the number of Internet access products with which it functions smoothly. If a complementor's good or service adds value to the sale of a firm's good or service, it is likely to create value for the firm. For instance, airlines are complementors to the hotel industry and engineering schools are complementors to high-tech industries.

Complementors can also harm firm competitiveness. For instance, poor airline performance can reduce the economic performance of hotels, theme parks, and other tourist destinations. Similarly, a reduction in the number of new homes built can negatively affect the furniture and home appliance industries as has been evident in recent years.

Interpreting Industry Analyses

Effective industry analyses are products of careful study and interpretation of data and information from multiple sources. A wealth of industry-specific data is available. Because of globalization, international markets and rivalries must be included in the firm's analyses. In fact, research shows that in some industries, international variables are more important than domestic ones as determinants of value creation. Furthermore, the development in international markets has enhanced the chances of success for new ventures as well as for more established firms.[126]

Following a study of the five forces of competition, the firm can develop the insights required to determine an industry's attractiveness regarding the potential to earn adequate or superior returns on its invested capital. In general, the stronger competitive forces are, the lower the profit potential for an industry's firms.

An unattractive industry has low entry barriers, suppliers and buyers with strong bargaining positions, strong competitive threats from product substitutes, and intense rivalry among competitors. These industry characteristics make it very difficult for firms to achieve value creation and earn above-average returns. Alternatively, an attractive industry has high entry barriers, suppliers and buyers with little bargaining power, few competitive threats from product substitutes, and relatively moderate rivalry.[127]

ANALYSIS OF DIRECT COMPETITORS

Evaluating the five forces helps firms understand the nature and level of competition in its industry, and thus its profit potential. Firms can then use this information to help them develop strategies for dealing with each of the forces. For instance, a firm may be able reduce the power of strong suppliers through joint ventures with a supplier company or through outright purchase. Also, a firm may be able to help erect higher entry barriers by building a large plant to produce economies of scale. Firms can also use a five forces analysis to gain information that is useful in understanding the positions, intentions, and performance of direct competitors. Some of the closest of these competitors fall into what is sometimes called a *strategic group*.

Strategic Groups

A set of firms emphasizing similar strategic dimensions to use a similar strategy is called a **strategic group**.[128] The competition between firms within a strategic group is greater than the competition between a member of a strategic group and companies outside that group. Thus, intra-strategic group competition is more intense than is inter-strategic group competition.[129]

Strategic dimensions—such as the extent of technological leadership, product quality, pricing policies, distribution channels, and customer service—are areas that firms in a strategic group emphasize in similar ways. Describing patterns of competition within strategic groups suggests that "organizations in a strategic group occupy similar positions in the market, offer similar goods to a similar set of customers, and may also use similar production technology and other organizational processes."[130] Thus, membership in a particular strategic group partially defines the essential characteristics of the firm's strategy.[131]

The notion of strategic groups can be useful for analyzing an industry's competitive structure. Such analyses can be helpful in diagnosing competition, positioning, and the profitability of firms within an industry.[132] Research has found that strategic groups differ in performance, suggesting that it is important to understand their differences.[133] Interestingly, research also suggests that strategic group membership remains relatively stable over time, making analysis easier and more useful.[134]

Using strategic groups to understand an industry's competitive structure requires the firm to plot companies' competitive actions and competitive responses along strategic dimensions such as pricing decisions, product quality, distribution channels, and so forth. Doing this shows the firm how certain companies are competing using similar strategic dimensions. For example, there are unique radio markets because consumers prefer different music formats and programming (news radio, talk radio, and so forth). Typically, a radio format is created through choices made regarding music or non-music style, scheduling, and announcer style.[135] It is estimated that approximately 30 different radio formats exist, suggesting that there are 30 strategic groups in this industry. The strategies within each of the 30 groups are similar, whereas the strategies across the total set of strategic groups are dissimilar. Thus, firms could increase their understanding of competition in the commercial radio industry by plotting companies' actions and responses in terms of important strategic dimensions.

Strategic groups have several implications. First, because firms within a group offer similar products to the same customers, the competitive rivalry among them can be intense. The more intense the rivalry, the greater is the threat to each firm's profitability. Second, the strengths of the five industry forces (the threats posed by new entrants, the power of suppliers, the power of buyers, product substitutes, and the intensity of rivalry among competitors) differ across strategic groups. Third, the more similar the strategies across the strategic groups, the greater is the likelihood of rivalry among the groups.

Understanding Competitors and Their Intentions

Competitor analysis focuses on each company with which a firm directly competes. The five forces analysis examines forces that influence the strength of rivalry among competitors, but it does not address their intentions. Airbus and Boeing and Sun Microsystems and Microsoft should be keenly interested in understanding each other's objectives, strategies, assumptions, and capabilities. Furthermore, the more intense the rivalry is in an industry, the greater the need to understand competitors. In a competitor analysis, the firm seeks to understand the following:

▶ What drives the competitor, as shown by its *future objectives*
▶ What the competitor is doing and can do, as revealed by its *current strategy and resources*
▶ What the competitor believes about the industry, as shown by its *assumptions*
▶ What the competitor's strengths and weaknesses are, as shown by its *capabilities*[136]

Information about these four components helps the firm prepare an anticipated *response profile* for each competitor (see Figure 3.3). Thus, the results of an effective competitor analysis help a firm understand, interpret, and predict its competitors' actions and responses.

Critical to an effective competitor analysis is gathering data and information that can help the firm understand its competitors' intentions and the strategic implications resulting from them.[137] **Competitor intelligence** is the set of data and information the firm gathers to better understand and better anticipate competitors' objectives, strategies, assumptions, and capabilities. In competitor analysis, the firm should gather intelligence not only about its competitors, but also regarding public policies in countries across the world. Intelligence about public policies "provides an early warning of threats and opportunities emerging from the global public

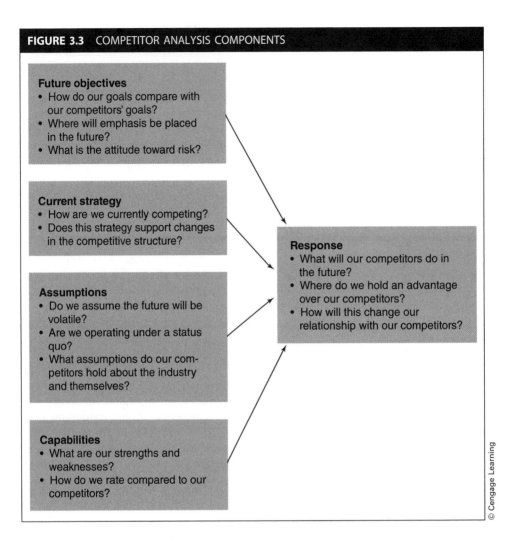

FIGURE 3.3 COMPETITOR ANALYSIS COMPONENTS

Future objectives
- How do our goals compare with our competitors' goals?
- Where will emphasis be placed in the future?
- What is the attitude toward risk?

Current strategy
- How are we currently competing?
- Does this strategy support changes in the competitive structure?

Assumptions
- Do we assume the future will be volatile?
- Are we operating under a status quo?
- What assumptions do our competitors hold about the industry and themselves?

Capabilities
- What are our strengths and weaknesses?
- How do we rate compared to our competitors?

Response
- What will our competitors do in the future?
- Where do we hold an advantage over our competitors?
- How will this change our relationship with our competitors?

© Cengage Learning

policy environment, and analyzes how they will affect the achievement of the company's strategy."[138] Through effective competitive and public policy intelligence, the firm gains the insights it needs to create a competitive advantage and to increase the quality of the strategic decisions it makes when determining how to compete against its rivals. Firms should follow generally accepted ethical practices in gathering competitor intelligence. Industry associations often develop such lists. Practices considered both legal and ethical include (1) obtaining publicly available information (such as court records, competitors' help-wanted advertisements, annual reports, financial reports of publicly held corporations, and Uniform Commerce Code filings), and (2) attending trade fairs and shows to obtain competitors' brochures, view their exhibits, and listen to discussions about their products.

In contrast, certain practices (including blackmail; trespassing; eavesdropping; and stealing drawings, samples, or documents) are widely viewed as unethical and often are illegal.[139] For instance, an employee of Coca-Cola, working with two others, stole information about a new Coke product, complete with a sample, and offered to sell it to Pepsi. Pepsi immediately informed Coke of the breach, and the perpetrators were apprehended. According to Pepsi spokesman Dave DeCecco: "We were just doing whatever any responsible company would do. Despite the fierce competition in this industry, it should also be fair."[140]

To protect themselves from digital fraud or theft that occurs through competitors' hacking into their employees' PCs, some companies buy insurance. Some competitor intelligence practices may be legal, but a firm must decide whether they are also ethical, given the image it desires as a corporate citizen. Especially with electronic transmissions, the line between legal and ethical practices can be difficult to determine. For example, a firm may develop Website addresses that are very similar to those of its competitors and thus occasionally receive e-mail transmissions that were intended for its competitors. According to legal experts, the legality of this "e-mail snagging" remains unclear.[141] Nonetheless, the practice is an example of the challenges companies face when deciding how to gather intelligence about competitors while simultaneously determining what to do to prevent competitors from learning too much about them. Open discussions of intelligence-gathering techniques can help a firm to ensure that people understand its convictions to follow ethical practices for gathering competitor intelligence. An appropriate guideline for competitor intelligence practices is to respect the principles of common morality and the right of competitors not to reveal certain information about their products, operations, and strategic intentions.[142]

Despite the importance of studying competitors, evidence suggests that only some firms use formal processes to collect and disseminate competitive intelligence. Other firms fail to analyze competitors' future objectives as they try to understand their current strategies, assumptions, and capabilities. This failure will yield incomplete insights about those competitors.

SUMMARY

▶ A firm's external environment can be challenging and complex. Because of the external environment's potential effect on performance, the firm must develop the skills required to identify opportunities and threats existing in that environment.

▶ The external environment has three major parts: (1) the general environment (elements in the broader society that affect industries and their firms), (2) the industry environment (factors that influence a firm, its competitive actions and responses, and the industry's profit potential), and (3) the competitor environment (each major competitor's future objectives, current strategies, assumptions, and capabilities).

▶ Analysis of the external environment has four steps: scanning, monitoring, forecasting, and assessing. Through environmental analysis, the firm identifies opportunities and threats.

▶ The general environment has seven segments: demographic, economic, political/legal, sociocultural, technological, global, and physical. For each segment, the firm attempts to determine the strategic relevance of environmental changes and trends.

- Compared with the general environment, the industry environment has a more direct effect on the firm's strategic actions. The five forces model of competition includes the threat of entry, the power of suppliers, the power of buyers, product substitutes, and the intensity of rivalry among competitors. Complementors (sometimes labeled a sixth force) can also influence industry competition. Complementors are companies that sell complementary goods or services compatible with the focal firm's own product or service. By studying these forces, the firm identifies a position in an industry where it can influence the forces to its benefit or where it can buffer itself from the power of the forces in order to earn above-average returns. Industries are populated with different strategic groups. A strategic group is a collection of firms that follow similar strategies and serve similar customers. Competitive rivalry is greater within a strategic group than it is among strategic groups.
- Competitor analysis informs the firm about the future objectives, current strategies, assumptions, and capabilities of the companies with which it competes directly.
- Different techniques are used to create competitor intelligence, which is defined as data, information, and knowledge that allow the firm to better understand its competitors and thereby predict their likely strategic and tactical actions. Firms should use only legal and ethical practices to gather intelligence. The Internet enhances firms' capabilities to gather insights about competitors and their strategic intentions.

ETHICS QUESTIONS

1. How can a firm use its "code of ethics" as it analyzes the external environment?
2. What ethical issues, if any, may be relevant to a firm's monitoring of its external environment? Does use of the Internet to monitor the environment lead to additional ethical issues? If so, what are they?
3. What is an ethical issue associated with each segment of a firm's general environment? Are firms across the globe doing enough to deal with this issue?
4. Why are ethical practices critical in the relationships between a firm and its suppliers?
5. In an intense rivalry, especially one that involves competition in the global marketplace, how can the firm gather competitor intelligence ethically while maintaining its competitiveness?
6. What do you believe determines whether an intelligence-gathering practice is or is not ethical? Do you see this changing as the world's economies become more interdependent? If so, why? Do you see this changing because of the Internet? If so, how?

NOTES

1. D. G. Sirmon, M. A. Hitt, & R. D. Ireland, 2007, Managing firm resources in dynamic environments to create value: Looking inside the black box, *Academy of Management Review*, 32: 273–292;

C. Williams & W. Mitchell, 2004, Focusing firm evolution: The impact of information infrastructure on market entry by U.S. telecommunications companies, 1984–1998, *Management Science*, 5: 1561–1575;

J. Song, 2002, Firm capabilities and technology ladders: Sequential foreign direct investments of Japanese electronics firms in East Asia, *Strategic Management Journal*, 23: 191–210.

2 D. K. Datta, J. P. Guthrie, D. Basuil, & A. Pandey, 2010, Causes and effects of employee downsizing: A review and synthesis, *Journal of Management*, 36: 281–348; J. A. Zuniga-Vicente & J. D. Vicente-Lorente, 2006, Strategic moves and organizational survival in turbulent environments: The case of Spanish banks(1983–97); J. Chattopadhyay, W. H. Glick, & G. P. Huber, 2001, Organizational actions in response to threats and opportunities, *Academy of Management Journal*, 44: 937–955.

3 R. A. D'Aveni, G. B. Dagnino, & K. G. Smith, 2010, The age of temporary advantage, *Strategic Management Journal*, 31: 1371–1385; C. M. Grimm, H. Lee, & K. G. Smith, 2005, *Strategy as Action: Competitive Dynamics and Competitive Advantages*, New York: Oxford University Press.

4 S. Shane, 2012, Reflections on the 2010 AMR decade award: Delivering on the promise of entrepreneurship as a field of research, *Academy of Management Review*, 37: 1020; K. E. Meyer, R. Mudambi, & R. Narula, 2001, Multinational enterprises and local contexts: The opportunities and challenges of multiple embeddedness, *Journal of Management Studies*, 48: 235–252; T. Pedersen & J. M. Shaver, 2011, Internationalization revisited: The big step hypothesis, *Global Strategy Journal*, 1: 263–274.

5 B. K. Boyd, K. T. Haynes, M. A. Hitt, D. D. Bergh, & D. J. Ketchen, 2012, Contingency hypotheses in strategic management research: Use, disuse or misuse? *Journal of Management*, 38: 278–313.

6 K. G. Smith, C. J. Collins, & K. D. Clark, 2005, Existing knowledge, knowledge creation capability, and the rate of new product introduction in high technology firms, *Academy of Management Journal*, 48: 346–357; R. M. Kanter, 2002, Strategy as improvisational theater, *MIT Sloan Management Review*, 43(2): 76–78.

7 J. Woolley, 2010, Technological emergence through entrepreneurship across multiple industries, *Strategic Entrepreneurship Journal*, 4: 1–21.

8 M. Song, C. Droge, S. Hanvanich, & R. Calantone, 2005, Marketing and technology resource complementarity: An analysis of their interaction effect in two environmental contexts, *Strategic Management Journal*, 26: 259–276; D. M. De Carolis, 2003, Competencies and imitability in the pharmaceutical industry: An analysis of their relationship with firm performance, *Journal of Management*, 29: 27–50.

9 L. Fahey, 1999, *Competitors*, New York: Wiley; B. A. Walters & R. L. Priem, 1999, Business strategy and CEO intelligence acquisition, *Competitive Intelligence Review*, 10(2): 15–22.

10 M.-J. Chen, H.-C. Lin, & J. G. Michel, 2010, Navigating in a hypercompetitive environment: The roles of action aggressiveness and TMT integration, *Strategic Management Journal*, 31: 1410–1430; D. G. Sirmon, M. A. Hitt, J.-L. Arrgele, & J. T. Campbell, 2010, The dynamic interplay of capability strengths and weaknesses: Investigating the bases of temporary competitive advantage, *Strategic Management Journal*, 31: 1386–1409.

11 M. W. Meyer, 2011, Is it capitalism? *Management and Organization Review*, 7: 5–18.

12 A. Moody, 2011, Research in motion: Multinationals moving R&D centers to China, *China Daily*, November 11–17: 1, 4–5.

13 V. Prior, 1999, The language of competitive intelligence: Part four, *Competitive Intelligence Review*, 10(1): 84–87.

14 M. A. Hitt, R. D. Ireland, S. M. Camp, & D. L. Sexton, 2001, Strategic entrepreneurship: Entrepreneurial strategies for wealth creation, *Strategic Management Journal*, 22(summer special issue): 479–491.

15 L. Rosenkopf & A. Nerkar, 2001, Beyond local search: Boundary-spanning exploration, and impact in the optical disk industry, *Strategic Management Journal*, 22: 287–306.

16 K. M. Patton & T. M. McKenna, 2005, Scanning for competitive intelligence, *Competitive Intelligence Magazine*, 8(2): 24–26; D. F. Kuratko, R. D. Ireland, & J. S. Hornsby, 2001, Improving firm performance through entrepreneurial actions: Acordia's corporate entrepreneurship strategy, *Academy of Management Executive*, 15(4): 60–71.

17 J. R. Hough & M. A. White, 2004, Scanning actions and environmental dynamism: Gathering information for strategic decision making, *Management Decision*, 42: 781–793; V. K. Garg, B. A. Walters, & R. L. Priem, 2003, Chief executive scanning emphases, environmental dynamism, and manufacturing firm performance, *Strategic Management Journal*, 24: 725–744.

18 R. Donkin, 1999, Too young to retire, *Financial Times*, July 2, 9.

19 C. Wei & Y. Lee, 2004, Event detection from online news documents for supporting environmental scanning, *Decision Support Systems*: 36: 385–401.

20 A. Cantes, 2011, Does your site comply with EU cookie legislation? Source Web Design, www.source design.co.uk, November 15.

21 Fahey, *Competitors*, 71–73.

22 S. Reddy, 2011, Latinos fuel growth in decade, *Wall Street Journal*, March 25, A2.

23 F. Dahlsten, 2003, Avoiding the customer satisfaction rut, *MIT Sloan Management Review*, 44(4): 73–77; Y. Luo & S. H. Park, 2001, Strategic alignment and performance of market-seeking MNCs in China, *Strategic Management Journal*, 22: 141–155.

24 K. Buysse & A. Verbeke, 2003, Proactive strategies: A stakeholder management perspective, *Strategic Management Journal*, 24: 453–470; I. M. Jawahar & G. L. McLaughlin, 2001, Toward a prescriptive stakeholder theory: An organizational life cycle approach, *Academy of Management Review*, 26: 397–414.

25 M. H. Zack, 2003, Rethinking the knowledge-based organization, *MIT Sloan Management Review*, 44(4): 67–71; H. Yli-Renko, E. Autio, & H. J. Sapienza, 2001, Social capital, knowledge acquisition, and knowledge exploitation in young technologically-based firms, *Strategic Management Journal*, 22(summer special issue): 587–613.

26 Fahey, *Competitors*.

27 The Associated Press, 2010, Procter, Colgate and Unilever profit as brands sell again, *New York Times*, www.nytimes.com, April 29.

28 K. M. Sutcliffe & K. Weber, 2003, The high cost of accurate knowledge, *Harvard Business Review*, 81(5): 74–82.

29 R. King, 2010, Consumer demographics: Use demographic resources to target specific audiences, *Journal of Financial Planning*, 23(12): S4–S6; L. Fahey & V. K. Narayanan, 1986, *Macroenvironmental Analysis for Strategic Management*, St. Paul, MN: West Publishing Co., 58.

30 2004, World population prospects: 2004 revision, www.un.org/esa/population/unpop.htm; D. Fishburn, 1999, The world in 1999, *The Economist Publications*, 9; 1999, Six billion … and counting, *Time*, October 4, 16.

31 2011, U.S. and world population, U.S. Census Bureau, http://www.census.gov.compendia/stayab/cats /population, January 23.

32 2011, U.S. Population projections, U.S. Census Bureau, http://www.census.gov/population/, January 23.

33 B. Ritholz, 2006, Wal-Mart's prescription drug plan could impact entire U.S. healthcare system, Seeking Alpha, http://retail.seekingalpha.com/article/17334, December 28.

34 D. Stipp, 1999, Hell no, we won't go! *Fortune*, July 19, 102–108; G. Colvin, 1997, How to beat the boomer rush, *Fortune*, August 18, 59–63.

35 S. Moffett, 2005, Fast-aging Japan keeps its elders on the job longer, *Wall Street Journal*, June 15, A1, A8.

36 U.S. Population projections, U.S. Census Bureau; C. Bryan, 2005, The south owes its growth to 20th-century invention, *Richmond Times-Dispatch*, July 24, E6.

37 R. Dobbs, S. Smit, J. Remes, J. Manyika, C. Roxburgh, & A. Restrepo, 2011, Urban world: Mapping the economic power of cities, Chicago: McKinsey Global Institute, March.

38 S. Reddy, 2011, Latinos fuel growth in decade, *Wall Street Journal*, March 25: A2.

39 2011. Hispanic and Asian population up 43%, UPI, http://www.upi.com, March 24.

40 G. Dessler, 1999, How to earn your employees' commitment, *Academy of Management Executive*, 13(2): 58–67; S. Finkelstein & D. C. Hambrick, 1996, *Strategic Leadership: Top Executives and Their Effect on Organizations*, Minneapolis, MN: West Publishing Co.

41 L. H. Pelled, K. M. Eisenhardt, & K. R. Xin, 1999, Exploring the black box: An analysis of work group diversity, conflict, and performance, *Administrative Science Quarterly*, 44: 1–28.

42 A. Mountford & H. Rapoport, 2011, The brain drain and the world distribution of income, *Journal of Development Economics*, 95: 4–17.

43 Dobbs, Smit, Remes, Manyika, Roxburgh, & Restrepo, Urban world.

44 Fahey & Narayanan, *Macroenvironmental Analysis*, 105.

45 H. Berument, N. B. Ceylan, & H. Olgun, 2007, Inflation uncertainty and interest rates: Is the Fisher relation universal? *Applied Economics*, 39: 53–73.

46 S. W. Bardley, H. Aldrich, D. A. Shepherd, & J. Wiklund, 2011, Resources, environmental change, and survival: Asymmetric paths of young independent and subsidiary organizations, *Strategic Management Journal*, 32: 486–509; P. Navarro, P. Bromiley, & P. Sottile, 2010, Business cycle management and firm performance, *Journal of Strategy and Management*, 3: 50–71.

47 R. McKinnon, 2006, The worth of the dollar, *Wall Street Journal*, June 13, A18.

48 M. A. Hitt, K. T. Haynes, & R. Serpa, 2010, Strategic leadership in the 21st century, *Business Horizons*, 53: 437–444; G. Chon, 2006, Kia's new U.S. plant advances sales push in North America, *Wall Street Journal*, October 23, B2; A. Chozick, 2006, Toyota lifts profit outlook, *Wall Street Journal*, November 8, A3.

49 P. Garnham, 2006, Dollar's rise loses momentum, *Financial Times*, December 22, 34.

50 J. P. Bonardi, A. J. Hillman, & G. D. Keim, 2005, The attractiveness of political markets: Implications for firm strategy, *Academy of Management Review*, 30: 397–413; G. Keim, 2001, Business and public policy: Competing in the political marketplace, in M. A. Hitt, R. E. Freeman, & J. S. Harrison (eds.), *Handbook of Strategic Management*, Oxford UK: Blackwell Publishers, 583–601.

51 A. G. Scherer & G. Palazzo, 2011, The new political role of business in a globalized world: A review of a new perspective on CSR and its implications for the firm, governance and democracy, *Journal of Management Studies*, 48: 899–931.

52 M. Jacoby, 2006, EU hits Microsoft with $358.3 million penalty, *Wall Street Journal*, July 13, A3.

53 M. D. Lord, 2003, Constituency building as the foundation for corporate political strategy, *Academy of Management Executive*, 17(1): 112–124; D. A. Schuler, K. Rehbein, & R. D. Cramer, 2003, Pursuing strategic advantage through political means: A multivariate approach, *Academy of Management Journal*, 45: 659–672; A. J. Hillman & M. A. Hitt, 1999, Corporate political strategy formulation: A model of approach, participation, and strategy decisions, *Academy of Management Review*, 24: 825–842.

54 M. Carson, 1998, *Global Competitiveness Quarterly*, March 9, 1.

55 2012, North American Free Trade Agreement, *Wikipedia*, http://en.wikipedia.org/wiki/North_American _Free_Trade_Agreement, January 24.

56 J. Jakobsen, 2010, Old problems remain, new ones crop up: Political risk in the 21st century, *Business Horizons*, 53: 481–490.

57 D. Stumpf, 2011, Oil-price forecast rises on Libyan unrest, *Wall Street Journal*, March 9, C10.

58 M. Ezrati, 2011, Europe's debt crisis continues, despite Ireland's resolved debt, *On Wall Street*, February, 35–36.

59 S. Li & S. Tallman, 2011, MNC strategies, exogenous shocks and performance outcomes, *Strategic Management Journal*, 32: 1119–1127.

60 A. Pe'er & O. Gottschalg, 2011, Red and blue: The relationship between the institutional context and the performance of leveraged buyout transactions, *Strategic Management Journal*, 32: 1356–1367.

61 L. Shao, C. C. Y. Kwok, & O. Guedhami, 2010, National culture and dividend policy, *Journal of International Business Studies*, 41: 1391–1414.

62 2012, U.S. government spending, http://www .usgovernmentspending.com, January 24.

63 C. Debaise, 2005, U.S. Workers start early on retirement savings, *Wall Street Journal*, January 20, D2.

64 B. Beck, 1999, The world in 1999: Executive, thy name is woman, *Economist*, November 6, 89; P. Thomas, 1995, Success at a huge personal cost: Comparing women around the world, *Wall Street Journal*, July 26, B1.

65 R. W. Fairlie, 2011, *Kauffman Index of Entrepreneurial Activity*, Kauffman the Foundation of Entrepreneurship, March.

66 G. Rubera, A. Ordanini, D. A. Griffith, 2011, Incorporating cultural values for understanding the influence of perceived product creativity on intention to buy: An examination in Italy and the U.S.; C. A. Bartlett & S. Ghoshal, 2002, Building competitive advantage through people, *MIT Sloan Management Review*, 43(2): 33–41.

67 E. Vaara, R. Sarala, G. K. Stahl, & I. Bjorkman, 2012, The impact of organizational and national cultural differences on social conflict and knowledge

transfer in international acquisitions, *Journal of Management Studies*, 49: 1–27.

[68] S. Brown-Philpot, 2012, The four-year career, *Fast Company*, February: 72–77.

[69] T. Fleming, 2003, Benefits of taking the superhighway to work, *Canadian HR Reporter*, 16(11): G7.

[70] M. J. McCarthy, 2004, New outposts: Granbury, Texas, isn't a rural town: it's a "micropolis"; Census bureau adopts term for main street America, and marketers take note; Beans, ribs and Starbucks, *Wall Street Journal*, June 3, A1.

[71] A. L. Porter & S. W. Cunningham, 2004, *Tech Mining Exploiting new Technologies for Competitive Advantage*, Hoboken, NJ: Wiley.

[72] M. A. Hitt, R. D. Ireland, D. G. Sirmon, & C. A. Trahms, 2011, Strategic entrepreneurship: Creating value for individuals, organizations & society, *Academy of Management Perspectives*, 25(2): 57–75; C. W. L. Hill & F. T. Rothaermel, 2003, The performance of incumbent firms in the face or radical technological innovation, *Academy of Management Review*, 28: 257–274; A. Afuah, 2002, Mapping technological capabilities into product markets and competitive advantage: The case of cholesterol drugs, *Strategic Management Journal*, 23: 171–179.

[73] N. Wingfield, 2003, Anytime, anywhere: The number of Wi-Fi spots is set to explode, bringing the wireless technology to the rest of us, *Wall Street Journal*, March 31, R6, R12.

[74] A. Andal-Ancion, P. A. Cartwright, & G. S. Yip, 2003, The digital transformation of traditional businesses, *MIT Sloan Review*, 44(4): 34–41; M. A. Hitt, R. D. Ireland, & H. Lee, 2000, Technological learning, knowledge management, firm growth and performance, *Journal of Technology and Engineering Management*, 17: 231–246.

[75] D. M. Sullivan & M. R. Marvel, 2011, Knowledge acquisition, Network reliance, and early-stage technology venture outcomes, *Journal of Management Studies*, 48: 1169–1193.

[76] Holmes, R. M. Jr., Miller, T., Hitt, M. A., & Salmador, M. P, 2012, The interrelationships among informal institutions, formal institutions, and inward foreign direct investment, *Journal of Management*, in press; W. P. Wan, 2005, Country resource environments, firm capabilities, and corporate diversification strategies, *Journal of Management Studies*, 42: 161–182.

[77] F. Vermeulen & H. Barkema, 2002, Pace, rhythm, and scope: Process dependence in building a multinational corporation, *Strategic Management Journal*, 23: 637–653.

[78] J. Lu & P. Beamish, 2004, International diversification and firm performance: The S-curve hypothesis, *Academy of Management Journal*, 47: 598–609; L. Tihanyi, R. A. Johnson, R. E. Hoskisson, & M. A. Hitt, 2003, Institutional ownership differences, and international diversification: The effects of boards of directors and technological opportunity, *Academy of Management Journal*, 46: 195–211.

[79] S. M. Puffer, D. J. McCarthy, & M. Boisot, 2009, Entrepreneurship in Russia and China: The impact of formal institutional voids, *Entrepreneurship Theory and Practice*, 34: 441–467; F. Balfour, 2006, Dipping a toe in the risk pool, *Business Week*, December 25, 83.

[80] R. D. Ireland, M. A. Hitt, S. M. Camp, & D. L. Sexton, 2001, integrating entrepreneurship and strategic management actions to create firm wealth, *Academy of Management Executive*, 15(1): 49–63.

[81] M. Subramaniam & N. Venkatraman, 2001, Determinants of transitional new product development capability: Testing the influence of transferring and deploying tacit overseas knowledge, *Strategic Management Journal*, 22: 359–378; P. J. Lane, J. E. Salk, & M. A. Lyles, 2001, Absorptive capacity, learning and performance in international joint ventures, *Strategic Management Journal*, 22: 1139–1161.

[82] Vermeulen & Barkema, Pace, rhythm, and scope.

[83] M. Fong, 2005, Unphased by barriers, retailers flock to China for clothes, *Wall Street Journal*, May 27, B1, B2.

[84] J. Fuerbringer & R. W. Stevenson, 2001, No bailout is planned for Argentina, *New York Times*, http://www.nytimes.com, July 14; K. L. Newman, 2000, Organizational transformation during institutional upheaval, *Academy of Management Review*, 25: 602–619.

[85] M. A. O'Grady, 2005, Americas: After the haircut, Argentina readies the shave, *Wall Street Journal*, May 27, A13.

[86] S. H. Park & Y. Luo, 2001, Guanxi and organizational dynamics: Organizational networking in Chinese firms, *Strategic Management Journal*, 22: 455–477; M. A. Hitt, M. T. Dacin, B. B. Tyler, & D. Park, 1997, Understanding the differences in Korean and U.S. executives' strategic orientations, *Strategic Management Journal*, 18: 159–167.

[87] M. A. Hitt, D. Ahlstrom, M. T. Dacin, E. Levitas, & L. Svobodina, 2004, The institutional effects on strategic alliance partner selection: China versus Russia, *Organization Science*, 15: 173–185.

[88] M.-J. Chen & D. Miller, 2011, The relational perspective as a business mindset, *Academy of Management Perspectives*, 25(3): 6–18.

[89] B. Flynn, 2010, Introduction to the special topic forum on global supply chain management, *Journal of Supply Chain Management*, 46(2): 3–4.

[90] J. Harris, 2011, Going green to stay in the black: Transnational capitalism and renewable energy, *Perspectives on Global Development and Renewable Energy*, 10(1): 41–59.

[91] M. Delmas, V. H. Hofmann, & M. Kuss, 2011, Under the tip of the iceberg: Absorptive capacity, environmental strategy and competitive advantage, *Business & Society*, 50(1): 116–154.

[92] I. Bonn & J. Fisher, 2011, Sustainability: The missing ingredient in strategy, *Journal of Business Strategy*, 32(1): 5–14; D. K. Nguyen & S. F. Slater, 2010, Hitting the sustainability sweet spot: Having it all, *Journal of Business Strategy*, 31(3): 5–11.

[93] C. de Vilhers, V. Naiker, & C. J. van Staden, 2011, The effect of board characteristics on firm environmental performance, *Journal of Management*, 37: 1636–1663.

[94] B. Kammel, 2011, How Siemens got its mojo back, *Bloomberg Businessweek*, http//:www.businessweek.com, April 4.

[95] D. Stanford, 2011, Why sustainability is winning over CEOs, *Bloomberg Businessweek*, http://www.businessweek.com, April 4.

[96] V. K. Narayanan & L. Fahey, 2005, The relevance of the institutional underpinnings of Porter's five forces framework to emerging economies: An epistemological analysis, *Journal of Management Studies*, 42: 207–223; N. Argyres & A. M. McGahan, 2002, An interview with Michael Porter, *Academy of Management Executive*, 16(2): 43–52; Y. E. Spanos & S. Lioukas, 2001, An examination into the causal logic of rent generation: Contrasting Porter's

competitive strategy framework and the resource-based perspective, *Strategic Management Journal*, 22: 907–934.

[97] M. A. Hitt, D. G. Sirmon, Y. Li, A. Ghobadian, & J.-L Arregle, 2012, Institutional polycentricity, resource orchestration and firm performance, paper presented at the Academy of Management Conference, Boston.

[98] W. McKinley, 2010, Organizational contexts for environmental construction and objectification activity, *Journal of Management Studies*, 48: 804–828.

[99] P. Sieger, T. Zellweger, R. S. Nason, & E. Clinton, 2011, Portfolio entrepreneurship in family firms: A resource-based perspective, *Strategic Entrepreneurship Journal*, 5: 327–351.

[100] J. C. Short, D. J. Ketchen Jr., T. B. Palmer, & G. T. M. Hult, 2007, Firm, strategic group and industry influences on performance, *Strategic Management Journal*, 28: 147–167.

[101] M. J. Ahn & A. S. York, 2011, Resource-based and institution-based approaches in biotechnology industry development in Malaysia, *Asia Pacific Journal of Management*, 28: 257–275.

[102] S. Zaheer & A. Zaheer, 2001, Market microstructure in a global b2b network, *Strategic Management Journal*, 22: 859–873.

[103] Hitt, Ricart, Costa, & Nixon, The new frontier.

[104] Y. Pan & P. S. K. Chi, 1999, Financial performance and survival of multinational corporations in China, *Strategic Management Journal*, 20: 359–374; G. R. Brooks, 1995, Defining market boundaries, *Strategic Management Journal*, 16: 535–549.

[105] J. Shamsie, 2003, The context of dominance: An industry-driven framework for exploiting reputation, *Strategic Management Journal*, 24: 199–215; K. C. Robinson & P. P. McDougall, 2001, Entry barriers and new venture performance; A comparison of universal and contingency approaches, *Strategic Management Journal*, 22(summer special issue): 659–685.

[106] J. C. Mahlich, 2010, Patents and performance in the Japanese pharmaceutical industry: An institution-based view, *Asia Pacific Journal of Management*, 27: 99–113.

[107] M. S. Giarratana & S. Torrisi, 2010, Foreign entry and survival in a knowledge-intensive market: Emerging economy countries' international linkages, technology competences, and firm experience, *Strategic Entrepreneurship Journal*, 4: 85–104.

[108] B. T. McCann & G. Vroom, 2010, Pricing response to entry and agglomeration effects, *Strategic Management Journal*, 31: 284–305.

[109] R. Makadok, 1999, Interfirm differences in scale economies and the evolution of market shares, *Strategic Management Journal*, 20: 935–952.

[110] B. J. Pine II, 2004, Mass customization: The new imperative, *Strategic Direction*, January, 2–3; R. Wise & P. Baumgartner, 1999, Go downstream: The new profit imperative in manufacturing, *Harvard Business Review*, 77(5): 133–141.

[111] R. Walker, 2012, Meet your maker, *Fast Company*, February: 90–96.

[112] M.-S. Cheung, M. B. Myers, & J. T. Mentzer, 2011, The value of relational learning in global buyer-supplier exchanges: A dyadic perspective and test of the pie-sharing premise, *Strategic Management Journal*, 32: 1061–1082.

[113] G. Walker, T. L. Madsen, & G. Carini, 2002, How does institutional change affect heterogeneity among firms? *Strategic Management Journal*, 23: 89–104.

[114] A. Reinhardt, 2005, The man who said no to Microsoft, *Business Week*, May 31, 49; 2002, The long shadow of big blue, *Economist*, November 9, 63–64.

[115] C. Dawson, 2001, Machete time: In a cost-cutting war with Nissan, Toyota leans on suppliers, *Business Week*, April 9, 42–43.

[116] M. van De Vijver, B. Vos, & H. Akkermans, 2011, A tale of two partnerships: Socialization in the development of buyer-supplier relationships, *Journal of Supply Chain Management*, 47(4): 23–43; R.-J. Jean, R. R. Sinkovics, & S. T. Cavusgil, 2010, Enhancing international customer-supplier relationships through IT resources: A study of Taiwanese electronics suppliers, *Journal of International Business Studies*, 41: 1218–1239.

[117] C. Bode, S. M. Wagner, K. J. Petersen, & L. M. Ellram, 2011, Understanding responses to supply chain disruptions: Insights from information processing and resource dependence perspectives, *Academy of Management Journal*, 54: 833–856.

[118] J. Singh, P. Lentz, & E. J. Nijssen, 2011, First and second-order effects of consumers' logics on firm-consumer relationships: A cross-market comparative analysis, *Journal of International Business Studies*, 42: 306–333.

[119] P. Rosenthal, 2011, New newspaper circulation figures beyond compare, thanks to new metrics, *Chicago Tribune*, http://newsblog.chicagotribune.com, May 3.

[120] D. G. Sirmon, M. A. Hitt, R. D. Ireland, & B. A. Gilbert, 2011, Resource orchestration to create competitive advantage: Breadth, depth, and life cycle effects, *Journal of Management*, 37: 1390–1412; S. Dutta, O. Narasimhan, & S. Rajiv, 2005, Conceptualizing and measuring capabilities: Methodology and empirical application, *Strategic Management Journal*, 26: 277–285.

[121] De Carolis, Competencies and imitability; D. L. Deephouse, 1999, To be different, or to be the same? It's a question (and theory) of strategic balance, *Strategic Management Journal*, 20: 147–166.

[122] S. Kukalis, 2010, Agglomeration economies and firm performance: The case of industry clusters, *Journal of Management*, 36: 453–481.

[123] A. T. Arikan & M. A. Schilling, 2011, Structure and governance in industrial districts: Implications for competitive advantage, *Journal of Management Studies*, 48: 772–803; L. Canina, C. A Enz, & J. S. Harrison, 2005. Agglomeration effects and strategic orientations: Evidence from the U.S. lodging industry, *Academy of Management Journal*, 48: 565–581.

[124] G. J. Kilduff, H. A Elfnbein, & B. M. Staw, 2010, The psychology of rivalry: A relationally dependent analysis of competition, *Academy of Management Journal*, 53: 943–969.

[125] A. Afuah, 2000, How much do your competitors' capabilities matter in the face of technological change? *Strategic Management Journal*, 21: 387–404; A. Brandenburger & B. Nalebuff, 1996, *Co-opetition*, New York: Currency Doubleday.

[126] K. D. Brouthers, L. E. Brouthers, & S. Werner, 2003, Transaction cost enhanced entry mode choices and firm performance, *Strategic Management Journal*, 24: 1239–1248; W. Kuemmerle, 2001, Home base and knowledge management in international ventures, *Journal of Business Venturing*, 17: 99–122.

[127] M. E. Porter, 1980, *Competitive Strategy*, New York: The Free Press.

[128] M. S. Hunt, 1972, Competition in the major home appliance industry, 1960–1970, doctoral dissertation,

Harvard University, Cambridge, MA; Porter, *Competitive Strategy*, 129.

129. F. Mas-Ruiz & F. Ruiz-Moreno, 2011, Rivalry within strategic groups and consequences for performance: The firm-size effects, *Strategic Management Journal*, 32: 1286–1308.

130. H. R. Greve, 1999, Managerial cognition and the mimetic adoption of market positions: What you see is what you do, *Strategic Management Journal*, 19: 967–988.

131. M. W. Peng, J. Tan, & T. W. Tong, 2004, Ownership types and strategic groups in an emerging economy, *Journal of Management Studies*, 41: 1105–1129; R. K. Reger & A. S. Huff, 1993, Strategic groups: A cognitive perspective, *Strategic Management Journal*, 14: 103–123.

132. M. Peteraf & M. Shanely, 1997, Getting to know you: A theory of strategic group identity, *Strategic Management Journal*, 18(special issue): 165–186.

133. Z. Guedri & J. McGuire, 2011, Multimarket competition, Mobility barriers and firm performance, *Journal of Management Studies*, 48: 857–890.

134. J. A. Zuniga-Vicente, J. M. de la Fuente Sabate, & I. S. Gonzalez, 2004, Dynamics of the strategic group membership-performance linkage in rapidly changing environments, *Journal of Business Research*, 57: 1378–1390; J. D. Osborne, C. I. Stubbart, & A. Ramaprasad, 2001, Strategic groups and competitive enactment: A study of dynamic relationships between mental models and performance, *Strategic Management Journal*, 22: 435–454.

135. Greve, Managerial cognition.

136. Porter, *Competitive Strategy*, 49.

137. P. M. Norman, R. D. Ireland, K. W. Artz, & M. A. Hitt, 2000, Acquiring and using competitive intelligence in entrepreneurial teams, paper presented at the Academy of Management, Toronto, Canada.

138. C. S. Fleisher, 1999, Public policy competitive intelligence, *Competitive Intelligence Review*, 10(2): 24.

139. A. Crane, 2005, In the company of spies: When competitive intelligence gathering becomes industrial espionage, *Business Horizons*, 48(3): 233–240.

140. C. Harlan, 2006, Trade secret plot pulls Coke, Pepsi together, *Pittsburgh Post-Gazette*, http://www.post-gazette.com/pg/06188/704045–28.stm, July 7.

141. M. Moss, 1999, Inside the game of e-mail hijacking, *Wall Street Journal*, November 9, B1, B4.

142. J. H. Hallaq & K. Steinhorst, 1994, Business intelligence methods: How ethical? *Journal of Business Ethics*, 13: 787–794.

Chapter 4

THE INTERNAL ORGANIZATION: RESOURCES, CAPABILITIES, AND CORE COMPETENCIES

KNOWLEDGE OBJECTIVES

Studying this chapter should provide you with the strategic management knowledge needed to:

1. Explain the need to study and understand the internal organization.

2. Define value creation and discuss its importance.

3. Describe the differences between tangible and intangible resources.

4. Define capabilities and discuss their development.

5. Describe four criteria used to determine if resources and capabilities are or are not core competencies.

6. Explain how value chain analysis is used to identify and evaluate resources and capabilities.

7. Define outsourcing and discuss reasons for its use.

8. Discuss why firms should prevent their core competencies from becoming core rigidities.

9. Explain several methods to measure firm performance and how firms can use multiple measures to balance stakeholder interests and enhance value creation.

As discussed in Chapter 1, rapidly developing technology and increasing globalization are making it increasingly difficult for firms to develop a sustainable competitive advantage.[1] For instance, an organization may develop a new process that cuts production costs 10 percent, only to discover that a competitor has developed a new technology that is superior to its newly-developed process. Or a medical products firm may create a new machine with some very attractive features only to have the value created by those features rapidly exceeded by a machine that a competitor in a country halfway around the world suddenly introduces. These are not unusual circumstances; in fact, they reflect the reality strategic decision makers face today.[2] As a result, competitive advantage tends to be more closely associated with intangible resources that are hard to imitate. Intel has historically competed on this basis, using its unique intangible resources and capabilities (including brand name and its R&D processes) as the foundation for trying to rapidly introduce new, innovative chips before competitors are able to duplicate the value created by the firm's current chips.

Firm resources provide a foundation for developing and implementing strategies. Possessing a unique bundle of resources puts a firm in a strong position to develop competitive advantage, leading to the creation of wealth for shareholders and other stakeholders.[3] The strategic management process helps a firm successfully identify and use sources of competitive advantage over time.[4]

This chapter shows how firms create value and earn high returns by using their resources and capabilities to form and then effectively leverage their unique core competencies to take advantage of opportunities in the external environment. Being able to do this consistently across time is critical in that the benefits of any firm's value-creating strategy can eventually be imitated by its competitors. In other words, all competitive advantages have a limited life.[5] In general, the sustainability of a competitive advantage is a function of three factors: (1) the rate of core competence obsolescence caused by environmental changes, (2) the availability of substitutes for the core competence, and (3) the imitability of the core competence.[6] Because of the reality of eventual imitation of competitive advantages, the challenge facing decision makers in all firms is to effectively manage current core competencies while simultaneously making the decisions that will lead to developing new ones at some point in the future.

In Chapter 3, we looked outside the firm to examine its general, industry, and competitor environments. In this chapter, we look inside the firm. By analyzing its internal organization, a firm determines what it *can do*—that is, the actions permitted by its unique resources, capabilities, and core competencies (see Figure 4.1). By matching what it *can do* with what it *might do* (a function of opportunities and threats in the external environment), a firm gains the insights required to select and implement its strategies.

We examine several topics in this chapter, beginning with the importance and challenge of studying the firm's internal organization. We then discuss the roles of resources, capabilities, and core competencies in developing sustainable competitive advantage. Included in this discussion are the techniques firms can use to identify and evaluate resources and capabilities and the criteria for selecting core competencies from among them. Resources, capabilities, and core competencies are not inherently valuable, but they create value when the firm uses them to perform certain activities that result in a competitive advantage. Accordingly, we also discuss the value chain concept and examine four criteria for evaluating core competences that establish competitive advantage.[7] The final section of this chapter examines the dimensions of firm performance from the perspective of all stakeholders. Measuring firm performance is an essential part of internal analysis.

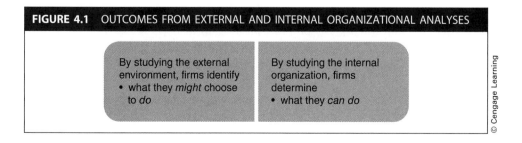

FIGURE 4.1 OUTCOMES FROM EXTERNAL AND INTERNAL ORGANIZATIONAL ANALYSES

By studying the external environment, firms identify
• what they *might* choose to *do*

By studying the internal organization, firms determine
• what they *can do*

© Cengage Learning

INTERNAL ANALYSIS AND VALUE CREATION

The decisions managers make regarding the firm's resources, capabilities, and core competencies significantly influence its performance.[8] Making these decisions—identifying, developing, deploying, and nurturing resources, capabilities, and core competencies—may appear to be relatively easy. In fact, however, this decision-making task is as challenging and difficult as any other with which managers are involved; moreover, it is increasingly internationalized and linked with the firm's success.[9] Market analysts expect that the pressure facing managers to pursue only strategies that help the firm meet the quarterly earning numbers can reduce their abilities to make objective, accurate assessments of the long-term potential of firm resources.[10] Recognizing a firm's core competencies is essential before the firm can make important strategic decisions, including those to enter or exit markets, invest in new technologies, build new or additional manufacturing capacity, or form strategic partnerships.[11]

The challenge and difficulty of making effective decisions are implied by preliminary evidence suggesting that one-half of organizational decisions fail.[12] Sometimes, mistakes are made as the firm analyzes its internal organization. For example, those making strategic decisions might choose to emphasize resources and capabilities that do not lead to forming a competitive advantage. When a mistake such as this occurs, decision makers must have the confidence to admit it and take corrective actions.[13] In fact, a firm can grow through well-intended errors in that the learning generated by making and correcting mistakes can be important to efforts to create new competitive advantages.[14] Moreover, firms can learn from the failure resulting from a mistake; that is, they can learn what *not* to do when seeking competitive advantage.[15]

Conditions Influencing Internal Analysis

In the global economy, traditional factors—such as labor costs, access to financial resources and raw materials, and protected or regulated markets—continue to be sources of competitive advantage for firms in some countries, but to a lesser degree than was previously the case. An important reason for this decline is that the advantages created by these sources can be duplicated through an international strategy (see Chapter 10). For instance, during the 1980s and early 1990s, Japanese auto manufacturers overcame the relative advantages that U.S. auto manufacturers used to enjoy, such as reduced transportation and importing costs, by building automobile assembly operations in the United States. The relatively free flow of resources throughout the global economy facilitates this trend. Consequently, those analyzing the firm's internal organization should adopt a **global mind-set,** which is the ability to study conditions inside a firm in ways that do not depend on the assumptions of a single country, culture, or context.[16]

Significant changes in the value-creating potential of a firm's resources and capabilities can occur in a rapidly changing global economy—an economy that is often characterized by a great deal of economic volatility. Because rapid changes affect a company's power and social structure, some may deny that change is necessary. *Denial* is an unconscious coping mechanism used to block out and prevent the taking of painful changes.[17] When encountering change-related denial, decision makers must remain committed to initiating changes that are needed to enhance the firm's ability to create value. A decision to involve people who deny the need for change in activities to bring about necessary change often reduces their resistance to change.

Effective strategic decisions are rarely reached on a consistent basis in firms that fail to change rapidly when conditions suggest the need to do so. Fostering an organizational setting in which experimentation and learning are expected and promoted is a key challenge to developing the ability to change rapidly.[18] The demands of 21st-century competition require top-level managers to rethink earlier concepts of the firm and competition. The inability to successfully do this may partially account for Kodak's filing for bankruptcy in 2012. Kodak started manufacturing cameras as its core product more than a century ago saying, "You press the button, we do the rest."[19] However, Kodak failed to maintain pace with the significant changes in consumer electronics such as the rapid movement to digital technologies and the cameras and related products associated with them. At the time of filing for bankruptcy, the firm's CEO had decided to base "... the firm's future on consumer and commercial inkjet printing." Analysts questioned this product focus as the source of Kodak's future success in that at the time, the firm was ranked only fifth worldwide in what was a highly competitive market.[20]

Managers with courage, self-confidence, integrity, the capacity to deal with uncertainty and complexity, and a willingness to hold people accountable for their work and to be held accountable themselves are better prepared to work with others to form the firm's core competencies as the foundation for developing value-creating strategies. The reason these managerial attributes and skills are helpful is that three challenging conditions—uncertainty, complexity, and intraorganizational conflicts—characterize decisions that managers make about the firm's resources, capabilities, and core competencies (see Figure 4.2).[21]

Managers face *uncertainty* from a number of sources, including those of new proprietary technologies, economic and political volatility, transformations in societal values, and shifts in customer demands.[22] *Complexity* results from the dependence firms have on one another and the large number of factors that influence firm performance. Furthermore, environmental uncertainty increases the complexity and range of issues the firm needs to examine when studying its internal

FIGURE 4.2 CONDITIONS AFFECTING MANAGERIAL DECISIONS ABOUT RESOURCES, CAPABILITIES, AND CORE COMPETENCIES

Conditions		
	Uncertainty	Uncertainty exists about the characteristics of the firm's general and industry environments and customers' needs.
	Complexity	Complexity results from the interrelationships among conditions shaping a firm.
	Intraorganizational Conflicts	Intraorganizational conflicts may exist among managers making decisions as well as among those affected by the decisions.

© Cengage Learning

organization. Managers must understand too that their biases about how to cope with uncertainty may affect their decisions about the resources and capabilities that will become the foundation of the firm's core competencies. Finally, *intraorganizational conflicts* often surface when decisions are made about which core competencies to nurture as well as how to nurture them.

The perspective that a firm is a bundle of heterogeneous resources, capabilities, and core competencies that can be used to create a unique market position is a critical characteristic of effective resource analysis.[23] This perspective suggests that a firm possesses at least some resources and capabilities that other companies do not—at least not in the same combination. Resources are the source of capabilities, some of which lead to the development of a firm's core competencies.[24] Figure 4.3 illustrates the relationships among resources, capabilities, and core competencies and shows how firms use the four criteria of sustainable competitive advantage and value chain analysis to identify sources of value and ultimately competitive advantage and strategic competitiveness.

The mind-set managers need to successfully deal with the uncertainty, complexity, and intraorganizational conflicts that often accompany their decisions is one through which they try to use their firm's resources and capabilities so the firm can simultaneously achieve operational effectiveness and uniqueness. Essentially, operational effectiveness means that the firm is able to do what competitors do, but better. Michael Porter argues that quests for productivity, quality, and speed depend on using a number of management techniques—total quality management (TQM), benchmarking, time-based competition, and reengineering. These quests help firms become operationally effective; and, being operationally effective is important in that the condition signals that the firm is using its resources and capabilities efficiently relative to competitors. However, operational effectiveness is not equivalent to establishing a unique strategic position. The firm with a unique strategic position creates value by doing things differently or by doing different things than competitors.[25] Over the long term, firms are able to consistently create value for stakeholders only by establishing a unique strategic position and implementing a strategy that takes advantage of that position. Evidence suggests that establishing a unique strategic position is as important to the success of social ventures—for example, strategic positions that seek to help countries or regions reach sustainability goals—as it is to the success of for-profit organizations.[26]

Creating Value

Firms create value for customers by exploiting core competencies and meeting the demanding standards of global competition.[27] This is important in that creating value for customers is the source of being able to subsequently create value for all other stakeholders. **Value** is measured by a product's performance characteristics and attributes for which customers are willing to pay.[28] Firms develop competitive advantages by providing more value to customers than competitors are able to provide.

Ultimately, creating customer value is the source of a firm's potential to earn above-average returns. The type of value a firm intends to create for customers affects its choice of business-level strategy and the organizational structure to use

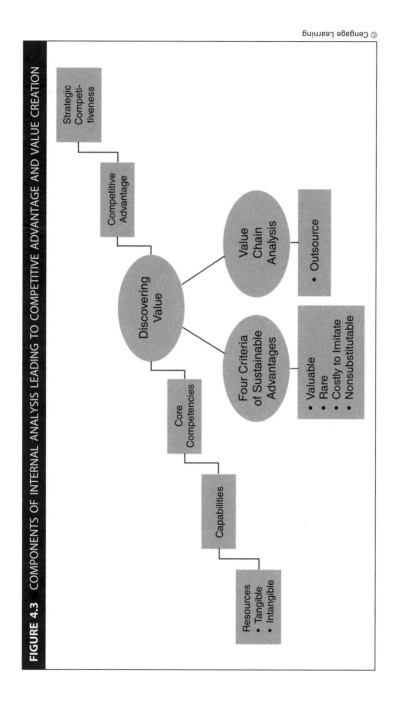

FIGURE 4.3 COMPONENTS OF INTERNAL ANALYSIS LEADING TO COMPETITIVE ADVANTAGE AND VALUE CREATION

© Cengage Learning

to implement that strategy.[29] As we explain in Chapter 5, value is created by a product's low cost, by its highly differentiated features, or by a combination of low cost and high differentiation compared with competitors' offerings. A business-level strategy is effective only when its use is grounded in exploiting the firm's current core competencies while actions are being taken to develop the core competencies that will be needed to effectively use "tomorrow's" business-level strategy. Thus, successful firms continuously examine the effectiveness of current and future core competencies.[30]

At one time, the strategic management process was concerned largely with understanding the characteristics of the industry in which a firm competed and, in light of those characteristics, determining the firm's position relative to competitors. Emphasizing an industry's characteristics as the primary determinant of a business-level strategy likely understated the role of the firm's resources and capabilities in developing competitive advantage. Today, core competencies, in combination with product-market positions, are recognized as the firm's most important sources of competitive advantage.[31] The core competencies of a firm, in addition to the results generated by studying its general, industry, and competitor environments, should drive the selection of strategies. Clayton Christensen speaks to this matter: "Successful strategists need to cultivate a deep understanding of the processes of competition and progress and of the factors that undergird each advantage. Only thus will they be able to see when old advantages are poised to disappear and how new advantages can be built in their stead."[32] By emphasizing core competencies when formulating strategies, companies learn to compete primarily on the basis of firm-specific resources that differ from their competitors' resources.

RESOURCES, CAPABILITIES, AND CORE COMPETENCIES

Resources, capabilities, and core competencies are the characteristics that provide the foundation for competitive advantage. Resources are the source of a firm's capabilities. Capabilities in turn are the source of a firm's core competencies, which are the basis of competitive advantages. As shown in Figure 4.3, resources and capabilities are combined to create core competencies. We now define and provide examples of these building blocks of competitive advantage.

Resources

Broad in scope, resources cover a spectrum of individual, social, and organizational phenomena.[33] Typically, any one resource, on its own, does not yield a competitive advantage; a competitive advantage normally is created through the unique bundling of several resources.[34] For example, the way Nike has uniquely combined its unique resources and capabilities has resulted in three core competencies: the power of the Nike brand, the company's relationships with athletes who are typically recognized throughout the world, and its signature performance-focused product design.[35]

Some of a firm's resources are tangible while others are intangible. **Tangible resources** are assets that can be observed and quantified, such as production equipment, manufacturing plants, and formal reporting structures. **Intangible resources** include assets that typically are rooted deeply in the firm's history and have accumulated over time. Because they are embedded in unique patterns of routines, intangible resources are relatively difficult for competitors to analyze and imitate. Knowledge, trust between managers and employees, ideas, the capacity for innovation, managerial capabilities, organizational routines (complex patterns of social interactions that allow firms to accomplish much of what they do), scientific capabilities, and the firm's reputation for its goods or services and how it interacts with people (such as employees, customers, and suppliers) are all examples of intangible resources.[36]

Tangible Resources. The four types of tangible resources are financial, organizational, physical, and technological (see Table 4.1). As tangible resources, a firm's financial assets and the status of its plant and equipment are visible. The value of many tangible resources can be recorded in financial statements; but, these statements do not account for the value of all of a firm's assets because they disregard some intangible resources.[37] As such, the exact nature of a firm's competitive advantages is rarely captured by financial statements. The value of tangible resources is also constrained because they are difficult to leverage—a firm generally cannot derive additional business or value from a tangible resource. For example, an airplane is a tangible resource or asset, but "You can't use the same airplane on five different routes at the same time. You can't put the same crew on five different routes at the same time. And the same goes for the financial investment you've made in the airplane."[38]

Although manufacturing assets are tangible, many of the processes for using these assets are intangible. Thus, the learning and potential proprietary processes associated with a tangible resource, such as manufacturing equipment, can have unique intangible attributes such as quality, just-in-time management practices, and unique manufacturing processes that develop over time and create competitive advantage.[39]

Intangible Resources. Human, innovation, and reputational are the three major types of intangible resources (see Table 4.2). As suggested in the preceding section, compared with tangible resources, intangible resources are a superior and more potent source

TABLE 4.1 TANGIBLE RESOURCES		
Financial Resources	▶	The firm's borrowing capacity
	▶	The firm's ability to generate internal funds
Organizational Resources	▶	The firm's formal reporting structure and its formal planning, controlling, and coordinating systems
Physical Resources	▶	Sophistication and location of a firm's plant and equipment
	▶	Access to raw materials
Technological Resources	▶	Stock of technology, such as patents, trademarks, copyrights, and trade secrets

SOURCES: Adapted from J. B. Barney, 1991, Firm resources and sustained competitive advantage, *Journal of Management*, 17: 101; R. M. Grant, 1991, *Contemporary Strategy Analysis*, Cambridge, U.K.: Blackwell Business, 100–102.

TABLE 4.2 INTANGIBLE RESOURCES

Human Resources	
	▶ Knowledge
	▶ Trust
	▶ Managerial capabilities
	▶ Organizational routines
Innovation Resources	
	▶ Ideas
	▶ Scientific capabilities
	▶ Capacity to innovate
Reputational Resources	
	▶ Reputation with customers
	▶ Brand name
	▶ Perceptions of product quality, durability, and reliability
	▶ Reputation with suppliers
	▶ For efficient, effective, supportive, and mutually beneficial interactions and relationships

SOURCES: Adapted from R. Hall, 1992, The strategic analysis of intangible resources, *Strategic Management Journal*, 13: 136–139; R. M. Grant, 1991, *Contemporary Strategy Analysis*, Cambridge, U.K.: Blackwell Business, 101–104.

of core competencies.[40] In fact, in the global economy, a firm's success rests more in its intellectual and systems capabilities than in its physical assets. Because of this, many firms are increasing their effort to nurture and develop their employees, especially those who are talented and fully engaged with their work and the firm.[41]

Because intangible resources are less visible and more difficult for competitors to understand, purchase, imitate, or substitute for, firms prefer to rely on them rather than on tangible resources as the foundation for their capabilities and core competencies. In fact, the more unobservable (that is, intangible) a resource is, the more sustainable will be the competitive advantage that is based on it. Another benefit of intangible resources is that, unlike most tangible ones, their use can be leveraged. With intangible resources, the larger the network of users, the greater is the benefit to each party.[42] For instance, sharing knowledge among employees does not diminish its value for any one person. On the contrary, two people sharing their individualized knowledge sets often can be leveraged to create additional knowledge that, although new to each of them, contributes to performance improvements for the firm.[43]

An intangible resource, *reputation* is an important source of competitive advantage for a number of companies including Google, Coca-Cola, and Southwest Airlines. Earned primarily through the firm's actions, products, and communications with its stakeholders, a value-creating reputation is a product of years of superior marketplace competence as perceived by stakeholders.[44] A reputation indicates the level of awareness a firm has been able to develop among stakeholders and the degree to which they hold the firm in high esteem.[45] A well-known and highly valued brand name is an application of reputation as a source of competitive advantage.

According to some, the most valuable global brands in 2011 were Apple, Google, IBM, McDonald's, and Microsoft. Brand names are a source of value creation as suggested by an analyst who said that "... brand valuations are a powerful measure of an organization's ability to create real and lasting value for shareholders."[46] The suggestion that the iPad name alone may be worth around $2 billion[47] suggests that the brand names Apple owns may indeed allow the firm to create value for stakeholders and perhaps particularly shareholders.

A firm's reputation is reciprocally interrelated with its *social capital*. A firm's social capital is its relationships with other organizations (e.g., suppliers, government units) that contribute to the creation of value.[48] Effective relationships allow firms to gain access to resources of partners that complement or supplement their resource base. Access to such resources helps them create additional amounts of value.

Decision makers must understand fully the strategic value of their firm's tangible and intangible resources. The *strategic value of resources* is indicated by the degree to which they can contribute to the development of capabilities, core competencies, and, ultimately, competitive advantage. For example, as a tangible resource, a distribution facility is assigned a monetary value on the firm's balance sheet. The real value of the facility, however, is grounded in a variety of factors, such as its proximity to raw materials and customers, but also in intangible factors such as the manner in which workers integrate their actions internally and with other stakeholders, including suppliers and customers.[49]

Capabilities

As a source of capabilities, tangible and intangible resources are a critical part of the pathway to developing a competitive advantage (as shown in Figure 4.3). **Capabilities** are the firm's capacity to deploy resources that have been purposely integrated to achieve a desired end state.[50] The glue binding an organization together, capabilities emerge over time through complex interactions between tangible and intangible resources. Critical to the forming of competitive advantages, capabilities are often based on developing, carrying, and exchanging information and knowledge through the firm's human capital.[51] Because a knowledge base is grounded in organizational actions that may not be explicitly understood by all employees, repetition and practice increase the value of a firm's capabilities.

Employees' skills and knowledge and often their functional expertise are the foundation for many of a firm's capabilities.[52] Because of this, the value of human capital in developing and using capabilities and, ultimately, core competencies cannot be overstated. Firms committed to continuously developing their people's capabilities are likely to sustain a competitive advantage longer than firms without such a commitment. Educational benefits and employee training can have immediate positive effects on the skill levels of employees and managers, as well as new ideas leading to technological innovation. Also, applicants are drawn to firms that have a reputation for excellent employee treatment, which can increase the quality of human resources in the firm.[53]

Fortune publishes a list annually of the best U.S. companies to work for. In 2011, SAS, Boston Consulting Group, Wegmans Food Markets, Google, and NetApp were the top five firms on the list. SAS has been on this list for 14 years and topped it for the second consecutive year in 2011. Describing this firm, a manager said that "People stay at SAS in large part because they are happy; but to dig a little deeper, I would argue that people don't leave SAS because they feel regarded—seen, attended to and cared for."[54] Thus, it seems that as a valued capability, SAS's human capital is a source of competitive advantage for the firm.

Increasingly, business leaders such as those at SAS support the view that the knowledge possessed by human capital is among the most significant of an organization's capabilities and may ultimately be at the root of all competitive advantages.[55] But firms must also be able to utilize the knowledge that they have and transfer it among their operating businesses.[56] For example, it has been suggested that "in the information age, things are ancillary, knowledge is central. A company's value derives not from things, but from knowledge, know-how, intellectual assets, competencies—all of it embedded in people."[57] Given this reality, the firm's challenge is to create an environment that allows people to fit their individual pieces of knowledge together so that collectively, employees possess as much organizational knowledge as possible.

To help develop an environment in which knowledge is widely shared, some organizations have created a new upper-level managerial position often referred to as chief learning officer (CLO). Establishing a CLO highlights a firm's belief that "future success will depend on competencies that traditionally have not been actively managed or measured—including creativity and the speed with which new ideas are learned and shared."[58] In general, the firm should manage knowledge in ways that will support its efforts to create value.

As illustrated in Table 4.3, capabilities are often developed in specific functional areas (such as manufacturing, R&D, and marketing) or in a part of a functional area (for example, advertising). Research suggests that a relationship exists between capabilities developed in functional areas and the firm's financial performance at both the corporate and business-unit levels,[59] suggesting the need to develop capabilities at all levels.

Core Competencies

Defined in Chapter 1, *core competencies* are resources and capabilities that serve as a source of a firm's competitive advantage. They distinguish a company competitively and reflect its personality. They emerge over time through an organizational process of accumulating and learning how to deploy different resources and capabilities.[60] As the capacity to take action, core competencies are "crown jewels of a company," the activities the company performs especially well compared with competitors, and through which the firm adds unique value to its products over a long period.[61]

Not all of a firm's resources and capabilities are *strategic assets*—that is, assets that have competitive value and the potential to serve as a source of competitive advantage.[62] Some resources and capabilities may result in competitive disadvantages, because they represent areas in which the firm is weak compared with competitors. Thus, some resources or capabilities cannot be developed into a core competence. Firms with substantial tangible resources such as financial capital

TABLE 4.3 EXAMPLES OF FIRMS' CAPABILITIES

FUNCTIONAL AREAS	CAPABILITIES	EXAMPLES OF FIRMS
Distribution	Effective use of logistics management techniques	Walmart
Human resources	Motivating, empowering, and retaining employees	AEROJET Starbucks
Management information systems	Effective and efficient control of inventories through point-of-purchase data collection methods	Walmart
Marketing	Effective promotion of brand-name products	Gillette Ralph Lauren Clothing McKinsey & Co.
	Effective customer service	Nordstrom Norwest Solectron Corporation Norrell Corporation
	Innovative merchandising	Crate & Barrel
Management	Ability to envision the future of clothing	Chanel
	Effective organizational structure	PepsiCo
Manufacturing	Design and production skills yielding reliable products	Komatsu
	Product and design quality	Toyota
	Production of technologically sophisticated automobile engines	Mazda
	Miniaturization of components and products	Sony
Research & development	Exceptional technological capability	Corning
	Development of sophisticated elevator control solutions	Motion Control Engineering Inc.
	Rapid transformation of technology into new products and processes	Chaparral Steel
	Digital technology	Thomson Consumer Electronics

(e.g., Google, Apple, and Walmart) may be able to purchase facilities or hire the skilled workers required to manufacture products that produce value for customers. However, firms without the financial capital needed to buy or build new capabilities have a weakness. To be successful, firms must locate external environmental opportunities that can be exploited through their core competencies, while avoiding competition in areas of weakness.[63]

An important question is "How many core competencies are required for the firm to have a sustainable competitive advantage?" McKinsey & Co. recommends that its clients identify three or four competencies around which their strategic actions can be framed.[64] Walmart's core competencies are commonly thought to be its (1) logistics systems, (2) information technology systems, (3) superior technology-based relationships with suppliers, and (4) low-cost culture. Supporting and nurturing more than four core competencies even for a firm as large and commercially successful as Walmart could prevent it from developing the focus needed to fully exploit its competencies in the marketplace.

Not all capabilities are core competencies. For instance, safety is a necessary capability in many industries including the airline industry. However, because most of the airlines in the world are arguably safe, this capability cannot be a source of competitive advantage. Similarly, it would be hard to use food safety as a distinguishing feature in the restaurant industry or room cleanliness in the luxury hotel industry. These are necessary but not sufficient capabilities for developing core competencies. Next, we explain how firms can understand which of their competencies constitute or will likely lead to competitive advantage.

BUILDING CORE COMPETENCIES

Firms can use two tools to identify and then build their core competencies. The first tool is the application of the four criteria of sustainable advantage to determine whether resources are or have the potential to be core competencies: whether they are valuable, rare, costly to imitate, and nonsubstitutable.[65] Because the capabilities shown in Table 4.3 have satisfied these four criteria, they are core competencies. Value chain analysis is the second tool. Firms use this tool to select the value-creating competencies that should be maintained, upgraded, or developed and those that should be outsourced.

Four Criteria of Sustainable Competitive Advantage

The four criteria of sustainable competitive advantage are presented in Table 4.4. Only capabilities that satisfy these four criteria are core competencies. Thus, as shown in Figure 4.4, every core competence is a capability, but not every capability is a core competence. For a capability to be a core competence, it must be "valuable and nonsubstitutable, from a customer's point of view, and unique and inimitable, from a competitor's point of view."[66]

A sustained competitive advantage is achieved only when competitors have failed in efforts to duplicate the benefits of a firm's strategy. For some period of time, the firm may earn a competitive advantage by using capabilities that are for example, valuable and rare but can be imitated.[67] In this instance, the length of

TABLE 4.4 FOUR CRITERIA FOR DETERMINING CORE COMPETENCIES		
Valuable Capabilities	▶	Help a firm neutralize threats or exploit opportunities
Rare Capabilities	▶	Are not possessed by many others
Costly-to-Imitate Capabilities	▶	Historical: A unique and a valuable organizational culture or brand name
	▶	Ambiguous cause: The causes and uses of a competence are unclear
	▶	Social complexity: Interpersonal relationships, trust, and friendship among managers, suppliers, and customers
Nonsubstitutable Capabilities	▶	No strategic equivalent

© Cengage Learning

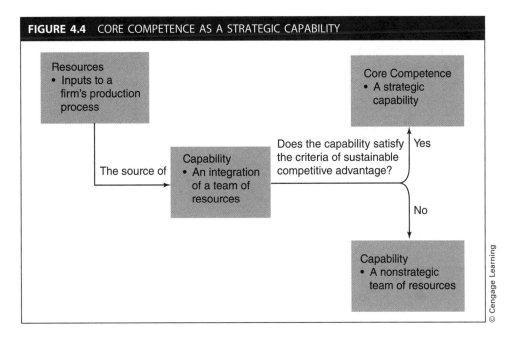

FIGURE 4.4 CORE COMPETENCE AS A STRATEGIC CAPABILITY

Resources
• Inputs to a firm's production process

The source of → Capability
• An integration of a team of resources

Does the capability satisfy the criteria of sustainable competitive advantage? — Yes

Core Competence
• A strategic capability

No

Capability
• A nonstrategic team of resources

© Cengage Learning

time a firm can expect to maintain its competitive advantage is a function of how quickly competitors can imitate it. Sustainable competitive advantage results only when all four criteria are satisfied.

Valuable. **Valuable capabilities** allow the firm to exploit opportunities or neutralize threats in its external environment. By effectively using capabilities to exploit opportunities, a firm creates value for its customers. For example, luxury-goods makers such as LVMH Moet Hennessy Louis Vuitton SA and Gucci owner PPR SA reported a 22 percent increase in 2011 sales compared to 2010, in spite of a difficult global economic environment. An analyst commented about the results saying that "the luxury-goods industry seems immune to the caution that has characterized many American and European shoppers…"[68] LVMH uses its valuable capabilities such as product design and brand name to produce a wide range of luxury-oriented products with the ability to take advantage of the opportunities the strong global demand for such products suggests.

Rare. **Rare capabilities** are possessed by few, if any, current or potential competitors. When evaluating this criterion, the most important question managers answer is, "Do rival firms possess these valuable capabilities, and if so, how many possess them?" Capabilities possessed by many rivals are unlikely to be a source of competitive advantage for any firm. Instead, valuable but common (i.e., not rare) resources and capabilities are sources of competitive parity.[69] Competitive advantage results only when firms develop and exploit capabilities that differ from those shared with competitors.

Costly to Imitate. **Costly-to-imitate capabilities** cannot easily be developed by other firms. Capabilities that are costly to imitate are created because of one or a combination of three reasons (see Table 4.4). First, a firm sometimes is able to develop capabilities because of *unique historical conditions.* "As firms evolve, they pick up skills, abilities and resources that are unique to them, reflecting their particular path through history."[70] That is, firms sometimes are able to develop capabilities because they were in the right place at the right time.[71]

A firm with a unique and valuable organizational culture that emerged in the early stages of the company's history "may have an imperfectly imitable advantage over firms founded in another historical period"[72]—one in which less valuable or less competitively useful values and beliefs strongly influenced the development of the firm's culture. This may be the case for McKinsey & Co. "It is that culture, unique to McKinsey and eccentric, which sets the firm apart from virtually any other business organization and which often mystifies even those who engage [its] services."[73] An organizational culture can be a source of advantage when employees are held together tightly by their belief in it.[74]

United Parcel Service (UPS) is a firm for which organizational culture is thought to be a source of competitive advantage. The firm's culture provides solid, consistent roots for everything the company does, including activities such as skills training and a strong commitment to technological innovation. In turn, influencing the firm's culture is the sense of mission founder Jim Casey established years ago that still fosters shared meaning for UPS employees.[75]

A second condition of being costly to imitate occurs when the link between the firm's capabilities and its competitive advantage is *causally ambiguous.*[76] In these instances, competitors can't clearly understand how a firm uses its capabilities as the foundation for competitive advantage. As a result, firms are uncertain what capabilities they should develop or how the capabilities they identify for a competitor create a competitive advantage. Thus, they cannot duplicate the benefits of a competitor's value-creating strategy. For years, firms have tried to duplicate the success of companies such as Southwest Airlines and Lincoln Electric (the world leader in arc welders). In both cases, most companies have failed because they do not understand how these firms' culture, technology, and human capital work together as a basis for competitive advantage.

Social complexity is the third reason capabilities can be costly to imitate. Social complexity exists when at least some and frequently many of the firm's capabilities are the product of complex social phenomena. Trust, interpersonal relationships, and friendships among managers and between managers and employees and a firm's reputation with suppliers and customers are examples of socially complex capabilities.

Nonsubstitutable. Nonsubstitutable capabilities lack strategic equivalents. This final criterion for a capability to be a source of competitive advantage "is that there must be no strategically equivalent valuable resources that are themselves either not rare or imitable. Two valuable firm resources (or two bundles of firm resources) are strategically equivalent when they each can be separately exploited to implement the same strategies."[77] In general, the strategic value of capabilities increases as they become more difficult to substitute.[78] The more invisible capabilities are, the more difficult it is for firms to find substitutes and the greater the challenge to competitors trying to imitate a firm's value-creating strategy. Firm-specific

TABLE 4.5 OUTCOMES FROM COMBINATIONS OF THE CRITERIA FOR SUSTAINABLE COMPETITIVE ADVANTAGE

IS THE RESOURCE OR CAPABILITY VALUABLE?	IS THE RESOURCE OR CAPABILITY RARE?	IS THE RESOURCE OR CAPABILITY COSTLY TO IMITATE?	IS THE RESOURCE OR CAPABILITY NONSUB-STITUTABLE?	COMPETITIVE CONSEQUENCES	PERFORMANCE IMPLICATIONS
No	No	No	No	Competitive disadvantage	Below-average returns
Yes	No	No	Yes/No	Competitive parity	Average returns
Yes	Yes	No	Yes/No	Temporary competitive advantage	Above-average returns to average returns
Yes	Yes	Yes	Yes	Sustainable competitive advantage	Above-average returns

© Cengage Learning

knowledge and trust-based working relationships between managers and nonmanagerial personnel are examples of capabilities that are difficult to identify and for which finding a substitute is challenging. However, causal ambiguity may make it difficult for the firm to learn and thus may stifle progress because the firm may not know how to improve processes that are not easily codified and thus ambiguous.[79]

In summary, sustainable competitive advantage is created only by using valuable, rare, costly-to-imitate, and nonsubstitutable capabilities. Table 4.5 shows the competitive consequences and performance implications resulting from combinations of the four criteria of sustainability. The analysis suggested by the table helps managers determine the strategic value of a firm's capabilities. The firm obviously would not want to emphasize resources and capabilities included in the first row in the table (that is, resources and capabilities that are neither valuable nor rare and that are imitable and for which strategic substitutes exist) for the purpose of choosing and then implementing a strategy. Capabilities yielding competitive parity and either temporary or sustainable competitive advantage, however, can and likely should be supported. Large competitors such as Coca-Cola and PepsiCo may have capabilities that can yield only competitive parity. In such cases, the firms will nurture these capabilities while simultaneously trying to develop capabilities that can yield either a temporary or sustainable competitive advantage.

Value Chain Analysis

Value chain analysis allows the firm to understand the parts of its operations that create value and those that do not. Understanding these issues is important because the firm earns high returns only when the value it creates is greater than the costs incurred to create that value.[80]

The value chain is a template that firms use to understand their cost position and to identify the multiple means they might use to facilitate implementation of a chosen

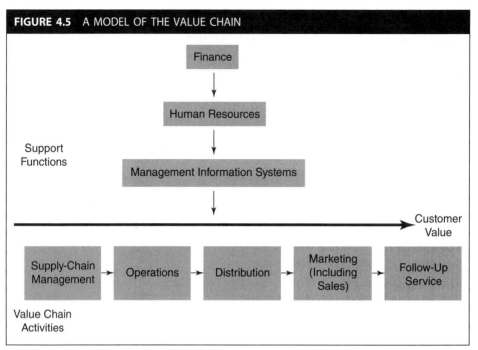

Finance

Human Resources

Management Information Systems

Support Functions

Customer Value

| Supply-Chain Management | Operations | Distribution | Marketing (Including Sales) | Follow-Up Service |

Value Chain Activities

SOURCE: © Copyrighted 2011 by Michael A. Hitt, R. Duane Ireland, and Robert E. Hoskisson.

business-level strategy.[81] As shown in Figure 4.5, a firm's value chain is segmented into value chain activities and support functions. **Value chain activities** are activities or tasks the firm completes in order to produce products and then sell, distribute, and service those products in ways that create value for customers. **Support functions** include the activities or tasks the firm completes in order to support the work being done to produce, sell, distribute, and service the products the firm is producing.

The value chain shows how a product moves from the supply-chain management stage (this stage includes the purchase and inventorying of raw materials) to the stage in which the firm provides follow-up service/support to its customer. For individual firms, the essential idea of the value chain "is to add as much value as possible as cheaply as possible and, most important, to capture that value."[82] In a globally competitive economy, the most valuable links on the chain tend to belong to people who have knowledge about customers.[83] This locus of value-creating possibilities applies similarly to retail and service firms and to manufacturers alike. Moreover, for organizations in all sectors, it has become increasingly necessary for companies to develop value-adding knowledge processes to compensate for the value and margin that the Internet (e-commerce) strips from physical processes.[84]

Figures 4.6 and 4.7 list the items to consider when assessing the value-creating potential of value chain activities and support functions, respectively. The intent in examining these activities and functions is to determine areas where the firm has the potential to create and capture value. All activities in both tables should be evaluated relative to competitors' capabilities. To be a source of competitive advantage, a resource or capability must allow the firm (1) to perform a value chain activity or a support function in a manner superior to the way competitors perform it or

FIGURE 4.6 CREATING VALUE THROUGH VALUE CHAIN ACTIVITIES

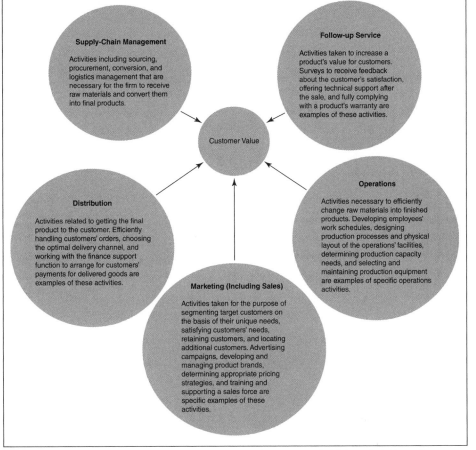

Supply-Chain Management

Activities including sourcing, procurement, conversion, and logistics management that are necessary for the firm to receive raw materials and convert them into final products.

Follow-up Service

Activities taken to increase a product's value for customers. Surveys to receive feedback about the customer's satisfaction, offering technical support after the sale, and fully complying with a product's warranty are examples of these activities.

Customer Value

Distribution

Activities related to getting the final product to the customer. Efficiently handling customers' orders, choosing the optimal delivery channel, and working with the finance support function to arrange for customers' payments for delivered goods are examples of these activities.

Operations

Activities necessary to efficiently change raw materials into finished products. Developing employees' work schedules, designing production processes and physical layout of the operations' facilities, determining production capacity needs, and selecting and maintaining production equipment are examples of specific operations activities.

Marketing (Including Sales)

Activities taken for the purpose of segmenting target customers on the basis of their unique needs, satisfying customers' needs, retaining customers, and locating additional customers. Advertising campaigns, developing and managing product brands, determining appropriate pricing strategies, and training and supporting a sales force are specific examples of these activities.

(2) to perform a value chain activity or a support function that competitors cannot perform. Only under these conditions does a firm create value for customers and have opportunities to capture that value.

Sometimes start-up firms create value by uniquely reconfiguring or recombining parts of the value chain. Federal Express (FedEx) changed the nature of the delivery business by reconfiguring the value chain activities of operations and distribution and the support function of human resources to originate the overnight delivery business, creating value in the process. The Internet has changed several aspects of the value chain for a number of firms. For instance, Amazon.com uses the Internet as a distribution channel for the purpose of selling an increasingly broad set of consumer products, including books and a large number of household items. Additionally, Twitter Inc. is beginning to market "… its ads to small medium-size merchants casting a wider net for advertising revenue as it steps up its efforts to turn more than 100 million monthly Twitter users into a business big enough to justify

FIGURE 4.7 CREATING VALUE THROUGH SUPPORT FUNCTIONS

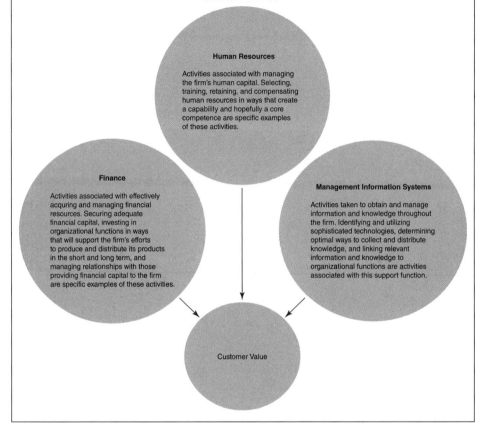

Human Resources

Activities associated with managing the firm's human capital. Selecting, training, retaining, and compensating human resources in ways that create a capability and hopefully a core competence are specific examples of these activities.

Finance

Activities associated with effectively acquiring and managing financial resources. Securing adequate financial capital, investing in organizational functions in ways that will support the firm's efforts to produce and distribute its products in the short and long term, and managing relationships with those providing financial capital to the firm are specific examples of these activities.

Management Information Systems

Activities taken to obtain and manage information and knowledge throughout the firm. Identifying and utilizing sophisticated technologies, determining optimal ways to collect and distribute knowledge, and linking relevant information and knowledge to organizational functions are activities associated with this support function.

Customer Value

SOURCE: © Copyrighted 2011 by Michael A. Hitt, R. Duane Ireland, and Robert E. Hoskisson.

its heady valuation."[85] Thus, Twitter is a new format that makes it possible for companies to present their products to those who "tweet" with their friends and colleagues.

Rating a firm's capability to execute its value chain activities and support functions is challenging. This may be the case for the newly-appointed CEO for Sony Corp. In examining the firm's portfolio of businesses as a means of determining how to improve the firm's overall performance, Kazuo Hirai said that "there are some businesses where we should make the hard decisions." Forming alliances with other companies to work with these businesses or selling them are examples of the hard decisions the new CEO believes must be made.[86]

Decision makers such as Sony Corp.'s CEO must use their judgment to identify and assess the value of a firm's resources and capabilities. Judgment is equally necessary for value chain analysis because no known accurate model or rule is available to help in the process. Nevertheless, firms that involve a heterogeneous group of managers in such activities are more likely to produce valuable results.[87]

Outsourcing

Managers sometimes determine that their firms lack capabilities in areas that are linked to competitive success. In such instances, outsourcing becomes a viable option for a firm to try to develop a competency inside the organization.

Concerned with how components, finished goods, or services will be obtained, **outsourcing** is the purchase of a value-creating activity from an external supplier.[88] Effective outsourcing allows firms to increase their flexibility, mitigate risks, and reduce their capital investments. In multiple global industries such as pharmaceuticals, the trend toward outsourcing continues at a rapid pace for a number of firms.[89] Moreover, in some industries, such as automobile manufacturing and consumer electronics, virtually all firms seek the value that can be captured through effective outsourcing.[90]

Outsourcing can be effective when few, if any, organizations possess the resources and capabilities required to achieve competitive superiority in all value chain activities and support functions. With respect to technologies, for example, research suggests that few companies can afford to develop internally all the technologies that might lead to competitive advantage.[91] By nurturing a smaller number of capabilities, a firm increases the probability of developing a competitive advantage because it does not become overextended. In addition, by outsourcing activities in which it lacks a core competence, the firm can fully concentrate on those areas in which it can create value.[92]

Intermediaries such as the Outsourcing Institute facilitate outsourcing by joining purchasers of outsourced goods and services with the firms that provide them.[93] With more than 70,000 members across the world, the Outsourcing Institute publishes annual buyers' guides, provides consulting and training on best practices, and facilitates networking among peers.

Other research suggests that outsourcing does not work effectively without extensive internal capabilities to effectively coordinate external sourcing as well as internal coordination of core competencies.[94] Furthermore, critics of outsourcing argue that too much outsourcing can lead to a decrease in a firm's ability to innovate.[95] Also, firms should be careful not to take advantage of suppliers once they have created a mutually dependent relationship with them. Taking advantage can include giving them lead times that are too short or making other unrealistic demands on them in the interest of cutting costs. Such behaviors can lead suppliers to integrate forward and become direct competitors to the firm they previously supplied.[96] Companies should be aware of all these risks and prepared to deal with them.

To verify that appropriate activities are outsourced, four skills are essential for managers: strategic thinking, deal making, partnership governance, and managing change.[97] Managers should understand whether and how outsourcing creates competitive advantage within their company—they need to be able to think strategically.[98] To complete effective outsourcing transactions, these managers must also be deal makers, to be able to secure rights from external providers that internal managers can fully use. They must be able to oversee and govern appropriately the relationship with the company to which the services were outsourced. Because outsourcing can significantly change how an organization operates, managers administering these programs must also be able to manage that change, including resolving employee resistance that accompanies any significant change effort.[99]

When Core Competencies Lose Their Value

Tools such as outsourcing can help a firm focus on its core competencies. However, evidence shows that the value-creating ability of core competencies should never be taken for granted,[100] nor should the ability of a core competence to be a permanent competitive advantage be assumed. One reason for these cautions is that core competencies have the potential to become *core rigidities*. As Leslie Wexner, founder and CEO of Limited Brands Inc., once said: "Success doesn't beget success. Success begets failure because the more that you know a thing works, the less likely you are to think that it won't work. When you've had a long string of victories, it's harder to foresee your own vulnerabilities."[101] Thus, each competence is a strength and a weakness—a strength because it is the source of competitive advantage and hence, value creation and a weakness because, if emphasized when it is no longer competitively relevant, it can be a seed of resistance to change.[102]

Events occurring in the firm's external environment create conditions through which core competencies can become core rigidities, generate resistance to change, and stifle innovation. "Often the flip side, the dark side, of core capabilities is revealed due to external events when new competitors figure out a better way to serve the firm's customers, when new technologies emerge, or when political or social events shift the ground underneath."[103] In the final analysis however, changes in the external environment do not cause core competencies to become core rigidities; rather, inflexibility on the part of managers stemming from the strength of their shared beliefs (strategic myopia) is the cause.[104]

This concludes our discussion of tools firms use to determine how their resources and value chain activities can lead to core competencies and sustainable competitive advantage. Evaluating firm performance is also an important part of internal analysis. We close this chapter with a discussion of this topic.

FIRM PERFORMANCE

Firms seek to develop and effectively use competitive advantages for the purpose of creating value for their shareholders and other stakeholders.[105] Firm performance is inherently multidimensional in that each stakeholder group expects those making strategic decisions in a firm to provide the leadership through which its valued objectives will be accomplished.[106] Stakeholders continue supporting a firm when its performance meets or exceeds their expectations. When performance falls below expectations, they may withdraw their support. For instance, shareholders may decide to sell their stock. Although a single stock sale rarely influences firm outcomes significantly, a trend of many shareholders or a shareholder that owns a significant percentage of a firm's total shares deciding to sell their stock can dramatically reduce the value of the firm's stock in the market. Also, large shareholders such as investment funds may have political power to persuade others to withdraw or withhold resources from the firm. In addition, stakeholders' rights are grounded in laws governing private property and private enterprise. Consequently, top managers tend to give shareholder needs high priority when making decisions.

Although organizations have dependency relationships with all of their primary stakeholders, they are not equally dependent on all stakeholders at all times; as a consequence, not every stakeholder has the same level of influence.[107] The more critical and valued a stakeholder's participation, the greater a firm's dependence on it. Greater dependence, in turn, gives the stakeholder more potential influence over a firm's commitments, decisions, and actions. Effective managers must find ways to either accommodate or insulate the organization from the demands of stakeholders controlling critical resources.[108]

Stakeholder Objectives and Power

Various stakeholders' objectives often differ from one another, sometimes placing managers in situations in which they must make trade-offs. Shareholders want the return on their investment (and, hence, their wealth) to be maximized. However, maximization of short-term returns sometimes is accomplished at the expense of investing in a firm's future. For instance, research has demonstrated that newly appointed CEOs of large companies tend to curtail R&D investments immediately after their appointment, resulting in short-term increases in profitability.[109] However, this short-term enhancement of shareholders' wealth can negatively affect the firm's future competitive ability, and sophisticated shareholders with diversified portfolios may sell their interests if a firm fails to invest in its future. Those making strategic decisions are responsible for a firm's survival in both the short and the long term.[110] Accordingly, it is not in the interests of any stakeholders for investments in the company to be unduly minimized.

In contrast to shareholders, another group of stakeholders—the firm's customers—could have their interests maximized when the quality and reliability of a firm's products are improved, but without a price increase. Employees, on the other hand, prefer that companies provide better working conditions and higher compensation and benefits. At the extreme, serving the needs and desires of customers and employees may come at the expense of lower returns for capital market shareholders.

Because of potential conflicts, each firm's decision makers are challenged when seeking to effectively manage stakeholder relationships. To deal with this challenge, decision makers must carefully prioritize the needs and desires of important stakeholders in case the firm lacks the resources to fully satisfy all of them at a point in time.

Power is the most critical criterion decision makers use to prioritize stakeholders. The level of stakeholder influence can come from economic power, political power, or formal power. **Economic power** comes from the ability to withhold economic support from the firm. **Political power** results from the ability to influence others to withhold economic support or to change the rules of the game, as in the example of a special interest group that lobbies a government body for legal changes.[111] **Formal power** involves laws or regulations that specify the legal relationship that exists between a firm and a particular stakeholder group.[112] For instance, firms have legal obligations to shareholders, and they are legally obligated to follow government regulations. Stakeholders can enjoy multiple sources of power.[113] Firms may also give a particular stakeholder group priority because of its strategic importance to future plans. For instance, a company may begin to build excellent community relations in a nearby community where it hopes to build a new plant. Or top executives may simply choose to give a stakeholder priority, as in the case of a firm that makes large donations to universities because top managers value education, even if the direct benefits to the firm are negligible.

When the firm earns high economic returns, the challenge of balancing stakeholder interests is lessened substantially. With the capability and flexibility provided by high returns, a firm can more easily satisfy multiple stakeholders simultaneously. When the firm is earning only average returns, however, managing stakeholders' varying needs may be more difficult given that with average returns, the firm is unable to maximize the interests of all stakeholders. The objective then becomes to at least minimally satisfy each stakeholder. Trade-off decisions are made in light of how dependent the firm is on the support of its stakeholder groups. A firm earning below-average returns does not have the capacity to minimally satisfy all stakeholders. The managerial challenge in this case is to make trade-offs that minimize the amount of support lost from stakeholders.

Measures of Firm Performance

Because various types of firm performance influence stakeholders differently, measures of firm performance can be divided into categories based on the three primary stakeholder groups defined in Chapter 1: capital market, product market, and organizational stakeholders. Table 4.6 shows examples of measures that are highly relevant to capital market stakeholders. Capital market stakeholders (shareholders and lenders) expect a firm to preserve and enhance the wealth they have entrusted to the firm. Shareholders are particularly interested in receiving high returns for the investment they have made in a company as demonstrated by their purchase of the firm's stock. Those returns may also be compared with the average return of all stocks in the market as a whole or in a designated industry for a particular period.

In addition, both shareholders and lenders expect returns that are commensurate with the degree of risk accepted with those investments (that is, lower returns are expected with low-risk investments, and higher returns are expected with high-risk investments). In this context, **risk** is an investor's uncertainty about the economic gains or losses that will result from a particular investment.[114] Strategic leaders must assess the risks involved in pursuing various courses of action.[115] Decisions that lead to lower variance in returns can enhance the value of an organization from the perspective of capital market stakeholders. Consequently, Table 4.6 contains a few common examples of measures that can be used to assess risk. These measures also can be used to adjust shareholder returns. Shareholders can deduct the average or market return for a particular period from the return that was actually received and then divide the result by the standard deviation of returns or beta.[116] Comparing this risk-adjusted return to the risk-adjusted return of other firms could provide a better sense of how well the stock is performing relative to the amount of risk the shareholder is assuming. Note also that lenders are interested

TABLE 4.6 FIRM PERFORMANCE FROM A CAPITAL MARKET PERSPECTIVE

STAKEHOLDER	NEEDS/DESIRES	EXAMPLES	MEASUREMENT
Capital Market			
Shareholders	High returns	Total shareholder return	$\dfrac{\text{(Share Price at Period End} - \text{Price at Start of Period)} + \text{Dividends}}{\text{Share Price at Start of Period}}$
	High relative returns	Adjusted for: Market return	Average return for other firms in market for same period
	High relative returns	Industry return	Average return for other firms in industry for same period
Lenders and shareholders	Low risk (variance)	Standard deviation	Standard deviation of shareholder return for the period
	Low risk (systematic)	Beta	Degree to which stock returns for the firm are correlated with stock returns for the whole market (systematic risk)
	High profitability	Return on assets	$\dfrac{\text{Net Profit after Taxes}}{\text{Total Assets}}$
		Return on equity	$\dfrac{\text{Net Profit after Taxes}}{\text{Shareholders' Equity}}$
	Growth	Growth in revenues	$\dfrac{\text{This Year Total Revenues} - \text{Last Year Total Revenues}}{\text{Last Year Total Revenues}}$
	Low financial risk	Debt-to-equity	$\dfrac{\text{Total Debt}}{\text{Shareholders' Equity}}$
		Debt-to-assets	$\dfrac{\text{Total Debt}}{\text{Total Assets}}$
	Internal efficiency	Current ratio	$\dfrac{\text{Current Assets}}{\text{Current Liabilities}}$
		Worker productivity	$\dfrac{\text{Sales}}{\text{Number of Employees}}$
		Asset turnover	$\dfrac{\text{Sales}}{\text{Total Assets}}$
		Inventory turnover	$\dfrac{\text{Sales}}{\text{Total Inventories}}$
		Collections period	$\dfrac{\text{Receivables} \times 365 \text{ Days}}{\text{Annual Credit Sales}}$

© Cengage Learning

in risk measures such as standard deviation or beta because they are indications of the financial stability of the firm.

In addition, capital market stakeholders are concerned about the growth of the firm because growth is so closely associated with other performance measures. They also become concerned when liquidity becomes too low or debt levels too high because these factors can influence a firm's ability to remain solvent. Furthermore, capital market stakeholders are interested in firm efficiency because of its influence

TABLE 4.7 OTHER MEASURES OF FIRM PERFORMANCE

STAKEHOLDER	NEEDS/DESIRES	EXAMPLES	MEASUREMENT
Product Market			
Primary customers	High-quality, reliable products at low prices	Satisfaction	Customer satisfaction survey
		Dissatisfaction	Product returns or customer complaints (for service firms)
Suppliers	High prices for goods and trustworthy, reliable behavior	Motivation to deliver	Delivery speed
		Availability of goods	Number of stockouts
		Fair contracts	Percentage of contract renewals; prices paid relative to competitors
Communities	Jobs, tax revenues, contributions to community, low negative influences	Job growth	Number of new jobs created in local community per year
		Philanthropy	Donations of time and money to community
		Dissatisfaction	Number of community complaints or legal suits
Unions	Job growth and security, high compensation, good working conditions	Compensation	Wages and other benefits relative to competitors
		Worker safety	Reports of injuries
Organizational			
Managers and other employees	High compensation, opportunities for advancement, job security, professional development, job satisfaction	Desire to stay	Manager or other employee turnover
		Education	Percentage of workforce receiving company-sponsored training per year
		Satisfaction with job	Employee or manager satisfaction survey
		Advancement opportunities	Percentage of upper-level positions filled internally

© Cengage Learning

on future profitability. Consequently, measures such as asset or inventory turnover and days receivable are also relevant.

Other stakeholders' needs and desires are also important to the firm's success; as such, managers should also establish measures that reflect how well the firm is responding to them. Table 4.7 contains a few examples of the types of measures firms might use for this purpose. Product market stakeholders include primary customers, suppliers, communities, and, where applicable, unions. Customers demand reliable products at the lowest possible prices. Firms can measure customer satisfaction with products and services as well as their perceptions of the value they are receiving relative to prices paid. Suppliers seek reliable customers who are willing to pay high prices for the goods and services they receive. Firms can measure success in supplier relationships in terms of the way suppliers serve them and their eagerness to engage in business. In measuring success, firms assume that suppliers are best motivated to serve a customer who is satisfying their needs. Also, although suppliers may desire the highest prices possible, they tend to be satisfied with fair prices and good treatment (reliable orders and payments). Consequently, from the buying firm's perspective, lower prices paid to suppliers might actually be an indication that the supplier perceives the firm in a favorable light, if the other indicators of supplier satisfaction support such a perspective.

Host communities want companies that are long-term employers and providers of tax revenues without placing excessive demands on public support services. They also turn to businesses, in part, to contribute money and time to help build the community. Union officials are interested in secure jobs, under highly desirable working conditions, for the employees they represent. Their demands typically are consistent with employees' needs. For instance, at the organizational level, managers and other employees want high levels of compensation and job security. They also desire professional development, job satisfaction, and advancement opportunities.[117]

Balancing Stakeholder Performance

As already noted, the needs and desires of both product market and organizational stakeholders at least partly conflict with each other and with those of capital market stakeholders. Resources a firm expends to satisfy one stakeholder group can reduce resources available for others. Optimal value creation means that the firm's decision makers must balance the interests of stakeholders to ensure that each of them is highly motivated to continue to contribute resources and energy to the firm. Trade-off decisions are made on the basis of how important the support of each stakeholder group is to the firm, which is also a function of the power each group possesses.[118]

Fortunately, stakeholders' goals are not completely in conflict with one another. For example, it is in the interest of all of an organization's stakeholders that a firm provides a steady and high return to shareholders because doing so reduces the cost of capital to the firm, thus increasing its ability to grow and prosper. Prosperity also means that more resources are available for all stakeholders. For instance, a prosperous firm can provide job security and higher compensation; the firm has more resources available to build innovative and reliable products that serve its customers well; and it has more resources to use to help foster excellent community relations. Even the most ardent supporters of a focus on shareholder wealth admit that other stakeholders are important for achieving high shareholder returns.[119]

Sustainable Development

We have focused on a firm's primary stakeholders rather than taking the broader perspective of social responsibility. A firm that provides safe and high-quality products, treats its suppliers fairly, adds positively to its community, treats employees and managers well, honors its financial obligations, and provides a higher-than-average and stable return to shareholders is well on its way to being what most people would call a socially responsible firm.[120] Also, obedience to laws and regulations is assumed, given that violations interfere with the firm's ability to create value. Nevertheless, there is one aspect of social performance that deserves separate attention because of its strategic importance. It is a firm's environmental performance.[121]

Evidence suggests that today, stakeholders are demanding more of firms with respect to environmental sustainability as a performance measure. McDonald's for example is responding positively to calls for it to push "… its pork suppliers to stop confining sows in small pens known as gestation stalls, thereby moving to address concerns raised by animal-welfare advocates."[122] A number of other restaurant chains such as Burger King and Chipotle Mexican Grill are also responding positively to demands to operate in more environmentally friendly and sustainable ways.

Sustainable development, defined as business growth that does not deplete the natural environment or damage society, results from firms' commitment to sustainability. Most organizations such as McDonald's, Burger King and Chipotle define their sustainability programs in terms of what they are doing to advance technology while at the same time protecting the environment and serving and protecting the communities and societies in which they operate. This is the case at Walmart as well. Andrea Thomas, Walmart's Senior Vice President for Sustainability, notes that the firm has a number of sustainability-related goals including zero waste, using 100 percent renewable energy, and selling only sustainable palm oil in its private label brands.[123]

Increasingly, companies throughout the world see sustainability as a competitive necessity. For example, results included in a recent study completed by MIT *Sloan Management Review* and the Boston Consulting Group indicate that two-thirds of the companies surveyed "… see sustainability as a competitive necessity in today's marketplace, up from 55 percent (in 2010).[124] One of the keys to sustainability is to transform value-creating activities so that they benefit society while advancing the other goals of the firm.[125] Corporate Knights, which is a Canadian and North American business magazine, prepares an annual list of the Global 100 Most Sustainable Corporations in the World. Based in Denmark, global healthcare company Novo Nordisk A/S held the top spot in the 2012 list.[126] This firm evaluates three issues or considerations when making its decisions: "is it financially, socially, and environmentally responsible?" Novo says that focusing on The Triple Bottom Line (as represented by the three considerations) is the foundation for how it conducts business. Moreover, Novo believes that "Doing business in a responsible and sustainable way, with a focus on improving public health, benefits patents, society and shareholders"[127] is appropriate.

One reason for including sustainability when measuring a firm's performance is to make sure that none of the firm's primary stakeholders are being neglected to such a point that they might withdraw their support from the organization. Of course, a more positive approach suggests that serving the needs of stakeholders above their minimum requirements brings substantial benefits to the firm, such as superior knowledge creation, an ability to acquire needed resources, reduced transaction costs, and higher stakeholder motivation levels. Another reason for using multiple measures of firm performance is that traditional financial measures may not reflect the full amount of value the firm is creating. Stakeholders other than shareholders who are powerful may acquire a disproportionate share of the value the firm is creating.[128] At least historically, powerful unions had the potential to absorb a large share of the value being created by companies competing in the automobile and airline industries. A powerful customer or buyer such as Walmart can reduce the amount of value a supplier can appropriate when selling its products to the giant retailer. The reasoning in both of these cases is consistent with the I/O model. Also, in firms that are predominantly owned by one family or by a business group, returns to shareholders may not account for a significant percentage of the total value the firm is creating.[129] Instead, value might be redistributed to other business ventures under control of the group or family or directly to family members in the form of wages, benefits, and perquisites.

SUMMARY

▶ In a new landscape of rapid technological change and globalization, a firm's resources, capabilities, and core competencies have a strong influence on its competitiveness. The most effective firms recognize that creating value and generating high returns for shareholders and other stakeholders is possible only when core competencies (critical strengths identified by analyzing the firm's internal organization) are matched with opportunities (determined by studying the firm's external environment).

▶ No competitive advantage lasts forever. Over time, rivals use their own unique resources, capabilities, and core competencies to form different value-creating propositions that duplicate the value-creating ability of the firm's competitive advantages. In general, the Internet's capabilities (e.g., rapid diffusion of information and knowledge) are reducing the sustainability of many competitive advantages. Thus, firms must exploit their current advantages while simultaneously using their resources and capabilities to form new advantages that can lead to future competitive success.

▶ Effectively managing core competencies requires careful analysis of the firm's resources (inputs to the production process) and capabilities (capacities for integrated bundles of resources to perform a task or activity).

▶ Single sets of resources are usually not a source of competitive advantage. Capabilities, which are groupings of tangible and intangible resources, are a more likely source of competitive advantages, especially relatively sustainable ones. A key reason for this is that the methods a firm uses to nurture and support core competencies that are based on capabilities are less visible to rivals and, as such, more complex and difficult to imitate.

▶ Only when a capability is valuable, rare, costly to imitate, and nonsubstitutable is it a core competence and a source of competitive advantage. Over time, core competencies must be nurtured and supported; but, they cannot be allowed to become core rigidities. Core competencies are a source of competitive advantage only when they allow the firm to create value by exploiting opportunities in the external environment. When this is no longer the case, attention shifts to selecting or forming other capabilities that meet the four criteria of sustainable competitive advantage.

▶ Value chain analysis can be used to identify and evaluate the competitive potential of resources and capabilities. By studying their skills relative to value chain activities and support functions, firms can understand their cost structure and identify the activities through which they can create value.

▶ When the firm cannot create value in either value chain activities or support function activities, outsourcing, or the purchase of a value-creating activity from an external supplier, is an option. The firm must outsource only to companies possessing a competitive advantage in the particular activity under consideration. In addition, the firm must continuously verify that it is not out-sourcing activities from which it has the ability to create value.

▶ Firm performance is inherently multidimensional. Each stakeholder group expects those making strategic decisions in a firm to provide the leadership through which its valued objectives will be accomplished. The priority given to each stakeholder group when making strategic decisions depends on its power and on its importance to the firm's strategies. When the firm earns superior economic returns on its investments, the challenge of balancing stake-holder interests is lessened substantially. Increasingly, sustainable development is an important measure stakeholders use to judge a firm's performance.

ETHICS QUESTIONS

1. Could efforts to develop sustainable competitive advantages result in employees using unethical practices? If so, what unethical practices might be used to compare a firm's core competencies with those held by rivals?

2. Do ethical practices affect a firm's ability to develop a brand name as a source of competitive advantage? If so, how does this happen? Identify some brands that are a source of competitive advantage in part because of the firm's ethical practices.

3. What is the difference between exploiting a firm's human capital and using that capital as a source of competitive advantage? Are there situations in which the exploitation of human capital can be a source of advantage? If so, can you name such a situation? If the exploitation of human capital can be a source of competitive advantage, is this a sustainable advantage? Why or why not?

4. Are there any ethical dilemmas associated with outsourcing? If so, what are they? How would you deal with those dilemmas?

5. What ethical responsibilities do managers have if they determine that a set of employees has skills that are valuable only to a core competence that is rapidly becoming a core rigidity for the firm?

6. Through postings to the Internet, firms sometimes make a vast array of data, information, and knowledge available to competitors as well as to customers and suppliers. What ethical issues, if any, are involved when the firm finds competitively relevant information on a competitor's Website?

7. To what extent does a firm have a moral obligation to distribute value to sta-keholders based on their relative contributions to its creation? Does a firm have any legal obligations to do so?

NOTES

1 M. D. Chari & P. David, 2012, Sustaining superior performance in an emerging economy: An empirical test in the Indian context, *Strategic Management Journal*, 33: 217–229; I. Hasan, N. Kobeissi, & H. Wang, 2011, Global equity offerings, corporate valuation, and subsequent international diversifica-tion, *Strategic Management Journal*, 32: 787–796.

2 J. C. Camillus, 2011, Organisational identity and the business environment: The strategic connection, *International Journal of Business Environment*, 4: 306–314; E. Vaara & J. Tienari, 2011, On the narrative construction of MNCs: An antenarrative analysis of legitimation and resistance in a cross-border merger, *Organization Science*, 22: 370–390.

3 N. J. Foss, K. Laursen, & T. Pedersen, 2011, Linking customer interaction and innovation: The mediat-ing role of new organizational practices, *Organiza-tion Science*, 22: 980–999; M. K. Srivastava &

D. R. Gnyawali, 2011, When do relational resources matter? Leveraging portfolio technological resources for breakthrough innovation, *Academy of Management Journal*, 54: 797–810.

4   L. Argote, 2011, Organizational learning: From experience to knowledge, *Organization Science*, 22: N. Kumar & P. Puranam, 2011, Have you restructured for global success? *Harvard Business Review*, 89(10): 123–128.

5   J. B. Barney, D. J. Ketchen, Jr., & M. Wright, 2011, The future of resource-based theory, *Journal of Management*, 37: 1299–1315; D. G. Sirmon, M. A. Hitt, R. D. Ireland, & B. A. Gilbert, 2011, Resource orchestration to create competitive advantage: Breadth, depth, and life cycle effects, *Journal of Management*, 37: 1390–1412.

6   A. Arora & A. Nandkumar, 2012, Insecure advantage? Markets for technology and the value of resources for entrepreneurial ventures, *Strategic Management Journal*, 33: 231–251; B. L. Connelly, D. J. Ketchen, & S. F. Slater, 2011, Toward a "theoretical toolbox" for sustainability research in marketing, *Journal of the Academy of Marketing Science*, 39: 86–100.

7   J. B. Barney, 2001, Is the resource-based "view" a useful perspective for strategic management research? Yes, *Academy of Management Review*, 26: 41–56.

8   J. G. Combs, D. J. Ketchen, Jr., R. D. Ireland, & J. W. Webb, 2011, The role of resource flexibility in leveraging strategic resources, *Journal of Management Studies*, 48: 1098–1125; J. B. Barney, 1999, How a firm's capabilities affect boundary decisions, *Sloan Management Review*, 40(3): 137–145.

9   I. Hasan, N. Kobeissi, & H. Wang, 2011, Global equity offerings, corporate valuation, and subsequent international diversification, *Strategic Management Journal*, 32: 787–796; W. Tsai, K.-H. Su, & M.-J. Chen, 2011, Seeing through the eyes of a rival: Competitor acumen based on rival-centric perceptions, *Academy of Management Journal*, 54: 761–778.

10 R. B. Adams, A. N. Licht, & L. Sagiv, 2011, Shareholders and stakeholders: How do directors decide? *Strategic Management Journal*, 32: 1331–1355; R. Garcia-Castro, M. A. Arino, & M. A. Canela, 2011, Over the long-run? Short-run impact and long-run consequences of stakeholder management, *Business & Society*, 50: 428–455.

11 G. Kenny, 2012, Diversification: Best practices of the leading companies, *Journal of Business Strategy*, 33: 12–20.

12 P. C. Nutt, 2002, *Why Decisions Fail*, San Francisco: Berrett-Koehler; P. C. Nutt, 1999, Surprising but true: Half the decisions in organizations fail, *Academy of Management Executive*, 13(4): 75–90.

13 A. Carmeli, A. Tishler, & A. C. Edmondson, 2012, CEO relational leadership and strategic decision quality in top management teams: The role of team trust and learning from failure, *Strategic Organization*, 10: 31–54; G. P. Hodgkinson & M. P. Healey, 2011, Psychological foundations of dynamic capabilities: Reflexion and reflection in strategic management, *Strategic Management Journal*, 32: 1500–1516.

14 K. Muehlfeld, P. R. Sahib, & A. Van Witteloostuijn, 2012, A contextual theory of organizational learning from failures and successes: A study of acquisition completion in the global newspaper industry, 1981–2008, *Strategic Management Journal*, in press; T. O. Salge & A. Vera, 2011, Small steps that matter: Incremental learning, slack resources and organizational

performance, *British Journal of Management*, in press; R. G. McGrath, 1999, Falling forward: Real options reasoning and entrepreneurial failure, *Academy of Management Review*, 24: 13–30.

15 E. Danneels, 2011, Trying to become a different type of company: Dynamic capability at Smith Corona, *Strategic Management Journal*, 32: 1–31; G. Gavetti & D. Levinthal, 2000, Looking forward and looking backward: Cognitive and experimental search, *Administrative Science Quarterly*, 45: 113–137.

16 S. Zaheer, M. S. Schomaker, & L. Nachum, 2012, Distance without direction: Restoring credibility to a much-loved construct, *Journal of International Business Studies*, 43: 18–27; C. V. Caprar, 2011, Foreign locals: A cautionary tale on the culture of MNC local employees, *Journal of International Business Studies* 42: 608–628.

17 I. J. Walsh & J. M. Bartunek 2011, Cheating the fates: Organizational foundings in the wake of demise, *Academy of Management Journal*, 54: 1017–1044; J. M. Mezias, P. Grinyer, & W. D. Guth, 2001, Changing collective cognition: A process model for strategic change, *Long Range Planning*, 34(1): 71–95.

18 L. Argote & E. Miron-Spektor, 2011, Organizational learning: From experience to knowledge, *Organization Science*, 22: 1123–1137; J. H. Moore & M. S. Kraatz, 2011, Governance form and organizational adaptation: Lessons from the savings and loan industry in the 1980s, *Organization Science*, 22: 850–868.

19 D. Mattioli, 2012, Kodak shutters camera business, *Wall Street Journal Online*, http://www.wsj.com, February 10.

20 M. Spector, D. Mattioli, & P. Brickley, 2012, Can bankruptcy filing save Kodak? *Wall Street Journal Online*, http://www.wsj.com, January 20.

21 M. J. Fern, L. B. Cardinal, & H. M. O'Neill, 2012, The genesis of strategy in new ventures: Escaping the constraints of founder and team knowledge, *Strategic Management Journal*, 33: 427–447; A. D. Henderson, M. E. Raynor, & M. Ahmed, 2012, How long must a firm be great to rule out chance? Benchmarking sustained superior performance without being fooled by randomness, *Strategic Management Journal*, 33: 387–406; R. Amit & P. J. H. Schoemaker, 1993, Strategic assets and organizational rent, *Strategic Management Journal*, 14: 33–46.

22 K. Muehlfeld, P. R. Sahib, & A. van Witteloostuijn, 2012, A contextual theory of organizational learning from failures and successes: A study of acquisition completion in the global newspaper industry, 1981–2008, *Strategic Management Journal*, 33: in press; R. E. Hoskisson & L. W. Busenitz, 2001, Market uncertainty and learning distance in corporate entrepreneurship entry mode choice, in M. A. Hitt, R. D. Ireland, S. M. Camp, & D. L. Sexton (eds.), *Strategic Entrepreneurship: Creating a New Integrated Mindset*, Oxford, UK: Blackwell Publishers, 151–172.

23 H. A. Ndofor & D. G. Sirmon, 2011, Firm resources, competitive actions and performance: Investigating a mediated model with evidence from the in-vitro diagnostics industry, *Strategic Management Journal*, 32: 640–657; V. P. Rindova & C. J. Fombrun, 1999, Constructing competitive advantage: The role of firm-constituent interactions, *Strategic Management Journal*, 20: 691–710; M. A. Peteraf, 1993, The cornerstones of competitive strategy: A resource-based view, *Strategic Management Journal*, 14: 179–191.

24. J. Brinckmann & M. Hoegl, 2011, Effects of initial teamwork capability and initial relational capability on the development of new technology-based firms, *Strategic Entrepreneurship Journal*, 5: 37–57; P. Sieger, T. Zellweger, R. S. Nason, & E. Clinton, 2011, Portfolio entrepreneurship in family firms: A resource-based perspective, *Strategic Entrepreneurship Journal*, 5: 327–351.

25. M. E. Porter, 2001, Strategy and the Internet, *Harvard Business Review*, 79(2): 63–78; M. E. Porter, 1996, What is strategy? *Harvard Business Review*, 74(6): 61–78.

26. S. Chen, 2012, Creating sustainable international social ventures, *Thunderbird International Business Review*, 54: 131–142.

27. C. C. Maurer, P. Bansal, & M. M. Crossan, 2011, Creating economic value through social venues: Introducing a culturally informed resource-based view, *Organization Science*, 22: 432–448; A. McWilliams & D. S. Siegel, 2011, Creating and capturing value: Strategic corporate social responsibility, resource-based theory, and sustainable competitive advantage, *Journal of Management*, 37: 1480–1495.

28. O. Chatain, 2011, Value creation, competition, and performance in buyer-supplier relationships, *Strategic Management Journal*, 32: 76–102; P. Schmitt, B. Skiera, & C. Van den Bulte, 2011, Referral programs and customer value, *Journal of Marketing*, 75: 46–59; 1998, Pocket Strategy, Value, *Economist Books*, 165.

29. V. Ambrosini, C. Bowman, & R. Schoenberg, 2011, Should acquiring firms pursue more than one value creation strategy? An empirical test of acquisition performance, *British Journal of Management*, 22: 173–185; M. Pynnonen, P. Ritala, & J. Hallikas, 2011, The new meaning of customer value: A systemic perspective, *Journal of Business Strategy*, 32: 51–57.

30. P. Waychal, R. P. Mohanty, & A. Verma, 2012, Determinants of innovation as a competence: An empirical study, *International Journal of Business Innovation and Research*, 5L 192–211; G. Vasudeva & J. Anand, 2011, Unpacking absorptive capacity: A study of knowledge utilization from alliance portfolios, *Academy of Management Journal*, 54: 611–623.

31. B. Clarysse, J. Bruneel, & M. Wright, 2011, Explaining growth paths of young technology-based firms: Structuring resource portfolios in different competitive environments, *Strategic Entrepreneurship Journal*, 5: 137–157; M. A. Hitt, R. D. Nixon, P. G. Clifford, & K. P. Coyne, 1999, The development and use of strategic resources, in M. A. Hitt, P. G. Clifford, R. D. Nixon, & K. P. Coyne (eds.), *Dynamic Strategic Resources*, Chichester, UK: Wiley, 1–14.

32. C. M. Christensen, 2001, The past and future of competitive advantage, *Sloan Management Review*, 42(2): 105–109.

33. F. Chirico, D. G. Sirmon, S. Sciascia, & P. Mazzola, 2011, Resource orchestration in family firms: Investigating how entrepreneurial orientation, generational involvement, and participative strategy affect performance, *Strategic Entrepreneurship Journal*, 5: 307–326; G. Ahuja & R. Katila, 2004, Where do resources come from? The role of idiosyncratic situations, *Strategic Management Journal*, 25: 887–907.

34. I. P. Mahmood, H. Zhu, & E. J. Zajac, 2011, Where can capabilities come from? Network ties and capability acquisition in business groups, *Strategic Management Journal*, 32: 820–848; S. Berman, J. Down, & C. Hill, 2002, Tacit knowledge as a source of

competitive advantage in the National Basketball Association, *Academy of Management Journal*, 45: 13–31.

35. C. Zook & J. Allen, 2011, The great repeatable business model, *Harvard Business Review*, 89(11): 107–114.

36. A. Fortune & W. Mitchell, 2012, Unpacking firm exit at the firm and industry levels: The adaptation and selection of firm capabilities, *Strategic Management Journal*, 33: in press; M. S. Feldman, 2000, Organizational routines as a source of continuous change, *Organization Science*, 11: 611–629.

37. J. Sydow & G. Schreyoegg, 2011, Organizing for fluidity? Dilemmas of new organizational forms, *Organization Science*, 21: 1251–1262; R. Lubit, 2001, Tacit knowledge and knowledge management: The keys to sustainable competitive advantage, *Organizational Dynamics*, 29(3): 164–178.

38. A. M. Webber, 2000, New math for a new economy, *Fast Company*, January–February, 214–224.

39. V. Rindova, E. Dalpiaz, & D. Ravasi, 2012, A cultural quest: A study of organizational use of new cultural resources in strategy formation, *Organization Science*, 22: in press; R. G. Schroeder, K. A. Bates, & M. A. Junttila, 2002, A resource-based view of manufacturing strategy and the relationship to manufacturing performance, *Strategic Management Journal*, 23: 105–117.

40. J. St-Pierre & J. Audet, 2011, Intangible assets and performance: Analysis on manufacturing SMEs, *Journal of Intellectual Capital*, 12: 202–223.

41. C. Fernandez-Araoz, B. Groysberg, & N. Nohria, 2011, How to hang on to your high potentials, *Harvard Business Review*, 89(10): 76–83; T. H. Davenport, J. Harris, & J. Shapiro, 2010, Competing on talent analytics, *Harvard Business Review*, 88(10): 52–58.

42. B. S. Anderson & Y. Eshima, 2012, The influence of firm age and intangible resources on the relationship between entrepreneurial orientation and firm growth among Japanese SMEs, *Journal of Business Venturing*, in press.

43. M. Reinholt, T. Pedersen, & N. J. Foss, 2011, Why a central network position isn't enough: The role of motivation and ability for knowledge sharing in employee networks, *Academy of Management Journal*, 54: 1277–1297; R. D. Ireland, M. A. Hitt, & D. Vaidyanath, 2002, Managing strategic alliances to achieve a competitive advantage, *Journal of Management*, 28: 413–434.

44. P. M. Lee, T. G. Pollock, & K. Jin, 2011, The contingent value of venture capitalist reputation, *Strategic Organization*, 9: 33–69; D. L. Deephouse, 2000, Media reputation as a strategic resource: An integration of mass communication and resource-based theories, *Journal of Management*, 26: 1091–1112.

45. A. P. Cowan & J. J. Marcel, 2011, Damaged goods: Board decisions to dismiss reputationally comprised directors, *Academy of Management Journal*, 54: 509–527; J. Shamsie, 2003, The context of dominance: An industry-driven framework for exploiting reputation, *Strategic Management Journal*, 24: 199–215.

46. I. Mansfield, 2011, Apple overtakes Google for most valuable brandname, *Cellular-News*, http://www.cellular-news.com, May 9.

47. I. Sherr, 2012, Price of the iPad name: $55,000 to $2 billion, *Wall Street Journal Online*, http://www.wsj.com, February 17.

48. D. Z. Levin, J. Walter, & J. K. Murnighan, 2011, Dormant ties: The value of reconnecting, *Organization*

Science, 22: 923–939; M. A. Hitt, H. Lee, & E. Yucel, 2002, The importance of social capital to the management of multinational enterprises: Relational networks among Asian and western firms, *Asia Pacific Journal of Management*, 19: 353–372.

49. U. Wassmer & P. Dussauge, 2012, Network resource stocks and flows: How do alliance portfolios affect the value of new alliance formations? *Strategic Management Journal*, 33: in press; J. M. Mol & N. M. Wkjnberg, 2011, From resources to value and back: Competition between and within organizations, *British Journal of Management*, 22: 77–95.

50. M. J. Mol & M. Kotabe, 2011, Overcoming inertia: Drivers of the outsourcing process, *Long Range Planning*, 44 (3): 160–178; C. E. Helfat & R. S. Raubitschek, 2000, Product sequencing: Co-evolution of knowledge, capabilities and products, *Strategic Management Journal*, 21: 961–979.

51. N. Argyres, 2011, Using organizational economics to study organizational capability development and strategy, *Organization Science*, 22: 1138–1143; M. A. Hitt, L. Bierman, K. Shimizu, & R. Kochhar, 2001, Direct and moderating effects of human capital on strategy and performance in professional service firms: A resource-based perspective, *Academy of Management Journal*, 44: 13–28; M. A. Hitt, R. D. Ireland, & H. Lee, 2000, Technological learning, knowledge management, firm growth and performance: An introductory essay, *Journal of Engineering and Technology Management*, 17: 231–246.

52. R. W. Coff, 2011, Drilling for micro-foundations of human capital-based competitive advantages, *Journal of Management*, 37: 1429–1443; N. W. Hatch & J. H. Dyer, 2004, Human capital and learning as a source of sustainable competitive advantage, *Strategic Management Journal*, 25: 1155–1178.

53. P. M. Wright & G. C. McMahan, 2011, Exploring human capital: Putting 'human' back into strategic human resource management, *Human Resource Management Journal*, 21: 93–104; D. B. Turban & D. W. Greening, 1996, Corporate social performance and organizational attractiveness to prospective employees, *Academy of Management Journal*, 40: 658–672.

54. 2011, 100 best companies to work for, CNNMoney.com, *Fortune*, http://www.cnnmoney.com/magazines /fortune, February 7.

55. A. Y. Lewin, S. Massini, & C. Peeters, 2011, Micro-foundations of internal and external absorptive capacity returns, *Organization Science*, 22: 81–98; S. Tallman & A. S. Chacar, 2011, Knowledge accumulation and dissemination in MNEs: A practice-based framework, *Journal of Management Studies*, 48: 278–304.

56. J. Cambra-Fierro, L. Florin, L. Perez, & J. Whitelock, 2011, Inter-firm market orientation as antecedent of knowledge transfer innovation and value creation in networks, *Management Decision*, 49: 444–467; R. A. Noe, J. A. Colquitt, M. J. Simmering, & S. A. Alvarez, 2003, Knowledge management: Developing intellectual and social capital, in S. E. Jackson, M. A. Hitt, & A. S. DeNisi (eds.), *Managing Knowledge for Sustained Competitive Advantage*, San Francisco: Jossey-Bass: 209–242; L. Argote & P. Ingram, 2000, Knowledge transfer: A basis for competitive advantage in firms, *Organizational Behavior and Human Decision Processes*, 82: 150–169.

57. G. G. Dess & J. C. Picken, 1999, *Beyond Productivity*, New York: AMACOM.

58. T. T. Baldwin & C. C. Danielson, 2000, Building a learning strategy at the top: Interviews with ten of America's CLOs, *Business Horizons*, 43(6): 5–14.

59. M. F. Wiersema & H. P. Bowen, 2011, The relationship between international diversification and firm performance: Why it remains a puzzle, *Global Strategy Journal*, 1: 152–170; M. A. Hitt & R. D. Ireland, 1985, Corporate distinctive competence, strategy, industry, and performance, *Strategic Management Journal*, 6: 273–293; M. A. Hitt, R. D. Ireland, & K. A. Palia, 1982, Industrial firms' grand strategy and functional importance, *Academy of Management Journal*, 25: 265–298; M. A. Hitt, R. D. Ireland, & G. Stadter, 1982, Functional importance and company performance: Moderating effects of grand strategy and industry type, *Strategic Management Journal*, 3: 315–330.

60. E. Rasmussen, S. Mosey, & M. Wright, 2011, The evolution of entrepreneurial competencies: A longitudinal study of university spin-off venture emergence, *Journal of Management Studies*, 48: 1312–1345; C. Zott, 2003, Dynamic capabilities and the emergence of intraindustry differential firm performance: Insights from a simulation study, *Strategic Management Journal*, 24: 97–125.

61. K. Hafeez, Y. B. Zhang, & N. Malak, 2002, Core competence for sustainable competitive advantage: A structured methodology for identifying core competence, *IEEE Transactions on Engineering Management*, 49(1): 28–35; C. K. Prahalad & G. Hamel, 1990, The core competence of the corporation, *Harvard Business Review*, 68(3): 79–93.

62. R. J. Arend & M. Levesque, 2010, Is the resource-based view a practical organizational theory? *Organization Science*, 21: 913–930; C. Bowman & V. Ambrosini, 2000, Value creation versus value capture: Towards a coherent definition of value in strategy, *British Journal of Management*, 11: 1–15; T. Chi, 1994, Trading in strategic resources: Necessary conditions, transaction cost problems, and choice of exchange structure, *Strategic Management Journal*, 15: 271–290.

63. D. H. Henard & M. A. McFadyen, 2012, Resource dedication and new product performance: A resource-based view, *Journal of Product Innovation Management*, 29: 193–204; C. Bowman, 2001, "Value" in the resource-based view of the firm: A contribution to the debate, *Academy of Management Review*, 26: 501–502.

64. C. Ames, 1995, Sales soft? Profits flat? It's time to rethink your business, *Fortune*, June 25, 142–146.

65. G. Ray, J. B. Barney, & W. A. Muhanna, 2004, Capabilities, business processes, and competitive advantage: Choosing the dependent variable in empirical tests of the resource-based view, *Strategic Management Journal*, 25: 23–37; J. B. Barney, 2001, Resource-based theories of competitive advantage: A ten-year retrospective on the resource-based view, *Journal of Management*, 27: 643–650; J. B. Barney, 1991, Firm resources and sustained competitive advantage, *Journal of Management*, 17: 99–120.

66. C. H. St. John & J. S. Harrison, 1999, Manufacturing-based relatedness, synergy, and coordination, *Strategic Management Journal*, 20: 129–145.

67. S. W. Bradley, D. A. Shepherd, & J. Wiklund, 2011, The importance of slack for new organizations facing 'tough' environments, *Journal of Management Studies*, 1071–1097; Barney, Firm resources and competitive advantage.

68 C. Passariello, 2012, New rich fuel luxury boom, *Wall Street Journal Online*, http://www.wsj.com, February 17.

69 A. Nair & D. D. Selover, 2012, A study of competitive dynamics, *Journal of Business Research*, 65: 355–361.

70 J. B. Barney, 1995, Looking inside for competitive advantage, *Academy of Management Executive*, 9(4): 49–60.

71 J. B. Barney, 1999, How a firm's capabilities affect boundary decisions, *Sloan Management Review*, 40(3): 137–145.

72 Barney, Firm resources and sustained competitive advantage, 108.

73 J. Huey, 1993, How McKinsey does it, *Fortune*, November 1, 56–81.

74 A. J. Bock, T. Opsahl, G. George, & D. M. Gann, 2012, The effects of culture and structure on strategic flexibility during business model innovation, *Journal of Management Studies*, 49: 279–305; D. Karreman, 2010, The power of knowledge: Learning from 'learning by knowledge-intensive firm,' *Journal of Management Studies*, 47: 1405–1416.

75 2012, Driving change, *The Greater Lansing Business Monthly*, http://www.lansingbusinessmonthly.com, February 17; L. Soupata, 2001, Managing culture for competitive advantage at United Parcel Service, *Journal of Organizational Excellence*, 20(3): 19–26.

76 A. W. King & C. P. Zeithaml, 2001, Competencies and firm performance: Examining the causal ambiguity paradox, *Strategic Management Journal*, 22: 75–99; R. Reed & R. DeFillippi, 1990, Causal ambiguity, barriers to imitation, and sustainable competitive advantage, *Academy of Management Review*, 15: 88–102.

77 Barney, Firm resources and sustained competitive advantage, 111.

78 U. Lichtenthaler & H. Ernst, 2012, Integrated knowledge exploitation: The complementarity of product development and technology licensing, *Strategic Management Journal*, in press; R. Amit & P. J. H. Schoemaker, 1993, Strategic assets and organizational rent, *Strategic Management Journal*, 14: 33–46.

79 G. Vasudeva & J. Anand, 2011, Unpacking absorptive capacity: A study of knowledge utilization from alliance portfolios, *Academy of Management Journal*, 54: 611–623; S. K. McEvily, S. Das, & K. McCabe, 2000, Avoiding competence substitution through knowledge sharing, *Academy of Management Review*, 25: 294–311.

80 M. E. Porter, 1985, *Competitive Advantage*, New York: The Free Press, 33–61.

81 S. Chattopadhyay, D. S. K. Chan & J. P. T. Mo, 2011, Modelling the disaggregated value chain—the new trend in China, *International Journal of Value Chain Management*, 6: 47–60; G. G. Dess, A. Gupta, J. F. Hennart, & C.W. L. Hill, 1995, Conducting and integrating strategy research at the international corporate and business levels: Issues and directions, *Journal of Management*, 21: 357–393.

82 J. Webb & C. Gile, 2001, Reversing the value chain, *Journal of Business Strategy*, 22(2): 13–17.

83 D. Ballantyne, P. Frow, R. J. Varey, & A. Payne, 2011, Value propositions as communication practice: Taking a wider view, *Industrial Marketing Management*, 40: 2–02–210; T. A. Stewart, 1999, Customer learning is a two-way street, *Fortune*, May 10, 158–160.

84 R. Amit & C. Zott, 2001, Value creation in E-business, *Strategic Management Journal*, 22(special issue): 493–520; M. E. Porter, 2001, Strategy and the Internet, *Harvard Business Review*, 79(3): 62–78.

85 S. Ovide, 2012, Twitter to pursue smaller ad clients, *Wall Street Journal Online*, http://www.wsj.com, February 17.

86 J. Osawa, 2012, Sony CEO: No 'sacred area,' *Wall Street Journal Online*, http://www.wsj.com, February 10.

87 J. S. Sidhu & H. W. Volberda, 2011, Coordination of globally distributed teams: A co-evolution perspective on offshoring, *International Business Review*, 20: 278–290; C. Pegels, Y. Song, & B. Yang, 2000, Management heterogeneity, competitive interaction groups, and firm performance, *Strategic Management Journal*, 21: 911–923.

88 C. Weigelt & M. B. Sarkar, 2012, Performance implications of outsourcing for technological innovations: Managing the efficiency and adaptability trade-off, *Strategic Management Journal*, 33: 189–216; Mol and Kotabe, Overcoming inertia.

89 2012, To outsource or not to outsource? That's the pharma R&D question, *Wall Street Journal Online*, http://www.wsj.com, February 7.

90 K. Sharda & L. Chatterjee, 2011, Configurations of outsourcing firms and organizational performance: A study of outsourcing industry in India, *Strategic Outsourcing: An International Journal*, 4: 152–178; A. Takeishi, 2001, Bridging inter- and intra-firm boundaries: Management of supplier involvement in automobile product development, *Strategic Management Journal*, 22: 403–433.

91 U. Lichtenthaler & H. Ernst, 2012, Integrated knowledge exploitation: The complementarity of product development and technology licensing, *Strategic Management Journal*, 33: in press; J. Yu, B. A. Gilbert, & B. M. Oviatt, 2011, Effects of alliances, time, and network cohesion on the initiation of foreign sales by new ventures, *Strategic Management Journal*, 32: 424–446.

92 E. Danneels, 2012, Second-order competences and Schumpeterian rents, *Strategic Entrepreneurship Journal* 6: in press; K. Hafeez, Y. B. Zhang, & N. Malak, 2002, Core competence for sustainable competitive advantage: A structured methodology for identifying core competence, *IEEE Transactions on Engineering Management*, 49(1): 28–35; C. K. Prahalad & G. Hamel, 1990, The core competence of the corporation, *Harvard Business Review*, 68(3): 79–93.

93 2012, The Outsourcing Institute: Gateway to the outsourcing marketplace, http://www.outsourcing.com, February 18.

94 R. Liu, D. J. Feils, & B. Scholnick, 2011, Why are different services outsourced to different countries? *Journal of International Business Studies*, 42: 558–571; M. J. Leiblein, J. J. Reuer, & F. Dalsace, 2002, Do make or buy decisions matter? The influence of organizational governance on technological performance, *Strategic Management Journal*, 23: 817–833.

95 J. Hsuan & V. Mahnke, 2011, Outsourcing R&D: A review, model, and research agenda, *R&D Management*, 41: 1–7; M. J. Mol, P. Pauwels, P. Matthyssens, & L. Quintens, 2004, A technological contingency perspective on the depth and scope of international outsourcing, *Journal of International Management*, 10: 287–305.

96 V. H. Villena, E. Revilla, & T. Choi, 2011, The dark side of buyer-supplier relationships: A social capital perspective, *Journal of Operations Management*, 29: 561–576; C. Rossetti & T. Y. Choi, 2005, On the

dark side of strategic sourcing: Experiences from the aerospace industry, *Academy of Management Executive*, 19(1): 46–60.

97 M. Useem & J. Harder, 2000, Leading laterally in company outsourcing, *Sloan Management Review*, 41(2): 25–36.

98 B. Vagadia, 2012, From tactical to strategic outsourcing, *Strategic outsourcing: Management for professionals*, 27–54; R. C. Insinga & M. J. Werle, 2000, Linking outsourcing to business strategy, *Academy of Management Executive*, 14(4): 58–70.

99 Mol and Kotabe, Overcoming inertia; M. Katz, 2001, Planning ahead for manufacturing facility changes: A case study in outsourcing, *Pharmaceutical Technology*, March, 160–164.

100 T. C. Powell, 2002, The philosophy of strategy, *Strategic Management Journal*, 23: 873–880.

101 G. G. Dess & J. C. Picken, 1999, Creating competitive (dis)advantage: Learning from Food Lion's freefall, *Academy of Management Executive*, 13(3): 97–111.

102 M. Hannan & J. Freeman, 1977, The population ecology of organizations, *American Journal of Sociology*, 82: 929–964.

103 D. Leonard-Barton, 1998, *Wellsprings of Knowledge*, Boston, MA.: Harvard Business Press, 30–31.

104 C. A. Siren, M. Kohtamaki, & A. Kuckertz, 2012, Exploration and exploitation strategies, profit performance, and the mediating role of strategic learning: Escaping the exploitation trap, *Strategic Entrepreneurship Journal*, 6: 18–41; Z. Zhou & Z. Chen, 2011, Formation mechanism of knowledge rigidity in firms, *Journal of Knowledge Management*, 15: 820–835.

105 P. Frow & A. Payne, 2011, A stakeholder perspective of the value proposition concept, *European Journal of Marketing*, 45: 223–240; J. Peloza & J. Shang, 2011, How can corporate social responsibility activities create value for stakeholders? A systematic review, *Journal of the Academy of Marketing Science*, 39: 117–135.

106 R. B. Adams, A. N. Licht, & L. Sagiv, 2011, Shareholders and stakeholders: How do directors decide? *Strategic Management Journal*, 32: 1331–1355; A. McWilliams & D. Siegel, 2001, Corporate social responsibility: A theory of the firm perspective, *Academy of Management Review*, 26: 117–127.

107 A. Habisch, L. Patelli, M. Pedrini, & C. Schwartz, 2011, Different talks with different folks: A comparative survey of stakeholder dialog in Germany, Italy, and the US, *Journal of Business Ethics*, 100: 381–404; J. M. Stevens, H. K. Steensma, D. A. Harrison, & P. L. Cochran, 2005, Symbolic or substantive document? The influence of ethics codes on financial executives' decisions, *Strategic Management Journal*, 26: 181–195.

108 F. Ackermann & C. Eden, 2011, Strategic management of stakeholders: Theory and Practice, *Long Range Planning*, 44: 179–196; R. E. Freeman & J. McVea, 2001, A stakeholder approach to strategic management, in M. A. Hitt, R. E. Freeman, & J. S. Harrison (eds.), *Handbook of Strategic Management*, Oxford, UK: Blackwell Publishers, 189–207.

109 J. S. Harrison & J. O. Fiet, 1999, New CEOs pursue their own self-interests by sacrificing stakeholder value, *Journal of Business Ethics*, 19: 301–308.

110 D. Souder & P. Bromiley, 2012, Explaining temporal orientation: Evidence from the durability of firms' capital investments, *Strategic Management Journal*, 33: in press.

111 D. C. Sprengel & T. Busch, 2011, Stakeholder engagement and environmental strategy—the case of climate change, *Business Strategy and the Environment*, 20: 351–364; J. Frooman, 1999, Stakeholder influence strategies, *Academy of Management Review*, 24: 191–205.

112 R. E. Freeman, 1984, *Strategic Management: A Stakeholder Approach*, Boston: Pitman.

113 A. G. Scherer & G. Palazzo, 2011, The new political roll of business in a globalized world: A review of a new perspective on CSR and its implications for the firm, governance, and democracy, *Journal of Management Studies*, 48: 899–931; R. K. Mitchell, B. R. Agle, & D. J. Wood, 1997, Toward a theory of stakeholder identification and salience: Defining the principle of who and what really count, *Academy of Management Review*, 22: 853–886.

114 Y. Deutsch, T. Keil, & T. Laamanen, 2011, A dual agency view of board compensation: The joint effects of outside director and CEO stock options on firm risk, *Strategic Management Journal*, 32: 212–227; P. Shrivastava, 1995, Ecocentric management for a risk society, *Academy of Management Review*, 20: 119.

115 D. Lovallo, C. Clarke, & C. Camerer, 2012, Robust analogizing and the outside view: Two empirical tests of case-based decision making, *Strategic Management Journal*, 33: in press; P. Bromiley, K. D. Miller, & D. Rau, 2001, Risk in strategic management research, in M. A. Hitt, R. E. Freeman, & J. S. Harrison (eds.), *Handbook of Strategic Management*, Oxford, UK: Blackwell Publishers, 259–288.

116 W. F. Sharpe, 1966, Mutual fund performance, *Journal of Business*, January, 119–138; J. L. Treynor, 1965, How to rate mutual fund performance, *Harvard Business Review*, January–February: 63–75.

117 A. B. Markle, 2011, Dysfunctional learning in decision processes: The case of employee reciprocity, *Strategic Management Journal*, 32: 1411–1425; K. Mossholder, H. A. Richardson, & R. P. Settoon, 2011, Human resource systems and helping in organizations: A relational perspective, *Academy of Management Review*, 36: 33–52.

118 M. Pirson & D. Malhotra, 2011, Foundations of organizational trust: What matters to different stakeholders? *Organization Science*, 22: 1087–1104; S. Maitlis, 2005, The social process of organizational sensemaking, *Academy of Management Journal*, 48: 21–49.

119 K. J. Murhpy & M. C. Jensen, 2011, CEO bonus plans: And how to fix them, Harvard Business School NOM unit working paper, http://www.ssrn.com/abstracct=1935654, November 19; M. C. Jensen, 2001, Value maximization, stakeholder theory, and the corporate objective function, *European Financial Management*, 7(3): 297–317.

120 S. Ansari, K. Munir, & T. Gregg, 2012, Impact at the 'bottom of the pyramid': The role of social capital in capability development and community empowerment, *Journal of Management Studies*, 49: in press; M. E. Porter & M. R. Kramer, 2006, Strategy and society: The link between competitive advantage and corporate social responsibility, *Harvard Business Review*, 84(12): 78–92.

121 E. M. Wong, M. E. Ormiston, & P. E. Tetlock, 2011, The effects of top management team integrative complexity and decentralized decision making on corporate social performance, *Academy of Management Journal*, 54: 1207–1228; G. Kassinis & N. Vafeas,

2006, Stakeholder pressures and environmental performance, *Academy of Management Journal*, 49: 145–159.

122. B. Tomson & J. Jargon, 2012, McDonald's asks farmers for a kinder McRib, *Wall Street Journal Online*, http://www.wsj.com, February 14.

123. A. Thomas, 2012, Walmart sustainability: The green room, http://www.walmart.com, February 18.

124. J. Kho, 2012, Report: More corporations turn to sustainability for competitive edge and profits, *Forbes*, http://www.forbes.com, January 24.

125. P. Capozucca & W. Sarni, 2012, Sustainability 2.0, *Deloitte Review*, Issue 10.

126. 2012, Global 100 Most sustainable corporations in the world, http://www.global100.org, February 1.

127. 2012, Our approach to sustainability, *Novo Nordisk A/S*, http://www.novonordisk.com, February 10.

128. J. A. Adegbesan & M. J. Higgins, 2011, The intra-alliance division of value created through collaboration, *Strategic Management Journal*, 32: 187–211; M. Blyler & R. W. Coff, 2003, Dynamic capabilities, social capital, and rent appropriation: Ties that split pies, *Strategic Management Journal*, 24: 677–686; R. Coff, 1999, When competitive advantage doesn't lead to performance: The resource-based view and stakeholder bargaining power, *Organization Science*, 10: 119–133.

129. G. T. Lumpkin & K. H. Brigham, 2011, Long-term orientation and intertemporal choice in family firms, *Entrepreneurship Theory and Practice*, 35: 1149–1169; S. J. Chang, 2003, Ownership structure, expropriation, and performance of group-affiliated companies in Korea, *Academy of Management Journal*, 46: 238–253.

PART 3

CREATING COMPETITIVE ADVANTAGE

CHAPTER 5   Business-Level Strategy   142
CHAPTER 6   Competitive Rivalry and Competitive Dynamics   172
CHAPTER 7   Cooperative Strategy   200
CHAPTER 8   Corporate-Level Strategy   225
CHAPTER 9   Acquisition and Restructuring Strategies   257
CHAPTER 10 International Strategy   284

Chapter **5**

BUSINESS-LEVEL STRATEGY

KNOWLEDGE OBJECTIVES

Studying this chapter should provide you with the strategic management knowledge needed to:

1. Define business-level strategies.

2. Discuss the relationship between customers and business-level strategies in terms of who, what, and how.

3. Explain the differences among business-level strategies.

4. Describe the relationships between strategy and structure.

5. Discuss the simple and functional structures used to implement business-level strategies.

6. Use the five forces model of competition to explain how value can be created through each business-level strategy.

7. Describe the risks of using each of the business-level strategies.

Strategy is concerned with making choices among two or more alternatives.[1] When choosing a strategy, the firm decides to pursue one course of action instead of others. Indeed, the main point of strategy is to help decision makers choose among the competing priorities and alternatives facing their firms. The choices are important, as an established link exists between a firm's strategies and its long-term performance. The fundamental objective of all strategies is to create value for stakeholders. Each strategy used should specify desired outcomes and how they are to be achieved.[2] Strategies are purposeful, precede the taking of actions to which they apply, and demonstrate a shared understanding of the firm's strategic intent and strategic mission.[3]

The chapters in this part of this book explore several types of strategies. **Business-level strategy**, the focus of this chapter, is an integrated and coordinated set of commitments and actions the firm uses to gain a competitive advantage by exploiting core competencies in specific product markets.[4] Consequently, every firm needs a business-level strategy for each of the markets in which it competes. Business-level strategy is described by five basic approaches that combine the scope of an organization's activities in the market (broad or narrow) with the primary source of its competitive advantage (low cost or uniqueness).[5] Business-level strategies provide a basic approach to the market; however, there is also a dynamic aspect of competitive strategy that is defined by the particular actions and reactions of firms in a market. Chapter 6 covers *competitive rivalry and competitive dynamics. Cooperative strategies* fall within the topic area of competitive dynamics, but they are so important in today's business environment that Chapter 7 is devoted to them.

Whereas, business-level strategies and competitive dynamics relate to competition in particular product markets, determining the markets in which a firm will compete is the domain of *corporate-level strategy*, the topic of Chapter 8. *Acquisitions and restructuring*, discussed in Chapter 9, are among the vehicles firms use to carry out a corporate-level strategy. For instance, if a firm decides to enter a new market, it might pursue an acquisition in that market. On the other hand, it might restructure to move out of certain products or markets. Finally, Chapter 10 deals with *international strategies*, which apply at both the business and corporate levels of a firm.

The strategies in these chapters can also be understood in terms of the five major elements of strategy described in Chapter 2.[6] (1) *Arenas* deal with the question, "Where will we be active (and with how much emphasis)?" This question is answered through a firm's corporate-level and international strategies. (2) *Vehicles* ask, "How will we get there?" Acquisition and restructuring strategies facilitate execution of the corporate-level strategy, whereas cooperative strategies are vehicles for business-level strategy. (3) *Differentiators*, described in depth in this chapter, address the issue of "How will we win?" (4) *Staging* deals with the question, "What will be our speed and sequence of moves?" Competitive rivalry and competitive dynamics address this important aspect of strategy. (5) Finally, *economic logic* asks, "How will we achieve above-average returns?" To some extent each of the strategies deals with this question because they share a common theme: how to create competitive advantage—a topic explored thoroughly in this chapter. Business-level strategy is based on the economic logic behind a firm's actions in a particular product market. In this sense, business-level strategy can be thought of as the firm's core strategy in each market or industry.[7]

This chapter begins with a discussion of the economic logic behind the selection of a business-level strategy. Because of the strategic importance of customers in the strategy selection process, we then focus on these stakeholders. Specifically, a business-level strategy determines (1) *who* will be served, (2) *what* customer needs the strategy will satisfy, and (3) *how* those needs will be satisfied. We then introduce how organizational structures are related to business-level strategy and discuss the five basic business-level strategies in detail. Our analysis of these strategies describes how the effective use of each strategy allows the firm to favorably position itself relative to the five competitive forces in the industry (see Chapter 3). We introduce and explain organizational structures that are linked with successful use of each business-level strategy, and then we use the value chain (see Chapter 4) to show examples of the primary and support activities that are needed to implement each one. We also describe the different risks firms may encounter when using one of these strategies.

ECONOMIC LOGIC AND BUSINESS-LEVEL STRATEGY

A business-level strategy reflects where and how the firm has an advantage over its rivals. An effectively formulated strategy marshals, integrates, and allocates the firm's resources, capabilities, and competencies so that it will be properly aligned with its external environment.[8] In the end, sound strategic choices that reduce the uncertainty a firm faces and facilitate its success are the foundations upon which successful strategies are built.[9] Only firms that continuously upgrade their capabilities (on which their competitive advantages are based) over time are able to achieve long-term success with their business-level strategies.[10] Accordingly, information about a host of variables, including markets, customers, technology, worldwide finance, and the changing world economy, must be collected and analyzed to properly form, use, and revise business-level strategies.[11]

Key issues the firm must address when choosing a business-level strategy are which good or service to offer customers, how to manufacture or create it, and how to distribute it to the marketplace. The essence of a firm's business-level strategy is "choosing to perform activities differently or to perform different activities than rivals."[12] Thus, the firm's business-level strategy is a deliberate choice about how it will perform the value chain's primary and support activities in ways that create unique value.[13] Value is delivered to customers when the firm is able to use the capabilities that serve as a base for competitive advantages resulting from the integration of activities.

Types of Business-Level Strategy

Firms choose from among five business-level strategies to establish and defend their desired strategic position against rivals: *cost leadership, differentiation, focused cost leadership, focused differentiation, and integrated cost leadership/differentiation* (see Figure 5.1). These five strategies are sometimes called generic because they can be used in any business and in any industry.[14] Each business-level strategy helps the firm to establish and exploit a competitive advantage within a particular competitive scope.

When selecting a business-level strategy, a firm evaluates two types of potential competitive advantage: "lower cost than rivals, or the ability to differentiate and command a premium price that exceeds the extra cost of doing so."[15] Having lower cost derives from the firm's ability to perform activities in ways that are more efficient than their rivals; being able to differentiate indicates the firm's capacity to perform different (and valuable) activities from those of rivals.[16] Competitive advantage is thus based on the lowest cost (often offering the lowest price) or on the distinctiveness of the product. In either case, they must offer superior value to the customer in order to have a competitive advantage.

The second dimension of the strategy is the target market, either a broad market or a narrow market (see Figure 5.1). Usually firms serving a broad market use their capabilities to create value for customers on an industry-wide basis. Alternatively, targeting a narrow market segment suggests that the firm is serving the needs of a narrowly-defined customer group. With focus strategies, the firm "selects a segment or group of segments in the industry and tailors its strategy to serving them to the exclusion of others."[17] As shown in Figure 5.1, the firm can also develop a combined low cost/distinctiveness approach to create value for customers in several market segments but not the whole industry. This approach is called an integrated cost leadership/differentiated strategy.

None of the five business-level strategies is inherently or universally superior to the others.[18] The effectiveness of each strategy is contingent both on the

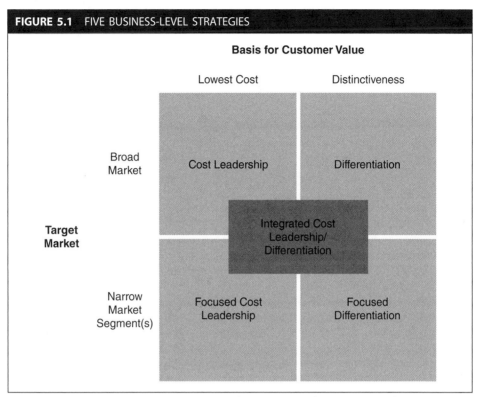

FIGURE 5.1 FIVE BUSINESS-LEVEL STRATEGIES

Basis for Customer Value

	Lowest Cost	Distinctiveness
Broad Market	Cost Leadership	Differentiation
	Integrated Cost Leadership/ Differentiation	
Narrow Market Segment(s)	Focused Cost Leadership	Focused Differentiation

(Target Market)

SOURCE: Based on M. E. Porter, 1998, *Competitive Advantage: Creating and Sustaining Superior Performance*, New York: The Free Press; D. G. Sirmon, M. A. Hitt, & R. D. Ireland, 2007, Managing firm resources in dynamic environments to create value: Looking inside the black box, *Academy of Management Review*, 32: 273–292; D. G. Sirmon, M. A. Hitt, R. D. Ireland & B. A. Gilbert, 2011, Resource orchestration to create competitive advantage: Breadth, depth and life cycles effects, *Journal of Management*, 37: 1390–1412. © Copyrighted 2011 by Michael A. Hitt, R. Duane Ireland, and Robert E. Hoskisson.

opportunities and threats in a firm's external environment and on the possibilities provided by the firm's unique resources, capabilities, and core competencies.[19] It is critical, therefore, for the firm to select an appropriate strategy in light of its opportunities, threats, and competencies.

Serving Customers

Orientation toward customers is the foundation of all successful business-level strategies. The "basis for customer value" deals with the question of whether firms will try to satisfy their customers through focusing on low costs (and presumably lower prices) or creating distinctive features that are highly attractive. Whereas, the target market examines the nature and size of the customer group the firm seeks.

Strategic competitiveness results only when the firm is able to satisfy a group of customers by using its capabilities to compete in individual product markets. Firms must satisfy customers through their business-level strategies because the returns earned from relationships with customers are the lifeblood of all organizations.[20] The most successful companies constantly seek to chart new competitive space in order to serve new customers as they simultaneously try to find ways to better serve existing customers. Since Howard Schultz reacquired the CEO position at Starbuck's, the company has introduced a steady stream of new ideas on better ways to serve existing customers and new products to capture and serve new customers.[21]

The firm's relationships with its customers are strengthened when it is committed to offering them superior value.[22] In business-to-business transactions, superior value is often created when the firm's product helps its customers to develop a new competitive advantage or to enhance the value of its existing competitive advantages. Receiving superior value enhances customers' loyalty to the firm that provides it. Evidence suggests that loyalty has a positive relationship with profitability. Norm Brodsky, a veteran entrepreneur who has had three businesses listed in *Inc.* magazine's list of the 500 fastest-growing companies, puts it this way: "There is a basic rule of business that's easy to forget, especially when you're competing for customers. Winning is not just about closing the sale. You win when you close the sale and also lay the foundation for a good relationship that will allow you to keep your customer for a long, long time."[23]

A number of companies have become skilled at the art of managing all aspects of their relationship with customers. In the fast-paced, technologically sophisticated global economy, firms that participate in e-commerce can understand their customers and manage their relationships with them more effectively than can companies without an Internet presence. The probability of successful competition increases when the firm carefully integrates Internet technology with its strategy, rather than using Internet technology on a "stand-alone basis."[24] Amazon.com fits this description quite well. It manages for the long term by trying to build customer satisfaction (using exciting new products such as the Kindle Fire) and loyalty by learning about its customers' needs and desires and providing opportunities to them (e.g., maintaining information on their purchasing behavior and offering new products and services in the same genre).[25] Effective management of customer relationships, especially in this era of e-commerce, helps the firm answer questions related to the issues of who, what, and how to serve.

From a business-level strategy perspective, customer relationships involve answering questions related to *who, what,* and *how.*

Who: Determining the Customers to Serve. A crucial decision related to a business-level strategy is the one a company makes about *who*, or which customers, to target for the firm's goods or services.[26] To make this decision, companies divide customers into groups based on differences in the customers' needs (discussed in the sections that follow). This process, called **market segmentation**, clusters people with similar needs into individual and identifiable groups.[27] As part of its business-level strategy, the firm develops a marketing program to effectively sell products to a target customer group.

Almost any identifiable human or organizational characteristic can be used to subdivide a market into segments that differ from one another on a given characteristic. Table 5.1 lists common characteristics on which customers' needs vary. On the basis of their core competencies and opportunities in the external environment, companies choose a business-level strategy to deliver value to target customers and satisfy their specific needs. For example, companies in the automobile industry

TABLE 5.1 BASIS FOR CUSTOMER SEGMENTATION

CONSUMER MARKETS
1. Demographic factors (age, income, sex, etc.)
2. Socioeconomic factors (social class, stage in the family life cycle)
3. Geographic factors (cultural, regional, and national differences)
4. Psychological factors (lifestyle, personality traits)
5. Consumption patterns (heavy, moderate, and light users)
6. Perceptual factors (benefit segmentation, perceptual mapping)

INDUSTRIAL MARKETS
1. End-use segments (identified by SIC code)
2. Product segments (based on technological differences or production economics)
3. Geographic segments (defined by boundaries between countries or by regional differences within them)
4. Common buying factor segments (cut across product market and geographic segments)
5. Customer size segments

SOURCE: From JAIN, Marketing Planning and Strategy, 6E. © 2000 Cengage Learning.

segment markets use demographic factors, such as income and age; socioeconomic factors, such as stage in family life cycle; and psychological factors, such as lifestyle. Rolls-Royce and Porsche both appeal to wealthy individuals; however, Rolls-Royce focuses on older people and Porsche appeals to the young at heart.[28] Most of the major automobile companies have created separate product lines, with associated business infrastructures, to appeal to different segments of the market. Toyota created its Lexus line and Honda its Acura line specifically to compete with BMW, Mercedes and Cadillac autos, which appeal to people with higher incomes.

What: Determining Which Customer Needs to Satisfy. As a firm decides who it will serve, it must simultaneously identify *what* the targeted customer group needs that its goods or services can satisfy.[29] The two generalized forms of value that products provide are low cost with acceptable features or highly differentiated features with acceptable cost. For instance, in the department store retail market, Walmart appeals to value-conscious consumers, whereas Saks Fifth Avenue seeks to appeal to consumers who expect the latest fashions and the highest quality merchandise.[30] Similarly, Apple Computer's strategy is to develop products that are highly differentiated. Its major competitors, such as Hewlett-Packard, Amazon, and Research in Motion (RIM), focus on differentiation as well but with some products also try to offer lower prices by managing costs to gain an advantage. Thus, the composition of competitors may lead to firms with similar capabilities earning different returns.[31] Providing value to customers involves several attributes including the quality of the service accompanying the product.[32]

How: Determining Core Competencies Necessary to Satisfy Customer Needs. *How* is addressed through core competencies, or the resources and capabilities that serve as a source of competitive advantage for the firm over its rivals (see Chapters 1 and 4). Firms use core competencies to implement value-creating strategies and thereby satisfy customers' needs. Only those firms with the capacity to continuously improve, innovate, and upgrade their competencies can expect to meet and, it is hoped, exceed customers' expectations across time.[33]

SAS Institute is the world's largest privately owned software company. Its programs are used for data warehousing, data mining, and decision support. Allocating more than 30 percent of revenues to R&D, the firm relies on its core competence in this area to satisfy the data-related needs of customers such as the Royal Bank of Canada, GE Healthcare, and a host of firms in other industries (e.g., communications, insurance, utilities).[34] All organizations, including SAS, must be able to use their core competencies (the *how*) to satisfy the needs (the *what*) of the target group of customers (the *who*) that the firm has chosen to serve by using its business-level strategy. Much of the success of any strategy, business-level or corporate-level (Chapter 8), depends on its implementation. Customers must believe that the firm can and does meet their needs (reputation).[35] But before we discuss each of the business-level strategies in detail, we introduce some of the structures that will be used to examine how each strategy can be implemented.

Strategy and Structure

Research shows that organizational structure and the controls that are a part of it affect firm performance.[36] In particular, when the firm's strategy is not matched with the most appropriate structure and controls, performance declines.[37] **Organizational structure** specifies the firm's formal reporting relationships, procedures, controls, and authority and decision-making processes.[38] Developing an organizational structure that will effectively support the firm's strategy is difficult, especially because of the uncertainty about cause–effect relationships in the global economy's rapidly changing and dynamic competitive environments. When a structure's elements (e.g., reporting relationships, procedures, and so forth) are properly aligned with one another, that structure facilitates effective implementation of the firm's strategies.[39]

Strategy and structure have a reciprocal relationship, with structure flowing from the selection of the firm's strategy.[40] Once in place, structure can influence current strategic actions as well as choices about future strategies. The general nature of the strategy–structure relationship means that changes to the firm's strategy create the need to change how the organization completes its work. Additionally, firms must be vigilant in their efforts to verify that the structural requirements for the completion of work are consistent with the implementation requirements of chosen strategies.

Three major types of organizational structures are used to implement strategies: simple structure, functional structure, and multidivisional structure. The **simple structure** is a structure in which the owner-manager makes all major decisions and monitors all activities while the staff serves as an extension of the manager's supervisory authority. Typically, the owner-manager actively works in the business on a daily basis. Informal relationships, few rules, limited task specialization, and modest information systems describe the simple structure. Frequent and informal communications between the owner-manager and employees make it relatively easy to coordinate the work that is to be done.

As the small firm grows and becomes more complex, managerial and structural challenges emerge, and firms tend to change from the simple structure to a functional organizational structure.[41] The **functional structure** consists of a chief executive officer and a limited corporate staff, with functional line managers in dominant organizational areas such as production, accounting, marketing, R&D, engineering, and human resources.[42] This structure allows for functional specialization, thereby facilitating active sharing of knowledge within each functional area.[43] Knowledge sharing facilitates career paths as well as the professional development of functional specialists. However, a functional orientation can have a negative effect on communication and coordination among those representing different organizational functions. Because of this, the CEO must work hard to verify that the decisions and actions of individual business functions promote the entire firm rather than a single function.[44] The functional structure supports implementation of the business-level strategies described in this chapter and some corporate-level strategies (e.g., single or dominant business, described in Chapter 8) with low levels of product diversification.

With continuing growth and success, firms often consider greater levels of diversification. Successful diversification requires analysis of growing amounts of data and information when the firm offers the same products in different markets (market or geographic diversification) or offers different products in several markets (product diversification). In addition, trying to manage high levels of diversification through functional structures creates serious coordination and control problems.[45] Thus, greater diversification often requires a different structural form.[46] The **multidivisional structure** (M-form) consists of operating divisions, each representing a separate business or profit center in which the top corporate officer delegates responsibilities for day-to-day operations and business-unit strategy to division managers. Each division represents a distinct, self-contained business with its own functional hierarchy. This structure and its variants in relationship to corporate-level strategy are described in Chapter 8.

We now discuss each business-level strategy and the structures they require.

COST LEADERSHIP STRATEGY

The **cost leadership strategy** is an integrated set of actions designed to produce or deliver goods or services with features that are acceptable to customers at the lowest cost, relative to that of competitors.[47] In terms of the two characteristics that define business-level strategies, basis for customer value and target market, low-cost leaders seek cost advantages while serving a broad customer segment. Europe's Ryanair Holdings is possibly *the* low-cost leader in passenger air travel. Ryanair makes its flight crew members buy their own uniforms and charges customers for a bottle of water. All passengers must check in online as no check-in counters are available at airports. Flight attendants use flight time to increase revenues by selling products such as digital cameras. Ryanair experienced a 10 percent increase to 72 million passengers in 2010. Overtime, the airline has enjoyed strong profitability as well.[48]

Successful Execution of the Cost Leadership Strategy

Firms using the cost leadership strategy sell no-frills, standardized goods or services to the industry's most typical customers. Although cost leadership implies keeping costs as low as possible, products and services provided by a firm pursuing cost leadership must still have qualities and features that customers find acceptable.[49] For instance, even the lowest cost automobiles must meet minimum standards for safety and include features that customers expect from all automobiles, such as a reliable radio, a spare tire, and some level of comfort. Indeed, emphasizing cost reductions while ignoring competitive features will be unsuccessful. At the extreme, concentrating only on reducing costs could result in very efficiently producing products that no customer wants to purchase. When the firm designs, produces, and markets a comparable product more efficiently than its rivals, it is likely using the cost leadership strategy.[50]

As described in Chapter 4, firms use value chain analysis to determine the parts of the company's operations that create value and those that do not. Cost leaders concentrate on finding ways to lower their costs relative to those of their competitors by constantly rethinking how to complete their primary and support activities to reduce costs further while still maintaining important features.[51] Figure 5.2 demonstrates the primary and support activities that allow a firm to create value through the cost leadership strategy. Companies unable to link the activities shown

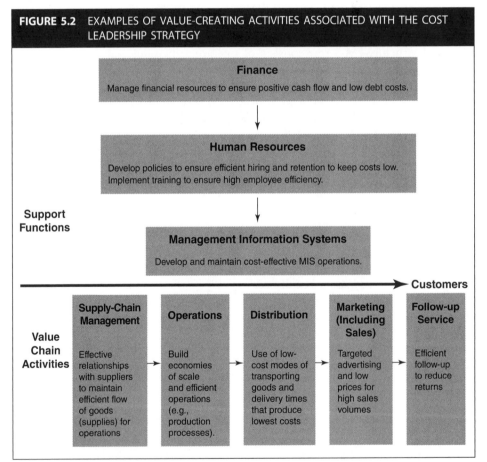

FIGURE 5.2   EXAMPLES OF VALUE-CREATING ACTIVITIES ASSOCIATED WITH THE COST LEADERSHIP STRATEGY

SOURCE: Based on M. E. Porter, 1998, *Competitive Advantage: Creating and Sustaining Superior Performance*, New York: The Free Press; D. G. Sirmon, M. A. Hitt & R. D. Ireland, 2007, Managing firm resources in dynamic environments to create value: Looking inside the black box, *Academy of Management Review*, 32: 273–292; D. G. Sirmon, M. A. Hitt, R. D. Ireland & B. A. Gilbert, 2011, Resource orchestration to create competitive advantage: Breadth, depth and life cycles effects, *Journal of Management*, 37: 1390–1412. © Copyrighted 2011 by Michael A. Hitt, R. Duane Ireland, and Robert E. Hoskisson.

in this figure typically lack the resources, capabilities, and core competencies needed to successfully use the cost leadership strategy.

As primary value chain activities, managing the relationships with suppliers, operating efficient processes (manufacturing or providing the service), distributing the products, marketing them, and providing follow-up service often account for significant portions of the total cost of the goods and services. Research suggests that having a competitive advantage in terms of the primary activities creates more value when using the cost leadership strategy than when using the differentiation strategy (discussed in the sections that follow).[52] Thus, cost leaders seeking to reduce costs to gain a competitive advantage may want to concentrate on the primary value chain activities.

Cost leaders also carefully examine all support activities to find additional sources of potential cost reductions. Management information systems can facilitate successful use of the cost leadership strategy. An example is the development of new systems for low cost and acceptable quality information required to perform and integrate all of the activities necessary to produce and distribute the firm's goods or services to its customers.

In recent times, a common means of reducing costs is by outsourcing one or more of the primary or secondary activities involved in the value chain. Although outsourcing may be the result of a planned strategy, it is more often based on a need to reduce costs in reaction to competitors' strategic moves.[53] In such cases, firms frequently search for outsourcing suppliers in countries with lower-cost labor and operations.[54] Thus, manufacturing may be outsourced to a Chinese company and information systems activities may be outsourced to an Indian company.[55]

Big Lots Inc. uses the cost leadership strategy. With its vision being "Helping people connect with their inner bargain self," Big Lots is the largest broad-line closeout discount chain in the United States. Operating under the format names of Big Lots, Big Lots Furniture, Wisconsin Toy, Consolidated International, Big Lots Capital, and Big Lots Wholesale, the firm strives constantly to maintain very low costs by relying on what some analysts see as a highly disciplined merchandise cost and inventory management system. The firm's stores sell name-brand products at prices that are 15 to 35 percent lower than those of discount retailers and roughly 70 percent lower than those of traditional retailers.[56]

Effective use of the cost leadership strategy allows a firm to create value despite the presence of strong competitive forces described in the five forces model of competition (see Chapter 3). We now turn to how firms are able to do this, examining each of the five forces.

Rivalry with Existing Competitors. Having the low-cost position is a valuable defense against rivals. Because of the cost leader's advantageous position, rivals hesitate to compete on the basis of price. Walmart is known for its ability to both control and reduce costs, making it difficult for firms to compete against it on the basis of price. Kmart's inability to compete against Walmart on the basis of cost led to its bankruptcy and eventually its merger with Sears. However, the new company continued to have difficulty competing with Walmart in terms of cost because of Walmart's comparative advantage in logistics. As a result, the corporation announced the closing of 81 Sears and Kmart stores in 2012.[57]

Bargaining Power of Buyers (Customers). Powerful customers can force a cost leader to reduce its prices, but not below the level at which the cost leader's next-most-efficient industry competitor can earn average returns. Although powerful customers might be able to force the cost leader to reduce prices even below this level, they probably would not choose to do so. Prices that are low enough to prevent the next-most-efficient competitor from earning average returns would force that firm to exit the market, leaving the cost leader with less competition and in a stronger position. Customers would thus lose their power and pay higher prices when they are forced to purchase from a single firm operating in an industry without competitive rivals.

Bargaining Power of Suppliers. The cost leader operates with margins greater than those of competitors. Among other benefits, higher margins relative to those of competitors make it possible for the cost leader to absorb its suppliers' price increases. When an industry faces substantial increases in the cost of its supplies, only the cost leader may be able to pay the higher prices and continue to earn either average or above-average returns. Alternatively, a powerful cost leader may be able to force its suppliers to hold down their prices, which reduce the suppliers' margins in the process.

Potential Entrants. Through continuous efforts to reduce costs to levels that are lower than those of its competitors, a cost leader becomes highly efficient. Because ever-improving levels of efficiency enhance profit margins, they serve as a significant entry barrier to potential competitors. New entrants must be willing and able to accept average to below-average returns until they gain the experience required to approach the cost leader's efficiency. To earn even average returns, new entrants must have the capabilities required to match the cost levels of competitors other than the cost leader. The low profit margins (relative to margins earned by firms implementing the differentiation strategy) make it necessary for the cost leader to sell large volumes of its products to create value. However, firms striving to be the cost leader must avoid pricing their products so low that their ability to operate profitably is reduced, even though volume increases.

Product Substitutes. Compared with its industry rivals, the cost leader also holds an attractive position in terms of product substitutes. A product substitute becomes an issue for the cost leader when its features and characteristics are potentially attractive to the firm's customers. When faced with possible substitutes, the cost leader has more flexibility than its competitors. To retain customers, it can reduce the price of its good or service. With still lower prices and competitive levels of differentiation, the cost leader increases the probability that customers will prefer its product rather than a substitute.

Using the Functional Structure to Implement the Cost Leadership Strategy

Different forms of the functional organizational structure are used to support implementation of the cost leadership, differentiation, and integrated cost leadership/differentiation strategies. The differences in these forms are accounted for primarily by different uses of three important structural characteristics or dimensions: *specialization* (concerned with the type and number of jobs required to complete work[58]), *centralization* (the degree to which decision-making authority is retained at higher managerial levels), and *formalization* (the degree to which formal rules and procedures govern work[59]).

Firms using the cost leadership strategy want to sell large quantities of standardized products to an industry's or a segment's typical customer. The following features characterize the cost leadership form of the functional structure: simple reporting relationships, few layers in the decision-making and authority structure, a centralized corporate staff, and a strong focus on process improvements through the manufacturing function rather than the development of new products through an emphasis on product R&D (see Figure 5.3).[60] This structure contributes to the emergence of a low-cost culture—a culture in which all employees constantly try to find ways to reduce the costs incurred to complete their work.

In terms of centralization, decision-making authority is centralized in a staff function to maintain a cost-reducing emphasis within each organizational function (for example, engineering, marketing, etc.). While encouraging continuous cost reductions, the centralized staff also verifies that further cuts in costs in one function will not adversely affect the productivity levels in other functions.

Jobs are highly specialized in the cost leadership functional structure. Job specialization is accomplished by dividing work into homogeneous subgroups.

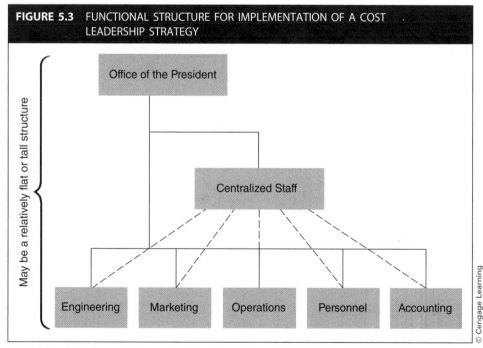

FIGURE 5.3   FUNCTIONAL STRUCTURE FOR IMPLEMENTATION OF A COST LEADERSHIP STRATEGY

May be a relatively flat or tall structure

Office of the President

Centralized Staff

Engineering   Marketing   Operations   Personnel   Accounting

© Cengage Learning

NOTES:
▸ Operations is the main function
▸ Process engineering is emphasized rather than new product R&D
▸ Relatively large centralized staff coordinates functions
▸ Formalized procedures allow for emergence of a low-cost culture
▸ Overall structure is mechanical; job roles are highly structured

Organizational functions are the most common subgroup, although work is sometimes batched on the basis of products produced or clients served. Specializing in their work allows employees to increase their efficiency, reducing the firm's costs as a result. Highly formalized rules and procedures, often emanating from the centralized staff, guide the work completed in the cost leadership form of the functional structure. Predictably following formal rules and procedures creates cost-reducing efficiencies.

Competitive Risks of the Cost Leadership Strategy

The cost leadership strategy is not risk free. One risk is that the processes the cost leader uses to produce and distribute its good or service could become obsolete because of innovations by its competitors. Obsolescence is even greater if the firm outsources major activities because they lose those capabilities, making it more difficult for them to innovate in the other activities that they keep.[61] Innovations may allow rivals to produce at costs lower than those of the original cost leader, or to provide additional differentiated features without increasing the product's price to customers.

A second risk is that the cost leader may focus on cost reductions at the expense of trying to understand customers' perceptions of "competitive levels of differentiation." As noted earlier, Walmart is known for constantly and aggressively reducing its costs. However, the firm must simultaneously remain focused on understanding when a cost-reducing decision to eliminate differentiated features that can create value in a low-cost environment (e.g., extended shopping hours, increases in the number of checkout counters to reduce customer waiting time) could create an unattractive value proposition for customers.

A final risk of the cost leadership strategy concerns imitation. Using their own core competencies (see Chapter 3), competitors sometimes learn how to successfully imitate the cost leader's strategy. In recent years, such imitation by foreign firms in emerging markets (sometimes referred to as emerging economy copycats) has been increasing because they have lower cost labor and lower costs of operation.[62] When this occurs, the cost leader must increase the value that its good or service provides to customers. Commonly, value is increased by selling the current product at an even lower price or by adding differentiated features that customers value while maintaining price.

Even cost leaders must be careful when reducing prices to a still lower level. If the firm prices its good or service at an unrealistically low level (a level at which it will be difficult to retain satisfactory margins), customers' expectations about a reasonable price become difficult to reverse.

DIFFERENTIATION STRATEGY

The **differentiation strategy** is an integrated set of actions designed by a firm to produce or deliver goods or services (at an acceptable cost) that customers perceive as being different in ways that are important to them.[63] The target market is still fairly broad, in that firms that pursue this strategy seek to sell their products to a broad group of customers. Nike follows a differentiation strategy. It continuously innovates to introduce new products and stay ahead of its competition. For example, it introduced its Foamposite Galaxy new shoe in 2012. This new outer-space themed shoe created excitement in the market. Almost 600 people lined up at a store in Indiana to be among the first to purchase the new shoe.[64]

Successful Execution of the Differentiation Strategy

While cost leaders serve an industry's typical customer, differentiators target customers who perceive that value is through the differentiated features of the firm's products. Firms must be able to produce differentiated products at competitive costs, however, to reduce upward pressure on the price customers pay for them. When a product's differentiated features are produced through noncompetitive costs, the price for the product can exceed what the firm's target customers are willing to pay. When the firm has a thorough understanding of what its target customers value, the relative importance they attach to the satisfaction of different needs, and for what they are willing to pay a premium, the differentiation strategy can be successfully used.[65] The key to success in a differentiation strategy is that customers must perceive that the additional cost of a product or service is more than offset by the value provided by its differentiating features.[66] Commonly recognized differentiated goods include Bose stereo equipment, Ralph Lauren clothing, and Caterpillar heavy-duty earth-moving equipment. McKinsey & Co., thought by some to be the world's most expensive and prestigious consulting firm, is a well-known example of a firm that offers differentiated services.

Through the differentiation strategy, the firm produces non-standardized products for customers who value differentiated features more than they value lowest possible cost. For example, superior product reliability and durability and high-performance sound systems are among the differentiated features of Toyota's Lexus products. The often-used Lexus promotional statement—"The Relentless Pursuit of Perfection"—suggests a strong commitment to overall product quality as a source of differentiation.[67] However, Lexus offers its vehicles to customers at a competitive purchase price. As with Lexus products, a good or service's unique attributes, rather than its purchase price, provide the value for which customers are willing to pay. A firm using the differentiation strategy seeks to be different from its competitors on as many dimensions as possible. The less similarity between a firm's goods or services and those of competitors, the more buffered it is from rivals' actions. A product can be differentiated in many ways. Unusual features, responsive customer service, rapid product innovations, technological leadership, perceived prestige and status, different tastes, and engineering design and performance are examples of approaches to differentiation.[68] The ability to sell a good or service at a price that substantially exceeds the cost of creating its differentiated features allows the firm to outperform rivals and create value.

A firm's value chain can be analyzed to determine whether the firm is able to link the activities required to create value by using the differentiation strategy. Figure 5.4 shows examples of value chain and support activities that are commonly used to differentiate a good or service. Companies without the core competencies needed to link these activities cannot expect to successfully use the differentiation

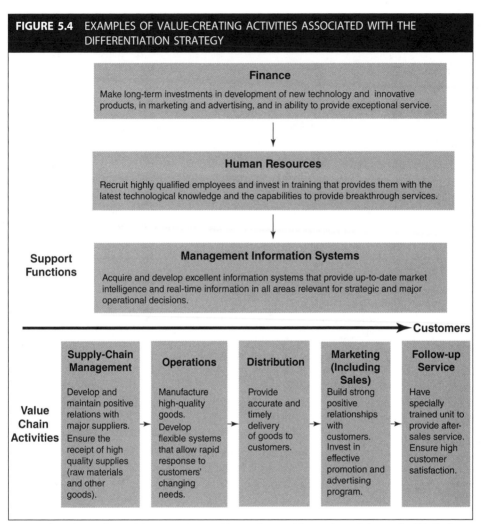

FIGURE 5.4 EXAMPLES OF VALUE-CREATING ACTIVITIES ASSOCIATED WITH THE DIFFERENTIATION STRATEGY

Finance

Make long-term investments in development of new technology and innovative products, in marketing and advertising, and in ability to provide exceptional service.

Human Resources

Recruit highly qualified employees and invest in training that provides them with the latest technological knowledge and the capabilities to provide breakthrough services.

Support Functions

Management Information Systems

Acquire and develop excellent information systems that provide up-to-date market intelligence and real-time information in all areas relevant for strategic and major operational decisions.

→ Customers

Value Chain Activities

Supply-Chain Management	Operations	Distribution	Marketing (Including Sales)	Follow-up Service
Develop and maintain positive relations with major suppliers. Ensure the receipt of high quality supplies (raw materials and other goods).	Manufacture high-quality goods. Develop flexible systems that allow rapid response to customers' changing needs.	Provide accurate and timely delivery of goods to customers.	Build strong positive relationships with customers. Invest in effective promotion and advertising program.	Have specially trained unit to provide after-sales service. Ensure high customer satisfaction.

SOURCE: Based on information from, M. E. Porter, 1998, *Competitive Advantage: Creating and Sustaining Superior Performance*, New York: The Free Press; D. G. Sirmon, M. A. Hitt, & R. D. Ireland, 2007, Managing firm resources in dynamic environments to create value: Looking inside the black box, *Academy of Management Review*, 32: 273–292; D. G. Sirmon, M. A. Hitt, R. D. Ireland, & B. A. Gilbert, 2011, Resource orchestration to create competitive advantage: Breadth, depth and life cycles effects, *Journal of Management*, 37: 1390–1412. © Copyrighted 2011 by Michael A. Hitt, R. Duane Ireland, and Robert E. Hoskisson.

strategy. Next, we explain how firms using the differentiation strategy can successfully position themselves in terms of the five forces of competition (see Chapter 3) to create value.

Rivalry with Existing Competitors. Customers tend to be loyal purchasers of products that are differentiated in ways that are meaningful to them. As their loyalty to a brand increases, their sensitivity to price increases is reduced. This is especially true of those purchasing high-end, big-ticket items (e.g., luxury automobiles and custom interior design services for the home and office). The relationship between brand loyalty and price sensitivity insulates a firm from competitive rivalry. Thus, McKinsey & Co. is insulated from its competitors, even on the basis of price, as long as it continues to satisfy the differentiated needs of its customer group. Bose is insulated from intense rivalry as long as customers continue to perceive that its stereo equipment offers superior sound quality at a competitive price.

Bargaining Power of Buyers (Customers). The uniqueness of differentiated goods or services reduces customers' sensitivity to price increases. Customers are willing to accept a price increase when a product still satisfies their perceived unique needs better than a competitor's offering can. Thus, the golfer whose needs are uniquely satisfied by Callaway golf clubs will likely continue buying those products even if their cost increases. Purchasers of brand-name items (e.g., Heinz ketchup and Kleenex tissues) will continue to purchase them even at higher prices than comparable products as long as they perceive that the extra value they are receiving from those products surpasses the additional costs.

Bargaining Power of Suppliers. Because the firm using the differentiation strategy charges a premium price for its products, suppliers must provide high-quality components, driving up the firm's costs. However, the high margins the firm earns in these cases partially insulate it from the influence of suppliers in that higher supplier costs can be paid through these margins. Alternatively, because of buyers' relative insensitivity to price increases, the differentiated firm might choose to pass the additional cost of supplies on to the customer by increasing the price of its unique product.

Potential Entrants. Customer loyalty and the need to overcome the uniqueness of a differentiated product present substantial entry barriers to potential entrants. Entering an industry under these conditions typically demands significant investments of resources (e.g., financial resources) and patience while seeking customers' loyalty.[69]

Product Substitutes. Firms selling brand-name goods and services to loyal customers are positioned effectively against product substitutes. In contrast, companies without brand loyalty face a higher probability of their customers switching either to products that offer differentiated features that serve the same function (particularly if the substitute has a lower price) or to products that offer additional features and perform more attractive functions.

Using the Functional Structure to Implement the Differentiation Strategy

Firms using the differentiation strategy produce products that customers perceive as different in ways that create value for them. With this strategy, the firm wants to sell nonstandardized products to customers with unique needs. The following features characterize the differentiation form of the functional structure: relatively complex and flexible reporting relationships, frequent use of cross-functional product development teams, and a strong focus on marketing and product R&D rather than manufacturing and process R&D (as with the cost leadership form of the functional structure), as shown in Figure 5.5.[70] This structure contributes to the emergence of a development-oriented culture—a culture in which employees try to find ways to further differentiate current products and to develop new, highly differentiated products.

Continuous product innovation demands that people throughout the firm be able to interpret and take action based on information that is often ambiguous, incomplete, and uncertain.[71] With a strong focus on the external environment to identify new opportunities, employees often gather this information from people outside the firm, such as customers and suppliers. Commonly, rapid responses to the possibilities indicated by the collected information are necessary, suggesting the need for decision-making responsibility and authority to be decentralized. To support creativity and the continuous pursuit of new sources of differentiation and new products, jobs in a functional structure are not highly specialized. This lack of specialization means that workers have a relatively large number of tasks in their job descriptions. Few formal rules and procedures are also characteristic of this structure. Low formalization, decentralization of decision-making authority and responsibility, and low specialization of work tasks combine to create a structure in which people interact frequently to exchange ideas about how to further differentiate current products while developing ideas for new products that can be differentiated to create value for customers.[72]

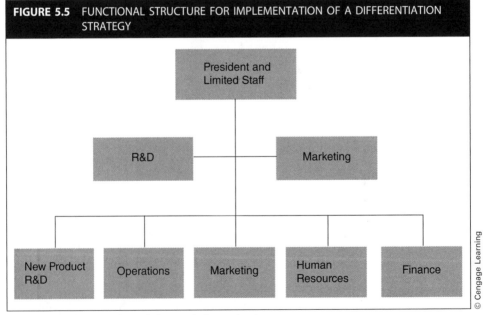

FIGURE 5.5 FUNCTIONAL STRUCTURE FOR IMPLEMENTATION OF A DIFFERENTIATION STRATEGY

© Cengage Learning

NOTES:
▶ Marketing is the main function for keeping track of new product ideas
▶ New product R&D is emphasized
▶ Most functions are decentralized, but R&D and marketing may have centralized staffs that work closely with each other
▶ Formalization is limited so that new product ideas can emerge easily and change is more readily accomplished
▶ Overall structure is organic; job roles are less structured

Competitive Risks of the Differentiation Strategy

As with the other business-level strategies, the differentiation strategy is not risk free. One risk is that customers might decide that the price differential between the differentiator's product and the cost leader's product is too large. In this instance, a firm may be offering differentiated features that exceed target customers' needs. The firm then becomes vulnerable to competitors that are able to offer customers a combination of features and price that is more consistent with their needs.

Another risk of the differentiation strategy is that a firm's means of differentiation may cease to provide value for which customers are willing to pay. A differentiated product becomes less valuable if imitation by rivals causes customers to perceive that competitors offer essentially the same good or service, but at a lower price.[73] For example, the Li Ning Company, the largest sporting goods firm in China, imitated the marketing strategies of its two major competitors, Nike and Addidas. Its slogan, "Anything is possible" is similar to Addidas' slogan "Impossible is nothing". Also Li Ning's logo is very similar to the Nike swoosh.[74]

A third risk of the differentiation strategy is that experience can narrow customers' perceptions of the value of a product's differentiated features. For example, the value of the IBM name provided a differentiated feature for the firm's personal computers for which some users were willing to pay a premium price in the early life cycle of the product. However, as customers familiarized themselves with the product's standard features, and as a host of other firms entered the personal computer market, IBM brand loyalty ceased to create value for which some customers were willing to pay. Competitors offered features similar to those found in the IBM product at a substantially lower price, reducing the attractiveness of IBM's product. Ultimately, IBM sold its PC business to China's Lenovo Group, although IBM kept a stake in the business.[75]

Counterfeiting is the differentiation strategy's fourth risk. Makers of counterfeit goods—products that attempt to convey differentiated features to customers at significantly reduced prices—are a concern for many firms using the differentiation strategy. For example, Callaway Golf Company's success has created great demand for counterfeited Callaway equipment. Companies such as Callaway work with government officials to encourage tighter import regulations to curb the flow of counterfeit products.

FOCUS STRATEGIES

Firms choose a **focus strategy** when they want their core competencies to serve the needs of a particular industry segment or niche at the exclusion of others. Examples of specific market segments that can be targeted by a focus strategy include (1) a particular buyer group (e.g., youths or senior citizens), (2) a different segment of a product line (e.g., products for professional painters or those for "do-it-yourselfers"), or (3) a different geographic market (e.g., the East or the West in the United States).[76] Thus, the focus strategy is an integrated set of actions designed to produce or deliver goods or services that serve the needs of a particular competitive segment.

Although the breadth of a target is clearly a matter of degree, the essence of the focus strategy "is the exploitation of a narrow target's differences from the balance of the industry."[77] Firms using the focus strategy intend to serve a particular segment of an industry more effectively than can industry-wide competitors. They succeed when they effectively serve a segment whose unique needs are so specialized that broad-based competitors choose not to serve that segment or when they satisfy the needs of a segment being served poorly by industry-wide competitors.

Through successful use of the focus strategy, firms gain a competitive advantage in specific market niches or segments, even though they do not possess an industry-wide competitive advantage. Firms can create value for customers in specific and unique market segments by using the *focused cost leadership strategy* or the *focused differentiation strategy*.

Focused Cost Leadership Strategy

Based in Sweden, IKEA, an international furniture retailer, follows the focused cost leadership strategy.[78] Young buyers desiring style at a low cost are Ikea's primary market segment. For these customers, Ikea offers home furnishings that combine good design, function, and acceptable quality with low prices. Instead of relying on third-party manufacturers, the firm's engineers design low-cost, modular furniture ready for assembly by customers. Ikea also displays its products in room-like settings, which reduces the need for sales associates or decorators to help the customer imagine how a batch of furniture will look when placed in the customer's home. This approach requires fewer sales personnel, allowing Ikea to keep its costs low. A third practice that keeps Ikea's costs low is expecting customers to transport their own purchases rather than providing delivery service. Ikea makes sure that its services and products "are uniquely aligned with the needs of (its) customers, who are young, are not wealthy, are likely to have children (but no nanny), and, because they work for a living, need to shop at odd hours."[79]

Focused Differentiation Strategy

Other firms implement the focused differentiation strategy in the pursuit of competitive advantage. As noted earlier, firms can differentiate their products in many ways. Harley-Davidson focuses on older consumers with an adventurous spirit. In fact, more than 60 percent of its sales are to buyers age 35 and older. Harley differentiates its motorcycles through quality and image rather than speed. It makes frequent improvements to existing models and introduces new models on a regular basis. Despite all these improvements, Harley's motorcycles still have the look and feel of a Harley. Despite their high price tags, Harley motorcycles are still growing in popularity. In 2011, sales grew in double digits, and even in Japan, home of rivals Honda and Suzuki, Harley owns the top spot in the big bike segment. In fact, the company projects that 40 percent of its sales will be outside the U.S. by 2014.[80]

Similar to the focused cost leadership strategy, the focused differentiation strategy also applies to service and to manufacturing firms. Firms must be able to complete various value chain and support activities in a competitively superior manner to achieve and sustain a competitive advantage and create value with a focus strategy. The activities required to use the focused cost leadership strategy are virtually identical to those shown in Figure 5.2, and the activities required to use the focused differentiation strategy are virtually identical to those shown in Figure 5.4. Similarly, each of the two focus strategies allows a firm to deal successfully with the five competitive forces in a manner parallel to that described with respect to the cost leadership strategy and the differentiation strategy. The only difference is that the target market changes from an industry-wide market to a narrow market segment. Thus, a review of Figures 5.2 and 5.4 and the text regarding the five competitive forces yields a description of the relationship between each of the two focus strategies and competitive advantage.

Using the Simple or Functional Structures to Implement Focus Strategies

The simple structure is matched with focus strategies as firms compete by offering a single product line in a single geographic market. Local restaurants, repair businesses, and other specialized enterprises are examples of firms relying on the simple structure to implement their strategy. However, as firms grow larger, a functional structure will be required. If they pursue a focused cost leadership or focused differentiation strategy, they will implement the functional structures as illustrated in Figure 5.3 or Figure 5.5, respectively.

Competitive Risks of Focus Strategies

With either focus strategy, the firm faces the same general risks as does the company using the cost leadership or the differentiation strategy on an industry-wide basis. However, focus strategies have three additional risks.

First, a competitor may be able to focus on a more narrowly defined competitive segment and "outfocus" the focuser. For example, Big Dog Motorcycles is trying to outfocus Harley-Davidson, which is pursuing a broader-focus differentiation strategy. While Harley focuses solely on producing heavyweight motorcycles, Big Dog builds motorcycles that target only the very high end of the heavyweight market—the high-end premium cruiser market—with names such as Pitbull, Wolf, Mastiff, and Bulldog. Big Dog is careful to differentiate its products from those of Harley-Davidson, citing its larger motors, fat rear tires, unique state-of-the-art electronics, and four-piston caliber brakes as examples of value-creating features. With additional value-creating differentiated features (e.g., performance capabilities made possible by larger engines), Big Dog may be able to better serve the unique needs of a narrow customer group.[81]

Second, a company competing on an industry-wide basis may decide that the market segment served by the focus strategy firm is attractive and worthy of competitive pursuit. For instance, Anne Fontaine specializes in designing, producing, and selling "uniquely feminine" white shirts for women through 70 of its own stores.[82] Gap, Inc.'s Forth & Towne retail concept, targeted at upscale women older than age 35, poses a direct threat to Anne Fontaine.[83]

The third risk involved with a focus strategy is that the needs of customers within a narrow competitive segment may become more similar to those of industry-wide customers as a whole. As a result, the advantages of a focus strategy are either reduced or eliminated. At some point, for example, Harley's customers may begin to focus more on speed and handling, areas where the other big motorcycle manufacturers have an advantage.

INTEGRATED COST LEADERSHIP/DIFFERENTIATION STRATEGY

Particularly in global markets, the firm's ability to integrate the means of competition necessary to implement the cost leadership and differentiation strategies may be critical to developing and sustaining competitive advantages. In fact, with globalization and technological advancements, many markets demand that firms not only "run harder" than competitors, they must also run differently and smarter.[84] Doing so requires the use of the **integrated cost leadership/differentiation strategy**. Compared with firms implementing one dominant business-level strategy, the company that successfully uses an integrated cost leadership/differentiation strategy should be in a better position to (1) adapt quickly to environmental changes, (2) learn new skills and technologies more quickly, and (3) effectively leverage its core competencies to compete effectively against its rivals.

Concentrating on the needs of its core customer group (higher-income, fashion-conscious discount shoppers), Target Corporation uses an integrated strategy. It relies on its relationships with Michael Graves in home, garden, and electronics products; Sonia Kashuk in cosmetics; Mossimo in apparel; and Eddie Bauer in camping and outdoor gear, among others, to offer differentiated products at discounted prices. Committed to presenting a consistent upscale image to its core customer group, the firm carefully studies trends to find new branded items that it believes can satisfy its customers' needs.[85]

Successful Execution of the Integrated Cost Leadership/Differentiation Strategy

Evidence suggests a relationship between successful use of the integrated strategy and above-average returns.[86] Thus, firms able to produce relatively differentiated products at relatively low costs can expect to perform well.[87] Researchers have discovered that "businesses which combined multiple forms of competitive advantage outperformed businesses that only were identified with a single form."[88]

Unlike Target, which uses the integrated cost leadership/differentiation strategy on an industry-wide basis, air-conditioning and heating-systems maker Aaon concentrates on a particular competitive scope. Thus, Aaon is implementing a focused integrated strategy. Aaon manufactures semi-customized rooftop air-conditioning systems for large retailers, including Walmart, Target, and Home Depot. The company positions its rooftop systems between low-priced commodity equipment and high-end customized systems. Aaon's objective is to provide products that perform beyond expectations and provide dependability at a reasonable cost. The firm's innovative manufacturing capabilities allow it to tailor a production line for units with special heat-recovery options unavailable on low-end systems. Combining custom features with assembly-line production methods results in significant cost savings. The firm's narrowly defined target customers receive some differentiated features (e.g., special heat-recovery options) at a low, but not the lowest, cost.[89]

The integrated cost leadership/differentiation strategy is an increasingly common strategy, although it is difficult to successfully implement. This difficulty is mainly caused by the fact that cost leadership and differentiation strategies emphasize different value chain and support activities. To achieve the low-cost position, emphasis is placed on production and process engineering, with infrequent product changes. To achieve a differentiated position, marketing and new-product R&D are emphasized, whereas production and process engineering are not. Thus, successful implementation of the integrated strategy requires a careful combination of activities designed to reduce costs with activities intended to create additional differentiation features. This balance requires a flexible organizational structure.

Using a Flexible Structure to Implement the Integrated Cost Leadership/Differentiation Strategy

As a result of the need to balance the various objectives associated with both cost leadership and differentiation, the type of functional structure needed for the integrated strategy must have flexible decision-making patterns that are partially centralized and partially decentralized. Additionally, jobs are less specialized than in a traditional functional structure so that workers are more sensitive to the need for a balance between low cost and differentiation. Some firms use modular products to create differentiation (easier customization) and simultaneously to hold down costs. Firms that use modular products often also use modular organizational structures to implement the strategy of modular products. Modular structures are more flexible and less hierarchical.[90]

A commitment to *strategic flexibility* (see Chapter 1) is necessary to effectively use the integrated cost leadership/differentiation strategy. Strategic flexibility results from developing systems, procedures, and methods that enable a firm to quickly and effectively respond to opportunities that reduce costs or increase differentiation. Because of the need for additional strategic flexibility, other system processes help to facilitate implementation of the integrated strategy. *Flexible manufacturing systems, information networks*, and *total quality management systems* are three sources of strategic flexibility that facilitate use of the integrated strategy. Valuable to the successful use of each business-level strategy, the strategic flexibility provided by these three tools is especially important to firms trying to balance the objectives of continuous cost reductions and continuous enhancements to sources of differentiation.

Flexible Manufacturing Systems. Modern information technologies have helped make flexible manufacturing systems (FMS) possible. These systems increase the "flexibilities of human, physical, and information resources" that the firm integrates to create differentiated products at low costs.[91] An FMS is a computer-controlled process used to produce a variety of products in moderate, flexible quantities with a minimum of manual intervention.[92] Particularly in situations where parts are too heavy for people to handle or when other methods are less effective in creating manufacturing and assembly flexibility, robots are integral to use of an FMS.[93]

The goal of an FMS is to eliminate the "low-cost-versus-product-variety" trade-off that is inherent in traditional manufacturing technologies. Firms use an FMS to change quickly and easily from making one product to making another. Used properly, an FMS allows the firm to respond more effectively to changes in its customers' needs, while retaining low-cost advantages and consistent product quality.[94] Because an FMS also enables the firm to reduce the lot size needed to manufacture a product efficiently, the firm increases its capacity to serve the unique needs of a narrow target market. Thus, FMS technology is a significant technological advance that allows firms to produce a wide variety of products at a relatively low cost. Levi Strauss, for example, uses an FMS to make jeans for women that fit their exact measurements. Customers of Andersen Windows can design their own windows using proprietary software the firm has developed. The effective use of an FMS is linked with a firm's ability to understand the constraints these systems can create (in terms of materials handling and the flow of supporting resources in scheduling, for example). FMS can also help a firm effectively integrate machines, computer systems, and people and to continuously build knowledge to adapt the system and products to best meet market needs.[95] In service industries, the processes used must be flexible enough to increase delivery speed and to satisfy changing customer needs. In industries of all types, effective integration of the firm's tangible assets (e.g., machines) and intangible assets (e.g., people's skills) facilitates implementation of complex competitive strategies, especially the integrated cost leadership/differentiation strategy.

Information Networks. By linking companies with their suppliers, distributors, and customers, information networks provide another source of strategic flexibility. Used correctly, these networks facilitate the firm's efforts to satisfy customer expectations in terms of product quality and delivery speed.[96] For instance, customer relationship management (CRM) is one form of an information-based network process that firms use to better understand customers and their needs. The effective CRM system provides a 360-degree view of the company's relationship with customers, encompassing all contact points, involving all business processes, and incorporating all communication media and sales channels.[97] The firm can then use this information to determine the trade-offs its customers are willing to make between differentiated features and low cost, which is vital for companies using the integrated cost leadership/differentiation strategy.

Information networks are also critical to the establishment and successful use of an enterprise resource planning (ERP) system. ERP is an information system used to identify and plan the resources required across the firm to receive, record, produce, and ship customer orders.[98] Aviall, an aircraft parts distributor, has approximately two million parts in inventory (worth approximately $1 billion). It uses a sophisticated ERP system to help maintain an up-to-date inventory of parts needed by its customers.[99] Growth in ERP applications such as the one used at Aviall has been significant. Full installations of an ERP system are expensive, running into the tens of millions of dollars for large-scale applications.

Improving efficiency on a company-wide basis is a primary objective of using an ERP system. Efficiency improvements result from the use of systems through which financial and operational data are moved rapidly from one department to another. Integrating data across parties that are involved with detailing product specifications and then manufacturing those products and distributing them in ways that are consistent with customers' unique needs enable the firm to respond with flexibility to customer preferences relative to cost and differentiation.

Total Quality Management Systems. In the 1970s and 1980s, executives in Western nations, including the United States, recognized that their firms' success and even survival in some industries (e.g., automobile manufacturing) depended on developing an ability to dramatically improve the quality of their goods and services while simultaneously reducing their cost structures. The relatively low costs of moderately high-quality products from a host of Japanese companies emphasized this message with resounding clarity.[100]

Focused on doing things right through increases in efficiency, total quality management (TQM) systems are used in firms across multiple nations and economic regions to increase their competitiveness. TQM systems incorporate customer definitions of quality focus and thereby guide the firm to the root causes of a problem rather than to its symptoms.[101] A key assumption underlying the use of a TQM system is that the costs of poor quality such as inspection, and lost customers are greater than the costs of developing high-quality products and services. Each TQM system implemented must be customized to the firm's resources, needs, and external environmental context.[102]

Firms use TQM systems to achieve several specific objectives, including (1) increasing customer satisfaction, (2) cutting costs, and (3) reducing the amount of time required to introduce innovative products to the marketplace.[103] Achieving these objectives improves a firm's flexibility and facilitates use of all business-level strategies. However, the outcomes suggested by these objectives are particularly important to firms implementing the integrated cost leadership/differentiation strategy. At least meeting (and perhaps exceeding) customers' expectations regarding quality is a differentiating feature, and eliminating process inefficiencies allows the firm to offer that quality at a relatively low cost. Thus, an effective TQM system helps the firm develop the flexibility needed to spot opportunities to simultaneously increase differentiation and/or reduce costs.

Competitive Risks of the Integrated Cost Leadership/Differentiation Strategy

The potential to create value by successfully using the integrated cost leadership/differentiation strategy is appealing. However, experience shows that substantial risk accompanies this potential. Selecting a business-level strategy requires the firm to make choices about how it intends to compete.[104] Achieving the low-cost position in an industry or a segment of an industry by using a focus strategy demands that the firm monitor its costs continuously relative to the costs of its competitors and reduce them if necessary. As shown in Figure 5.1, the use of the differentiation strategy, with either an industry-wide (broad target) or a focused (narrow target) competitive scope, requires the firm to provide its customers with differentiated goods or services they value and for which they are willing to pay a premium price. Such a strategy often requires regular innovation to maintain a differentiated product that provides the necessary value to customers.[105]

The firm that uses the integrated strategy yet fails to establish a leadership position risks becoming "stuck in the middle."[106] Being in this position prevents the firm from dealing successfully with the competitive forces in its industry and from having a distinguishable competitive advantage. The firm will not be able to create value, and it will be limited to earning average returns only when the structure of the industry in which it competes is highly favorable or if its competitors are in the same position.[107] Without these conditions, the firm will earn below-average returns. Thus, companies implementing the integrated cost leadership/differentiation strategy, such as Target and Aaon, must be certain that their competitive actions allow them both to offer some differentiated features that their customers value and to provide them with products at a relatively low cost.

No research evidence shows that the attributes of the cost leadership and differentiation strategies cannot be effectively integrated. The integrated strategy therefore is an appropriate strategic choice for firms with the core competencies required to produce somewhat differentiated products at relatively low costs. It is also important that the appropriate structure with additional processes be used to facilitate proper implementation of the strategy.

SUMMARY

- A business-level strategy is an integrated and coordinated set of commitments and actions the firm uses to gain a competitive advantage by exploiting core competencies in specific product markets. This chapter examines five business-level strategies: cost leadership, differentiation, focused cost leadership, focused differentiation, and integrated cost leadership/differentiation. A firm's strategic competitiveness is enhanced when it is able to develop and exploit new core competencies faster than competitors can mimic the competitive advantages yielded by the firm's current competencies.

- Customers are the foundation of successful business-level strategies. When considering customers, a firm simultaneously examines *who* to serve (which customer groups), *what* they want (the needs the firm seeks to satisfy), and *how* to serve them (the core competencies that will meet those needs). Increasing market segmentation throughout the global economy creates opportunities for firms to identify unique customer needs.

- Strategy and structure influence each other, although strategy has an overall stronger influence on structure. Research indicates that firms tend to change structure when declining performance forces them to do so. Effective managers anticipate the need for structural change, quickly modifying structure to better accommodate the firm's strategy implementation needs when evidence calls for that action.

- Business-level strategies are commonly implemented using the functional structure. The cost leadership strategy requires a centralized functional structure in which manufacturing efficiency and process engineering are emphasized. The differentiation strategy's functional structure decentralizes implementation-related decisions, especially those concerned with marketing, and emphasizes those involved with individual organizational functions. Focus strategies, often used in small firms, require a simple structure until such time that the firm diversifies in terms of products and/or markets. The integrated low cost/differentiation strategy requires a functional structure with well-developed processes to manage partial centralization and jobs that are semi-specialized. Thus, it requires a structure that allows a flexible decision-making approach.

▶ Firms seeking competitive advantage through the cost leadership strategy produce no-frills, standardized products for an industry's typical customer. These low-cost products must be offered with competitive levels of differentiation. Above-average returns are earned when firms continuously maintain their costs at a level lower than those of their competitors, while providing customers with products that have low prices and acceptable levels of differentiated features. In recent years, an increasing number of firms have used outsourcing as a means of reducing their costs in order to seek or maintain a competitive advantage based on cost.

▶ Competitive risks associated with the cost leadership strategy include (1) a loss of competitive advantage to newer technologies, (2) a failure to detect changes in customers' needs, and (3) the ability of competitors to imitate the cost leader's competitive advantage through their own unique strategic actions.

▶ The differentiation strategy enables firms to provide customers with products that have different (and valued) features. Differentiated products must be sold at a cost that customers believe is competitive, given the product's features as compared with the cost–feature combination available through competitors' offerings. Because of their uniqueness, differentiated goods or services are sold at a premium price. Products can be differentiated along any dimension that some customer group values. Firms using this strategy seek to differentiate their products from competitors' goods or services along as many dimensions as possible. The less similarity with competitors' products, the more buffered a firm is from competition with its rivals.

▶ Risks associated with the differentiation strategy include (1) a customer group's decision that the differences between the differentiated product and the cost leader's good or service are no longer worth a premium price, (2) the inability of a differentiated product to create the type of value for which customers are willing to pay a premium price, (3) the ability of competitors to provide customers with products that have features similar to those associated with the differentiated product, but at a lower cost, and (4) the threat of counterfeiting, whereby firms produce a cheap imitation of a differentiated good or service.

▶ Through the cost leadership and the differentiated focus strategies, firms serve the needs of a narrow market segment (e.g., a buyer group or geographic area). This strategy is successful when firms have the core competencies required to provide value to a narrow market segment that exceeds the value available from firms serving customers on an industry-wide basis.

▶ The competitive risks of focus strategies include (1) a competitor's ability to use its core competencies to "outfocus" the focuser by serving an even more narrowly defined competitive segment, (2) decisions by industry-wide competitors to serve a customer group's specialized needs that the focuser has been serving, and (3) a reduction in differences of the needs between customers in a narrow market segment and the industry-wide market.

▶ Firms using the integrated cost leadership/differentiation strategy strive to provide customers with relatively low-cost products that have some valued differentiated features. In recent times, it has become a more commonly used strategy and can be valuable. But, a primary risk of this strategy is that a firm might produce products that do not offer sufficient value in terms of either low cost or differentiation. When this occurs, the company is "stuck in the middle," competing at a disadvantage and unable to earn more than average returns.

ETHICS QUESTIONS

1. Can a commitment to ethical conduct on issues such as the environment, product quality, and fulfilling contractual agreements affect a firm's competitive advantage? If so, how?
2. Is there more incentive for differentiators or cost leaders to pursue stronger ethical conduct?
3. Can an overemphasis on cost leadership or differentiation lead to ethical challenges?
4. Creating brand image is one way a firm can differentiate its good or service. However, many questions are now being raised about the effect brand images have on consumer behavior. For example, considerable concern has arisen about brand images that are managed by tobacco firms and their effect on the smoking habits of teenagers. Should firms be concerned about how they form and use brand images? Why or why not?
5. To what extent should an individual manager be concerned about the accuracy of the claims the company makes about its products in its advertisements?

NOTES

1. G. Gavetti, D. A. Levinthal, & J. W. Rivkin, 2005, Strategy making in novel and complex worlds: The power of analogy, *Strategic Management Journal*, 26: 691–712.
2. F. Chirco, D. G. Sirmon, S. Sciascia, & P. Mazzola, 2011, Resource orchestration in family firms: Investigating how entrepreneurial orientation, generational involvement, and participative strategy affect performance, *Strategic Entrepreneurship Journal*, 5: 307–326; R. S. Kaplan & D. P. Norton, 2001, *The Strategy-Focused Organization*, Boston: Harvard Business School Press, 90.
3. D. J. Ketchen Jr., C. C. Snow, & V. L. Street, 2004, Improving firm performance by matching strategic decision-making processes to competitive dynamics, *Academy of Management Executive*, 18(4): 29–43; R. D. Ireland, M. A. Hitt, S. M. Camp, & D. L. Sexton, 2001, Integrating entrepreneurship and strategic management actions to create firm wealth, *Academy of Management Executive*, 15(1): 49–63.
4. N. Park, J. M. Mezias, & J. Song, 2004, Increasing returns, strategic alliances, and the values of E-commerce firms, *Journal of Management*, 30: 7–27; V. P. Rindova & C. J. Fombrun, 1999, Constructing competitive advantage: The role of firm-constituent interactions, *Strategic Management Journal*, 20: 691–710.
5. M. E. Porter, 1980, *Competitive Strategy*, New York: The Free Press.
6. D. C. Hambrick & J. W. Fredrickson, 2001, Are you sure you have a strategy? *Academy of Management Executive*, 15(4): 48–59.
7. C. B. Dobni & G. Luffman, 2003, Determining the scope and impact of market orientation profiles on strategy implementation and performance, *Strategic Management Journal*, 24: 577–585.
8. A. Cuervo-Cazurra & C. A. Un, 2010, Why some firms never invest in R&D, *Strategic Management Journal*, 31: 759–779; K. Shimizu & M. A. Hitt, 2004, Strategic flexibility: Organizational preparedness to reverse ineffective strategic decisions, *Academy of Management Executive*, 18(4): 44–59.
9. R. D. Ireland & C. C. Miller, 2005, Decision-making and firm success, *Academy of Management Executive*, 18(4): 8–12; J. J. Janney & G. G. Dess, 2004, Can real-options analysis improve decision making? Promises and pitfalls, *Academy of Management Executive*, 18(4): 60–75.
10. E. Danneels, 2012, Second-order competences and Schumpeterian rents, *Strategic Entrepreneurship Journal*, 6: 42–58.
11. L. Tihanyi, A. E. Ellstrand, C. M. Daily, & D. R. Dalton, 2000, Composition of top management team and firm international diversification, *Journal of Management*, 26: 1157–1177; P. F. Drucker, 1999, *Management in the 21st Century*, New York: Harper Business.
12. M. E. Porter, 1996, What is strategy? *Harvard Business Review*, 74(6): 61–78.

[13] M. E. Porter, 1985, *Competitive Advantage*, New York: The Free Press, 26.

[14] Porter, *Competitive Strategy*.

[15] M. E. Porter, 1994, Toward a dynamic theory of strategy, in R. P. Rumelt, D. E. Schendel, & D. J. Teece (eds.), *Fundamental Issues in Strategy*, Boston: Harvard Business School Press, 423–461.

[16] Porter, What is strategy? 62.

[17] Porter, *Competitive Advantage*, 15.

[18] G. G. Dess, G. T. Lumpkin, & J. E. McGee, 1999, Linking corporate entrepreneurship to strategy, structure, and process: Suggested research directions, *Entrepreneurship: Theory & Practice*, 23(3): 85–102; P. M. Wright, D. L. Smart, & G. C. McMahan, 1995, Matches between human resources and strategy among NCAA basketball teams, *Academy of Management Journal*, 38: 1052–1074.

[19] L. E. Brouthers, E. O'Donnell & J. Hadjimarcou, 2005, Generic product strategies for emerging market exports into triad nation markets: A mimetic isomorphism approach, *Journal of Management Studies*, 42: 225–245.

[20] F. E. Webster Jr., A. J. Malter, & S. Ganesan, 2005, The decline and dispersion of marketing competence, *MIT Sloan Management Review*, 6(4): 35–43; L. L. Berry, 2001, The old pillars of new retailing, *Harvard Business Review*, 79(4): 131–137.

[21] J. Gertner, 2012, Starbucks for infusing a steady stream of new ideas to revive its business, *Fast Company*, March, 112–113.

[22] M. A. Hitt, R. D. Ireland, D. G. Sirmon, & C. A. Trahms, 2011, Strategic entrepreneurship: Creating value for individuals, organizations and society, *Academy of Management Perspectives*, 25(2): 57–75.

[23] N. Brodsky, 2006, It's hard to make Inc. 500 if you're always churning clients, *Inc.* magazine, September, 57.

[24] M. E. Porter, 2001, Strategy and the Internet, *Harvard Business Review*, 79(3): 62–78.

[25] Amazon for playing the long game, 2012, *Fast Company*, March, 81.

[26] R. F. Lusch, 2011, Reframing supply chain management: A service-dominant logic, *Journal of Supply Chain Management*, 47(1): 14–18; A. Reed II & L. E. Bolton, 2005, The complexity of identity, *MIT Sloan Management Review*, 46(3): 18–22.

[27] C. W. Lamb Jr., J. F. Hair Jr., & C. McDaniel, 2006, *Marketing*, 8th ed., Mason, OH: Thomson/South-Western, 224; A. Dutra, J. Frary, & R. Wise, 2004, Higher-order needs drive new growth in mature consumer markets, *Journal of Business Strategy*, 25(5): 26–34; W. D. Neal & J. Wurst, 2001, Advances in market segmentation, *Marketing Research*, 13(1): 14–18; S. C. Jain, 2000, *Marketing Planning and Strategy*, Cincinnati: South-Western, 104–125.

[28] 2012, Porsche, http://www.porsche.com/usa, February 24; 2012, Rolls-Royce, http://www.rolls-royce.com, February 24.

[29] A. W. Joshi, 2010, Salesperson influence on product development: Insights from a study of small manufacturing organizations, *Journal of Marketing*, 74: 94–107; D. A. Aaker, 1998, *Strategic Marketing Management*, 5th ed., New York: Wiley, 20.

[30] 2007, Saks Fifth Avenue, http://www.saksfifthavenue.com, January 30.

[31] O. Chatain, 2010, Value creation, competitors and performance in buyer-supplier relationships, *Strategic Management Journal*, 32: 76–102.

[32] M. Pynnonen, P. Ritala, & J. Halikas, 2011, The new meaning of customer value: A systemic perspective, *Journal of Business Strategy*, 32: 51–57.

[33] K. Z. Zhou & F. Wu, 2010, Technological capability, strategic flexibility and product innovation, *Strategic Management Journal*, 32: 547–561; T. Sheng & C. Lui, 2010, An empirical study on the effect of e-service quality on online customer satisfaction and loyalty, *Nankai Business Review Journal*, 1: 273–283.

[34] 2012, SAS Institute, Customer success, http://www.sas .com, February 24; C. A. O'Reilly III & J. Pfeffer, 2000, *Hidden Value: How Great Companies Achieve Extraordinary Results with Ordinary People*, Boston: Harvard Business School Press, 102.

[35] G. Davies, R. Chun, & M. A. Kamins, 2010, Reputation gaps and the performance of service organizations, *Strategic Management Journal*, 31: 530–546.

[36] T. Burns & G. M. Stalker, 1961, *The Management of Innovation*, London: Tavistok; P. R. Lawrence & J. W. Lorsch, 1967, *Organization and Environment*, Homewood, IL: Richard D. Irwin; J. Woodward, 1965, *Industrial Organization: Theory and Practice*, London: Oxford University Press.

[37] W. D. Sine, H. Mitsuhashi, & D. A. Kirsch, 2006, Revisiting Burns and Stalker: Formal structure and new venture performance in emerging economy sectors, *Academy of Management Journal*, 49: 121–132; H. Kim, R. E. Hoskisson, L. Tihanyi, & J. Hong, 2004, Evolution and restructuring of diversified business groups in emerging markets: The lessons from chaebols in Korea, *Asia Pacific Journal of Management*, 21: 25–48; P. Jenster & D. Hussey, 2001, *Company Analysis: Determining Strategic Capability*, Chichester, UK: Wiley, 135–171.

[38] B. Keats & H. O'Neill, 2001, Organizational structure: Looking through a strategy lens, in M. A. Hitt, R. E. Freeman, & J. S. Harrison (eds.), *Handbook of Strategic Management*, Oxford, UK: Blackwell Publishers, 520–542; J. R. Galbraith, 1995, *Designing Organizations*, San Francisco: Jossey-Bass, 6.

[39] H. Barth, 2003, Fit among competitive strategy, administrative mechanisms, and performance: A comparative study of small firms in mature and new industries, *Journal of Small Business Management*, 41(2): 133–147.

[40] M. Sengul, 2001, Divisionalization: Strategic effects of organizational structure, paper presented during the 21st Annual Strategic Management Society Conference, San Francisco, October.

[41] J. J. Chrisman, A. Bauerschmidt, & C. W. Hofer, 1998, The determinants of new venture performance: An extended model, *Entrepreneurship: Theory & Practice*, 23(3): 5–29; H. M. O'Neill, R. W. Pouder, & A. K. Buchholtz, 1998, Patterns in the diffusion of strategies across organizations: Insights from the innovation diffusion literature, *Academy of Management Review*, 23: 98–114.

[42] Galbraith, *Designing Organizations*, 25.

[43] Keats & O'Neill, Organizational structure, 539.

[44] Lawrence & Lorsch, *Organization and Environment*.

[45] O. E. Williamson, 1975, *Markets and Hierarchies: Analysis and Anti-trust Implications*, New York: The Free Press.

[46] A. Chandler, 1962, *Strategy and Structure*, Cambridge, MA: MIT Press.

[47] Porter, *Competitive Strategy*, 35–40.

[48] Ryanair, 2012, *Wikipedia*, http://en.wikipedia.org/ wiki/Ryanair, February 24.

[49] P. Bromiley & M. Washburn, 2011, Cost reduction vs. innovation search in R&D, *Journal of Strategy and Management*, 4: 196–214.

[50] D. G. Sirmon, M. A. Hitt, R. D. Ireland & B. A. Gilbert, 2011, Resource orchestration to create

competitive advantage: Breadth, depth and life-cycle effects, *Journal of Management*, 37: 1390–1412.

51. C. Malburg, 2000, Competing on costs, *Industry Week*, October 16, 31.

52. D. F. Lynch, S. B. Keller, & J. Ozment, 2000, The effects of logistics capabilities and strategy on firm performance, *Journal of Business Logistics*, 21(2): 47–68.

53. J. J. Mohr, S. Sengupta, & S. F. Slater, 2011, Mapping the outsourcing landscape, *Journal of Business Strategy*, 32: 42–50.

54. B. Flynn, 2010, Introduction to the special topic forum on global supply chain management, *Journal of Supply Chain Management*, 46(2): 3–4.

55. H. Wang & C. Kimble, 2010, Low-cost strategy through product architecture: Lessons from China, *Journal of Business Strategy*, 31(3): 12–20.

56. 2012, Big Lots, About our company, http://www .biglotscorporate.com, February 25.

57. J. Greenberg, 2012, Sears closing list 2012, *International Business times*, http://www.ibtimes.com, February, 24.

58. R. H. Hall, 1996, *Organizations: Structures, Processes, and Outcomes*, 6th ed., Englewood Cliffs, NJ: Prentice Hall, 13; S. Baiman, D. F. Larcker, & M. V. Rajan, 1995, Organizational design for business units, *Journal of Accounting Research*, 33: 205–229.

59. Hall, *Organizations*, 64–75.

60. J. B. Barney, 2002, *Gaining and Sustaining Competitive Advantage*, 2nd ed., Upper Saddle River, NJ: Prentice Hall, 257.

61. M. Reitzig & S. Wagner, 2010, The hidden costs of outsourcing: Evidence from patent data, *Strategic Management Journal*, 31: 1183–1201.

62. Y. Luo, J. Sun, & S. l. Wang, 2011, Emerging economy copycats: Capability, environment and strategy, *Academy of Management Perspectives*, 25(2): 37–56.

63. Porter, *Competitive Strategy*, 35–40.

64. J. Gresko, 2012, New Nike shoe with outer space theme causes frenzy, *ABC News*, http://abcnews.go .com, February 24.

65. Porter, *Competitive Strategy*, 35–40.

66. Sirmon, Hitt, Ireland, & Gilbert, Resource orchestration to create competitive advantage.

67. 2012, Lexus, http://www.lexus.com, February 25.

68. D. Dunlap-Hinkler, M. Kotabe, & R. Mudambi, 2010, A story of breakthrough versus incremental innovation: Corporate entrepreneurship in the global pharmaceutical industry, *Strategic Entrepreneurship Journal*, 4: 106–127; E. Levitas & T. Chi, 2010, A look at the value creation effects of patenting and capital investment though the real options lens: The moderating role of uncertainty, *Strategic Entrepreneurship Journal*, 4: 212–233.

69. C. Camison & A. Villar-Lopez, 2010, Effect of SMEs' international experience on foreign intensity and economic performance: The mediating role of internationally exploitable assets and competitive strategy, *Journal of Small Business Management*, 48: 116–151.

70. M. M. Crosan & M Apaydin, 2010, A multidimensional framework of organizational innovation: A systematic review of the literature, *Journal of Management Studies*, 47: 1154–1191.

71. M. K. Srivastava & D. R. Gnyawali, 2011, When do relational resources matter? Leveraging portfolio technological resources for breakthrough innovation, *Academy of Management Journal*, 54: 797–810.

72. A. M. Hess & F. T. Rothaermel, 2011, When are assets complementary? Star scientists, strategic alliances, and innovation in the pharmaceutical industry, *Strategic Management Journal*, 32: 895–909.

73. M. Semadeni & B. S. Anderson, 2010, The follower's dilemma: Innovation and imitation in the professional services industry, *Academy of Management Journal*, 53: 1175–1193.

74. Luo, Sun & Wang, Emerging economy copycats.

75. M. Williams & P. Kallendar, 2004, China's Lenovo to buy IBM's PC business, *IDG News*, December 7.

76. Porter, *Competitive Strategy*, 98.

77. Porter, *Competitive Advantage*, 15.

78. 2012, Ikea, The Ikea concept and History, http:// www.ikea.com, February 26.

79. Porter, What is strategy? 65.

80. 2012, Harley-Davidson, Investor Relations, http:// investor.harley-davidson.com, February 26.

81. 2012, Big Dog Motorcycles, http://www.bigdogmotor cycles.com, February 26.

82. 2012, Anne Fontaine, http://www.annefontaine.com, February 26.

83. 2012, Forth & Towne, http://ww2.forthandtowne .com, February 26.

84. J. R De La Torre & A. Chacar, 2012, Network coordination and performance among MNEs in Latin America, *Global Strategy Journal*, 2: 3–25.

85. 2012. Target corporation, *Hoovers*, http://www .hoovers.com/company/Target_Corporation; 2012, Target Corporation, http://sites.target.com/site/en/ company/page.

86. A. Arora & A. Nandkumar, 2012, Insecure advantage? Markets for technology and the value of resources for entrepreneurial ventures, *Strategic Management Journal*, 33: 231–251; G. G. Dess, G. T. Lumpkin, & J. E. McGee, 1999, Linking corporate entrepreneurship to strategy, structure, and process: Suggested research directions, *Entrepreneurship: Theory & Practice*, 23(3): 89.

87. M. Makri, M. A. Hitt, & P. J. Lane, 2010, Complementary technologies, knowledge relatedness, and invention outcomes in high technology mergers and acquisitions, *Strategic Management Journal*, 31: 602–628; P. Ghemawat, 2001, *Strategy and the Business Landscape*, Upper Saddle River, NJ: Prentice Hall, 56.

88. G. G. Dess, A. Gupta, J. F. Hennart, & C. W. L. Hill, 1995, Conducting and integrating strategy research at the international, corporate, and business levels: Issues and directions, *Journal of Management*, 21: 357–393.

89. 2012, Aaon Inc. About Us, http://www.aaon.com, February 26.

90. G. Hoetker, 2006, Do modular products lead to modular organizations? *Strategic Management Journal*, 27: 501–518.

91. R. Sanchez, 1995, Strategic flexibility in product competition, *Strategic Management Journal*, 16(summer special issue): 140.

92. A. Faria, P. Fenn, & A. Bruce, 2005, Production technologies and technical efficiency: Evidence from Portuguese manufacturing industry, *Applied Economics*, 37: 1037–1046.

93. R. Olexa, 2001, Flexible parts feeding boosts productivity, *Manufacturing Engineering*, 126(4): 106–114.

94. M. K. Malhotra & A. W. Mackelprang, 2012, Are internal manufacturing and external supply chain flexibilities complementary capabilities? *Journal of Operations Management*, in press.

95. P. C. Patel, S. Terjesen, & D. Li, 2012, Enhancing effects of manufacturing flexibility through absorptive capacity and operational ambidexterity, *Journal of Operations Management*, in press; M. Savsar, 2005, Performance analysis of an FMS operating under different failure rates and maintenance policies, *International Journal of Flexible Manufacturing Systems*, 16: 229–249.

96. P. Theodorou & G. Florou, 2008, Manufacturing strategies and financial performance—the effect of advanced information technology:CAD/CAM sytems, *Omega*, 36: 107–121; A. McAfee, 2003, When too much IT knowledge is a dangerous thing, *McKinsey Quarterly*, 44(2): 83–89.

97. D. Elmuti, H. Jia, & D. Gray, 2009, Customer relationship management strategic application and organizational effectiveness: An empirical investigation, *Journal of Strategic Marketing*, 17: 75–96.

98. E. Bendoly & M. Cotteleer, 2008, Understanding behavioral sources of process variation following enterprise system deployment, *Journal of Operations Management*, 26: 23–44.

99. 2012. Aviall, Company Information, http://www.avial.com, February 27.

100. D. Chatterji & J. M. Davidson, 2001, Examining TQM's legacies for R&D, *Research Technology Management*, 44(1): 10–12.

101. J. Pfeffer, 1998, *The Human Equation: Building Profits by Putting People First*, Boston: Harvard Business School Press, 156.

102. D. Zhang, K. Linderman & R. G. Schroeder, 2012, The moderating role of contextual factors on quality management practice, *Journal of Operations Management*, in press.

103. V. W. S. Yeung & R. W. Armstrong, 2003, A key to TQM benefits: Manager involvement in customer processes, *International Journal of Services Technology and Management*, 4(1): 14–29.

104. De Kluyver, *Strategic Thinking*, 3; C. H. St. John & J. S. Harrison, 1999, Manufacturing-based relatedness, synergy, and coordination, *Strategic Management Journal*, 20: 129–145.

105. N. Dorner, 2011, Service innovation: Why is it so difficult to accomplish? *Journal of Business Strategy*, 32(3): 37–46; M. L. Mors, 2010, Innovation in a global consulting firm: When the problem is too much diversity, *Strategic Management Journal*, 31: 841–872.

106. Porter, *Competitive Advantage*, 16.

107. Ibid., 17.

Chapter **6**

COMPETITIVE RIVALRY AND COMPETITIVE DYNAMICS

KNOWLEDGE OBJECTIVES

Studying this chapter should provide you with the strategic management knowledge needed to:

1. Define competitors, competitive rivalry, competitive behavior, and competitive dynamics.

2. Describe market commonality and resource similarity as the building blocks of a competitor analysis.

3. Explain awareness, motivation, and ability as drivers of competitive behavior.

4. Discuss factors affecting the likelihood a competitor will take competitive actions.

5. Discuss factors affecting the likelihood a competitor will respond to actions taken against it.

6. Explain competitive dynamics in slow-cycle, fast-cycle, and standard-cycle markets.

Continuous increases in globalization and technological change are altering the fundamental nature of competition in many of the world's industries.[1] Additional complexity in the form of interdependencies between the firm and its competitors is a key result of these changes.[2] As noted in Chapter 1, *hypercompetitive* is a term some use to capture the nature of the competitive environments firms face today. A team of experts say the following about the nature of competition and rivalry in such environments:

> The new age of competition is distinct because of the dramatic increase in competitive actions and reactions between firms. As a consequence of the accelerating rate of actions and reactions, the time firms have to make decisions has decreased, and the speed with which new ideas are created and brought to market has increased. Above all, the speed at which data, information, and knowledge pulse between competitors has skyrocketed. In this new age of competition, fast companies generate advantages and market power while faster ones generate more advantages and greater market power, and no one's advantages are guaranteed to last long.[3]

The speed and strength of the actions and reactions between competitors are easy to see in technologically advanced, global industries such as handheld communications devices where new products and features are introduced at an astounding rate. However, it seems that globalization and rapid technology changes are affecting the nature of competition in most industries, even those in which relative stability might be expected, such as the food industry; but, "stable" no longer describes this industry either. In the recent past, for example, competitors Campbell Soup and Heinz have experienced declines in their U.S. sales revenue. Economic conditions accounted for some of the declines, while increased competition from other competitors, as well as against each other, is another contributor. In response to declines in their U.S. sales revenue, the firms are competing against each other as they try to expand internationally. Heinz is expanding sales of its products in developing markets such as China, Russia, and Latin America while Campbell "... is also working to expand its international reach."[4] Thus, competition in virtually all industries today is dynamic and intense.

This chapter focuses on competitive rivalry and competitive dynamics. **Competitors** are firms operating in the same market, offering similar products and targeting similar customers.[5] For instance, FedEx and UPS compete against each other in several product markets, including package delivery by both land and air and emerging e-commerce and logistics markets. **Competitive rivalry** is the ongoing set of competitive actions and competitive responses occurring between competitors as they contend with each other for an advantageous market position. Competitive rivalry influences a firm's ability to gain and sustain competitive advantages[6] and affects the scope and nature of its operations.[7] Rivalry results from firms both initiating their own competitive actions and responding to actions their competitors take.[8]

Competitive behavior is the set of competitive actions and competitive responses the firm takes to build or defend its competitive advantages and to improve its market position.[9] Through competitive behavior, the firm tries to successfully position itself relative to the five forces of competition (see Chapter 3) and to defend and use current competitive advantages while building advantages for the future (see Chapter 4). **Competitive dynamics** describe the total set of actions and responses all firms competing within a market take. Figure 6.1 shows the relationships among competitors, competitive rivalry, and competitive dynamics.

Another way of highlighting competitive rivalry's effect on the firm's strategies is to say that a strategy's success is determined not only by its initial competitive actions, but also by how well it anticipates competitors' responses to them, and by how well the firm anticipates and responds to its competitors' initial actions (also called *attacks*).[10] Although competitive rivalry affects all types of strategies, its most dominant influence is on business-level strategies in that these strategies are concerned with what the firm intends to do to successfully use its competitive advantages in specific product markets (see Chapter 5). Firms with business-level strategies, allowing them to be different from competitors in ways that create value for customers, are positioned to successfully engage in competitive rivalry.[11]

The essence of these important topics is that a firm's strategies are dynamic in nature. Actions one firm takes elicit responses from competitors that in turn typically result in responses from the firm that took the initial action.[12] Increasingly, competitors engage in competitive actions and responses in more than one market.[13] Firms competing against each other in several product or geographic markets are engaged in **multimarket competition**.[14] Boeing and the European Aeronautic Defence and Space Company N.V. (EADS) compete against each other in countries throughout the world to manufacture and sell both commercial and military

FIGURE 6.1 FROM COMPETITORS TO COMPETITIVE DYNAMICS

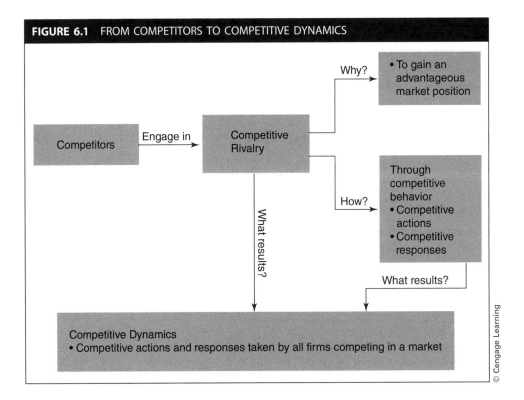

airplanes. Similarly, Brazil's Embraer and Canada's Bombardier dominate the regional jet market.[15] The implication for each pair of these competitors is that actions one of these airplane manufacturers takes in one geographic market may affect its competitor's response in a different market in which they both compete.

The current trend for firms to expand their geographic scope is one reason the number of companies involved with multimarket competition continues to increase. Because of this, firms trying to predict their pattern of competitive rivalry should anticipate that in the future, they are likely to encounter a larger number of increasingly diverse competitors. This trend also suggests that firms should expect competitive rivalry to have a stronger effect on their strategies' success than historically has been the case.[16] Furthermore, research shows that intensified rivalry within an industry can result in decreased financial performance.[17]

We begin this chapter by presenting an integrative model of competitive rivalry at the firm level. We then describe market commonality and resource similarity as the building blocks of a competitor analysis. Next, we discuss the effects of three organizational characteristics—awareness, motivation, and ability—on the firm's competitive behavior. We then examine competitive rivalry in detail by describing the factors that affect the likelihood a firm will take a competitive action and the factors that affect the likelihood a firm will respond to a competitor's action. In the chapter's final section, we turn our attention to competitive dynamics to describe how market characteristics affect competitive rivalry in slow-cycle, fast-cycle, and standard-cycle markets.

A MODEL OF COMPETITIVE RIVALRY

Competitive rivalry at the firm level is modeled in Figure 6.2. Of course, firm rivalry tends to be more dynamic and complex than the model indicates;[18] nevertheless, the model provides a useful framework for discussing competitive rivalry. Rivalry is studied at the firm level because the competitive actions and responses the firm takes are the foundation for successfully building and using its competitive advantages to gain an advantageous market position.[19] Thus, we use the model in Figure 6.2 to explain competition between a particular firm and each of its competitors. The sum of all individual rivalries (as shown in Figure 6.2) occurring in a particular market reflects the competitive dynamics in that market.

Over time, the firm is involved with many competitive actions and competitive responses.[20] Competitive rivalry evolves from this pattern of action and response as

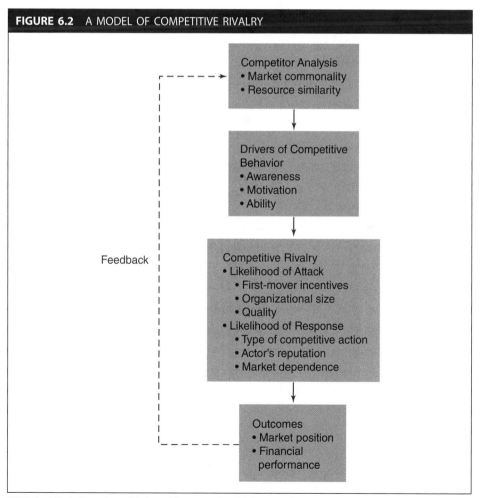

FIGURE 6.2 A MODEL OF COMPETITIVE RIVALRY

Competitor Analysis
• Market commonality
• Resource similarity

Drivers of Competitive Behavior
• Awareness
• Motivation
• Ability

Feedback

Competitive Rivalry
• Likelihood of Attack
  • First-mover incentives
  • Organizational size
  • Quality
• Likelihood of Response
  • Type of competitive action
  • Actor's reputation
  • Market dependence

Outcomes
• Market position
• Financial performance

SOURCE: Republished with permission of Academy of Management, from M.J. Chen, 1996, Competitor Analysis and Interfirm Rivalry: Toward a Theoretical Integration, *Academy of Management Review*, vol. 21, pp. 100–134; permission conveyed through Copyright Clearance Center, Inc.

one firm's competitive actions noticeably affect a competitor's, eliciting competitive responses from that firm.[21] This pattern shows that firms are mutually interdependent, that they feel each other's actions and responses, and that marketplace success is a function of both individual strategies and the consequences of their use.[22]

The intensity of rivalry within a market is affected by many factors, including the total number of competitors, market characteristics, and the quality of individual firms' strategies. On a global scale, firms that develop and use effective business-level strategies tend to outperform competitors in particular product markets, even when experiencing intense competitive rivalry.[23] This appears to be the case for Google as it implements a differentiation strategy at the business level. Although the Internet is sometimes thought to be "the ultimate level playing field," Google continues to outperform a group of different competitors including "search engines like Microsoft's Bing, specialized review and listing sites like Help, comparison shopping sites like Nextag, online merchants like Amazon and social networks like Facebook."[24] We now turn directly to Figure 6.2 as our foundation for further discussion of competitive rivalry.

COMPETITOR ANALYSIS

A *competitor analysis* is the first step the firm takes to predict the extent and nature of its rivalry with each competitor. Recall that a competitor is a firm operating in the same market, offering similar products, and targeting similar customers. The number of markets in which firms compete against each other and the similarity in their resources (called *market commonality* and *resource similarity,* respectively, as defined in this chapter) determine the extent to which the firms are competitors. Firms with high market commonality and highly similar resources are "clearly direct and mutually acknowledged competitors."[25] However, being direct competitors does not necessarily mean that the rivalry between the firms will be intense. The *drivers of competitive behavior*—as well as factors influencing the likelihood that a competitor will initiate competitive actions and will respond to its competitor's competitive actions—influence the intensity of rivalry, even for direct competitors.[26]

In Chapter 3, we discussed competitor analysis as a technique firms use to understand their competitive environment, which, along with the general and industry environments, is part of the firm's external environment. We described how firms use competitor analysis to help them understand their competitors. This understanding results from studying competitors' future objectives, current strategies, assumptions, and capabilities. In this chapter, the discussion of competitor analysis is extended to describe what firms study as the first step to being able to predict competitors' behavior in the form of their competitive actions and responses. The discussions of competitor analysis in Chapter 3 and this chapter are complementary in that firms must first understand competitors before their competitive actions and competitive responses can be predicted.

Market Commonality

Each industry is composed of various markets. The financial services industry, for instance, has markets for insurance, brokerage services, banks, and so forth. By concentrating on the needs of different unique customer groups, markets can be further subdivided. The insurance market can be broken into market segments (such as commercial and consumer), product segments (such as health insurance and life insurance), and geographic markets (such as Western Europe and Southeast Asia).

In general, competitors agree about the different characteristics of individual markets that form an industry.[27] For example, in the transportation industry, there is an understanding that the commercial air travel market differs from the ground transportation market that is served by firms such as U.S.-based Yellow Freight System, Arkansas Best, and Con-way Inc. Although differences exist, most industries' markets are somewhat related in terms of technologies used or core competencies needed to develop a competitive advantage.[28] For example, different types of transportation companies need to provide reliable and timely service. Commercial airline carriers such as Southwest Airlines and Singapore Airlines must therefore develop service competencies to satisfy their passengers, while Yellow Freight System, Arkansas Best, and Con-way Inc. must develop such competencies to serve the needs of those using their fleets to ship goods.

Firms competing in several or even many markets, some of which may be in different industries, are likely to come into contact with a particular competitor several times,[29] a situation called market commonality. **Market commonality** is concerned with the number of markets with which the firm and a competitor are jointly involved and the degree of importance of the individual markets to each.[30] Firms competing against one another in several or many markets engage in multimarket competition.[31] For example, McDonald's and Burger King compete against each other in multiple geographic markets around the world, whereas Prudential and CIGNA compete against each other in several market segments (institutional and retail) as well as product markets (such as life insurance and health insurance). Airlines, chemicals, pharmaceuticals, and consumer foods are other industries in which firms often simultaneously engage each other in multiple market competitions.

Firms competing in several markets have the potential to respond to a competitor's actions not only within the market in which the actions are taken, but also in other markets in which they compete with the rival. This potential complicates the rivalry between competitors. In fact, research suggests that "a firm with greater multimarket contact is less likely to initiate an attack, but more likely to move (respond) aggressively when attacked."[32] Thus, in general, multimarket competition reduces competitive rivalry.[33]

Resource Similarity

Resource similarity is the extent to which the firm's tangible and intangible resources are comparable to a competitor's in terms of type and amount.[34] Firms with similar types and amounts of resources are likely to have similar strengths and weaknesses and use similar strategies.[35] Such is the case with some of the major and large hotel chains. Marriott, Accor, Hilton, and Intercontinental, the top hospitality companies, all have high brand recognition, advanced information and reservations systems, and strong marketing programs.[36] Furthermore, they all have a strong international presence and draw their managers from many of the same hospitality schools, located mainly in the United States and Europe. It is not uncommon for a manager to work for several different hotel companies during a career, which adds to the similarity of human resources across the major companies. Also, all of the major hospitality companies are highly vulnerable to global economic conditions, changes in information technology, and sociocultural shifts, such as changing demographics.[37]

When performing a competitor analysis, a firm analyzes each competitor in terms of resource similarity and market commonality. Assessing market commonality is easier than assessing resource similarity, particularly when critical resources are intangible, such as brand name, knowledge, trust, and the capacity to innovate. In contrast, the following resources are tangible: access to raw materials and a competitor's ability to borrow capital. A competitor's intangible resources are difficult to identify and understand, making an assessment of their value challenging. Marriott and Hilton can easily determine the market segments and geographic locations in which they are competing; but, determining if any intangible resources (such as knowledge and trust among employees) are a source of competitive advantage is more difficult.

The results of a firm's competitor analyses can be mapped for visual comparisons. In Figure 6.3, we show different hypothetical intersections between the firm and individual competitors in terms of market commonality and resource similarity. These intersections indicate the extent to which the firm, and those to which it has compared itself, are competitors.[38] For example, the firm and its competitor displayed in quadrant I have similar types and amounts of resources and use them to compete against each other in many markets that are important to each. These conditions lead to the conclusion that the firms modeled in quadrant I are direct and mutually acknowledged competitors. FedEx and UPS would fall into quadrant I, as would Marriott and Hilton. In contrast, the firm and its competitor shown in quadrant III share few markets and have little similarity in their resources,

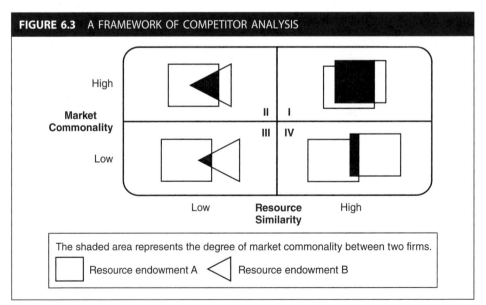

FIGURE 6.3 A FRAMEWORK OF COMPETITOR ANALYSIS

The shaded area represents the degree of market commonality between two firms.

Resource endowment A ◁ Resource endowment B

SOURCE: Republished with permission of Academy of Management, from M.J. Chen, 1996, Competitor Analysis and Interfirm Rivalry: Toward a Theoretical Integration, *Academy of Management Review*, vol. 21, pp. 100–134; permission conveyed through Copyright Clearance Center, Inc.

indicating that they are not direct and mutually acknowledged competitors. The firm's mapping of its competitive relationship with rivals is fluid as firms enter and exit markets and as companies' resources change in type and amount. Thus, the companies with which the firm is a direct competitor change over time.

DRIVERS OF COMPETITIVE ACTIONS AND RESPONSES

As shown in Figure 6.2, market commonality and resource similarity influence the drivers of competitive behavior (awareness, motivation, and ability). In turn, the drivers influence the firm's competitive behavior, as shown by the actions and responses it takes while engaging in competitive rivalry.[39]

Awareness, which is a prerequisite to any competitive action or response being taken by the firm or its competitor, refers to the extent to which competitors recognize the degree of their mutual interdependence that results from market commonality and resource similarity.[40] A lack of awareness can lead to excessive competition, resulting in a negative effect on all competitors' performance.[41] Awareness tends to be greatest when firms have highly similar resources (in terms of types and amounts) to use while competing against each other in multiple markets. Oil field service companies Baker Hughes, Halliburton, and Schlumberger are fully aware of each other as are pharmaceutical competitors Abbott Laboratories, Johnson & Johnson, Bristol-Myers Squibb, and French-based Sanofi. Similarly aware are entertainment competitors Netflix, Hulu, and Vudu. Competing in a niche market space, Canada's two ice hotels (Hotel de Glace and Snow Village) are also fully aware of each other and understand the likely consequences of their competitive actions and responses[42]—realities reflecting the essence of awareness as a driver of competitive actions and responses.

Motivation, which concerns the firm's incentive to take action or to respond to a competitor's attack, relates to perceived gains and losses. Thus, a firm may be aware of competitors, but may not be motivated to engage in rivalry with them if it perceives that its position will not improve as a result of doing so, or that its market position will not be damaged if it does not respond.[43]

Walmart may not be as motivated today to engage directly with major competitor Carrefour. Although rivals for years, these firms' current performances are quite different in that Carrefour is struggling. The decline in the value of Carrefour's shares by almost two-thirds between 2007 and 2011 demonstrates the firm's struggles, as does the fact that in 2011 on a per employee per year basis, Walmart earned $7,804 in profits, whereas Carrefour earned only $1,260. What contributed to Carrefour's problems? "Its rapid international expansion intended to offset slow growth in France stretched the company too thin as it entered 24 countries between 1994 and 2004."[44] Because of poor results, Carrefour has sold off operations in 10 countries in the past few years. Although certainly aware of Carrefour, its competitor's current struggles may reduce Walmart's motivation to respond immediately to competitive actions the firm may take.

In contrast, the motivation for firms such as India's Alibaba Group to take competition actions against Walmart may be increasing. Walmart's recent decision to buy a majority stake in Chinese e-commerce company Yihaodian as a means of increasing its presence in the rapidly growing online shopping patterns occurring in

China is the key reason for this.[45] Walmart's size, skills, and expansion-oriented move into China's online shopping markets could incentivize Alibaba Group to react competitively to its competitor's actions.

Market commonality affects a firm's perceptions and resulting motivation. For example, all else being equal, the firm is more likely to attack the rival with which it has low market commonality than the one with which it competes in multiple markets. The primary reason is that high stakes are involved when seeking a more advantageous position over a rival with whom the firm shares many markets. As mentioned earlier, multimarket competition can find a competitor responding to the firm's action in a market different from the one in which the initial action was taken. Actions and responses of this type can cause both firms to lose focus on core markets and to battle each other with resources that had been allocated for other purposes. Because of the high stakes of competition under the condition of market commonality, the probability is high that the attacked firm will respond to its competitor's action in an effort to protect its position in one or more markets.[46]

In some instances, the firm may be aware of the large number of markets it shares with a competitor and may be motivated to respond to an attack by that competitor, but it lacks the ability to do so. *Ability* relates to each firm's resources and the flexibility they provide. Without available resources (such as financial capital and people), the firm lacks the ability to attack a competitor or respond to its actions. However, similar resources suggest similar abilities to attack and respond. When a firm faces a competitor with similar resources, it must carefully study a possible attack before initiating it because the similarly resourced competitor is likely to respond to that action.[47]

Resource dissimilarity also influences competitive actions and responses between firms. The greater the "resource imbalance" between a firm and its competitors, the longer it will take the firm with a resource disadvantage to respond.[48] For example, Walmart initially used its cost leadership business-level strategy to compete only in small communities (those with a population of 25,000 or less). Using sophisticated logistics systems and efficient purchasing practices as competitive advantages, among others, Walmart created what was at that time a new type of value (primarily in the form of wide selections of products at the lowest competitive prices) for customers in small retail markets. Local stores, facing resource deficiencies relative to Walmart, lacked the ability to marshal resources at the pace required to respond quickly and effectively. However, even when facing competitors with greater resources (greater ability) or more attractive market positions, firms should eventually respond, no matter how daunting doing so seems.[49] Choosing not to respond can ultimately result in failure, as happened with at least some local retailers who did not respond to Walmart's competitive actions.

COMPETITIVE RIVALRY

As noted, *competitive rivalry* is the ongoing set of competitive actions and competitive responses occurring between competing firms for an advantageous market position. Because the ongoing competitive action-response sequence between a firm and a competitor affects the performance of both firms,[50] it is important for companies to carefully study competitive rivalry to successfully use their strategies. Understanding a competitor's awareness, motivation, and ability helps the firm predict the likelihood of an attack by that competitor and how likely it is that a competitor will respond to the actions taken against it.

As described previously, the predictions drawn from the study of competitors in terms of awareness, motivation, and ability are grounded in market commonality and resource similarity. These predictions are fairly general. The value of the final set of predictions the firm develops about each of its competitor's competitive actions and competitive responses is enhanced by studying the "likelihood of attack" factors (such as first-mover incentives and organizational size) and the "likelihood of response" factors (such as the actor's reputation) that are shown in Figure 6.2. Studying these factors allows the firm to develop a deeper understanding of its competitor for the purpose of refining its predictions about that competitor's actions and responses.

Strategic and Tactical Actions

When engaging in competitive rivalry, firms use both strategic and tactical actions to form their competitive actions and competitive responses.[51] A **competitive action** is a strategic or tactical action the firm takes to build or defend its competitive advantages or improve its market position. A **competitive response** is a strategic or tactical action the firm takes to counter the effects of a rival's competitive action. A strategic action or a strategic response is a market-based move that involves a significant commitment of organizational resources and is difficult to implement and reverse. A **tactical action** or a **tactical response** is a market-based move that is taken to fine-tune a strategy; it involves fewer resources than a competitive response and is relatively easy to implement and reverse.

Based in San Francisco, CA, construction and engineering firm URS Corp. acquired Canadian-based Flint Energy Services Ltd. for $1.25 billion in a strategic action designed to enter the expanding drilling market in North America.[52] Similarly, UPS bid $6.4 billion in early 2012 to buy Dutch package shipper TNT Express NV. If completed, this strategic action would provide UPS "… with a leading position in Europe's fragmented package-and-logistics market and boost (its) existing footprints in China, India and Brazil."[53] The fine-tuning of the price for a firm's product is a tactical action. Airline companies, for example, fine-tune the pricing of their services on essentially a "real-time basis" for the purpose of matching the supply of seats on individual flights with the demand for those seats. Dunkin' Donuts recently formed a franchise agreement with Delhi-based Jubilant FoodWorks to open its first store in India. Starbucks' decision to form a joint venture with Tata Global Beverages Ltd. to enter India just a few months after the Dunkin' Donuts entry is an example of a strategic response.[54] A firm's decision to use short-term rebates in response to rebates offered by competitors is an example of a tactical response.

LIKELIHOOD OF ATTACK

In addition to market commonality, resource similarity, and the drivers of awareness, motivation, and ability, other factors also affect the likelihood a competitor will use strategic actions and tactical actions to attack its competitors. Three of these factors are first-mover incentives, organizational size, and quality.

First-Mover Incentives

A **first mover** is a firm that takes an initial competitive action to build or defend its competitive advantages or to improve its market position. Superior R&D skills are often the foundation of the first mover's competitive success.[55] The first-mover concept has been influenced by the work of the famous economist Joseph Schumpeter, who argued that firms achieve competitive advantage by taking innovative actions[56] (we define and fully describe innovation in Chapter 12). In general, first movers "allocate funds for product innovation and development, aggressive advertising, and advanced research and development."[57]

The benefits of being a successful first mover can be substantial. Especially in fast-cycle markets (discussed later in this chapter) where changes occur rapidly and where it is virtually impossible to sustain a competitive advantage for any period of time, "a first mover may experience five to ten times the valuation and revenue of a second mover."[58] This evidence suggests that although first-mover benefits are never absolute, they are often critical to firm success in industries experiencing rapid technological developments and relatively short product life cycles.[59] In addition to earning above-average returns until its competitors respond to its successful competitive action, the first mover has a chance to (1) gain the loyalty of customers who may become committed to the products of the firm that first made them available, (2) set or influence industry standards, and (3) gain market share that can be difficult for competitors to take during future competitive rivalry.

First movers tend to be aggressive and willing to experiment with innovation and take higher, yet reasonable levels of risk.[60] To be a first mover, the firm must have readily available the amount of resources required to significantly invest in R&D as well as to rapidly and successfully produce and market a stream of innovative products. Organizational slack makes it possible for firms to have the ability (as measured by available resources) to be first movers. *Slack* is the buffer or cushion actual or obtainable resources provide that are not currently in use and that are in excess of the minimum resources needed to produce a certain level of output.[61] Thus, slack represents liquid resources that the firm can quickly allocate to support the actions such as R&D investments and aggressive marketing campaigns that lead to first-mover benefits. Slack allows a competitor to take aggressive competitive actions to continuously introduce innovative products.[62] Furthermore, a first mover will try to rapidly gain market share and customer loyalty in order to earn above-average returns until its competitors are able to effectively respond to its first move.

Being a first mover also carries risk. For example, it is difficult to accurately estimate the returns that will be earned from introducing product innovations.[63] Additionally, the first mover's cost to develop a product innovation can be substantial, reducing the slack available to support further innovation. Also, research suggests that in some cases, a first mover is less likely to make the conversion to the product design that eventually becomes the dominant design in the industry.[64] In such cases, a first mover enjoys most of the benefits from its new product in the period before adoption of a dominant design. These risks mean that a firm should carefully study the results a competitor achieves as a first mover. Continuous success by the competitor suggests additional product innovations, whereas lack of product acceptance over the course of the competitor's innovations may indicate less willingness in the future to accept the risks of being a first mover.

A **second mover** is a firm that responds to the first mover's competitive action, typically through imitation. More cautious than the first mover, the second mover studies customers' reactions to product innovations. In the course of doing so, the second mover also tries to find any mistakes the first mover made so that it can avoid the resulting problems. Often, successful imitation of the first mover's innovations allows the second mover "to avoid both the mistakes and the huge spending of the pioneers (first movers)."[65] Second movers also have the time to develop processes and technologies that are more efficient than those the first mover used.[66] Greater efficiencies could result in lower costs for the second mover. Overall, the outcomes of the first mover's competitive actions may provide an effective blueprint for second and even late movers (as described in the sections that follow) as they determine the nature and timing of their competitive responses.[67]

Texas Instruments (TI) tends to be a second mover to its cutting-edge rival Intel in chip manufacturing. Consequently, Intel's chips typically are the most advanced and sought after in the PC industry. However, keeping that first-mover position also means that Intel spends more than any of its competitors on R&D. TI, on the other hand, has used its less costly position as a second mover to make impressive inroads into markets such as cell phones, consumer electronics, and medical devices.[68]

Determining that a competitor thinks of itself as an effective second mover allows the firm to expect that competitor to respond quickly to first movers' successful, innovation-based market entries. If the firm itself is a first mover, then it can expect a successful second-mover competitor to study its market entries and to respond to them quickly. As a second mover, the competitor will try to respond with a product that creates customer value exceeding the value provided by the product that the firm introduced initially as a first mover. The most successful second movers are able to rapidly and meaningfully interpret market feedback to respond quickly, yet productively, to the first mover's innovations.[69]

A **late mover** is a firm that responds to a competitive action, but only after considerable time has elapsed after the first mover's action and the second mover's response. Typically, a late response is better than no response at all, although any success achieved from the late competitive response tends to be slow in coming and considerably less than that achieved by first and second movers. Thus, the firm competing against a late mover can expect that competitor to enter a particular market only after both the first and second movers have achieved success. Moreover, on a relative basis, the firm can predict that the late mover's competitive action will allow it to earn even average returns only when enough time has elapsed for it to understand how to create value that is more attractive to customers than is the value offered by the first and second movers' products. Although exceptions do exist, the firm can predict that the late mover's competitive actions will be relatively ineffective, certainly as compared with those initiated by first movers and second movers.

Organizational Size

An organization's size affects the likelihood, types, and timing of competitive actions it will take.[70] In general, compared with large companies, small firms are nimble and flexible competitors who rely on speed and surprise to defend their competitive advantages or develop new ones while engaged in competitive rivalry, especially with large companies, to gain an advantageous market position.[71] Small firms' flexibility and nimbleness allow them to develop greater *variety* in their competitive actions relative to larger firms.[72] Nevertheless, because they tend to have more slack resources, large firms are likely to initiate *more* competitive and strategic actions during a given time.[73] Thus, the competitive actions a firm is likely to encounter from competitors larger than it is are different from the competitive actions it will encounter from competitors who are smaller.

Relying on a limited variety of competitive actions (which is the large firm's tendency) can lead to reduced competitive success across time, partly because competitors learn how to effectively respond to a predictable set of competitive actions taken by a firm. In contrast, remaining flexible and nimble (which is the small firm's tendency) in order to develop and use a wide variety of competitive actions contributes to success against rivals.

Quality

Quality has many definitions, including well-established ones relating it to the production of goods or services with zero defects[74] and to a never-ending cycle of continuous improvement.[75] **Quality** exists when the firm's goods or services meet or exceed customers' expectations. Thus, in the eyes of customers, quality involves doing the right things relative to performance measures that are important to them.[76] Some evidence suggests that quality is one of the most critical components of being able to satisfy a firm's customers.[77]

Customers may be interested in measuring the quality of a firm's products against a broad range of dimensions. Table 6.1 shows sample quality dimensions

---

TABLE 6.1 QUALITY DIMENSIONS OF PRODUCTS

PRODUCT QUALITY DIMENSIONS
1. *Performance*—Operating characteristics
2. *Features*—Important special characteristics
3. *Flexibility*—Meeting operating specifications over some period of time
4. *Durability*—Amount of use before performance deteriorates
5. *Conformance*—Match with pre-established standards
6. *Serviceability*—Ease and speed of repair
7. *Aesthetics*—How a product looks and feels
8. *Perceived quality*—Subjective assessment of characteristics (product image)

SERVICE QUALITY DIMENSIONS
1. *Timeliness*—Performed in the promised period of time
2. *Courtesy*—Performed cheerfully
3. *Consistency*—Giving all customers similar experiences each time
4. *Convenience*—Accessibility to customers
5. *Completeness*—Fully serviced, as required
6. *Accuracy*—Performed correctly each time

SOURCE: Adapted from J. W. Dean, Jr., & J. R. Evans, 1994, *Total Quality: Management, Organization and Society*, St. Paul, MN: West Publishing Company; H. V. Roberts & B. F. Sergesketter, 1993, *Quality Is Personal*, New York: The Free Press; D. Garvin, 1988, *Managed Quality: The Strategic and Competitive Edge*, New York: The Free Press.

---

for products in which customers commonly express an interest. Quality is possible only when top-level managers support it and when its importance is part of the organizational culture.[78] When employees and managers value quality, they become vigilant about continuously finding ways to improve it.[79]

Quality is a universal theme in the global economy and is a necessary but not sufficient condition for competitive success.[80] Without quality, a firm's products lack credibility, meaning that customers do not think of them as viable options. Indeed, customers will not consider buying a product until they believe that it can satisfy at least their base-level expectations in terms of quality dimensions that are important to them. For example, quality was an issue for Jaguar automobiles for years as the carmaker endured frequent complaints from drivers about poor quality. This is no longer the case, as suggested by the following comments: "Many might not know it, but Jaguar is the third best ranked brand by the most trusted dependability survey (J. D. Power) in the world... It's fair to say that the brand's past reliability issues may still linger in the minds of some, but the Jaguar of today is not the Jaguar of old. It still carries with it a British heart and soul, but has refined its manufacturing processes to be world class."[81]

Quality affects competitive rivalry. The firm studying a competitor producing products that suffer from poor quality can predict that the competitor's costs are high and that its sales revenue likely will decline until the quality issues are resolved. In addition, the firm can predict that the competitor likely will not be aggressive in terms of taking competitive actions, given that its quality problems must be corrected in order to gain credibility with customers. Once the problems are corrected however, that competitor is likely to take competitive actions emphasizing significant product quality improvements.

Hyundai's experiences illustrate these expectations. Immediately upon becoming CEO of the company in March 1999, Chung Mong Koo started touring the firm's manufacturing facilities and then announced that improving product quality was an immediate and critical objective. Actions taken to improve quality included establishing a quality-control unit and allocating significant resources (more than $1 billion annually) to R&D in order to build cars that could compete on price and deliver on quality. Outcomes from Hyundai's focus on quality improvements are impressive. For example, the Hyundai Genesis was the highest-ranked model in the midsize premium car category in the 2012 J.D. Power and Associates Vehicle Dependability Study. Overall, the Genesis received more than 20 top honors during its first three years of availability.[82]

LIKELIHOOD OF RESPONSE

So far in this chapter, we have examined how market commonality, resource similarity, awareness of mutual interdependence, motivation to act based on perceived gains and losses, and the ability of a firm to take action can influence competitive behavior. We have also described how first-mover incentives, organizational size, and a firm's emphasis on quality can help it predict whether a competitor will pursue a competitive action. These same factors should also be evaluated to help a firm predict whether a competitor will respond to an action it is considering.

We describe other factors that a firm should consider when predicting competitive responses from one or more competitors in this section.

The success of a firm's competitive action is affected both by the likelihood a competitor will respond to it and by the type (strategic or tactical) and effectiveness of that response. As noted earlier, a competitive response is a strategic or tactical action the firm takes to counter the effects of a competitor's competitive action. In general, a firm is likely to respond to a competitor's action when it either significantly strengthens the position of the competitor or significantly weakens the focal firm's competitive position.[83] For instance, the actions of a competitor may lead to better use of its capabilities to create competitive advantages or an improved market position. Alternatively, a competitor's actions could damage the firm's own ability to use its capabilities to create or maintain an advantage or make its market position less defensible.

Next, we discuss the three factors that can help a firm predict how a competitor is likely to respond to competitive actions: the type of competitive action, reputation, and market dependence.

Type of Competitive Action

Competitive responses to strategic actions differ from responses to tactical actions. These differences allow the firm to predict a competitor's likely response to a competitive action that has been launched against it. Of course, a general prediction is that strategic actions receive strategic responses, whereas tactical responses are taken to counter the effects of tactical actions.

In general, strategic actions elicit fewer total competitive responses.[84] The reason for this is that as with strategic actions, strategic responses involve a significant commitment of resources and are difficult to implement and reverse. Moreover, the time needed for a strategic action to be implemented and its effectiveness assessed delays the competitor's response to that action.[85] In contrast to the time required to respond to a strategic action, a competitor likely will respond quickly to a tactical action, such as when an airline company almost immediately matches a competitor's tactical action of reducing prices in certain markets. Either strategic actions or tactical actions that target a large number of a rival's customers are likely to be targeted with strong responses.[86] In fact, if the effects of a competitor's action on the focal firm are significant (e.g., loss of market share, loss of major resources such as critical employees), a response is likely to be swift and strong.[87]

Actor's Reputation

In the context of competitive rivalry, an *actor* is the firm taking an action or response; *reputation* is "the positive or negative attribute ascribed by one rival to another based on past competitive behavior."[88] A positive reputation may be a source of competitive advantage and high returns, especially for producers of consumer goods.[89] Because of this, firms act aggressively to protect their reputation as Johnson & Johnson (J&J) has demonstrated. In early 2012, J&J "recalled its entire U.S. supply of infants' Tylenol—about 574,000 bottles—due to a design flaw that has not caused harm but sets back the health-products giant's efforts to regain sales following a string of earlier recalls."[90] Given the importance of earning and maintaining a reputation for high product quality for drug manufacturers, J&J's newly-appointed CEO Alex Gorsky was expected to deal aggressively with the firm's quality issues especially in light of the fact that surveys were showing that "J&J's reputation (was) retreating." In this regard, it was learned in 2012 that "for the first time in 13 years of the Harris Poll Reputation Quotient study, J&J (was not) ranked first or second among companies—it (was) seventh."[91]

To predict the likelihood of a competitor's response to a current or planned action, the firm examines the competitor's reputation for how it responds when attacked—past behavior is assumed to be a reasonable predictor of future behavior. Procter & Gamble, for example, has a reputation for being an aggressive competitor when attacked by rivals.[92] As suggested by comments stated previously, competitors such as Abbott Laboratories, Baxter International, and Pfizer among others could expect strong competitive reactions if they were to attack Johnson & Johnson on the basis of product quality issues.

Competitors are more likely to respond to either strategic or tactical actions when those actions are taken by a market leader.[93] In particular, successful actions will be quickly imitated. For example, Apple was the dominant manufacturer of personal computers when IBM, the market leader in the computer industry, devoted significant resources to enter the market. When IBM was immediately successful in this endeavor, competitors such as Dell, Compaq, and Gateway responded with strategic actions to enter the market. IBM's reputation as well as its successful strategic action strongly influenced entry by these competitors. Once the market became saturated and the product became more standardized, IBM's reputation was no longer a significant source of competitive advantage relative to the cost advantages of competitors. Intense competitive rivalry in this industry has resulted in other changes over the years including IBM's decision to sell its PC business to China's Lenovo Group, Hewlett-Packard's decision to acquire Compaq, and Acer's acquisition of Gateway.

In contrast to a firm with a strong reputation, such as IBM, competitors are less likely to respond to companies with reputations for competitive behavior that is risky, complex, and unpredictable. For instance, a firm with a reputation as a price predator (an actor that frequently reduces prices to gain or maintain market share) generates few responses to its tactical actions. This is because price predators, which typically increase prices once their market share objective is reached, lack credibility with their competitors.[94] On the other hand, a firm with a reputation for pricing integrity, such as Walmart, is much more likely to receive a competitive response to its pricing policies.[95]

Dependence on the Market

Market dependence denotes the extent to which a firm's revenues or profits are derived from a particular market.[96] In general, firms can predict that competitors with high market dependence are likely to respond strongly to attacks threatening their market position.[97] For example, firms that depend almost exclusively on one market, such as the Wrigley Company (chewing gum), Lincoln Electric (arc welders), or United Airlines (airline transportation) are much more likely to exhibit strong reactions to the strategic and tactical actions of competitors. Interestingly, the threatened firm in these instances may not respond quickly, but rather take more of a calculated approach to increase the effectiveness of its response.

The ninth largest tire manufacturer in the world, Cooper Tire & Rubber Co., is one of only two U.S.-owned tire manufacturers. Cooper sells tires exclusively to the replacement market both in North America (66 percent of 2011 revenues) and internationally (34 percent of 2011 revenues), which means that it has a high degree of market dependence. The firm is strongly committed to continuously developing innovative products that serve the needs of those buying replacement tires. Thus, Cooper carefully studies competitors' products and competitive actions as the foundation for developing innovative replacement tires as a foundation for seeking to outperform its rivals.[98]

COMPETITIVE DYNAMICS

Whereas competitive rivalry concerns the ongoing actions and responses between a firm and its competitors for an advantageous market position, *competitive dynamics* concerns the ongoing actions and responses taking place among *all* firms competing within a market for advantageous positions.

To explain competitive rivalry, we described (1) factors that determine the degree to which firms are competitors (market commonality and resource similarity), (2) the drivers of competitive behavior for individual firms (awareness, motivation, and ability), and (3) factors affecting the likelihood a competitor will act or attack (first-mover incentives, organizational size, and quality) and respond (type of competitive action, reputation, and market dependence). Building and sustaining competitive advantages are at the core of competitive rivalry, in that advantages are the link to an advantageous market position.

To explain competitive dynamics, we discuss the effects of varying rates of competitive speed in different markets (called slow-cycle, fast-cycle, and standard-cycle markets) on the behavior (actions and responses) of all competitors within a given market. Competitive behaviors, as well as the reasons or logic for taking them, are similar within each market type, but differ across market types.[99] Thus, competitive dynamics differs in slow-cycle, fast-cycle, and standard-cycle markets. The sustainability of the firm's competitive advantages is an important difference among the three market types.

As noted in Chapter 1, firms want to sustain their advantages for as long as possible, although no advantage is permanently sustainable. The degree of sustainability is affected by how quickly competitive advantages can be imitated and how costly it is to do so.

Slow-Cycle Markets

Slow-cycle markets are markets in which the firm's competitive advantages are shielded from imitation for what are commonly long periods of time and where imitation is costly.[100] Competitive advantages are relatively sustainable in slow-cycle markets.

Building a one-of-a-kind competitive advantage that is proprietary leads to competitive success in a slow-cycle market. This type of advantage is difficult for competitors to understand. As discussed in Chapter 4, a difficult-to-understand and costly-to-imitate advantage results from unique historical conditions, causal ambiguity, and/or social complexity. Copyrights, geography, patents, and ownership of an information resource are examples of what leads to one-of-a-kind advantages.[101] Once a proprietary advantage is developed, the firm's competitive behavior in a slow-cycle market is oriented to protecting, maintaining, and extending that advantage. Thus, the competitive dynamics in slow-cycle markets involve all firms concentrating on competitive actions and responses that enable them to protect, maintain, and extend their proprietary competitive advantage.

Walt Disney Co. continues to extend its proprietary characters, such as Mickey Mouse, Minnie Mouse, and Goofy. These characters have a unique historical development as a result of Walt and Roy Disney's creativity and vision for entertaining people. Products based on the characters seen in Disney's animated cartoons and films are sold through Disney's theme park shops as well as self-standing retail outlets called Disney Stores. The list of character-based products is extensive, including everything from the characters to clothing decorated with the characters' images. Patents shield the use of these characters, so the proprietary nature of Disney's advantage in terms of animated characters protects the firm from imitation by competitors.

Consistent with another attribute of competition in a slow-cycle market, Disney remains committed to protecting its exclusive rights to its characters and their use as shown by the fact that "the company once sued a day-care center, forcing it to remove the likeness of Mickey Mouse from a wall of the facility."[102] As with all firms competing in slow-cycle markets, Disney's competitive actions (such as building theme parks in France, Japan, and Hong Kong) and responses (such as lawsuits to protect its right to fully control use of its animated characters) maintain and extend its proprietary competitive advantage while protecting it. Disney has been able to establish through actions and defend through responses an advantageous market position as a result of its competitive behavior.

In the pharmaceutical industry, patent laws and regulatory requirements, such as those in the United States requiring approval by the Federal Food and Drug Administration (FDA) to launch new products, shield pharmaceutical companies' positions. Once a patent expires, the firm is no longer shielded from competition, a situation that has severe financial implications. Consequently, competitors in this market try to extend patents on their drugs to maintain advantageous positions that the patents provide.

Pfizer's patent for Lipitor was incredibly important to the firm's success for many years. Lipitor is the world's best-selling drug ever, accounting for over $106 billion in sales revenue for Pfizer between 2002 and 2011 alone. A cholesterol medication, Lipitor went off patent on November 30, 2011. Anticipating significant revenue and earnings' declines as a result of the loss of this patent, Pfizer is taking actions to deal with these issues. For a period of time, Pfizer intended to offer insured patients a discount card allowing them to buy Lipitor for $4 per month.[103] Additionally, Pfizer formed a profit-sharing agreement with Watson Pharmaceuticals to make an authorized generic version of Lipitor[104] while India-based Ranbaxy Laboratories received approval from the U.S. Food and Drug Administration in December, 2011 to sell

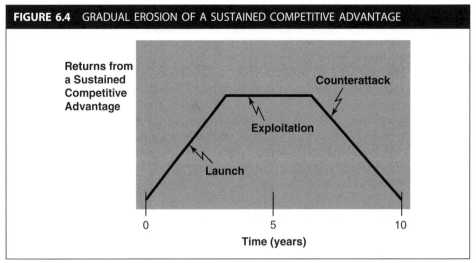

FIGURE 6.4 GRADUAL EROSION OF A SUSTAINED COMPETITIVE ADVANTAGE

SOURCE: Republished with permission of Academy of Management, from I. C. MacMillan, 1988, Controlling Competitive Dynamics by Taking Strategic Initiative, *Academy of Management Executive*, II(2), pp. 111–118.; permission conveyed through Copyright Clearance Center, Inc.

Atorvastatin, its generic version of Lipitor, in the United States.[105] Laws permit only limited generic competition in the first six months of a patent's expiration. As such, Pfizer expected a larger number of generic versions of Lipitor to enter the market as of May 31, 2012.

Figure 6.4 shows the competitive dynamics generated by firms competing in slow-cycle markets. In slow-cycle markets, firms launch a product (e.g., a new drug) that has been developed through a proprietary advantage (e.g., R&D) and then exploit it for as long as possible while the product is shielded from competition. Eventually, competitors respond to the action with a counterattack. In markets for drugs, this counterattack commonly occurs as patents expire, creating the need for another product launch by the firm seeking a shielded market position.

Fast-Cycle Markets

Fast-cycle markets are markets in which the firm's capabilities that contribute to competitive advantages are not shielded from imitation and where imitation is often rapid and inexpensive. Thus, competitive advantages are not sustainable in fast-cycle markets. Firms competing in fast-cycle markets recognize the importance of speed; these companies appreciate that "time is as precious a business resource as money or head count—and that the costs of hesitation and delay are just as steep as going over budget or missing a financial forecast."[106] Such high-velocity environments place considerable pressures on top managers to make strategic decisions quickly, but they must also be effective decisions.[107] The often substantial competition and technology-based strategic focus make the strategic decisions complex, increasing the need for a comprehensive approach integrated with decision speed.[108]

Reverse engineering and the rate of technology diffusion in fast-cycle markets facilitate rapid imitation. A competitor uses reverse engineering to quickly gain the knowledge required to imitate or improve the firm's products, usually in only a few months. Technology is diffused rapidly in fast-cycle markets, making it available to competitors in a short period of time. The technology often used by fast-cycle competitors is not proprietary, nor is it protected by patents, as in slow-cycle markets. For example, only a few hundred parts, which are readily available on the open market, are required to build a personal computer. Patents protect only a few of these parts, such as microprocessor chips.[109]

Fast-cycle markets are more volatile than slow-cycle markets and standard-cycle markets. Indeed, the pace of competition in fast-cycle markets is almost frenzied, as companies rely on ideas and the innovations resulting from them as growth engines. Because prices fall rapidly in these markets, companies need to profit quickly from their product innovations. For example, rapid declines in the prices of microprocessor chips produced by Intel and Advanced Micro Devices, among others, make it possible for PC manufacturers to continuously reduce their prices to end users. Imitation of many fast-cycle products is relatively easy, as demonstrated by a host of PC manufacturers. All of these firms have partly or largely imitated IBM's initial PC design to create their products. Continuous declines in the costs of parts, as well as the fact that the information and knowledge required to assemble a PC is not especially complicated and is readily available, make it possible for additional competitors to enter this market without significant difficulty.[110]

Fast-cycle market characteristics make it virtually impossible for companies in this type of market to develop sustainable competitive advantages. Recognizing this, firms avoid "loyalty" to any of their products, preferring to cannibalize their current product by launching a new product before competitors learn how to do so through successful imitation. This emphasis creates competitive dynamics that differ substantially from those in slow-cycle markets. Instead of concentrating on protecting, maintaining, and extending competitive advantages, as is the case for firms in slow-cycle markets, companies competing in fast-cycle markets focus on learning how to rapidly and continuously develop new competitive advantages that are superior to those they replace. In fast-cycle markets, firms do not concentrate on trying to protect a given competitive advantage because they understand that the advantage will not exist long enough to extend it.

Figure 6.5 shows the competitive behavior of firms competing in fast-cycle markets. Competitive dynamics in this market type finds firms taking actions and responses in the course of competitive rivalry that are oriented to rapid and continuous product introductions and the use of a stream of ever-changing competitive advantages. The firm launches a product as a competitive action and then exploits the advantage associated with it for as long as possible. However, the firm also tries to move to another temporary competitive action before competitors can respond to the first one. Thus, competitive dynamics in fast-cycle markets, in which all firms seek to establish a new competitive advantage before their competitors learn how to effectively respond to current ones, often result in rapid product upgrades as well as quick product innovations.[111]

As our discussion suggests, innovation has a dominant effect on competitive dynamics in fast-cycle markets. For individual firms, this means that innovation is a key source of competitive advantage. Through innovation, the firm can cannibalize its own products before competitors successfully imitate them.[112]

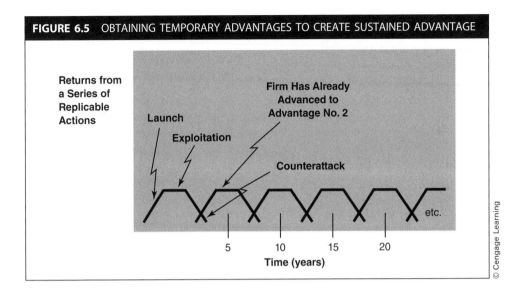

FIGURE 6.5 OBTAINING TEMPORARY ADVANTAGES TO CREATE SUSTAINED ADVANTAGE

© Cengage Learning

Standard-Cycle Markets

Standard-cycle markets are those in which the firm's competitive advantages are moderately shielded from imitation and where imitation is moderately costly. Competitive advantages are partially sustainable in standard-cycle markets, but only when the firm is able to continuously upgrade the quality of its competitive advantages. The competitive actions and responses that form a standard-cycle market's competitive dynamics find firms seeking large market shares, trying to gain customer loyalty through brand names, and carefully controlling their operations to consistently provide the same positive experience for customers.[113]

Companies competing in standard-cycle markets serve many customers. Because the capabilities on which their competitive advantages are based are less specialized, imitation is faster and less costly for standard-cycle firms than for those competing in slow-cycle markets. However, imitation is less quick and more expensive in these markets than in fast-cycle markets. Thus, the competitive dynamics in standard-cycle markets rest midway between the characteristics of dynamics in slow-cycle and fast-cycle markets. The quickness of imitation is reduced and becomes more expensive for standard-cycle competitors when a firm is able to develop economies of scale by combining coordinated and integrated design and manufacturing processes with a large sales volume.

Because of large volumes, the size of mass markets, and the need to develop scale economies, the competition for market share is intense in standard-cycle markets. This form of competition is readily evident in the battles between Coca-Cola and PepsiCo, as these firms compete against each other in markets throughout the world. These firms are aware of each other and possess the motivation and ability to engage in aggressive competition. Recently, sustainability has become another dimension on which Coke and PepsiCo are competing and are launching multiple initiatives to do so. PepsiCo, for example, purchased its first renewable energy certificates in 2007. The firm used these certificates to buy more than 1.1 billion kilowatt-hours of renewable energy between 2007 and 2010. According to analysts, this was "enough to offset the electricity use of all of its U.S. manufacturing, distribution and administrative offices" during this time period.[114] In 2011, Coca-Cola appointed a person to the newly-created position of Chief Sustainability Officer. Among other objectives, the firm seeks to use water more efficiently, reduce its global carbon emissions, and "to replace 100 percent petroleum-based PET plastic with PET plastic that contains up to 30 percent material derived from plants."[115] Thus, both firms envision sustainability as an important objective and as a means of learning how to outcompete a key rival.

In the final analysis, innovation substantially influences competitive dynamics as it affects the actions and responses of all companies competing in a slow-cycle, fast-cycle, or standard-cycle market.[116] We have emphasized innovation's importance to the firm's value creation in earlier chapters and will do so again in Chapter 12. Our discussion of innovation in terms of competitive dynamics extends the earlier discussions by showing its importance in all types of markets in which firms compete.

SUMMARY

▶ Competitors are firms competing in the same market, offering similar products, and targeting similar customers. Competitive rivalry is the ongoing set of competitive actions and competitive responses occurring between competitors as they compete against each other for an advantageous market position. The outcomes of competitive rivalry influence the firm's ability to sustain its competitive advantages as well as the level (below average, average, or above average) of its financial returns.

▶ The set of competitive actions and responses the firm takes while engaged in competitive rivalry is called competitive behavior. Competitive dynamics is the set of actions all firms competing within a particular market take.

▶ A firm studies competitive rivalry to be able to predict the competitive actions and responses that each of its competitors likely will take. Competitive actions are either strategic or tactical in nature. The firm takes competitive actions to defend or build its competitive advantages or improve its market position. Competitive responses are taken to counter the effects of a competitor's competitive action. A strategic action or a strategic response requires a significant commitment of organizational resources, is difficult to successfully implement, and is hard to reverse. A tactical action or a tactical response requires fewer organizational resources and is easier to implement and reverse.

▶ A competitor analysis is the first step the firm takes to be able to predict its competitors' actions and responses. In their analysis, firms study market commonality (the number of markets with which competitors are jointly involved and their importance to each) and resource similarity (how comparable competitors' resources are in terms of type and amount). In general, the greater the market commonality and resource similarity, the more firms acknowledge that they are direct competitors.

▶ Market commonality and resource similarity shape the firm's awareness (the degree to which it and its competitor understand their mutual interdependence), motivation (the firm's incentive to attack or respond), and ability (the quality of the resources available to the firm to attack and respond). Having knowledge of a competitor in terms of these characteristics increases the quality of the firm's predictions about a competitor's actions and responses.

- First-mover incentive is another factor that affects the likelihood of a competitor taking competitive actions. First movers, those firms taking an initial competitive action, often earn above-average returns until competitors can successfully respond to their action and gain loyal customers. Not all firms can be first movers in that they may lack the awareness, motivation, or ability required to engage in this type of competitive behavior. Moreover, some firms prefer to be a second mover (the firm responding to the first mover's action). One reason for this is that second movers, especially those acting quickly, can successfully compete against the first mover. By studying the first mover's good or service, customers' reactions to it, and the responses of other competitors to the first mover, the second mover can often avoid the early entrant's mistakes and find ways to improve upon the value created for customers by the first mover's good or service. Late movers (those that respond a long time after the original action was taken) commonly are less successful.
- Large organizational size tends to reduce the number of different types of competitive actions that large firms launch; smaller competitors use a wide variety of actions. Ideally, the firm would like to initiate a large number of diverse actions when engaged in competitive rivalry.
- Poor product quality dampens a firm's ability to take competitive actions, in that it is a base denominator to successful competition in the global economy.
- The type of action (strategic or tactical) the firm takes, the competitor's reputation for the nature of its competitor behavior, and its dependence on the market in which the action is taken are studied to predict a competitor's response. In general, the number of tactical responses exceeds the number of strategic responses. Competitors respond more frequently to the actions taken by the firm with a reputation for predictable and understandable competitive behavior, especially if that firm is a market leader. In general, the firm can predict that when its competitor is highly dependent for its revenue and profitability in the market in which the firm takes a competitive action, that competitor is likely to launch a strong response. However, firms that are more diversified across markets are less likely to respond to a particular action that affects only one of the markets in which they compete.
- Competitive dynamics concerns the ongoing competitive behavior occurring among all firms competing in a market for advantageous positions. Market characteristics affect the set of actions and responses firms take while competing in a market as well as the sustainability of firms' competitive advantages. In slow-cycle markets, where competitive advantages can be maintained, competitive dynamics finds firms taking actions and responses that are intended to protect, maintain, and extend their proprietary advantages. In fast-cycle markets, competition is almost frenzied as firms concentrate on developing a series of temporary competitive advantages. This emphasis is necessary because firms' advantages in fast-cycle markets are not proprietary and, as such, are subject to rapid and relatively inexpensive imitation. In standard-cycle markets, firms

are moderately shielded from competition as they use competitive advantages that are moderately sustainable. Competitors in standard-cycle markets serve mass markets and try to develop economies of scale to enhance their profitability. Innovation is vital to competitive success in each of these market types.

ETHICS QUESTIONS

1. When competing against one another, firms jockey for a market position that is advantageous, relative to competitors. In this jockeying, what are the ethical implications associated with the way competitor intelligence is gathered?

2. Second movers often respond to a first mover's competitive actions through imitation. Is there anything unethical about a company imitating a competitor's good or service as a means of engaging in competition?

3. The standards for competitive rivalry differ in countries throughout the world. What should firms do to cope with these differences? What guidance should a firm give to employees as they deal with competitive actions and competitive responses that are ethical in one country, but unethical in others?

4. In slow-cycle markets, effective competitors are able to shield their competitive advantages from imitation by competitors for relatively long periods of time. However, this is not the case in fast-cycle markets. Do these conditions have implications in terms of ethical business practices? Do ethical standards in slow-cycle markets differ from those in fast-cycle markets?

5. Is it ethical for the firm competing against a competitor in several markets to launch a competitive response in a market that differs from the one in which that competitor took a competitive action against the local firm? Why or why not?

NOTES

1. P. L. Drnevich & A P. Kriauciunas, 2011, Clarifying the conditions and limits of the contributions of ordinary and dynamic capabilities to relative firm performance, *Strategic Management Journal*, 32: 254–279; G. J. Castrogiovanni, 2002, Organization task environments: Have they changed fundamentally over time? *Journal of Management*, 28: 129–150.

2. F. Polidoro & P. K. Toh, 2011, Letting rivals come close or warding them off? The effects of substitution threat on imitation deterrence, *Academy of Management Journal*, 54: 369–392; G. Sargut & R. G. McGrath, 2011, Learning to live with complexity, *Harvard Business Review*, 89(9): 68–76.

3. C. M. Grimm, H. Lee, & K. G. Smith, 2006, *Strategy as Action: Competitive Dynamics and Competitive Advantage*, Oxford, UK: Oxford University Press.

4. P. Ziobro, 2012, Campbell Soup's profit falls 14%, *Wall Street Journal Online*, http://www.wsj.com, February 17; P. Ziobro, 2012, Heinz squeezes growth from emerging markets *Wall Street Journal Online*, http://www.wsj.com, February 17.

5. M.-J. Chen, 1996, Competitor analysis and interfirm rivalry: Toward a theoretical integration, *Academy of Management Review*, 21: 100–134.

6. J. A. Clougherty, 2011, Using rival effects to identify synergies and improve merger typologies, *Strategic Organization*, 9: 310–335; J. J. Marcel, P. S. Barr, & I. M. Duhaime, 2011, The influence of executive cognition on competitive dynamics, *Strategic Management Journal*, 32: 115–138.

7. D. G. Sirmon, M. A. Hitt, R. D. Ireland, & B. A. Gilbert, 2011, Resource orchestration to create competitive advantage: Breadth, depth, and life cycle effects, *Journal of Management*, 37: 1390–1412; W. Tsai, K.-H. Su, & M.-J. Chen, 2011, Seeing through the eyes of a rival: Competitor acumen based on rival-centric perceptions, *Academy of Management Journal*, 54: 761–778.

8. R. E. Caves, 1984, Economic analysis and the quest for competitive advantage, in *Papers and Proceedings of the 96th Annual Meeting of the American Economic Association*, 127–132.

9. Grimm, Lee, & Smith, *Strategy as Action*; G. Young, K. G. Smith, C. M. Grimm, & D. Simon, 2000, Multimarket contact and resource dissimilarity: A competitive dynamics perspective, *Journal of Management*, 26: 1217–1236; C. M. Grimm & K. G. Smith, 1997, *Strategy as Action: Industry Rivalry and Coordination*, Cincinnati: South-Western, 53–74.

10. F. Polidoro, G. Ahuja, & W. Mitchell, 2011, When the social structure overshadows competitive incentives: The effects of network embeddedness on joint

venture dissolution, *Academy of Management Journal,* 54: 203–223; H. D. Hopkins, 2003, The response strategies of dominant U.S. firms to Japanese challengers, *Journal of Management,* 29: 5–25.

[11] H. Hilman & Z. A. Mohamed, 2011, Strategic role of sourcing strategy in the relationships between competitive strategies and organisational performance, *Journal for International Business and Entrepreneurship Development,* 6: 75–82.

[12] M.-J. Chen & D. Miller, 2012, Competitive dynamics: Themes, trends, and a prospective research platform, *Academy of Management Annals,* 6: 1–89; G. Young, K. G. Smith, & C. M. Grimm, 1996, "Austrian" and industrial organization perspectives on firm-level competitive activity and performance, *Organization Science,* 73: 243–254.

[13] Z. Guedri & J. McGuire, 2011, Multimarket competition, mobility barriers, and firm performance, *Journal of Management Studies,* 48: 857–890; H. A. Haveman & L. Nonnemaker, 2000, Competition in multiple geographic markets: The impact on growth and market entry, *Administrative Science Quarterly,* 45: 232–267.

[14] J. Gimeno, 2011, A retrospective of "hyper-competition' in a multimarket environment," In G. D. Markham & P. H. Phan (eds.), *The competitive dynamics of entrepreneurial market entry,* Northampton, MA.: Edward Elgar Publishing, 85–123; L. Fuentelsaz & J. Gomez, 2006, Multipoint competition, strategic similarity and entry into geographic markets, *Strategic Management Journal,* 27: 477–499; K. G. Smith, W. J. Ferrier, & H. Ndofor, 2001, Competitive dynamics research: Critique and future directions, in M. A. Hitt, R. E. Freeman, & J. S. Harrison (eds.), *Handbook of Strategic Management,* Oxford, UK: Blackwell Publishers, 326.

[15] W. H. Thome, 2012, Bombardier versus Embraer on battlefield—East Africa, *TN Global Travel Industry News,* http://www.eturbonews.com, January 5; 2011, Boeing versus Airbus: The fight for flight intensifies, *CNNMoney,* http://www.cnnmoney.com, July 5.

[16] J. Haleblian, G. McNamara, K. Kolev, & B. J. Dykes, 2012, Exploring firm characteristics that differentiate leaders from followers in industry merger waves: A competitive dynamics perspective, *Strategic Management Journal,* 33: in press; G. Young, K. G. Smith, C. M. Grimm, & D. Simon, 200, Multimarket contact and resource dissimilarity: A competitive dynamics perspective, *Journal of Management,* 26: 1230–1233.

[17] F. Mas-Ruiz & F. Ruiz-Moreno, 2011, Rivalry within strategic groups and consequences for performance: The firm-size effects, *Strategic Management Journal,* 32: 1286–1308; K. Ramaswamy, 2001, Organizational ownership, competitive intensity, and firm performance: An empirical study of the Indian manufacturing sector, *Strategic Management Journal,* 22: 989–998; K. Cool, L. H. Roller, & B. Leleux, 1999, The relative impact of actual and potential rivalry on firm profitability in the pharmaceutical industry, *Strategic Management Journal,* 20: 1–14.

[18] H. A. Ndofor, D. G. Sirmon, & X. He, 2011, Firm resources, competitive actions and performance: Investigating a mediated model with evidence from the in-vitro diagnostics industry, *Strategic Management Journal,* 32: 640–657; D. R. Gnyawali & R. Madhavan, 2001, Cooperative networks and competitive dynamics: A structural embeddedness

perspective, *Academy of Management Review,* 26: 431–445.

[19] S.-H. Lee, S. B. Bach, & Y.-S. Baik, 2011, The impact of ipos on the values of directly competing incumbents, *Strategic Entrepreneurship Journal,* 5: 158–177; M. E. Porter, 1991, Towards a dynamic theory of strategy, *Strategic Management Journal,* 12: 95–117.

[20] F. Bridoux, K. G. Smith, & C. M. Grimm, 2012, The management of resources: Temporal effects of different types of actions on performance, *Journal of Management,* in press; K. G. Smith, C. M. Grimm, G. Young, & S. Wally, 1997, Strategic groups and rivalrous firm behavior: Toward a reconciliation, *Strategic Management Journal,* 18: 149–157.

[21] J. E. McGee & M. J. Rubach, 2011, Responding to increased environmental hostility: A study of the competitive behavior of small retailers, *Journal of Applied Business Research* 13: 83–94; D. Simon, 2005, Incumbent pricing responses to entry, *Strategic Management Journal,* 26: 1229–1248; W. J. Ferrier, 2001, Navigating the competitive landscape: The drivers and consequences of competitive aggressiveness, *Academy of Management Journal,* 44: 858–877; M. E. Porter, 1980, *Competitive Strategy,* New York: The Free Press.

[22] K.-H. Kim & W. Tsai, 2012, Social comparison among competing firms, *Strategic Management Journal,* 33: 115–136; Smith, Ferrier, & Ndofor, Competitive dynamics research, 319.

[23] J. R. De La Torre & A. Chacar, 2012, Network coordination and performance among MNEs in Latin American, *Global Strategy Journal,* 2: 3–25.

[24] S. Lohr, 2011, Google's competitors square off against its leader, *The New York Times Online,* http://www.nytimes.com, September 21.

[25] Chen, Competitor analysis and interfirm rivalry, 108.

[26] Ibid., 109.

[27] S. Kaplan, 2011, Research in cognition and strategy: Reflections on two decades of progress and a look to the future, *Journal of Management Studies,* 48: 665–695; E. Abrahamson & C. J. Fombrun, 1994, Macrocultures: Determinants and consequences, *Academy of Management Review,* 19: 728–755.

[28] C. Salter, 2002, On the road again, *Fast Company,* January, 50–58.

[29] Young, Smith, Grimm, & Simon, Multimarket contact and resource dissimilarity, 1219.

[30] G. J. Kilduff, H. A. Elfenbein, & B. M. Staw, 2010, The psychology of rivalry: A relationally dependent analysis of competition, *Academy of Management Journal,* 53: 943–969; Chen, Competitor analysis and interfirm rivalry, 106.

[31] H. R. Greve, J. A. C. Baum, H. Mitsuhashi, & T. J. Rowley, 2010, Built to last but falling apart: Cohesion, friction, and withdrawal from interfirm alliances, *Academy of Management Journal,* 53: 302–322; L. Fuentelsaz & J. Gomez, 2006, Multipoint competition, strategic similarity and entry into geographic markets, *Strategic Management Journal,* 27: 477–499; J. Gimeno & C. Y. Woo, 1999, Multimarket contact, economies of scope, and firm performance, *Academy of Management Journal,* 42: 239–259.

[32] Young, Smith, Grimm, & Simon, Multimarket contact and resource dissimilarity, 1230.

[33] C.-H. Lee, N. Venkatraman, H. Tanriverdi, & B. Iyer, 2010, Complementarity-based hypercompetition in the software industry: Theory and empirical test,

1990-2002, *Strategic Management Journal*, 31: 1431–1456; J. Gimeno, 1999, Reciprocal threats in multimarket rivalry: Staking out "spheres of influence" in the U.S. airline industry, *Strategic Management Journal*, 20: 101–128; N. Fernandez & P. L. Marin, 1998, Market power and multimarket contact: Some evidence from the Spanish hotel industry, *Journal of Industrial Economics*, 46: 301–315.

34. J. Min & H. Mitsuhashi, 2012, Dynamics of unclosed triangles in alliance networks: Disappearance of brokerage positions and performance consequences, *Journal of Management Studies*, 49: in press; Chen, Competitor analysis and interfirm rivalry, 107.

35. M. H. Kunc & J. D. W. Morecroft, 2010, Managerial decision making and firm performance under a resource-based paradigm, *Strategic Management Journal*, 31: 1164–1182; J. Gimeno & C. Y. Woo, 1996, Hypercompetition in a multimarket environment: The role of strategic similarity and multimarket contact on competitive de-escalation, *Organization Science*, 7: 322–341.

36. L. Canina, C. A. Enz, & J. S. Harrison, 2005, Agglomeration effects and strategic orientations: Evidence from the U.S. lodging industry, *Academy of Management Journal*, 48: 565–581.

37. Q. Xiao, J. W. O'Neill, & A. S. Mattila, 2012, The role of hotel owners: The influence of corporate strategies on hotel performance, *International Journal of Contemporary Hospitality Management*, 24: 122–139; J. W. O'Neill & A. S. Mattila, 2006, Strategic hotel development and positioning: The effects of revenue drivers on profitability, *Cornell Hotel and Restaurant Administration Quarterly*, 47(2): 146–155.

38. Chen, Competitor analysis and interfirm rivalry, 107–108.

39. Ibid., 110.

40. Ibid.; R. A. D'Aveni, G. B. Dagnino, & K. G. Smith, 2010, The age of temporary advantage, *Strategic Management Journal*, 31: 1371–1385.

41. T. C. Powell, D. Lovallo, & C. R. Fox, 2011, Behavioral strategy, *Strategic Management Journal*, 32: 1369–1386; S. Tallman, M. Jenkins, N. Henry, & S. Pinch, 2004, Knowledge, clusters and competitive advantage, *Academy of Management Review*, 29: 258–271.

42. W. Connors, 2012, Competition heats up in Canada's ice hotel market, *The Wall Street Journal*, http://www.wsj.com, February 17.

43. L. Zucchini & T. Kretschmer, 2011, Competitive pressure: Competitive dynamics as reactions to multiple rivals, http://www.ssrn.com/abstract=1919509; S. H. Park & D. Zhou, 2005, Firm heterogeneity and competitive dynamics in alliance formation, *Academy of Management Review*, 30: 531–554; Smith, Ferrier, & Ndofor, Competitive dynamics research, 320.

44. A. Roberts & C. Matlack, 2011, Once Wal-Mart's equal, Carrefour falls behind, *Bloomberg BusinessWeek Online*, http://www.businessweek.com, October 20.

45. L. Burkitt, 2012, Wal-Mart ups stake in China e-commerce, *The Wall Street Journal Online*, http://www.wsj.com, February 19.

46. Chen, Competitor analysis and interfirm rivalry, 113.

47. R. Reed & S.F. Stourred-Barnes, 2011, Patenting as a competitive tactic in multipoint competition, *Journal of Strategy and Management*, 4: 365–383;

R. Belderbos & L. Sleuwaegen, 2005, Competitive drivers and international plant configuration strategies: A product-level test, *Strategic Management Journal*, 26: 577–593.

48. G. M. Giaglis & K. G. Fouskas, 2011,The impact of managerial perceptions on competitive response variety *Management Decision*, 49: 1257–1275; Grimm & Smith, *Strategy as Action*, 125.

49. S.-J. Chang & J. H. Rhee, 2011, Rapid FDI expansion and firm performance, *Journal of International Business Studies*, 42: 979–994; D. B. Yoffie & M. Kwak, 2001, Mastering strategic movement at Palm, *MIT Sloan Management Review*, 43(1): 55–63.

50. R. Makadok, 2011, The four theories of profit and their joint effects, *Journal of Management*, 37: 1316–1334; K. G. Smith, W. J. Ferrier, & C. M. Grimm, 2001, King of the hill: Dethroning the industry leader, *Academy of Management Executive*, 15(2): 59–70.

51. W. J. Ferrier & H. Lee, 2003, Strategic aggressiveness, variation, and surprise: How the sequential pattern of competitive rivalry influences stock market returns, *Journal of Managerial Issues*, 14: 162–180; G. S. Day, 1997, Assessing competitive arenas: Who are your competitors? in G. S. Day & D. J. Reibstein (eds.), *Wharton on Competitive Strategy*, New York: Wiley, 25–26.

52. R. Dezember, 2012, Construction firm expands in oil drilling, *The Wall Street Journal Online*, http://www. wsj.com, February 21.

53. B. Sechler & R. van Dallen, 2012, UPS makes grab for Europe rival, *The Wall Street Journal Online*, http://www.wsj.com, February 18.

54. R. Ahmed, 2012, First Dunkin' Donuts outline in India by June, *The Wall Street Journal Online*, http://www.wsj.com, February 21.

55. A. Perez-Luno, J. Wiklund, & R. V. Cabrera, 2011, The dual nature of innovative activity: How entrepreneurial orientation influences innovation generation and adoption, *Journal of Business Venturing*, 26: 555–571; W. T. Robinson & J. Chiang, 2002, Product development strategies for established market pioneers, early followers, and late entrants, *Strategic Management Journal*, 23: 855–866.

56. J. Schumpeter, 1934, *The Theory of Economic Development*, Cambridge, MA: Harvard University Press.

57. J. L. C. Cheng & I. F. Kesner, 1997, Organizational slack and response to environmental shifts: The impact of resource allocation patterns, *Journal of Management*, 23: 1–18.

58. F. Wang, 2000, Too appealing to overlook, *America's Network*, December, 10–12.

59. J. Kim & C.-Y. Lee, 2011, Technological regimes and the persistence of first-mover advantages, *Industrial and Corporate Change*, 20: 1305–1333; D. P. Forbes, 2005, Managerial determinants of decision speed in new ventures, *Strategic Management Journal*, 26: 355–366.

60. J. G. Combs, D. J. Ketchen, Jr., R. D. Ireland, & J. W. Webb, 2011, The role of resource flexibility in leveraging strategic resources, *Journal of Management Studies*, 48: 1098–1125; A. Srivastava & H. Lee, 2005, Predicting order and timing of new product moves: The role of top management in corporate entrepreneurship, *Journal of Business Venturing*, 20: 459–481; A. Nerer & P. W. Roberts, 2004, Technological and product-market experience and the success of new product introductions in the

pharmaceutical industry, *Strategic Management Journal*, 25: 779–799.

[61] C. A. Siren, M. Kohtsmski, & A. Kuckertz, 2012, Exploration and exploitation strategies, profit performance, and the mediating role of strategic learning: Escaping the exploitation trap, *Strategic Entrepreneurship Journal*, 6: 18–41; S. W. Geiger & L. H. Cashen, 2002, A multidimensional examination of slack and its impact on innovation, *Journal of Managerial Issues*, 14: 68–84; L. J. Bourgeois III, 1981, On the measurement of organizational slack, *Academy of Management Review*, 6: 29–39.

[62] S. W. Bradley, D. A. Shepherd, & J. Wiklund, 2011, The importance of slack for new organizations facing 'tough' environments, *Journal of Management Studies*, 48: 1071–1097; T. Gantumur & A. Stephan, 2011, Mergers & acquisitions and innovation performance in the telecommunications equipment industry, *Industrial and Corporate Change*, in press.

[63] C. C. Phelps, 2010, A longitudinal study of the influence of alliance network structure and composition on firm exploratory innovation, *Academy of Management Journal*, 53: 890–913; M. Semadeni & B. S. Anderson, 2010, The follower's dilemma: Innovation and imitation in the professional services industry, *Academy of Management Journal*, 53: 1175–1193; M. B. Lieberman & D. B. Montgomery, 1988, First-mover advantages, *Strategic Management Journal*, 9: 41–58.

[64] G. Dowell & A. Swaminathan, 2006, Entry timing, exploration, and firm survival in the early U.S. bicycle industry, *Strategic Management Journal*, 27: 1159–1182.

[65] 2001, Older, wiser, webbier, *Economist*, June 30, 10.

[66] W. Zhu & X. Xu, 2011, Second-mover advantages with asymmetric costs and information updates: A product life perspective, *Managerial and Decision Economics*, 32: 527–533; W. Boulding & M. Christen, 2001, First-mover disadvantage, *Harvard Business Review*, 79(9): 20–21.

[67] D. Levinson & F. Xie, 2011, Does first last? The existence and extent of first mover advantages on spatial networks, *Journal of Transport and Land Use*, 4: 47–69; J. Gimeno, R. E. Hoskisson, B. B. Beal, & W. P. Wan, 2005, Explaining the clustering of international expansion moves: A critical test in the U.S. telecommunications industry, *Academy of Management Journal*, 48: 297–319.

[68] C. Edwards, 2006, To see where tech is headed, watch TI, *Business Week*, November 6, 74.

[69] J. Pettit & E. Darner, 2012, The myth of first mover advantage, http://www.ssrn.com/abstract=1989078, January 24; H. R. Greve, 1998, Managerial cognition and the mimetic adoption of market positions: What you see is what you do, *Strategic Management Journal*, 19: 967–988.

[70] S. D. Dobrev & G. R. Carroll, 2003, Size (and competition) among organizations: Modeling scale-based selection among automobile producers in four major countries, 1885–1981, *Strategic Management Journal*, 24: 541–558; Smith, Ferrier, & Ndofor, Competitive dynamics research, 327.

[71] W. S. Desarbo, R. Grewal, & J. Wind, 2006, Who competes with whom? A demand-based perspective for identifying and representing asymmetric competition, *Strategic Management Journal*, 27: 101–129; F. K. Pil & M. Hoiweg, 2003, Exploring scale: The advantage of thinking small, *McKinsey Quarterly*, 44(2): 33–39; M.-J. Chen & D. C. Hambrick, 1995, Speed, stealth and selective attack: How small firms differ from large firms in competitive behavior, *Academy of Management Journal*, 38: 453–482.

[72] D. Miller & M.-J. Chen, 1996, The simplicity of competitive repertoires: An empirical analysis, *Strategic Management Journal*, 17: 419–440.

[73] Young, Smith, & Grimm, "Austrian" and industrial organization perspectives.

[74] J. C. de Oliveira Matias & D. A. Coelho, 2011, Integrated total quality management: Beyond zero defects theory and towards innovation, *Total Quality Management & Business Excellence*, 22: 891–910; P. B. Crosby, 1980, *Quality Is Free*, New York: Penguin.

[75] P. Ingeolsson, M. Eriksson, & J. Lilja, 2012, Can selecting the right values help TQM implementation? A case study about organisational homogeneity at the Walt Disney Company, *Total Quality Management & Business Excellence*, in press; W. E. Deming, 1986, *Out of the Crisis*, Cambridge, MA: MIT Press.

[76] N. Plambeck, 2011, The development of new products: The role of firm context and managerial cognition, *Journal of Business Venturing*, R. S. Kaplan & D. P. Norton, 2001, *The Strategy-Focused Organization*, Boston: Harvard Business School Press.

[77] S. Raithel, M. Sarstedt, S. Scharf, & M. Schwaiger, 2012, On the value of customer satisfaction: Multiple drivers and multiple markets, *Journal of the Academy of Marketing Science*, in press; L. B. Crosby, R. DeVito, & J. M. Pearson, 2003, Manage your customers' perception of quality, *Review of Business*, 24(1): 18–24.

[78] L. Yarbrough, N. A. Morgan, & D. W. Vorhies, 2011, The impact of product market strategy-organizational culture fit on business performance, *Journal of the Academy of Marketing Science*, 39: 555–573.

[79] J. W. Webb, R. D. Ireland, M. A. Hitt, G. M. Kistruck, & L. Tihanyi, 2011, Where is the opportunity without the customer? An integration of marketing activities, the entrepreneurship process, and institutional theory, *Journal of the Academy of Marketing Science*, 39: 537–554; K. E. Weick & K. M. Sutcliffe, 2001, *Managing the Unexpected*, San Francisco: Jossey-Bass, 81–82.

[80] J. Dyer & W. Chu, 2011, The determinants of trust in supplier-automaker relations in the US, Japan, and Korea: A retrospective, *Journal of International Business Studies*, 42: 28–34; G. Yeung & V. Mok, 2005, What are the impacts of implementing ISOs on the competitiveness of manufacturing industry in China, *Journal of World Business*, 40: 139–157.

[81] 2011 Jaguar XF review, *Car Advice*, http://www.caradvice.com/au, July 5.

[82] 2012, Hyundai Genesis named most dependable midsize premium car by J.D. Power and Associates, *PR Newswire*, http://www.prnewswire.com, February 15.

[83] F. Mas-Ruiz & F. Ruiz-Moreno, 2011, Rivalry within strategic groups and consequences for performance: The firm-size effects, *Strategic Management Journal*, 32: 1286–1308; J. Schumpeter, 1950, *Capitalism, Socialism and Democracy*, New York: Harper; Smith, Ferrier, & Ndofor, Competitive dynamics research, 323.

[84] M. Carney, E. R. Gedajiovic, P. M. A. R. Heugens, M. van Essen, & J. van Oosterhout, 2011, Business group affiliation, performance, context, and strategy: A meta-analysis, *Academy of Management Journal*, 54: 437–460; M.-J. Chen & I. C. MacMillan, 1992,

Nonresponse and delayed response to competitive moves, *Academy of Management Journal,* 35: 539–570; Smith, Ferrier, & Ndofor, Competitive dynamics research, 335.

85. A. M. L. Raes, M. G. Heijitjes, U. Glunk, & R. A. Roe, 2011, The interface of the top management team and middle managers: A process model, *Academy of Management Review,* 36: 102–126; M.-J. Chen, K. G. Smith, & C. M. Grimm, 1992, Action characteristics as predictors of competitive responses, *Management Science,* 38: 439–455.

86. M.-J. Chen, 2009, Competitive dynamics research: An insider's odyssey, *Asia Pacific Journal of Management,* 26: 5–25; M.-J. Chen & D. Miller, 1994, Competitive attack, retaliation and performance: An expectancy-valence framework, *Strategic Management Journal,* 15: 85–102.

87. T. Gardner, 2005, Interfirm competition for human resources: Evidence from the software industry, *Academy of Management Journal,* 48: 237–258; N. Huyghebaert & L. M. van de Gucht, 2004, Incumbent strategic behavior in financial markets and the exit of entrepreneurial startups, *Strategic Management Journal,* 25: 669–688.

88. Smith, Ferrier, & Ndofor, Competitive dynamics research, 333.

89. M. D. Pfarrer, T. G. Pollock, & V. P. Rindova, 2010, A tale of two assets: The effects of firm reputation and celebrity on earnings surprises and investors' reactions, *Academy of Management Journal,* 53: 1131–1152; P. W. Roberts & G. R. Dowling, 2003, Corporate reputation and sustained superior financial performance, *Strategic Management Journal,* 24: 1077–1093; J. Shamsie, 2003, The context of dominance: An industry-driven framework for exploiting reputation, *Strategic Management Journal,* 24: 199–215.

90. J. D. Rockoff, 2012, J&J recalls infants' Tylenol, *The Wall Street Journal Online,* http://www.wsj.com, February 18.

91. J. D. Rockoff & J. S. Lublin, 2012, New J&J chief to face repair jobs, *The Wall Street Journal Online,* http://www.wsj.com, February 23, 2012.

92. J. Neff, 2010, P&G gets aggressive with 'one company' approach, *Advertising Age,* http://www.adage.com, December 16.

93. F. Karakaya & P. Yannopoulos, 2011, Impact of market entrant characteristics on incumbent reactions to market entry, *Journal of Strategic Marketing,* 19: 171–185; W. J. Ferrier, K. G. Smith, & C. M. Grimm, 1999, The role of competitive actions in market share erosion and industry dethronement: A study of industry leaders and challengers, *Academy of Management Journal,* 42: 372–388.

94. Smith, Grimm, & Gannon, *Dynamics of Competitive Strategy.*

95. C. Jordan, J. Zhang, A. Krishna, & M. W. Kruger, 2011, When Wal-Mart enters: How incumbent retailers react and how this affects their sales outcomes, *Journal of Marketing Research,* 47: 577–593.

96. A. Karnani & B. Wernerfelt, 1985, Research note and communication: Multiple point competition, *Strategic Management Journal,* 6: 87–97.

97. Smith, Ferrier, & Ndofor, Competitive dynamics research, 330.

98. 2012, Cooper Tires, http://www.coopertire.com, February 22; 2012, Cooper Tire & Rubber Co., *Standard & Poor's Stock Reports,* http://www.standardandpoors.com, February 18.

99. C. Zhang, P. Song, & Z. Qu, 2011, Competitive action in the diffusion of Internet technology products in emerging markets: Implications for global marketing managers, *Journal of International Marketing,* 19(4): 40–60; A. Kalnins & W. Chung, 2004, Resource-seeking agglomeration: A study of market entry in the lodging industry, *Strategic Management Journal,* 25: 689–699; J. R. Williams, 1999, *Renewable Advantage: Crafting Strategy through Economic Time,* New York: The Free Press.

100. J. W. Park & R. Madhaven, 2011, Do opposites attract? The uncertainty spread as a predictor of diversification, mergers and acquisitions, http://ssrn.com/abstract=1887584, July 17; J. R. Williams, 1992, How sustainable is your competitive advantage? *California Management Review* 34(3): 29–51.

101. Williams, *Renewable Advantage,* 6.

102. Ibid., 57.

103. 2011, KABC Los Angeles, Generic versions of Lipitor coming to market, http://abclocal.go.com, November 30.

104. D. Wilson, 2011, Plan would delay sales of generic for Lipitor, *The New York Times Online,* http://www.nytimes.com, November 11.

105. S. Mehdudia, 2011, Ranbaxy launches generic version of Lipitor in U.S. market, *The Hindu,* http://www.thehindu.com, December 1.

106. 2003, How fast is your company? *Fast Company,* June, 18.

107. J. R. Mitchell, D.A. Shepherd, & M. P. Sharfman, 2011, Erratic strategic decisions: When and why managers are inconsistent in strategic decision making, *Strategic Management Journal,* 32: 683–704; T. Talaulicar, J. Grundei, & A. V. Werder, 2005, Strategic decision making in start-ups: The effect of top management team organization and processes on speed and comprehensiveness, *Journal of Business Venturing,* 20: 519–541.

108. M. H. Kune & J. D. W. Morecroft, 2010, Managerial decision making and firm performance under a resource-based paradigm, *Strategic Management Journal,* 31: 1164–1182; M. Song, C. Droge, S. Hanvanich, & R. Calantone, 2005, Marketing and technology resource complementarity: An analysis of their interaction effect in two environmental contexts, *Strategic Management Journal,* 26: 259–276.

109. Williams, *Renewable Advantage,* 8.

110. Ibid.

111. R. Sanchez, 1995, Strategic flexibility in production competition, *Strategic Management Journal,* 16(summer special issue): 9–26.

112. Schumpeter, *The Theory of Economic Development.*

113. Williams, *Renewable Advantage,* 7.

114. L. Laitinen, 2007, Coke vs. Pepsi: A battle to be green, *Green@work,* http://www.greenatworkmag.com, July/August.

115. 2010/2011 Sustainability report, Coca-Cola Home page, http://www.cocacola.com, February, 2011.

116. D. R. Gynawali & B.-J. Park, 2011, Co-opetition between giants: Collaboration with competitors for technological innovation, *Research Policy,* 40: 650–663.

Chapter 7

COOPERATIVE STRATEGY

KNOWLEDGE OBJECTIVES

Studying this chapter should provide you with the strategic management knowledge needed to:

1. Define cooperative strategies and explain why they are important in the current competitive environment.

2. Explain how the primary reasons for the use of cooperative strategy differ depending on market context (fast cycle, slow cycle, or standard cycle).

3. Define and discuss equity and nonequity strategic alliances.

4. Discuss the types of cooperative strategies that are formed primarily to reduce costs or increase differentiation.

5. Identify and describe cooperative strategies that help a firm address forces in the external environment.

6. Explain the cooperative strategies that firms use primarily to foster growth.

7. Discuss the risks associated with cooperative strategies.

8. Describe how firms can effectively implement and manage their cooperative strategies.

Globalization and rapid technological changes have created a business environment in which interorganizational cooperation is required for success.[1] Typically firms do not possess all of the knowledge, abilities, and resources they need to be successful in today's competitive environment.[2] In addition to developing new resources and abilities in-house or buying what they need through arms-length business transactions, an increasing number of firms are forming cooperative relationships with other organizations to develop new sources of competitive advantage.[3] A **cooperative strategy** is a strategy in which firms work together to achieve a shared objective.[4] A **relational advantage** exists when a firm's relationships with other firms put it at an advantage relative to rival firms.[5] Firms that use cooperative strategies successfully gain relational advantages that allow them to out-perform their rivals in terms of strategic competitiveness and above-average returns.[6]

We examine several topics in this chapter. First, we discuss some of the reasons cooperative strategies are important in the current competitive environment.

We examine these reasons in general and also by market type: slow cycle, fast cycle, or standard cycle. We then offer examples of various types of cooperative strategies on the basis of their primary strategic objectives: to increase differentiation or reduce costs, to deal with forces in the external environment, or to grow and diversify. Many of the examples fall into the category of strategic alliances because they are the most frequently used form of cooperative strategy. A **strategic alliance** is a cooperative strategy in which firms combine resources and capabilities to create a competitive advantage.[7] The chapter closes with discussions of the risks of using cooperative strategies as well as how effective management of them can reduce those risks and enhance performance.

THE IMPORTANCE OF COOPERATIVE STRATEGY

Cooperative strategies have become an integral part of the competitive landscape and are now quite important to many companies.[8] Firms use cooperative strategies to leverage their own resources and capabilities as well as to develop new resources and capabilities, and to do so more quickly than they could if they were acting independently.[9] Because cooperative strategies do not tend to be permanent arrangements, they can also enhance strategic flexibility. That is, it is relatively easier for a firm to move in and out of cooperative strategies due to changes in the environment or its strategies than it is to start up or shut down parts of its own internal operations.

Cooperative strategies are consistent with the stakeholder perspective introduced in Chapter 1. The stakeholder approach suggests that the primary role of managers is to coordinate a network of cooperative relationships, both inside and outside the firm.[10] The underlying assumption is that organizations are inherently cooperative systems.[11] Because of their cooperative nature, organizations are inclined to form partnerships with stakeholders to achieve common objectives.

Cooperative relationships can be powerful mechanisms for aligning stakeholder interests and can also help a firm reduce environmental uncertainty.[12] For example, much of a firm's success in the automobile industry depends on the strength of its suppliers. But just as an automobile manufacturer depends on its suppliers, so do its suppliers depend on the manufacturer. Their fortunes are closely aligned, and thus much of the uncertainty they face depends on the strategic and tactical actions each takes.[13] Mutual dependence suggests that manufacturers and their suppliers should form strong partnerships in order to reduce uncertainty and enhance joint value creation.[14] A senior executive of a firm that supplies Toyota described the relationship in simple terms: "Toyota helped us dramatically improve our production system."[15] The payoff to Toyota is a better, and more loyal, supplier.

Increasingly, cooperative strategies are formed by firms who also compete against one another, a situation called **co-opetition**.[16] For instance, rivals Samsung Electronics and Sony Corporation simultaneously pursue competition and collaboration to help address major technological challenges. Their co-opetition, in turn, encourages co-opetition among other firms in the industry.[17] In spite of the potential advantages of cooperating with a competitor, some research suggests that doing so may be associated with lower levels of ground-breaking innovation in the service sector. Specifically, one study found that service firms that use information from their own research and development processes as well as firms that are involved in science-based product innovation collaborations are more likely to introduce new-to-the-market innovations than firms that rely primarily on information coming from competitors.[18] This is not all that surprising because firms are probably unlikely to release genuinely novel ideas and technologies to their closest rivals.

In some industries, alliance versus alliance is becoming more prominent than firm against firm as a point of competition. In the global airline industry, for example, the Star Alliance (i.e., United Airlines, SAS, Singapore Airlines, and South African Airways) competes against the SkyTeam Alliance (i.e., Delta Airlines, Air France, Middle East Airlines, and Aeroflot) and the Oneworld alliance (i.e. American Airlines, British Airways, and Japan Airlines).[19] Each of these alliances is active in recruiting new companies and defections also occur, as in the case of Star partner Shanghai Airlines moving to Skyteam.

The individually unique competitive conditions of slow-cycle, fast-cycle, and standard-cycle markets (discussed in Chapter 6) find firms using cooperative strategies for slightly different reasons (see Table 7.1).[20] Slow-cycle markets are markets where the firm's competitive advantages are shielded from imitation for relatively long periods and where imitation is costly. These markets have close to monopolistic conditions. Railroads and, historically, telecommunications, utilities, and financial services are examples of industries characterized as slow-cycle markets. In fast-cycle markets the firm's competitive advantages are not shielded from imitation, thereby preventing their long-term sustainability. Competitive advantages are moderately shielded from imitation in standard-cycle markets, typically allowing them to be sustained for a longer time compared with fast-cycle market situations, but for a shorter

TABLE 7.1 REASONS FOR STRATEGIC ALLIANCES BY MARKET TYPE	
MARKET	**REASON**
Slow Cycle	▶ Gain access to a restricted market ▶ Establish a franchise in a new market ▶ Maintain market stability (e.g., establishing standards)
Fast Cycle	▶ Speed up development of new goods or services ▶ Speed up new market entry ▶ Maintain market leadership ▶ Form an industry technology standard ▶ Share risky R&D expenses ▶ Overcome uncertainty
Standard Cycle	▶ Gain market power (reduce industry overcapacity) ▶ Gain access to complementary resources ▶ Establish better economies of scale ▶ Overcome trade barriers ▶ Meet competitive challenges from other competitors ▶ Pool resources for very large capital projects ▶ Learn new business techniques

time than in slow-cycle markets. In this chapter, we focus specifically on the most common form of cooperative strategy, strategic alliances, to describe how purposes tend to vary across the three types of markets.

Strategic Alliances in Slow-Cycle Markets

Firms in slow-cycle markets often use strategic alliances to enter restricted markets or to establish franchises in new markets. Strategic alliances may allow firms to enter markets more quickly because partner firms already have experience in a market of interest.[21]

The alliance partner better understands conditions in the new market, including sociocultural, legal, regulatory, economic, and industry influences, and provides knowledge of and relationships with customers and suppliers. CSX is one of the Big Four railroads that control approximately 90 percent of rail revenues in the United States. Although their own route system is limited to 23 Eastern states and some areas in Canada, CSX also has access to Pacific ports through alliances with railroads in the Western United States.[22]

Slow-cycle markets are becoming rare in the 21st-century competitive landscape for several reasons, including the privatization of industries and economies, the rapid expansion of the Internet's capabilities in terms of the quick dissemination of information, and the speed with which advancing technologies make quickly imitating even complex products possible.[23] Firms competing in slow-cycle markets should recognize the future likelihood that they'll encounter situations in which their competitive advantages become partially sustainable (in the case of a standard-cycle market) or unsustainable (in the case of a fast-cycle market). Cooperative strategies can be helpful to firms making the transition from relatively sheltered markets to more competitive ones.[24]

Strategic Alliances in Fast-Cycle Markets

Fast-cycle markets tend to be unstable, unpredictable, and complex.[25] These three conditions virtually preclude the establishment of long-lasting competitive advantages, forcing firms to constantly seek sources of new competitive advantages while creating value by using current ones. Alliances between firms with current excess resources and capabilities and those with promising capabilities help companies competing in fast-cycle markets to make an effective transition from the present to the future and also to gain rapid entry to new markets.

The information technology (IT) industry is a fast-cycle market. The IT landscape continues to change rapidly as businesses are becoming more and more focused on selecting a handful of strategic partners to help drive down costs, integrate technologies that provide significant business advantages or productivity gains, and aggressively look for applications that can be shifted to more flexible and cost-effective platforms. For example, IBM uses a global network of alliance partners to enhance its IT services for its customers. Specifically, the company works with its partners to "optimize IT infrastructure efficiency, decrease operational and management costs, enhance workforce productivity and effectiveness, and extend ROI on existing IT investment."[26]

Strategic Alliances in Standard-Cycle Markets

In standard-cycle markets, which are often large and oriented toward economies of scale (e.g., the commercial aerospace industry, beverages), alliances are more likely to be made by partners with complementary resources and capabilities. One of the most important motives for alliances in these markets is to gain market power. For example, PepsiCo acquired an equity stake in Tingyi-Asahi Beverages Holding, a joint venture with massive distribution links across China, in an effort to increase its expansion in one of the fastest growing soft drinks markets in the world. Pepsi hopes to close in on the market leader Coca-Cola Company.[27]

Cooperative strategies may also be important in standard-cycle markets because they allow firms to learn new business techniques and new technologies. Firms can and should learn from each of their alliance partners.[28] Indeed, learning from alliances may be most critical in standard-cycle markets, but it can also help firms in slow-cycle and fast-cycle markets.

Types of Alliances and Other Cooperative Strategies

Strategic alliances can be divided into two basic types on the basis of their legal form, depending on whether they involve equity. An **equity strategic alliance** is an alliance in which two or more firms own a portion of the equity in the venture they have created. Many direct foreign investments are completed through equity strategic alliances.[29] Sometimes they take the form of purchase of stock in an existing company, as when BMW AG purchased a 15 percent stake in SGL Carbon SE, a supplier of lightweight carbon fibers and composites, in an effort to share the costs of developing new components and secure access to the technologies it needs to build electric and hybrid vehicles.[30]

A **joint venture** is a strategic alliance in which two or more firms create a legally independent company to share resources and capabilities to develop a competitive advantage.[31] Joint ventures also involve equity. Typically, partners in a joint venture own equal percentages and contribute equally to its operations. For example, Walter Energy, a U.S.-based metallurgical coal producer for the global steel industry, has a 50 percent joint venture with Peace River Coal of Canada to develop properties in British Columbia.[32] Because joint ventures result in sharing of resources, costs, and risks associated with a particular venture, they are an attractive way for firms to deal with uncertain competitive conditions such as economic downturns.[33]

Joint ventures are effective in establishing long-term relationships and in transferring **tacit knowledge**, which is knowledge that is complex and hard to codify. These characteristics mean that tacit knowledge is learned through experiences, such as those taking place when people from partner firms work together in a joint venture.[34] Tacit knowledge is an important source of competitive advantage for many firms because it is hard for rivals to duplicate.[35]

A **nonequity strategic alliance** is an alliance in which two or more firms develop a contractual relationship to share some of their unique resources and capabilities to create a competitive advantage. Licensing agreements, supply contracts, outsourcing, and distribution agreements are examples of nonequity strategic alliances. In this type of strategic alliance, firms do not establish a separate independent

FIGURE 7.1 STRATEGIC OBJECTIVES OF COOPERATIVE STRATEGIES

Primary Intention	Type of Strategy
Enhance differentiation or reduce costs.	Complementary strategic alliances Network cooperative strategies
Effectively address forces in the external environment.	Competitive response alliances Uncertainty-reducing alliances Competition-reducing cooperative strategies Associations and consortia
Promote growth and/or diversification.	Diversifying strategic alliances Franchising International cooperative strategies

company and therefore do not take equity positions. Consequently, nonequity strategic alliances are less formal and demand fewer partner commitments than joint ventures and equity strategic alliances, and generally do not foster an intimate relationship between partners; nevertheless, research evidence suggests that they can still create value for the firms involved.[36] The relative informality and lower commitment levels characterizing nonequity strategic alliances make them less suitable for complex projects in which success requires effective transfers of tacit knowledge between partners.[37]

Many other forms of cooperative strategy exist. For instance, trade groups, associations, and research consortia combine firms in common purposes. Also, firms may cooperate in other ways, either formally (e.g., a cartel or *keiretsu*, which is a group of firms tied together by cross-shareholdings) or informally (e.g., collusion). Equity, nonequity, and other forms of alliances and cooperative strategies can be divided into categories based on their primary strategic objectives. Figure 7.1 lists the most common types of cooperative strategies based on whether they are primarily intended to enhance differentiation or reduce costs, help the firm deal more effectively with forces in its external environment, or increase the firm's growth and diversification. Obviously, any particular alliance can have two or more of these objectives; however, dividing them on the basis of their primary strategic objective will facilitate this discussion.

COOPERATIVE STRATEGIES THAT ENHANCE DIFFERENTIATION OR REDUCE COSTS

Cooperative strategies are used at the business level to help improve a firm's performance in individual product markets. As discussed in Chapter 5, business-level strategy details what the firm intends to do to gain a competitive advantage in specific product markets. Thus, the firm forms a business-level cooperative strategy when it believes that combining its resources and capabilities with those of one or more partners will create competitive advantages that it cannot create by itself and that will lead to success in a specific product market. Chapter 5 described two primary means of creating above-normal value for customers in product markets: producing goods or services at lower costs or differentiating a good or service so that customers prefer it.[38] Cooperative strategies that are intended to achieve these objectives fall into two general categories: complementary strategic alliances and network cooperative strategies.

Complementary Strategic Alliances

Complementary strategic alliances are business-level alliances in which firms share some of their resources and capabilities in complementary ways to develop competitive advantages.[39] There are two types of complementary strategic alliances—vertical and horizontal.

Vertical Complementary Strategic Alliances. In a *vertical complementary strategic alliance*, firms share their resources and capabilities from different stages of the value chain to create a competitive advantage. Recall that the value chain refers to the sequence of activities that ultimately results in the satisfaction of customer needs. Frequently vertical alliances mean that an organization creates an alliance with one of its suppliers or customers, often in an effort to innovate as a response to environmental changes.[40] For example, in response to a slumping dairy industry made even more competitive by industry consolidation and an inability to differentiate their products, Australian dairy producers are using alliances to move up the value chain toward consumers. A case in point is the alliance between Murray Goulburn Co-operative (MGC) and the French giant Danone that focuses on yogurts and other processed food items that allow for greater brand recognition.[41]

Horizontal Complementary Alliances. A *horizontal complementary strategic alliance* is an alliance in which firms share some of their resources and capabilities from the same stage of the value chain to create a competitive advantage.[42] Commonly, firms use this type of alliance to focus on long-term product development and distribution opportunities.[43] Research on the worldwide aircraft industry demonstrates that companies are more likely to form horizontal alliances than to try to develop new products on their own when resource requirements are great and the resources available to any one firm are limited. In these circumstances, a firm may not possess all of the resources it needs.[44]

Although complementary alliances may require similar levels of investment from the partners, the benefits tend to be different. There are several potential reasons for the imbalance of benefits.[45] Frequently, the partners have different opportunities as a result of the alliance. Partners may learn at different rates and have different capabilities to leverage the complementary resources provided by the alliance. Some firms are more effective at managing alliances and deriving the benefits from them.[46] The partners may also have different reputations in the market, thus enhancing or limiting the effects of actions they might take as a result of the knowledge or other resources they receive through an alliance.

Network Cooperative Strategies

Increasingly, firms are engaging in several cooperative strategies simultaneously. In addition to forming their own alliances with individual companies, a growing number of firms are joining forces in multiple networks.[47] A **network cooperative strategy** is a cooperative strategy in which multiple firms agree to form partnerships to achieve shared objectives. A network cooperative strategy is particularly effective when it is formed by geographically clustered firms, such as those in California's Silicon Valley or Singapore's Silicon Island.[48] Networks facilitate matching firms that have complementary markets and compatible resources.[49]

The set of strategic alliance partnerships resulting from the use of a network cooperative strategy is commonly called an *alliance network*. Firms involved in alliance networks gain information and knowledge from multiple sources, which include both their partners and their "partners' partners."[50] They can use this heterogeneous knowledge to produce more and better innovation.[51] As noted throughout this chapter, having access to multiple collaborations increases the likelihood that additional competitive advantages will be formed as the set of resources and capabilities being shared expands.[52] In turn, increases in competitive advantages further stimulate the development of product innovations that are critical to value creation in the global economy.[53] Consequently, firms involved in alliance networks tend to be more innovative.[54] One example is the Lockheed Martin Cyber Security Alliance, which "combines the strengths of market leading companies' solutions and integrates their best practices, hardware, software, and tools within a unique new research, development, and collaboration center called the NexGen Cyber Innovation and Technology Center."[55] The alliance includes leading innovators such as Cisco, Dell, Intel, Symantec, Microsoft, McAfee, and EMC Corporation.

Effective social relationships and interactions among partners while sharing their resources and capabilities make it more likely that a network cooperative strategy will be successful.[56] Also important is having an effective *strategic center firm*, which is at the core of an alliance network and around which the network's cooperative relationships revolve (see Figure 7.2). Strategic center firms outsource and partner often with network members and encourage other members to do so as well. They also foster the development of core competencies and competitive advantages within and across network members so that all members of the network can benefit from them. In addition, they serve as gatekeepers with regard to exchange of information among members.[57]

Research evidence suggests that the positive financial effects of network cooperative strategies will continue to make these strategies important to the success of both suppliers and buyers.[58] However, one of the disadvantages to belonging to an alliance network is that a firm can be locked into its partners, precluding the development of alliances with others. Also, in certain types of networks, such as a Japanese *keiretsu*, firms in the network are expected to help other firms in the network whenever they need aid. Such expectations can become a burden to the firm rendering assistance, thus reducing its performance.[59]

Alliance networks vary by industry condition and goal orientation. A *stable alliance network* is formed in mature industries in which demand is relatively constant and predictable. Through a stable alliance network, firms try to extend their

FIGURE 7.2 A STRATEGIC NETWORK

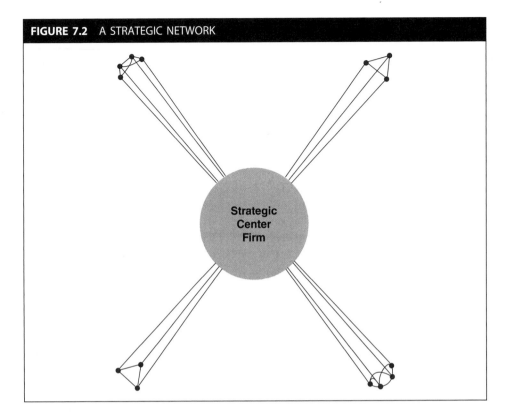

competitive advantages to other settings while continuing to profit from operations in their core, relatively mature industry. Thus, stable networks are built for exploitation of the economies (scale and/or scope) available between firms.[60] These economies can help reduce a firm's cost structure.

Dynamic alliance networks are used in industries characterized by frequent product innovations and short product life cycles.[61] For instance, the pace of innovation in the IT industry is too fast for any one company to maintain success over time. Therefore, the ability to develop and nurture strategic partnerships can make the difference between success and failure in the industry. In dynamic alliance networks, partners typically explore new ideas and possibilities with the potential to lead to product innovations, entries to new markets, and the development of new markets.[62] In some cases these networks even take the form of "open innovation," composed of collaborators and competitors who share knowledge in the pursuit of co-development of new technologies. Members of these alliances can come and go as they please. For instance, open innovation alliances are used frequently by firms operating in the mobile phone industry, where consumer needs and requirements change rapidly.[63]

Participation in stable alliance networks tends to be directed primarily toward producing products at low cost, while that in dynamic alliance networks is directed more toward continuing to produce goods and services that are highly attractive to customers. However, membership in a dynamic alliance network can also help a firm deal with uncertainty in the external environment by keeping firm managers abreast of important technological and other changes.

COOPERATIVE STRATEGIES THAT ADDRESS FORCES IN THE EXTERNAL ENVIRONMENT

As discussed previously, the external environment of most firms is increasingly complex and ever changing. One of the great challenges managers face is helping their firms to prosper in their respective environments. Several types of cooperative strategies can assist managers in this task. *Competitive response alliances* help firms deal with the actions of competitors. *Uncertainty-reducing alliances* help firms take some of the uncertainty out of the environments they are facing. *Competition-reducing cooperative strategies* give the partnering firms differential advantages in their markets. Finally, *associations and consortia* can strengthen member firms in dealing with external stakeholders such as legislators, suppliers, and customers.

Competitive Response Alliances

As discussed in Chapter 6, competitors initiate competitive actions to attack rivals and launch competitive responses to their competitors' actions. Strategic alliances can be used to respond to competitors' attacks. Because they can be difficult to reverse and expensive to operate, strategic alliances are formed to primarily respond to major strategic actions of competitors rather than as rapid responses to their tactical actions. For example, Nokia and Microsoft formed an alliance in which Microsoft software is used on Nokia's phones in an effort to offer a viable alternative to RIM, whose Black-Berry system controls one-third of the enterprise smartphone market.[64]

Uncertainty-Reducing Alliances

Cooperative strategies can be a powerful mechanism for responding to the strategic actions of competitors, but they can also be used to hedge against risk and reduce environmental uncertainty, especially in fast-cycle markets where technology changes rapidly and new products must be developed quickly.[65] Also, they are used where uncertainty exists, such as in entering new product markets or emerging economies. For example, the international legal firm Davies Arnold Cooper (DAC) LLP signed a formal alliance deal with Chilean legal firm Seguros Lex as a part of its strategy to increase operations in Latin America. A senior partner at DAC explained the move as follows: "If this works well we'll look to make it a DAC office. We'll be sending people out from time to time, but our strategy is to find local lawyers who know the local market. It's a strategy that has been successful in Mexico and Madrid."[66]

Competition-Reducing Cooperative Strategies

Virtually all cooperative strategies between or among competitors have the effect of reducing competition in an industry. Simply put, as competitors work together, competition is reduced. Alliance networks, in particular, provide advantages to member firms that make it hard for nonmember firms to compete. For example, in an effort to reduce costs in drug development and commercialization, the major pharmaceutical companies have established networks of preferred suppliers, especially in the area of contract research. Firms that are not in one of these networks are at a severe competitive disadvantage.[67]

Another common and more direct competition-reducing cooperative strategy is *collusion*. Collusive strategies often are illegal. There are two types of collusive strategies—explicit collusion and tacit collusion. *Explicit collusion* means that two or more competing firms negotiate directly to jointly agree about the amount to produce as well as the prices that will be charged for what is produced.[68] Explicit collusion strategies are illegal in the United States and most developed economies (except in regulated industries). Therefore, firms that use such strategies may face litigation and may be found guilty of noncompetitive actions.

Tacit collusion exists when several firms in an industry indirectly coordinate their production and pricing decisions by observing each other's competitive actions and responses.[69] Firms that engage in tacit collusion recognize that they are interdependent and that their competitive actions and responses significantly affect competitors' behaviors toward them. Tacit collusion results in less than fully competitive production levels and prices that are higher than they might otherwise be. Firms engaging in tacit collusion do not directly negotiate output and pricing decisions, as they do in explicit collusion. This type of competition-reducing strategy is more common in industries that are highly concentrated, such as breakfast cereals and airlines. Research suggests that tacit collusion in the airline industry is related to poor on-time performance and service quality.[70]

Mutual forbearance is a form of tacit collusion in which competition is reduced because firms fear responses to competitive attacks from competitors with whom they compete in multiple markets.[71] Rivals learn a great deal about each other when engaging in multimarket competition, including how to deter the effects of their rivals' competitive attacks and responses. For example, researchers discovered that competitors in the personal computer industry mutually forbear in price and new product introductions.[72] Specifically, firms might respond to competitive attacks by introducing new products but they do not use pricing to retaliate.

Governments in free market economies need to determine how rivals can collaborate to increase their competitiveness without violating established regulations.[73] It is challenging to reach this determination when evaluating collusive strategies, particularly tacit ones. For example, it is difficult to determine where to draw the line when evaluating global pharmaceutical and biotechnology firms that must collaborate in order to stay competitive. Some regulation is necessary to maintain an effective balance between collaboration and competition; however, sometimes regulation can interfere with efficient markets.

Associations and Consortia

Because they are inherently cooperative systems, organizations are inclined to form coalitions with stakeholders to achieve common objectives.[74] These coalitions can take a variety of forms, including associations, trade groups, industry and labor panels, and research consortia. Firms join associations to gain access to information and to obtain legitimacy, acceptance, and influence.[75] Associations and consortia can also enhance creative efforts leading to innovation.[76] And, of course, these forms of cooperation can help firms deal with changes in their environment.

One pervasive trend is the "green" movement; that is, efforts among governments, non-governmental organizations, and business firms to protect the natural environment.[77] A key element of this movement is sustainability, or the notion that firms should adopt strategies that allow them to continue their operations indefinitely without exhausting the resources they use. The Sustainability Consortium involves dozens of companies from around the world, including Alcoa, Cargill, L'Oréal, Disney, Fundación Chile, SAP, and Unilever. Their objective is to deal with the increasing pressure to reduce environmental and social impacts associated with global consumption through collaborations that increase understanding, standardization of best practices, and informed decision making.[78]

Often one of the primary purposes of associations and consortia is to provide a common voice when dealing with an important external stakeholder, such as the government. For instance, many trade groups employ lobbyists at the federal, state, regional, or local level. These lobbyists work to ensure that government legislation is as favorable as possible to the member firms. Trade group representatives may also work directly with government leaders and representatives to enhance business relationships.

COOPERATIVE STRATEGIES THAT PROMOTE GROWTH AND/OR DIVERSIFICATION

So far we have described cooperative strategies that help firms enhance differentiation, reduce costs, or effectively address trends and forces in their external environments. Cooperative strategies can also be used to promote growth or diversification (or both). Growth is a primary goal in most organizations.

Firms can decide to pursue growth through a variety of internal strategies, such as new product development or market development. Other firms pursue growth externally through mergers and acquisitions, the topic of Chapter 9. However, cooperative strategies are sometimes an attractive alternative to mergers and acquisitions as a vehicle for growth.[79] Cooperative strategies can be more attractive than mergers and acquisitions because typically they require fewer resource commitments and permit greater strategic flexibility because they are not as permanent.[80] In fact, an alliance can be used as a way to determine if the partners might benefit from a future merger or acquisition between them. This "testing process" often characterizes alliances formed to combine firms' unique technological resources and capabilities. For instance, the previously-mentioned alliance deal between Davies Arnold Cooper LLP and Seguros Lex is expected ultimately to end in a merger of the two companies.[81] Cooperative strategies that frequently are used to stimulate growth include diversifying strategic alliances, franchising, and international cooperative strategies. These strategies may also promote market diversification (increased market scope) and sometimes product diversification.

Diversifying Strategic Alliances

A **diversifying strategic alliance** is a cooperative strategy in which firms share some of their resources and capabilities to diversify into new product or market areas. (Product diversification will be explored more comprehensively in Chapter 8.) For example, Nasdaq OMX formed an alliance with Bolsa Electronica de Chile (BEC) to provide advisory services and technology to the Latin American exchange. Fernando Canas, president of BEC explained, "Our alliance with Nasdaq OMX will support areas of BEC strategic development like technology implementation and partnerships for new products."[82] This deal is part of an overall strategy by Nasdaq to diversify its businesses. The company provides infrastructure to 70 exchanges worldwide and competes head-to-head with NYSE Euronext in trying to control as much of the global exchange services market as possible.

Franchising

Franchising is a cooperative strategy in which a firm (the *franchisor*) uses a franchise as a contractual relationship to describe and control the sharing of its resources and capabilities with partners (the *franchisees*).[83] A **franchise** is a "contractual agreement between two legally independent companies whereby the franchisor grants the right to the franchisee to sell the franchisor's product or do business under its trademarks in a given location for a specified period of time."[84] McDonald's, Hilton Worldwide, and UPS are well-known examples of firms that use the franchising corporate-level cooperative strategy.[85] Recent estimates set the number of franchise businesses in the U.S. alone at approximately 825,000 across 300 different businesses. Franchise businesses generate nearly 18 million jobs and contribute more than $2.1 trillion to the economy.[86] Already a hallmark of well-developed economies around the globe, franchising is also expected to contribute significantly to growth in emerging economies in the 21st century.[87]

In the most successful franchising strategies, the partners (the franchiser and the franchisees) work closely together.[88] A primary responsibility of the franchisor is to develop programs to transfer to the franchisees the knowledge and skills that they need to compete successfully at the local level.[89] In return, franchisees should provide feedback to the franchisor regarding how their units could become more effective and efficient.[90] Working cooperatively, the franchisor and its franchisees find ways to strengthen the core company's brand name, which is often the most important competitive advantage for franchisees operating in their local markets.[91] Research indicates that franchising is especially efficient if franchisees are allowed to own multiple outlets.[92]

Franchising is a particularly attractive strategy in fragmented industries, such as retailing and commercial printing. In such industries, a large number of small and medium-sized firms compete as rivals; however, no firm or small set of firms has a dominant share, making it possible for a company to gain a large market share by consolidating independent companies through contractual relationships. This is why franchising is such a common cooperative strategy in food chains.

International Cooperative Strategies

A **cross-border strategic alliance** is an international cooperative strategy in which firms with headquarters in different nations combine some of their resources and capabilities to create a competitive advantage. For example, several years ago General Electric established a memorandum of understanding with Newcom LLC, a Mongolian investment company that also runs an airline and a cellular phone network, to explore alliances in energy, water, mining, aviation, railway, lighting, and health care. One result of the alliance is a deal to supply 31 huge turbines to a wind-farm project in Mongolia, where air pollution from traditional power plants is a growing problem.[93] In virtually all industries, the number of cross-border alliances being completed continues to increase.[94]

There are several reasons for the widespread use of cross-border strategic alliances. A firm may form cross-border strategic alliances to leverage core competencies that are the foundation of its domestic success to expand into international markets.[95] For example, Japan's Ajinomoto Company entered into a global R&D alliance with Kellogg to jointly develop new health and nutrition products in the areas of weight management, sugar reduction, and sodium reduction. Kellogg is the largest cereal producer in the world. Ajinomoto has strengths in development of new technologies and ingredients. According to Masatoshi Ito Ajinomoto, President and CEO, "The potential for synergy between Kellogg's strong marketing and product development capabilities combined with Ajinomoto's excellence in basic and applied research is unique and exciting."[96]

Limited domestic growth opportunities and governmental economic policies are additional reasons firms use cross-border alliances. Local ownership is an important national policy objective in some nations. In India and China, for example, governmental policies reflect a strong preference to license local companies. Indeed, investment by foreign firms in these countries may be allowed only through a partnership with a local firm, such as in a cross-border alliance. A cross-border strategic alliance can also be helpful to foreign partners from an operational perspective, because the local partner has significantly more information about factors contributing to competitive success such as local markets, sources of capital, legal procedures, and cultural and institutional norms.[97] In spite of these advantages, cross-border alliances tend to be more complex and risky than domestic strategic alliances, especially if they are used in emerging markets.[98]

Because firms often have multiple alliances in different geographical regions, alliance networks are frequently formed to implement international cooperative strategies.[99] Differences among countries' regulatory environments increase the challenge of managing international networks and verifying that, at a minimum, the network's operations comply with all legal requirements.[100] *Distributed alliance networks* are often the organizational structure used to manage international cooperative strategies. As shown in Figure 7.3, several regional strategic center firms are included in the distributed network to manage partner firms' multiple cooperative arrangements.

Strategic centers for Ericsson (telecommunications exchange equipment) are located in countries throughout the world, instead of only in Sweden where the firm is headquartered. Ericsson is active in over 100 countries and employs more than 100,000 people around the world. It manages networks that serve more than 250 million customers. To achieve these impressive results, the company is involved in several major alliance networks and has formed cooperative agreements with companies throughout the world through each network. For example, as a

FIGURE 7.3   A DISTRIBUTED STRATEGIC NETWORK

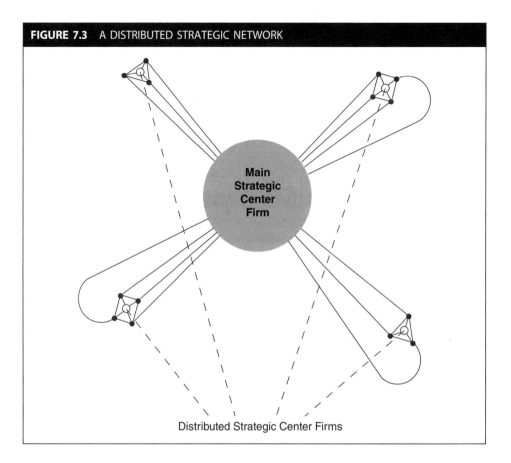

Distributed Strategic Center Firms

founding member of the Ethernet alliance (Intel, AT&T, Oracle, and Cisco are also members), Ericsson acts as the strategic center firm for a cooperative arrangement that promotes open industry standards and provides interoperability testing for its members.[101]

COMPETITIVE RISKS OF COOPERATIVE STRATEGIES

Although their use by firms has increased significantly, many cooperative strategies fail.[102] For example, some research has demonstrated that although the stock market response to corporate strategic alliances tends to be positive, about half of them lead to reductions in shareholder returns.[103] Other evidence is even more pessimistic, demonstrating that two-thirds of cooperative strategies have serious problems in their first two years and that as many as 70 percent of them fail.[104]

Prominent risks of cooperative strategy are shown in the top box of Figure 7.4 (the rest of the figure is explained later in this chapter). One is that a partner may act opportunistically, which means taking advantage of a firm's vulnerabilities.[105] Opportunistic behaviors surface either when formal contracts fail to prevent them or when an alliance is based on a false perception of partner trustworthiness. Not infrequently, the

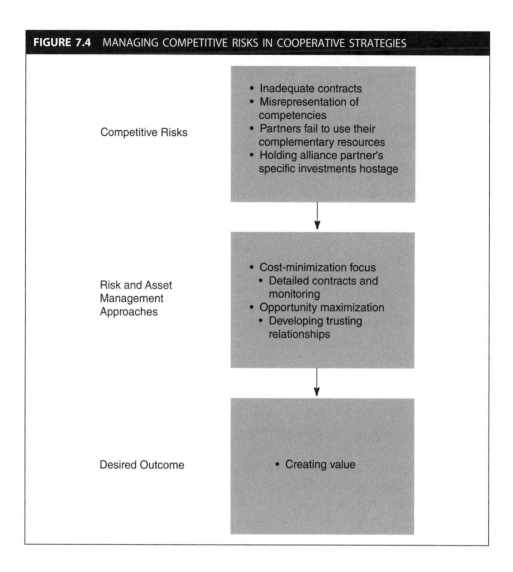

FIGURE 7.4 MANAGING COMPETITIVE RISKS IN COOPERATIVE STRATEGIES

Competitive Risks
- Inadequate contracts
- Misrepresentation of competencies
- Partners fail to use their complementary resources
- Holding alliance partner's specific investments hostage

Risk and Asset Management Approaches
- Cost-minimization focus
- Detailed contracts and monitoring
- Opportunity maximization
- Developing trusting relationships

Desired Outcome
- Creating value

opportunistic firm wants to acquire as much of its partner's tacit knowledge as it can.[106] Full awareness of what a partner wants in a cooperative strategy reduces the likelihood that a firm will suffer from another's opportunistic actions.[107]

Some cooperative strategies fail when it is discovered that a firm has *misrepresented the competencies* it can bring to the partnership. This risk is more common when the partner's contribution is grounded in some of its intangible assets. Superior knowledge of local conditions is an example of an intangible asset that partners often fail to deliver. Asking the partner to provide evidence that it does possess the resources and capabilities it is to share in the cooperative strategy (even when they are largely intangible) may be an effective way to deal with this risk.[108]

Another risk is that a firm fails to make available to its partners the complementary resources and capabilities (such as its most sophisticated technologies) that it committed to the cooperative strategy. This risk surfaces most commonly when firms form an international cooperative strategy.[109] In these instances, dissimilar cultures can result in different interpretations of contractual terms or trust-based expectations.

A final risk is that the firm may make investments that are specific to the alliance while its partner does not. For example, the firm might commit resources and capabilities to develop manufacturing equipment that can be used only to produce items coming from the alliance. If the partner is not also making alliance-specific investments, the firm is at a relative disadvantage in terms of returns earned from the alliance compared with investments made to earn the returns.

IMPLEMENTING AND MANAGING COOPERATIVE STRATEGIES

As this chapter has demonstrated, cooperative strategies are an important option for firms competing in the global economy. However, they are also complex and prone to failure. Firms gain the most benefits from cooperative strategies when they are effectively managed. Because the ability to effectively implement and manage cooperative strategies is unevenly distributed across organizations, superior skills in these areas may be a source of competitive advantage.[110]

Learning from the experiences associated with both successful and unsuccessful cooperative strategies is important to the success of future cooperative strategies.[111] Learning is more likely to happen when experiences are internalized. In other words, those involved with forming and using cooperative strategies should make a deliberate attempt to use these experiences to develop useful knowledge about how to succeed in the future.[112] To gain maximum value from this knowledge, firms should organize it and verify that it is always properly distributed to those involved with forming and using cooperative strategies. Firms must also learn how to manage both the tangible and intangible assets (such as knowledge) that are associated with a cooperative arrangement.[113] In fact, since one of the primary reasons for cooperative agreements is to gain knowledge, partnering firms should have explicit systems and processes in place to record and disseminate venture-related knowledge within their organizations.[114]

In addition, specific managers or teams should be assigned to oversee the firm's portfolio of alliances in general and the specific learning associated with particular ventures.[115] Maintaining an alliance portfolio comes with both benefits and costs (such as the costs of administering them), so the net benefits to an organization depend on how effectively a portfolio is managed.[116] Those responsible for managing the firm's set of cooperative strategies coordinate activities, categorize knowledge learned from previous experiences, and make certain that what the firm knows about how to effectively form and use cooperative strategies is in the hands of the right people at the right time. They should visualize their firms' portfolios in the context of the entire industry rather than as a series of individual alliances.[117] Firms can also increase the performance of their alliance portfolios by including alliances with companies from a variety of different value chain activities, which provides more opportunities to acquire knowledge they do not already possess.[118] In addition, firms may benefit from experience associated with repeated relationships with the same partners.[119]

Firms generally use one of two primary approaches to manage cooperative strategies: cost minimization and opportunity maximization[120] (see Figure 7.4). In the *cost minimization* management approach, the firm develops formal contracts with its partners. These contracts specify how the cooperative strategy is to be monitored and how partner behavior is to be controlled. The goal of this approach is to minimize the cooperative strategy's cost and to prevent opportunistic behavior by a partner. The focus of the second managerial approach—*opportunity maximization*—is on maximizing a partnership's value-creation opportunities. In this case, partners are prepared to take advantage of unexpected opportunities to learn from each other and to explore additional marketplace possibilities. Less formal contracts, with fewer constraints on partners' behaviors, make it possible for partners to explore how they can share their resources and capabilities in multiple value-creating ways.

Firms can successfully use either approach to manage cooperative strategies. However, the costs to monitor the cooperative strategy are greater with cost minimization, in that writing detailed contracts and using extensive monitoring mechanisms are expensive, even though the approach is intended to reduce alliance costs. Although monitoring systems may prevent partners from acting in their own best interests, they also preclude positive responses to those situations in which opportunities to use the alliance's competitive advantages surface unexpectedly.[121] Thus, formal contracts and extensive monitoring systems tend to stifle partners' efforts to gain maximum value from their participation in a cooperative strategy and require significant resources to be put into place and used.[122]

The relative lack of detail and formality that is a part of the contract developed by firms using opportunity maximization means that firms need to trust each other to act in the partnership's best interests. A psychological state, *trust* involves a willingness to be vulnerable because of the expectations of positive behavior from the firm's alliance partner. When partners trust each other, there is less need to write detailed formal contracts to specify each firm's alliance behaviors, and the cooperative relationship tends to be more stable.[123] On a relative basis, trust tends to be more difficult to establish in international cooperative strategies compared with domestic ones.[124] Differences in trade policies, cultures, laws, and politics that are part of cross-border alliances account for the increased difficulty. When trust exists, partners' monitoring costs are reduced and opportunities to create value are maximized. In these cases, the firms have established social capital; that is, they have a stronger position in the social network of firms that jointly create value.[125]

Research showing that trust between partners increases the likelihood of alliance success highlights the benefits of the opportunity maximization approach to managing cooperative strategies.[126] Trust may also be the most efficient way to influence and control alliance partners' behaviors. Consistent with the stakeholder perspective that is one of the foundations of this book, research indicates that trust can be a source of competitive advantage.[127] Simply stated, firms that are known to be trustworthy may have a competitive advantage in terms of how they develop and use cooperative strategies. This is partly because it is impossible to specify all the operational details of a cooperative strategy in a formal contract. When a firm has confidence that its partner can be trusted, its concern about the inability to contractually control all alliance details is reduced.

SUMMARY

▸ A cooperative strategy is one in which firms work together to achieve a shared objective. Strategic alliances, which are cooperative strategies in which firms combine some of their resources and capabilities to create a competitive advantage, are the primary form of cooperative strategy.

▸ Strategic alliances can be divided into two basic legal forms: equity strategic alliances (in which firms own different shares of a newly created venture) and nonequity strategic alliances (in which firms cooperate through a contractual relationship). Joint ventures are a type of equity alliance in which firms create and own shares of a new business venture that is intended to develop competitive advantages.

▸ Co-opetition describes a situation in which cooperative strategies are formed by firms who also compete against one another.

▸ Firms in slow-cycle markets often use strategic alliances to enter restricted markets or to establish franchises in new markets. In standard-cycle markets, alliances are more likely to be made by partners with complementary resources and capabilities. Companies also may cooperate in standard-cycle markets to gain market power or to learn new business techniques and new technologies. Alliances between firms with current excess resources and capabilities and those with promising capabilities help companies competing in fast-cycle markets to make an effective transition from the present to the future and also to gain rapid entry to new markets.

▸ Some cooperative strategies are used at the business level to help improve a firm's performance in individual product markets, either through reducing costs or increasing differentiation. Cooperative strategies that are intended to achieve these objectives fall into two general categories: complementary strategic alliances (vertical or horizontal) and network cooperative strategies.

▸ In a network cooperative strategy, several firms agree to form multiple partnerships to achieve shared objectives. One of the primary benefits of this strategy is the firm's opportunity to gain access to its partner's other partnerships. The probability of this happening improves when a strategic center firm facilitates partner relationships that provide unique ways to share resources and capabilities to form competitive advantages.

▸ Firms can also use cooperative strategies to deal with an environment that is increasingly complex and ever changing. Competitive response alliances help firms deal with the actions of competitors. Competition-reducing cooperative strategies give the partnering firms differential advantages in their markets. Uncertainty-reducing alliances help firms take some of the uncertainty out of the environments they are facing. Finally, associations and consortia can strengthen member firms in dealing with external stakeholders such as legislators, suppliers, and customers.

▸ Diversifying alliances, franchising, and international cooperative strategies tend to promote firm growth. These cooperative strategies are sometimes an attractive alternative to mergers and acquisitions because typically they require fewer resource commitments and permit greater strategic flexibility because they are not as permanent.

- Cooperative strategies are not risk free. If a contract is not developed appropriately, or if a partner misrepresents its competencies or fails to make them available, failure is likely. Furthermore, a firm may be held hostage through asset-specific investments made in conjunction with a partner, which may be exploited.
- Cooperative strategies are more likely to be successful if they are effectively implemented and managed. Consequently, firms should devote resources to learning from their cooperative strategies, assign responsibility for cooperative strategies to high-level executives, and decide on a cost minimization or opportunity maximization approach.
- Trust is another important aspect of successful cooperative strategies. Firms recognize the value of partnering with companies known for their trustworthiness. When trust exists, a cooperative strategy is managed to maximize the pursuit of opportunities between partners. Without trust, formal contracts and extensive monitoring systems are used to manage cooperative strategies. In this case, the interest is to minimize costs rather than to maximize opportunities by participating in a cooperative strategy.

ETHICS QUESTIONS

1. From an ethical perspective, how much information is a firm obliged to provide to a potential complementary alliance partner about what it expects to learn from a cooperative arrangement?
2. "A contract is necessary because most firms cannot be trusted to act ethically in a cooperative venture such as a strategic alliance." In your opinion, is this statement true or false? Why? Does the answer vary by country? Why?
3. Ventures in foreign countries without strong contract law are risky because managers may be subjected to bribery attempts once their firms' assets have been invested in the country. How can managers deal with these problems?
4. This chapter mentions international strategic alliances being formed by the world's airline companies. Do these companies face any ethical issues as they participate in multiple alliances? If so, what are the issues? Are they different for airline companies headquartered in the United States than for those with European home bases? If so, what are the differences, and what accounts for them?
5. Firms with a reputation for ethical behavior in strategic alliances are likely to have more opportunities to form cooperative strategies than companies that have not earned this reputation. What actions can firms take to earn a reputation for behaving ethically as a strategic alliance partner?

NOTES

1. V. Navickas & V. Mykolaityte, 2010, The alternation of the strategic alliances paradigm in the global economy, *Economics and Management*, 15: 155–158.
2. M. Mickeviciene & L. Zitkus, 2011, Competitive ability as an instrument for ex-ante evaluation of enterprise's competitiveness, *Engineering Economics*, 22: 423–433.

3. M. Garbuio, A. W. King, & D. Lovallo, 2011, Looking inside: Psychological influences on structuring a firm's portfolio of resources, *Journal of Management*, 37: 1444–1463; G. Zaefarian, S. C. Henneberg, & P. Naudé, 2011, Resource acquisition strategies in business relationships, *Industrial Marketing Management*, 40: 862–874; G. Soda, 2011, The management

of firms' alliance network positioning: Implications for innovation, *European Management Journal*, 29: 377–388.

4 H. Yang, Z. Lin, & Y. Lin, 2010, A multilevel framework of firm boundaries: Firm characteristics, dyadic differences, and network attributes, *Strategic Management Journal*, 31: 237–261; T. A. Hemphill, 2003, Cooperative strategy, technology innovation and competition policy in the United States and the European Union, *Technology Analysis & Strategic Management*, 1: 93–101.

5 C. R. Allred, S. E. Fawcett, C. Wallin, & G. M. Magnan, 2011, A dynamic collaboration capability as a source of competitive advantage, *Decision Sciences*, 4: 129–161.

6 R. J. Jiang, Q. T. Tao, & M. D. Santoro, 2010, Alliance portfolio diversity and firm performance, *Strategic Management Journal*, 31: 1136–1144.

7 Y. Chao, 2011, Decision-making biases in the alliance life cycle: Implications for alliance failure, *Management Decision*, 49: 350–364; R. D. Ireland, M. A. Hitt, & D. Vaidyanath, 2002, Alliance management as a source of competitive advantage, *Journal of Management*, 28: 413–446.

8 H. Adobor, 2011, Alliances as competitive regimes, *Competitiveness Review*, 21(1): 66–88; Y. Awazu, 2006, Managing technology alliances: The case for knowledge management, *International Journal of Information Management*, 26: 484–498.

9 L. Nachum & S. Song, 2011, The MNE as a portfolio: Interdependencies in MNE growth trajectory, *Journal of International Business Studies*, 42: 381–405; J. Oxley & T. Wada, 2009, Alliance structure and the scope of knowledge transfer: Evidence from U.S.-Japan agreements, *Management Science*, 55: 635–649; B. R. Barringer & J. S. Harrison, 2000, Walking a tightrope: Creating value through interorganizational relationships, *Journal of Management*, 26: 367–404.

10 E. Garriga, 2009, Cooperation in stakeholder networks: Firms' 'tertius iungens'role, *Journal of Business Ethics*, 90: 623–637; C. W. L. Hill & T. M. Jones, 1992, Stakeholder-agency theory, *Journal of Management Studies*, 29: 131–154; R. E. Freeman, 1984, *Strategic Management: A Stakeholder Approach*, Boston, MA: Pitman.

11 R. E. Freeman, J. S. Harrison, A. C. Wicks, B. Parmar, S. de Colle, 2010, *Stakeholder Theory: The State of the Art*, Cambridge, MA: Cambridge University Press; A. A. Lado, N. G. Boyd, & S. C. Hanlon, 1997, Competition, cooperation and the search for economic rents: A syncretic model, *Academy of Management Review*, 22: 110–141; C. Barnard, 1938, *The Functions of the Executive*, Cambridge, MA: Harvard University Press.

12 J. S. Harrison, D. A. Bosse, & R. A. Phillips, 2010, Managing for stakeholders, stakeholder utility functions and competitive advantage, *Strategic Management Journal*, 31: 58–74; J. S. Harrison & C. H. St. John, 1996, Managing and partnering with external stakeholders, *Academy of Management Executive*, 10(2): 46–59.

13 J. H. Dyer & W. Chu, 2011, The determinants of trust in supplier-automaker relationships in the U.S., Japan and Korea, *Journal of International Business Studies*, 42: 10–27.

14 Harrison & St. John, Managing and partnering with external stakeholders.

15 J. K. Liker & T. Y. Choi, 2004, Building deep supplier relationships, *Harvard Business Review*, 82(12): 104.

16 J. Zhang & G. Frazier, 2011, Strategic alliance via co-opetition: Supply chain partnership with a competitor, *Decision Support Systems*, 51: 853–863.

17 D. R. Gnyawali & B.-J. Park, 2011, Co-opetition between giants: Collaboration with competitors for technological innovation, *Research Policy*, 40: 650–663.

18 A.-L. Mention, 2011, Co-operation and co-opetition as open innovation practices in the service sector: Which influence on innovation novelty? *Technovation*, 31(1): 44–53.

19 S. Mills, 2011, Airline alliance survey, *Airline Business*, 27(9): 32–47.

20 J. R. Williams, 1998, *Renewable Advantage: Crafting Strategy through Economic Time*, New York, NY: The Free Press.

21 D. Lavie, P. Haunschild, & P. Khanna, 2012, Organizational differences, relational mechanisms, and alliance performance, *Strategic Management Journal*, in press.

22 M. Kimes, 2011, Showdown on the railroad, *Fortune*, September 26: 161–172.

23 P. Savetpanuvong, U. Tanlamai, & C. Lursinap, 2011, Sustaining innovation in information technology entrepreneurship with a sufficiency economy philosophy, *International Journal of Innovation Science*, 3(2): 69–82.

24 H. Ouyang, 2010, Imitator-to-innovator S curve and chasms, *Thunderbird International Business Review*, 52L 31–44; I. Filatotchev, M. Wright, K. Uhlenbruck, L. Tihanyi, & R. E. Hoskisson, 2003, Governance, organizational capabilities, and restructuring in transition economies, *Journal of World Business*, 38(4): 331–347.

25 B. Bowonder, A. Dabal, S. Kumar, & A. Shirodkar, 2010, Innovation strategies for creating competitive advantage, *Research-Technology Management*, 53(3): 19–32.

26 IBM, 2012, Alliances, http://www-935.ibm.com/services/us/en/it-services/alliances-eus.html, accessed February 17.

27 Business Monitor International, 2012, *Bahrain Food & Drink Report*, Quarter 2: 14.

28 J. Oxley & T. Wada, 2009, Alliance structure and the scope of knowledge transfer: Evidence from U.S.-Japan agreements, *Management Science*, 55, 635–649; D. C. Mowery, J. E. Oxley, & B. S. Silverman, 1996, Strategic alliances and interfirm knowledge transfer, *Strategic Management Journal*, 17: 77–91.

29 A.-W. Harzing, 2002, Acquisitions versus Greenfield investments: International strategy and management of entry modes, *Strategic Management Journal*, 23: 211–227; S. J. Chang & P. M. Rosenzweig, 2001, The choice of entry mode in sequential foreign direct investment, *Strategic Management Journal*, 22: 747–776.

30 C. Rauwald, 2011, BMW makes bet on carbon maker, *Wall Street Journal Online*, November 19.

31 M. V. S. Kumar, 2011, Are joint ventures positive sum games? The relative effects of cooperative and noncooperative behavior, *Strategic Management Journal*, 32: 32–54.

32 Business Monitor International, 2012, *Canada Mining Report*, Quarter 2: 41.

33 M. S. Jiang, R. Chu, & Y. Pan, 2011, Anticipated duration of international joint ventures, *Journal of International Management*, 17: 175–183; X. Lin & C. L. Wang, 2008, Enforcement and performance: The role of ownership, legalism and trust in

international joint ventures, *Journal of World Business*, 43: 340–351.

34 S. Tallman & A. S. Chacar, 2011, Communities, alliances, networks and knowledge in multinational firms: A micro-analytic approach, *Journal of International Management*, 17: 201–210; S. L. Berman, J. Down, & C. W. L. Hill, 2002, Tacit knowledge as a source of competitive advantage in the National Basketball Association, *Academy of Management Journal*, 45: 13–31.

35 H. Hoang & F. T. Rothaermel, 2005, The effect of general and partner specific alliance experience on joint R&D project performance, *Academy of Management Journal*, 48: 332–345.

36 J. J. Reuer, E. Klijn, F. A. J. van den Bosch, & H. W. Volberda, 2011, Bringing corporate governance to international joint ventures, *Global Strategy Journal*, 1: 54–66; S. Das, P. K. Sen, & S. Sengupta, 1998, Impact of strategic alliances on firm valuation, *Academy of Management Journal*, 41: 27–41.

37 J. Schweitzer & S. P. Gudergan, 2011, Contractual complexity, governance and organisational form in alliances, *International Journal of Strategic Business Alliances*, 2: 26–40; C. Weigelt, 2009, The impact of outsourcing new technologies on integrative capabilities and performance, *Strategic Management Journal*, 30: 595–616.

38 M. E. Porter, 1994, Toward a dynamic theory of strategy, in R. P. Rumelt, D. E. Schendel, & D. J. Teece (eds.), *Fundamental Issues in Strategy*, Boston, MA: Harvard Business School Press, 423–461.

39 W. Shi & J. E. Prescott, 2011, Sequence patterns of firms' acquisition and alliance behavior and their performance implications, *Journal of Management Studies* 48: 1044–1070; J. S. Harrison, M. A. Hitt, R. E. Hoskisson, & R. D. Ireland, 2001, Resource complementarity in business combinations: Extending the logic to organizational alliances, *Journal of Management*, 27: 679–699.

40 M. Meuleman, A. Lockett, S. Manigart & M. Wright, 2010, Partner selection decisions in interfirm collaborations: The paradox of relational embeddedness, *Journal of Management Studies*, 47: 995–1019; J. Zhang & C. Baden-Fuller, 2010, The influence of technological knowledge base and organizational structure on technology collaboration, *Journal of Management Studies*, 47: 679–704; S. M. Mudambi & S. Tallman, 2010, Make, buy or ally? Theoretical perspectives on knowledge process outsourcing through alliances, *Journal of Management Studies*, 47: 1434–1456.

41 Consolidation in Australian dairy sector to intensify, 2012, *Austria Food and Drink Report*, Quarter 2, Business Monitor International LTD: 52.

42 M. Makri, M. A. Hitt, & J. P. Lane, 2010, Complementary technologies, knowledge relatedness, and invention outcomes in high technology mergers and acquisitions, *Strategic Management Journal*, 31: 602–628; R. Cairo, 2006, Co-opetition and strategic business alliances in telecommunications, *Business Review*, 5: 147–154.

43 R. W. Cooper & T. W. Ross, 2009, Sustaining cooperation with joint ventures, *Journal of Law, Economics and Organization*, 25(1): 31–54.

44 B. Garrette, X. Castañer, & P. Dussauge, 2009, Horizontal alliances as an alternative to autonomous production: product expansion mode choice in the worldwide aircraft industry, 1945–2000, *Strategic Management Journal*, 30, 885–894.

45 P. Dussauge, B. Garrette, & W. Mitchell, 2004, Asymmetric performance: The market share impact of scale and link alliances in the global auto industry, *Strategic Management Journal*, 25: 701–711.

46 O. Chatain & P. Zemsky, 2011, Value creation and value capture with frictions, *Strategic Management Journal*, 32: 1206–1231.

47 D. Lavie, 2009, Capturing value from alliance portfolios, *Organizational Dynamics*, 38(1): 26–36; Z. Zhao, J. Anand, & W. Mitchell, 2005, A dual networks perspective on inter-organizational transfer of R&D capabilities: International joint ventures in the Chinese automotive industry, *Journal of Management Studies*, 42: 127–160.

48 A. T. Arkan & M. A. Schilling, 2011, Structure and governance in industrial districts: Implications for competitive advantage, *Journal of Management Studies*, 48: 772–803; L. Canina, C. A. Enz, & J. S. Harrison, 2005, Agglomeration effects and strategic orientations: Evidence from the U.S. lodging industry, *Academy of Management Journal*, 48: 565–581; S. S. Cohen & G. Fields, 1999, Social capital and capital gains in Silicon Valley, *California Management Review*, 41(2): 108–130.

49 H. Mitsuhashi & H. R. Greve, 2009, A matching theory of alliance formation and organizational success: Complementarity and compatibility, *Academy of Management Journal*, 52: 975–995.

50 C. C. Phelps, 2010, A longitudinal study of the influence of alliance network structure and composition on firm exploratory innovation, *Academy of Management Journal*, 53: 890–913; J. H. Dyer & N. W. Hatch, 2006, Relation-specific capabilities and barriers to knowledge transfers: Creating advantage through network relationships, *Strategic Management Journal*, 27: 701–719.

51 I. P. Mahmood, H. Zhu, & E. J. Zajac, 2011, Where can capabilities come from? Network ties and capability acquisition in business groups, *Strategic Management Journal*, 32: 820–848.

52 A. V. Shipilov, 2009, Firm scope experience, historic multimarket contact with partners, centrality, and the relationship between structural holes and performance, *Organization Science*, 20: 85–106; D. Lavie, 2006, The competitive advantage of interconnected firms: An extension of the resource-based view, *Academy of Management Review*, 31: 638–658.

53 A. M. Joshi & A. Nerkar, 2011, When do strategic alliances inhibit innovation by firms? Evidence from patent pools in the global optical disc industry, *Strategic Management Journal*, 32: 1139–1160; G. J. Young, M. P. Charns, & S. M. Shortell, 2001, Top manager and network effects on the adoption of innovative management practices: A study of TQM in a public hospital system, *Strategic Management Journal*, 22: 935–951.

54 G. G. Bell, 2005, Clusters, networks, and firm innovativeness, *Strategic Management Journal*, 26: 287–295.

55 Lockheed Martin, 2012, Cyber security, http://www.lockheedmartin.com/us/what-we-do/information-technology/cyber-security.html, accessed February 17.

56 J. Wincent, S. Anokhin, D. Ortqvist, & E. Autio, 2010, Quality meets structure: Generalized reciprocity and firm-level advantage in strategic networks, *Journal of Management Studies*, 47: 597–624.

57 P.-H. Soh, 2010, Network patterns and competitive advantage before the emergence of a dominant design, *Strategic Management Journal*, 31: 438–461; P. Dussauge, B. Garrette, & W. Mitchell, 2000, Learning from competing partners: Outcomes and duration of scale and link alliances in Europe,

North America and Asia, *Strategic Management Journal*, 21: 99–126.

58 A. Echols & W. Tsai, 2005, Niche and performance: The moderating role of network embeddedness, *Strategic Management Journal*, 26: 219–238; S. Chung & G. M. Kim, 2003, Performance effects of partnership between manufacturers and suppliers for new product development: The supplier's standpoint, *Research Policy*, 32: 587–604.

59 H. Kim, R. E. Hoskisson, & W. P. Wan, 2004, Power, dependence, diversification strategy and performance in keiretsu member firms, *Strategic Management Journal*, 25: 613–636.

60 F. T. Rothaermel, 2001, Complementary assets, strategic alliances, and the incumbent's advantage: An empirical study of industry and firm effects in the biopharmaceutical industry, *Research Policy*, 30: 1235–1251.

61 G. Soda, 2011; The management of firms' alliance network positioning: Implications for innovation, *European Management Journal*, 29, 377–388; V. Shankar & B. L. Bayus, 2003, Network effects and competition: An empirical analysis of the home video game industry, *Strategic Management Journal*, 24: 375–384.

62 A. Capaldo & A. M. Petruzzelli, 2011, In search of alliance-level relational capabilities: Balancing innovation, value creation, and appropriability in R&D alliances, *Scandinavian Journal of Management*, 27: 273–286; A.E. Leiponen, 2008, Competing through cooperation: The organization of standard setting in wireless communications, *Management Science*, 54: 1904–1919.

63 K. Han, W. Oh, K. S. Im, R. M. Chang, H. Oh, & A. Pinsonneault, 2012, Value cocreation and wealth spillover in open innovation alliances, *MIS Quarterly*, 36: 291–316.

64 M. Lev-Ram, 2011, Can Nokia and Microsoft win in the workplace? *Fortune*, March 21, 48.

65 C. Lopez-Duarte & M. M. Vidal-Suarez, 2010, External uncertainty and entry mode choice: Cultural distance, political risk and language diversity, *International Business Review*, 19: 575–588; J. J. Reuer & R. Ragozzino, 2006, Agency hazards and alliance portfolios, *Strategic Management Journal*, 27: 27–43; J. J. Reuer & T. W. Tong, 2005, Real options in international joint ventures, *Journal of Management*, 31: 403–423.

66 K. Dowell, 2010, DAC forms alliance with Chilean firm, *The Lawyer*, November 29, 3.

67 P. Van Arnum, 2012, Strategies for preferred-provider partnerships, *Pharmaceutical Technology*, February, 6–12.

68 M. Escrihuela-Villar, 2011, On collusion and industry size, *Annals of Economics and Finance*, 12(1): 31–40.

69 Y. Lu & J. Wright, 2010, Tacit collusion with price-matching punishments, *International Journal of Industrial Organization*, 28: 298–306; D. Leahy & S. Pavelin, 2003, Follow-my-leader and tacit collusion, *International Journal of Industrial Organization*, 21(3): 439–454.

70 J. T. Prince & D. H. Simon, 2009, Multi-market contact and service quality: Evidence from on-time performance in the U.S. airline industry, *Academy of Management Journal*, 52: 336–354.

71 T. Yu, M. Subramaniam & A. A. Cannella, Jr., 2009, Rivalry deterrence in international markets: Contingencies governing the mutual forbearance

hypothesis, *Academy of Management Journal*, 52: 127–147.

72 W. Kang, B. L. Bayus, & S. Balasubramanian, 2010, The strategic effects of multimarket contact: Mutual forbearance and competitive response in the personal computer industry, *Journal of Marketing Research*, 47: 415–427; S. Jayachandran, J. Gimeno, & P. Rajan, 1999, Theory of multimarket competition: A synthesis and implications for marketing strategy, *Journal of Marketing*, 63(3): 49–66.

73 P. Massey & M. McDowell, 2010, Joint dominance and tacit collusion: Some implications for competition and regulatory policy, *European Competition Journal*, 6: 427–444.

74 R. E. Freeman, J. S. Harrison, & A. C. Wicks, 2007, *Managing for Stakeholders: Survival, Reputation and Success*, New Haven, CT: Yale University Press.

75 M. T. Dacin, C. Oliver, & J.-P. Roy, 2007, The legitimacy of strategic alliances: An institutional perspective, *Strategic Management Journal*, 28: 169–182; W. R. Scott, 1992, *Organizations: Rational, Natural, and Open Systems*, 3rd ed., Englewood Cliffs, NJ: Prentice Hall.

76 S. Rangan, R. Samhi, & L. N. Van Wassenhove, 2006, Constructive partnerships: When alliances between private firms and public actors can enable creative strategies, *Academy of Management Review*, 31: 738–751.

77 K. K. Dhanda & P. J. Murphy, 2011, the new Wild West is green: Carbon offset markets, transactions and providers, *Academy of Management Perspectives*, November: 37–49; A. A. Marcus, & A. R. Fremeth, 2009, Green management matters regardless, *Academy of Management Perspectives*, August: 17–26.

78 About the consortium, 2012, The Sustainability Consortium, http://www.sustainabilityconsortium.org/why-we-formed/, accessed February 24, 2012.

79 J. H. Dyer, P. Kale, & H. Singh, 2004, When to ally and when to acquire, *Harvard Business Review*, (July–August): 109–115.

80 J. L. Johnson, R. P.-W. Lee, A. Saini, & B. Grohmann, 2003, Market-focused strategic flexibility: Conceptual advances and an integrative model, *Academy of Marketing Science Journal*, 31: 74–90; C. Young-Ybarra & M. Wiersema, 1999, Strategic flexibility in information technology alliances: The influence of transaction cost economics and social exchange theory, *Organization Science*, 10: 439–459.

81 K. Dowell, 2010, DAC forms alliance with Chilean firm, *The Lawyer*, November 29, 3.

82 P. Stafford, 2011, Nasdaq OMX in deal with Chile's BEC, FT.com, published by The Financial Times LTD, London, U.K., October 21, accessed February 25, 2012.

83 J. G. Combs, D. J. Ketchen, Jr., C. L. Shook, & J. C. Short, 2011, Antecedents and consequences of franchising: Past accomplishments and future challenges, *Journal of Management*, 37: 99–126; J. G. Combs & D. J. Ketchen Jr., 2003, Why do firms use franchising as an entrepreneurial strategy? A meta-analysis, *Journal of Management*, 29: 427–443.

84 F. Lafontaine, 1999, Myths and strengths of franchising, *Financial Times*, Mastering Strategy (Part 9), November 22, 8–10.

85 J. Daley, 2012, The top 10 franchises, *Entrepreneur*, 40(1), 84–95; E. A. McCrea & G. M. Torres-Baumgarten, 2011, Mail Boxes Etc. or The UPS Store?

A decision from a franchisee's perspective, *Entrepreneurship: Theory and Practice*, 35: 595–610.

[86] L. Fenwick, 2011, Franchises aren't running on empty, *Franchising World*, July, 68.

[87] G. M. Kistruct, J. W. Webb, C. J. Sutter, & R. D. Ireland, 2011, Microfranchising in base-of-the-pyramid markets: Institutional challenges and adaptations to the franchise model, *Entrepreneurship: Theory and Practice*, 35: 503–531.

[88] J. McDonnell, A. Gaetson, & C.-H. Huang, 2011, Investigating relationships between relationship quality, customer loyalty and cooperation: An empirical study of convenience stores' franchise chain systems, *Asia Pacific Journal of Marketing and Logistics*, 23: 367–385; S. C. Michael, 2002, Can a franchise chain coordinate? *Journal of Business Venturing*, 17: 325–342.

[89] T. M. Nisar, 2011, Intellectual property securitization and growth capital in retail franchising, *Journal of Retailing*, 87: 393–405; M. Gerstenhaber, 2000, Franchises can teach us about customer care, *Marketing*, March 16, 18.

[90] W. R. Meek, B. Davis-Sramek, M. S. Baucus, & R. N. Germain, 2011, Commitment in franchising: The role of collaborative communication and a franchisee's propensity to leave, *Entrepreneurship: Theory and Practice*, 35: 559–581.

[91] T. W. K. Leslie & L. S. McNeill, 2010, Towards a conceptual model for franchise perceptual equity, *Journal of Brand Management*, 18: 21–33; S. C. Michael, 2002, First mover advantage through franchising, *Journal of Business Venturing*, 18: 61–68.

[92] A. A. Perrryman & J. G. Combs, 2012, Who should own it? An agency-based explanation for multi-outlet ownership and co-location in plural form franchising, *Strategic Management Journal*, 33: 368–386.

[93] J. Areddy, 2011, Wind farm will use GE turbines, *Wall Street Journal*, November 18, B6.

[94] L. D. Qiu, 2010, Cross-border mergers and strategic alliances: *European Economic Review*, 54: 818–831; H. Ren, B. Gray, & H. Kim, 2009, Performance of international joint ventures: What factors really make a difference and how? *Journal of Management*, 35: 805–832.

[95] J. Yu, B. A. Gilbert, & B. M. Oviatt, 2010, Effects of alliances, time, and network cohesion on the initiation of foreign sales by new ventures, *Strategic Management Journal*, 32: 424–446; H. K. Steensma, L. Tihanyi, M. A. Lyles, & C. Dhanaraj, 2005, The evolving value of foreign partnerships in transitioning economies, *Academy of Management Journal*, 48: 213–235.

[96] Ajinomoto and Kellogg Company create research and development alliance, 2012, Ajinomoto Co., Inc., http://www.ajinomoto.com/about/press/g2010_07_12.html, accessed February 25.

[97] M. Meuleman & M. Wright, 2011, Cross-border private equity syndication: Institutional context and learning, *Journal of Business Venturing*, 26: 35–48; J. W. Lu & P. W. Beamish, 2006, Partnering strategies and performance of SMEs' international joint ventures, *Journal of Business Venturing*, 21: 461–480.

[98] L.-Y. Huang & Y.-J. Hsieh, 2012; Examining the antecedents to inter-partner credible threat in international joint ventures, *International Business Research*, 5(1), 49–60; W. J. Henisz & B. A. Zelner, 2010, The hidden risks in emerging markets, *Harvard Business Review*, April, 88(4): 88–95.

[99] S. Tallman & A. S. Chacar, 2011, Communities, alliances, networks and knowledge in multinational firms: A micro-analytic framework, *Journal of International Management*, 17: 201–210; C. Jones, W. S. Hesterly, & S. P. Borgatti, 1997, A general theory of network governance: Exchange conditions and social mechanisms, *Academy of Management Review*, 22: 911–945.

[100] A. Goerzen, 2005, Managing alliance networks: Emerging practices of multinational corporations, *Academy of Management Executive*, 19(2): 94–107; J. M. Mezias, 2002, Identifying liabilities of foreignness and strategies to minimize their effects: The case of labor lawsuit judgments in the United States, *Strategic Management Journal*, 23: 229–244.

[101] 2012, Member roster, Ethernet Alliance, http://www.ethernetalliance.org/about-us/member-roster/, accessed February 22; 2012, Facts and figures, http://www.ericsson.com/thecompany/company_facts/facts_figures, accessed February 22; 2009, Ericsson launches Connected Home Gateway software enabling multimedia services to the home, February 12, http://www.ericsson.com/news/1289807, accessed February 22; 2006, Ethernet alliance develops further, *Competitive Response Newsletter*, June 7, 1; 2002, Ericsson NewsCenter, http://www.ericsson.com, February 10.

[102] H. R. Greve, J. A. C. Baum, H. Mitsuhashi, & T. J. Rowley, 2010, Built to last but falling apart: Cohesion, friction, and withdrawal from interfirm alliances, *Academy of Management Journal*, 53: 302–322; D. C. Hambrick, J. Li, K. Xin, & A. S. Tsui, 2001, Compositional gaps and downward spirals in international joint venture management groups, *Strategic Management Journal*, 22: 1033–1053.

[103] T. R. Keasler & K. C. Denning, 2009, A re-examination of corporate strategic alliances: New market responses, *Quarterly Journal of Finance & Accounting*, 48: 21–47.

[104] R. D. Ireland, M. A. Hitt, & D. Vaidyanath, 2002, Alliance management as a source of competitive advantage, *Journal of Management*, 28: 413–446; A Madhok & S. B. Tallman, 1998, Resources, transactions and rents: Managing value through interfirm collaborative relationships, *Organization Science*, 9: 326–339.

[105] T. Das & N. Rahman, 2010, Determinants of partner opportunism in strategic alliances: A conceptual framework, *Journal of Business & Psychology*, 25: 55–74; T. K. Das, 2006, Strategic alliance temporalities and partner opportunism, *British Journal of Management*, 17(1): 1–20.

[106] R. Agarwal, D. Audretsch, & M. B. Sarkar, 2010, Knowledge spillovers and strategic entrepreneurship, *Strategic Entrepreneurship Journal*, 4: 271–283; P. M. Norman, 2002, Protecting knowledge in strategic alliances: Resource and relational characteristics, *Journal of High Technology Management Research*, 13(2): 177–202.

[107] T. K. Das, 2011, Regulatory forces and opportunism in the alliance development process, *Journal of Management*, 37: 682–708; J. Connell & R. Voola, 2007, Strategic alliances and knowledge sharing: Synergies or silos? *Journal of Knowledge Management*, 11: 52–66.

[108] M. S. Giarratana & S. Torrisi, 2010, Foreign entry and survival in a knowledge-intensive market: Emerging economy countries' international linkages, technology competencies, and firm experience, *Strategic Entrepreneurship Journal*, 4: 85–104.

[109] F. Lumineau, M. Frechet, & D. Puthod, 2011, An organizational learning perspective on the contracting process, *Strategic Organization*, 9: 8–32; P. Lane, J. E. Salk, & M. A. Lyles, 2001, Absorptive capacity, learning, and performance in international joint ventures, *Strategic Management Journal*, 22: 1139–1161.

[110] K. Sluyts, P. Matthyssens, R. Martens, & S. Streukens, 2011, Building capabilities to manage strategic alliances, *Industrial Marketing Management*, 40: 875–886; J. Sammer, 2006, Alliances: How to get desired outcomes, *Business Finance*, 12(4): 38–40; J. H. Dyer, P. Kale, & H. Singh, 2001, How to make strategic alliances work, *MIT Sloan Management Review*, 42(4): 37–43.

[111] G. Vasudeva & J. Anand, 2011, Unpacking absorptive capacity: A study of knowledge utilization from alliance portfolios, *Academy of Management Journal*, 54, 611–623; R. C. Sampson, 2005, Experience effects and collaborative returns in R&D alliances, *Strategic Management Journal*, 26: 1009–1030; J. H. Dyer & N. W. Hatch, 2004, Using supplier networks to learn faster, *MIT Sloan Management Review*, 45(1): 57–63.

[112] Y. Awazu, 2006, Managing technology alliances: The case for knowledge management, *International Journal of Information Management*, 26: 484–498.

[113] C. C. Chung & P. W. Beamish, 2010, The trap of continual ownership change in international equity joint ventures, *Organization Science*, 21: 995–1015.

[114] B. I. Park, 2011, Knowledge transfer capacity of multinational enterprises and technology acquisition in international joint ventures, *International Business Review*, 20, 75–87; O. Mohama, T. Ramayah, & N. Hathaivaseawong, 2010, Transfer of marketing knowledge in Thai international joint venture firms, *Asian Academy of Management Journal*, 15: 197–216;

[115] K. H. Heimeriks, E. Klijn, & J. J. Reuer, 2009, Building capabilities for alliance portfolios, *Long Range Planning*, 42(1): 96–114.

[116] U. Wassmer, 2010, Alliance portfolios: A review and research agenda, *Journal of Management*, 36: 141–171; P. Kale & H. Singh, 2009, Managing strategic alliances: What do we know now, and where do we go from here? *Academy of Management Perspectives*, August: 45–62.

[117] P. Ozcan & K. M. Eisenhardt, 2009, Origin of alliance portfolios: Entrepreneurs, network strategies and firm performance, *Academy of Management Journal*, 52: 246–279.

[118] A. M. Hess & F. T. Rothaermel, 2011, When are assets complementary? Star scientists, strategic alliances, and innovation in the pharmaceutical industry, *Strategic Management Journal*, 32: 895–909; R. J. Jiang, Q. T. Tao, & Mi. D. Santoro, 2010, Alliance portfolio diversity and firm performance, *Strategic Management Journal*, 31: 1136–1144.

[119] R. Gulati, D. Lavie, & H. Singh, 2009, The nature of partnering experience and the gains from alliances, *Strategic Management Journal*, 30, 1213–1233.

[120] M. H. Hansen, R. E. Hoskisson, & J. B. Barney, 2007, Competitive advantage in alliance governance: Resolving the opportunism minimization–gain maximization paradox, *Managerial and Decision Economics*, 28: 191–208.

[121] J. J. Reuer & A. Arino, 2002, Contractual renegotiations in strategic alliances, *Journal of Management*, 28: 47–68.

[122] R. P. Lee & J. L. Johnson, 2010, Managing multiple facets of risk in new product alliances, *Decision Sciences*, 41: 271–300; J. H. Dyer & C. Wujin, 2003, The role of trust-worthiness in reducing transaction costs and improving performance: Empirical evidence from the United States, Japan, and Korea, *Organization Science*, 14: 57–69.

[123] J. J. Li, L. Poppo, & K. Z. Zhou, 2010, Relational mechanisms, formal contracts, and local knowledge acquisition by international subsidiaries, *Strategic Management Journal*, 31: 349–370; Y. Luo, 2005, How important are shared perceptions of procedural justice in cooperative alliances? *Academy of Management Journal*, 48: 695–709; V. Perrone, A. Zaheer, & B. McEvily, 2003, Free to be trusted? Boundary constraints on trust in boundary spanners, *Organization Science*, 14: 422–439.

[124] P. W. Beamish & N. C. Lupton, 2009, Managing joint ventures, *Academy of Management Perspectives*, May: 75–94.

[125] J. Aarstad, S. A. Haugland, & A. Greve, 2010, Performance spillover effects in entrepreneurial networks: Assessing a dyadic theory of social capital, *Entrepreneurship: Theory and Practice*, 34: 1003–1019; G. Dokko & L. Rosenkropf, 2010, Social capital for hire? Mobility of technical professionals and firm influence in wireless standards committees, *Organization Science*, 21: 677–695.

[126] C. R. Reutzel, J. D. Worthington, & J. D. Collins, 2012, Strategic alliance poker: Demonstrating the importance of complementary resources and trust in strategic alliance management, *Decision Sciences Journal of Innovative Education*, 10: 105–115; R. Krishnan, X. Martin, & N. G. Noorderhaven, 2006, When does trust matter to alliance performance? *Academy of Management Journal*, 49: 894–917; J. B. Barney & M. H. Hansen, 1994, Trustworthiness: Can it be a source of competitive advantage? *Strategic Management Journal*, 15(special winter issue): 175–203.

[127] B. L. Parmar, R. E. Freeman, J. S. Harrison, A. C. Wicks, L. Purnell, & S. de Colle, 2010, Stakeholder theory: The state of the art, *Academy of Management Annals*, 3: 403–445; C. C. Phelps, 2010, A longitudinal study of the influence of alliance network structure and composition on firm exploratory innovation, *Academy of Management Journal*, 53: 890–913; J. H. Davis, F. D. Schoorman, R. C. Mayer, & H. H. Tan, 2000, The trusted general manager and business unit performance: Empirical evidence of a competitive advantage, *Strategic Management Journal*, 21: 563–576.

Chapter 8

CORPORATE-LEVEL STRATEGY

KNOWLEDGE OBJECTIVES

Studying this chapter should provide you with the strategic management knowledge needed to:

1. Define corporate-level strategy and discuss its importance to the diversified firm.

2. Describe the advantages and disadvantages of single and dominant business strategies.

3. Explain three primary reasons why firms move from single and dominant business strategies to more diversified strategies to enhance value creation.

4. Describe the multidivisional structure (M-form) and controls and discuss the difference between strategic controls and financial controls.

5. Describe how related diversified firms create value by sharing or transferring core competencies.

6. Explain the two ways value can be created with an unrelated diversification strategy.

7. Explain the use of the three versions of the multidivisional structure (M-form) to implement different diversification strategies.

8. Discuss the incentives and resources that encourage diversification.

9. Describe motives that can be incentives for managers to diversify a firm too much.

Our discussions of business-level strategies (Chapter 5) and the rivalry and competitive dynamics associated with them (Chapter 6) concentrated on firms competing in a single industry or product market. However, some of the cooperative strategies described in Chapter 7 move firms beyond their traditional markets and industries, resulting in diversification. A *diversification strategy* allows a firm to use its knowledge, skills, and resources to pursue opportunities for value creation in new business areas while also seeking to develop new capabilities and acquire new resources through participating in those areas.[1] **Corporate-level strategy** specifies actions a firm takes to gain a competitive advantage by selecting and managing a portfolio of businesses that compete in different product markets or industries. With regard to the five major elements of strategy described in Chapter 2, corporate-level strategy answers the question regarding arenas: in what product markets and businesses should the firm compete and how should corporate head-quarters manage those businesses?[2]

Like a firm's business-level and cooperative strategies, corporate-level strategies are intended to help a firm create value leading to high performance.[3] Some suggest that few corporate-level strategies actually create value.[4] A corporate-level strategy's value is ultimately determined by the degree to which "the businesses in the portfolio are worth more under the management of the company than they would be under any other ownership."[5] Thus, one way to measure the success of a corporate-level strategy is to determine whether the aggregate returns across all of a firm's business units exceed what those returns would be without the overall corporate strategy, in terms of the firm's ability to create value and achieve high performance.[6]

Product diversification, a primary form of corporate-level strategy, concerns the scope of the industries and markets in which the firm competes as well as "how managers buy, create and sell different businesses to match skills and strengths with opportunities presented to the firm."[7] Successful diversification is expected to reduce variability in the firm's profitability in that its earnings are generated from several different business units.[8] Because firms incur development and monitoring costs when diversifying, the ideal business portfolio balances diversification's costs and benefits.[9] CEOs and their top management team are ultimately responsible for determining the ideal portfolio of businesses for the firm.[10]

We begin the chapter by examining different levels (from low to high) of diversification. Value-creating reasons for firms to use a corporate-level strategy are explored next, along with vertical integration strategy as a means to gain power over competitors. Two types of diversification strategies denoting moderate to very high levels of diversification—related and unrelated—are then examined. The specific structural design that is often used to facilitate implementation of each corporate-level strategy is presented. Finally, the chapter explores value-neutral incentives to diversify as well as managerial motives for diversification, which can be destructive because of too much diversification.

LEVELS OF DIVERSIFICATION

Diversified firms vary according to their level of diversification and the connections between and among their businesses.[11] Figure 8.1 defines five categories of diversification. In addition to the *single* and *dominant* business categories, which denote relatively low levels of diversification, more fully diversified firms are classified into *related* and *unrelated* categories. A firm is related through its diversification when there are several links between its business units; for example, units may share products or services, technologies, or distribution channels. The more links among businesses, the more constrained is the relatedness of diversification. Unrelatedness refers to the absence of direct links between businesses.

Low Levels of Diversification

A firm pursing a low level of diversification uses either a single or a dominant corporate-level diversification strategy. A *single business strategy* is a corporate-level strategy in which the firm generates 95 percent or more of its sales revenue

FIGURE 8.1 LEVELS AND TYPES OF DIVERSIFICATION

Low Levels of Diversification

Single business: More than 95% of revenue comes from a single business. (A)

Dominant business: Between 70% and 95% of revenue comes from a single business. (A) (B)

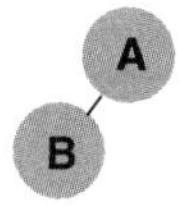

Moderate to High Levels of Diversification

Related constrained: Less than 70% of revenue comes from the dominant business, and all businesses share product, technological, and distribution linkages. (A) (B—C)

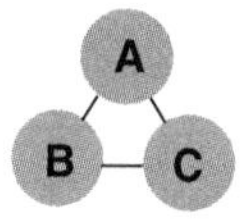

Related linked (mixed related and unrelated): Less than 70% of revenue comes from the dominant business, and there are only limited links between businesses. (A) (B—C)

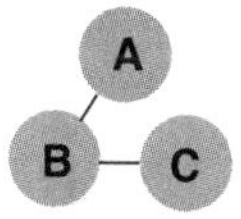

Very High Levels of Diversification

Unrelated: Less than 70% of revenue comes from the dominant business, and there are no common links between businesses. (A) (B) (C)

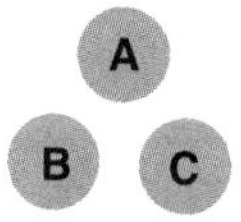

SOURCE: Based on R. P. Rumelt, 1974, *Strategy, Structure and Economic Performance*, Boston: Harvard Business School.

from its core business area.[12] For example, Medifast concentrates exclusively on manufacturing and marketing prepackaged meals that are sold through a network of salespeople called health coaches.[13]

With the *dominant business diversification strategy*, the firm generates between 70 and 95 percent of its total revenue within a single business area. United Parcel Service (UPS) uses this strategy. Recently, UPS generated 60 percent of its revenue from its U.S. package delivery business and 18 percent from its international package business, with the remaining revenues coming from the firm's nonpackage business.[14] Although the U.S. package delivery business currently generates the largest percentage of the firm's sales revenue, UPS anticipates that in the future its international and nonpackage businesses will account for the majority of its growth in revenues. This expectation suggests that UPS may become more diversified, in terms of both the goods and services it offers and the number of countries in which those goods and services are offered. If this happens, UPS would likely be classified as a moderately diversified firm.

Moderate and High Levels of Diversification

A firm generating more than 30 percent of its sales revenue outside a dominant business and whose businesses are related to each other in some manner uses a *related diversification strategy*. When the links between the diversified firm's businesses are rather direct, a *related constrained diversification strategy* is being used. A related constrained firm shares a number of resources and activities among its businesses. The Campbell Soup Company, Procter & Gamble, and Merck & Co. use a related constrained strategy. With a related constrained strategy, resources and activities are shared among a firm's businesses.

A diversified company that has a portfolio of businesses with only a few links between them is combining related and unrelated approaches and is using the *related linked diversification strategy*. Compared with related constrained firms, related linked firms share fewer resources and assets among their businesses, instead concentrating on transferring knowledge and competencies among the businesses. Johnson & Johnson and General Electric follow this corporate-level diversification strategy. Johnson & Johnson, for example, has more than 200 operating companies that manufacture and market thousands of branded health care products in a variety of categories.[15] Despite the diversity of the company's products, the products are still "linked" by a focus on health care. As with firms using each type of diversification strategy, companies implementing the related linked strategy constantly adjust the mix in their portfolio of businesses as well as decisions about how to manage their businesses.

A highly diversified firm, which has no well-defined relationships between its businesses, follows an *unrelated diversification strategy*. These types of firms are also referred to as *conglomerates*. United Technologies, Textron, and Samsung are examples of firms using this type of corporate-level strategy. Samsung's major operating companies, for instance, include electronics, machinery and heavy industries, chemicals, and financial services, but the company also operates hotels and resorts, an engineering company, and a medical center.[16]

Research evidence suggests that a curvilinear relationship may exist between level of diversification and firm performance.[17] As illustrated in Figure 8.2, the dominant business and unrelated business strategies are expected to have lower

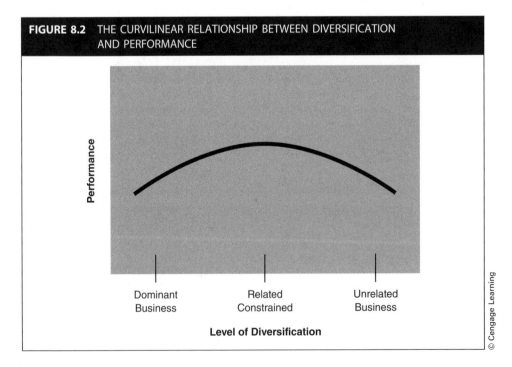

FIGURE 8.2 THE CURVILINEAR RELATIONSHIP BETWEEN DIVERSIFICATION AND PERFORMANCE

© Cengage Learning

　　　　PART 3 CREATING COMPETITIVE ADVANTAGE

performance than the related constrained diversification strategy. The related linked strategy would fall somewhere between the related constrained and the unrelated diversification strategies; the single business strategy is not included in the figure because it does not involve a significant level of diversification. There are many reasons why a diversification strategy that involves a portfolio of closely related firms is likely to be higher performing than other types of diversification strategies. These reasons will become evident as this chapter unfolds. However, it is important to note two caveats to this pattern of diversification and performance: first, some firms are successful with each type of diversification strategy; second, some research suggests that *all* diversification leads to trade-offs and a certain level of suboptimization.[18]

REASONS FOR DIVERSIFICATION

There are many reasons firms use a corporate-level diversification strategy.[19] Table 8.1, which lists many of these reasons, will serve as an outline for much of the rest of this chapter. Most often corporate-level managers use a diversification strategy in an attempt to improve the firm's overall performance (*value-creating diversification* in Table 8.1). Value is created through related diversification when the strategy allows a company's business units to increase revenues or reduce costs while implementing their business-level strategies. If the businesses in the corporate portfolio are related to each other (related diversification), then firms might seek to increase performance through economies of scope; that is, through economies that result from sharing activities or transferring core competencies across the related businesses.[20] Related diversification can also lead to increased market power (power from size or strength in the market).[21] Unrelated diversification, on the other hand, may lead to financial economies because

---

TABLE 8.1 REASONS FOR DIVERSIFICATION

VALUE-CREATING DIVERSIFICATION
- Economies of scope (related diversification)
  —Sharing activities
  —Transferring core competencies
- Market power (related diversification)
  —Blocking competitors through multimarket competition
  —Vertical integration
- Financial economies (unrelated diversification)
  —Efficient internal capital allocation
  —Business restructuring

VALUE-NEUTRAL DIVERSIFICATION
- Antitrust regulation
- Tax laws
- Low performance
- Uncertain future cash flows
- Risk reduction for firm
- Tangible resources
- Intangible resources

VALUE-REDUCING DIVERSIFICATION
- Diversifying managerial employment risk
- Increasing managerial compensation

© Cengage Learning

---

of efficient internal capital allocation or the restructuring of a firm's businesses.[22] All of these concepts will receive further elaboration in the pages that follow.

Value-neutral diversification does not necessarily guide the firm toward any particular type of value-creating diversification strategy. Value-neutral reasons for diversifying include government-induced stimuli such as antitrust regulation and tax laws, as well as particular concerns managers may have about a firm's low performance, uncertainty of future cash flows, or other types of risk. In addition, the firm may possess tangible or intangible resources that would facilitate diversification. The prevailing logic of diversification suggests that the firm should diversify into additional markets when it has excess resources, capabilities, and core competencies with multiple value-creating uses.[23] Although these factors might push a firm toward diversification, hopefully its managers will actually pursue a type of diversification that will add value to the firm.

Other reasons for using a diversification strategy may not increase the firm's value; in fact, diversification may increase costs or reduce a firm's revenue and its value (*value-reducing diversification* in Table 8.1).[24] These situations tend to be driven by the personal motivations of the managers who are guiding the firm's diversification strategy. Diversification rationales such as reduced employment risk, increased compensation, and empire building will be discussed in a later section.

Operational relatedness and *corporate relatedness* are two ways diversification strategies can create value (see Figure 8.3). Study of these independent relatedness

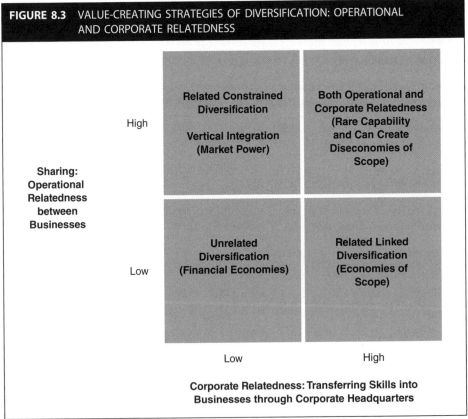

FIGURE 8.3 VALUE-CREATING STRATEGIES OF DIVERSIFICATION: OPERATIONAL AND CORPORATE RELATEDNESS

© Cengage Learning

dimensions shows the importance of resources and key competencies.[25] The vertical dimension of Figure 8.3 indicates sharing activities (operational relatedness), and its horizontal dimension depicts corporate capabilities for transferring knowledge (corporate relatedness). The firm with a strong capability in managing operational synergy, especially in sharing assets between its businesses, falls in the upper-left quadrant, which also represents vertical sharing of assets through vertical integration. The lower-right quadrant represents a highly developed corporate capability for transferring a skill across businesses. This capability is located primarily in the corporate office. The use of either operational relatedness or corporate relatedness is based on a knowledge asset that the firm can either share or transfer.[26] Unrelated diversification is shown in Figure 8.3 in the lower-left quadrant. The unrelated diversification strategy creates value through financial economies rather than through either operational relatedness or corporate relatedness among business units.

DIVERSIFICATION AND THE MULTIDIVISIONAL STRUCTURE

In Chapter 5, we introduced the idea that value can be created by effectively using an organizational structure—a simple structure, functional structure, or flexible structure—to facilitate implementation of one of the business-level strategies. By definition, corporate-level diversification strategies are multi-business and therefore a different type of structure is appropriate when implementing these strategies.[27] In Chapter 5, the *multidivisional structure* (M-form) was described as consisting of several operating divisions, each representing a separate business or profit center in which the top corporate officer delegates responsibilities for day-to-day operations and business-unit strategy to division managers. Each division represents a distinct, self-contained business with its own business-level structure.[28] The M-form ties all those divisions together. Diversification is a dominant corporate-level strategy in the global economy, resulting in extensive use of the M-form.[29] Proper use of the M-form in a diversified firm can lead to value creation.[30]

Alfred Chandler viewed the M-form as an innovative response to coordination and control problems that surfaced during the 1920s in the functional structures then used by large firms such as DuPont and General Motors.[31] As initially designed, the M-form was thought to have three major benefits: "(1) it enabled corporate officers to more accurately monitor the performance of each business, which simplified the problem of control; (2) it facilitated comparisons between divisions, which improved the resource allocation process; and (3) it stimulated managers of poorly performing divisions to look for ways of improving performance."[32] Active monitoring of performance through the M-form increases the likelihood that decisions made by managers heading individual units will be in the shareholders' best interests. The M-form may be used to support implementation of both related and unrelated diversification strategies.[33] It helps firms successfully manage the many demands of diversification, including those related to processing vast amounts of information.[34]

Organizational controls are an important aspect of the M-form. They guide the use of strategy, indicate how to compare actual results with expected results, and suggest corrective actions to take when the difference between actual and expected results is unacceptable.[35] Firms rely on two types of organizational controls, strategic controls and financial controls, to enhance the ability of the M-form structure to support their strategies.

Strategic controls are largely subjective criteria intended to verify that the firm is using appropriate strategies for the conditions in the external environment and the company's competitive advantages. They deal with the content of strategic actions as opposed to their outcomes. Thus, strategic controls are concerned with examining the fit between what the firm *might* do (as suggested by opportunities in its external environment) and what it *can* do (as indicated by its competitive advantages) (see Chapters 2 and 4). Effective strategic controls help the firm understand what it takes to be successful and set appropriate strategic goals, as well as monitor goal achievement.[36] They demand rich and frequent communications between top managers responsible for evaluating overall firm performance and those with primary responsibility for implementing the firm's strategies in its divisions.

Partly because strategic controls are difficult to use with extensive diversification, **financial controls** are emphasized to evaluate the performance of business units in unrelated diversified firms. Financial controls are largely objective criteria used to measure the firm's performance against previously established quantitative standards.[37] Accounting-based measures, such as return on investment and return on assets, and market-based measures, such as economic value added, are examples of financial controls.

As explained below, a corporate-wide emphasis on sharing among business units (as called for by the related constrained diversification strategy) results in an emphasis on strategic controls while financial controls are emphasized for strategies in which activities or capabilities aren't shared (e.g., unrelated diversification). Part of the reason for the superiority of strategic controls in a related constrained versus an unrelated setting is because they require that corporate-level managers understand each of their businesses very well, and this is much more likely when the businesses are related to each other.

RELATED DIVERSIFICATION

With the related diversification corporate-level strategy, the firm builds upon or extends its resources, capabilities, and core competencies to create value.[38] The company using the related diversification strategy wants to develop and exploit economies of scope between its business units. Available to companies operating in multiple industries or product markets, **economies of scope** are cost savings that the firm creates by successfully transferring some of its capabilities and competencies that were developed in one of its businesses to another of its businesses.[39] **Synergy** exists when the value created by business units working together exceeds the value those same units create working independently.[40]

As illustrated in Figure 8.3, firms seek to create value from economies of scope through two basic kinds of operational economies: sharing activities (operational relatedness) and transferring skills or corporate core competencies (corporate relatedness). The difference between sharing activities and transferring competencies is based on how separate resources are jointly used to create economies of scope. To create economies of scope, tangible resources, such as plant and equipment or other business-unit physical assets, often must be shared. Less tangible resources, such as manufacturing know-how, also can be shared.[41] However, know-how transferred between separate activities with no physical or tangible resources involved is a transfer of a corporate-level core competence and not an operational sharing of activities.

Operational Relatedness: Sharing Activities

Firms can create operational relatedness by sharing either a primary activity such as inventory delivery systems or a support activity such as purchasing practices (see discussion of the value chain in Chapter 4). Sharing activities is quite common, especially among related constrained firms. Firms expect activity sharing among units to result in increased value creation and improved financial returns.[42]

Several issues affect the degree to which activity sharing creates positive outcomes. Research has shown that firms that are successful in creating economies of scope in their related businesses often demonstrate a corporate passion for pursuing appropriate coordination mechanisms, including information systems.[43] On the other hand, activity sharing can be risky because business-unit ties create links between outcomes. For instance, if demand for one business's product is reduced, there may not be sufficient revenues to cover the fixed costs required to operate the facilities being shared. Moreover, one business-unit manager may feel that another unit is receiving a disproportionate share of the gains being accrued through activity sharing. Such perceptions can create conflicts between division managers. Coordination challenges such as these must be carefully managed for sharing of activities to be effective.[44]

Managing the interdependencies between related business lines increases coordination costs, so synergy will only lead to improved performance through economies of scope if the benefits exceed the costs.[45] In spite of the additional costs, research shows that related diversification can create value. For example, studies that examined acquisitions of firms in the same industry (called *horizontal acquisitions*), such as the banking industry, have found that sharing resources and activities and thereby creating economies of scope contributed to post-acquisition increases in performance and higher returns to shareholders.[46] Additionally, firms that sold related units in which resource sharing was a possible source of economies of scope have been found to produce lower returns than those that sold businesses unrelated to the firms' core businesses.[47] Still other research discovered that firms with more related units had lower risk.[48] These results suggest that gaining economies of scope by sharing activities across a firm's businesses may be important in reducing risk and creating value. Furthermore, more attractive results are obtained through activity sharing when a strong corporate office facilitates it.[49]

Using the Cooperative Form of the Multidivisional Structure to Implement the Related Constrained Strategy

The **cooperative form** is a structure in which horizontal integration is used to bring about interdivisional cooperation. The divisions in the firm using the related constrained diversification strategy commonly are formed around products and markets, or both. In Figure 8.4, we use product divisions as part of the representation

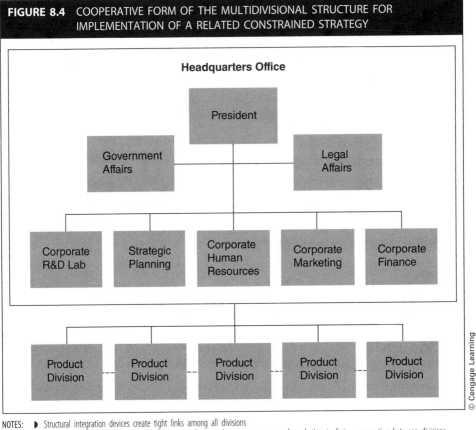

FIGURE 8.4 COOPERATIVE FORM OF THE MULTIDIVISIONAL STRUCTURE FOR IMPLEMENTATION OF A RELATED CONSTRAINED STRATEGY

Headquarters Office

President

Government Affairs

Legal Affairs

Corporate R&D Lab

Strategic Planning

Corporate Human Resources

Corporate Marketing

Corporate Finance

Product Division — Product Division — Product Division — Product Division — Product Division

© Cengage Learning

NOTES:
▶ Structural integration devices create tight links among all divisions
▶ Corporate office emphasizes centralized strategic planning, human resources, and marketing to foster cooperation between divisions
▶ R&D is likely to be centralized
▶ Rewards are subjective and tend to emphasize overall corporate performance in addition to divisional performance
▶ Culture emphasizes cooperative sharing

of the cooperative form of the M-form, although market divisions could be used instead of or in addition to product divisions to develop the figure. All of the divisions of the related constrained firm share one or more corporate strengths, such as production competencies, marketing competencies, or channel dominance.[50] Interdivisional sharing of competencies in the cooperative form helps the firm create economies of scope.[51] Increasingly, it is important that the links resulting from effective use of integration mechanisms support the cooperative sharing of both intangible resources (such as knowledge) and tangible resources (such as facilities and equipment).[52]

Different characteristics of structure are used as integrating mechanisms by the cooperative structure to facilitate interdivisional cooperation.[53] *Centralization* is one of these mechanisms (see Chapter 5). Centralizing some organizational functions (human resource management, R&D, marketing, or finance) at the corporate level allows the linking of activities among divisions. Work completed in these centralized functions is managed by the firm's central office with the purpose of exploiting common strengths among divisions by sharing competencies. Other helpful integrating mechanisms include *standardization*, which involves adoption of uniform processes and procedures, and *formalization*, the process through which a firm documents rules and procedures.

The success of the cooperative M-form is significantly affected by how well information is processed among divisions.[54] But because cooperation among divisions implies a loss of managerial autonomy, division managers may not readily commit themselves to the type of integrative information-processing activities that this structure demands. Moreover, coordination among divisions sometimes results in an unequal flow of positive outcomes to divisional managers. In other words, when managerial rewards are based partly on the performance of individual divisions, the manager of the division that is able to benefit the most by the sharing of corporate competencies might be viewed as receiving gains at the expense of others. Strategic controls are important in these instances, as divisional managers' performance can be evaluated at least partly on the basis of how well they have facilitated interdivisional cooperative efforts. Furthermore, using reward systems that emphasize overall company performance, besides financial outcomes achieved by individual divisions, helps overcome problems associated with the cooperative form.

Corporate Relatedness: Transferring of Core Competencies

Over time, the firm's intangible resources, such as its know-how, become the foundation of core competencies. **Corporate-level core competencies** are complex sets of resources and capabilities that link different businesses, primarily through managerial and technological knowledge, experience, and expertise.[55] Related linked firms (see Figure 8.3) often transfer competencies across businesses, thereby creating value in at least two ways.[56] First, because the expense of developing a competence has been incurred in one unit, transferring it to a second business unit eliminates the need for the second unit to allocate resources to develop the competence.[57] Resource intangibility is a second source of value creation through corporate relatedness. Intangible resources are difficult for competitors to understand and imitate; therefore, the unit receiving a transferred competence often gains an immediate competitive advantage over its rivals.[58]

A number of firms have successfully transferred some of their resources and capabilities across businesses. For example, the food giant Cargill has transferred its expertise in food processing into a diverse array of businesses. It is the largest beef producer in the United States (number eight in pork and number three in turkey), has grain storage capacity of 531 million bushels, runs a $50 billion food additives business, and generates 60 percent of its income outside the United States.[59] On the service side, Catholic Health Initiatives, operator of hundreds of hospitals, medical centers, and nursing homes in the United States, uses its expertise in research and testing to build its presence in the outpatient market.[60]

Using the Strategic Business-Unit Form of the Multidivisional Structure to Implement the Related Linked Strategy

As noted previously, when the firm has fewer links or less constrained links among its divisions, the related linked diversification strategy is used. The **strategic business-unit form** of the M-form supports implementation of this strategy and

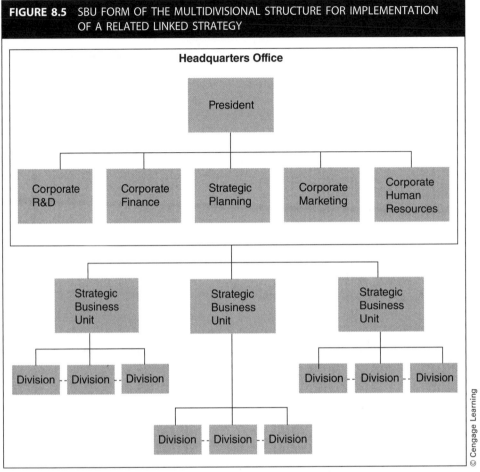

FIGURE 8.5 SBU FORM OF THE MULTIDIVISIONAL STRUCTURE FOR IMPLEMENTATION OF A RELATED LINKED STRATEGY

Headquarters Office

President

Corporate R&D | Corporate Finance | Strategic Planning | Corporate Marketing | Corporate Human Resources

Strategic Business Unit | Strategic Business Unit | Strategic Business Unit

Division -- Division -- Division

Division -- Division -- Division

Division -- Division -- Division

© Cengage Learning

NOTES:
▶ Structural integration among divisions within SBUs, but independence across SBUs
▶ Strategic planning may be the most prominent function in headquarters for managing the strategic planning approval process of SBUs for the president
▶ Each SBU may have its own budget for staff to foster integration
▶ Corporate headquarters staff serve as consultants to SBUs and divisions, rather than having direct input to product strategy as in the cooperative form

consists of three levels: corporate headquarters, strategic business units (SBUs), and divisions within each of the SBUs (see Figure 8.5). For example, General Electric (GE), a related linked firm, has six major SBUs, each with multiple divisions.[61] They include Energy, Capital, Home and Business Solutions, Healthcare, Aviation, and Transportation. In addition, the company has a vice chairman at the same level in the organizational structure as the SBU managers. He is responsible for overseeing Global Growth and Operations.

The divisions within SBUs are related in terms of shared products or markets or both, but the divisions of one SBU have little in common with the divisions of the other SBUs. Divisions within each SBU share product or market competencies to develop economies of scope and possibly economies of scale. In the SBU structure, each SBU is a profit center that is controlled and evaluated by the headquarters office. Although both financial and strategic controls are important, on a relative basis, financial controls are more vital to headquarters' evaluation of each SBU; strategic controls are critical when the heads of SBUs evaluate their divisions' performance. Strategic controls are also critical to the headquarters' efforts to determine whether the company has chosen an effective portfolio of businesses and whether those businesses are being effectively managed.[62] Therefore, there is need for strategic structures that promote exploration to identify new products and markets, but also for actions that exploit the current product lines and markets.[63]

One way managers facilitate the transfer of competencies is to move key people into new management positions.[64] Thus, managers with the ability to facilitate the transfer of a core competence may come at a premium. However, several circumstances may make transfers problematic. A business-unit manager of an older division may be reluctant to transfer key people who have accumulated knowledge and experience critical to the business unit's success. In another situation, the key people involved may not want to transfer, especially if the transfer involves relocation to a distant location such as a different country.[65] Additionally, the top-level managers from the transferring division may not want the competencies transferred to a new division to fulfill the firm's diversification objectives.

Market Power through Multipoint Competition and Vertical Integration

Related diversification can also be used to gain market power. **Market power** exists when a firm is able to sell its products above the existing competitive level, or to reduce the costs of its primary and support activities below the competitive level, or both.[66] Two avenues firms might pursue to increase their market power through diversification are *multipoint competition* and *vertical integration.*

Introduced in Chapter 6 as a strategy that influences competitive rivalry, **multipoint** (also called **multimarket**) **competition** exists when two or more diversified firms simultaneously compete in the same product or geographic markets.[67] For example, the major hospitality companies Marriott and Hilton compete in virtually every segment of the industry. For example, in the premium market Marriott has Ritz-Carlton, and Hilton has a chain of hotels inspired by the Waldorf Astoria. In the upscale market both companies have their namesake hotels (Marriott and Hilton), and in the value segment Marriott's Courtyard and Fairfield Inn compete directly with Hilton's Hampton Inn. They also compete directly in other markets, including vacation timeshares. By virtue of the fact that they compete in the same service markets and often in the same geographic markets, they are less likely to take aggressive competitive actions against each other (i.e., drastic price reductions). This is often called *mutual forbearance.*[68]

Some firms choose to create value by using vertical integration to gain market power (see Figure 8.3). **Vertical integration** exists when a company produces its own inputs (*backward integration*) or owns its own source of distribution of outputs (*forward integration*). For example, Hanwha SolarOne is a vertically integrated solar company. It produces polysilicon, as well as solar wafers, cells, and modules. The company also handles project development for solar applications.[69]

In some instances, firms partially integrate their operations, producing and selling their products by using both company business units and outside sources.[70] **Taper integration,** as this strategy is sometimes called, "arises when a firm sources inputs externally from independent suppliers as well as internally within the boundaries of the firm, or disposes of its outputs through independent outlets in addition to company-owned distribution channels."[71] Research has shown that carefully balancing vertical integration and strategic outsourcing provides competitive benefits leading to superior performance when a high level of innovation is required for success.[72]

Vertical integration is commonly used in the firm's core business to gain market power over rivals. Market power is gained as the firm develops the ability to save money on its operations, avoid market costs, improve product quality, and, possibly, protect its technology from imitation by rivals.[73] Market power also is created when firms have strong ties between their assets for which no market prices exist. Establishing a market price would result in high search and transaction costs, so firms seek to vertically integrate rather than remain separate businesses.[74] When they do, a cooperative M-form similar to that described in association with the related constrained firm is implemented (see Figure 8.4).

Vertical integration does have limits. For example, an outside supplier may produce the product at a lower cost. As a result, internal transactions from vertical integration may be expensive and reduce profitability relative to competitors.[75] Also, bureaucratic costs may be present with vertical integration.[76] And, because vertical integration can require substantial investments in specific technologies, it may reduce the firm's flexibility, especially when technology changes quickly. Finally, changes in demand create capacity balance and coordination problems. If one division is building a part for another internal division, but achieving economies of scale requires the first division to manufacture quantities that are beyond the capacity of the internal buyer to absorb, it would be necessary to sell the parts outside the firm as well as to the internal division. Thus, although vertical integration can create value, especially through market power, it is not without risks and costs.[77]

Many manufacturing firms no longer pursue vertical integration as a means of gaining market power. In fact, reducing vertical integration is the focus of most manufacturing firms, such as Intel and Dell, and even among large automobile companies, such as Ford and General Motors, as they develop independent supplier networks.[78] Flextronics, a contract manufacturer specializing in supply-chain services and high-tech products, represents a new breed of large contract manufacturers that is helping to foster this revolution in supply-chain management.[79] Such firms often manage their customers' entire product lines and offer services ranging from inventory management to delivery and after-sales service.

Simultaneous Operational Relatedness and Corporate Relatedness

As Figure 8.3 suggests, some firms simultaneously seek operational and corporate forms of economies of scope.[80] Simultaneously creating economies of scope by sharing activities (operational relatedness) and transferring core competencies (corporate relatedness) may be difficult to achieve. If the costs associated with managing both types of relatedness exceed the benefits, then firms may experience what might be called "diseconomies" of scope.[81] However, firms that are successful may be able to achieve a sustainable competitive advantage because it will be difficult for competitors to imitate their success.

The Walt Disney Company uses a related diversification strategy to simultaneously create economies of scope through operational and corporate relatedness. Within the firm's studio entertainment business, for example, Disney can gain economies of scope by sharing activities among its different movie distribution companies, such as Touchstone Pictures, Hollywood Pictures, and Dimension Films, among others. Broad and deep knowledge about its customers is a capability on which Disney relies to develop corporate-level core competencies in terms of marketing and distribution. With these competencies, Disney is able to create economies of scope through corporate relatedness as it cross-sells products that are highlighted in its movies through the distribution channels that are part of its theme parks, media, resorts, and consumer products businesses. Thus, characters created in cartoons and movies become figures that are promoted on the Disney Channel and sold in Disney's stores and resorts. In addition, themes found in movies frequently become rides or shows at theme parks. Or, in the case of *Pirates of the Caribbean*, a theme park ride inspired a movie and several sequels.[82]

Either cooperative or SBU M-forms are likely to be implemented with this dual strategy, depending on the degree of diversification (i.e., more diversification would likely require the SBU form). However, with this strategy more process mechanisms to facilitate integration and coordination may be required. For example, more frequent, direct contact between division managers may be essential. This integrating mechanism encourages and supports cooperation and the sharing of either competencies or resources that have the possibility of being used to create new advantages.

Liaison roles sometimes are established in each division to reduce the amount of time division managers spend integrating and coordinating their unit's work with the work taking place in other divisions. Temporary teams or task forces may be formed around projects for which success depends on sharing competencies that are embedded within several divisions. Formal integration departments might be established in firms that frequently use temporary teams or task forces. Ultimately, a matrix organization may evolve in firms implementing this dual strategy. A **matrix organization** is an organizational structure in which a dual structure combines both functional specialization and business product or project specialization.[83] Although complicated, an effective matrix structure can lead to improved coordination among a firm's divisions that seek to simultaneously implement operational and corporate relatedness.[84]

UNRELATED DIVERSIFICATION

Firms do not seek either operational relatedness or corporate relatedness when using the unrelated diversification corporate-level strategy. An unrelated diversification strategy (see Figure 8.3) can create value through two types of financial economies. **Financial economies** are cost savings realized through improved allocations of financial resources based on investments inside or outside the firm.[85]

Efficient internal capital allocations lead to financial economies.[86] One way they do this is by reducing total corporate risk through creation of a portfolio of businesses with different risk profiles. The second type of financial economy is concerned with purchasing other corporations and restructuring their assets. Here, the diversified firm buys another firm, restructures that company's assets in ways that allow it to operate more profitably, and then sells it for a profit in the external market.[87] These two types of financial economies will now be discussed in greater detail.

Efficient Internal Capital Market Allocation

In a market economy, capital markets are thought to allocate capital efficiently. Efficiency results from investors purchasing firm equity shares (ownership) that have high future cash-flow values. Capital is also allocated through debt as bondholders and financiers try to improve the value of their investments by taking stakes in businesses with high growth prospects.

In large diversified firms, the corporate office distributes capital to business divisions to create value for the overall company. Because corporate managers have access to more detailed and accurate information about the businesses in which the firm operates, they should be expected to make distributions that result in gains that exceed those that might be available if capital were allocated by the capital market.[88] Compared with corporate office personnel, external investors have relatively limited access to internal information and can only estimate divisional performance and future business prospects. Information provided to capital markets through annual reports and other sources may not include negative information, instead emphasizing positive prospects and outcomes. Even external shareholders who have access to information have no guarantee of full and complete disclosure.[89] Also, external sources of capital have limited ability to understand the dynamics inside large organizations.

If intervention from outside the firm is required to make corrections to capital allocations, only significant changes are possible, such as forcing the firm into bankruptcy or changing the top management team. Alternatively, in an internal capital market, the corporate office can fine-tune its corrections, by choosing, for example, to adjust managerial incentives or suggesting strategic changes in one of the firm's businesses.[90] Thus, capital can be allocated according to more specific criteria than is possible with external market allocations. Because it has less accurate information, the external capital market may fail to allocate resources adequately to high-potential investments compared with corporate office investments. The corporate office of a diversified company can more effectively perform tasks such as disciplining underperforming management teams through resource allocations.[91]

Research suggests, however, that in efficient capital markets, the unrelated diversification strategy may be discounted.[92] "For years, stock markets have applied a 'conglomerate discount': they value diversified manufacturing conglomerates at 20 percent less, on average, than the value of the sum of their parts. The discount still applies, in good economic times and bad. Extraordinary manufacturers (like GE) can defy it for a while, but more ordinary ones (like Philips and Siemens) cannot."[93] One reason for this discount could be that firms sometimes substitute acquisitions for innovation.[94] In these instances, too many resources are allocated to analyzing and completing acquisitions to further diversify a firm instead of allocating an appropriate amount of resources to nurturing internal innovation.

Despite the challenges associated with unrelated diversification, some firms still use it.[95] Large diversified business groups are found in many European countries, where the number of firms using the conglomerate or unrelated diversification strategy has actually increased, and throughout emerging economies as well.[96] For example, conglomerates continue to dominate the private sector in Latin America, China, Korea, and Taiwan.[97] Typically family controlled, these corporations also account for the greatest percentage of private firms in India.[98] Some research suggests that an unrelated diversification strategy may work better in developing economies, perhaps because managers are more efficient at allocating capital where it can be put to good use than the financial markets in those countries.[99]

The Achilles heel of the unrelated diversification strategy is that conglomerates in developed economies have a fairly short life cycle because financial economies are more easily duplicated than are the gains derived from operational relatedness and corporate relatedness. This is less of a problem in emerging economies, where the absence of a "soft infrastructure" (including effective financial intermediaries, sound regulations, and contract laws) supports and encourages use of the unrelated diversification strategy.[100] In fact, in emerging economies, such as those in India and Chile, diversification increases the performance of firms affiliated with large diversified business groups.[101]

Restructuring

Financial economies can also be created when firms learn how to create value by buying, restructuring, and then selling other companies' assets in the external market.[102] As in the real estate business, buying assets at low prices, restructuring them, and selling them at a price exceeding their cost generates a positive return on the firm's invested capital. Some conglomerates have pursued value creation through restructuring firms in this way. Today, this strategy is often pursued by private equity firms, which are like an unrelated diversified firm in that they have large portfolios of acquired businesses that they buy, restructure, and sell, either to another company or through a public offering.[103]

Creating financial economies by acquiring and restructuring other companies' assets requires an understanding of significant trade-offs. Success usually calls for a focus on mature, low-technology businesses because of the uncertainty of demand for high-technology products. In high-technology businesses, decisions about resource allocation become too complex, creating information-processing overload on the small corporate staffs of unrelated diversified firms. Furthermore, high-technology businesses often depend on human resources; these people can leave or demand higher pay and thus appropriate or deplete the value of an acquired firm.[104] Service businesses with a client orientation are also difficult to buy and sell in this way because of their client-based sales orientation and the mobility of sales people.[105] This is especially so in professional service businesses such as accounting, law, advertising, consulting, and investment banking.

Using the Competitive Form of the Multidivisional Structure to Implement the Unrelated Diversification Strategy

As noted previously, firms using the unrelated diversification strategy want to create value through efficient internal capital allocations or by buying, restructuring, and selling businesses.[106] The competitive form of the M-form structure supports implementation of this strategy. The **competitive form** is a structure in which the firm's divisions are completely independent (see Figure 8.6). Unlike the divisions in the cooperative structure (see Figure 8.4), the divisions that are part of the competitive structure do not share common corporate strengths (e.g., marketing competencies or channel dominance). Because strengths aren't shared in the competitive structure, integrating devices aren't developed for the divisions to use.

An efficient internal capital market, which is the foundation for successful use of the unrelated diversification strategy, requires organizational arrangements that emphasize divisional competition rather than cooperation.[107] Three benefits are expected from the internal competition that the competitive form of the M-form facilitates. First, internal competition creates flexibility—corporate headquarters can have divisions working on different technologies to identify those with the greatest future potential. Resources can then be allocated to the division that is working with the most promising technology to fuel the entire firm's success.[108]

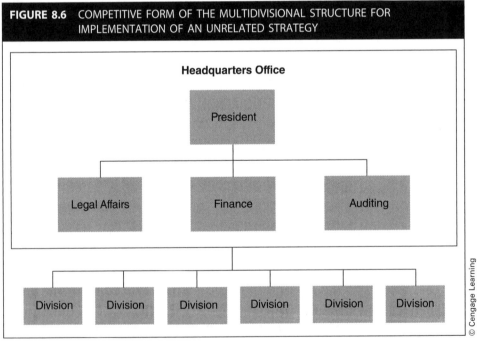

FIGURE 8.6 COMPETITIVE FORM OF THE MULTIDIVISIONAL STRUCTURE FOR IMPLEMENTATION OF AN UNRELATED STRATEGY

Headquarters Office

President

Legal Affairs   Finance   Auditing

Division   Division   Division   Division   Division   Division

© Cengage Learning

NOTES:
▶ Corporate headquarters has a small staff
▶ Finance and auditing are the most prominent functions in the headquarters office to manage cash flow and assure the accuracy of performance data coming from divisions
▶ The legal affairs function becomes important when the firm acquires or divests assets
▶ Divisions are independent and separate for financial evaluation purposes
▶ Divisions retain strategic control, but cash is managed by the corporate office
▶ Divisions compete for corporate resources

Second, internal competition challenges the status quo and inertia, because division heads know that future resource allocations are a product of excellent current performance as well as superior positioning of their division in terms of future performance. Last, internal competition motivates effort. The challenge of competing against internal peers can be as great as the challenge of competing against external marketplace competitors.[109]

Independence among divisions, as shown by a lack of sharing of corporate strengths and the absence of integrating devices, allows the firm using the unrelated diversification strategy to form specific profit performance expectations for each division to stimulate internal competition for future resources. The benefits of internal capital allocations or restructuring cannot be fully realized unless divisions are held accountable for their own independent performance. In the competitive structure, organizational controls (primarily financial controls) are used to emphasize and support internal competition among separate divisions and to form the basis for allocating corporate capital based on their individual performance.

To emphasize competitiveness among divisions, the headquarters office maintains an arms-length relationship with them and does not intervene in divisional affairs, except to audit operations and discipline managers whose divisions perform poorly. In this situation, the headquarters office relies on strategic controls to set rate-of-return targets and financial controls to monitor divisional performance relative to those targets. The headquarters office then allocates cash flow on a competitive basis, rather than automatically returning cash to the division that produced it. Thus, the focus of the headquarters' work is on performance appraisal, resource allocation, and legal aspects related to acquisitions to verify that the firm's portfolio of businesses will lead to financial success.[110]

VALUE-NEUTRAL DIVERSIFICATION: INCENTIVES AND RESOURCES

The objectives described in the last two sections on related and unrelated diversification are all focused on helping the firm create value through its corporate-level strategy. However, diversification is sometimes pursued with value-neutral rather than value-creating objectives in mind.

Incentives to Diversify

Incentives to diversify come from both the external environment and a firm's internal organization. External incentives include antitrust regulations and tax laws. Internal incentives include low performance, uncertain future cash flows, and an overall reduction of risk for the firm. Diversification strategies taken in light of these various incentives sometimes increase the firm's ability to create value, but often the effect is neutral.

Antitrust Regulation. Government antitrust policies and tax laws provided incentives for U.S. firms to diversify in the 1960s and 1970s.[111] Antitrust laws against mergers that created increased market power (via either vertical or horizontal integration) were stringently enforced during that period.[112] As a result, many of the mergers during that time were unrelated, involving companies pursuing different lines of business. Thus, the merger wave of the 1960s was "conglomerate" in character. Merger activity that produced conglomerate diversification was encouraged primarily by the Celler-Kefauver Act, which discouraged horizontal and vertical mergers. For example, in the 1973–1977 period, 79.1 percent of all mergers were conglomerate.[113]

During the 1980s, antitrust enforcement lessened, resulting in more and larger horizontal mergers (acquisitions of target firms in the same line of business, such as a merger between two oil companies).[114] In addition, investment bankers became more open to the kinds of mergers they tried to facilitate; as a consequence, hostile takeovers increased to unprecedented numbers.[115] The conglomerates or highly diversified firms of the 1960s and 1970s became more "focused" in the 1980s and early 1990s as merger constraints were relaxed and restructuring was implemented.[116]

Starting in the late 1990s, however, antitrust concerns emerged again with the large volume of mergers and acquisitions (see Chapter 9).[117] Thus, mergers and acquisitions are receiving more scrutiny. Partially as a result of the trend toward increased scrutiny, the U.S. government enacted the Antitrust Modernization Act of 2002. As a result of this act, the Antitrust Modernization Commission was created to examine whether antitrust laws need to be modernized, to solicit the views of all of the parties concerned with regard to operation of the antitrust laws, to evaluate relevant proposals for changes, and to prepare a report for the president and Congress. In early 2007, a bill to extend the existence of the commission passed both houses of Congress.[118] The effect of this commission on the diversification strategies of U.S. firms will be a topic for future research, but it is unlikely that firms will ever revert to the levels of unrelated diversification observed during the conglomerate era of the 1960s.

Tax Laws. The tax effects of diversification stem from both individual tax rates and corporate tax changes. Some companies (especially mature ones) generate more cash from their operations than they can reinvest profitably. Some argue that *free cash flows* (liquid financial assets for which investments in current businesses are no longer economically viable) should be redistributed to shareholders as dividends.[119] However, in the 1960s and 1970s, dividends were taxed more heavily than capital gains. As a result, before 1980, shareholders wanted firms to diversify by buying and building companies in high-performance industries rather than giving back the cash in the form of dividends.

Under the 1986 Tax Reform Act, however, the top individual ordinary income tax rate was reduced from 50 to 28 percent, and the special capital-gains tax was also changed, treating capital gains as ordinary income. These changes meant that shareholders were not as interested in having firms retain funds for purposes of diversification. These changes in the tax law also influenced an increase in divestitures of unrelated business units after 1986. Thus, while individual tax rates for capital gains and dividends created a shareholder incentive to increase diversification before 1986, they encouraged less diversification after 1986.

Corporate tax laws also affect diversification because acquisitions typically increase a firm's depreciable asset allowances. This happens because the acquiring firm takes on the acquired firm's assets (and thus their depreciation). Depreciation produces lower taxable income, thereby providing an additional incentive for acquisitions. Before 1986, acquisitions may have been the most attractive means for securing tax benefits,[120] but the 1986 Tax Reform Act diminished some of the corporate tax advantages of diversification.[121]

Low Performance. Some research shows that low returns are related to greater levels of diversification.[122] Firms may be willing to take higher risks or engage in unusual types of diversification in an effort to improve performance.[123] For example, the Australian media and investment company Seven Network Ltd. was merged with heavy-equipment provider WesTrac Pty. Ltd. to become Seven Group Holdings. The deal came after Seven Network was unable to find lucrative ways to invest in the Australian media and telecommunications sector after it raised a significant amount of cash by selling a half stake in the company to Kohlberg Kravis Roberts & Co. Analysts were skeptical when the deal was announced. Angus Gluskie, portfolio manager at White Funds Management, said, "It will totally transform the company, given it takes it into a very different industry but WesTrac has been a good business, it has got some interesting exposures and it's going to make the new Seven Group a very interesting creature for investment markets." [124] Managers in the two companies had to admit that there were limited synergies from the merger.

Uncertain Future Cash Flows. As a firm's product line matures or is threatened, a firm may diversify as an important defensive strategy.[125] Diversifying into other product markets or into other businesses can reduce uncertainty about a firm's future cash flows. For instance, PepsiCo has a long history of diversification through acquisitions, including Frito Lay, Tropicana, and Quaker Oats.[126] At one time, the company even owned several fast food restaurant chains, including Pizza Hut, Kentucky Fried Chicken, and Taco Bell. More recently, the firm acquired Brazilian biscuit maker Mabel in a deal valued at about $520 million.[127] For PepsiCo, while the demand for one of its business lines might decline at any time, demand for one or more of its businesses might increase.

Smaller firms also may find it necessary to diversify simply to survive.[128] In the intensely competitive commercial real estate brokerage market, BGC Partners Inc. acquired both Newmark Knight Frank and Grubb & Ellis Co. These acquisitions add significant size to BGC, but analysts are still wondering if the company will be big enough to compete with industry giants like CBRE Group, which is ten times larger.[129]

Synergy and Firm Risk Reduction. As mentioned previously, firms may pursue economies of scope among their diversified business units in an effort to realize synergy. Synergy is more likely to be produced if the firm's business units are highly related and if managers take steps to integrate activities across the firm.[130] But as a firm increases its relatedness and integration between business units, it also increases its risk of large-scale performance problems, because synergy produces interdependence among business units that can reduce a firm's flexibility to respond to changes in its external environment. Also, the businesses can become so tightly linked that difficulties in one part of the firm reverberate across the entire firm. Concerns like these may increase the risk aversion tendencies of managers, sometimes resulting in decisions to constrain the level of activity sharing among business units or to diversify the firm into other businesses that are not as closely related to the existing businesses of the firm.[131]

Resources and Diversification

As we have discussed, there are several value-neutral incentives for firms to diversify as well as value-creating incentives, such as the ability to create economies of scope. However, even when incentives to diversify exist, a firm must have the types and levels of resources and capabilities needed to successfully use a corporate-level diversification strategy.[132] Although financial, intangible, and tangible resources can all facilitate successful diversification, they vary in their ability to create value. Indeed, the degree to which resources are valuable, rare, costly to imitate, and nonsubstitutable (see Chapter 4) influences their ability to create value through diversification. For instance, free cash flows are a financial resource that may be used to diversify the firm. These types of financial resources tend to be highly visible to competitors and thus more imitable and less likely to create value over the long term.[133] On the other hand, intangible resources that can be used to help with diversification, such as knowledge, skills, and relationships with stakeholders, tend to be more valuable because they are hard for competitors to recognize or imitate.

Tangible resources usually include the plant and equipment necessary to produce a good or service and tend to be less flexible assets. Any excess capacity often can be used only for closely related products, especially those requiring highly similar manufacturing technologies. Excess capacity of other tangible resources, such as a sales force, can be used to diversify more easily. Again, excess capacity in a sales force is more effective with related diversification, because it may be utilized to sell similar products. The sales force would be more knowledgeable about the characteristics, customers, and distribution channels of related products.[134] Tangible resources may create resource interrelationships in production, marketing, procurement, and technology, defined earlier as activity sharing. Intangible resources are more flexible than tangible physical assets in facilitating diversification. Although the sharing of tangible resources may induce diversification, intangible resources such as tacit knowledge could encourage even more diversification.[135]

VALUE-REDUCING DIVERSIFICATION: MANAGERIAL MOTIVES TO DIVERSIFY

Managerial motives for diversification may exist independently of value-neutral reasons (i.e., incentives and resources) and value-creating reasons (e.g., economies of scope).[136] One motive that can drive diversification is the desire of top executives to increase their compensation. Because diversification and firm size are highly correlated, as size increases, so does executive compensation.[137] Furthermore, top executives may diversify a firm in order to reduce their own employment risk;[138] that is, managers may have a perception that firms that are diversified are less likely to experience performance peaks and valleys that could lead to job loss. Of course, top executives may also experience increases in personal satisfaction and power from running a larger or more complex organization, a phenomenon referred to as "empire building."[139]

The desire for increased compensation, reduced managerial risk, and empire building can motivate top managers to engage in diversification that is not in the best interests of shareholders or other stakeholders. Consequently, internal governance mechanisms are used to limit managers' tendencies to pursue too much diversification.[140] These mechanisms, such as the board of directors, monitoring by owners (especially those that hold large ownership positions, such as investment funds), and long-term oriented executive compensation, are discussed in detail in Chapter 11. In addition, the top managers' desires to retain strong reputations can reduce their propensity to engage in self-serving but value-destroying diversification, in part because they may want to be considered for even better or more lucrative positions in other firms.[141]

When internal governance mechanisms such as board of director vigilance or owner monitoring are not strong, the external market for corporate control may act as a disciplining force for top managers. For instance, loss of adequate internal governance may result in poor performance, thereby triggering a threat of takeover.[142] A takeover may improve efficiency by replacing ineffective managerial teams; however, if current managers feel vulnerable to this sort of discipline they may pursue defensive tactics, sometimes called "poison pills," to fend off the acquisition and thus preserve their jobs. One example of a poison pill is the "golden parachute," which provides high compensation to managers of the acquired firm as they leave the firm after a takeover (other defensive tactics are discussed in Chapter 11).[143] Therefore, a threat of external governance, although restraining managers, does not flawlessly control managerial motives for diversification.[144]

As shown in Figure 8.7, the level of diversification that can be expected to have the greatest positive effect on performance is based partly on how the interaction of value-creating influences, value-neutral influences, and value-reducing influences affects the adoption of particular diversification strategies. As indicated earlier, the greater the incentives and the more flexible the resources, the higher the level of expected diversification. Financial resources (the most flexible) should have a stronger relationship to the extent of diversification than either tangible or intangible resources. Tangible resources (the most inflexible) are useful primarily for related diversification.

As discussed in this chapter, firms can create more value by effectively using diversification strategies; however, diversification must be kept in check by internal corporate governance (see Chapter 11). Also, the governing effects of the capital market (i.e., threat of a takeover) and the external market for managerial talent help keep in check value-reducing motivations of top executives to diversify.

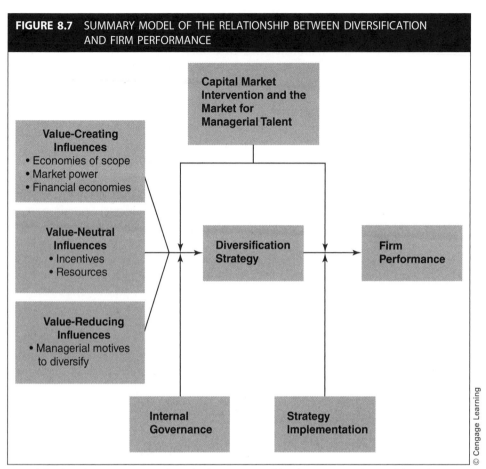

FIGURE 8.7 SUMMARY MODEL OF THE RELATIONSHIP BETWEEN DIVERSIFICATION AND FIRM PERFORMANCE

Capital Market Intervention and the Market for Managerial Talent

Value-Creating Influences
• Economies of scope
• Market power
• Financial economies

Value-Neutral Influences
• Incentives
• Resources

Value-Reducing Influences
• Managerial motives to diversify

Diversification Strategy

Firm Performance

Internal Governance

Strategy Implementation

© Cengage Learning

SOURCE: R. E. Hoskisson & M. A. Hitt, 1990, Antecedents and performance outcomes of diversification: A review and critique of theoretical perspectives, *Journal of Management*, 16: 498.

Appropriate strategy implementation tools, such as the organizational structures discussed in this chapter, are also important.

SUMMARY

▶ A single or dominant business corporate-level strategy may be preferable to a more diversified strategy, unless a corporation can develop economies of scope or financial economies between businesses, or unless it can obtain market power through additional levels of diversification. These economies and market power are the main sources of value creation when the firm diversifies.

▶ Strategic controls (largely subjective criteria) and financial controls (largely objective criteria) are the two types of organizational controls used to successfully implement the firm's chosen corporate-level strategy within the M-form. Both types of controls are critical, although their degree of emphasis varies on the basis of individual matches between strategy and structure.

▶ Related diversification creates value through the sharing of activities or the transfer of core competencies. Sharing activities usually involves sharing tangible resources between businesses. Transferring core competencies involves transferring core competencies developed in one business to another. It also may involve transferring competencies between the corporate office and a business unit.

▶ Sharing activities is usually associated with the corporate-level related constrained diversification strategy. Activity sharing is costly to implement and coordinate, may create unequal benefits for the divisions involved in the sharing, and may lead to fewer managerial risk-taking behaviors.

▶ Transferring core competencies is often associated with related linked (or mixed related) diversification, although firms pursuing both sharing activities and transferring core competencies can use it.

▶ Efficiently allocating resources or restructuring a target firm's assets and placing them under rigorous financial controls are two ways to accomplish successful unrelated diversification. These methods focus on obtaining financial economies.

▶ Unique combinations of different forms of the M-form are matched with different corporate-level diversification strategies to properly implement these strategies. The cooperative M-form, used to implement the related constrained corporate-level strategy, has a centralized corporate office and extensive integrating mechanisms. Divisional incentives are linked to overall corporate performance. The related linked SBU M-form establishes separate profit centers within the diversified firm. Each profit center may have divisions offering similar products, but the centers are unrelated to each other. The competitive M-form, used to implement the unrelated diversification strategy, is highly decentralized, lacks integrating mechanisms, and utilizes objective financial criteria to evaluate each unit's performance.

▶ The primary reason a firm diversifies is to create more value. However, diversification is sometimes pursued because of incentives from tax and governmental antitrust policies, performance disappointments, and uncertainties about future cash flow or to reduce risk.

▶ Managerial motives to diversify (including to increase compensation) can lead to too much diversification and a reduction in the firm's value-creating ability. On the other hand, managers may also be effective stewards of the firm's assets, and the desire to retain a strong personal reputation as well as corporate governance mechanisms can encourage responsible behavior.

▶ Decision makers should pay attention to their firm's internal organization and external environment when making decisions about the optimal level of diversification for their company. Internal resources are important determinants of the direction that diversification should take. However, opportunities in the firm's external environment may facilitate additional levels of diversification, as might unexpected threats from competitors.

ETHICS QUESTIONS

1. Assume that you overheard the following statement: "Those managing an unrelated diversified firm face far more difficult ethical challenges than do those managing a dominant business firm." Based on your reading of this chapter, do you believe this statement true or false? Why?

2. Is it ethical for managers to diversify a firm rather than return excess earnings to shareholders? Provide reasoning to support your answer.

3. Are ethical issues associated with the use of strategic controls? With the use of financial controls? If so, what are they?

4. Are ethical issues involved in implementing the cooperative and competitive M-forms? If so, what are they? As a top-level manager, how would you deal with them?

5. What unethical practices might occur when a firm restructures the assets it has acquired through its diversification efforts? Explain.

6. Do you believe that ethical managers are unaffected by the managerial motives to diversify discussed in this chapter? If so, why? In addition, do you believe that ethical managers should help their peers learn how to avoid making diversification decisions on the basis of the managerial motives to diversify (e.g., increased compensation)? Why or why not?

NOTES

1. H-Y. Liu & C-W. Hsu, 2011, Antecedents and consequences of corporate diversification, *Management Decision*, 49: 1510–1534.
2. M. E. Raynor, 2007, What is corporate strategy, really? *Ivey Business Journal*, 71(8): 1–3; D. C. Hambrick & J. W. Fredrickson, 2005, Are you sure you have a strategy? *Academy of Management Executive*, 19(4): 54; M. E. Porter, 1987, From competitive advantage to corporate strategy, *Harvard Business Review*, 65(3): 43–59.
3. W. P. Wan, R. E. Hoskisson, J. C. Short, & D. W. Yiu, 2011, Resource-based theory and corporate diversification: Accomplishments and opportunities, *Journal of Management*, 1335–1368; M. D. R. Chari, S. Devaraj, & P. David, 2008, The impact of information technology investments and diversification strategies on firm performance, *Management Science*, 54: 224–234; R. A. Burgelman & Y. L. Doz, 2001, The power of strategic integration, *MIT Sloan Management Review*, 42(3): 28–38.
4. K. Lee, M. W. Peng, & K. Lee, 2008, From diversification premium to diversification discount during institutional transitions, *Journal of World Business*, 43(1): 47–65; C. C. Markides & P. J. Williamson, 1996, Corporate diversification and organizational structure: A resource-based view, *Academy of Management Journal*, 39: 340–367.
5. A. Campbell, M. Goold, & M. Alexander, 1995, Corporate strategy: The question for parenting advantage, *Harvard Business Review*, 73(2): 120–132.
6. D. Collis, D. Young & M. Goold, 2007, The size, structure, and performance of corporate headquarters, *Strategic Management Journal*, 28: 383–405; T. H. Brush, P. Bromiley, & M. Hendrickx, 1999,

The relative influence of industry and corporation on business segment performance: An alternative estimate, *Strategic Management Journal*, 20: 519–547.
7. D. D. Bergh, 2001, Diversification strategy research at a crossroads: Established, emerging and anticipated paths, in M. A. Hitt, R. E. Freeman, & J. S. Harrison (eds.), *Handbook of Strategic Management*, Oxford, UK: Blackwell Publishers, 363.
8. H. C. Wang & J. B. Barney, 2006, Employee incentives to make firm-specific investments: Implications for resource-based theories of corporate diversification, *Academy of Management Journal*, 31: 466–476; W. Lewellen, 1971, A pure financial rationale for the conglomerate merger, *Journal of Finance*, 26: 521–537.
9. A.-W. Harzing, 2002, Acquisitions versus greenfield investments: International strategy and management of entry modes, *Strategic Management Journal*, 23: 211–227; J. D. Fisher & Y. Liang, 2000, Is sector diversification more important than regional diversification? *Real Estate Finance*, 17(3): 35–40.
10. J. J. Marcel, 2009, Why top management team characteristics matter when employing a chief operating officer: A strategic contingency perspective, *Strategic Management Journal*, 30: 647–658; Hambrick & Fredrickson, Are you sure you have a strategy?
11. R. George & R. Kabir, 2012, Heterogeneity in business groups and the corporate diversification-firm performance relationship, *Journal of Business Research*, 65: 412–420; E. Fang, R. W. Palmatier, & R. Grewal, 2011, Effects of customer and innovation asset configuration strategies on firm performance, *Journal of Marketing Research*, 48: 587–602;

12. R. P. Rumelt, 1974, *Strategy, Structure, and Economic Performance*, Boston: Harvard Business School Press; L. Wrigley, 1970, Divisional autonomy and diversification, doctoral dissertation, Harvard University, Cambridge, MA.

13. P. Graham, 2010, What it takes, *Forbes*, November 8, 81.

14. 2011, United Parcel Service Annual Report, http://www.ups.com, accessed February 28, 2012.

15. 2012, Johnson & Johnson, Our products, http://www.jnj.com/connect/healthcare-products/, February 28.

16. 2012, Samsung, Company, Corporate profile, http://www.samsung/corporateprofile/affiliatedcompanies.html, utc.com/units/com.htm, February 28.

17. Z.-F. Guo, 2012, An analysis of the degree of diversification and performance, *International Journal of Business & Finance Research*, 6(2): 53–58; L. E. Palich, L. B. Cardinal, & C. C. Miller, 2000, Curvilinearity in the diversification-performance linkage: An examination of over three decades of research, *Strategic Management Journal*, 21: 155–174.

18. L. You & R. T. Daigler, 2010, Is international diversification really beneficial, *Journal of Banking & Finance*, 34: 163–173; E. Stickel, 2001, Uncertainty reduction in a competitive environment, *Journal of Business Research*, 51: 169–177; S. Chatterjee & J. Singh, 1999, Are tradeoffs inherent in diversification moves? A simultaneous model for type of diversification and mode of expansion decisions, *Management Science*, 45: 25–41.

19. R. Guo, 2011, What drives firms to be more diversified? *Journal of Finance & Accountancy*, 6: 1–10; C.-J. Huang & J.-R. Lin, 2011, Financial liberalization and banking performance: An analysis of Taiwan's former 'top 10 banks,' *Applied Economics Letters*, 12: 1111–1120.

20. A. Bakay, A. Elkassabgi, & Mu. Moqbel, 2011, Resource allocation, level of international diversification and firm performance, *International Journal of Business & Management*, 6(12): 87–93.

21. D. K. Chronopoulos, C. Giardone, & J. C. Nankervis, 2011, Are there any cost and profit efficiency gains in financial conglomeration? Evidence from the accession countries, *European Journal of Finance*, 17: 603–621.

22. G. Colak, 2010, Diversification, refocusing and firm value, *European Financial Management*, 16: 422–448.

23. Wan, Hoskisson, Short, & Yiu, Resource-based theory and corporate diversification; B. S. Silverman, 1999, Technological resources and the direction of corporate diversification: Toward an integration of the resource-based view and transaction cost economics, *Administrative Science Quarterly*, 45: 1109–1124.

24. Guo, What drives firms to be more diversified?

25. D. G. Sirmon, M. A. Hitt, R. D. Ireland, & B. A. Gilbert, 2011, Resource orchestration to create competitive advantage: Breadth, depth and life cycle effects, *Journal of Management*, 37: 1390–1412; W. S. DeSarbo, C. A. Di Benedetto, M. Song, & I. Sinha, 2005, Revisiting the Miles and Snow strategic framework: Uncovering interrelationships between strategic types, capabilities, environmental uncertainty, and firm performance, *Strategic Management Journal*, 26: 47–74.

26. S. F. Matusik & M. A. Fitza, 2012, Diversification in the venture capital industry: Leveraging knowledge under uncertainty, *Strategic Management Journal*, 33: 407–426; R. E. Hoskisson & L. W. Busenitz,

2002, Market uncertainty and learning distance in corporate entrepreneurship entry mode choice, in M. A. Hitt, R. D. Ireland, S. M. Camp, & D. L. Sexton (eds.), *Strategic Entrepreneurship: Creating a New Mindset*, Oxford, UK: Blackwell Publishers, 150–172; S. K. McEvily & B. Chakravarthy, 2002, The persistence of knowledge-based advantage: An empirical test for product performance and technological knowledge, *Strategic Management Journal*, 23: 285–305.

27. Y. Spiegel, 2009, Managerial overload and organization design, *Economics Letters*, 105(1): 53–55; A. Chandler, 1962, *Strategy and Structure*, Cambridge, MA: MIT Press.

28. J. Greco, 1999, Alfred P. Sloan, Jr. (1875–1966): The original organizational man, *Journal of Business Strategy*, 20(5): 30–31.

29. H. Zhou, 2005, Market structure and organizational form, *Southern Economic Journal*, 71: 705–719; H. Itoh, 2003, Corporate restructuring in Japan, Part I: Can M-form organization manage diverse businesses? *Japanese Economic Review*, 54: 49–73.

30. S. Karim, 2006, Modularity in organizational structure: The reconfiguration of internally developed and acquired business units, *Strategic Management Journal*, 27: 799–823.

31. O. E. Williamson, 1994, Strategizing, economizing, and economic organization, in R. P. Rumelt, D. E. Schendel, & D. J. Teece (eds.), *Fundamental Issues in Strategy*, Cambridge, MA: Harvard Business School Press, 361–401; Chandler, *Strategy and Structure*.

32. R. E. Hoskisson, C. W. L. Hill, & H. Kim, 1993, The multidivisional structure: Organizational fossil or source of value? *Journal of Management*, 19: 269–298.

33. J. I. Galan & M. J. Sanchez-Bueno, 2009, The continuing validity of the strategy-structure nexus: New findings 1993–2003, *Strategic Management Journal*, 30: 1234–1243.

34. Spiegel, Managerial overload and organization design; A. D. Chandler, 1994, The functions of the HQ unit in the multibusiness firm, in R. P. Rumelt, D. E. Schendel, & D. J. Teece (eds.), *Fundamental Issues in Strategy*, Cambridge, MA: Harvard Business School Press, 327.

35. J. S. Harrison & C. H. St. John, 2010, *Foundations in Strategic Management*, 5th ed., Mason, Ohio: South-Western Cengage Learning.

36. L.-C. Hsu & H.-C. Chang, 2011, The role of behavioral strategic controls in family firm innovation, *Industry & Innovation*, 18: 709–727.

37. I. Bostan, 2010, Performance of financial control, *Theoretical and Applied Economics*, 17: 77–86; L. He, 2010, On financial control and corporate governance structures, *International Journal of Business & Management*, 5: 215–218.

38. R. A. D'Aveni, G. B. Dagnino, & K. G. Smith, 2010, The age of temporary advantage, *Strategic Management Journal*, 31: 1371–1385; H. Tanriverdi & N. Venkatraman, 2005, Knowledge relatedness and the performance of multibusiness firms, *Strategic Management Journal*, 26: 97–119.

39. J.-P. Chavas, B. Barham, J. Foltz, & K. Kim, 2012, Analysis and decomposition of scope economies: R&D at U.S. research universities, *Applied Economics*, 44: 1387–1404; M. E. Porter, 1985, *Competitive Advantage*, New York: The Free Press, 328.

40. B. Melnikas, 2011, Knowledge economy: Synergy effects, interinstitutional interaction and internationalization processes, *Engineering Economics*, 22: 367–379;

G. Hoberg & G. Phillips, 2010, Product market synergies and competition in mergers and acquisitions: A text-based analysis, *Review of Financial Studies*, 23: 3773–3811.

41 Ravichandran, Liu, Han, & Hasan, Diversification and firm performance; J. W. Lu & P. W. Beamish, 2004, International diversification and firm performance: The S-curve hypothesis, *Academy of Management Journal*, 47: 598–609; R. G. Schroeder, K. A. Bates, & M. A. Junttila, 2002, A resource-based view of manufacturing strategy and the relationship to manufacturing performance, *Strategic Management Journal*, 23: 105–117.

42 A. Pehrsson, 2006, Business relatedness and performance: A study of managerial perceptions, *Strategic Management Journal*, 27: 265–282; D. Gupta & Y. Gerchak, 2002, Quantifying operational synergies in a merger/acquisition, *Management Science*, 48: 517–533.

43 C. W. Moon, 2011, Information sharing as source of synergy creation in corporate diversification: An empirical analysis of Korean banking industry, *International Business & Economics Research*, 10(8): 35–44; C. H. St. John & J. S. Harrison, 1999, Manufacturing-based relatedness, synergy, and coordination, *Strategic Management Journal*, 20: 129–145.

44 Zhou, Synergy, coordination costs, and diversification choices; M. L. Marks & P. H. Mirvis, 2000, Managing mergers, acquisitions, and alliances: Creating an effective transition structure, *Organizational Dynamics*, 28(3): 35–47.

45 Ibid.

46 Ibid; C. Park, 2003, Prior performance characteristics of related and unrelated acquirers, *Strategic Management Journal*, 24: 471–480; G. Delong, 2001, Stockholder gains from focusing versus diversifying bank mergers, *Journal of Financial Economics*, 2: 221–252; T. H. Brush, 1996, Predicted change in operational synergy and post- acquisition performance of acquired businesses, *Strategic Management Journal*, 17: 1–24; H. Zhang, 1995, Wealth effects of U.S. bank takeovers, *Applied Financial Economics*, 5: 329–336.

47 D. D. Bergh, 1995, Size and relatedness of units sold: An agency theory and resource-based perspective, *Strategic Management Journal*, 16: 221–239.

48 M. Lubatkin & S. Chatterjee, 1994, Extending modern portfolio theory into the domain of corporate diversification: Does it apply? *Academy of Management Journal*, 37: 109–136.

49 G. Kenny, 2012, Diversification: Best practices of the leading companies, *Journal of Business Strategy*, 33(1): 12–20; E. Dooms & A. A. Van Oijen, 2008, The balance between tailoring and standardizing control, *European Management Review*, 5(4): 245–252; T. Kono, 1999, A strong head office makes a strong company, *Long Range Planning*, 32(2): 225.

50 Rumelt, *Strategy, Structure and Economic Performance*.

51 E. Doving & P. N. Gooderham, 2008, Dynamic capabilities as antecedents of the scope of related diversification: The case of small firm accountancy practices, *Strategic Management Journal*, 29: 841–857; Zhou, Synergy, coordination costs, and diversification choices.

52 A. Renzi & C. Simone, 2011, Innovation, tangible and intangible resources: The 'space of slacks interaction,' *Strategic Change*, 20(1/2): 59–71; J. Surroca,

J. A. Tribo, & S. Waddock, 2010, Corporate responsibility and financial performance: The role of intangible resources, *Strategic Management Journal*, 31: 463–490; J. Robins & M. F. Wiersema, 1995, A resource-based approach to the multibusiness firm: Empirical analysis of portfolio interrelationships and corporate financial performance, *Strategic Management Journal*, 16: 277–299.

53 R. L. Daft, 2010, *Organization Theory and Design*, 10th Ed., Independence, KY: Cengage Learning

54 H.-C. Lai, Y.-C. Chiu, Y-C. Liaw, & T.-Y. Lee, 2010, Technological diversification and organizational divisionalization: The moderating role of complementary assets, *British Journal of Management*, 21: 983–995.

55 I.-C. Hsu & Y.-S. Wang, 2008, A model of intraorganizational knowledge sharing: Development and initial test, *Journal of Global Information Management*, 16(3): 45–73; M. Kotabe, X. Martin, & H. Domoto, 2003, Gaining from vertical partnerships: Knowledge transfer, relationship duration, and supplier performance improvement in the U.S. and Japanese automotive industries, *Strategic Management Journal*, 24: 293–316; L. Capron, P. Dussauge, & W. Mitchell, 1998, Resource redeployment following horizontal acquisitions in Europe and the United States, 1988–1992, *Strategic Management Journal*, 19: 631–661.

56 H.-Y. Liu & F. H. Liu, 2011, The process of competence leveraging in related diversification: A case of technology management at a composite-material company, *Technology Analysis & Strategic Management*, 23: 193–211; L. Capron & N. Pistre, 2002, When do acquirers earn abnormal returns? *Strategic Management Journal*, 23: 781–794.

57 D. J. Miller, 2006, Technological diversity, related diversification and firm performance, *Strategic Management Journal*, 27: 601–619.

58 J. W. Spencer, 2003, Firms' knowledge-sharing strategies in the global innovation system: Empirical evidence from the flat panel display industry, *Strategic Management Journal*, 24: 217–233.

59 D. Whitford & D. Burke, 2011, Inside the quiet giant that rules the food business, *Fortune*, November 7, 165–178.

60 2012, Catholic Health Initiatives, http://www.catholichealthinit.org/, March 2.

61 2012, GE Company Organizational Chart, http://www.ge.com/pdf/company/ge_organization_chart.pdf, March 1.

62 Kenny, Diversification: Best practices of the leading companies.

63 B. Keats & H. O'Neill, 2001, Organizational structure: Looking through a strategy lens, in M. A. Hitt, R. E. Freeman, & J. S. Harrison (eds.), *Handbook of Strategic Management*, Oxford, UK: Blackwell Publishers, 520–542.

64 G. Stalk Jr., 2005, Rotate the core, *Harvard Business Review*, 83(3): 18–19; C. Zellner & D. Fornahl, 2002, Scientific knowledge and implications for its diffusion, *Journal of Knowledge Management*, 6(2): 190–198.

65 R. Konopaske, C. Robie, & J. M. Ivancevich, 2009, Managerial willingness to assume traveling, short-term and long-term global assignments, *Management International Review*, 49: 359–387.

66 A. Pehrsson, 2010, Business-relatedness and the strategy of moderations: Impacts on foreign subsidiary performance, *Journal of Strategy and*

Management, 3: 110–133; M. Ceccagnoli, 2009, Appropriabililty, preemption, and firm performance, Strategic Management Journal, 30: 81–98.

[67] Y. Xu, 2011, Competitive network and competitive behavior: A study of the U.S. airline industry, Academy of Strategic Management Journal, 10: 45–63; J. Gimeno & C. Y. Woo, 1999, Multimarket contact, economies of scope, and firm performance, Academy of Management Journal, 42: 239–259.

[68] T. Yu, M. Subramaniam, & A. A. Canella, Jr., 2009, Rivalry deterrence in international markets: Contingencies governing the mutual forbearance hypothesis, Academy of Management Journal, 52: 127–147; H. R. Greve, 2008, Multimarket contact and sales growth: Evidence from insurance, Strategic Management Journal, 29: 229–249.

[69] 2012, The direction of vertically integrated: Downstream, Greentech Solar, http://www.greentechmedia.com/articles/read/the-direction-of-the-vertically-integrated-downstream/, March 2.

[70] I. Geyskens, J.-B. E. M. Steenkamp, & N. Kumar, 2006, Make, buy, or ally: A transaction cost theory meta-analysis, Strategic Management Journal, 49: 519–543; R. Gulati, P. R. Lawrence, & P. Puranam, 2005, Adaptation in vertical relationships: Beyond incentive conflict, Strategic Management Journal, 26: 415–440.

[71] F. T. Rothaermel, M. A. Hitt, & L. A. Jobe, 2006, Balancing vertical integration and strategic outsourcing: Effects on product portfolio, product success, and firm performance, Strategic Management Journal, 27: 1033.

[72] Ibid.

[73] L. Diestre & N. Rajagopalan, 2011, An environmental perspective on diversification: The effects of chemical relatedness and regulatory sanctions, Academy of Management Journal, 54: 97–115; S. J. Forbes & M. Lederman, 2010, Does vertical integration affect firm performance? Evidence from the airline industry, RAND Journal of Economics, 41: 765–790.

[74] R. Carter & G. M. Hodgson, 2006, The impact of empirical tests of transactions costs economics on the debate on the nature of the firm, Strategic Management Journal, 27: 461–476; O. E. Williamson, 1996, Economics and organization: A primer, California Management Review, 38(2): 131–146.

[75] S. Novak & S. Stern, 2008, How does outsourcing affect performance dynamics? Evidence from the automobile industry, Management Science, 54(12), 1963–1979.

[76] E. Rawley, 2010, Diversification, coordination costs and organizational rigidity: Evidence from microdata, Strategic Management Journal, 31: 873–891.

[77] M. G. Jacobides, 2005, Industry change through vertical disintegration: How and why markets emerged in mortgage banking, Academy of Management Journal, 48: 465–498.

[78] W.-M. Lu & S.-W. Hung, 2010, Assessing the performance of a vertically disintegrated chain by the DEA approach, International Journal of Production Research, 48: 1155–1170; T. Hutzschenreuter & F. Gröne, 2009, Changing vertical integration strategies under pressure from foreign competition: The case of U.S. and German multinationals, Journal of Management Studies, 46: 269–307.

[79] 2012, Flextronics, http://www.flextronics.com/about_us/default.aspx, March 1.

[80] P. David, J. P. O'Brien, T. Yoshikawa, & A. Delios, 2010, Do shareholders or stakeholders appropriate the rents from corporate diversification? The influence of ownership structure, Academy of Management Journal, 53: 636–654; K. M. Eisenhardt & D. C. Galunic, 2000, Coevolving: At last, a way to make synergies work, Harvard Business Review, 78(1): 91–111.

[81] R. Schoenberg, 2001, Knowledge transfer and resource sharing as value creation mechanisms in inbound continental European acquisitions, Journal of Euro-Marketing, 10: 99–114.

[82] 2012, Disney, Company overview, http://corporate.disney.go.com/corporate/overview.html, March 1.

[83] L. Davidovitch, A. Parush, & A. Shtub, 2010, Simulator-based team training to share resources in a matrix structure organization, IEEE Transactions on Engineering Management, 57: 288–300.

[84] 2009, Design your governance model to make the matrix work, People & Strategy, 32(4), 16–25; J. G. March, 1994, A Primer on Decision Making: How Decisions Happen, New York: The Free Press, 117–118; J. G. Galbraith & R. K. Kazanjian, Strategy Implementation: Structure, Systems, and Processes, St. Paul, MN: West Publishing Co.

[85] D. Lee & R. Madhaven, 2010, Divestiture and firm performance: A meta-analysis, Journal of Management, 36: 1345–1371; C. W. L. Hill, 1994, Diversification and economic performance: Bringing structure and corporate management back into the picture, in R. P. Rumelt, D. E. Schendel, & D. J. Teece (eds.), Fundamental Issues in Strategy, Boston: Harvard Business School Press, 297–321.

[86] J.-M. Gaspar & M. Massa, 2011, The role of commonality between CEO and divisional managers in internal capital markets, Journal of Financial & Quantitative Analysis, 46: 841–869.

[87] M. E. Porter, 1985, Competitive Advantage, New York: The Free Press.

[88] O. E. Williamson, 1975, Markets and Hierarchies: Analysis and Antitrust Implications, New York: Macmillan Free Press.

[89] R. Aggarwal & N. A. Kyaw, 2009, International variations in transparency and capital markets: Evidence from European firms, Journal of International Financial Management & Accounting, 20(1): 1–34; C. Botosan & M. Harris, 2000, Motivations for changes in disclosure frequency and its consequences: An examination of voluntary quarterly segment disclosure, Journal of Accounting Research, 38: 329–353.

[90] A. Capezio, J. Shields, & M. O'Donnell, 2011, Too good to be true: Board structural independence as a moderator of CEO pay-for-performance, Journal of Management Studies, 48: 487–513.

[91] D. Miller, R. Eisenstat, & N. Foote, 2002, Strategy from the inside out: Building capability-creating organizations, California Management Review, 44(3): 37–54; P. Taylor & J. Lowe, 1995, A note on corporate strategy and capital structure, Strategic Management Journal, 16: 411–414.

[92] J. Shyu & Y-L. Chen, 2009, Diversification, performance, and the corporate life cycle, Emerging Markets Finance & Trade, 45(6): 57–68; J. M. Campa & S. Kedia, 2002, Explaining the diversification discount, Journal of Finance, 57: 1731–1762; O. A. Lamont & C. Polk, 2001, The diversification discount: Cash flows versus returns, Journal of Finance, 56: 1693–1721; R. Rajan, H. Servaes, & L. Zingales, 2001, The cost of diversity: The

diversification discount and inefficient investment, *Journal of Finance*, 55: 35–79.

[93] 2001, Spoilt for choice, *Economist* online, http://www.economist.com, July 5.

[94] R. D. Banker, S. Wattal, & J. M. Plehn-Dujowich, 2011, R&D versus acquisitions: Role of diversification in the choice of innovation strategy by information technology firms, *Journal of Management Information Systems*, 28: 109–144.

[95] T. R. Eisenmann, 2002, The effects of CEO equity ownership and firm diversification on risk taking, *Strategic Management Journal*, 23: 513–534; D. J. Denis, D. K. Denis, & A. Sarin, 1999, Agency theory and the reference of equity ownership structure on corporate diversification strategies, *Strategic Management Journal*, 20: 1071–1076; R. Amit & J. Livnat, 1988, A concept of conglomerate diversification, *Journal of Management*, 14: 593–604.

[96] W. P. Wan & R. E. Hoskisson, 2003, Home country environments, corporate diversification strategies, and firm performance, *Academy of Management Journal*, 46: 27–45; T. Khanna & K. Palepu, 1997, Why focused strategies may be wrong for emerging markets, *Harvard Business Review*, 75(4): 41–50.

[97] A. N. Berger, I. Hasan, & M. Zhou, 2010, The effects of focus versus diversification on bank performance: Evidence from Chinese banks, *Journal of Banking & Finance*, 34: 1417–1435; A. Mishra & M. Akbar, 2007, Empirical examination of diversification strategies in business groups: Evidence from emerging markets, *International Journal of Emerging Markets*, 2: 22–38; C. Chung, 2006, Beyond Guanxi: Network contingencies in Taiwanese business groups, *Organization Studies*, 27: 461–480; S. J. Chang & J. Hong, 2002, How much does the business group matter in Korea? *Strategic Management Journal*, 23: 265–274; C. Chung, 2001, Markets, culture and institutions: The emergence of large business groups in Taiwan, 1950s–1970s, *Journal of Management Studies*, 38: 719–745.

[98] 2011, Too big for India, *The Economist*, August 13, 61–61; N. Lakshman, 2007, Private equity invades India, *Business Week*, January 8, 40; S. Manikutty, 2000, Family business groups in India: A resource-based view of the emerging trends, *Family Business Review*, 13: 279–292.

[99] S. Purkayastha, T. S. Manolova, & L. F. Edelman, 2012, Diversification and performance in developed and emerging market contexts: A review of the literature, *International Journal of Management Reviews*, 14: 18–38; Wan & Hoskisson, Home country environments.

[100] S. L. Sun, X. Zhoa, & H. Yang, 2010, Executive compensation in Asia: A critical review, *Asia Pacific Journal of Management*, 27: 775–802; T. Khanna, K. G. Palepu, & J. Sinha, 2005, Strategies that fit emerging markets, *Harvard Business Review*, 83(6): 63–76; T. Khanna & J. W. Rivkin, 2001, Estimating the performance effects of business groups in emerging markets, *Strategic Management Journal*, 22: 45–74.

[101] Lee, Park, & Shin, Disappearing internal capital markets; T. Khanna & K. Palepu, 2000, Is group affiliation profitable in emerging markets? An analysis of diversified Indian business groups, *Journal of Finance*, 55: 867–892; T. Khanna & K. Palepu, 2000, The future of business groups in emerging markets: Long-run evidence from Chile, *Academy of Management Journal*, 43: 268–285.

[102] D. D. Bergh, R. A. Johnson, & R. L. Dewitt, 2008, Restructuring through spin-off or sell-off: Transforming information asymmetries into financial gain, *Strategic Management Journal*, 29: 133–148; H. G. Barkema & M. Schijven, 2008, Toward unlocking the full potential of acquisitions: The role of organizational restructuring, *Strategic Management Journal*, 51: 696–722; R. E. Hoskisson, R. A. Johnson, D. Yiu, & W. P. Wan, 2001, Restructuring strategies and diversified business groups: Differences associated with country institutional environments, in M. A. Hitt, R. E. Freeman, & J. S. Harrison (eds.), *Handbook of Strategic Management*, Oxford, UK: Blackwell Publishers, 433–463.

[103] H. Gospel, A. Pendleton, S. Vitols, & P. Wilke, 2011, New investment funds, restructuring and labor outcomes: A European perspective, *Corporate Governance: An International Review*, 19: 276–289.

[104] R. Coff, 2003, Bidding wars over R&D-intensive firms: Knowledge, opportunism, and the market for corporate control, *Academy of Management Journal*, 46: 74–85.

[105] S. Nambisan, 2001, Why service businesses are not product businesses, *MIT Sloan Management Review*, 42(4): 72–80; T. A. Doucet & R. M. Barefield, 1999, Client base valuation: The case of a professional service firm, *Journal of Business Research*, 44: 127–133.

[106] J.-G. Gaspar & M. Massa, 2011, The role of commonality between CEO and divisional managers in internal capital markets, *Journal of Financial & Quantitative Analysis*, 46: 841–869; M. F. Wiersema & H. P. Bowen, 2008, Corporate diversification: The impact of foreign competition, industry globalization, and product diversification, *Strategic Management Journal*, 29: 115–132; Hoskisson, Hill, & Kim, The multidivisional structure.

[107] M. C. Jensen & W. H. Meckling, 2009, Specific knowledge and divisional performance measurement, *Journal of Applied Corporate Finance*, 21(2): 49–57; Hill, Hitt, & Hoskisson, Cooperative versus competitive structures, 512.

[108] S. Agarwal, I.-M. Chiu, V. Souphom, & G. M. Yamashiro, 2011, The efficiency of internal capital markets: Evidence from the Annual Capital Expenditure Survey, *Quarterly Review of Economics & Finance*, 51: 162–172.

[109] S. Lee, K. Park, & H.-H. Shin, 2009, Disappearing internal capital markets: Evidence from diversified business groups in Korea, *Journal of Banking & Finance*, 33: 326–334; J. Birkinshaw, 2001, Strategies for managing internal competition, *California Management Review*, 44(1): 21–38.

[110] J. A. Doukas & O. B. Kan, 2008, Investment decision and internal capital markets: Evidence from acquisitions, *Journal of Banking & Finance*, 32: 1484–1498; T. R. Eisenmann & J. L. Bower, 2000, The entrepreneurial M-form: Strategic integration in global media firms, *Organization Science*, 11: 348–355.

[111] M. Lubatkin, H. Merchant, & M. Srinivasan, 1997, Merger strategies and shareholder value during times of relaxed antitrust enforcement: The case of large mergers during the 1980s, *Journal of Management*, 23: 61–81.

[112] D. P. Champlin & J. T. Knoedler, 1999, Restructuring by design? Government's complicity in corporate restructuring, *Journal of Economic Issues*, 33(1): 41–57.

[113] R. M. Scherer & D. Ross, 1990, *Industrial Market Structure and Economic Performance*, Boston: Houghton Mifflin.

[114] A. Shleifer & R. W. Vishny, 1994, Takeovers in the 1960s and 1980s: Evidence and implications, in R. P. Rumelt, D. E. Schendel, & D. J. Teece (eds.), *Fundamental Issues in Strategy*, Boston: Harvard Business School Press, 403–422.

[115] S. Chatterjee, J. S. Harrison, & D. D. Bergh, 2003, Failed takeover attempts, corporate governance and refocusing, *Strategic Management Journal*, 24: 87–96; Lubatkin, Merchant, & Srinivasan, Merger strategies and shareholder value; D. J. Ravenscraft & R. M. Scherer, 1987, *Mergers, Sell-Offs and Economic Efficiency*, Washington, DC: Brookings Institution, 22.

[116] D. A. Zalewski, 2001, Corporate takeovers, fairness, and public policy, *Journal of Economic Issues*, 35: 431–437; P. L. Zweig, J. P. Kline, S. A. Forest, & K. Gudridge, 1995, The case against mergers, *Business Week*, October 30, 122–130; J. R. Williams, B. L. Paez, & L. Sanders, 1988, Conglomerates revisited, *Strategic Management Journal*, 9: 403–414.

[117] E. J. Lopez, 2001, New anti-merger theories: A critique, *Cato Journal*, 20: 359–378; 1998, The trustbusters' new tools, *Economist*, May 2, 62–64.

[118] A. A. Foer, 2009, The antitrust modernization commission: A retrospective from the perspective of the American Antitrust Institute, *Antitrust Bulletin*, 54: 305–326.

[119] M. C. Jensen, 1986, Agency costs of free cash flow, corporate finance, and takeovers, *American Economic Review*, 76: 323–329.

[120] R. Gilson, M. Scholes, & M. Wolfson, 1988, Taxation and the dynamics of corporate control: The uncertain case for tax motivated acquisitions, in J. C. Coffee, L. Lowenstein, & S. Rose-Ackerman (eds.), *Knights, Raiders, and Targets: The Impact of the Hostile Takeover*, New York: Oxford University Press, 271–299.

[121] C. Steindel, 1986, Tax reform and the merger and acquisition market: The repeal of the general utilities, *Federal Reserve Bank of New York Quarterly Review*, 11(3): 31–35.

[122] T. Afza, C. Slahudin, & M. S. Nazir, 2008, Diversification and corporate performance: An evaluation of Pakistani firms, *South Asian Journal of Management*, 15(3): 7–18; C. Park, 2002, The effects of prior performance on the choice between related and unrelated acquisitions: Implications for the performance consequences of diversification strategy, *Journal of Management Studies*, 39: 1003–1019; Y. Chang & H. Thomas, 1989, The impact of diversification strategy on risk-return performance, *Strategic Management Journal*, 10: 271–284.

[123] D. A. Levinthal & B. Wu, 2010, Opportunity costs and non-scale free capabilities: Profit maximization, corporate scope and profit margins, *Strategic Management Journal*, 31: 780–801; M. N. Nickel & M. C. Rodriguez, 2002, A review of research on the negative accounting relationship between risk and return: Bowman's paradox, *Omega*, 30(1): 1–18; E. H. Bowman, 1982, Risk seeking by troubled firms, *Sloan Management Review*, 23: 33–42.

[124] L. McFarland, 2010, Australian mogul consolidates units, *Wall Street Journal*, February 23, B2.

[125] D. G. Sirmon, M. A. Hitt, & R. D. Ireland, 2007, Managing firm resources in dynamic environments to create value: Looking inside the black box,

Academy of Management Review, 32: 273–292; A. E. Bernardo & B. Chowdhry, 2002, Resources, real options, and corporate strategy, *Journal of Financial Economics*, 63: 211–234.

[126] 2012, Brands, Pepsico, http://www.pepsico.com/Brands.html, March 3.

[127] 2012, EM Expansion—Focus on Brazil, China, Turkey, *Australia Food & Drink Report, Quarter 2*, 16.

[128] W. H. Tsai, Y. C. Kuo, & J.-H. Hung, 2009, Corporate diversification and CEO turnover in family businesses: Self-entrenchment or risk reduction? *Small Business Economics*, 32(1): 57–76; C. G. Smith & A. C. Cooper, 1988, Established companies diversifying into young industries: A comparison of firms with different levels of performance, *Strategic Management Journal*, 9: 111–121.

[129] L. Kusisto, 2012, Inside the brokerage biz: Cantor makes a big splash, *Wall Street Journal*, February 27, A20.

[130] P. Danese & P. Romano, 2011, Supply chain integration and efficiency performance: A study on the interactions between customer and supplier integration, *Supply Chain Management*, 16: 220–230; A. Nagurney, 2010, Multi-product supply chain horizontal network integration: Models, theory and computational results, *International Transactions in Operational Research*, 17: 333–349.

[131] T. B. Folta & J. P. O'Brien, 2008, Determinants of firm-specific thresholds in acquisition decisions, *Managerial and Decision Economics*, 29(2/3): 209–225; N. M. Kay & A. Diamantopoulos, 1987, Uncertainty and synergy: Towards a formal model of corporate strategy, *Managerial and Decision Economics*, 8: 121–130.

[132] Wan, Hoskisson, Short & Yiu, Resource-based theory and corporate diversification; D. G. Sirmon, S. Gove, & M. A. Hitt, 2008, Resource management in dyadic competitive rivalry: The effects of resource bundling and deployment, *Academy of Management Journal*, 51: 919–935; J. G. Matsusaka, 2001, Corporate diversification, value maximization, and organizational capabilities, *Journal of Business*, 74: 409–432; S. J. Chatterjee & B. Wernerfelt, 1991, The link between resources and type of diversification: Theory and evidence, *Strategic Management Journal*, 12: 33–48.

[133] E. N. Kim, S. S. Das, & A. Das, 2009, Diversification strategy, capital structure, and the Asian financial crisis (1997–1998): Evidence from Singapore firms, *Strategic Management Journal*, 30: 577–594; W. Keuslein, 2003, The Ebitda folly, *Forbes*, March 17, 165–167.

[134] L. Capron & J. Hulland, 1999, Redeployment of brands, sales forces, and general marketing management expertise following horizontal acquisitions: A resource-based view, *Journal of Marketing*, 63(2): 41–54.

[135] M. V. S. Kumar, 2009, The relationship between product and international diversification: The effects of short-run constraints and endogeneity, *Strategic Management Journal*, 30: 99–116; A. M. Knott, D. J. Bryce, & H. E. Pose, 2003, On the strategic accumulation of intangible assets, *Organization Science*, 14: 192–207; R. D. Smith, 2000, Intangible strategic assets and firm performance: A multi-industry study of the resource-based view, *Journal of Business Strategies*, 17(2): 91–117.

[136] A. J. Nyberg, I. S. Fulmer, B. Gerhart, & M. A. Carpenter, 2010, Agency theory revisited:

CEO return and shareholder interest alignment, *Academy of Management Journal*, 53: 1029–1049.

137 J. E. Core & W. R. Guay, 2010, Is CEO pay too high and are incentives too low? A wealth-based contracting framework, *Academy of Management Perspectives*, 24(1): 5–19; I. Filatotchev & D. Allcock, 2010, Corporate governance and executive remuneration: A contingency framework, *Academy of Management Perspectives*, 24(1): 20–33; S. W. Geiger & L. H. Cashen, 2007, Organizational size and CEO compensation: The moderating effect of diversification in downscoping organizations, *Journal of Managerial Issues*, 19: 233–252.

138 L. L. Lan & L. Heracleous, 2010, Rethinking agency theory: The view from law, *Academy of Management Review*, 35: 294–315; W.-H. Tsai, Y.-C. Kuo, & J.-H. Hung, 2009, Corporate diversification and CEO turnover in family businesses: Self-entrenchment or risk reduction? *Small Business Economics*, 32(1): 57–76; M. Goranova, T. M. Alessandri, P. Brandes, & R. Dharwadkar, 2007, Managerial ownership and corporate diversification: A longitudinal view, *Strategic Management Journal*, 28: 211–225.

139 O.-K. Hope & W. B. Thomas, 2008, Managerial empire building and firm disclosure, *Journal of Accounting Research*, 46: 591–626.

140 A. J. Wowak & D. C. Hambrick, 2010, A model of person-pay interaction: How executives vary in their responses to compensation arrangements, *Strategic Management Journal*, 31: 803–821.

141 E. F. Fama, 1980, Agency problems and the theory of the firm, *Journal of Political Economy*, 88: 288–307.

142 J. J. Janney, 2002, Eat or get eaten? How equity ownership and diversification shape CEO risk-taking, *Academy of Management Executive*, 14(4): 157–158; J. W. Lorsch, A. S. Zelleke, & K. Pick, 2001, Unbalanced boards, *Harvard Business Review*, 79(2): 28–30; R. E. Hoskisson & T. Turk, 1990, Corporate restructuring: Governance and control limits of the internal market, *Academy of Management Review*, 15: 459–477.

143 M. Kahan & E. B. Rock, 2002, How I learned to stop worrying and love the pill: Adaptive responses to takeover law, *University of Chicago Law Review*, 69(3): 871–915.

144 R. C. Anderson, T. W. Bates, J. M. Bizjak, & M. L. Lemmon, 2000, Corporate governance and firm diversification, *Financial Management*, 29(1): 5–22; J. D. Westphal, 1998, Board games: How CEOs adapt to increases in structural board independence from management, *Administrative Science Quarterly*, 43: 511–537; J. K. Seward & J. P. Walsh, 1996, The governance and control of voluntary corporate spin offs, *Strategic Management Journal*, 17: 25–39; J. P. Walsh & J. K. Seward, 1990, On the efficiency of internal and external corporate control mechanisms, *Academy of Management Review*, 15: 421–458.

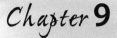

Chapter 9

ACQUISITION AND RESTRUCTURING STRATEGIES

KNOWLEDGE OBJECTIVES

Studying this chapter should provide you with the strategic management knowledge needed to:

1. Explain the popularity of acquisition strategies.

2. Discuss reasons firms use an acquisition strategy to create value.

3. Describe seven problems that work against developing a competitive advantage using an acquisition strategy.

4. Name and describe attributes of effective acquisitions.

5. Define the restructuring strategy and distinguish among its common forms.

6. Explain the short- and long-term outcomes of the different types of restructuring strategies.

In Chapter 8, we studied corporate-level strategies, focusing on types and levels of product diversification strategies that can build core competencies and create competitive advantage. As noted in the previous chapter, diversification allows a firm to create value by productively using excess resources.[1] However, as is the case for each strategy examined in Part 3 of this book, a diversification strategy can be expected to enhance performance only when the firm has the competitive advantages required to successfully use the strategy. In the case of diversification strategies, the firm should possess the competitive advantages needed to form and manage an effective portfolio of businesses and to restructure that portfolio as necessary.[2]

In this chapter, we explore mergers and acquisitions, often combined with a diversification strategy, as a major strategy that firms use throughout the world. Merger and acquisition strategies are developed as a part of the decisions top-level managers make during the strategic management process.[3] In the latter half of the 20th century, mergers and acquisitions became a popular strategy used by major corporations. Even smaller and more focused firms began employing merger and acquisition strategies to grow and enter new markets.[4] However, these strategies are not without problems, and many acquisitions fail. Thus, the focus of this chapter is on how mergers and acquisitions can be used to produce value for the firm's stakeholders while avoiding the pitfalls of the acquisition process.[5]

Before describing attributes associated with effective mergers and acquisitions, we examine the most significant problems companies experience when pursuing these strategies. For example, when a merger or acquisition contributes to poor performance, a firm may deem it necessary to restructure its operations. Closing the chapter are descriptions of three restructuring strategies, as well as the short- and long-term outcomes resulting from their use. Setting the stage for these topics is an examination of the popularity of mergers and acquisitions and a discussion of the differences among mergers, acquisitions, and takeovers.

THE POPULARITY OF MERGER AND ACQUISITION STRATEGIES

The acquisition strategy has been popular among United States firms for many years. Some believe that this strategy has played a central role in an effective restructuring of United States businesses over the past few decades.[6] Increasingly, acquisition strategies are becoming more popular with firms in other nations and economic regions, including Europe, Asia, and Latin America.[7] In fact, a large percentage of acquisitions in recent years have been made across country borders (i.e., a firm headquartered in one country acquiring a firm headquartered in another country).[8] Many of these have been made by emerging economies such as China and Brazil.[9] For example, Marfrig, a Brazilian meat packer, acquired Keystone Foods for $1.25 billion. Keystone is a top supplier to American fast food chains such as Subway and McDonald's. JBS, now the world's largest meat packer, bought Pilgrim's Pride for $800 million as well as Swift for $1.4 billion. Both of these acquired firms are meat packing operations, which now gives JBS significant exposure in the United States. These acquisitions in large part were made possible by Brazil's national development bank (BNDES), which supports Brazilian firms in developing their international operations.[10]

As the worldwide economy improved after the deep recession in 2008, acquisition activity increased,[11] but it was not near the pre-recession levels. For example, in 2007, global M&A activity reached a record $4.4 trillion. And, in this same year the value of M&As in Europe outstripped the value in the United States.[12] The 2006 level also was at a new record of approximately $3.44 trillion.[13] Much of this early activity was due to the high availability of corporate cash and increased involvement by private equity firms.[14] However, global value of M&A deals shrank in 2011 to $2.7 trillion.[15]

Strategic decisions regarding the use of a merger or acquisition strategy are complex because of a highly uncertain global economy. However, these strategies are sometimes used precisely because of this uncertainty. A firm may make an acquisition to increase its market power because of a competitive threat, to enter a new market because of the opportunity available in that market, or to spread the risk due to the uncertain environment.[16] In addition, as volatility brings undesirable changes to its primary markets, a firm may acquire other companies as options that allow the firm to shift its core business into different markets.[17]

A merger or acquisition strategy should be used only when the acquiring firm will be able to increase its economic value through ownership and the use of an acquired firm's assets.[18] Evidence suggests, however, that, at least for acquiring firms, acquisition strategies may not result in these desirable outcomes.[19] Researchers have found that shareholders of acquired firms often earn above-average returns from an acquisition, while shareholders of acquiring firms are less likely to do so, typically earning returns from the transaction that are close to zero, although unanticipated bidders receive more of a premium.[20] In approximately two-thirds of all acquisitions, the acquiring firm's stock price falls immediately after the intended transaction is announced.[21] When Google announced it would acquire Motorola Mobility, Google's share price dropped 1.5 percent compared with an increase of 56 percent in Motorola Mobility's stock.[22] Although this response is near normal, a more negative response for the bidding firm would be an indication of investor skepticism about the likelihood that the acquirer will be able to achieve the synergies required to justify the premium paid.

Mergers, Acquisitions, and Takeovers: What Are the Differences?

Before examining the reasons firms engage in mergers and acquisitions, the problems they encounter, and the keys to success, we should define a few terms that will make the discussion easier to follow. A **merger** is a strategy through which two firms agree to integrate their operations on a relatively co-equal basis. A merger of relative equals took place when, in 2010, United merged with Continental Airlines to form the world's largest airline.[23] There are not many true mergers, however, because one party is usually dominant. For example, the DaimlerChrysler merger was originally envisioned as a combination of equals, but Daimler executives quickly became dominant.

We define an **acquisition** as a strategy through which one firm buys a controlling, 100 percent interest in another firm with the intent of making the acquired firm a subsidiary business within its portfolio or melding with another division. *Partial acquisitions* occur when the acquiring firm obtains less than 100 percent of the target firm. To avoid confusion, the word *acquisition* will always refer to a complete acquisition for the remainder of this book. In the case of an acquisition, the management of the acquired firm reports to the management of the acquiring firm.

While most mergers are friendly transactions, acquisitions include unfriendly takeovers. A **takeover** is a special type of acquisition strategy wherein the target firm did not solicit the acquiring firm's bid. Oftentimes, takeover bids spawn bidding wars. For example, Houston-based Southern Union, which owns pipelines that bring gas from Texas and the Gulf Coast to markets in Florida and the Midwest, agreed to a takeover deal with Energy Transfer Equity LP for $33 per share in stock. Shortly after, Williams Company countered with a price of $39 a share in cash. In response, Energy Transfer offered $40 a share. Ultimately, Williams dropped out, and Energy Transfer is taking over the Southern Union assets, but at a much higher price than it originally agreed because of the bidding war between the two firms.[24] As this example points out, the bidding process is one reason why it is difficult for the acquiring firm to create value in an acquisition.

Hostile takeovers are not only unexpected, but undesired by the target firm's managers. According to the chief financial officer of a bidding firm, the hostile bid "might not have been friendly to members of the board or management, [but] our proposal was very friendly to shareholders."[25] Acquisitions are much more common than mergers and takeovers; as a result, this chapter focuses on acquisitions.

REASONS FOR ACQUISITIONS

Several reasons support the use of an acquisition strategy. Although each reason can provide a legitimate rationale for an acquisition, the acquisition may not necessarily lead to a competitive advantage.

Increase Market Power

A primary reason for acquisitions is to achieve greater market power. *Market power* (defined in Chapter 8) exists when a firm is able to sell its goods or services above competitive levels or when the costs of its primary or support activities are below those of its competitors. Market power usually is derived from the size of the firm and its resources and capabilities to compete in the marketplace. It is also affected by the firm's share of the market. Therefore, most acquisitions designed to achieve greater market power entail buying a competitor, a supplier, a distributor, or a business in a highly related industry to allow exercise of a core competence and to gain competitive advantage in the acquiring firm's primary market. One goal in achieving market power is to become a market leader. For example, in the merger noted previously between United and Continental, the combined company became the market leader in market share in not only the United States, but also the world airline market.

Firms use horizontal, vertical, and related acquisitions to increase their market power.

Horizontal Acquisitions. The acquisition of a company competing in the same industry in which the acquiring firm competes is referred to as a *horizontal acquisition*. As noted previously, JBS Company is a Brazilian meat packing firm, which through acquisitions, has become the largest meat producer. In years 2007 to 2011, JBS has participated in 13 transactions, including the acquisitions of United States meat producers Swift, Smithfield Beef, and Pilgrim's Pride. Although few Americans have heard of JBS, it is now responsible for 22 percent of the United States beef supply. JBS started with regional acquisitions in Brazil and then moved to areas in South America; since that time, it has moved into Australia and, as noted, the United States. It has diversified not only into beef, but also chicken and pork. For instance, JBS is the world's second-largest poultry producer. Since it has diversified into these three areas, it can hedge prices of these different commodities. Also, when the European Union restricted Brazilian beef, because of its international diversification, it took advantage of its Australian subsidiary to export into Europe. Although no Brazilian meat producers export finished cuts into the United States, JBS has its own United States subsidiaries. One can see the advantage of the horizontal acquisition moves that JBS has made in the meat packing industry.[26]

Horizontal acquisitions increase a firm's market power by exploiting cost-based and revenue-based synergies.[27] Research suggests that horizontal acquisitions of firms with similar characteristics result in higher performance than when firms with dissimilar characteristics combine their operations.[28] Examples of important similar characteristics include strategy, managerial styles, and resource allocation patterns. Similarities in these characteristics make the integration of the two firms proceed more smoothly.[29] Horizontal acquisitions are often most effective when the acquiring firm integrates the acquired firm's assets with its assets, but only after evaluating and divesting excess capacity and assets that do not complement the newly combined firm's core competencies.[30]

Vertical Acquisitions. A *vertical acquisition* refers to a firm acquiring a supplier or distributor of one or more of its goods or services.[31] A firm becomes vertically integrated through this type of acquisition, in that it controls additional parts of the value chain (see Chapter 4). Oracle acquired Sun Microsystems, a computer hardware producer (backward vertical integration), in 2010. With the deal, Sun also gained significant software expertise that is important for developing cloud computing expertise. The intent is to pursue combination hardware and software systems to establish a platform on which to run the various products that are needed in the cloud and establish a standard that client firms can depend on for running their large networks.[32] Oracle has also made vertical acquisitions (forward vertical integration) of application software producers in particular markets which facilitate distribution into industries in which it does not have a strong presence; for example, Oracle "got into healthcare through its purchase of Relsys, a maker of analytics applications for the life sciences industry."[33]

Related Acquisitions. The acquisition of a firm in a highly related industry is called a *related acquisition*. Bristol-Myers Squibb recently acquired hepatitis C drug developer Inhibitex for $2.5 billion ($26 a share in cash). They have bought other small biotech producers to help with producing antiviral medicines which can be taken orally. With the all-oral hepatitis C treatment, it expects "better cure rates, shorter duration of the therapy, and lower toxicity than the current standard of care," which is provided through an injectable syringe rather than orally. A competitor, Gilead Sciences, has also purchased a biotech firm, Pharmasset, and is likewise seeking to produce a hepatitis C drug. These acquisitions are related acquisitions because they are in the same sector but are complementary and needed to produce a new type of drug that has not been previously produced by the acquiring firms.[34]

Acquisitions intended to increase market power are subject to regulatory review and to analysis by financial markets. Besides the other meat packing operations purchased by Brazilian firm JBS, they had targeted National Beef Packing, fourth-largest United States beef processor. However, regulators in Washington filed an antitrust lawsuit indicating the acquisition would impose a "fundamental restructuring of the United States beef-packing industry" and "eliminate head-to-head competition."[35] As such, JBS abandoned the deal. The proposed merger between AT&T and T-Mobile was disapproved by the United States Justice Department.[36] Thus, firms seeking growth and market power through acquisitions must understand the political/legal segment of the general environment (see Chapter 3) in order to successfully use an acquisition strategy.

Overcome Entry Barriers

Barriers to entry (introduced in Chapter 3) are factors associated with the market or with the firms currently operating in it that increase the expense and difficulty new ventures face as they try to enter that particular market. For example, well-established competitors may have substantial economies when manufacturing their products. In addition, enduring relationships with customers often create product loyalties that are difficult for new entrants to overcome. When facing differentiated products, new entrants typically must spend considerable resources to advertise their goods or services and may find it necessary to sell at a price below competitors' to entice customers.

Facing the entry barriers created by economies of scale and differentiated products, a new entrant may find the acquisition of an established company to be more effective than entering the market as a competitor while offering a new good or service that is unfamiliar to current buyers. In fact, the higher the barriers to market entry, the greater the probability that a firm will acquire an existing firm to overcome them. Although an acquisition can be expensive, it does provide the new entrant with immediate market access.

Firms trying to enter international markets often face quite steep entry barriers. In response, acquisitions are commonly used to overcome those barriers. At least for large multinational corporations, another indicator of the importance of entering and then competing successfully in international markets is the fact that five emerging markets (China, India, Brazil, Mexico, and Indonesia) are among the 12 largest economies in the world, with a combined purchasing power that is already over half that of the Group of Seven industrial nations (United States, Japan, Britain, France, Germany, Canada, and Italy). Likewise, firms from these emerging economies are pursuing substantive cross-border acquisitions as illustrated by the JBS acquisitions in Latin America, United States, and Australia.[37]

Acquisitions made between companies with headquarters in different countries are called *cross-border acquisitions*. These acquisitions are often made to overcome entry barriers. Compared with a cross-border alliance (discussed in Chapter 10), a cross-border acquisition gives a firm more control over its international operations.[38] Acquisitions often represent the fastest means to enter international markets and help firms overcome the liabilities associated with such strategic moves.[39] Takeda, a large Japanese pharmaceutical company, recently acquired Swiss drug maker Nycomed for $13.7 billon. Buying Nycomed makes Takeda a major player in European markets. More significantly, the acquisition broadens Takeda's distribution capability in emerging markets "at a time when pharmaceutical firms world-wide are wrestling with the impact on revenue from the expiration of patents." In fact, the Nycomed deal will increase Takeda's sales in China around fourfold.[40]

Reduce Costs and Risks Associated with New Product Development

Developing new products internally and successfully introducing them into the marketplace often require significant investments of a firm's resources, including time, making it difficult to quickly earn a profitable return.[41] Also of concern to firms' managers is achieving adequate returns from the capital invested to develop and commercialize new products—an estimated 88 percent of innovations fail to achieve adequate returns. Perhaps contributing to these less-than-desirable rates of return is the successful imitation of approximately 60 percent of innovations within four years after the patents are obtained. Because of outcomes such as these, managers often perceive internal product development as a costly, high-risk activity.[42]

Acquisitions are another means a firm can use to gain access to new products and to current products that are new to the firm. Compared to internal product development processes, acquisitions provide more predictable returns. Because of this, managers may view acquisitions as lowering risk.[43] Possibly for this reason, acquisitions that involve extensive bidding wars are common in high-technology industries.[44]

Acquisition activity is also extensive throughout the pharmaceutical industry, in which firms frequently use acquisitions to overcome the high costs of developing products internally and to increase the predictability of returns on their investments. High acquisition prices are also common. For instance, the Bristol-Myers Squibb acquisition of hepatitis C drug developer Inhibitex, as well as Gilead Sciences' purchase of biotech Pharmasset, as noted previously, are cases in point.[45]

While acquisitions have become a common means of avoiding risky internal ventures (and therefore risky R&D investments), they may also become a substitute for innovation.[46] This can be a problem because innovation is so vital to the future competitiveness of firms.[47] Furthermore, as mentioned previously, acquisitions can depress firm performance. Thus, acquisitions are not a risk-free alternative to entering new markets.

Increase Speed to Market

Compared with internal product development, acquisitions result in more rapid market entries.[48] Entry speed is important, in that quick market entries are critical to successful competition in the highly uncertain, complex global environment.[49] Acquisitions provide rapid access both to new markets and to new capabilities. For instance, Google's acquisition of Motorola Mobility gave the company entry into the mobile phone hardware segment plus a strong set of patents.[50] Similarly, iRobot, a top robotics company, which sells a mix of consumer products like the Roomba robotic vacuum cleaner and military gear, made an acquisition in 2008 of Nekton Research which focuses on undersea robots. One analyst noted that "the acquisition is likely to speed up iRobot's entry into the underwater market by 12 to 18 months."[51]

Increase Diversification and Reshape the Firm's Competitive Scope

Firms also use acquisitions to diversify. Based on experience and the insights resulting from it, firms typically find it easier to develop and introduce new products in markets they currently serve. In contrast, it is difficult for companies to develop products that differ from their current lines for markets in which they lack experience. Thus, it is uncommon for a firm to develop new products internally to diversify its product lines. Using acquisitions to diversify a firm is the quickest and, typically, the easiest way to change a firm's portfolio of businesses.[52]

Both related and unrelated diversification strategies can be implemented through acquisitions.[53] However, research has shown that the more related the acquired firm is to the acquiring firm, the greater the probability that the acquisition will be successful.[54] Thus, horizontal acquisitions (through which a firm acquires a competitor) and other types of related acquisitions tend to contribute more to the firm's ability to create value than acquiring a company that operates in quite different product markets from those in which the firm competes.[55] For example, firms in the financial services industry have become more diversified over time, often through acquisitions. One study suggests that these firms are diversifying not only to provide a more complete line of products for their customers but also to create strategic flexibility. In other words, they diversify into some product lines to provide options for future services they may wish to emphasize. As noted earlier, such acquisitions are a means of dealing with an uncertain competitive environment.[56]

Firms may use diversifying acquisitions to alter the scope of their activities. Scope falls within the major strategy element of arenas, defined in Chapter 2 as the breadth of a firm's activities across products, markets, geographic regions, core technologies, and value-creation stages.[57] A firm may desire to alter its scope if the intensity of competitive rivalry in an industry is affecting profitability.[58] To reduce the negative effect of an intense rivalry on their financial performance, firms may use acquisitions to reduce their dependence on one or more products or markets. For example, music retailers began to diversify as CD sales started to decline. By the end of 2009, CD sales had declined by about 50 percent over their largest number. Best Buy started to sell musical instruments in 2008 in response to the deficit in CD sales. Best Buy continues to sell music CDs but adds other products to make up for the loss in revenue from CDs.[59] Many years ago, General Electric reduced its emphasis on electronics markets by making acquisitions in the financial services industry. Today, GE gets about half of its revenues and profits from service businesses.[60]

Learn and Develop New Capabilities

Some acquisitions are made to gain capabilities that the firm does not possess. For example, acquisitions may be used to acquire a special technological capability.[61] Furthermore, acquisitions may be used to learn in different ways in different cultures and institutional backgrounds such as in the United States versus China.[62] Research has shown that firms can broaden their knowledge base and reduce inertia through acquisitions.[63] Therefore, acquiring other firms with skills and capabilities that differ from its own helps the acquiring firm learn and remain agile.[64] Using new capabilities to pioneer new products and to enter markets quickly can create advantageous market positions.[65]

Of course, firms are better able to learn these capabilities if they share some similar properties with the firm's current capabilities. Thus, firms should seek to acquire companies with different but related and complementary capabilities in order to build their own knowledge base.[66] For example, Li & Fung Ltd., based in Hong Kong, is a sourcing company that designs and transports products for manufacturers including many apparel and durable-goods manufacturers in the United States. It has a highly refined distribution network in North America and Europe which has made it one of the largest suppliers of toys and clothes to retailers. Much of its success has come through acquisitions of small competitors. Each deal broadens and deepens its sourcing network, already one of the most extensive worldwide. These acquisitions bring Li & Fung more revenue, new manufacturing customers, and at the same time added expertise in a new product area. "In 2010 and 2011, for instance, Li & Fung bought leading suppliers of leather goods, health and beauty products, denim products, and toys, along with onshore sourcing companies in the United States and Western Europe."[67]

PROBLEMS IN ACHIEVING ACQUISITION SUCCESS

Acquisition strategies based on legitimate reasons described in this chapter can increase value and help firms to earn above-average returns. However, acquisition strategies are not risk free. Figure 9.1 shows reasons for the use of acquisition strategies and potential problems with such strategies.

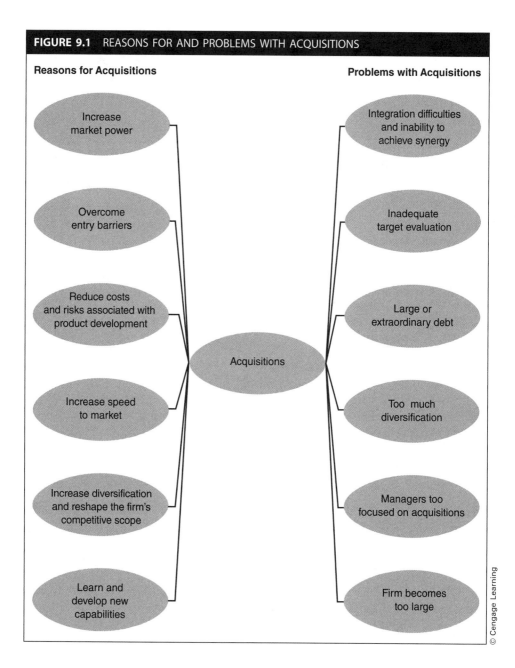

FIGURE 9.1   REASONS FOR AND PROBLEMS WITH ACQUISITIONS

Research suggests that perhaps 20 percent of all mergers and acquisitions are successful, approximately 60 percent produce disappointing results, and the remaining 20 percent are clear failures.[68] Successful acquisitions generally involve a well-conceived strategy in selecting the target, avoiding too high of a premium, and an effective integration process.[69] As shown in Figure 9.1, several problems may prevent successful acquisitions.

Integration Difficulties and an Inability to Achieve Synergy

The importance of a successful integration should not be underestimated. Without it, an acquisition is unlikely to produce positive returns. As suggested by a researcher studying the process, "managerial practice and academic writings show that the post-acquisition integration phase is probably the single most important determinant of shareholder value creation (and equally of value destruction) in mergers and acquisitions."[70]

Integration is complex and involves a large number of activities. Integration challenges include melding two disparate corporate cultures, linking different financial and control systems, building effective working relationships (particularly when management styles differ), and resolving problems regarding the status of the newly acquired firm's executives.[71] As this list suggests, many of the important integration activities revolve around people. It is especially important to focus on effective management of human capital in the target firm after an acquisition because that is where much of an organization's knowledge is contained.[72] Turnover of key personnel from the acquired firm can have a negative effect on the performance of the merged firm. The loss of key personnel, such as critical managers, weakens the acquired firm's capabilities and reduces its value. If implemented effectively, the integration process can have a positive effect on target firm managers and reduce the probability that key human resources will leave.[73]

If the potential for synergy exists between an acquired and a target firm, the potential is released primarily during the integration stage.[74] Defined in Chapter 8, *synergy* refers to the value created by business units working together that would not have been created in those same units working independently. That is, synergy exists when assets are worth more when used in conjunction than when used separately. Synergy is created by the efficiencies derived from economies of scale and economies of scope and by sharing resources (e.g., human capital and knowledge) across the businesses of the combined firm.[75] Externally acquired capabilities do not always integrate well with the acquiring firm's internal processes and procedures—a reality necessitating committed effort during the integration stage.[76]

A firm develops a competitive advantage through an acquisition strategy only when a transaction generates private synergy.[77] *Private synergy* is created when the combination and integration of the acquiring and acquired firms' assets yield capabilities and core competencies that could not be developed by combining and integrating either firm's assets with another company. Private synergy is possible when firms' assets are complementary in unique ways; that is, the unique type of asset complementarity is not possible by combining either company's assets with another firm's assets.[78] Because of its uniqueness, private synergy is difficult for competitors to understand and imitate. However, private synergy is difficult to create.

Even if the potential for private synergy exists, and managers work diligently to realize it during the integration process, it is still possible that the net effect of an acquisition on firm value will be negative because the costs exceed the benefits. Beyond the purchase price, a firm's ability to account for costs that are necessary to create anticipated revenue- and cost-based synergies affects the acquisition's success. Firms experience several types of expenses when trying to create private synergy through acquisitions. Called *transaction costs*, these expenses are incurred when firms use acquisition strategies to create synergy.[79] Transaction costs may be direct or indirect. Direct costs include legal fees and charges from investment bankers who complete due diligence for the acquiring firm. Indirect costs include managerial time to evaluate target firms and then to complete negotiations, as well as the loss of key managers and employees after an acquisition. Another type of cost involves the actual time and resources used for integration processes, such as the time managers spend in meetings and the cost of integrating information systems, manufacturing systems, R&D processes, and retirement systems. Firms tend to underestimate these costs when determining the value of the synergy that may be created by combining and integrating the acquired firm's assets with the acquiring firm's assets. This may help explain why so many acquisitions fail to live up to expectations.

Inadequate Evaluation of Target

Due diligence is a process through which a potential acquirer evaluates a target firm for acquisition. In an effective due-diligence process, hundreds of items are examined in areas as diverse as the financing for the intended transaction, differences in cultures between the acquiring and target firm, tax consequences of the transaction, and actions that would be necessary to successfully meld the two workforces. Due diligence is commonly performed by investment bankers, accountants, lawyers, and management consultants specializing in that activity, although firms actively pursuing acquisitions may form their own internal due-diligence team.[80]

The failure to complete an effective due-diligence process may easily result in the acquiring firm paying an excessive premium for the target company. In fact, research shows that without due diligence, "the purchase price is driven by the pricing of other 'comparable' acquisitions rather than by a rigorous assessment of where, when, and how management can drive real performance gains. [In these cases], the price paid may have little to do with achievable value."[81]

Many firms once used investment banks to perform their due diligence, but in the post-Enron era the process is increasingly performed in-house. While investment bankers such as Credit Suisse, First Boston, and Citibank still play a significant role in due diligence for large mergers and acquisitions, their role in smaller mergers and acquisitions seems to be decreasing. A growing number of companies are building their own internal operations to offer advice about mergers and how to finance them. However, although investment banks are playing a lesser role, there will always be the need for an outside opinion for a company's board of directors—to reassure them about a planned merger and reduce their liability.

Large or Extraordinary Debt

To finance a number of acquisitions completed during the 1980s and 1990s, some companies significantly increased their levels of debt. A financial innovation called junk bonds helped make this possible. *Junk bonds* are a financing option through which risky acquisitions are financed with money (debt) that provides a large potential return to lenders (bondholders). Because junk bonds are unsecured obligations that are not tied to specific assets for collateral, interest rates for these high-risk debt instruments sometimes reached between 18 and 20 percent during the 1980s.[82] Some prominent financial economists viewed debt as a means to discipline managers, causing them to act in shareholders' best interests.[83] Junk bonds are now used less frequently to finance acquisitions, and the conviction that debt disciplines managers is less strong.

As mentioned earlier, the large Brazilian meat processor, JBS, bought several United States firms' brands including Swift, Pilgrim's Pride, and Smithfield Beef. Due to these and other acquisitions, its debt had grown to $6.9 billion. Although Moody's (a debt rating agency) has had a positive outlook on JBS since 2009, "the company's debt-constrained cash flow" has kept its debt rating low.[84] It will be difficult to do more deals until its debt burden is lowered.

High debt can have several negative effects on the firm. For example, because high debt increases the likelihood of bankruptcy, it can lead agencies such as Moody's and Standard & Poor's to downgrade the firm's credit rating.[85] In addition, high debt may preclude needed investment in activities that contribute to the firm's long-term success, such as R&D, human resource training, and marketing.[86] Still, use of leverage can be a positive force in a firm's development, allowing it to take advantage of attractive expansion opportunities. Too much leverage (such as extraordinary debt), however, can lead to negative outcomes, including postponing or eliminating investments, such as critical R&D expenditures that are necessary to create value over the long term.

Too Much Diversification

As explained in Chapter 8, diversification strategies can lead to improved firm performance. In general, firms using related diversification strategies outperform those using unrelated diversification strategies. However, conglomerates, formed by using an unrelated diversification strategy, can be successful. United Technologies and General Electric are examples of highly diversified firms that have been very successful with their unrelated acquisition strategies.[87]

At some point, however, firms become over-diversified. The level at which over-diversification occurs varies across companies because each firm has different capabilities to manage diversification. Recall from Chapter 8 that related diversification requires more information processing than does unrelated diversification. The need for related diversified firms to process more information of greater diversity is such that they become over-diversified with a smaller number of business units, compared with firms using an unrelated diversification strategy.[88] Regardless of the type of diversification strategy implemented, however, declines in performance result from over-diversification, after which business units are often divested.[89]

Even when a firm is not over-diversified, a high level of diversification can have a negative effect on the firm's long-term performance. For example, the scope created by additional amounts of diversification often causes managers to rely on financial rather than strategic controls to evaluate business units' performances. Top-level executives often rely on financial controls to assess the performance of business units when they do not have a rich understanding of business units' objectives and strategies. Use of financial controls, such as return on investment (ROI), causes individual business-unit managers to focus on short-term outcomes at the expense of long-term investments. When long-term investments are reduced to increase short-term profits, a firm's overall ability to create value may be harmed.[90]

Another problem resulting from too much diversification is the tendency for acquisitions to become substitutes for innovation. Earlier in this chapter, we mentioned that sometimes firms make acquisitions in order to avoid the costs and risks associated with new product development. In other words, they buy innovation instead of producing it internally. This problem is magnified in firms that over-diversify because a reinforcing cycle evolves. Costs associated with acquisitions may result in fewer allocations to activities, such as R&D, that are linked to innovation. Without adequate support, a firm's innovation skills begin to atrophy. Without internal innovation skills, the only option available to a firm is to make still additional acquisitions to gain access to innovation. Evidence suggests that firms that use acquisitions as a substitute for internal innovation eventually encounter performance problems.[91]

Managers Too Focused on Acquisitions

Typically, a fairly substantial amount of managerial time and energy is required for acquisition strategies to enhance the firm's value. Activities with which managers become involved include (1) searching for viable acquisition candidates, (2) completing effective due-diligence processes, (3) preparing for negotiations, and (4) managing the integration process after the acquisition is completed.

Top-level managers do not personally gather all data and information required to make acquisitions. However, these executives do make critical decisions about the firms to be targeted, the nature of the negotiations, and so forth. Company experiences show that participating in and overseeing the activities required for making acquisitions can divert managerial attention from other matters that are necessary for long-term competitive success, such as identifying and taking advantage of other opportunities and interacting with important external stakeholders. Evidence suggests that the acquisition process can create a short-term perspective and a greater aversion to risk among top-level executives in a target firm.[92]

Both theory and research suggest that managers can become overly involved in the process of making acquisitions.[93] One observer suggested: "The urge to merge is still like an addiction in many companies: doing deals is much more fun and interesting than fixing fundamental problems. So, as in dealing with any other addiction or temptation, maybe it is best to just say no."[94] When acquisitions do fail, leaders are tempted to blame failure on others or on unforeseen circumstances rather than on their excessive involvement in the acquisition process.[95] An active board that questions decisions regarding acquisitions can help counteract the tendency for managers to become too involved in acquisitions.[96]

Firm Becomes Too Large

Most acquisitions create a larger firm that should help increase its economies of scale. These economies can then lead to more efficient operations; for example, the two sales organizations can be integrated using fewer sales representatives because a sales representative can sell the products of both firms (particularly if the products of the acquiring and target firms are highly related).

There is a managerial incentive to grow larger through acquisitions because size serves as a defense against takeovers, at least in the United States.[97] Also, many firms seek increases in size because of the potential economies of scale and enhanced market power (discussed earlier). At some level, however, the additional costs required to manage the larger firm will exceed the benefits of the economies of scale and additional market power. In addition, the complexities generated by the larger size often lead managers to implement more bureaucratic controls to manage the combined firm's operations.

Bureaucratic controls are formalized supervisory and behavioral rules and policies designed to ensure that decisions and actions across different units of a firm are consistent. However, through time, formalized controls often lead to relatively rigid and standardized managerial behavior.[98] Certainly, in the long run, the diminished flexibility that accompanies rigid and standardized managerial behavior may produce less innovation as well as fewer searches for entrepreneurial opportunities (see Chapter 12). Because of innovation's importance to competitive success, the bureaucratic controls resulting from a large organization (that is, built by acquisitions) can have a detrimental effect on performance.[99]

EFFECTIVE ACQUISITIONS

Earlier in the chapter, we noted that acquisition strategies do not consistently produce above-average returns for the acquiring firm's shareholders. Nonetheless, some companies are able to create value when using an acquisition strategy.[100] Results from a research study shed light on the differences between unsuccessful and successful acquisition strategies and suggest that there is a pattern of actions and attributes that can improve the probability of acquisition success.[101] Table 9.1 summarizes the attributes and actions and the results of successful acquisitions.

TABLE 9.1 ATTRIBUTES AND RESULTS OF SUCCESSFUL ACQUISITIONS

ATTRIBUTES	RESULTS
1. Acquired firm has assets or resources that are complementary to the acquiring firm's core business	1. High probability of synergy and competitive advantage by maintaining strengths
2. Acquisition is friendly	2. Faster and more effective integration and possibly lower premiums
3. Acquiring firm conducts effective due diligence to select target firms and evaluate the target firm's health (financial, cultural, and human resources)	3. Firms with strongest complementarities are acquired and overpayment is avoided
4. Acquiring firm has financial slack (cash or a favorable debt position)	4. Financing (debt or equity) is easier and less costly to obtain
5. Merged firm maintains a low to moderate debt position	5. Lower financing cost, lower risk (e.g., of bankruptcy), and avoidance of trade-offs that are associated with high debt
6. Sustained and consistent emphasis on R&D and innovation	6. Maintain long-term competitive advantage in markets
7. Has experience with change and is flexible and adaptable	7. Faster and more effective integration facilitates achievement of synergy

© Cengage Learning

First, the study shows that when the target firm's assets *complement* the acquired firm's assets, an acquisition is more successful. With complementary assets, integrating two firms' operations has a higher probability of creating synergy. In fact, integrating two firms with complementary assets frequently produces unique capabilities and core competencies. With complementary assets, the acquiring firm can maintain its focus on core businesses and leverage the complementary assets and capabilities from the acquired firm. Oftentimes, targets were selected and "groomed" by establishing a working relationship sometime before the acquisition. As discussed in Chapter 7, strategic alliances are sometimes used to test the feasibility of a future merger or acquisition.[102]

The study's results also show that *friendly acquisitions*—in which firms work together to find ways to integrate their operations to create synergy—facilitate integration of the firms involved in an acquisition.[103] In hostile takeovers, animosity often results between the two top management teams, a condition that in turn affects working relationships in the newly created firm. As a result, more key personnel in the acquired firm may be lost, and those who remain may resist the changes necessary to integrate the two firms.[104] With effort, cultural clashes can be overcome, and fewer key managers and employees will become discouraged and leave.[105] Efficient and effective integration helps produce the desired synergy in the newly created firm.

Additionally, *effective due-diligence processes* involving the deliberate and careful selection of target firms and an evaluation of the relative health of those firms (financial health, cultural fit, and the value of human resources) contribute to successful acquisitions. Firms that take a capabilities perspective do better as well when examining target fit; that is, how well does the target firm match, extend, or complement the acquiring firm's capabilities?[106] *Financial slack* in the form of debt equity or cash in both the acquiring and acquired firms also has frequently contributed to success in acquisitions. While financial slack provides access to financing for the acquisition, it is still important to maintain a *low or moderate level of debt* after the acquisition to keep debt costs low. When substantial debt was used to finance the acquisition, companies with successful acquisitions reduced the debt quickly, partly by selling off assets from the acquired firm, especially noncomplementary or poorly performing assets. For these firms, debt costs do not prevent long-term investments such as R&D, and managerial discretion in the use of cash flow is relatively flexible.

Another attribute of successful acquisition strategies is an *emphasis on innovation*, as demonstrated by continuing investments in R&D activities. Significant R&D investments show a strong managerial commitment to innovation and can help offset the tendency to substitute acquisitions for innovation. Innovation is increasingly important to overall competitiveness, as well as acquisition success.

Flexibility and adaptability are the final two attributes of successful acquisitions. When executives of both the acquiring and target firms have experience in managing change and learning from acquisitions, they will be more skilled at adapting their capabilities to new environments.[107] As a result, they will be more adept at integrating the two organizations, which is particularly important when firms have different organizational cultures.

Cisco Systems is an example of a firm that appears to pay close attention to the attributes of Table 9.1 when using its acquisition strategy. In fact, Cisco is admired for its ability to complete successful acquisitions and integrate them quickly, although, as noted, this has created a larger firm.[108] A number of other network companies pursued acquisitions to build up their ability to sell into the network equipment binge, but only Cisco retained much of its value in the post-bubble era. Many firms, such as Lucent, Nortel, and Ericsson, teetered on the edge of bankruptcy after the dot-com bubble burst. When it makes an acquisition, "Cisco has gone much further in its thinking about integration. Not only is retention important, but Cisco also works to minimize the distractions caused by an acquisition. This is important, because the speed of change is so great, that even if the target firm's product development teams are distracted, they will be slowed, contributing to acquisition failure. So, integration must be rapid and reassuring."[109] For example, Cisco facilitates acquired employees' transitions to their new organization through a link on its Website called "Cisco Acquisition Connection." This Website has been specifically designed for newly acquired employees and provides up-to-date materials tailored to their new jobs.

RESTRUCTURING

Restructuring is a strategy through which a firm changes its set of businesses or its financial structure.[110] Restructuring is a global phenomenon.[111] From the 1970s into the 2000s, divesting businesses from company portfolios and downsizing accounted for a large percentage of firms' restructuring strategies. Commonly, firms focus on a fewer number of products and markets following restructuring. The words of an executive describe this typical outcome: "Focus on your core business, but don't be distracted, let other people buy assets that aren't right for you."[112]

Although restructuring strategies are generally used to deal with acquisitions that are not reaching expectations, firms sometimes use these strategies because of changes they have detected in their external environment.[113] For example, opportunities sometimes surface in a firm's external environment that a diversified firm can pursue because of the capabilities it has formed by integrating firms' operations. In such cases, restructuring may be appropriate to position the firm to create more value for stakeholders, given the environmental changes.[114] This seems to be the case with the restructuring of Citigroup noted in the Strategic Focus example.

The failure of an acquisition strategy sometimes precedes a restructuring strategy. In other instances, however, firms purposefully pursue a restructuring strategy because their external or internal environments change.[115] For example, opportunities sometimes surface in the external environment that are particularly attractive to the diversified firm in light of its core competencies. Similarly, the firm may find ways to use its competitive advantages to create new products or to enter new markets. In such cases, restructuring may be appropriate to position the firm to create more value for stakeholders, given the environmental changes.[116]

As discussed next, firms use three predominant restructuring strategies: downsizing, downscoping, and leveraged buyouts.

Downsizing

Once thought to be an indicator of organizational decline, downsizing is now recognized as a legitimate restructuring strategy.[117] *Downsizing* is a reduction in the number of a firm's employees and, sometimes, in the number of its operating units, but it may or may not change the composition of businesses in the company's portfolio. To increase the probability that downsizing will result in increased performance, it should be an intentional, proactive management strategy, rather than a strategy forced on the firm as a result of involuntary decline.[118]

Firms use downsizing as a restructuring strategy for different reasons. Downsizing is more likely to produce desired performance outcomes if a firm has a high level of slack, as indicated by insufficiently used resources.[119] If there is not much slack, then downsizing can cut into the core of a firm's operations and competencies, thus reducing overall long-term performance. Downsizing is often used when the acquiring firm paid too high of a premium (reducing slack resources) to acquire the target firm.[120] Managers should remember that as a strategy, downsizing will be far more effective when they consistently use human resource practices that ensure procedural justice and fairness in downsizing decisions.[121]

Downscoping

Downscoping—which refers to a divestiture, spin-off, or some other means of eliminating businesses that are unrelated to a firm's core businesses—has a more positive effect on firm performance than downsizing.[122] Commonly, downscoping is described as a set of actions that cause a firm to strategically refocus on its core businesses.[123] Houston-based ConocoPhillips plans to spin off its pipelines and refining operations (downstream businesses) from the upstream business focused on energy exploration and production. The company believes that the exploration company, in particular, is undervalued by Wall Street analysts. In preparation for the spin-off in 2012, ConocoPhillips has been shedding nonessential assets. The upstream business will be called ConocoPhillips, while the downstream business will be labeled Phillips-66. Such company split-ups are called for by financial analysts when the current level and type diversification does not add significant value.[124]

A firm that downscopes often also downsizes simultaneously. However, it does not eliminate key employees from its primary businesses in the process, because such action could lead to a loss of one or more core competencies. Instead, a firm that is simultaneously downscoping and downsizing becomes smaller by reducing the diversity of businesses in its portfolio.[125] By refocusing on its core businesses, the firm can be managed more effectively by the top management team. Managerial effectiveness increases because the firm has become less diversified, allowing the management team to better understand and manage the remaining businesses.[126] Interestingly, sometimes the divested unit can also take advantage of unforeseen opportunities not recognized while under the leadership of the parent firm.[127]

In general, United States firms use downscoping as a restructuring strategy more frequently than do companies in other regions of the world. The trend in Europe, Latin America, and Asia has been to build conglomerates. In Latin America, these conglomerates are called *grupos*. However, many Asian and Latin American conglomerates have begun to adopt Western corporate strategies in recent years and have been refocusing on their core businesses. This downscoping has occurred simultaneously with increasing globalization and with more open markets, which have greatly enhanced the competition. By downscoping, these firms have been able to focus on their core businesses and improve their competitiveness.[128]

Leveraged Buyouts

Leveraged buyouts are commonly used as a restructuring strategy to correct for managerial mistakes or because the firm's managers are making decisions that primarily serve their own interests rather than those of shareholders.[129] A *leveraged buyout* (LBO) is a restructuring strategy whereby a party buys all of a firm's assets in order to take the firm private (that is, the firm's stock will no longer be traded publicly). Firms that facilitate or engage in taking public firms private are called *private equity firms*. Private equity firms may also be involved in taking business units of a public company private.

For example, BankRate, provides information on CDs, mortgagees, car loans and insurance from a variety of company-specific Websites. As such, they generate revenue by providing advertising and customer leads for the companies that list information on the BankRate Website. However, they experienced a severe downturn in 2009 during the financial crisis. At the time, they were a publicly traded firm. CEO Thomas Evans decided to seek to take the firm private through the help of a private equity firm, Apax Partners. While private, the firm made several acquisitions, CreditCards.com for $145 million and NetQuote for $205 million, which allowed them to expand their reach in credit-card and insurance segments. Thus, not only did they restructure their debt and their capital, but also added potential market reach. Due to the restructuring, the company was able to go public again in 2011, much sooner than they had anticipated. At the time of the IPO, Apax Partners was paid handsomely because the market cap was three times what the cost was in taking the firm private. Although not all deals are as successful as this one, it does demonstrate what private equity firms seek to do with taking a firm private. Furthermore, the firm has more debt than it did previously, but it is also more successful.[130]

Usually, significant amounts of debt are incurred to finance the buyout; hence the buyout is "leveraged." LBOs typically fall into one of three general categories: management buyouts, employee buyouts, and whole-firm buyouts, in which a company or partnership purchases an entire company instead of a part of it. To support debt payments and to downscope the company to concentrate on the firm's core businesses, the new owners may immediately sell a number of assets.[131] It is not uncommon for those buying a firm through an LBO to restructure the firm to the point that it can be sold at a profit within five to eight years as in the BankRate example.

Very high debt brings with it significant risks, which can dramatically influence the performance of an LBO. For example, TGP, a private equity firm, partnered with KKR to a take a large Texas utility, TXU, private, for $43.2 billion, renaming it Energy Future Holdings (EFH). To this point in time, this was the largest public to private deal ever undertaken and marked the high point of private equity deal volume just before the financial crisis in 2007. Until TGP restructured EFG's debt in 2010, there was significant speculation that EFG might default on its large debt position during the deep recession.[132]

In part because of managerial incentives, management buyouts, more so than employee buyouts and whole-firm buyouts, have been found to lead to downscoping, an increased strategic focus, and improved performance.[133] In fact, research has shown that management buyouts can also lead to greater entrepreneurial activity and growth.[134] There may be different reasons for a buyout; one is to protect against a capricious financial market, allowing the owners to focus on developing innovations and bringing them to the market. As such, buyouts can represent a form of firm rebirth to facilitate entrepreneurial efforts and stimulate effective growth.[135]

Outcomes from Restructuring

Figure 9.2 shows the short-term and long-term outcomes resulting from the three restructuring strategies. Although downsizing may reduce labor costs in the short term, it does not commonly lead to higher firm performance. In fact, research has shown that downsizing contributes to lower returns for firms using this form of restructuring.[136] Stock market participants in many nations tend to evaluate downsizing negatively, an indication that investors believe that downsizing will have a negative effect on companies' ability to create value in the long term. One reason for their pessimism could be that downsizing results in a loss of valuable human capital.[137] Losing employees with many years of experience with the firm represents a major loss of knowledge. Research also suggests that such loss of human capital can also spill over into dissatisfaction of customers.[138] As noted in Chapter 4, knowledge is vital to competitive success in the global economy. Investors may also assume that downsizing occurs as a consequence of other problems in a company. Thus, in general, research evidence and corporate experience suggest that downsizing may be of more tactical (or short-term) value than strategic (or long-term) value.[139]

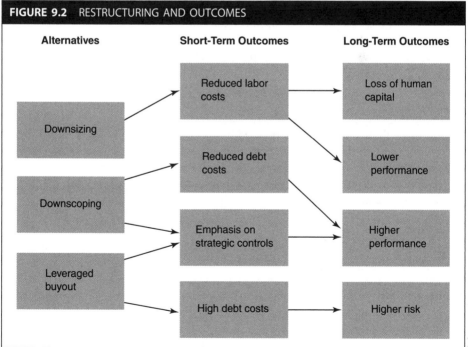

FIGURE 9.2   RESTRUCTURING AND OUTCOMES

© Cengage Learning

As Figure 9.2 indicates, downscoping generally leads to more positive outcomes in both the short and the long term than do downsizing and engaging in a leveraged buyout. Downscoping's desirable long-term outcome of higher performance is a product of reduced debt costs and the emphasis on strategic controls derived from concentrating on the firm's core businesses. With this reduction in debt costs and increased emphasis on strategic controls, the refocused firm should be able to increase its ability to compete.[140]

Although whole-firm LBOs have been hailed as a significant innovation in the financial restructuring of firms, there can be negative trade-offs. First, the resulting large debt increases the financial risk of the firm, as evidenced by the number of companies that filed for bankruptcy in the 1990s after executing a whole-firm LBO. Sometimes, the intent of the owners to increase the efficiency of the bought-out firm and then sell it within five to eight years creates a short-term and risk-averse managerial focus. As a result, these firms may fail to invest adequately in R&D or take other major actions designed to maintain or improve the company's core competence. Research also suggests that in firms with an entrepreneurial mind-set, buyouts can lead to greater innovation, especially if the debt load is not too great.[141] However, because buyouts more often result in significant debt, most LBOs have taken place in mature industries in which stable cash flows are possible. This enables the buying firm to meet the recurring debt payments, which can mitigate some of the risk associated with a buyout.

SUMMARY

▶ Acquisition strategies are increasingly popular. Because of globalization, deregulation of multiple industries in many different economies, and favorable legislation, domestic and cross-border mergers and acquisitions remain a viable strategy for global competitors pursuing value creation.

▶ Firms use acquisition strategies to: (1) increase market power; (2) overcome entry barriers to new markets or regions; (3) reduce the costs and risks associated with developing new products; (4) increase the speed of entering a new market; (5) become more diversified and reshape the firm's competitive scope; and (6) enhance learning, thereby adding to the firm's knowledge base.

▶ Among the problems associated with use of an acquisition strategy are: (1) the difficulty of effectively integrating the firms involved, leading to an inability to achieve synergy; (2) inadequately evaluating the target firm's value relative to the costs of acquisition; (3) creating debt loads that preclude adequate long-term investments (e.g., in R&D); (4) creating a firm that is too diversified; (5) creating an internal environment in which managers devote increasing amounts of their time and energy to analyzing and completing acquisitions; and (6) developing a combined firm that is too large, necessitating extensive use of bureaucratic, rather than strategic, controls.

▶ Effective acquisitions have the following attributes: (1) the acquiring and target firms have complementary resources that can be the basis of core competencies in the newly created firm; (2) the acquisition is friendly, thereby facilitating integration of the two firms' resources; (3) the target firm is selected and purchased based on a thorough due-diligence process; (4) the acquiring and target firms have considerable slack in the form of cash or debt capacity; (5) the merged firm maintains a low or moderate level of debt by selling off portions of the acquired firm or some of the acquiring firm's poorly performing units; (6) R&D and innovation are emphasized in the new firm; and (7) the acquiring and acquired firms have experience in terms of adapting to change.

▶ Restructuring is used to improve a firm's performance by correcting for problems created by ineffective management. Restructuring by downsizing involves reducing the number of employees and hierarchical levels in the firm. Although it can lead to short-term cost reductions, they may be realized at the expense of long-term success because of the loss of valuable human resources (and knowledge).

▶ The goal of restructuring through downscoping is to reduce the firm's level of diversification. Often, the firm divests unrelated businesses to achieve this goal. Eliminating unrelated businesses makes it easier for the firm and its top-level managers to refocus on the core businesses.

▶ Another restructuring strategy is the leveraged buyout (LBO), through which a firm is purchased so that it can become a private firm. LBOs usually are financed largely through debt, which creates substantial risks. Management buyouts, employee buyouts, and whole-firm buyouts are the three types of LBOs. Because they provide clear managerial incentives, management buyouts have been the most successful of the three. Often, the intent of a buyout is to improve efficiency and performance to the point at which the firm can be sold successfully within five to eight years.

▶ Commonly, restructuring's primary goal is gaining or reestablishing effective strategic control of the firm. Of the three restructuring strategies, downscoping is aligned the most closely with establishing and using strategic controls.

ETHICS QUESTIONS

1. What are the ethical issues associated with takeovers, if any? Are mergers more or less ethical than takeovers? Why or why not?

2. One of the outcomes associated with market power is that the firm is able to sell its good or service above competitive levels. Is it ethical for firms to pursue market power? Does your answer to this question differ by the industry in which the firm competes? For example, are the ethics of pursuing market power different for firms producing and selling medical equipment compared with those producing and selling sports clothing?

3. What ethical considerations are associated with downsizing decisions? If you were part of a corporate downsizing, would you feel that your firm had acted unethically? If you believe that downsizing has an unethical component to it, what should firms do to avoid using this technique?

4. What ethical issues are involved with conducting a robust due-diligence process?

5. Some evidence suggests that there is a direct relationship between a firm's size and the level of compensation its top executives receive. If this is so, what inducement does this relationship provide to top-level managers? What can be done to influence this relationship so that it serves shareholders' best interests?

NOTES

1. W. P. Wan, R. E. Hoskisson, J. C. Short, and D. W. Yiu, 2011, Resource-based theory and corporate diversification: Accomplishments and opportunities, *Journal of Management*, 37(5): 1335–1368; J. Anand, 2004, Redeployment of corporate resources: A study of acquisition strategies in the US defense industries, 1978–1996, *Managerial and Decision Economics*, 2S: 383–400.

2. M. Marks & P. H. Mirvis, 2011, A framework for the human resources role in managing culture in mergers and acquisitions, *Human Resource Management*, 50(6): 859–877; M. Kwan, 2002, Maximizing value through diversification, *MIT Sloan Management Review*, 43(2): 10.

3. C. Öberg, 2011, Acquiring once, acquiring twice–Lessons learned from repeated acquisitions of innovative firms, *International Journal of Innovation Management*, 15(6): 1243–1269; M. Farjoun, 2002, Towards an organic perspective on strategy, *Strategic Management Journal*, 23: 561–594.

4. B. Park & P. N. Ghauri, 2011, Key factors affecting acquisition of technological capabilities from foreign acquiring firms by small and medium sized local firms, *Journal of World Business*, 46(1): 116–125.

5. C. M. Christensen, R. Alton, C. Rising, & A. Waldeck, 2011, The new M&A playbook, *Harvard Business Review*, 89(3): 48–57; M. A. Hitt, J. S. Harrison, & R. D. Ireland, 2001, *Mergers and Acquisitions: A Guide to Creating Value for Stakeholders*, New York: Oxford University Press.

6. D. S. Siegel & K. L. Simons, 2010, Assessing the effects of mergers and acquisitions on firm performance, plant productivity, and workers: New evidence from matched employer-employee data, *Strategic Management Journal*, 31(8): 903–916; B. E. Chappuis, K. A. Frick, & P. J. Roche, 2004, High-tech mergers take shape, *McKinsey Quarterly*, (1): 60–69; G. K. Deans, F. Kroeger, & S. Zeisel, 2002, The consolidation curve, *Harvard Business Review*, 80(12): 20–21; 2000, How M&As will navigate the turn into a new century, *Mergers & Acquisitions*, January, 29–35.

7. 2011, Mergers soar. *OECD Observer*, September, 10.

8. O. Hope, W. Thomas, & D. Vyas, 2011, A cost of pride: Why do firms from developing countries bid higher? *Journal of International Business Studies*, 42(1): 128–151.

9. J. Zhang, C. Zhou, & H. Ebbers, 2011, Completion of Chinese overseas acquisitions: Institutional perspectives and evidence, *International Business Review*, 20(2): 226–238.

10. R. Buchanan, 2011, Burst of M&A activity keeps bankers busy, *Latin Trade*, January, 57–59.

11. G. Chon, A. Das, & D. Cimilluca, 2011, Urge to merge not seen fading, *Wall Street Journal*, April, C11.

12. C. Moschieri & J. M. Campa, 2009, The European M&A industry: A market in the process of construction, *Academy of Management Perspectives*, 23(4): 71–87.

13. J. Weber, 2007, An irresistible urge to merge, *Business Week*, January 1, 72–73.

14. E. Thornton, 2006, What's behind the buyout binge? *Business Week*, December 4, 38.

15. J. Hodgson, 2011, Goldman Sachs tops league as M&A value shrinks, *Market Watch*, www.marketwatch.com, December 20.

16. J. A. Clougherty & T. Duso, 2011, Using rival effects to identify synergies and improve merger typologies, *Strategic Organization*, 9(4): 310–335.

17. T. W. Tong & Y. Li, 2011, Real options and investment mode: Evidence from corporate venture capital and acquisition, *Organization Science*, 22(3): 659–674.

18. P. J. Williamson & A. P. Raman, 2011, How China reset its global acquisition agenda, *Harvard Business Review*, 89(4): 109–114; G. Cullinan, J.-M. Le Roux, & R.-M. Weddigen, 2004, When to walk away from a deal, *Harvard Business Review*, 82(4): 96–104; L. Selden & G. Colvin, 2003, M&A needn't be a loser's game, *Harvard Business Review*, 81(6): 70–73.

19. J. J. Reuer, 2005, Avoiding lemons in M&A deals, *MIT Sloan Management Review*, 46(3): 15–17.

20. M. Cornett, B. Tanyeri, & H. Tehranian, 2011, The effect of merger anticipation on bidder and target firm announcement period returns, *Journal of Corporate Finance*, 17(3): 595–611; M. C. Jensen, 1988, Takeovers: Their causes and consequences, *Journal of Economic Perspectives*, 1(2): 21–48.

21. A. Rappaport & M. L. Sirower, 1999, Stock or cash? *Harvard Business Review*, 77(6): 147–158.

22. P. Taylor & R. Waters, 2011. Google in $12.5bn Motorola phone deal, *Financial Times*, August 16, 1.

23. D. Bennett & M. Credeur, 2012, Marriage at 30,000 feet, *Bloomberg Businessweek*, February 6–12, 58–63.

24. A. Fontevecchia, 2011, All out bidding war for Southern Union: Energy Transfer tries to block Williams' offer, *Forbes*, http://www.forbes.com, June 27; S. M. Davidoff, 2011, The fizzled-out bidding war for Southern Union, *New York Times*, http://nytimes.com, October 14.

25. E. Thornton, 2007, Unsolicited aggression, *Business Week*, January 1, 34.

26. K. Blankfeld, 2011, All you can eat, *Forbes*, May 9, 170–172.

27. S. Bhattacharyya & A. Nain, 2011, Horizontal acquisitions and buying power: A product market analysis, *Journal of Financial Economics*, 99(1): 97–115; L. Capron, 1999, Horizontal acquisitions: The benefits and risks to long-term performance, *Strategic Management Journal*, 20: 987–1018.

28. C. Chung & E. Tostão, 2012, Effects of horizontal consolidation under bilateral imperfect competition between processors and retailers, *Applied Economics*, 44(26): 3379–3389; C. E. Fee & S. Thomas, 2004, Sources of gains in horizontal mergers: Evidence from customer, supplier, and rival firms, *Journal of Financial Economics*, 74: 423–460.

29. C. Jiang, R. Chua, M. Kotabe, & J. Murray, 2011, Effects of cultural ethnicity, firm size, and firm age on senior executives' trust in their overseas business partners: Evidence from China, *Journal of International Business Studies*, 42(9): 1150–1173; K. Ramaswamy, 1997, The performance impact of strategic similarity in horizontal mergers: Evidence from the U.S. banking industry, *Academy of Management Journal*, 40: 697–715.

30. L. Capron, W. Mitchell, & A. Swaminathan, 2001, Asset divestiture following horizontal acquisitions: A dynamic view, *Strategic Management Journal*, 22: 817–844.

31. S. Kedia, S. A. Ravid, & V. Pons, 2011, When do vertical mergers create value? *Financial Management*,

40(4): 845–877; S. Chatterjee, 1991, Gains in vertical acquisitions and market power: Theory and evidence, *Academy of Management Journal*, 34(2): 436–448.

[32] S. Prasso, 2011, Oracle's bold moves, *Fortune*, April 11, 27.

[33] K. MacFadyen, 2010, Strategic buyer of the year: Shrewd Larry, *Mergers & Acquisitions Report*, 23(14): 19.

[34] M. Herper, 2012, Bristol's purchase of Inhibitex caps amazing run for some biotech stocks, *Forbes*, http://www.forbes.com, January 7.

[35] Blankfeld, All you can eat.

[36] T. Catan, B. Kendall, & A. Schatz, 2011, After AT&T: The new antitrust era, *Wall Street Journal*, December 21, B1, B6.

[37] M. Turner, 2011, Emerging markets M&A surges, *Wall Street Journal*, http://www.wsj.com, May 19.

[38] K. Boeh, 2011, Contracting costs and information asymmetry reduction in cross-border M&A, *Journal of Management Studies*, 48(3): 568–590; K. Shimizu, M. A. Hitt, D. Vaidyanath, & V. Pisano, 2004, Theoretical foundations of cross-border mergers and acquisitions: A review of current research and recommendations for the future, *Journal of International Management*, 10: 307–353; Hitt, Harrison, & Ireland, *Mergers and Acquisitions*, Chapter 10.

[39] J. W. Lu & P. W. Beamish, 2001, The internationalization and performance of SMEs, *Strategic Management Journal*, 22(special issue): 565–586.

[40] K. Inagaki & J. Osawa, 2011, Takeda, Toshiba make $16 billion M&A push, *Wall Street Journal*, http://www.wsj.com, May 20; K. Inagaki, 2011, Takeda buys Nycomed for $14 billion, *Wall Street Journal*, http://www.wsj.com, May 20.

[41] G. K. Lee & M. B. Lieberman, 2010, Acquisition vs. internal development as modes of market entry, *Strategic Management Journal*, 31(2): 140–158; V. Bannert & H. Tschirky, 2004, Integration planning for technology intensive acquisitions, *R&D Management*, 34(5): 481–494.

[42] H. K. Ellonen, P. Wilstrom, & A. Jantunen, 2009, Linking dynamic-capability portfolios and innovation outcomes, *Technovation*, 29: 753–762; M. Song & C. A. De Benedetto, 2008, Supplier's involvement and success of radical new product development in new ventures, *Journal of Operations Management*, 26: 1–22; Hitt, Harrison, & Ireland, *Mergers and Acquisitions*.

[43] G. Ahuja & R. Katila, 2001, Technological acquisitions and the innovation performance of acquiring firms: A longitudinal study, *Strategic Management Journal*, 22: 197–220; M. A. Hitt, R. E. Hoskisson, R. A. Johnson, & D. D. Moesel, 1996, The market for corporate control and firm innovation, *Academy of Management Journal*, 39: 1084–1119.

[44] A. Kaul, 2012, Technology and corporate scope: Firm and rival innovation as antecedents of corporate transactions, *Strategic Management Journal*, 33(4): 347–367; R. Coff, 2003, Bidding wars over R&D intensive firms: Knowledge, opportunism and the market for corporate control, *Academy of Management Journal*, 46: 74–85.

[45] Herper, Bristol's purchase of Inhibitex caps amazing run for some biotech stocks.

[46] Hitt, Hoskisson, Johnson, & Moesel, The market for corporate control; M. A. Hitt, R. E. Hoskisson, & R. D. Ireland, 1990, Mergers and acquisitions and managerial commitment to innovation in M-form firms, *Strategic Management Journal*, 11(summer special issue): 29–47.

[47] W. Park & S. Sonenshein, 2012, Impact of horizontal mergers on research & development and patenting: Evidence from merger challenges in the U.S., *Journal of Industry, Competition & Trade*, 12(1): 143–167; M. A. Hitt, R. E. Hoskisson, R. D. Ireland, & J. S. Harrison, 1991, Effects of acquisitions on R&D inputs and outputs, *Academy of Management Journal*, 34: 693–706.

[48] P. Kale & P. Puranam, 2004, Choosing equity stakes in technology sourcing relationships: An integrative framework, *California Management Review*, 46(3): 77–99; T. Yoshikawa, 2003, Technology development and acquisition strategy, *International Journal of Technology Management*, 25: 666–674; K. F. McCardle & S. Viswanathan, 1994, The direct entry versus takeover decision and stock price performance around takeovers, *Journal of Business*, 67: 1–43.

[49] K. M. Eisenhardt, 2002, Has strategy changed? *MIT Sloan Management Review*, 43(2): 88–91.

[50] Waters, Google in $12.5bn Motorola phone deal.

[51] K. Schachter, 2008, iRobot Dives into M&A, *Red Herring*, September 8, 4.

[52] M. Nippa, U. Pidun, & H. Rubner, 2011, Corporate portfolio management: Appraising four decades of academic research, *Academy of Management Perspectives*, 25(4): 50–66; Capron, Mitchell, & Swaminathan, Asset divestiture following horizontal acquisitions; D. D. Bergh, 1997, Predicting divestiture of unrelated acquisitions: An integrative model of ex ante conditions, *Strategic Management Journal*, 18: 715–731.

[53] C. E. Helfat & K. M. Eisenhardt, 2004, Intertemporal economies of scope, organizational modularity, and the dynamics of diversification, *Strategic Management Journal*, 25: 1217–1232; C. Park, 2003, Prior performance characteristics of related and unrelated acquirers, *Strategic Management Journal*, 24: 471–480.

[54] Hitt, Harrison, & Ireland, *Mergers and Acquisitions*.

[55] K. M. Ellis, T. H. Reus, B. T. Lamont, & A. L. Ranft, 2011, Transfer effects in large acquisitions: How size-specific experience matters, *Academy of Management Journal*, 54(6): 1261–1276.

[56] 2012, M&A activity reflects an unsettled market, *Financial Executive*, 28(1): 55–56; M. Song, R. J. Calantone, & C. Anthony, 2002, Competitive forces and strategic choice decisions: An experimental investigation in the United States and Japan, *Strategic Management Journal*, 23: 969–978.

[57] D. C. Hambrick & J. W. Fredrickson, 2005, Are you sure you have a strategy? *Academy of Management Executive*, 19(4): 51–62, reprinted from 15(4).

[58] W. H. Tsai, Y. C. Kuo, & J.-H. Hung, 2009, Corporate diversification and CEO turnover in family businesses: Self- entrenchment or risk reduction? *Small Business Economics*, 32(1): 57–76; W. J. Ferrier, 2001, Navigating the competitive landscape: The drivers and consequences of competitive aggressiveness, *Academy of Management Journal*, 44: 858–877.

[59] J. Plambeck, 2010, As CD sales wane, music retailers diversify, *New York Times*, http://www.nytimes.com, May 30.

[60] 2011, Business: Operating Segments, General Electric 2011 Annual Report, http://www.ge.com/ar2012, March 1; R. E. Hoskisson & M. A. Hitt, 1994, *Downscoping: How to Tame the Diversified Firm*, New York: Oxford University Press.

61. S. Ransbotham & S. Mitra, 2010, Target age and the acquisition of innovation in high-technology industries, *Management Science*, 56(11): 2076–2093; P. Puranam, H. Singh, & M. Zollo, 2006, Organizing for innovation: Managing the coordination-autonomy dilemma in technology acquisitions, *Academy of Management Journal*, 49: 263–280.

62. H. Yang, S. L. Sun, Z. Lin, & M. W. Peng, 2011, Behind M&As in China and the United States: Networks, learning, and institutions, *Asia Pacific Journal of Management*, 28(2): 239–255.

63. M. Wagner, 2011, To explore or to exploit? An empirical investigation of acquisitions by large incumbents, *Research Policy*, 40(9): 1217–1225; F. Vermeulen & H. Barkema, 2001, Learning through acquisitions, *Academy of Management Journal*, 44: 457–476.

64. K. Uhlenbruck, M. A. Hitt, & M. Semadeni, 2006, Market value effects of acquisitions involving Internet firms: A resource-based analysis, *Strategic Management Journal*, 27: 899–913; F. Vermeulen, 2005, How acquisitions can revitalize firms, *MIT Sloan Management Review*, 46(4): 45–51; M. L. A. Hayward, 2002, When do firms learn from their acquisition experience? Evidence from 1990–1995, *Strategic Management Journal*, 23: 21–39.

65. P. Desyllas & A. Hughes, 2010, Do high technology acquirers become more innovative? *Research Policy*, 39(8): 1105–1121; G. Ahuja & C. Lampert, 2001, Entrepreneurship in the large corporation: A longitudinal study of how established firms create breakthrough inventions, *Strategic Management Journal*, 22(special issue): 521–543.

66. M. Makri, M. A. Hitt, & P. J. Lane, 2010, Complementary technologies, knowledge relatedness, and invention outcomes in high technology M&As, *Strategic Management Journal*, 31: 602–628; J. S. Harrison, M. A. Hitt, R. E. Hoskisson, & R. D. Ireland, 2001, Resource complementarities in business combinations: Extending the logic to organizational alliances, *Journal of Management*, 27: 679–690.

67. A. Adolph, C. Mainardi, & J. Nelly, 2012, The capabilities premium in M & A, *Strategy + Business*, Spring, 9.

68. Williamson & Raman, How China reset its global acquisition agenda; J. A. Schmidt, 2002, Business perspective on mergers and acquisitions, in J. A. Schmidt (ed.), *Making Mergers Work*, Alexandria, VA: Society for Human Resource Management, 23–46.

69. S. Teerikangas, P. Véry, & V. Pisano, 2011, Integration managers' value-capturing roles and acquisition performance, *Human Resource Management*, 50(5): 651–683; M. Zollo & H. Singh, 2004, Deliberate learning in corporate acquisitions: Post-acquisition strategies and integration capability in U.S. bank mergers, *Strategic Management Journal*, 25: 1233–1256.

70. M. Zollo, 1999, M&A—The challenge of learning to integrate, Mastering strategy (part eleven), *Financial Times*, December 6, 14–15.

71. C. C. Lakshman, 2011, Postacquisition cultural integration in mergers & acquisitions: A knowledge-based approach, *Human Resource Management*, 50(5): 605–623; R. A. Weber & C. F. Camerer, 2003, Cultural conflict and merger failure: An experimental approach, *Management Science*, 49: 400–415; D. K. Datta, 1991, Organizational fit and acquisition performance: Effects of post-acquisition integration, *Strategic Management Journal*, 12: 281–297.

72. J. A. Krug & W. Shill, 2008, The big exit: Executive churn in the wake of M&As, *Journal of Business Strategy*, 29(4): 15–21; J. A. Krug, 2003, Why do they keep leaving? *Harvard Business Review*, 81(2): 14–15.

73. S. Chreim & M. Tafaghod, 2012, Contradiction and sensemaking in acquisition integration, *Journal of Applied Behavioral Science*, 48(1): 5–32; K. Marmenout, 2010, Employee sensemaking in mergers: How deal characteristics shape employee attitudes, *Journal of Applied Behavioral Science*, 46(3): 329–359.

74. Y. M. Zhou, 2011, Synergy, coordination costs, and diversification choices, *Strategic Management Journal*, 32: 624–639; J. M. Shaver, 2006, A paradox of synergy: Contagion and capacity effects in mergers and acquisitions, *Academy of Management Review*, 31: 962–976.

75. G. Hoberg & G. Phillips, 2010, Product market synergies and competition in mergers and acquisitions: A text-based analysis, *Review of Financial Studies*, 23: 3773–3811; T. Saxton & M. Dollinger, 2004, Target reputation and appropriability: Picking and deploying resources in acquisitions, *Journal of Management*, 30: 123–147.

76. R. Ashkenas, S. Francis, & R. Heinick, 2011, The merger dividend, *Harvard Business Review*, 89(7/8): 126–133; S. A. Zahra & A. P. Nielsen, 2002, Sources of capabilities, integration and technology commercialization, *Strategic Management Journal*, 23: 377–398.

77. J. B. Barney, 1988, Returns to bidding firms in mergers and acquisitions: Reconsidering the relatedness hypothesis, *Strategic Management Journal*, 9(summer special issue): 71–78.

78. C. W. Moon, 2011, Information sharing as source of synergy creation in corporate diversification: An empirical analysis of Korean banking industry, *International Business & Economics Research*, 10(8): 35–44; Makri, Hitt, & Lane, Complementary technologies, knowledge relatedness, and invention outcomes in high technology M&As.

79. C. Shapiro, 2010, A tribute to Oliver Williamson: Antitrust economics, *California Management Review*, 52(2): 138–146; O. E. Williamson, 1999, Strategy research: Governance and competence perspectives, *Strategic Management Journal*, 20: 1087–1108.

80. Cullinan, Le Roux, & Weddigen, When to walk away from a deal.

81. Rappaport & Sirower, Stock or cash? 149.

82. G. Yago, 1991, *Junk Bonds: How High Yield Securities Restructured Corporate America*, New York: Oxford University Press, 146–148.

83. M. C. Jensen, 1986, Agency costs of free cash flow, corporate finance, and takeovers, *American Economic Review*, 76: 323–329.

84. Blankfeld, All you can eat.

85. L. D. Purda, 2011, Assessing credit or determining quantity? The evolving role of rating agencies, *Journal of Applied Finance*, 21(2): 20–37; M. A. Hitt & D. L. Smart, 1994, Debt: A disciplining force for managers or a debilitating force for organizations? *Journal of Management Inquiry*, 3: 144–152.

86. B. Seifert & H. Gonenc, 2012, Creditor rights and R&D expenditures, *Corporate Governance: An International Review*, 20(1): 3–20; Hitt, Harrison, & Ireland, *Mergers and Acquisitions*.

[87] 2012, United Technologies, http://www.utc.com, March 3, 2012, General Electric, http://www.ge .com, March 3, 2012.

[88] E. Rawley, 2010, Diversification, coordination costs and organizational rigidity: Evidence from micro-data, *Strategic Management Journal*, 31: 873–891; C. W. L. Hill & R. E. Hoskisson, 1987, Strategy and structure in the multiproduct firm, *Academy of Management Review*, 12: 331–341.

[89] A. Khorana, A. Shivdasani, C. Stendevad, & S. Sanzhar, 2011, Spin-offs: Tackling the conglomerate discount, *Journal of Applied Corporate Finance*, 23(4): 90–101; R. A. Johnson, R. E. Hoskisson, & M. A. Hitt, 1993, Board of director involvement in restructuring: The effects of board versus managerial controls and characteristics, *Strategic Management Journal*, 14(special issue): 33–50; C. C. Markides, 1992, Consequences of corporate refocusing: Ex ante evidence, *Academy of Management Journal*, 35: 398–412.

[90] L. Yuan, L. Xiyao, L. Yi, & B. R. Barnes, 2011, Knowledge communication, exploitation and endogenous innovation: The moderating effects of internal controls in SMEs, *R&D Management*, 41(2): 156–172; Hitt, Harrison, & Ireland, *Mergers and Acquisitions*; R. E. Hoskisson & R. A. Johnson, 1992, Corporate restructuring and strategic change: The effect on diversification strategy and R&D intensity, *Strategic Management Journal*, 13: 625–634.

[91] J. Haleblian, J.-J. Kim, & N. Rajagopalan, 2006, The influence of acquisition experience and performance on acquisition behavior: Evidence from the U.S. commercial banking industry, *Academy of Management Journal*, 49: 357–370.

[92] C. Moschieri & J. Mair, 2011, Adapting for innovation: Including divestitures in the debate, *Long Range Planning*, 44(1): 4–25; R. E. Hoskisson, M. A. Hitt, & R. D. Ireland, 1994, The effects of acquisitions and restructuring (strategic refocusing) strategies on innovation, in G. von Krogh, A. Sinatra, & H. Singh (eds.), *Management of Corporate Acquisitions*, London: Macmillan, 144–169.

[93] J. Martin & K. Davis, 2010, Learning or hubris? Why CEOs create less value in successive acquisitions, *Academy of Management Perspectives*, 24(1): 79–81; M. L. A. Hayward & D. C. Hambrick, 1997, Explaining the premiums paid for large acquisitions: Evidence of CEO hubris, *Administrative Science Quarterly*, 42: 103–127; R. Roll, 1986, The hubris hypothesis of corporate takeovers, *Journal of Business*, 59: 197–216.

[94] J. Pfeffer, 2003, The human factor: Curbing the urge to merge, *Business 2.0*, July, 58.

[95] Weber & Camerer, Cultural conflict and merger failure.

[96] Hayward, When do firms learn from their acquisition experience?

[97] M. L. Humphery-Jenner & R. G. Powell, 2011, Firm size, takeover profitability, and the effectiveness of the market for corporate control: Does the absence of anti-takeover provisions make a difference? *Journal of Corporate Finance*, 17(3): 418–437.

[98] H. R. Greve, 2011, Positional rigidity: Low performance and resource acquisition in large and small firms, *Strategic Management Journal*, 32(1): 103–114.

[99] Hitt, Harrison, & Ireland, *Mergers and Acquisitions*.

[100] M. Graebner, K. Eisenhardt, & P. Roundy, 2010, Success and failure in technology acquisitions: Lessons for buyers and sellers, *Academy of Management Perspectives*; 24(3): 73–92; Uhlenbruck, Hitt, & Semadeni, Market value effects of acquisitions involving Internet firms; Hitt, Harrison, & Ireland, *Mergers and Acquisitions*.

[101] M. A. Hitt, R. D. Ireland, J. S. Harrison, & A. Best, 1998, Attributes of successful and unsuccessful acquisitions of U.S. firms, *British Journal of Management*, 9: 91–114.

[102] H. Yang, Z. Lin, & M. W. Peng, 2011, Behind acquisitions of alliance partners: Exploratory learning and network embeddedness, *Academy of Management Journal*, 54(5): 1069–1080; P. Porrini, 2004, Can a previous alliance between an acquirer and a target affect acquisition performance? *Journal of Management*, 30: 545–562.

[103] T. Hamza, 2011, Determinants of short-term value creation for the bidder: Evidence from France, *Journal of Management & Governance*, 15(2): 157–186; R. J. Aiello & M. D. Watkins, 2000, The fine art of friendly acquisition, *Harvard Business Review*, 78(6): 100–107.

[104] M. Marks & M. Philip, 2011, Merge ahead: A research agenda to increase merger and acquisition success, *Journal of Business & Psychology*, 26(2): 161–168; P. Gwynne, 2002, Keeping the right people, *MIT Sloan Management Review*, 43(2): 19; D. D. Bergh, 2001, Executive retention and acquisition outcomes: A test of opposing views on the influence of organizational tenure, *Journal of Management*, 27: 603–622.

[105] A. E. Rafferty & S. L. D. Restubog, 2010, The impact of change process and context on change reactions and turnover during a merger, *Journal of Management*, 36(5): 1309–1338; R. W. Coff, 2002, Human capital, shared expertise, and the likelihood of impasse in corporate acquisitions, *Journal of Management*, 28: 107–128; M. L. Marks & P. H. Mirvis, 2001, Making mergers and acquisitions work: Strategic and psychological preparation, *Academy of Management Executive*, 15(2): 80–92.

[106] G. Adolph, C. Mainardi, & J. Neely, 2012, The capabilities premium in M&A, *Strategy + Business*, Spring, 1–10.

[107] J. Jwu-Rong, H. Chen-Jui, & L. Hsieh-Lung, 2010, A matching approach to M&A, R&D, and patents: Evidence from Taiwan's listed companies, *International Journal of Electronic Business Management*, 8(3): 273–280; J. Haleblian, J.-J. Kim, & N. Rajagopalan, The influence of acquisition experience and performance on acquisition behavior; L. Markoczy, 2001, Consensus formation during strategic change, *Strategic Management Journal*, 22: 1013–1031.

[108] R. Myers, 2011, Integration Acceleration, *CFO*, 27(1): 52–57.

[109] D. Mayer & M. Kenney, 2004, Economic action does not take place in a vacuum: Understanding Cisco's acquisition and development strategy, *Industry and Innovation*, 11(4): 299–325.

[110] D. Lee & R. Madhaven, 2010, Divestiture and firm performance: A meta-analysis, *Journal of Management*, 36: 1345–1371; D. D. Bergh & E. N.-K. Lim, 2008, Learning how to restructure: Absorptive capacity and improvisational views of restructuring actions and performance, *Strategic Management Journal*, 29: 593–616.

[111] Y. Zhou, X. Li, & J. Svejnar, 2011, Subsidiary divestiture and acquisition in a financial crisis: Operational focus, financial constraints, and ownership,

Journal of Corporate Finance, 17(2): 272–287; Y. G. Suh & E. Howard, 2009, Restructuring retailing in Korea: The case of Samsung-Tesco, *Asia Pacific Business Review*, 15: 29–40; Z. Wu & A. Delios, 2009, The emergence of portfolio restructuring in Japan, *Management International Review*, 49: 313–335.

112 S. Thurm, 2008, Who are the best CEOs of 2008? *Wall Street Journal Online*, http://www.wsj.com, December 15.

113 L. Diestre & N. Rajagopalan, 2011, An environmental perspective on diversification: The effects of chemical relatedness and regulatory sanctions, *Academy of Management Journal*, 54: 97–115.

114 J. L. Morrow, Jr., D. G. Sirmon, M. A. Hitt, & T. R. Holcomb, 2007, Creating value in the face of declining performance: Firm strategies and organizational recovery, *Strategic Management Journal*, 28: 271–283; J. L. Morrow, Jr., R. A. Johnson, & L. W. Busenitz, 2004, The effects of cost and asset retrenchment on firm performance: The overlooked role of a firm's competitive environment, *Journal of Management*, 30: 189–208.

115 A. Praet, 2011, Voluntary firm restructuring: Why do firms sell or liquidate their subsidiaries? *Annals of Finance*, 7(4): 449–476; M. Brauer, 2006, What we have acquired and what should we acquire in diversification research? A review and research agenda, *Journal of Management*, 32: 751–785.

116 Siegel & Simons, Assessing the effects of mergers and acquisitions on firm performance, plant productivity, and workers; Morrow, Jr., Johnson, & Busenitz, The effects of cost and asset retrenchment on firm performance; T. A. Kruse, 2002, Asset liquidity and the determinants of asset sales by poorly performing firms, *Financial Management*, 31(4): 107–129.

117 F. Muñoz-Bullon & M. J. Sanchez-Bueno, 2010, Downsizing implementation and financial performance, *Management Decision*, 48(8): 1181–1197; R. D. Nixon, M. A. Hitt, H.-U. Lee, & E. Jeong, 2004, Market reactions to announcements of corporate downsizing actions and implementation strategies, *Strategic Management Journal*, 25: 1121–1129.

118 P. Galagan, 2010, The biggest losers: The perils of extreme downsizing, *T + D*, November, 27–29; W. McKinley, J. Zhao, & K. G. Rust, 2000, A sociocognitive interpretation of organizational downsizing, *Academy of Management Review*, 25: 227–243.

119 E. G. Love & N. Nohria, 2005, Reducing slack: The performance consequences of downsizing by large industrial firms, 1977–1993, *Strategic Management Journal*, 26: 1087–1108.

120 H. A. Krishnan, M. A. Hitt, & D. Park, 2007, Acquisition premiums, subsequent workforce reductions and post-acquisition performance, *Journal of Management Studies*, 44: 709–732.

121 R. Iverson & C. Zatzick, 2011, The effects of downsizing on labor productivity: The value of showing consideration for employees' morale and welfare in high-performance work systems, *Human Resource Management*, 50(1): 29–43; C. O. Trevor & A. J. Nyberg, 2008, Keeping your headcount when all about you are losing theirs: Downsizing, voluntary turnover rates, and the moderating role of HR practices, *Academy of Management Journal*, 51: 259–276.

122 D. D. Bergh & E. N.-K. Lim, 2008, Learning how to restructure: Absorptive capacity and improvisational views of restructuring actions and performance, *Strategic Management Journal*, 29: 593–616; Hoskisson & Hitt, *Downscoping*.

123 L. Dranikoff, T. Koller, & A. Schneider, 2002, Divestiture: Strategy's missing link, *Harvard Business Review*, 80(5): 74–83.

124 A. Fontevecchia, 2012, ConocoPhillips selling assets left and right, preparing for spin off, *Forbes*, http://www.forbes.com, January 26.

125 U. Pidun, H. Rubner, M. Krühler, R. Untiedt, & M. Nippa, 2011, Corporate portfolio management: Theory and practice, *Journal of Applied Corporate Finance*, 23(1): 63–76; M. Rajand & M. Forsyth, 2002, Hostile bidders, long-term performance, and restructuring methods: Evidence from the UK, *American Business Review*, 20(1): 71–81.

126 Y. Zhou, X. Li, & J. Svejnar, 2011, Subsidiary divestiture and acquisition in a financial crisis: Operational focus, financial constraints, and ownership, *Journal of Corporate Finance*, 17(2): 272–287; Johnson, Hoskisson, & Hitt, Board of director involvement in restructuring; R. E. Hoskisson & M. A. Hitt, 1990, Antecedents and performance outcomes of diversification: A review and critique of theoretical perspectives, *Journal of Management*, 16: 461–509.

127 C. Moschieri, 2011, The implementation and structuring of divestitures: The unit's perspective, *Strategic Management Journal*, 32: 368–401.

128 Khorana, Shivdasani, Stendevad, & Sanzhar, Spin-offs: Tackling the conglomerate discount; R. E. Hoskisson, R. A. Johnson, L. Tihanyi, & R. E. White, 2005, Diversified business groups and corporate refocusing in emerging economies, *Journal of Management*, 31: 941–965; Hoskisson, R. E., Johnson, R. A., Yiu, D., & Wan, B. 2001. Restructuring strategies of diversified business groups: Differences associated with country institutional environments. In M. Hitt, E. Freeman, & J. Harrison (Eds.), *The Blackwell handbook of strategy*: 433–463. Oxford, UK: Basil Blackwell.

129 M. Schneider & A. Valenti, 2010, The effects of "going private" using private equity: The newly private corporation and the dimensions of corporate performance, *Business & Society*, 115(1): 75–106; C. C. Markides & H. Singh, 1997, Corporate restructuring: A symptom of poor governance or a solution to past managerial mistakes? *European Management Journal*, 15: 213–219.

130 E. Savitz, 2011, BankRate: An IPO day chat with CEO Tom Evans, *Forbes*, http://www.forbes.com, June 17.

131 S. Guo, E. S. Hotchkiss, & W. Song, 2011, Do buyouts (still) create value? *Journal of Finance*, 66(2): 479–517; M. F. Wiersema & J. P. Liebeskind, 1995, The effects of leveraged buyouts on corporate growth and diversification in large firms, *Strategic Management Journal*, 16: 447–460.

132 J. Kelly, 2011, The operators, *Bloomberg Businessweek*, February 21, 62–67; 2010, EFH seeks cheaper longer debt with exchange, *Power Finance and Risk*, August 2, 5.

133 H. Aslan & P. Kumar, 2011, Lemons or cherries? Growth opportunities and market temptations in going public and private, *Journal of Financial & Quantitative Analysis*, 46(2): 489–526; R. Harris, D. S. Siegel, & M. Wright, 2005, Assessing the impact of management buyouts on economic efficiency: Plant-level evidence from the United Kingdom, *Review of Economics and Statistics*, 87: 148–153; P. H. Phan & C. W. L. Hill, 1995, Organizational restructuring and economic performance

in leveraged buyouts: An ex-post study, *Academy of Management Journal*, 38: 704–739.

134 C. M. Daily, P. P. McDougall, J. G. Covin, & D. R. Dalton, 2002, Governance and strategic leadership in entrepreneurial firms, *Journal of Management*, 3: 387–412.

135 J. Lerner, M. Sorensen, & P. Strömberg, 2011, Private equity and long-run investment: The case of innovation, *Journal of Finance*, 66(2): 445–477; M. Wright, R. E. Hoskisson, & L. W. Busenitz, 2001, Firm rebirth: Buyouts as facilitators of strategic growth and entrepreneurship, *Academy of Management Executive*, 15(1): 111–125.

136 E. G. Love & M. Kraatz, 2009, Character, conformity, or the bottom line? How and why downsizing affected corporate reputation, *Academy of Management Journal*, 52: 314–335; J. P. Guthrie & D. K. Datta, 2008, Dumb and dumber: The impact of downsizing on firm performance as moderated by industry conditions, *Organization Science*, 19: 108–123; H. A. Krishnan & D. Park, 2002, The impact of work force reduction on subsequent performance in major mergers and acquisitions: An exploratory study, *Journal of Business Research*, 55(4): 285–292; P. M. Lee, 1997, A comparative analysis of layoff announcements and stock price reactions in the United States and Japan, *Strategic Management Journal*, 18: 879–894.

137 K. Kostopoulos & N. Bozionelos, 2010, Employee reactions to forms of downsizing: Are there any lesser evils? *Academy of Management Perspectives*, 24(4): 95–96; W. F. Casio, 2005, Strategies for responsible restructuring, *Academy of Management Executive*, 19(4): 39–50.

138 P. Williams, K. M. Sajid, & N. Earl, 2011, Customer dissatisfaction and defection: The hidden costs of downsizing, *Industrial Marketing Management*, 40(3): 405–413.

139 H. Sitlington & V. Marshall, 2011, Do downsizing decisions affect organisational knowledge and performance? *Management Decision*, 49(1): 116–129.

140 Moschieri & Mair, Adapting for innovation: Including divestitures in the debate; K. Shimizu & M. A. Hitt, 2005, What constrains or facilitates divestitures of formerly acquired firms? The effects of organizational inertia, *Journal of Management*, 31: 50–72.

141 Lerner, Sorensen, & Strömberg, Private equity and long-run investment: The case of innovation; M. Wright, R. E. Hoskisson, L. W. Busenitz, & J. Dial, 2000, *Academy of Management Review*, 25(3): 591–601.

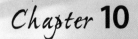

Chapter 10

INTERNATIONAL STRATEGY

KNOWLEDGE OBJECTIVES

Studying this chapter should provide you with the strategic management knowledge needed to:

1. Explain the primary reasons for firms pursuing international diversification.

2. Explain the factors that influence decisions regarding the international scope of a firm's activities.

3. Define the three international corporate-level strategies along with the structures associated with each strategy.

4. Explain the relationship between international corporate-level strategy and the selection of business-level corporate strategies within business units, countries, or global regions.

5. Identify the factors that contribute to the advantage of firms in a dominant global industry and associated with a specific country or regional environment.

6. Name and describe the five modes for entering international markets.

7. Explain the effects of international diversification on firm returns and innovation.

8. Name and describe three major risks of international diversification.

9. Explain why the positive outcomes from international expansion are limited.

The global competitive environment has evolved from one dominated by a few large developed countries to one with many more centers of economic activity.

Firms now exist in a vastly changed global economy. And in the 21st century, Brazil, Russia, India and China (BRIC) represent large and growing economies and major international market opportunities for firms from many countries, including the United States, Japan, Korea, and the European Union.[1] In the not-too-distant past, the primary economic decision making body was composed of 6 countries (G-6). Today, it is composed of 20 countries (G-20). China has the second largest economy in the world, and by 2050 it is predicted that the BRIC countries will have economies among the largest six in the world.[2] This chapter covers various aspects of **international diversification,** a strategy through which a firm expands the sales of its goods or services across the borders of global regions and countries into different geographic locations or markets. We examine opportunities that firms identify as they seek to develop and exploit core competencies by diversifying geographically into global markets.[3] In addition, we discuss different problems, complexities, and threats that might accompany use of the firm's international strategies. Although national boundaries, cultural differences, and geographical distances all pose barriers to entry into many markets, significant opportunities draw businesses into the international arena.[4]

A firm that plans to operate globally must formulate a successful strategy to take advantage of these global opportunities. Furthermore, to mold their firms into truly global companies, managers must develop a global mind-set, which was defined in Chapter 4 as the ability to study an internal environment in ways that do not depend on the assumptions of a single country, culture, or context.[5] As firms move into international markets, they develop relationships with suppliers, customers, and partners and then learn from these relationships. Especially with regard to managing human resources, traditional means of operating, with little cultural diversity and without global sourcing, are no longer effective.[6]

Figure 10.1, which serves as an outline for this chapter, provides an overview of the various incentives, choices, and outcomes associated with international strategy. This chapter first focuses on the reasons firms internationalize. After a firm decides to compete internationally, it must select its strategy and a structure to help implement that strategy. The chapter outlines both international business- and corporate-level strategies and structures and then provides rationales for choosing a mode of entry into international markets. Entry may be accomplished by exporting from domestic-based operations, licensing products or services, forming strategic alliances with international partners, acquiring a foreign-based firm, or establishing a new subsidiary. International diversification can lead to increased strategic

FIGURE 10.1 REASONS FOR, SELECTION OF, AND OUTCOMES FROM INTERNATIONAL STRATEGIES

Reasons for International Strategy	Selection of International Strategies	Selection of Mode of Entry		Desired Strategic Competitiveness Outcomes
Increase market size	*Corporate-level strategy*	Exporting		
Increase return on investment	• Multidomestic	Licensing	Management difficulties	Higher performance
Seek economies of scale, scope, and learning	• Global • Transnational	Strategic alliances		
		Acquisitions	Risks	
Obtain resources and achieve other location advantages	*Business-level strategy* (overall or by market)	New wholly owned subsidiary		Innovation

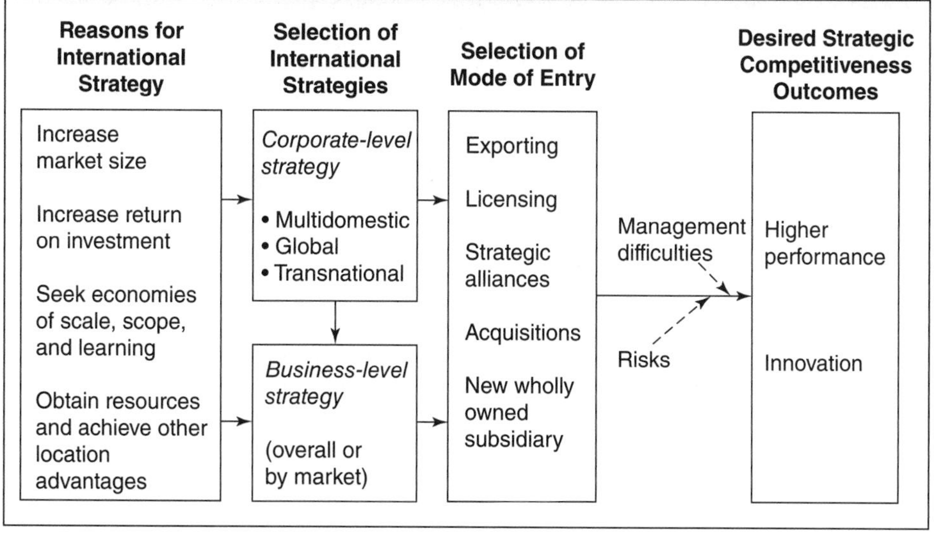

© Cengage Learning

competitiveness by extending product life cycles, providing incentives for more innovation, and ultimately producing higher firm performance. These benefits are tempered by political, economic, and other formal institutional risks and the problems of managing a complex international firm with operations in multiple countries.

INCENTIVES FOR USING AN INTERNATIONAL STRATEGY

An **international strategy** is a strategy through which the firm sells its goods or services outside its domestic market.[7] An international strategy results in international diversification. Firms pursue an international strategy (as opposed to a purely domestic strategy) to seek new opportunities to create value in international markets. When successful, firms can derive four basic benefits from using international strategies: (1) increased market size; (2) greater returns on major capital investments or on investments in new products and processes; (3) greater economies of scale, scope, or learning; and (4) a competitive advantage through location (for example, access to low-cost labor or critical resources).

Increased Market Size

Firms can expand the size of their potential market—sometimes dramatically—by moving into international markets. New large-scale, emerging markets, such as China and India, provide a strong internationalization incentive because of the potential demand for consumer products and services.[8] Because of currency fluctuations, firms may also choose to distribute their operations across many countries, including emerging ones, in order to reduce the risk of devaluation in one country. However, the uniqueness of emerging markets presents both opportunities and challenges.[9] India, for example, offers a huge potential market and its government is becoming more supportive of foreign direct investment.[10] Nevertheless, India differs from Western countries in many respects, including culture, politics, and the precepts of its economic system. The differences between India and Western countries pose serious challenges to Western competitive paradigms; these challenges emphasize the skills needed to manage financial, economic, and political risks.[11]

A large majority of U.S.-based companies' international business is in European markets.[12] The most attractive countries in Europe are Great Britain, Germany, and Spain. But, the recent economic crises have reduced the direct investments made in Europe by foreign multinational firms.

Companies seeking to internationalize their operations in Asia, Europe, or elsewhere need to understand the pressure on them to respond to local, national, or regional customs, especially where goods or services require customization because of cultural differences or effective marketing to entice customers to try a different product.[13] Although changing consumer tastes and practices linked to cultural values or traditions is not simple, following an international strategy is a particularly attractive option to firms competing in domestic markets that have limited growth opportunities.

The size of an international market also affects a firm's willingness to invest in R&D to build competitive advantages in that market.[14] Larger markets usually offer higher potential returns and thus pose less risk for a firm's investments.

The strength of the science base in the country in question also can affect a firm's foreign R&D investments. Most firms prefer to invest more heavily in those countries with the scientific knowledge and talent needed to produce value-creating products and processes from their R&D activities.[15] The United States and Germany have strong reputations in R&D, and China is also making very large investments to increase its innovative prowess. International diversification can help extend a product's life cycle.[16] Typically, a firm discovers an innovation in its home-country market. Some demand for the product may then develop in other countries, and exports are provided by domestic operations. Increased demand in foreign countries justifies direct foreign investment in production capacity abroad, especially because foreign competitors also organize to meet increasing demand. As the product becomes standardized, the firm may rationalize its operations by moving production to a region with low manufacturing costs.[17]

Return on Investment

Large markets may be crucial for earning a return on significant investments, such as plant and capital equipment or R&D. Therefore, most R&D-intensive industries, such as electronics, are international. In addition to the need for a large market to recoup heavy investment in R&D, the development pace for new technology is increasing. As a result, new products become obsolete more rapidly, and therefore investments need to be recouped more quickly. Moreover, firms' abilities to develop new technologies are expanding; and, because of different patent laws across country borders, imitation by competitors is more likely. Through reverse engineering, competitors are able to take apart a product, learn the new technology, and develop a similar product that imitates the new technology. Because their competitors can imitate the new technology relatively quickly, firms need to recoup new product development costs even more rapidly. Consequently, the larger markets provided by international expansion are particularly attractive in many industries, such as computer hardware, because they expand the opportunity for the firm to recoup a large capital investment and large-scale R&D expenditures.[18]

However, the primary reason for making investments in international markets is to generate higher returns than firms would achieve on investments made in their domestic markets.[19] For example, Gruma, Mexico's leading corn flour producer, has had difficulty earning high returns in its home market because of government price controls on both flour and tortillas. However, Gruma has used this dominant position in Mexico to buy new brands and build plants in other countries. Its margins are significantly better in its international operations than they are in Mexico. It operates in 105 countries and had sales of $4.2 billion in 2011.[20]

Economies of Scale, Scope, and Learning

By expanding their markets, firms may be able to enjoy economies of scale, particularly in their manufacturing operations. To the extent that a firm can standardize its products across country borders and use the same or similar production facilities, thereby coordinating critical resource functions, it is more likely to achieve optimal economies of scale.[21]

In some industries, technology drives globalization because the economies of scale necessary to reduce costs to the lowest level often require an investment greater than that needed to meet domestic market demand. There is also pressure for cost reductions, achieved by purchasing from the lowest-cost global suppliers. For example, economies of scale are critical in the global auto industry. Ford, Honda, General Motors (GM), and Volkswagen are each producing an economy car to compete with the existing cars in China. Because of global economies of scale, these companies have obtained market share in China, but GM has the largest market share of 13 percent.[22] The Chinese government–owned Shanghai Automotive Industry Corp. (SAIC) has helped these foreign car companies achieve significant success in manufacturing cars in China. SAIC has joint ventures, for example, with both GM and Volkswagen. SAIC has developed into a major global corporation with sales of more than four million autos in 2011 for total revenue of $54.3 billion. As such it is ranked among the *Fortune* Global 500 corporations.[23]

Economies of scope are also an incentive for international expansion. Firms may be able to exploit core competencies in international markets through sharing resources and knowledge between units across country borders.[24] This sharing generates synergy, which helps the firm produce higher-quality goods or services at lower cost.

In addition, working across international markets provides the firm with new learning opportunities.[25] Multinational firms have substantial occasions to learn from the different practices they encounter in international markets. Moreover, R&D expertise for emerging products and businesses may not exist in the domestic market.[26] To take advantage of international R&D investments, firms need to already have a strong R&D system in place to absorb the knowledge. Likewise, local companies can learn from foreign multinational firms that enter their markets, depending on the local firm's ability to absorb the knowledge.[27]

Obtain Resources and Achieve Other Location Advantages

Another traditional motive for firms to become multinational is to secure needed resources, whether in the form of scarce factors of production or lower costs.[28] Key supplies of raw material, especially minerals and energy, are important in some industries. For instance, aluminum producers need a supply of bauxite, tire firms need rubber, and oil companies scour the world to find new petroleum reserves. Other industries, such as the garment, electronics, and watch-making industries, seek low-cost factors of production and have moved portions of their operations to foreign locations in pursuit of lower costs.

Some countries provide access to lower-cost labor, energy, or other natural resources. In North America, Mexico has well-developed infrastructures and a skilled, though inexpensive, labor force, and it has received significant amounts of foreign direct investment. The costs of locating in Mexico are significantly lower than in other countries regionally. Location advantages can be influenced by the needs of intended customers as well as by costs.[29] For example, dozens of Chinese and Taiwanese companies have made significant investments in production facilities in Central Europe to be closer to wealthy European customers. Additionally, the Czech Republic is becoming a major distribution center for international companies because of its central location. Deutsche Post DHL Worldwide Express is among the firms to establish distribution centers near Prague.[30] In addition, firms often follow competitors into markets not only because of access to customers but also because of access to other important stakeholders or resources (e.g., suppliers).[31]

Cultural influences may also affect location advantages and disadvantages. If there is a strong match between the cultures in which international transactions are carried out, the liabilities associated with being a foreigner are lower than if the cultures are very different.[32] Research also suggests that regulatory differences influence the level of ownership multinational firms are willing to undertake in a foreign business venture as well as their strategies for managing expatriate human resources.[33]

Assuming that the reasons for expanding their strategic entry into international markets are sufficient, firms must make several decisions regarding how to proceed. As discussed in Chapters 5 and 8, firms expect to create value through the implementation of a business-level strategy and a corporate-level strategy. Consequently, they must decide whether they will follow an international corporate-level strategy that emphasizes a different approach to each international market, a standardized approach, or something in between. They must also determine how to use their distinctive competencies to create advantages in international markets through a business-level strategy. In addition, they have to choose a mode for entering new markets.

INTERNATIONAL CORPORATE-LEVEL STRATEGY

International corporate-level strategy focuses on the scope of a firm's operations through both product and geographic diversification.[34] The firm must select which products or services will be provided to various regions around the world. Consequently, international corporate-level strategy is similar to the corporate-level strategy described in Chapter 8 because it involves the decision of where a firm should compete. International corporate-level strategy adds an international dimension to the diversification decisions firms make. Although large firms have tended to reduce the scope of their product diversification over the past two decades, the trend toward refocusing on core activities has been accompanied by an increase in the scope of international operations.[35]

The essence of international corporate-level strategy is to allow firms to use their core competencies to pursue opportunities in the external environment. To create competitive advantage, each strategy must realize a core competence based on difficult-to-duplicate resources and capabilities.[36]

International Scope: Worldwide Presence or Regionalization

Because a firm's location can affect its value creation, it must decide whether to compete in all or many global markets, or to focus on a particular region.[37] Competing in all markets provides the potential for economies because of the combined market size. Also, firms may be influenced to expand their global reach because competing in risky emerging markets can lead to higher performance.[38] However, a firm that competes in industries in which the international markets differ greatly may wish to narrow its focus to a particular region of the world.

Regionalization. Firms have been motivated to develop strategies that focus on particular regions by countries developing trade agreements and institutions that enhance the attractiveness of their regions.[39] The European Union (EU) and the Organization of American States (OAS) in South America are associations that developed trade agreements to promote the flow of trade across country boundaries within their respective regions.[40] Many European firms acquire and integrate their businesses in Europe to better coordinate pan-European brands as the EU creates more unity in European markets.[41] Similarly, the North American Free Trade Agreement (NAFTA), signed by the United States, Canada, and Mexico, facilitates free trade across country borders in North America. NAFTA loosens restrictions on international strategies within the region and provides greater opportunity for international strategies. A treaty called the Central American Free Trade Agreement (CAFTA) was signed by President George W. Bush in 2005 and was ratified by many Central American countries in 2006. It is now frequently called CAFTA-DR because of the addition of the Dominican Republic. Similar to other such agreements, the intention is to reduce trade barriers across borders and encourage trade in the region.[42]

Firms that pursue regionalization can better understand the cultures, legal and social norms, and other factors that are important for effective competition in those markets. For example, a firm may focus only on Far East markets rather than compete simultaneously in the Middle East, Europe, and the Far East. Or, the firm may choose a region of the world where the markets are more similar and some coordination and sharing of resources would be possible. In this way, the firm may be able not only to better understand the markets in which it competes, but also to achieve some economies. In large countries, firms also select subnational regions in which to compete. For example, China has a massive population and land mass. There are substantial differences across some of its regions, and some foreign firms choose to locate and compete only in selected regions (e.g., in large metropolitan areas such as Shanghai and Beijing).[43]

Most firms enter regional markets sequentially, beginning in markets with which they are more familiar. They also introduce their largest and strongest lines of business into these markets first, followed by their other lines of business once the first lines are successful. They also usually invest in the same area as their original investment location.[44]

Liability of Foreignness. In addition to the trend toward regionalization, another important factor that influences the scope of a firm's international operations is the liability of foreignness. Liabilities associated with being a foreign business in a highly different business environment can make competing on a worldwide scale risky and expensive.[45]

A variety of factors make operating a business in a foreign country difficult. Employment contracts and labor forces differ significantly in international markets. For example, it is more difficult to lay off employees in Europe than in the United States because of differences in employment contracts. Also, in many cases, host governments demand joint ownership, which allows the foreign firm to avoid tariffs. Furthermore, host governments frequently require a high percentage of procurements, manufacturing, and R&D to use local sources.[46] These issues increase the need for local investment and responsiveness compared with seeking global economies of scale.[47]

Some of the biggest difficulties associated with liability of foreignness have to do with an inability to understand customers in international markets. Walmart discovered this when it tried to enter the German market. The company assumed that Germans would want to be treated as Americans are in Walmart stores; when Walmart staff greeted customers brightly and helped pack their purchases, Germans fled. The company did not know that many Germans regard shop assistants who try to help them with suspicion.[48] In 2006 Walmart sold its German stores to Metro, a local rival.

In the 21st century, regionalization and the liability of foreignness may lead some firms to focus more on regional adaptation rather than global markets.[49] After a firm has decided where it will compete, whether in a particular global region or across multiple regions, one of the most important decisions corporate-level managers must make is the degree to which headquarters will guide the strategy of businesses outside the home country. Some firms pursue corporate strategies that give individual country units the authority to develop their own business-level strategies, while other firms dictate what their business-level strategies will be in order to standardize the firm's products and sharing of resources across countries.[50] The three basic approaches to international corporate-level strategy are multidomestic (products adapted to each market), global (one product for the whole world), and transnational (a combination of multidomestic and global). As illustrated in Figure 10.2, two factors

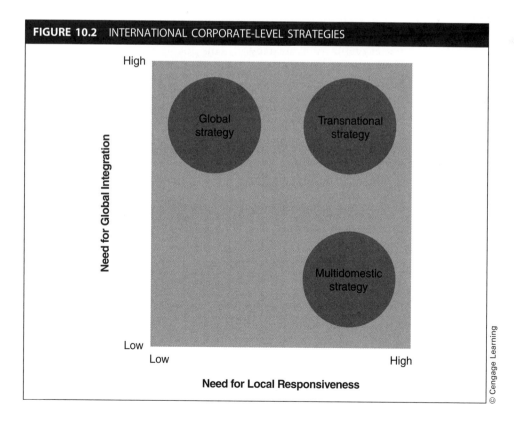

FIGURE 10.2   INTERNATIONAL CORPORATE-LEVEL STRATEGIES

© Cengage Learning

that influence the decision regarding the type of corporate-level strategy are the need for global integration and the need for local responsiveness.

Multidomestic Strategy

A **multidomestic strategy** is an international strategy in which strategic and operating decisions are decentralized to the strategic business unit in each country to allow that unit to tailor products to the local market.[51] A multidomestic strategy focuses on competition within each country. It assumes that the markets differ and therefore are segmented by country boundaries. In other words, consumer needs and desires, industry conditions (e.g., the number and type of competitors), political and legal structures, and social norms vary by country. With multidomestic strategies, the firm can customize its products to meet the specific needs and preferences of local customers. Therefore, these strategies should maximize a firm's competitive response to the idiosyncratic requirements of each market. The use of multidomestic strategies usually expands the firm's local market share because the firm can pay attention to the needs of the local clientele.[52]

The multidomestic strategy decentralizes the firm's strategic and operating decisions to business units in each country so that product characteristics can be tailored to local preferences.[53] Firms using this strategy try to isolate themselves from global competitive forces by establishing protected market positions or by competing in industry segments that are most affected by differences among local countries. Also, the need for local repair and service capabilities can influence a firm to be responsive to local country conditions through its internationalization strategy.[54] This localization may even affect industries that are seen as needing more global economies of scale, such as home appliances.

The **worldwide geographic area structure,** which emphasizes national interests and facilitates the firm's efforts to satisfy local or cultural differences, is used to implement the multidomestic strategy (see Figure 10.3). Because using the multidomestic strategy requires little coordination between different country markets, integrating mechanisms among divisions in the worldwide geographic area structure aren't needed. Hence, formalization is low, and coordination among units in the structure is often informal.

The worldwide geographic area structure evolved as a natural outgrowth of the multicultural European marketplace. Friends and family members of the main business, who were sent as expatriates into foreign countries to develop the independent country subsidiary, often implemented this type of structure for the main business. The relationship to corporate headquarters by divisions took place through informal communication among "family members."[55]

One disadvantage of the multidomestic strategy with a worldwide geographic area structure is the inability to create global efficiency. For instance, multidomestic strategies make it more difficult to achieve economies of scale. Also, the use of these strategies results in more uncertainty for the corporation as a whole because of the differences across markets and thus the different strategies used by local country units.

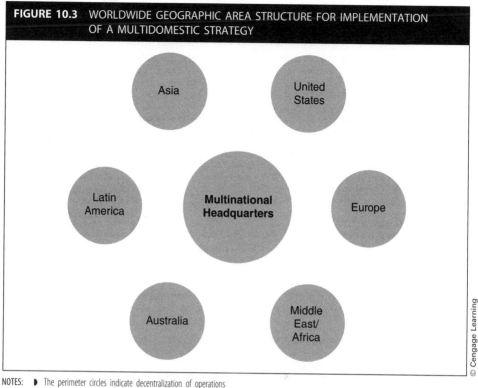

FIGURE 10.3 WORLDWIDE GEOGRAPHIC AREA STRUCTURE FOR IMPLEMENTATION OF A MULTIDOMESTIC STRATEGY

Asia

United States

Latin America

Multinational Headquarters

Europe

Australia

Middle East/ Africa

© Cengage Learning

NOTES:
▶ The perimeter circles indicate decentralization of operations
▶ Emphasis is on differentiation by local demand to fit an area or country culture
▶ Corporate headquarters coordinates financial resources among independent subsidies
▶ The organization is like a decentralized federation

Global Strategy

In contrast to a multidomestic strategy, a **global strategy** is an international strategy through which the firm offers standardized products across country markets, with the competitive strategy being dictated by the home office.[56] The strategic business units operating in each country are assumed to be interdependent, and the home office attempts to achieve integration across these businesses.[57] A global strategy emphasizes economies of scale and offers greater opportunities to utilize innovations developed at the corporate level or in one country in other markets. Many Japanese firms have successfully used the global strategy.[58]

Pressure has increased for global integration of operations, mostly driven by more universal product demand. As nations industrialize, the demand for some products and commodities appears to become more similar. This "nationless," or borderless, demand for globally branded products may be due to similarities in lifestyle in developed nations. For instance, the Swedish firm IKEA International has become a global brand by selling company-designed furniture through about 287 stores in 38 countries. To cut transportation costs, IKEA uses flat packaging; customers assemble the products at home. About 49 percent of its sales occur in five countries—Germany, United States, France, Italy and Sweden. About two thirds of its suppliers are located in Europe but the country providing the greatest amount of its supplies is China at 22 percent.[59] IKEA sells by mail order and online, and its stores also feature Swedish cuisine restaurants and playrooms for children.

While a global strategy produces lower risk, the firm may forgo growth opportunities in local markets, either because those markets are less likely to identify opportunities or because opportunities require that products be adapted to the local market.[60] The global strategy is not as responsive to local markets and is difficult to manage because of the need to coordinate strategies and operating decisions across country borders. In addition, a global strategy can reduce the effectiveness of learning processes in a multinational firm because of the pressure to conform to a standard way of doing things.[61]

Achieving efficient operations with a global strategy requires the sharing of resources and coordination and cooperation across country boundaries, which in turn require centralization and headquarters control. The **worldwide product divisional structure** supports use of the global strategy (see Figure 10.4). In this kind of structure, decision-making authority is centralized in the worldwide division headquarters to coordinate and integrate decisions and actions among divisional business units. This structure is often used in rapidly growing firms seeking to manage their diversified product lines effectively, as in Japan's Kyowa Hakko.[62]

FIGURE 10.4 WORLDWIDE PRODUCT DIVISIONAL STRUCTURE FOR IMPLEMENTATION OF A GLOBAL STRATEGY

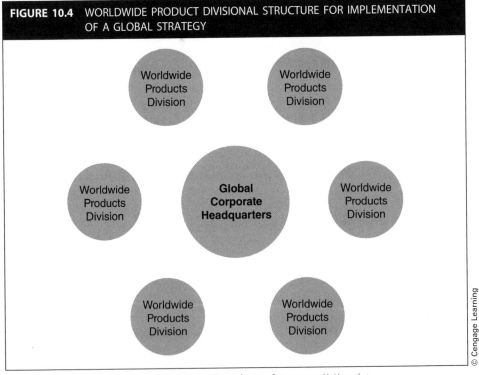

© Cengage Learning

NOTES:
▶ The headquarters' circle indicates centralization to coordinate information flow among worldwide products
▶ Corporate headquarters uses many intercoordination devices to facilitate global economies of scale and scope
▶ Corporate headquarters also allocates financial resources in a cooperative way
▶ The organization is like a centralized federation

With businesses in pharmaceuticals, biochemicals, and advanced medical equipment, this company uses the worldwide product divisional structure to facilitate its decisions about how to successfully compete in what it believes are rapidly shifting global competitive environments.

Integrating mechanisms are important for effective use of the worldwide product divisional structure. Direct contact between managers, liaison roles between departments, and "extensive and formal use of task forces and operating committees to supplement communication and coordination of worldwide operations" are examples of these mechanisms.[63] The evolution of a shared vision of the firm's strategy, and how structure supports its implementation, is one of the important outcomes resulting from the effective use of these mechanisms. The disadvantages of the combination of the global strategy and worldwide structure are the difficulty involved with coordinating decisions and actions across country borders and the inability to quickly respond to local needs and preferences.

Transnational Strategy

A **transnational strategy** is an international strategy through which the firm seeks to achieve both global efficiency and local responsiveness.[64] Realizing these goals is difficult: the first requires close global coordination and the second requires local flexibility. "Flexible coordination"—building a shared vision and individual commitment through an integrated network—is needed to implement the transnational strategy.[65] Such integrated networks allow a firm to manage its connections with customers, suppliers, partners, and other parties more efficiently, rather than using arm's-length transactions.[66] In reality, it is difficult to successfully use the transnational strategy because of its conflicting goals. On the positive side, effective implementation of a transnational strategy often produces higher performance than does implementation of either the multidomestic or global international corporate-level strategies.[67]

The worldwide combination structure is used to implement the transnational strategy. The **worldwide combination structure** draws characteristics and mechanisms from both the worldwide geographic area structure and the worldwide product divisional structure. The fit between the multidomestic strategy and the worldwide geographic area structure, and between the global strategy and the worldwide product divisional structure, are apparent. However, when a firm wants to implement both the multidomestic and the global strategies simultaneously through a combination structure, the appropriate integrating mechanisms for the two structures are less obvious.

Some assets and operations of the worldwide combination structure are centralized and others are decentralized. In addition, some functions are integrated and others are nonintegrated. These seemingly opposite characteristics must be managed by an overall structure that is capable of encouraging all employees to understand the effects of cultural diversity on a firm's operations. Consequently, a blend of formal and informal relationships and various mechanisms—including meetings, conference calls, subsidiary visits, cross-national teams, rotations and transfer of employees, and task forces that use inputs from across the firm—is developed throughout the organization to leverage both efficiency and flexibility.[68] Within a worldwide combination structure, some subsidiaries may be given a *global mandate,* which means that they are responsible for supplying a particular good or service to all parts of the organization throughout the world. Others may make a *specialized contribution* to an interdependent network of subsidiaries.[69] For instance, a subsidiary may be assigned the responsibility for one part of a production process. Still other subsidiaries within the structure may be responsible only for *local implementation,* which means that they play a well-defined role in the value chain, such as marketing and service in a single country.[70]

The requirements of a combination structure highlight the need for a strong educational component to change the whole culture of the organization. If the cultural change is effective, the combination structure should allow the firm to learn how to gain competitive benefits in local economies by adapting its core competencies, which often have been developed and nurtured in less culturally diverse competitive environments. As firms globalize and move toward the transnational strategy, the idea of a corporate headquarters has become increasingly important in fostering leadership and a shared vision to create a stronger company identity.[71] But fostering multiple and dispersed capabilities is also a challenge. Firms have been effectively managing "centers of excellence" as they emerge in foreign subsidiaries to help with this challenge.[72]

An example would be firms in the global automobile industry, which are choosing the transnational strategy to deal with global trends. Many of these companies produce automobiles with a basic design that is standard throughout the world but also a variety of models that reflect local markets. Standard designs help create efficiencies in engineering and production, while customized models appeal to individual markets. Also, automobile companies are increasing their production of models in the countries where they are sold. Although the transnational strategy is difficult to implement, emphasis on global efficiency is increasing as more industries begin to experience global competition.[73] To add to the problem, emphasis on local requirements is also increasing: global goods and services often require some customization to meet government regulations within particular countries or to fit customer tastes and preferences. In addition, most multinational firms desire coordination and sharing of resources across country markets to hold down costs. Furthermore, some products and industries may be more suited than others for standardization across country borders.

As a result, most large multinational firms with diverse products employ a multidomestic strategy with certain product lines and a global strategy with others. Many multinational firms may require this type of flexibility if they are to be strategically competitive, partly because of trends such as regionalization and the liability of foreignness.

INTERNATIONAL BUSINESS-LEVEL STRATEGY

In addition to a corporate-level international strategy, firms must also determine the business-level strategies that will be pursued in each business and international location. The generic business-level strategies discussed in Chapter 5 include cost leadership, differentiation, focused cost leadership, focused differentiation, and integrated cost leadership/differentiation. A firm must also respond to competitive rivalry and competitive dynamics within international markets, as discussed in Chapter 6.

International business-level strategies depend in part on the type of international corporate-level strategy the firm selects. If the firm adopts a global corporate-level strategy, then subsidiaries within particular countries may have very little liberty to choose their own business-level strategies because the essential characteristics of the product are already established. In these cases, the subsidiary would play the role of local implementer. The local implementer simply fine-tunes a strategy that is determined by international headquarters.

The cost leadership strategy is most closely associated with a global corporate-level strategy because global corporate-level strategies tend to produce standard products for the whole world, thus facilitating economies of scale. If the firm's international corporate-level strategy is multidomestic or to some extent transnational, then each international subsidiary will have more control over its own approach to its domestic market. For example, Bausch & Lomb has different approaches to its various international markets in sunglasses as well as other eye care products.[74] Production and marketing policies are determined in individual markets, although the company does have some international plants to enhance production efficiency. Thus, its transnational corporate-level strategy allows some freedom to determine business-level strategies in individual markets.

In an international business-level strategy, the home country of operation is often the most important source of competitive advantage.[75] The resources and capabilities established in the home country frequently allow the firm to pursue the strategy into markets in other countries. Based on work by Michael Porter, Figure 10.5 presents the factors contributing to the advantage of firms in a dominant global

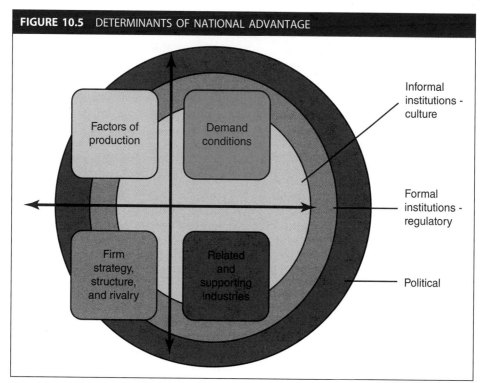

FIGURE 10.5 DETERMINANTS OF NATIONAL ADVANTAGE

SOURCE: © Copyrighted 2011 by Michael A. Hitt, R. Duane Ireland, and Robert E. Hoskisson.

industry and associated with a specific country or regional environment.[76] As shown in the figure, these factors must be managed within a context of formal institutions (e.g., laws and regulations), informal institutions (e.g., culture), and political system (e.g., degree of democracy).

The first dimension, *factors of production,* refers to the inputs necessary to compete in any industry—labor, land, natural resources, capital, and infrastructure (such as transportation, postal, and communication systems). Factors are basic (e.g., natural and labor resources) or advanced (e.g., digital communication systems and a highly educated workforce). Other factors are generalized (e.g., physical infrastructure exemplified by highway systems) and specialized (skilled personnel in a specific industry, such as the workers in a port who specialize in handling bulk chemicals). If a country has both advanced and specialized production factors, it is likely to serve an industry well by spawning strong home-country competitors that also can be successful global competitors.

Ironically, countries often develop advanced and specialized factors because they lack critical basic resources. For example, some Asian countries, such as South Korea, lack abundant natural resources but offer a strong work ethic, a large number of engineers, and systems of large firms to create an expertise in manufacturing. Similarly, Germany developed a strong chemical industry, partially because Hoechst and BASF spent years creating a synthetic indigo dye to reduce their dependence on imports, unlike Britain, whose colonies provided large supplies of natural indigo.[77]

The second dimension, *demand conditions,* is characterized by the nature and size of buyers' needs in the home market for the industry's goods or services. The sheer size of a market segment can produce the demand necessary to create scale-efficient facilities. This efficiency can also lead to domination of the industry in other countries. Specialized demand may create opportunities beyond national boundaries. For example, Swiss firms have long led the world in tunneling equipment because of the need to tunnel through mountains for rail and highway passage in Switzerland. Japanese firms have created a niche market for compact, quiet air conditioners, which are important in Japan because homes are often small and located close together.[78]

Related and supporting industries is the third dimension. Italy has become the leader in the shoe industry because of related and supporting industries; a well-established leather-processing industry provides the leather needed to construct shoes and related products. Also, many people travel to Italy to purchase leather goods, providing support in distribution. Supporting industries in leather-working machinery and design services also contribute to the success of the shoe industry. In fact, the design services industry supports its own related industries, such as ski boots, fashion apparel, and furniture. In Japan, the popular cartoons and the animation sector, integrated with technological knowledge from the consumer electronics industry, facilitated the emergence of a successful video game industry.[79]

Firm strategy, structure, and rivalry compose the final dimension and also foster the growth of certain industries. This dimension varies greatly across nations. For instance, because of the excellent technical training system in Germany, firms strongly emphasize methodical product and process improvements. In Japan, unusual cooperative and competitive systems have facilitated the cross-functional management of complex assembly operations. In Italy, the national pride of the country's designers has spawned strong industries in sports cars, fashion apparel, and furniture. In the United States, competition among computer software producers has favored the development of this industry.

The four dimensions presented in Figure 10.5 also must be managed within the country's institutional environment to include structural attributes of a national economy and the political system in order to achieve a national advantage. Government policies and regulations can also strongly influence the ability of firms in a country to compete successfully on a global scale. Airbus was originally formed as a multinational European consortium to challenge the dominant position of U.S. aircraft manufacturers. Now one of the two largest aircraft makers, Airbus has received much support from multiple European governments over its history.[80]

Although each firm must create its own success, not all firms will survive to become global competitors—not even those operating with the same country factors that spawned the successful firms. Furthermore, research indicates that as a firm continues its growth into multiple international locations, the country of origin is less important for competitive advantage except in certain industries (e.g., pharmaceuticals).[81] The actual strategic choices managers make may be the most compelling reason for success or failure. Accordingly, the dimensions illustrated in Figure 10.5 are likely to produce competitive advantages only when the firm develops and implements an appropriate strategy that takes advantage of distinct country factors. Thus, these distinct country factors are necessary to consider when analyzing business-level strategies (i.e., cost leadership, differentiation, focused cost leadership, focused differentiation, and integrated cost leadership/differentiation) in an international context.

CHOICE OF INTERNATIONAL ENTRY MODE

After the firm selects its international strategies and decides whether to employ them in regional or world markets, it must choose a market entry mode. International expansion is accomplished by exporting products, licensing arrangements, strategic alliances, acquisitions, and establishing new wholly owned subsidiaries (see Figure 10.6). Each means of market entry has its advantages and disadvantages. Furthermore, the timing of international entry can influence its success.[82] Thus, choosing the appropriate mode or path to enter international markets affects the firm's performance in those markets.[83]

Exporting

Many industrial firms begin their international expansion by exporting goods or services to other countries.[84] Exporting does not require the expense of establishing operations in host countries, but exporters must establish some means of marketing and distributing their products. Usually, exporting firms develop contractual arrangements with host-country firms.

The disadvantages of exporting include the often high costs of transportation and possible tariffs placed on incoming goods. Furthermore, the exporter has less

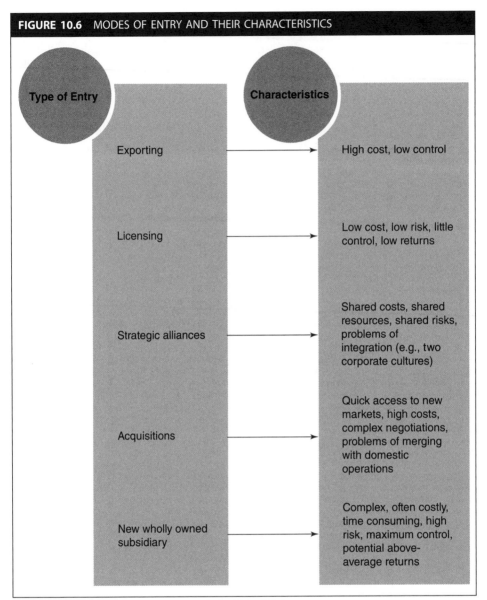

FIGURE 10.6 MODES OF ENTRY AND THEIR CHARACTERISTICS

Type of Entry

Characteristics

Exporting	→	High cost, low control
Licensing	→	Low cost, low risk, little control, low returns
Strategic alliances	→	Shared costs, shared resources, shared risks, problems of integration (e.g., two corporate cultures)
Acquisitions	→	Quick access to new markets, high costs, complex negotiations, problems of merging with domestic operations
New wholly owned subsidiary	→	Complex, often costly, time consuming, high risk, maximum control, potential above-average returns

SOURCE: © Copyrighted 2011 by Michael A. Hitt, R. Duane Ireland, and Robert E. Hoskisson

control over the marketing and distribution of its products in the host country and must either pay the distributor or allow the distributor to mark up the price to recoup its costs and earn a profit.[85] As a result, it may be difficult to market a competitive product through exporting or to provide a product that is customized to each international market.[86] However, evidence suggests that cost leadership strategies enhance the performance of exports in developed countries, whereas differentiation strategies are more successful in emerging economies.[87]

Firms export mostly to countries that are closest to their facilities because of the lower transportation costs and the usually greater similarity between geographic neighbors. For example, U.S. NAFTA partners Mexico and Canada account for more than half of the goods exported from Texas. The Internet has also made exporting easier. Even small firms can access critical information about foreign markets, examine a target market, research the competition, and find lists of potential customers.[88] Governments also use the Internet to facilitate applications for export and import licenses. Small businesses are most likely to use the exporting mode of international entry.[89] However, currency exchange rates are a significant problem for small businesses. Larger firms have specialists that manage the exchange rates, but small businesses rarely have this expertise. Changes in exchange rates can dramatically alter a firm's success in international markets.

Licensing

Licensing is one form of organizational network that is becoming common, particularly among smaller firms.[90] A licensing arrangement allows a foreign firm to purchase the right to manufacture and sell the firm's products within a host country or set of countries.[91] The licenser is normally paid a royalty on each unit produced and sold. The licensee takes the risks and makes the monetary investments in facilities for manufacturing, marketing, and distributing the goods or services. As a result, licensing is possibly the least costly form of international expansion.

Philip Morris International (PMI), Altria Group's international cigarette business, has seven of the top international cigarette brands in its portfolio, including the best-selling Marlboro. While its international sales have been strong and increasing, PMI wanted to enter the Chinese market because China accounts for almost one-third of the cigarettes smoked globally. Nevertheless, U.S.-owned cigarette companies had trouble entering the highly attractive Chinese market because state-owned tobacco companies lobbied against such entry. To overcome this problem, PMI formed a licensing agreement with the China National Tobacco Corporation (CNTC). Under the terms of the agreement, CNTC has the right to sell cigarettes under the Marlboro brand name.[92]

Licensing is also a way to expand returns based on older innovations.[93] Even if product life cycles are short, licensing may be a useful tool. For instance, because the toy industry faces relentless change and unpredictable buying patterns, licensing is used and contracts are often completed in foreign markets where labor may be less expensive.

Licensing also has disadvantages. For example, with a licensing agreement, the firm has very little control over the manufacture and marketing of its products in other countries, so structuring a licensing agreement properly is very important. In addition, licensing provides the lowest potential returns, because returns must be shared between the licenser and the licensee. Worse, the international firm may learn the technology and produce and sell a similar competitive product after the license expires. Komatsu, for example, first licensed much of its technology from International Harvester, Bucyrus International, and Cummins to compete against Caterpillar in the earth-moving equipment business. Komatsu then dropped these licenses and developed its own products using the technology it had gained from the U.S. companies.[94]

In addition, if a firm wants to move to a different ownership arrangement, licensing may create some inflexibility. Thus, it is important that a firm thinks ahead and considers sequential forms of entry into international markets.[95] The key is to create needed flexibility in a licensing agreement so that a firm can pursue other means of approaching the market as conditions change.

Strategic Alliances

In recent years, strategic alliances have become a popular means of international expansion.[96] Strategic alliances allow firms to share the risks and resources required to enter international markets. Moreover, strategic alliances can facilitate the development of new core competencies that contribute to the firm's future strategic competitiveness.[97] Consequently, because their resources are so limited, alliances are an especially attractive way for small and medium-sized firms to enter international markets.[98]

Most strategic alliances are formed with a host-country firm that knows and understands the competitive conditions, legal and social norms, and cultural idiosyncrasies of the country. This helps the expanding firm produce and market a competitive product. For example, McDonald's formed a venture with China's largest gas retailer, the state-owned Sinopec, to create a chain of "Drive-Thru" restaurants at Sinopec gas stations. The agreement gives McDonald's the ability to expand rapidly along highways and in fast-growing suburbs of China's large cities. We learned earlier in the example of SAIC that China has become a very large auto market. With the sales of cars booming and an increasing number of Chinese driving, this alliance should significantly enhance McDonald's sales revenues in China over time. Based on its successful alliance with Sinopec and the growing number of Chinese driving their own cars, McDonald's introduced other drive-thru restaurants in China.[99]

Often, firms in emerging economies want to form international alliances and ventures to gain access to sophisticated technologies that are new to them. This type of arrangement can benefit the firm from the non-emerging economy as well, in that it gains access to a new market and doesn't have to pay tariffs to do so (because it is partnering with a local company).[100] In return, the host-country firm may find its new access to the expanding firm's technology and innovative products attractive. Each partner in an alliance brings knowledge or resources to the partnership. Indeed, partners often enter an alliance with the purpose of learning new capabilities, such as technological skills.[101]

Not all alliances are successful, however; in fact, many fail.[102] The primary reasons for failure—even more common than market changes—include incompatible partners and conflict between partners.[103] International strategic alliances are especially difficult to manage.[104] Several factors may cause a relationship to sour. Trust between the partners is critical and is affected by at least four fundamental issues: the initial condition of the relationship, the negotiation process used to arrive at an agreement, partner interactions, and external events. Trust is also influenced by the cultures of the countries involved in the alliance or joint venture.[105] The legal form of an international alliance depends on the nature of the alliance. Research has shown that equity-based alliances, over which a firm has more control, tend to produce more positive returns than non-equity–based alliances.[106] Research suggests that alliances are more favorable than acquisitions in the face of high uncertainty, where cooperation is needed to bring out the knowledge dispersed between partners, and where strategic flexibility is important, such as with small and medium-sized firms.[107] Acquisitions are better in situations that need less strategic flexibility and when the transaction is used to maintain economies of scale or scope.[108] Also, if conflict in a strategic alliance or joint venture will not be manageable, an acquisition may be a better option.

Acquisitions

As free trade has continued to expand in global markets, cross-border acquisitions have also been increasing significantly. In recent years, such acquisitions have comprised more than 45 percent of all acquisitions completed worldwide.[109] As explained in Chapter 9, acquisitions can provide quick access to a new market. In fact, acquisitions may provide the fastest, and often the largest, initial international expansion of any of the alternatives.[110] When the acquiring and acquired firms are effectively integrated, each can share knowledge with the other. The synergy created is one of the major values of acquisitions in addition to providing a means of entering a foreign market.[111]

Although acquisitions have become a popular mode of entering international markets, they are not without costs. International acquisitions carry some of the disadvantages of domestic acquisitions, such as integration difficulties leading to an inability to achieve synergy (see Chapter 9). Like domestic acquisitions, they can be expensive and often require debt financing, which increases costs associated with the deal. In addition, negotiations for international acquisitions are generally more complicated than those for domestic acquisitions.[112] Dealing with the legal and regulatory requirements in the target firm's country and obtaining appropriate information to negotiate an agreement frequently present significant problems.

Finally, the problems of merging the new firm into the acquiring firm often are more complex than in domestic acquisitions. The acquiring firm must deal not only with different corporate cultures, but also with potentially different social cultures and practices.[113] Therefore, while international acquisitions have been popular because of the rapid access to new markets that they provide, they also carry with them large costs and high risks.[114]

New Wholly-Owned Subsidiary

The establishment of a new wholly owned subsidiary is called a *greenfield venture*. The process of establishing a greenfield venture is often complex and potentially costly, but it gives the firm maximum control and has the most potential to provide above-average returns. This potential is especially true of firms with strong intangible capabilities that might be leveraged through a greenfield venture.[115] For instance, Walmart generally tries to draw on the strength of its brand name when it enters new geographic or product markets. It did this when it entered the banking industry in Mexico. The Mexican market is especially attractive because 80 percent of Mexicans have never had a bank account and the existing big banks charge significantly higher interest rates and fees than banks in the United States. And,

Walmart attracts many to its stores and can use the stores to make the banking services available to its retail customers. In November of 2007, Walmart opened 16 banking branches in 5 different Mexican states.[116]

A firm maintains full control of its operations with a greenfield venture, which is especially advantageous if the firm has proprietary technology. Research also suggests that "wholly-owned subsidiaries and expatriate staff are preferred" in service industries where "close contact with end customers" and "high levels of professional skills, specialized knowhow, and customization" are required.[117] Other research suggests that greenfield investments are more prominent where physical capital–intensive plants are planned and that acquisitions are more likely preferred when a firm is human capital–intensive—that is, where a strong local degree of unionization and significant cultural differences would cause difficulty in transferring knowledge to a host nation through a greenfield approach.[118]

The risks are also high for a greenfield venture because of the costs of establishing a new business operation in a foreign country. The firm may have to acquire the knowledge and expertise of the existing market by hiring either host-country nationals, possibly from competitors, or consultants, which can be costly. Still, the firm maintains control over the technology, marketing, and distribution of its products. Alternatively, the company would have to build new manufacturing facilities, establish distribution networks, and learn and implement appropriate marketing strategies to compete in the new market.[119]

Research shows that changes in government policies can influence whether a firm decides on a joint venture or a wholly owned approach. For instance, after the Asian financial crisis of the late 1990s, many countries had to change their institutional policies to allow for more foreign ownership. As the institutional policy changed, many firms chose to go with a wholly owned approach rather than a joint venture.[120]

Dynamics of Mode of Entry

A number of factors affect a firm's choice of mode of entry into international markets.[121] Initially, market entry will often be achieved through export, which requires no foreign manufacturing expertise and investment only in distribution. Licensing similarly requires relatively few resources, as in the case of Philip Morris International's entry into China. Both exporting and licensing are effective early entrance strategies.

Strategic alliances are popular because they allow a firm to connect with an experienced partner already in the targeted market. Strategic alliances also reduce risk through the sharing of costs. Consequently, a strategic alliance is often used in more uncertain situations, such as an emerging economy.[122] However, if intellectual property rights in the emerging economy are not well-protected, if the number of firms in the industry is growing quickly, and if the need for global integration is high, the greenfield entry mode is preferred.[123]

To secure a stronger presence in international markets, acquisitions or greenfield ventures may be required. For example, several Japanese automobile manufacturers, such as Honda, Nissan, and Toyota, gained a presence in the United States through both greenfield ventures and joint ventures.[124] Toyota has particularly strong intangible production capabilities that it transferred to the United States through greenfield ventures.[125]

Both acquisitions and greenfield ventures are more likely to be used at later stages in the development of an international strategy. In addition, both of these strategies tend to be more successful when the firm making the investment possesses valuable core competencies that it can transfer.[126] Large diversified business groups, often found in emerging economies, not only gain resources through diversification, but also have specialized abilities in managing differences in inward and outward flows of foreign direct investment. In particular, Korean *chaebols,* a form of business conglomerate, have been adept at making acquisitions in emerging economies.[127]

Thus, to enter a global market, a firm selects the entry mode that is best suited to the situation at hand. In some instances, the various options will be followed sequentially, beginning with exporting and ending with greenfield ventures. In other cases, the firm may use several, but not all, of the different entry modes, each in different markets. The decision regarding which entry mode to use is primarily a result of the industry's competitive conditions, the country's situation and government policies, and the firm's unique set of resources, capabilities, and core competencies.

STRATEGIC COMPETITIVENESS OUTCOMES

After a firm has chosen its international strategy and mode of entry, it turns its attention to implementation. Implementation is very important because, as explained next, international expansion is risky and may not result in a competitive advantage which helps to produce positive returns. The probability the firm will achieve success with an international strategy increases when that strategy is effectively implemented.

International Diversification and Returns

As noted earlier, firms have many reasons for diversifying internationally. Because of its potential advantages, international diversification should be related positively to firms' returns. In fact, researchers have found that international diversification can lead to greater operational efficiency, which ultimately leads to higher financial performance.[128] A firm's returns may decrease at first as international diversification increases, but then returns increase as the firm learns to manage its international expansion.[129]

The stock market is particularly sensitive to investments in international markets. Firms that are broadly diversified into multiple international markets usually achieve the most positive returns, especially when they diversify geographically into core business areas.[130] There are many reasons for the positive effects of international diversification, such as potential economies of scale and experience, location advantages, increased market size, and the opportunity to stabilize returns, which helps reduce a firm's overall risk.[131] All of these outcomes can be achieved by both smaller and newer ventures and larger and more established firms. New ventures can also enjoy higher returns when they learn new technologies through their international diversification.[132]

Firms in the Japanese automobile industry have found that international diversification may allow them to better exploit their core competencies because sharing knowledge resources between operations can produce synergy. Also, a firm's returns may affect its decision to diversify internationally. For example, poor returns in a domestic market may encourage a firm to expand internationally in order to enhance its profit potential. In addition, internationally diversified firms may have access to more flexible labor markets, as the Japanese do in the United States, and may thereby benefit from global scanning for competition and market opportunities. Also, through global networks with assets in many countries, firms can develop more flexible structures to adjust to changes that might occur.[133] "Offshore outsourcing," or *offshoring*, has allowed for significant value-creating opportunities for firms engaged in it, especially as firms move into regions with more flexible labor markets. Furthermore, offshoring increases exports for the firms that receive the contract.[134]

Multinational firms with efficient and competitive operations are more likely than solely domestic firms to produce above-average returns for their investors and better products for their customers. However, as explained later, international diversification can be carried too far.

International Diversification and Innovation

In Chapter 1, we noted that the development of new technology is at the heart of value creation. A nation's competitiveness partly depends on the capacity of its industry to innovate. Eventually and inevitably, competitors outperform firms that fail to innovate and improve their operations and products. Therefore, the only way to sustain a competitive advantage is to upgrade it continually.[135]

International diversification provides the potential for firms to achieve greater returns on their innovations (through larger or more numerous markets) and lowers the often substantial risks of R&D investments. In addition, firms moving into international markets are exposed to new products and processes. If they learn about those products and processes and integrate this knowledge into their operations, they can develop further innovation.[136] Therefore, international diversification provides incentives for firms to innovate.[137] However, for firms to take advantage of R&D investment, they must have a well-developed capacity for knowledge absorption.[138]

International diversification may also be necessary to generate the resources required to sustain a large-scale R&D operation. An environment of rapid technological obsolescence makes it difficult for a firm to invest in new technologies and the capital-intensive operations required to take advantage of such investments. Firms operating solely in domestic markets may find such high-level investments problematic because of the length of time required to recoup the original costs. If that time is extended, it may not even be possible to recover the investment before the technology becomes obsolete.[139] As a result, international diversification improves a firm's ability to appropriate additional and necessary returns from innovation before competitors can overcome the initial competitive advantage created by the innovation. For instance, research suggests that Japanese foreign direct investment in developing countries is focused more on market-seeking and labor cost-saving purposes, whereas investment in developed economies is more focused on strategy development as well as market-seeking purposes. In these firms, a relatively strong ownership advantage is evident compared with firms in developing economies.[140]

The relationship among international diversification, innovation, and returns is complex. Researchers generally agree that technological and organizational learning through international diversification ultimately leads to higher financial performance.[141] However, some level of performance is necessary to provide the resources to generate international diversification, which in turn provides incentives and resources to invest in R&D. The latter, if done appropriately, should enhance the returns of the firm, which then provides more resources for continued international diversification and investment in R&D.[142] But as with many types of investments, higher returns mean higher risks.

Risks in an International Environment

International strategy carries risks that are not associated with a purely domestic strategy.[143] Because of these risks, international expansion is difficult to implement, and it is difficult to manage after implementation. The chief risks are political, economic, and other formal institutional risks. Taking these risks into account, highly internationally diversified firms are accustomed to market conditions yielding competitive situations that differ from what was predicted. Sometimes, these situations contribute to the firm's value creation; on other occasions, they negatively affect the firm's efforts.

Political Risks. Political risks are related to instability in national governments and to war, both civil and international. Instability in a national government creates numerous problems, including economic risks and uncertainty created by government regulations; the existence of many, possibly conflicting, legal authorities; and the potential nationalization of private assets.

Government corruption can have a very negative effect on business. Firms don't like to invest where corruption is prevalent because corruption leads to instability, sometimes in the form of protests, revolts, or revolutions.[144] Often these actions are associated with changes in national leadership, which could also mean changes in economic policies. According to Transparency International's annual corruption index, the five least corrupt governments in the world in 2011 were in New Zealand, Denmark, Finland, Sweden and Singapore. The United States government was also among the least corrupt. North Korea, Somalia, Iraq and Haiti were among the most corrupt governments in the ranking.[145]

Changes in government policies can dramatically influence the attractiveness of direct foreign investment. For example, China's government at times has created hurdles for foreign investors, with increased scrutiny of foreign-backed mergers and proposed restrictions in areas from banking to retailing to manufacturing. Such changes can limit the attractiveness of foreign investment. On the other hand, some firms are able to achieve a favored position with the government in a particular country. In this case, they face less investment risk, which can put them at a competitive advantage relative to other firms.[146]

Economic Risks. Foremost among the economic risks of international diversification are the differences and fluctuations in the value of different currencies.[147] The value of the dollar relative to other currencies determines the value of the international assets and earnings of U.S. firms. For example, an increase in the value of the U.S. dollar can reduce the value of U.S. multinational firms' international assets and earnings in other countries. Furthermore, the value of different currencies can also, at times, dramatically affect a firm's competitiveness in global markets because of its effect on the prices of goods manufactured in different countries.[148] An increase in the value of the dollar can harm U.S. firms' exports to international markets because of the price differential of the products. It can also affect economies of other countries.

Economic and political risks are interdependent. Besides the fact that political instability in the Middle East has caused a great deal of political turmoil elsewhere, Middle Eastern problems influence oil prices. Because the global economy is so dependent on oil, these fluctuations can have serious economic consequences. For example, due to western countries' restrictions placed on Iranian exports and financial assets because of concerns about its development of nuclear capabilities, the price of oil increased dramatically in 2012.

The terrorism that has grown out of militant political groups in the region also poses a huge risk for businesses around the globe.[149] The predictable economic effect of terrorism is an increase in insurance and risk-management costs, which results in enhanced production prices, forcing companies to reanalyze the risks of doing business in countries where security risks are higher. Other economic costs and risks—such as the risk associated with damage to a country or region's infrastructure or financial system in the aftermath of a major disaster—are not easy to predict or measure.

Other Formal Institutional Risks. There are other formal institutional risks in addition to political and economic risks. These include heavy formal regulations and weak or ineffective legal protections, often referred to as institutional voids. Formal, burdensome regulations are likely to discourage foreign firms from investing in the country.[150] In fact, some of those burdensome regulations may be directed toward potential foreign investors to protect domestic rival firms. Such protective laws and regulations can occur in emerging economy countries such as China (as discussed previously) and in developed economies such as the United States.

Institutional voids such as weak or nonexistent intellectual property protection laws and enforcement discourage foreign investors as well. Such institutional voids have created concerns for technology based firms considering entering the Chinese and Russian markets, for example. In fact, these voids have also limited entrepreneurial activity in these sectors in those countries.[151] Weaknesses in formal educational systems necessary to provide needed human capital to staff businesses also create concerns. These institutional risks often prevent or limit firms' direct investments in countries where these risks are high.[152]

Country institutional environments are complex. As already suggested, there are multiple formal institutions related to the political environment (e.g., degree of democracy and stability of the government), the economy (e.g., fiscal policies) and the regulatory environment (e.g., laws, regulations and their enforcement). All of these are interrelated and often exist at different levels (e.g., national, state, municipal). For example, the country has national laws and regulations, states have their own laws and regulations, and cities also have laws and regulations. Foreign companies that have subsidiaries in the country must understand and work within the limitations of all of them.[153] These risks are more challenging for companies that have their home bases in countries with formal institutions that are well developed and thus are quite different from these. Thus, these institutional environments pose hazards for foreign firms' capabilities to navigate and manage effectively in them.[154]

Complexity of Managing Multinational Firms

Although firms can realize many benefits by implementing an international strategy, doing so is complex and can produce greater risks.[155] Risk levels increase even more when a firm operates in several different countries. Because of this increased complexity and risk, firms can grow only so large and diverse before becoming unmanageable or before the costs of managing them exceed their benefits.[156]

Returns on international diversification tend to level off and become negative as the diversification increases past some point.[157] There are several reasons for the limits to the positive effects of international diversification. First, greater geographic dispersion across country borders increases the costs of coordination between units and the distribution of products. Second, trade barriers, logistical costs, cultural diversity, and other differences by country (e.g., access to raw materials and different employee skill levels) greatly complicate the implementation of an international diversification strategy.[158]

Institutional and cultural factors can present strong barriers to the transfer of a firm's competitive advantages from one country to another.[159] In fact, some now recommend that multinational firms must take an ambicultural approach to management whereby they adopt the best managerial practices from several cultures.[160] Also, marketing programs often have to be redesigned and new distribution networks established when firms expand into new countries. In addition, firms may encounter different labor costs and capital charges. In general, it is difficult to effectively implement, manage, and control a firm's international operations.[161]

The amount of international diversification that can be managed will vary from firm to firm and according to the abilities of each firm's managers. The problems of central coordination and integration are mitigated if the firm diversifies into more friendly countries that are geographically close and have cultures similar to its own country's culture. In that case, there are likely to be fewer trade barriers, the laws and customs are better understood, and the product is easier to adapt to local markets.[162] For example, U.S. firms may find it less difficult to expand their operations into Mexico, Canada, and Western European countries than into Asian countries.

Management must also be concerned with the relationship between the host government and the multinational corporation. Although government policy and regulations are often barriers, many firms, such as Toyota and General Motors, have turned to strategic alliances to overcome those barriers.[163] By forming interorganizational networks, such as strategic alliances, firms can share resources and risks but also build flexibility. However, large networks can be difficult to manage.

Evidence suggests that more culturally diverse top management teams often have a greater knowledge of international markets and their idiosyncrasies[164] (see Chapter 2 for a discussion of top management teams). Moreover, an in-depth understanding of diverse markets among top-level managers facilitates intrafirm coordination and the use of long-term, strategically relevant criteria for evaluating the performance of managers and their units. In turn, this approach improves innovation and performance.[165]

SUMMARY

▶ The use of international strategies is increasing. Firms are pursuing international diversification to (1) increase market size; (2) increase return on investment; (3) seek economies of scale, scope, and learning; and (4) obtain resources and achieve other location advantages.

▶ Firms that pursue an international strategy must decide whether to compete in all or many global markets, or to focus on a particular region. Competing in all markets provides the potential for economies because of the combined market size. Also, firms may be influenced to expand their global reach because competing in emerging markets can lead to higher performance. However, a firm that competes in industries in which the international markets differ greatly may wish to narrow its scope because of the liability of foreignness. Factors such as differences in labor forces or an inability to understand customers in a particular market can lead to disadvantages for firms competing outside their primary domestic markets. Also, the trend toward regionalization is supported by governments that have developed trade agreements to increase the economic power of their regions.

▶ There are three types of international corporate-level strategies. A *multidomestic strategy* focuses on competition within each country in which the firm competes. Firms using a multidomestic strategy, implemented through the worldwide geographic area structure, decentralize strategic and operating decisions to the business units operating in each country so that each unit can tailor its goods and services to the local market.

▶ A *global strategy* assumes more standardization of products across country boundaries. The worldwide product divisional structure is used to implement the global strategy. This structure is centralized in order to coordinate and integrate different functional activities so as to gain global economies of scope and scale. Decision-making authority is centralized in the firm's worldwide division headquarters.

▶ A *transnational strategy* seeks to combine aspects of both multidomestic and global strategies in order to emphasize both local responsiveness and global integration and coordination. It is implemented through the combination structure. Because it must be simultaneously centralized and decentralized, integrated and nonintegrated, and formalized and nonformalized, the combination structure is difficult to organize and manage successfully. It requires an integrated network and a culture of individual commitment where training is continually emphasized.

- Although the transnational strategy's implementation is a challenge, environmental trends are causing many multinational firms to consider the need for both global efficiency and local responsiveness. Many large multinational firms, particularly those with multiple diverse products, use a multidomestic strategy with some product lines and a global strategy with others.
- International business-level strategies partly depend on the type of international corporate-level strategy the firm has selected. The cost leadership strategy is most closely associated with a global corporate-level strategy because global corporate-level strategies tend to produce standard products for the whole world, thus facilitating economies of scale. If the firm's international corporate-level strategy is multidomestic or transnational, then each international subsidiary will have more control over its own approach to its domestic market. An international business unit, whether in a particular country or a region, adopts an approach based on one of the generic business-level strategies, which are cost leadership, differentiation, focused cost leadership, focused differentiation, and integrated cost leadership/differentiation.
- International business-level strategies are usually grounded in one or more home-country advantages. There are four important dimensions: factors of production; demand conditions; related and supporting industries; and patterns of firm strategy, structure, and rivalry.
- Firms may enter international markets in one of several ways, including undertaking exporting or licensing, forming strategic alliances, making acquisitions, and establishing new wholly owned subsidiaries, often called greenfield ventures. Most firms begin with exporting or licensing, because of their lower costs and risks, but later may expand to strategic alliances and acquisitions. Establishing a new wholly owned subsidiary is the most expensive and risky means of entering a new international market. However, such subsidiaries provide the advantages of maximum control by the firm and, if they are successful, the greatest returns.
- In general, international diversification is related to above-average returns, but this assumes that the diversification is effectively implemented and the firm's international operations are well-managed. International diversification provides greater economies of scope and learning, which, along with greater innovation, help produce above-average returns.
- International diversification facilitates innovation in a firm because it provides a larger market and faster returns from investments in innovation. In addition, international diversification may generate the resources necessary to sustain a large-scale R&D program.
- Among the risks involved with managing multinational operations are political risks (e.g., instability of national governments), economic risks (e.g., fluctuations in the value of a country's currency), and other formal institutional risks (e.g., heavy or negative regulations, weak or nonexistent legal protections).
- There are limits to the ability of a firm to effectively manage international expansion. International diversification increases coordination and distribution costs, and management problems are exacerbated by trade barriers, logistical costs, and cultural diversity, among other factors.

ETHICS QUESTIONS

1. As firms internationalize, they may be tempted to locate facilities where product liability laws are lax in testing new products. Is this an acceptable practice? Why or why not?

2. Regulation and laws regarding the sale and distribution of tobacco products are stringent in the U.S. market. What are the ethical implications of U.S. firms pursuing marketing strategies for tobacco products in other countries that would be illegal in the United States?

3. Some companies outsource production to firms in foreign countries to save money. To what extent is a company morally responsible for the way workers are treated by the firms in those countries to which they outsource production?

4. Global and multidomestic strategies call for different competitive approaches. What ethical concerns might surface when firms try to market standardized products globally? When should firms develop different products or approaches for each local market?

5. Are companies morally responsible to support the U.S. government as it imposes trade sanctions on other countries, such as China, because of human rights violations? What if a significant amount of its international business is in one of those countries?

6. Latin America has been experiencing significant changes in both political orientation and economic development. What strategies should foreign international businesses implement, if any, to influence government policy in these countries? Can businesses realistically expect to influence political changes?

NOTES

1. 2012, BRIC countries—Background, latest statistics and original articles, Global Sherpa, http://www.globalsherpa.org, March 9; I. Hasan, N. Koissa, & H. Wang, 2011, Global equity offerings, corporate valuation, and subsequent international diversification, *Strategic Management Journal*, 32: 787–796.

2. Ibid.

3. A. H. Kirca, G. T. M. Hult, S. Deligonul, M. Z. Perryy, & S. T. Cavusgil, 2012, A multilevel examination of the drivers of firm multinationality: A meta-analysis, *Journal of Management*, 38: 502–530; W. P. Wan, 2005, Country resource environments, firm capabilities, and corporate diversification strategies, *Journal of Management Studies*, 42: 161–182.

4. M. A. Hitt, L. Tihanyi, T. Miller, & B. Connelly, 2006, International diversification: Antecedents, outcomes and moderators, *Journal of Management*, 32: 831–867; M. Wright, I. Filatotchev, R. E. Hoskisson, & M. W. Peng, 2005, Strategy research in emerging economies: Challenging the conventional wisdom, *Journal of Management Studies*, 42: 1–30.

5. M. Javidan, R. M. Steers, & M. A. Hitt (eds.), 2007, *The Global Mindset: Advances in International Management*, Vol. 19, Amsterdam: Elsevier Science; T. M. Begley & D. P. Boyd, 2003, The need for a corporate global mind-set, *MIT Sloan Management Review*, 44(2): 25–32; A. K. Gupta & V. Govindarajan, 2002, Cultivating a global mindset, *Academy of Management Executive*, 16(1): 116–126.

6. V. Mok & G. Yeung, 2005, Employee motivation, external orientation and the technical efficiency of foreign-financed firms in China: A stochastic frontier analysis, *Managerial and Decision Economics*, 26(3): 175–190; R. L. Mecham III, 2003, Success for the new global manager: What you need to know to work across distances, countries, and cultures, *Leadership Quarterly*, 14: 347–352; A. McWilliams, D. D. Van Fleet, & P. M. Wright, 2001, Strategic management of human resources for global competitive advantage, *Journal of Business Strategies*, 18(1): 1–24.

7. C. Camison & A. Villar-Lopez, 2010, Effect of SMEs' international experience on foreign intensity and economic performance: The mediating role of internationally exploitable assets and competitive strategy, *Journal of Small Business Management*, 48: 116–151; S. Tallman, 2001, Global strategic management, in M. A. Hitt, R. E. Freeman, & J. S. Harrison (eds.), *Handbook of Strategic Management*, Oxford, UK: Blackwell Publishers, 462–490; C. W. L. Hill, 2000, *International Business: Competing in the Global Marketplace*, 3rd ed., Boston: McGraw-Hill/Irwin, 378–380.

8. Global Sherba, BRIC countries.

9. V. Govindarajan & R. Ramamurthi, 2011, Reverse innovation, emerging markets and global strategy, *Global Strategy Journal*, 1: 191–205.

10. 2006, Setting up shop in India, *Economist*, November 4, 73–74.

11 P. Cappelli, H. Singh, J. Singh, & M. Useem, 2010, The India way: Lessons for the U.S., *Academy of Management Perspectives*, 24(2): 6–24.

12 2005, EU economy: Building transatlantic bridges, *EIU Views Wire*, May 27; T. Aeppel, 2003, Manufacturers spent much less abroad last year—U.S. firms cut investing overseas by estimated 37 percent; the "high-wage paradox," *Wall Street Journal*, May 9, A8; J. P. Quinlan, 1998, Europe, not Asia, is corporate America's key market, *Wall Street Journal*, January 12, A20.

13 J. R. Ramsey, J. N. Leonel, G. Z. Gomes, & P. R. R. Monteiro, 2011, Cultural intelligence's influence on international business travelers' stress, *Cross Cultural Management*, 18: 21–37; W. Kuemmerle, 2001, Go global—or not? *Harvard Business Review*, 79(6): 37–49.

14 A. Di Minin & M. Bianchi, 2011, Safe nests in global nets: Internationalization and appropriability of R&D in wireless telecom, *Journal of International Business Studies*, 42: 910–934.

15 D. Dunlap-Hinkler, M. Kotabe, & R. Mudambi, 2010, A story of breakthrough versus incremental innovation: Corporate entrepreneurship in the global pharmaceutical industry, *Strategic Entrepreneurship Journal*, 4: 106–127.

16 D. G. Sirmon, M. A. Hitt, R. D. Sirmon, & B. A. Gilbert, 2011, Resource orchestration to create competitive advantage: Breadth, depth, and life cycle effects, *Journal of Management*, 37: 1390–1412; R. Vernon, 1996, International investment and international trade in the product cycle, *Quarterly Journal of Economics*, 80: 190–207.

17 J. M.-S. Cheng, C. Blankson, P. C. S. Wu, & S. S. M. Chen, 2005, A stage model of an international brand development: The perspectives of manufacturers from two newly industrialized economies—South Korea and Taiwan, *Industrial Marketing Management*, 34: 504–514; S. Andersson, 2004, Internationalization in different industrial contexts, *Journal of Business Venturing*, 19: 851–875.

18 C. A. Lin, 2011, The advantage of foreignness in innovation, *Strategic Management, Journal*, 32: 1232–1242; F. Jiang, 2005, Driving forces of international pharmaceutical firms' FDI into China, *Journal of Business Research*, 22(1): 21–39; W. Shan & J. Song, 1997, Foreign direct investment and the sourcing of technological advantage: Evidence from the biotechnology industry, *Journal of International Business Studies*, 28: 267–284.

19 S.-J. Chang & J. H. Rhee, 2011, Rapid R&D expansion and firm performance, *Journal of International Business Studies*, 4: 979–994.

20 2012, Company overview, Gruma Corporation, http://www.gruma.com, March 9; G. Smith, 2007, Wrapping the globe in tortillas, *Business Week*, February 26, 54.

21 K. J. Petersen, R. B. Handfield, & G. L. Ragatz, 2005, Supplier integration into new product development: Coordinating product, process and supply chain design, *Journal of Operations Management*, 23: 371–388; S. A. J. Mauri & A. V. Phatak, 2001, Global integration as inter-area product flows: The internalization of ownership and location factors influencing product flows across MNC units, *Management International Review*, 41(3): 233–249.

22 S. Zaheer & L. Nachum, Sense of place: From Location resources to MNE locational capital, *Global Strategy Journal*, 1: 96–108.

23 2012, Shanghai Automotive Industry Corp., http://www.saicgroup.com, March 9.

24 Y. Fang, G.-L. F. Jiang, S. Makino, & P. W. Beamish, 2010, Multinational firm knowledge, use of expatriates, and foreign subsidiary performance, *Journal of Management Studies*, 47: 27–54; A. Inkpen & K. Ramaswamy, 2006, *Global Strategy: Creating and Sustaining Advantage across Borders*, New York: Oxford University Press.

25 R. Salomon & B. Jin, 2010, Do leading or lagging firms learn more from exporting, *Strategic Management Journal*, 31: 1088–1113; Hitt, Tihanyi, Miller, & Connelly, International diversification.

26 S. Tallman & A. S. Chacar, 2011, Knowledge accumulation and dissemination in MNEs: A practice-based framework, *Journal of Management Studies*, 48: 278–304; D. Rigby & C. Zook, 2003, Open-market innovation, *Harvard Business Review*, 89(10): 80–89.

27 Y. Zhang, H. Li, Y. Li, & L.-A. Zhou, 2010, FDI spillovers in an emerging market: The role of foreign firms' country of origin diversity and domestic firms' absorptive capacity, *Strategic Management Journal*, 31: 969–989.

28 J. Alcacer & W. Chung, 2011, Benefiting from location: Knowledge retrieval, *Global Strategy Journal*, 1: 233–236; J. Bernstein & D. Weinstein, 2002, Do endowments predict the location of production? Evidence from national and international data, *Journal of International Economics*, 56(1): 55–76.

29 R. Tahir & J. Larimo, 2004, Understanding the location strategies of the European firms in Asian countries, *Journal of American Academy of Business*, 5: 102–110.

30 2012, Company Portrait, Deutsche Post DHL, http://www.dhl.com, March 9.

31 H. Zhu, L. Eden, S. R. Miller, D. E. Thomas, & P. Fields, 2012, Host-country location decisions of early movers and latecomers: The role of local density and experiential learning, *International Business Review*, 21: 145–155.

32 O. Shenkar, 2012, Cultural distance revisited: Towards a more rigorous conceptualization and measurement of cultural differences, *Journal of International Business Studies*, 43: 1–11; D. A. Waldman, A. S. de Luque, N. Washburn, R. J. House, et al., 2006, Cultural and leadership predictors of corporate social responsibility values of top management: A GLOBE study of 15 countries, *Journal of International Business Studies*, 37: 823–837.

33 D. Xu, Y. Pan, & P. W. Beamish, 2004, The effect of regulative and normative distances on MNE ownership and expatriate strategies, *Management International Review*, 44(3): 285–307.

34 W. P. Wan & R. E. Hoskisson, 2003, Home country environments, corporate diversification strategies and firm performance, *Academy of Management Journal*, 46: 27–45; J. M. Geringer, S. Tallman, & D. M. Olsen, 2000, Product and international diversification among Japanese multinational firms, *Strategic Management Journal*, 21: 51–80.

35 H. P. Bowen & M. F. Wiersema, 2005, Foreign-based competition and corporate diversification strategy, *Strategic Management Journal*, 26: 1153–1171.

36 D. Degravel, 2011, Managing organizational capabilities: The keystone step, *Journal of Strategy and Management*, 4: 251–274; S. Tallman & K. Fladmoe-Lindquist, 2002, Internationalization, globalization, and capability-based strategy, *California Management Review*, 45(1): 116–135;

D. A. Griffith & M. G. Harvey, 2001, A resource perspective of global dynamic capabilities, *Journal of International Business Studies*, 32: 597–606.

[37] A. Rugman & A. Verbeke, 2004, A perspective on regional and global strategies of multinational enterprises, *Journal of International Business Studies*, 35: 3–18; B. Elango, 2004, Geographic scope of operations by multinational companies: An exploratory study of regional and global strategies, *European Management Journal*, 22(4): 431–441.

[38] C. Pantzalis, 2001, Does location matter? An empirical analysis of geographic scope and MNC market valuation, *Journal of International Business Studies*, 32: 133–155.

[39] J.-L. Arregle, T. Miller, M. A. Hitt, & P. W. Beamish, 2012, Do regions matter? An integrated institutional and semi-globalization perspective on the internationalization of MNEs, *Strategic Management Journal*, in press.

[40] R. D. Ludema, 2002, Increasing returns, multinationals and geography of preferential trade agreements, *Journal of International Economics*, 56: 329–358.

[41] 2006, Other EU candidates: A very long engagement, *Economist*, November 11: 56–57.

[42] 2007, Office of the United States Trade Representative, Central America-Dominican Republic Free Trade agreement, http://www.ustr.gov/Trade_Agreements, February 20.

[43] C. M. Chan, S. Makino, & T. Isobe, 2010, Does subnational region matter? Foreign affiliate performance in the United States and China, *Strategic Management Journal*, 31: 1226–1243.

[44] W. Chung & J. Song, 2004, Sequential investment, firm motives, and agglomeration of Japanese electronics firms in the United States, *Journal of Economics and Management Strategy*, 13: 539–560; D. Xu & O. Shenkar, 2002, Institutional distance and the multinational enterprise, *Academy of Management Review*, 27(4): 608–618.

[45] R. G. Bell, I. Filatotchev, & A. A. Rasheed, 2012, The liability of foreignness in capital markets: Sources and remedies, *Journal of International Business Studies*, 43: 107–122; L. Eden & S. Miller, 2004, Distance matters: Liability of foreignness, institutional distance and ownership strategy, in M. Hitt & J. L. Cheng (eds.), *Advances in International Management*. Oxford, UK: JAI/Elsevier, 187–221.

[46] G. A. Shinkle & A. P. Kriauciunas, 2012, The impact of current and founding institutions on the strength of competitive aspirations in transition economies, *Strategic Management Journal*, 33: 448–458; J. W. Spencer, T. P. Murtha, & S. A. Lenway, 2005, How governments matter to new industry creation, *Academy of Management Review*, 30: 321–337.

[47] L. Nachum, 2010, When is foreignness an asset or a liability? Explaining the performance differential between foreign and local firms, *Journal of Management*, 36: 714–739; P. Ghemawat, 2001, Distance still matters: The hard reality of global expansion, *Harvard Business Review*, 79(8): 137–147.

[48] 2006, Global retailing: Trouble at till, *Economist*, November 4, 18.

[49] A. Rugman & R. Hodgetts, 2001, The end of global strategy, *European Management Journal*, 19(4): 333–343.

[50] J. Birkinshaw, 2001, Strategies for managing internal competition, *California Management Review*, 44(1): 21–38.

[51] L. Li, 2005, Is regional strategy more effective than global strategy in the U.S. service industries? *Management International Review*, 45: 37–57; B. B. Alred & K. S. Swan, 2004, Global versus multidomestic: Culture's consequences on innovation, *Management International Review*, 44: 81–105.

[52] Y. Luo, 2001, Determinants of local responsiveness: Perspectives from foreign subsidiaries in an emerging market, *Journal of Management*, 27: 451–477.

[53] Inkpen & Ramaswamy, *Global Strategy*.

[54] O. Gadiesh, 2004, Risk-proofing your brand, *European Business Forum*, summer, 82.

[55] C. A. Bartlett & S. Ghoshal, 1989, *Managing across Borders: The Transnational Solution*, Boston: Harvard Business School Press.

[56] E. Wood, L. Khavul, E. Perez-Nordtvedt, S. Prakhya, R. V. Dabrowski, & C. Zheng, 2011, Strategic commitment and timing of internationalization from emerging markets: Evidence from China, India, Mexico and South Africa, *Journal of Small Business Management*, 49: 252–282; L. Li, 2005, Is regional strategy more effective than global strategy in the U.S. service industries? *Management International Review*, 45: 37–57.

[57] I. C. MacMillan, A. B. van Putten, & R. G. McGrath, 2003, Global gamesmanship, *Harvard Business Review*, 81(5): 62–71.

[58] H. D. Hopkins, 2003, The response strategies of dominant US firms to Japanese challengers, *Journal of Management*, 29: 5–25; S. Massini, A. Y. Lewin, T. Numagami, & A. Pettigrew, 2002, The evolution of organizational routines among large Western and Japanese firms, *Research Policy*, 31(8,9): 1333–1348; M. W. Peng, S. H. Lee, & J. J. Tan, 2001, The keiretsu in Asia: Implications for multilevel theories of competitive advantage, *Journal of International Management*, 7: 253–276; A. Bhappu, 2000, The Japanese family: An institutional logic for Japanese corporate networks and Japanese management, *Academy of Management Review*, 25: 409–415.

[59] 2012, Yearly summary—2011, Ikea, http://www.ikea.com, March 10.

[60] A. Yaprak, 2002, Globalization: Strategies to build a great global firm in the new economy, *Thunderbird International Business Review*, 44(2): 297–302; D. G. McKendrick, 2001, Global strategy and population level learning: The case of hard disk drives, *Strategic Management Journal*, 22: 307–334.

[61] M. Zellmer-Bruhn & C. Gibson, 2006, Multinational organization context: Implications for team learning and performance, *Academy of Management Journal*, 49: 501–518.

[62] 2012, Kyowa, http://www.kyowa.co.jp/english/, March 10.

[63] T. W. Malnight, 2002, Emerging structural patterns within multinational corporations: Toward process-based structures, *Academy of Management Journal*, 44: 1187–1210.

[64] Inkpen & Ramaswamy, *Global Strategy*.

[65] Bartlett & Ghoshal, *Managing across Borders*.

[66] J. Xia, 2011, Mutual dependence, partner substitutability, and repeated partnership: The survival of cross-border alliances, *Strategic Management Journal*, 32: 229–253; T. B. Lawrence, E. A. Morse, & S. W. Fowler, 2005, Managing your portfolio of connections, *MIT Sloan Management Review*, 46(2): 59–65.

[67] A. Abbott & K. Banerji, 2003, Strategic flexibility and firm performance: The case of US based transnational corporations, *Global Journal of Flexible Systems Management*, 4(1/2): 1–7; J. Child & Y. Van,

2001, National and transnational effects in international business: Indications from Sino-foreign joint ventures, *Management International Review*, 41(1): 53–75.

68 Inkpen & Ramaswamy, *Global Strategy*, 69.

69 J. Cantwell & R. Mudambi, 2005, MNE competence-creating subsidiary mandates, *Strategic Management Journal*, 26: 1109–1128.

70 Inkpen & Ramaswamy, *Global Strategy*; J. M. Birkinshaw & A. J. Morrison, 1995, Configurations of strategy and structure in subsidiaries of multinational corporations, *Journal of International Business Studies*, 26: 729–754.

71 R. J. Kramer, 1999, Organizing for global competitiveness: The corporate headquarters design, *Chief Executive Digest*, 3(2): 23–28.

72 T. S. Frost, J. M. Birkinshaw, & P. C. Ensign, 2002, Centers of excellence in multinational corporations, *Strategic Management Journal*, 23: 997–1018.

73 Inkpen & Ramaswamy, *Global Strategy*.

74 2012, Bausch & Lomb, http://www.bausch.com, March 10.

75 J. Gimeno, R. E. Hoskisson, B. D. Beal, & W. P. Wan, 2005, Explaining the clustering of international expansion moves: A critical test in the U.S. telecommunications industry, *Academy of Management Journal*, 48: 297–319.

76 M. E. Porter, 1990, *The Competitive Advantage of Nations*, New York: The Free Press.

77 Ibid., 84.

78 Ibid., 89.

79 C. Storz, 2008, Dynamics in innovation systems: Evidence from Japan's game software industry, *Research Policy*, 37: 1480–1491.

80 2012, The success story of Airbus, http://www.airbus.com/company/history, March 10.

81 J.C. Mahlich, 2010, Patents and performance in the Japanese pharmaceutical industry: An institution-based view, *Asia Pacific Journal of Management*, 27: 99–113; L. Nachum, 2001, The impact of home countries on the competitiveness of advertising TNCs, *Management International Review*, 41(1): 77–98.

82 H. J. Sapienza, E. Autio, G. George, & S. A. Zahra, 2006, A capabilities perspective on the effects of early internationalization on firm survival and growth, *Academy of Management Review*, 31: 914–933.

83 J.-F. Hennart, 2011, A theoretical assessment of the empirical literature on the impact of multinationality on performance, *Global Strategy Journal*, 1: 135–151.

84 C. Lages, C. R. Lages, & L. F. Lages, 2005, The RELQUAL scale: A measure of relationship quality in export market ventures, *Journal of Business Research*, 58: 1040–1048; R. Isaak, 2002, Using trading firms to export: What can the French experience teach us? *Academy of Management Executive*, 16(4): 155–156.

85 Y. Chui, 2002, The structure of the multinational firm: The role of ownership characteristics and technology transfer, *International Journal of Management*, 19(3): 472–477.

86 Luo, Determinants of local responsiveness.

87 J. M. Shaver, 2011, The benefits of geographic sales diversification: How exporting facilitates capital investment, *Strategic Management Journal*, 32: 1046–1060; M. A. Raymond, J. Kim, & A. T. Shao, 2001, Export strategy and performance: A comparison of exporters in a developed market and an

emerging market, *Journal of Global Marketing*, 15(2): 5–29.

88 A. Haahti, V. Madupu, U. Yavas, & E. Babakus, 2005, Cooperative strategy, knowledge intensity and export performance of small and medium sized enterprises, *Journal of World Business*, 40(2): 124–138.

89 P. Westhead, M. Wright, & D. Ucbasaran, 2001, The internationalization of new and small firms: A resource-based view, *Journal of Business Venturing*, 16: 333–358.

90 D. Kline, 2003, Sharing the corporate crown jewels, *MIT Sloan Management Review*, 44(3): 83–88; M. A. Hitt & R. D. Ireland, 2000, The intersection of entrepreneurship and strategic management research, in D. L. Sexton & H. Landstrom (eds.), *Handbook of Entrepreneurship*, Oxford, UK: Blackwell Publishers, 45–63.

91 A. Arora & A. Fosfuri, 2000, Wholly owned subsidiary versus technology licensing in the worldwide chemical industry, *Journal of International Business Studies*, 31: 555–572.

92 N. Byrnes & F. Balfour, 2009, Philip Morris unbound, *BusinessWeek*, May 4, 38–42; 2007, The China National Tobacco Corporation and Philip Morris International announce the establishment of a long-term strategic cooperative partnership, http://www.altria.com/media, February 22.

93 Y. J. Kim, 2005, The impact of firm and industry characteristics on technology licensing, *S.A.M. Advanced Management Journal*, 70(1): 42–49.

94 2012, Komatsu, company information: Products and applications, http://www.komatsu.com, March 10; C. A. Bartlett & S. Rangan, 1992, Komatsu limited, in C. A. Bartlett & S. Ghoshal (eds.), *Transnational Management: Text, Cases and Readings in Cross-Border Management*, Homewood, IL: Irwin, 311–326.

95 J. J. Reuer & T. W. Tong, 2005, Real options in international joint ventures, *Journal of Management*, 31: 403–423; B. Petersen, D. E. Welch, & L. S. Welch, 2000, Creating meaningful switching options in international operations, *Long Range Planning*, 33(5): 688–705.

96 S.H. Wen & C.-M. Chuang, 2010, To teach or to compete? A strategic dilemma of knowledge owners in international alliances, *Asia Pacific Journal of Management*, 27: 697–726; R. Larsson, K. R. Brousseau, M. J. Driver, & M. Homqvist, 2003, International growth through cooperation: Brand-driven strategies, leadership, and career development in Sweden, *Academy of Management Executive*, 17(1): 7–21.

97 M. A. Hitt, D. Ahlstrom, M. T. Dacin, E. Levitas, & L. Svobodina, 2004, The institutional effects on strategic alliance partner selection in transition economies: China versus Russia, *Organization Science*, 15: 173–185; M. Peng, 2001, The resource-based view and international business, *Journal of Management*, 27: 803–829.

98 J. W. Lu & P. W. Beamish, 2006, Partnering strategies and performance of SMEs' international joint ventures, *Journal of Business Venturing*, 21: 461–480.

99 W. Griffith, 2008, McDonald's has a big appetite for China, MSNBC, http://www.msnbc.msn.com, August 15; G. Fairclough & G. A. Fowler, 2006, Drive-through tips for China, *Wall Street Journal*, June 20, B1.

100 M. Bener & K.W. Glaister, 2010, Determinants of performance in international joint ventures, *Journal of Strategy and Management*, 3: 188–214.

101 F. J. Contractor, J. A. Woodley, & A. Piepenbrink, 2011, How tight an embrace? Choosing the optimal degree of partner interaction in alliances based on risk, technology characteristics and agreement provisions, *Global Strategy Journal*, 1: 67–85; A. T. Mohr & J. F. Puck, 2005, Managing functional diversity to improve the performance of international joint ventures, *Long Range Planning*, 38(2): 163–182.

102 M. W. Peng & O. Shenkar, 2002, Joint venture dissolution as corporate divorce, *Academy of Management Executive*, 16(2): 92–105; O. Shenkar & A. Van, 2002, Failure as a consequence of partner politics: Learning from the life and death of an international cooperative venture, *Human Relations*, 55: 565–601.

103 J. A. Robins, S. Tallman, & K. Fladmoe-Lindquist, 2002, Autonomy and dependence of international cooperative ventures: An exploration of the strategic performance of U.S. ventures in Mexico, *Strategic Management Journal*, 23(10): 881–901; Y. Gong, O. Shenkar, Y. Luo, & M.-K. Nyaw, 2001, Role conflict and ambiguity of CEOs in international joint ventures: A transaction cost perspective, *Journal of Applied Psychology*, 86: 764–773.

104 P. K. Jagersma, 2005, Cross-border alliances: Advice from the executive suite, *Journal of Business Strategy*, 26(1): 41–50; D. C. Hambrick, J. Li, K. Xin, & A. S. Tsui, 2001, Compositional gaps and downward spirals in international joint venture management groups, *Strategic Management Journal*, 22: 1033–1053; M. T. Dacin, M. A. Hitt, & E. Levitas, 1997, Selecting partners for successful international alliances: Examination of U.S. and Korean firms, *Journal of World Business*, 32: 3–16.

105 L. Huff & L. Kelley, 2003, Levels of organizational trust in individualist versus collectivist societies: A seven-nation study, *Organization Science*, 14(1): 81–90; A. Arino, J. de la Torre, & P. S. Ring, 2001, Relational quality: Managing trust in corporate alliances, *California Management Review*, 44(1): 109–131.

106 D. Li, L. E. Eden, M. A. Hitt, & R. D. Ireland, 2008, Friends, acquaintances or strangers? Partner selection in R&D alliances, *Academy of Management Journal*, 51: 315–334; Y. Pan & D. K. Tse, 2000, The hierarchical model of market entry modes, *Journal of International Business Studies*, 31: 535–554;.

107 J. J. Reuer, 2005, Avoiding lemons in M&A deals, *MIT Sloan Management Review*, 46(3): 15–17; G. A. Knight & P. W. Liesch, 2002, Information internalisation in internationalising the firm, *Journal of Business Research*, 55(12): 981–995.

108 B. Aybar & A. Ficici, 2009, Cross-border acquisitions and firm value: An analysis of emerging-market multinationals, *Journal of International Business Studies*, 40: 1317–1338; J. H. Dyer, P. Kale, & H. Singh, 2004, When to ally and when to acquire, *Harvard Business Review*, 82(7): 108–117.

109 K. Shimizu, M. A. Hitt, D. Vaidyanath, & V. Pisano, 2004, Theoretical foundations of cross-border mergers and acquisitions: A review of current research and recommendations for the future. *Journal of International Management*, 10: 307–353; M. A. Hitt, J. S. Harrison, & R. D. Ireland, 2001, *Creating Value through Mergers and Acquisitions*, New York: Oxford University Press.

110 M. D. R. Chari & K. Chang, 2009, Determinants of the share of equity sought in cross-border acquisitions, *Journal of International Business Studies*, 40: 1277–1297; M. A. Hitt & V. Pisano, 2003, The

cross-border merger and acquisition strategy, *Management Research*, 1: 133–144.

111 J. Birkinshaw, H. Bresman, & R. Nobel, 2010, Knowledge transfer in international acquisitions: A retrospective, *Journal of International Business Studies*, 41: 21–26.

112 Y. Y. Chen & M. N. Young, 2010, Cross-border mergers and acquisitions by Chinese listed companies: A principal—principal perspective, *Asia Pacific Journal of Management*, 27: 523–539.

113 T. H. Reus & B. T. Lamont, 2009, The double-edged sword of cultural distance in international acquisitions, *Journal of International Business Studies*, 40: 1298–1316; P. Quah & S. Young, 2005, Post-acquisition management: A phases approach for cross-border M&As, *European Management Journal*, 23(1): 65–80.

114 S. R. Gubbi, P. S. Aulakh, S. Ray, M. B. Sarkar, & R. Chittoor, 2010, Do international acquisitions by emerging-economy firms create shareholder value? The case of Indian firms, *Journal of International Business Studies*, 41: 397–418.

115 A. H. L. Slangen, 2011, A communication-based theory of the choice between Greenfield and acquisition entry, *Journal of Management Studies*, 48: 1699–1726; K. E. Meyer, S. Estrin, S. K. Bhaumik, & M.W. Peng, 2009, Institutions, resources, and entry strategies in emerging economies, *Strategic Management Journal*, 30: 61–80.

116 2012, Walmart, Walmart de Mexico fact sheet, http://www.walmart.com/About us. March 11.

117 C. Bouquet, L. Hebert, & A. Delios, 2004, Foreign expansion in service industries: Separability and human capital intensity, *Journal of Business Research*, 57: 35–46.

118 B. Elango, 2005, The influence of plant characteristics on the entry mode choice of overseas firms, *Journal of Operations Management*, 23(1): 65–79.

119 R. Belderbos, 2003, Entry mode, organizational learning, and R&D in foreign affiliates: Evidence from Japanese firms, *Strategic Management Journal*, 34: 235–259.

120 J.-P. Roy, 2012, IJV partner trustworthy behavior: The role of host country governance and partner selection criteria, *Journal of Management Studies*, 49: 332–355; K. E. Meyer & H. V. Nguyen, 2005, Foreign investment strategies in subnational institutions in emerging markets: Evidence from Vietnam, *Journal of Management Studies*, 42: 63–93; J. Reuer, O. Shenkar, & R. Ragozzino, 2004, Mitigating risks in international mergers and acquisitions: The role of contingent payouts, *Journal of International Business Studies*, 35: 19–32.

121 S. J. Chang & P. Rosenzweig, 2001, The choice of entry mode in sequential foreign direct investment, *Strategic Management Journal*, 22: 747–776.

122 Roy, IJV partner trustworthy behavior; K. E. Myer, 2001, Institutions, transaction costs, and entry mode choice in Eastern Europe, *Journal of International Business Studies*, 32: 357–367.

123 S. Li, 2004, Why are property rights protections lacking in China? An institutional explanation, *California Management Review*, 46(3): 100–115; Y. Luo, 2001, Determinants of entry in an emerging economy: A multilevel approach, *Journal of Management Studies*, 38: 443–472.

124 A. Takeishi, 2001, Bridging inter- and intra-firm boundaries: Management of supplier involvement in automobile product development, *Strategic Management Journal*, 22: 403–433.

125 2012, Toyota increasing U.S. transmission production, Toyota, http://www.toyota.com, March 1; D. K Sobek II, A. C. Ward, & J. K. Liker, 1999, Toyota's principles of set-based concurrent engineering, *Sloan Management Review*, 40(2): 53–83.

126 A. H. Kirca. G. T. M. Hult, K. Roth, S. T. Cavusgil, M. Z. Perryy, M. B. Ardeniz, S. Z. Deligonul, J. A. Mena, W. A. Pollitte, J. J. Hoppner, J. C. Miller & R. C. White, 2011, Firm-specific assets, multinationality and financial performance: A meta-analytic review and theoretical integration, *Academy of Management Journal*, 54: 47–72; J. Hagedoorn & G. Dysters, 2002, External sources of innovative capabilities: The preference for strategic alliances or mergers and acquisitions, *Journal of Management Studies*, 39: 167–188.

127 J. E. Garten, 2005, A new threat to America, Inc., *Business Week*, July 25, 114; Hoskisson, Kim, Tihanyi, & White, A framework; S. J. Chang & J. Hong, 2002, How much does the business group matter in Korea? *Strategic Management Journal*, 23: 265–274.

128 K. Ito & E. L. Rose, 2010, The implicit return on domestic and international sales: An empirical analysis of US and Japanese firms, *Journal of International Business Studies*, 41: 1074–1089; Hitt, Tihanyi, Miller, & Connelly, International diversification.

129 M. F. Wiersema & H. P. Bowen, 2011, The relationship between international diversification and firm performance: Why it remains a puzzle, *Global Strategy Journal*, 1: 152–170; J. W. Lu & P. W. Beamish, 2004, International diversification and firm performance: The S-curve hypothesis, *Academy of Management Journal*, 47: 598–609.

130 S.-C. Chang & C.-F. Wang, 2007, The effect of product diversification strategies on the relationship between international diversification and firm performance, *Journal of World Business*, 42: 61–77; S. E. Christophe & H. Lee, 2005, What matters about internationalization: A market-based assessment, *Journal of Business Research*, 58: 536–543.

131 S. Li & S. Tallman, 2011, MNC strategies, exogenous shocks, and performance outcomes, *Strategic Management Journal*, 32: 1119–1127; J. M. Geringer, P. W. Beamish, & R. C. daCosta, 1989, Diversification strategy and internationalization: Implications for MNE performance, *Strategic Management Journal*, 10: 109–119.

132 S. A. Zahra, R. D. Ireland, & M. A. Hitt, 2000, International expansion by new venture firms: International diversity, mode of market entry, technological learning, and performance, *Academy of Management Journal*, 43: 925–950.

133 T. R. Holcomb & M. A. Hitt, 2007, Toward a model of strategic outsourcing, *Journal of Operations Management*, 25: 464–481; U. Andersson, M. Forsgren, & U. Holm, 2002, The strategic impact of external networks: Subsidiary performance and competence development in the multinational corporation, *Strategic Management Journal*, 23: 979–996; Malnight, Emerging structural patterns.

134 D. Farrell, 2005, Offshoring: Value creation through economic change, *Journal of Management Studies*, 42: 675–683; J. P. Doh, 2005, Offshore outsourcing: Implications for international business and strategic management theory and practice, *Journal of Management Studies*, 42: 695–704.

135 R. A. D'Aveni, G. B. Dagnino, & K. G. Smith, 2010, The age of temporary advantage, *Strategic Management Journal*, 31: 1371–1385.

136 J. Penner-Hahn & J. M. Shaver, 2005, Does international research and development increase patent output? An analysis of Japanese pharmaceutical firms, *Strategic Management Journal*, 26: 121–140; I. Zander & O. Solvell, 2000, Cross border innovation in the multinational corporation: A research agenda, *International Studies of Management and Organization*, 30(2): 44–67.

137 L. Tihanyi, R. A. Johnson, R. E. Hoskisson, & M. A. Hitt, 2003, Institutional ownership differences and international diversification: The effects of board of directors and technological opportunity, *Academy of Management Journal*, 46: 195–211.

138 Penner-Hahn & Shaver, Does international research increase patent output?

139 B. Ambos, 2005, Foreign direct investment in industrial research and development: A study of German MNCs, *Research Policy*, 34: 395–410; F. Bradley & M. Gannon, 2000, Does the firm's technology and marketing profile affect foreign market entry? *Journal of International Marketing*, 8(4): 12–36.

140 S. Makino, P. W. Beamish, & N. B. Zhao, 2004, The characteristics and performance of Japanese FDI in less developed and developed countries, *Journal of World Business*, 39(4): 377–392.

141 Hitt, Tihanyi, Miller, & Connelly, International diversification, 854.

142 B. Cassiman & E. Golovko, 2011, Innovation and internationalization through exports, *Journal of International Business Studies*, 42: 56–75; O. E. M. Janne, 2002, The emergence of corporate integrated innovation systems across regions: The case of the chemical and pharmaceutical industry in Germany, the UK and Belgium, *Journal of International Management*, 8: 97–119; N. J. Foss & T. Pedersen, 2002, Transferring knowledge in MNCs: The role of sources of subsidiary knowledge and organizational context, *Journal of International Management*, 8: 49–67.

143 Y. Paik, 2005, Risk management of strategic alliances and acquisitions between western MNCs and companies in central Europe, *Thunderbird International Business Review*, 47(4): 489–511; A. Delios & W. J. Henisz, 2003, Policy uncertainty and the sequence of entry by Japanese firms, 1980–1998, *Journal of International Business Studies*, 34: 227–241.

144 C. J. P. Chen, Y. Ding, & C. Kim, 2010, High-level politically connected firms, corruption, and analysts forecast accuracy around the world, *Journal of International Business Studies*, 41: 1505–1524.

145 2011, Demands for better government must be heeded, Transparency International, http://cpi.transparency.org, accessed March 11, 2012.

146 G. L. F. Holburn & B. A. Zelner, 2010, Political capabilities, political risk, and international investment strategy: Evidence from the global electric power generation industry, *Strategic Management Journal*, 31: 1290–1315; J. G. Frynas, K. Mellahi, & G. A. Pigman, 2006, First mover advantages in international business and firm-specific political resources, *Strategic Management Journal*, 27: 321–345.

147 T. Vestring, T. Rouse, & U. Reinert, 2005, Hedging your offshoring bets, *MIT Sloan Management Review*, 46(3): 26–29; L. L. Jacque & P. M. Vaaler, 2001, The international control conundrum with exchange risk: An EVA framework, *Journal of International Business Studies*, 32: 813–832.

148 T. G. Andrews & N. Chompusri, 2005, Temporal dynamics of crossvergence: Institutionalizing MNC

integration strategies in post-crisis ASEAN, *Asia Pacific Journal of Management*, 22(1): 5–22; S. Mudd, R. Grosse, & J. Mathis, 2002, Dealing with financial crises in emerging markets, *Thunderbird International Business Review*, 44(3): 399–430.

[149] Inkpen & Ramaswamy, *Global Strategy*.

[150] R. M. Holmes, T. Miller, M. A. Hitt, & M. P. Salmador, 2012, The interrelationships among informal institutions, formal institutions and inward foreign direct investment, *Journal of Management*, in press.

[151] S. M. Puffer & D. J. McCarthy, 2011, Two decades of Russian business and management research: An institutional theory perspective, *Academy of Management Perspectives*, 25(2): 21–36; S. M. Puffer, D. J. McCarthy, & M. Boisot, 2010, Entrepreneurship in Russia and China: The impact of formal institutional voids, *Entrepreneurship Theory and Practice*, 34: 441–467.

[152] C. Schwens, J. Eiche, & R. Kabst, 2011, *Journal of Management Studies*, 48: 330–351.

[153] B. Batjargal, M. A. Hitt, A. S. Tsui, J.-L. Arregle, J. W. Webb, & T. Miller, 2013, Institutional polycentricism, entrepreneurs' social networks and new venture growth, *Academy of Management Journal*, in press; B. Batjargal, 2010, The effects of network's structural holes, polycentric institutions, and new venture growth in China and Russia, *Strategic Entrepreneurship Journal*, 4: 146–163.

[154] H. Berry, M. F. Guillen, & N. Zhou, 2010, In institution approach to cross-national distance, *Journal of International Business Studies*, 41: 1460–1480; A. H. L. Slangen & S. Beugelsdijk, 2010, The impact of institutional hazards on foreign multinational activity: A contingency perspective, *Journal of International Business Studies*, 41: 980–995.

[155] Y. Li, L. Li, Y. Liu, & L. Wang, 2005, Linking management control systems with product development and process decisions to cope with environment complexity, *International Journal of Production Research*, 43: 2577–2591; J. Child, L. Chung, & H. Davies, 2003, The performance of cross-border units in China: A test of natural selection, strategic choice and contingency theories, *Journal of International Business Studies*, 34: 242–254.

[156] Y.-H. Chiu, 2003, The impact of conglomerate firm diversification on corporate performance: An empirical study in Taiwan, *International Journal of Management*, 19: 231–237; Y. Luo, 2003, Market-seeking MNEs in an emerging market: How parent-subsidiary links shape overseas success, *Journal of International Business Studies*, 34: 290–309.

[157] Wan & Hoskisson, Home country environments; M. A. Hitt, R. E. Hoskisson, & H. Kim, 1997, International diversification: Effects on innovation and firm performance in product-diversified firms, *Academy of Management Journal*, 40: 767–798;

S. Tallman & J. Li, 1996, Effects of international diversity and product diversity on the performance of multinational firms, *Academy of Management Journal*, 39: 179–196.

[158] P. Scott & P. T. Gibbons, 2011, Emerging threats for MNC subsidiaries and the cycle of decline, *Journal of Business Strategy*, 32: 34–41; B. Shimoni & H. Bergmann, 2006, Managing in a changing world: From multiculturalism to hybridization—the production of hybrid management cultures in Israel, Thailand, and Mexico, *Academy of Management Perspectives*, 20(3): 76–89;.

[159] Holmes, Miller, Hitt & Salmador, the interrelationships between informal institutions, formal institutions and inward foreign direct investments; I. Bjorkman, W. Barner-Rasmussen, & L. Li, 2004, Managing knowledge transfer in MNCs: The impact of headquarters control mechanisms, *Journal of International Business Studies*, 35: 443–455.

[160] M.-J. Chen & D. Miller, 2010, West meets east: Toward an ambicultural approach to management, *Academy of Management Perspectives*, 24: 17–24.

[161] I. M. Manev & W. B. Stevenson, 2001, Nationality, cultural distance, and expatriate status: Effects on the managerial network in a multinational enterprise, *Journal of International Business Studies*, 32: 285–303.

[162] P. S. Barr & M. A. Glynn, 2004, Cultural variations in strategic issue interpretation: Relating cultural uncertainty avoidance to controllability in discriminating threat and opportunity, *Strategic Management Journal*, 25: 59–67; D. E. Thomas & R. Grosse, 2001, Country-of-origin determinants of foreign direct investment in an emerging market: The case of Mexico, *Journal of International Management*, 7: 59–79.

[163] 2012, General Motors to take 7% of Peugeot in strategic alliance, *The Economic Times*, http://www.economictimes.com, February 29; J Addison, 2011, Ford and Toyota strategic alliance for hybrid trucks and SUVs, *Clean Tech Blog*, http://www.cleantechblog.com, August 23.

[164] D. S. Elenkov, W. Judge, & P. Wright, 2005, Strategic leadership and executive innovation influence: An international multi-cluster comparative study, *Strategic Management Journal*, 26: 665–682; M. Carpenter & J. Fredrickson, 2001, Top management teams, global strategic posture, and the moderating role of uncertainty, *Academy of Management Journal*, 44: 533–545; S. Finkelstein & D. C. Hambrick, 1996, *Strategic Leadership: Top Executives and Their Effects on Organizations*, St. Paul, MN: West Publishing Co.

[165] E. Golovko & G. Valenti, 2011, Exploring the complementarity between innovation and export for SMEs' growth, *Journal of International Business Studies*, 42: 362–380; Hitt, Hoskisson, & Kim, International diversification.

PART 4

MONITORING AND CREATING ENTREPRENEURIAL OPPORTUNITIES

CHAPTER 11 Corporate Governance   320
CHAPTER 12 Strategic Entrepreneurship   351
CHAPTER 13 Strategic Flexibility and Real Options Analysis   372

Chapter **11**

CORPORATE GOVERNANCE

KNOWLEDGE OBJECTIVES

Studying this chapter should provide you with the strategic management knowledge needed to:

1. Define corporate governance and explain why it is used to monitor and control managers' strategic decisions.

2. Explain how ownership came to be separated from managerial control in the modern corporation.

3. Define an agency relationship and managerial opportunism and describe their strategic implications.

4. Explain how three internal governance mechanisms—ownership concentration, the board of directors, and executive compensation—are used to monitor and control managerial decisions.

5. Discuss trends among the three types of compensation executives receive and their effects on strategic decisions.

6. Describe how the external corporate governance mechanism—the market for corporate control—acts as a restraint on top-level managers' strategic decisions.

7. Discuss the use of corporate governance in international settings, in particular in Germany and Japan.

8. Describe how corporate governance fosters ethical strategic decisions and the importance of such behaviors on the part of top-level executives.

Corporate governance is an increasingly important part of the strategic management process.[1] If the board of directors makes the wrong decision in compensating the firm's key strategic leader, the CEO, the whole firm suffers, as do its shareholders. Compensation is used to motivate CEOs to act in the best interests of the firm—in particular, the shareholders. When they do, the firm's value should increase.

What are a CEO's actions worth? The amount of compensation paid to CEOs suggests that they are worth a significant amount in the United States. While some critics argue that U.S. CEOs are paid too much,[2] the hefty increases in their compensation in recent years ostensibly have come from linking their pay to their firms' performance, and until recently, U.S. firms performed better than many firms in other countries. Research suggests that CEOs receive excessive compensation when corporate governance is the weakest.[3] The use of stock options, in particular, may have been abused by some boards because of the excessive amount of options awarded to CEOs and a tendency to re-price them at a lower level whenever the stock price falls.[4] However, although there are governance concerns about repricing, research also notes that some repricing can be beneficial in a steep downturn to maintain appropriate incentive for maintaining competitive innovation and performance.[5]

Corporate governance is the set of mechanisms used to manage the relationships among stakeholders and to determine and control the strategic direction and performance of organizations.[6] At its core, corporate governance is concerned with ensuring that strategic decisions are made effectively.[7] Governance can also be thought of as a means corporations use to establish effective relationships between parties (such as the firm's owners and its top-level managers) whose interests may be in conflict. Thus, corporate governance reflects and enforces the company's values.[8] In modern corporations—especially those in the United States and the United Kingdom—a primary objective of corporate governance is to ensure that the interests of top-level managers are aligned with the interests of the shareholders. Corporate governance involves oversight in areas in which owners, managers, and members of boards of directors may have conflicts of interest. These areas include the election of directors, the general supervision of CEO pay and more focused supervision of director pay, and the corporation's overall structure and strategic direction.[9] The primary goal is to ensure that the firm performs well and creates value for the shareholders.

Corporate governance has been emphasized in recent years because corporate governance mechanisms occasionally fail to adequately monitor and control top-level managers' decisions, as evidenced in scandals such as those at Enron and more recently the financial crisis and associated deep recession. This situation has resulted in changes in governance mechanisms in corporations throughout the world, especially with respect to efforts intended to improve the performance of boards of directors.[10] These changes often cause confusion about the proper role of the board. Some boards are only seeking to comply with the regulations, whereas others are making fundamental changes in the way they govern. A second and more positive reason for this interest is that evidence suggests that a well-functioning corporate governance and control system can create a competitive advantage for a firm.[11] For example, one governance mechanism—the board of directors—has been suggested to be rapidly evolving into a major strategic force in U.S. business firms.[12] Thus, in this chapter, we describe actions designed to implement strategies that focus on monitoring and controlling mechanisms, which can help to ensure that top-level managerial actions contribute to the firm's ability to create value and earn above-average returns.

Effective corporate governance is also of interest to nations.[13] As stated by one scholar, "Every country wants the firms that operate within its borders to flourish and grow in such ways as to provide employment, wealth, and satisfaction, not only to improve standards of living materially but also to enhance social cohesion. These aspirations cannot be met unless those firms are competitive internationally in a sustained way, and it is this medium- and long-term perspective that makes good corporate governance so vital."[14]

Corporate governance, then, reflects company standards, which in turn collectively reflect societal standards.[15] In many corporations, shareholders hold top-level managers accountable for their decisions and the results they generate. As with these firms and their boards, nations that effectively govern their corporations may gain a competitive advantage over rival countries. In a range of countries, but especially in the United States and the United Kingdom, the fundamental goal of business organizations is to maximize shareholder value.[16] Traditionally, shareholders are treated as the firm's key stakeholders because they are the company's legal owners. The firm's owners expect top-level managers and others influencing the corporation's actions (for example, the board of directors) to make decisions that will result in the maximization of the company's value and, hence, of the owners' wealth.

In the first section of this chapter, we describe the relationship providing the foundation on which the corporation is built: that between owners and managers. The majority of this chapter is used to explain various mechanisms owners use to govern managers and to ensure that they comply with their responsibility to maximize shareholder value.

The modern corporation uses three internal governance mechanisms and a single external one (see Table 11.1). The three internal governance mechanisms we describe in this chapter are (1) ownership concentration, as represented by types of shareholders and their different incentives to monitor managers; (2) the board of directors; and (3) executive compensation. We then consider the external corporate governance mechanism: the market for corporate control. Essentially, this market is a set of potential owners seeking to acquire undervalued firms and earn above-average returns on their investments by replacing ineffective top-level management teams.[17] The chapter's focus then shifts to the issue of international corporate governance. We briefly describe governance approaches used in German and Japanese firms in which traditional governance structures are being affected by global competition. In part, this discussion suggests the possibility that the structures used to govern global companies in many different countries, including Germany, Japan, the United Kingdom, and the United States, are becoming more, rather than less,

---

TABLE 11.1 CORPORATE GOVERNANCE MECHANISMS

INTERNAL GOVERNANCE MECHANISMS

Ownership Concentration
▶ Relative amounts of stock owned by individual shareholders and institutional investors

Board of Directors
▶ Individuals responsible for representing the firm's owners by monitoring top-level managers' strategic decisions

Executive Compensation
▶ Use of salary, bonuses, and long-term incentives to align managers' decisions with shareholders' interests

EXTERNAL GOVERNANCE MECHANISM

Market for Corporate Control
▶ The purchase of a company that is underperforming relative to industry rivals in order to improve the firm's strategic competitiveness

© Cengage Learning

similar. We also cover the importance of corporate governance international settings, including in emerging economies. Closing our analysis of corporate governance is a consideration of the need for these control mechanisms to encourage and support ethical behavior in organizations.

Importantly, the mechanisms discussed in this chapter can positively influence the governance of the corporation, which has placed significant responsibility and authority in the hands of top-level managers. The most effective managers understand their accountability for the firm's performance and respond positively to corporate governance mechanisms.[18] In addition, the firm's owners should not expect any single mechanism to remain effective over time. Rather, the use of several mechanisms allows owners to govern the corporation in ways that maximize value creation and increase the financial value of their firm. With multiple governance mechanisms operating simultaneously, however, it is also possible for some of the mechanisms to conflict.[19] Later, we review how these conflicts can occur.

SEPARATION OF OWNERSHIP AND MANAGERIAL CONTROL

Historically, founder-owners and their descendants managed U.S. firms. In these cases, corporate ownership and control resided in the same people. As firms grew larger, "the managerial revolution led to a separation of ownership and control in most large corporations, where control of the firm shifted from entrepreneurs to professional managers while ownership became dispersed among thousands of unorganized stockholders who were removed from the day-to-day management of the firm."[20] These changes created the modern public corporation, which is based on the efficient separation of ownership and managerial control. Supporting the separation is a basic legal premise suggesting that the primary objective of a firm's activities is to increase the corporation's profit and thereby the financial gains of the owners (the shareholders).[21]

The separation of ownership and managerial control allows shareholders to purchase stock, which entitles them to income (residual returns) from the firm's operations after paying expenses. This right, however, requires that they also take a risk that the firm's expenses may exceed its revenues. To manage this investment risk, shareholders maintain a diversified portfolio by investing in several companies to reduce their overall risk.[22] As shareholders diversify their investments over a number of corporations, their risk declines. The poor performance or failure of any one firm in which they invest has less overall effect. Thus, shareholders specialize in managing their investment risk.

In small firms, managers often are high-percentage owners, so there is less separation between ownership and managerial control. In fact, ownership and managerial control are not separated in a large number of family-owned firms. In the United States, at least one-third of Standard and Poor's top 500 firms have substantial family ownership, holding on average about 18 percent of the outstanding equity. And family-owned firms perform better when a member of the family is the CEO than when the CEO is an outsider.[23]

In many countries outside the United States, such as in Latin America, Asia, and some European countries, family-owned firms represent the dominant business organization form. There are at least two critical issues for family-controlled firms as they grow. First, owner-managers may not have access to all of the skills needed to effectively manage the growing firm and maximize its returns for the family. Thus, they may need outsiders to help improve management of the firm. Second, they may need to seek outside capital and thus give up some of the ownership control. In these cases, protection of the minority owners' rights becomes important.[24]

To avoid these potential problems, when these firms grow and become more complex, their owner-managers may contract with managerial specialists. As decision-making specialists, managers are agents of the firm's owners and are expected to use their decision-making skills to operate the owners' firm in ways that will maximize the return on the owners' investment.[25]

Without owner (shareholder) specialization in bearing risk and management specialization in making decisions, a firm probably would be limited by the abilities of its owners to manage and make effective strategic decisions. Thus, the separation and specialization of ownership (risk bearing) and managerial control (decision making) should produce the highest returns for the firm's owners.

Agency Relationships

The separation between owners and managers creates an agency relationship. An **agency relationship** exists when one or more people (the *principal* or principals) hire another person or people (the *agent* or agents) as decision-making specialists to perform a service. Thus, an agency relationship exists when one party delegates decision-making responsibility to a second party for compensation (see Figure 11.1).

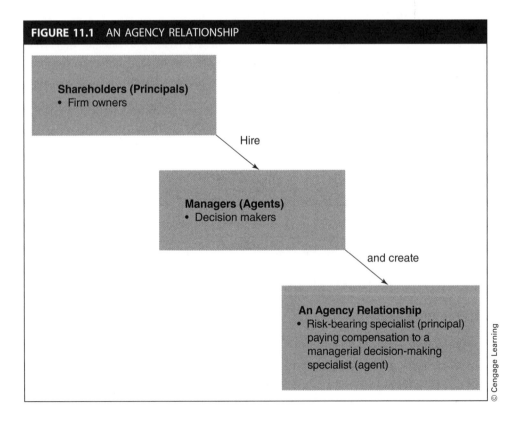

FIGURE 11.1 AN AGENCY RELATIONSHIP

Shareholders (Principals)
• Firm owners

Hire

Managers (Agents)
• Decision makers

and create

An Agency Relationship
• Risk-bearing specialist (principal) paying compensation to a managerial decision-making specialist (agent)

© Cengage Learning

In addition to shareholders and top executives, other examples of agency relationships are consultants and clients and insured and insurer. Moreover, within organizations, an agency relationship exists between managers and their employees, as well as between top executives and the firm's owners. In the modern corporation, managers must understand the links between these relationships and the firm's effectiveness.[26] Although the agency relationship between managers and their employees is important, in this chapter we focus on the agency relationship between the firm's owners (the principals) and top-level managers (the principals' agents) because this relationship is related directly to how the firm's strategies are implemented.

The separation between ownership and managerial control can be problematic. Research evidence documents a variety of agency problems in the modern corporation. Problems can surface because the principal and the agent have different interests and goals, or because shareholders lack direct control of large publicly traded corporations. Problems also arise when an agent makes decisions that result in the pursuit of goals that conflict with those of the principals. Thus, the separation of ownership and control potentially allows divergent interests (between principals and agents) to surface, which can lead to managerial opportunism.

Managerial opportunism is the seeking of self-interest with guile (i.e., cunning or deceit).[27] Opportunism is both an attitude (e.g., an inclination) and a set of behaviors (i.e., specific acts of self-interest).[28] It is not possible for principals to know beforehand which agents will or will not act opportunistically. The reputations of top executives are an imperfect predictor, and opportunistic behavior is usually evident only after it has occurred. Thus, principals establish governance and control mechanisms to prevent agents from acting opportunistically, even though only a few are likely to do so. Interestingly, research suggests that when CEOs feel constrained by governance mechanisms, they are more likely to seek external advice that in turn helps them to make better strategic decisions.[29]

Product Diversification as an Example of an Agency Problem

As explained in Chapter 8, a corporate-level strategy to diversify the firm's product lines can enhance a firm's value creation and increase its returns, both of which serve the interests of shareholders and top executives. However, product diversification can result in two benefits to managers that shareholders do not enjoy, so top executives may prefer more product diversification than do shareholders.[30] First, diversification usually increases the size of a firm, and size is positively related to executive compensation. Also, diversification increases the complexity of managing a firm and its network of businesses and may therefore require more pay because of this complexity.[31] Thus, increased product diversification provides an opportunity for top executives to increase their compensation.

Second, product diversification and the resulting diversification of the firm's portfolio of businesses can reduce top executives' employment risk.[32] Managerial employment risk includes the risk of managers losing their jobs, compensation, or reputations.[33] These risks are reduced with increased diversification because a firm and its upper-level managers are less vulnerable to the reduction in the demand that is associated with a single or limited number of product lines or businesses.

Another concern that may represent an agency problem is a firm's free cash flows over which top executives have control. *Free cash flows* are resources remaining after the firm has invested in all projects that have positive net present values within its current businesses.[34] In anticipation of positive returns, managers may decide to invest these funds in products that are not associated with the firm's current lines of business to increase the firm's level of diversification. The managerial decision to use free cash flows to overdiversify the firm is an example of self-serving and opportunistic managerial behavior. Shareholders, for instance, may prefer that free cash flows be distributed to them as dividends, so they can control how the cash is invested.[35]

Curve S in Figure 11.2 depicts the shareholders' optimal level of diversification. Owners seek the level of diversification that reduces the risk of the firm's failure while simultaneously increasing the company's value through the development of economies of scale and scope (see Chapter 8). Of the four corporate-level diversification strategies shown in Figure 11.2, shareholders likely prefer the diversified position noted by point A on curve S—a position that is located between the dominant business and related-constrained diversification strategies. Of course, the optimal level of diversification owners seek varies from firm to firm.[36] Factors that affect shareholders' preferences include the firm's primary industry, the intensity of rivalry among competitors in that industry, and the top management team's experience with implementing diversification strategies.

Upper-level executives—as agents—also seek an optimal level of diversification. Declining performance resulting from too much product diversification increases the probability that corporate control of the firm will be acquired in the market. After a firm is acquired, the employment risk for the firm's top executives increases substantially. Furthermore, a manager's employment opportunities in the external managerial labor market (discussed in Chapter 2) are affected negatively by a firm's poor performance. Therefore, top executives prefer diversification, but not to a point at which it increases their employment risk and reduces their employment opportunities.[37] Curve M in Figure 11.2 shows that executives prefer higher levels of product diversification than shareholders. Top executives might prefer the level of diversification shown by point B on curve M.

In general, shareholders prefer riskier strategies and more focused diversification. They reduce their risk through holding a diversified portfolio of equity investments. Alternatively, managers obviously cannot balance their employment risk by working for a diverse portfolio of firms. Therefore, top executives may prefer a level of diversification that maximizes firm size and their compensation and that reduces their employment risk. Product diversification, therefore, is a potential agency problem that could result in principals incurring costs to control their agents' behaviors.

Agency Costs and Governance Mechanisms

The potential conflict illustrated by Figure 11.2, coupled with the fact that principals do not know which managers might act opportunistically, demonstrates why principals establish governance mechanisms. However, such mechanisms incur costs. **Agency costs** are the sum of incentive costs, monitoring costs, enforcement costs, and individual financial losses incurred by principals, because governance

FIGURE 11.2 MANAGER AND SHAREHOLDER RISK AND DIVERSIFICATION

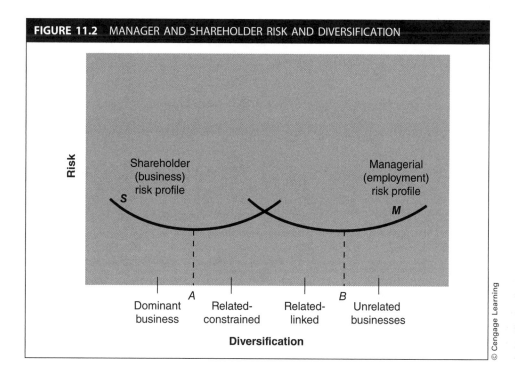

mechanisms cannot guarantee total compliance by the agent. If a firm is diversified, governance costs increase because it is more difficult to monitor actions inside the firm.[38] In general, managerial interests are more likely to prevail when governance mechanisms are weak because managers have a significant amount of autonomy to make strategic decisions. If, however, the board of directors controls managerial autonomy, or if other strong governance mechanisms are used, the firm's strategies should better reflect stakeholders' and certainly shareholders' interests.[39]

More recently, however, observers of firms' governance practices have been concerned about more egregious behavior beyond ineffective corporate strategies such as fraudulent behaviors discovered at companies, including Enron and WorldCom. Partly in response to these behaviors, the U.S. Congress enacted the Sarbanes-Oxley (SOX) Act in 2002 and passed the Dodd-Frank Wall Street Reform and Consumer Protection Act (Dodd-Frank) in mid-2010.

An outcome of these two acts is that corporate governance mechanisms receive greater scrutiny.[40] While the implementation of SOX has been controversial to some, most believe that its use has led to generally positive outcomes in terms of protecting stakeholders and certainly shareholders' interests. For example, section 404 of SOX, which prescribes significant transparency improvement on internal controls associated with accounting and auditing, has arguably improved the internal auditing scrutiny and thereby trust in firms' financial reporting. Moreover, research suggests that internal controls associated with Section 404 increase shareholder value.[41] Nonetheless, some argue that the Act, especially Section 404, creates excessive costs for firms. In addition, a decrease in foreign firms' listing on U.S. stock exchanges occurred at the same time as listing on foreign exchanges increased.

In part, this shift may be because of the costs SOX generates for firms seeking to list on U.S. exchanges.

Although the details of its implementation remain uncompleted, Dodd-Frank is recognized as the most sweeping set of financial regulatory reforms in the United States since the Great Depression. The Act is intended to align financial institutions' actions with society's interests. Dodd-Frank includes provisions related to the categories of consumer protection, systemic risk oversight, executive compensation, and capital requirements for banks. Some legal analysts offer the following description of the Act's provisions: "[Dodd-Frank] creates a Financial Stability Oversight Council headed by the Treasury Secretary, establishes a new system for liquidation of certain financial companies, provides for a new framework to regulate derivatives, establishes new corporate governance requirements, and regulates credit rating agencies and securitizations. The Act also establishes a new consumer protection bureau and provides for extensive consumer protection in financial services."[42]

More intensive application of governance mechanisms as mandated by legislation such as Sarbanes-Oxley and Dodd-Frank affect firms' choice of strategies. For example, more intense governance might find firms choosing to pursue fewer risky projects, possibly decreasing shareholder wealth as a result. In considering how some provisions associated with Dodd-Frank that deal with banks might be put into practice, a U.S. federal regulator said that "To put it plainly, my view is that we are in danger of trying to squeeze too much risk and complexity out of banking."[43] As this comment suggests, determining governance practices that strike an appropriate balance between protecting stakeholders' interests and allowing firms to implement strategies with some degree of risk is difficult.

We now turn to the effects of different governance mechanisms on the decisions managers make and on the use of the firm's strategies.

OWNERSHIP CONCENTRATION

Ownership concentration is defined by both the number of large-block shareholders and the total percentage of shares they own. **Large-block shareholders** typically own at least 5 percent of a corporation's issued shares. Ownership concentration as a governance mechanism has received considerable interest because large-block shareholders are increasingly active in their demands that corporations adopt effective governance mechanisms to control managerial decisions.[44]

In general, diffuse ownership (a large number of shareholders with small holdings and few, if any, large-block shareholders) produces weak monitoring of managers' decisions. Among other problems, diffuse ownership makes it difficult for owners to effectively coordinate their actions. Diversification of the firm's product lines beyond the shareholders' optimal level might result from weak monitoring of managers' decisions. Higher levels of monitoring could encourage managers to avoid strategic decisions that do not increase shareholder value. In fact, research evidence shows that ownership concentration is associated with lower levels of firm product diversification.[45] Thus, with high degrees of ownership concentration, the probability is greater that managers' strategic decisions will increase shareholder value. In recent years, the number of individuals who are large-block shareholders has declined. Institutional owners (discussed below) have replaced individuals as large-block shareholders.

In general, diffuse ownership (a large number of shareholders with small holdings and few, if any, large-block shareholders) produces weak monitoring of managers' decisions. One reason for this is that diffuse ownership makes it difficult for owners to effectively coordinate their actions. As noted earlier, diversification beyond the shareholders' optimum level can result from ineffective monitoring of managers' decisions. Higher levels of monitoring could encourage managers to avoid strategic decisions that harm shareholder value such as too much diversification. Supporting this possibility is research evidence suggesting that ownership concentration is associated with lower levels of firm product diversification.[46] Thus, with high degrees of ownership concentration, the probability is greater that managers' decisions will be designed to maximize shareholder value.[47]

In general, but not in every case, ownership concentration's influence on strategies and firm performance is positive. For example, when large-block shareholders have a high degree of wealth, they have power relative to minority shareholders to appropriate the firm's wealth; this is particularly the case when they are in managerial positions. Excessive appropriation at the expense of minority shareholders is somewhat commonly found in countries such as Korea where minority shareholder rights are not as protected as they are in the United States.[48] The importance of having a board of directors to mitigate excessive appropriation of minority shareholder value has been found in firms with strong family ownership wherein family members have incentives to appropriate shareholder wealth, especially in the second generation after the founder has departed.[49]

Influence of Institutional Owners

A classic work published in the 1930s argued that the "modern" corporation had become characterized by a separation of ownership and control.[50] This change occurred primarily because growth prevented founder-owners from maintaining their dual positions in their increasingly complex companies. More recently, another shift has occurred: ownership of many modern corporations is now concentrated in the hands of institutional investors rather than individual shareholders.

Institutional owners are financial institutions such as stock mutual funds and pension funds that control large-block shareholder positions. Because of their prominent ownership positions, institutional owners, as large-block shareholders, are a powerful governance mechanism. Institutions of these types now own more than 73 percent of the stock in large U.S. corporations.[51]

These ownership percentages suggest that as investors, institutional owners have both the size and the incentive to discipline ineffective top-level managers and can significantly influence a firm's choice of strategies and overall strategic decisions.[52] Research evidence indicates that institutional and other large-block shareholders are becoming more active in their efforts to influence a corporation's strategic decisions. Initially, these shareholder activists and institutional investors concentrated on the performance and accountability of CEOs and contributed to the ouster of a number of them. They are now targeting what they believe are ineffective boards of directors, especially in regard to CEO pay.

For example, one provision of the Dodd-Frank Financial Reform Act passed in 2010 gives investors a vote on top executive compensation at least once every three years. Although the votes are non-binding, they do give investors a "say on pay." Although shareholder advocates were disappointed by the votes in "say on pay" in 2011, only 1.6 percent of the roughly 3,000 saw their pay policies rejected, and shareholder advocates do pressure boards to make sure that their pay is justified. Furthermore, some of the shareholder activists are using the votes as evidence in court cases to show that boards are not meeting their fiduciary duties as they should.[53]

Activists often target the actions of boards more directly via proxy vote proposals that are intended to give shareholders more decision rights because they believe board processes have been ineffective.[54] A rule approved by the U.S. Securities and Exchange Commission allowing large shareholders (owning one to five percent of a company's stock) to nominate up to 25 percent of a company's board of directors may enhance shareholders' decision rights. The impact of such regulation might have a significant impact on corporate governance, shareholder activism and, in fact, overall corporate investor relations.[55]

Established in 1932, CalPERS is a large institutional owner providing retirement and health coverage to more than 1.6 million California public employees, retirees, and their families. In 2011, CalPERS was the largest public employee pension fund in the United States. However, the recent economic crisis resulted in the fund encountering a loss of 24 percent of its invested assets in 2009. By mid-2011, though, much of that loss had been recovered.[56] As a large institutional owner, CalPERS is thought to aggressively promote governance decisions and actions that it believes will enhance shareholder value in companies in which it invests. One action CalPERS takes is to annually develop its Shareowner/Corporate Engagement Program to engage "underperforming public stock companies through private contacts and proxy actions rather than by posting a public 'name-and-shame' List."[57] Previously, CalPERS published a Focus List that included companies it felt acted in ways demonstrating very poor governance practices. Commenting about the change to its new program, the president of CalPERS' board noted that "The Focus List has served us well by calling public attention to some of the worst market players, but the time has come for a more effective approach."[58] Regardless of the actions taken, CalPERS is recognized as an effective steward of shareholders' best interests when interacting with companies in which it has invested.

To date, research suggests that institutional activism may not have a strong direct effect on firm performance. But evidence does suggest that institutional activism may indirectly influence a targeted firm's strategic decisions, including those concerned with international diversification and innovation. Thus, to some degree at least, institutional investor activism has the potential to discipline managers and to enhance the likelihood of a firm taking future actions that are in shareholders' best interests.[59]

BOARD OF DIRECTORS

Typically, shareholders monitor the managerial decisions and actions of a firm through the board of directors. The **board of directors** is a group of shareholder-elected individuals whose primary responsibility is to act in the owners' interests by formally monitoring and controlling the corporation's top-level executives.[60] Boards of directors can positively influence both managers and the companies they serve. Furthermore, research indicates that the composition of the board of directors is particularly important during crisis situations, such as bankruptcies or takeovers. Thus, an effective board of directors can be a source of competitive advantage.[61]

Those who are elected to the board of directors are expected to oversee managers and to ensure that the corporation is operated in ways that will maximize its shareholders' wealth. Unfortunately, some boards of directors have not been highly effective in monitoring and controlling top management's actions.[62] Because of their relatively ineffective performance and in light of the recent financial crisis, and, as noted earlier, boards are experiencing increasing pressure from shareholders, lawmakers, and regulators to become more forceful in their oversight role to prevent top-level managers from acting in their own best interests.

Generally, board members (often called *directors*) are classified into one of three groups based on their relationship to the firm (see Table 11.2). *Insiders* are active top-level managers in the corporation who are elected to the board because they are a source of information about the firm's day-to-day operations.[63] *Related outsiders* have some relationship with the firm, contractual or otherwise, that may create questions about their independence, but these individuals are not involved with the corporation's day-to-day activities. *Outsiders* provide independent counsel to the firm and may hold top-level managerial positions in other companies or may have been elected to the board before the beginning of the current CEO's tenure.[64]

Managers have been suspected of using their power to select and compensate directors in order to exploit their personal ties with them. One important signal of managerial power on a board of directors is the situation in which an individual holds both the CEO and Chair of the board title. This is labeled *CEO duality*. Governance activists often see this as a possible abuse of managerial power. For example, Institutional Shareholder Services Inc., an investor advisory service, recently recommended against the election of four board members at Walt Disney Company because of the board's decision to let the CEO, Robert Iger, also serve as the board's chairman.[65] Yet, having a board that actively monitors top-level managers' decisions and actions does not ensure high performance. However, boards with members having significant relevant experience and knowledge are the most likely to help the firm formulate and implement effective strategies.[66]

TABLE 11.2   CLASSIFICATIONS OF BOARDS OF DIRECTORS' MEMBERS

INSIDERS

▶   The firm's CEO and other top-level managers

RELATED OUTSIDERS

▶   Individuals not involved with the firm's day-to-day operations, but who have a relationship with the company

OUTSIDERS

▶   Individuals who are independent of the firm in terms of day-to-day operations and other relationships

© Cengage Learning

In the early 1980s the SEC proposed that board committees responsible for firm audits be made up of outside directors. These requirements were instituted more generally after SOX was passed, and policies of the New York Stock Exchange as well as the American Stock Exchange now require that boards be composed primarily of outsiders and that audit committees are fully independent. Thus one can clearly see that corporate governance is becoming more intense through the board of directors' mechanism.

Alternatively, having a large number of outside board members can also create problems. For example, because outsiders typically do not have contact with the firm's day-to-day operations and do not have ready access to detailed information about managers and their skills, they lack the insights required to fully and perhaps effectively evaluate their decisions and initiatives.[67] Insiders possess such information by virtue of their organizational positions. Without this type of information provided by insiders, outsider-dominated boards may emphasize the use of financial, as opposed to strategic, controls to gather information to evaluate the performance of managers and business units. A virtually exclusive reliance on financial evaluations shifts risk to top-level managers, who, in turn, may make decisions to maximize their own interests and reduce their employment risk. Reductions in R&D investments, additional diversification of the firm, and the pursuit of greater levels of compensation are some of the results of managers' actions to achieve financial goals set by outsider-dominated boards.[68]

Board Effectiveness

Because of the importance of boards of directors in corporate governance and as a result of increased scrutiny from shareholders—in particular, large institutional investors—the performance of individual board members and of entire boards is being evaluated more formally and with greater intensity.[69] Given the financial crisis and greater demands for greater accountability and improved performance, many boards have initiated voluntary changes in addition to the changes required by SOX.[70] Trends among boards include (1) increases in the diversity of the backgrounds of board members (for example, a greater number of directors from public service, academic, and scientific settings; a greater percentage on boards of ethnic minorities and women;[71] and members from different countries on boards of U.S. firms); (2) the establishment and consistent use of formal processes to evaluate the board's performance; (3) the creation of a "lead director" role that has strong powers with regard to the setting of the board's agenda and oversight of the activities of non-management board members; (4) modifications of the compensation of directors, especially reducing or eliminating stock options as a part of the package; and (5) requirements that directors own significant stakes in the company in order to keep them focused on shareholder interests.[72]

In addition to monitoring the behavior of the CEO and other top managers, outside directors can provide social network ties that act as linkages to external stakeholders.[73] In addition, they can advise managers regarding strategies and the strategic direction of the firm. Consequently, boards composed of highly successful executives from a wide variety of industries will be able to provide a broader perspective to top management. As noted above, boards are also appointing lead outside directors. Once appointed, a lead outside director should seek effectiveness through three linked sets of behaviors: the nonexecutive lead director should (1) become engaged in the firm, but not try to micromanage it; (2) challenge the reasoning behind decisions, but still support them when they are made; and (3) provide an independent perspective on important decisions.[74] At times, the lead director will also have to manage the succession process in selecting a new CEO.

EXECUTIVE COMPENSATION

The compensation of top-level managers, and especially of CEOs, generates a great deal of interest and strongly held opinions. Some believe that CEOs are paid appropriately for the risk and complexity of their work,[75] while others feel that CEOs are paid significantly more than they are worth and that executive compensation systems are not as closely associated to firm performance outcomes as they should be.[76]

One reason for the widespread interest in executive compensation is the natural curiosity about extremes and excesses. For example, the CEO of Apple, Timothy Cook, received a total compensation package worth nearly $378 million in 2011. He earned a salary of roughly $900,000 while the rest was made up in a grant of restricted stock. Comparatively, Steve Jobs, the former CEO, received an annual salary of $1. Mr. Cook's compensation vests over a 10-year period; the method of compensation is an indication by the board that they want to keep their leadership team in place to continue Apple's success. Interestingly, at the time of the grant, Apple's share price was $376 per share; however, it briefly reached $600 in March of 2012, making his compensation package worth much more than when originally established.[77]

Shareholders, angry about seemingly excessive executive pay, have increasingly sought a voice in regard to executive compensation. As noted above, "say on pay" regulations for proxy votes have increased downward pressure on excess pay by CEOs. Although there were not a large number of activist campaigns on proxy votes focused on executive compensation soon after the regulatory change, the results have been significant according to research. Research examining 134 Vote-No campaigns related to executive pay between 1997 and 2007 found that CEOs experienced a $7.3 million average reduction in pay. According to this evidence, shareholder pay campaigns by activists, usually fostered by governance and union pension funds, are having an effect on lowering CEO pay.[78]

Another reason for interest in executive compensation stems from a more substantive view that CEO pay is tied, in an indirect but very tangible way, to the fundamental governance processes in large corporations.[79] From this perspective, **executive compensation** is a governance mechanism that seeks to align the interests of top managers and owners through salaries, bonuses, and long-term incentive compensation, such as restricted stock awards and stock options. Research suggests that firms with a smaller pay gap between the CEO and other top executives perform better, especially when collaboration among top management team members is more important.[80] The performance improvement is attributed to better cooperation among top management team members.

Increasingly, long-term incentive plans are becoming a critical part of compensation packages in U.S. firms. The use of longer-term pay helps firms cope with or avoid potential agency problems by linking managerial wealth to the wealth of common shareholders. Because of this, the stock market generally reacts positively to the introduction of a long-range incentive plan for top executives, but the reaction increases with institutional ownership and decreases with longer CEO tenure.[81] Nevertheless, sometimes the use of a long-term incentive plan prevents major stockholders (e.g., institutional investors) from pressing for changes in the composition of the board of directors because they assume that the long-term incentives will ensure that top executives will act in shareholders' best interests. Alternatively, stockholders largely assume that top-executive pay and the performance of a firm are more closely aligned when firms have boards that are dominated by outside members, so there is often a substitution effect between governance mechanisms (long-term compensation and number of outside directors[82]).

Effectively using executive compensation as a governance mechanism is particularly challenging to firms implementing international strategies. For example, the interests of owners of multinational corporations may be best served when there is less uniformity among the compensation plans of the firm's foreign subsidiaries.[83] Developing an array of unique compensation plans requires additional monitoring and increases the firm's agency costs. Importantly, pay levels vary by regions of the world. For example, managers receive the highest compensation in the United States, while managerial pay is much lower in Asia. Compensation is lower in India partly because many of the largest firms are owned and controlled by families.[84] As corporations acquire firms in other countries, the managerial compensation puzzle becomes more complex and may cause additional executive dissatisfaction with pay consideration.[85]

The Effectiveness of Executive Compensation

For several reasons, executive compensation—especially long-term incentive compensation—is complicated. First, the strategic decisions that top-level managers make are typically complex and non-routine, so it is difficult to evaluate the quality of those decisions. As a result, the board of directors often links the compensation of top-level managers to measurable outcomes, such as the firm's financial performance. Second, an executive's decision often affects a firm's financial outcomes over an extended period, making it difficult to assess the effect of current decisions on the corporation's performance. In fact, strategic decisions are more likely to have long-term rather than short-term effects on a company's strategic outcomes. Third, a number of other factors affect a firm's performance besides top-level managerial decisions and behavior. Unpredictable economic, social, or legal changes (see Chapter 3) make it difficult to discern the effects of strategic decisions. Thus, although performance-based compensation may provide incentives to top management teams to make decisions that best serve shareholders' interests, such compensation plans alone are imperfect in their ability to monitor and control managers.[86] Still, incentive compensation represents a significant and increasing portion of many executives' total pay.

Even incentive compensation plans that are intended to increase the value of a firm in line with shareholder expectations are subject to managerial manipulation. For instance, annual bonuses may provide incentives for managers to pursue short-run objectives at the expense of the firm's long-term interests. Supporting this conclusion, some research has found that bonuses based on annual performance were negatively related to R&D investments when the firm was highly diversified, which may affect the firm's long-term strategic competitiveness.[87]

Although long-term performance-based incentives may reduce the temptation to underinvest in the short run, they increase executive exposure to risks associated with uncontrollable events, such as market fluctuations and industry decline. The longer the focus of incentive compensation, the greater are the long-term risks top-level managers bear. Also, because long-term incentives tie a manager's overall wealth to the firm in a way that is inflexible, such incentives and ownership may not be valued as highly by a manager as by outside investors who have the opportunity to diversify their wealth in a number of other financial investments.[88] Thus, firms may have to overcompensate managers using long-term incentives.

Such long-term incentives also broaden the temptation for CEOs to manage earnings in a way that facilitates their wealth versus that of shareholders.[89] For example, such incentive compensation has also been shown to have some unintended consequences. Because of the temptation to manage earnings, stock options are more associated with earnings restatements, which lead to a reduction in share price.[90] Research also shows that stock options can lead to excessive risk taking and that options can increase the performance of highly talented people but worsen performance for leaders of lower ability.[91]

Although some stock option-based compensation plans are well-designed, with option strike prices (the prices at which the options become attractive) substantially higher than current stock prices, too many have been designed simply to give executives more wealth that will not immediately show up on the balance sheet. Furthermore, stock option *repricing,* in which the strike price value of the option is lowered from its original position, is very common. Research suggests that repricing occurs more frequently in high-risk situations to restore the incentive effect for innovation to remain competitive.[92] However, because of the large number of options granted in recent years and the increasingly common practice of repricing them, public pressure increased to adjust accounting rules so that the actual value given to executives was reflected in accounting statements. A new rule issued by the Financial Accounting Standards Board (FASB) required the firm to record stock options as an expense beginning in July 2005. Another practice that has caused a great deal of controversy is *backdating,* in which an options grant is dated earlier than it was actually drawn up to ensure an attractive exercise price for managers holding the options. In early 2007, a U.S. federal court in Delaware ruled that directors who approved stock option backdating could be sued for breach of fiduciary duty.[93]

MARKET FOR CORPORATE CONTROL

Practices such as options repricing and backdating are evidence that internal governance mechanisms are an imperfect means of ensuring that the interests of top-level managers are aligned with the interests of the shareholders. When weak internal governance leads to suboptimal firm performance, sometimes external corporate governance mechanisms are needed. Primary among these is the market for corporate control.

The **market for corporate control** is an external governance mechanism that becomes active when a firm's internal controls fail.[94] It is composed of individuals and firms that buy ownership positions in or take over potentially undervalued corporations so they can form new divisions in established diversified companies or merge two previously separate firms. Because the undervalued firm's executives are assumed to be responsible for formulating and implementing the strategy that produced the poor performance, that team is usually replaced. Thus, when the market for corporate control operates effectively, it ensures that managers who are ineffective or act opportunistically are disciplined.[95]

The market for corporate control was very active in the 1980s. Then, because of government legislation to discourage hostile takeovers and the collapse of the high-yield (junk) bond market in 1990, takeovers became less popular. However, there was a resurgence of activity in the United States and elsewhere from 2002 to 2008, as relatively easy access to financing encouraged private equity firms to increase their involvement in acquisitions. However, this activity was dampened by the financial crisis.[96]

The market for corporate control is often viewed as a "court of last resort."[97] This suggests that the takeover market as a source of external discipline is used only when internal governance mechanisms are relatively weak and have proved to be ineffective. Alternatively, other research suggests that the rationale for takeovers as a corporate governance strategy is not as strong as the rationale for takeovers as an ownership investment in target candidates that are performing well.[98] In support of this view, a study of active corporate raiders in the 1980s showed that takeover attempts often were focused on firms with above-average performance in their industries.[99] Consequently, although some takeovers are best explained in terms of their investment potential, others are indicative of external market discipline.

The market for corporate control as a governance mechanism should be triggered by a firm's poor performance relative to industry competitors. A firm's poor performance, often demonstrated by earning below-average returns, is an indicator that internal governance mechanisms have failed; that is, they did not result in managerial decisions that maximized shareholder value. This market has been active for some time. As noted in Chapter 9, the 1990s produced a surge in the number and value of mergers and acquisitions. During the short lull in merger and acquisition activity during the economic downturn of 2001–2002, unsolicited takeover bids increased, an indication that during a recession, poorly managed firms are more easily identified.[100] After this period, the number and size of deals were increasing until the financial crisis in 2008. Furthermore, takeovers and even hostile takeovers involving firms from two countries, are increasing. In Europe, boards have much less influence regarding takeover bids than in the United States. In fact, typically in Europe, all bids must be subjected to a shareholder vote. In the United States, boards are given much greater freedom to act on behalf of the shareholders.

Most hostile takeover attempts are due to the target firm's poor performance. Therefore, target firm managers and members of the board of directors are highly sensitive about hostile takeover bids because they frequently mean that managers and directors have not managed the company effectively. If they accept the offer, they are likely to lose their jobs because the acquiring firm will appoint its own management. Even if they fend off the takeover attempt, they must improve the performance of the firm or risk losing their jobs anyway.[101] We now turn to the methods managers use to defend their companies against takeovers.

Managerial Defense Tactics

Firms targeted for hostile takeovers may use multiple defense tactics to fend off the takeover attempt (see Table 11.3). Historically, the increased use of the market for corporate control as a governance mechanism has enhanced the sophistication and variety of such defense tactics.[102] The market for corporate control tends to increase risk for managers. As a result, managerial pay is often augmented indirectly through *golden parachutes*, wherein a CEO can receive up to three years' salary if his or her firm is taken over. Among other outcomes, takeover defenses

TABLE 11.3 HOSTILE TAKEOVER DEFENSE STRATEGIES

DEFENSE STRATEGY	SUCCESS AS A STRATEGY	EFFECTS ON SHAREHOLDER WEALTH
Capital structure change Dilution of the target firm's stock, making it more costly for an acquiring firm to continue purchasing the target's shares. Employee stock option plans (ESOPs), recapitalization, issuance of additional debt, and share buybacks are actions associated with this strategy.	Medium	Inconclusive
Corporate charter amendment An amendment to the target firm's charter for the purpose of staggering the elections of members to its board of directors so that not all are elected during the same year. This change to the firm's charter prevents a potential acquirer from installing a completely new board in a single year.	Very low	Negative
Golden parachute A lump-sum payment of cash that is given to one or more top-level managers when the firm is acquired in a takeover bid.	Low	Negligible
Greenmail The repurchase of the target firm's shares of stock that were obtained by the acquiring firm at a premium in exchange for an agreement that the acquirer will no longer target the company for takeover.	Medium	Negative
Litigation Lawsuits that help the target firm stall hostile takeover attempts. Antitrust charges and inadequate disclosure are examples of the grounds on which the target firm could file.	Low	Positive
Poison pill An action the target firm takes to make its stock less attractive to a potential acquirer.	High	Positive
Standstill agreement A contract between the target firm and the potential acquirer specifying that the acquirer will not purchase additional shares of the target firm for a specified period of time in exchange for a fee paid by the target firm.	Low	Negative

SOURCES: R. Campbell, C. Ghosh, M. Petrova, & C. C. Sirmans, 2011, Corporate governance and performance in the market for corporate control: The case of REITS, *Journal of Real Estate Finance & Economics*, 42: 451–480; M. Ryngaert & R. Scholten, 2010, Have changing takeover defense rules and strategies entrenched management and damaged shareholders? The case of defeated takeover bids, *Journal of Corporate Finance*, 16: 16–37; M. Ruiz-Mallorqui & D. J. Santana-Martin, 2009, Ultimate institutional owner and takeover defenses in the controlling versus minority shareholders context, *Corporate Governance: An International Review*, 17: 238–254; J. A. Pearce II & R. B. Robinson, Jr., 2004, Hostile takeover defenses that maximize shareholder wealth, *Business Horizons*, 47(5): 15–24.

increase the costs of making the acquisition, causing the incumbent management to become entrenched, while reducing the chances of introducing a new management team.[103] Some defense tactics require asset restructuring, created by divesting one or more divisions in the diversified firm's portfolio. Others necessitate changes in only the financial structure of the firm, such as repurchasing shares of the firm's outstanding stock. Another similar takeover defense strategy is known as a "poison pill." This strategy usually allows shareholders (other than the acquirer) to convert "shareholders' rights" into a large number of common shares if an individual or company acquires beyond a set amount of the target firm's stock (typically 10 to 20 percent). This process increases the number of shareholders friendly to the target firm who have concentrated ownership, which makes it more difficult for the acquiring firm to buy up all the shares necessary to take over the target firm. In addition, this process increases the total number of outstanding shares diluting the potential acquirer's existing stake, which means that to maintain or expand its ownership position, the potential acquirer must buy additional shares at premium prices. The additional purchases increase the potential acquirer's costs. Some firms amend the corporate charter so board member elections are staggered, resulting in only one-third of members being up for reelection each year. Research shows that this results in managerial entrenchment and reduced vulnerability to hostile take-overs.[104] Some tactics, such as reincorporation of the firm in another state, require shareholder approval. On the other hand, the *greenmail tactic,* wherein money is used to repurchase stock from a corporate raider to avoid the takeover of the firm, requires no approval. Defensive tactics are controversial, and the research on their effects is inconclusive. However, most institutional investors oppose the use of defense tactics.[105]

A potential problem with the market for corporate control is that it may not be entirely efficient. A study of several of the most active corporate raiders in the 1980s showed that approximately 50 percent of their takeover attempts targeted firms with above-average performance in their industry—corporations that were neither undervalued nor poorly managed.[106] The targeting of high-performance businesses may lead to acquisitions at premium prices and to decisions by managers of the targeted firm to establish costly takeover defense tactics to protect their corporate positions.[107]

Although the market for corporate control lacks the precision of internal governance mechanisms, the fear of acquisition and influence by corporate raiders is an effective constraint on the managerial-growth motive. The market for corporate control has been responsible for significant changes in many firms' strategies and, when used appropriately, has served shareholders' interests.[108] But this market and other means of corporate governance vary by region of the world and by country. Accordingly, we next address the topic of international corporate governance.

INTERNATIONAL CORPORATE GOVERNANCE

This chapter has focused on governance structures found in the United States, which are similar to those found in the United Kingdom. However, understanding the corporate governance structures only in these countries is inadequate for a multinational firm in today's global economy.[109] Although the similarities among governance structures in industrialized nations are increasing, there are differences, and firms using an international strategy must understand these differences in order to operate effectively in different international markets.[110]

This section discusses some of the essential features associated with governance structures in Germany and Japan. Although the stability associated with German and Japanese governance structures historically has been viewed as an asset, the governance systems in these countries are changing, as they are changing in other parts of the world.[111] These changes are partially the result of multinational firms operating in many different countries and attempting to develop a more global governance system.[112]

Corporate Governance in Germany

In many private German firms, the owner and manager may still be the same individual. In these instances, there is no agency problem. Even in publicly traded German corporations, there is often a dominant shareholder. Thus, the concentration of ownership is an important means of corporate governance in Germany, as it is in the United States.

Historically, banks have been at the center of the German corporate governance structure, as is also the case in many other European countries, such as Italy and France. As lenders, banks become major shareholders when companies they finance seek funding on the stock market or default on loans. Although the stakes are usually less than 10 percent, the only legal limit on how much of a firm's stock banks can hold is that a single ownership position cannot exceed 15 percent of the bank's capital. Through their shareholdings, and by casting proxy votes for individual shareholders who retain their shares with the banks, three banks in particular— Deutsche Bank, Dresdner Bank, and Commerzbank—exercise significant power. Although shareholders can tell the banks how to vote their ownership position, they generally do not do so. A combination of their own holdings and their proxies results in majority positions for these three banks in many German companies. These banks, along with others, monitor and control managers, both as lenders and as shareholders, by electing representatives to supervisory boards. Interestingly, research suggests that CEO compensation often depends on demographic and social similarities between CEOs and board chairs.[113]

German firms with more than 2,000 employees are required to have a two-tiered board structure that places the responsibility for monitoring and controlling managerial (or supervisory) decisions and actions in the hands of a separate group. Although all the functions of direction and management are the responsibility of the management board (the *Vorstand*), appointment to the Vorstand is the responsibility of the supervisory tier (the *Aufsichtsrat*). In large public companies, the supervisory board must contain an equal number of employee-elected and shareholder-elected representatives.[114]

Proponents of the German structure suggest that it helps prevent corporate wrongdoings and rash decisions by "dictatorial CEOs." However, critics maintain that it slows decision making and often ties a CEO's hands. In Germany the power sharing may have gone too far because it includes representation from the community as well as unions. Accordingly, the framework of corporate governance in Germany has made it difficult for companies to be restructured as quickly as they can be in the United States when their performance suffers.[115]

Corporate governance in Germany is changing, at least partly, because of the increasing globalization of business. Many German firms are beginning to gravitate toward the U.S. system. Recent research suggests that the traditional system produced some agency costs because of a lack of external ownership power.[116] Alternatively, firms with stronger external ownership power were less likely to undertake governance reforms. Firms that adopted governance reforms often divested poorly performing units and achieved higher levels of market performance.[117]

Corporate Governance in Japan

Attitudes toward corporate governance in Japan are affected by the cultural concepts of obligation, family, and consensus.[118] In Japan, an obligation "may be to return a service for one rendered. Or an obligation may derive from a more general relationship, for example, to one's family, to fellow alumni, or to one's company, ministry, or country. This sense of particular obligation is common elsewhere but it feels stronger in Japan."[119] As part of a company with a strong culture, individuals are members of a unit that envelops their lives; such strong company cultures command the attention and allegiance of parties throughout such corporations. Moreover, a *keiretsu* (a group of firms tied together by cross-shareholdings) is more than an economic concept; it, too, is a family. A keiretsu firm usually owns less than 2 percent of any other member firm; however, each company typically has a stake in every firm in the keiretsu. As a result, somewhere between 30 and 90 percent of a firm is owned by other members of the keiretsu. Cross-shareholding is a manifestation of the close relationships that exist among a company and its primary stakeholders, including affiliates, suppliers, and customers. These close relationships "can decrease economic efficiency by preventing companies from doing business with the optimal suppliers or customers."[120] Cross-shareholding rates in Japan have been falling in recent years.

Consensus, an important influence in Japanese corporate governance, calls for the expenditure of significant amounts of energy to win the hearts and minds of people whenever possible, as opposed to top executives issuing edicts.[121] Consensus is highly valued, even when it results in a slow and cumbersome decision-making process. This system of governance places more importance on satisfying the needs of the group of stakeholders than of the shareholders. However, there are calls for changes in this system and attempts to achieve more balance in satisfying the stakeholders and increasing shareholder value.[122]

As in Germany, banks in Japan play an important role in financing and monitoring large public firms. The main bank—the one owning the largest share of stocks and the largest amount of debt—has the closest relationship with the company's top executives. It provides financial advice to the firm and also closely monitors managers. Thus, Japan's corporate governance structure is bank-based, whereas that in the United States is market-based. Aside from lending money, a Japanese bank can hold up to five percent of a firm's total stock; a group of related financial institutions can hold up to 40 percent. In many cases, main-bank relationships are part of a horizontal keiretsu.

Japan's corporate governance practices are changing. For example, because of Japanese banks' continuing development as economic organizations, their role in the monitoring and control of managerial behavior and firm outcomes is less significant than in the past.[123] Also, deregulation in the financial sector has reduced the cost of mounting hostile takeovers.[124] As such, deregulation facilitated additional activity in Japan's market for corporate control, which was nonexistent in past years. Interestingly, however, recent research shows that CEOs of both public and private companies in Japan receive similar levels of compensation, and their compensation is tied closely to observable performance goals.[125]

Global Corporate Governance

As noted earlier, a relatively uniform governance structure is evolving in developed economies throughout the world. Even in Asia, as markets become more global and customer demands more similar, shareholders are becoming the focus of managers' efforts. Furthermore, investors are becoming more and more active throughout the world.

Even in transition economies, such as those of China and Russia, changes in corporate governance are occurring.[126] For example, there has been a gradual decline in China in the equity held in state-owned enterprises and the number and percentage of private firms have grown; but, the state still relies on direct and/or indirect controls to influence the strategies firms use. In terms of long-term success, these conditions may affect firms' performances in that research results show that firms with higher state ownership tend to have lower market value and more volatility in those values across time. This is likely because of agency conflicts between internal management and government objectives for the firms; the executives may not seek to maximize shareholder returns given that they must also seek to satisfy social goals placed on them by the government.[127] This suggests a potential conflict between the principals, particularly the state owner and the private equity owners of the state-owned enterprises.[128]

GOVERNANCE MECHANISMS, STAKEHOLDER MANAGEMENT, AND ETHICAL BEHAVIOR

The governance mechanisms described in this chapter are designed to ensure that the agents of the firm's owners—the corporation's top executives—make strategic decisions that best serve the interests of the entire group of stakeholders, as described in Chapters 1 and 2. In the United States, governance mechanisms focus on the control of managerial decisions to ensure that shareholders' interests will be served, but product market stakeholders (e.g., customers, suppliers, and host communities) and organizational stakeholders (e.g., managerial and non-managerial employees) are important as well.[129]

As discussed in Chapters 1 and 2, excellent stakeholder relationships based on trust and mutual satisfaction of goals can enhance firm competitiveness by allowing the firm to obtain superior knowledge upon which to base strategic decisions[130] and by enhancing implementation of strategies due to higher levels of commitment among stakeholders.[131] Firms with trustworthy reputations also draw customers, suppliers, and business partners to them, thus enhancing strategic opportunities. Dissatisfied stakeholders may withdraw their support from one firm and provide it to another. For example, dissatisfied customers are likely to purchase products from a supplier offering an acceptable substitute. Furthermore, neglect of stakeholders can lead to negative outcomes such as adverse regulation, legal suits and penalties, consumer retaliation, strikes, walkouts, and bad press. Consequently, a firm creates more value when its governance mechanisms take into consideration the interests of all stakeholders.[132]

Companies that design and use governance mechanisms intended to encourage serving the interests of all stakeholders are also less likely to find themselves in situations in which their actions are considered unethical. The Enron, WorldCom, HealthSouth, and Tyco International scandals illustrate the devastating effect of poor ethical behavior not only on a firm's stakeholders, but also on other firms. These crises have influenced governance not only in the United States, but in other countries as well.

The decisions and actions of a corporation's board of directors can be effective deterrents to unethical behavior and encourage socially responsible behavior.[133] For example, research has found that firms with a CEO pay structure that has a long-term focus are more socially responsible than firms with a short-term pay focus.[134] Some believe that the most effective boards actively work to set boundaries for their firms' business ethics and values.[135] Once formulated, the board's expectations regarding the ethical decisions and actions of all of the firm's stakeholders must be clearly communicated to its top-level managers. Moreover, as shareholders' agents, these managers must understand that the board will hold them fully accountable for the development and support of an organizational culture that results in ethical decisions and behaviors. As explained in Chapter 2, CEOs can be positive role models for ethical behavior.

Ethical behavior on the part of top executives is important, and effective governance systems are required to monitor it.[136] However, if the governance systems become too strong, they may eliminate the flexibility managers need to be creative, produce innovations, and respond quickly to changes in the firm's competitive environment. So, while too little or weak governance produces an internal environment whereby managerial opportunism can flourish, too much or overly strong governance may significantly reduce or eliminate managerial risk taking and the ability to adapt to changing environmental conditions.[137] Firms need to have effective governance mechanisms and simultaneously be able to be entrepreneurial.

SUMMARY

▷ Corporate governance is a relationship among stakeholders that is used to determine a firm's direction and control its performance. How firms monitor and control top-level managers' decisions and actions affects how they formulate and implement strategies. Effective governance that aligns managers' decisions with shareholders' interests can contribute to a competitive advantage.

▷ There are three internal governance mechanisms in the modern corporation: ownership concentration, the board of directors, and executive compensation. The market for corporate control is the single external governance mechanism influencing managers' decisions and the outcomes resulting from them.

- Ownership is separated from control in the modern corporation. Owners (principals) hire managers (agents) to make decisions that maximize the firm's value. As risk-bearing specialists, owners diversify their risk by investing in multiple corporations with different risk profiles. As decision-making specialists, owners expect their agents (the firm's top-level managers) to make decisions that lead to maximizing the firm's value. Thus, modern corporations are characterized by an agency relationship that is created when one party (the firm's owners) hires and pays another party (top-level managers) to use its decision-making skills.

- Separation of ownership and control creates an agency problem when an agent pursues goals that conflict with principals' goals. Principals establish and use governance mechanisms to control this potential problem.

- Ownership concentration is based on the number of large-block shareholders and the percentage of shares they own. With significant ownership percentages, such as those held by large mutual funds and pension funds, institutional investors often are able to influence top executives' strategic decisions and actions. Thus, unlike diffuse ownership, which often results in relatively weak monitoring and control of managerial decisions, concentrated ownership produces more active and effective monitoring. An increasingly powerful force in the United States and, to a lesser degree, the United Kingdom, institutional investors actively use their positions of concentrated ownership to force managers and boards of directors to make decisions that maximize a firm's value.

- In the United States and the United Kingdom, a firm's board of directors, composed of insiders, related outsiders, and outsiders, is a governance mechanism that shareholders expect to represent their collective interests. The percentage of outside directors on many boards now exceeds the percentage of inside directors. Outsiders are expected to be more independent of a firm's top-level managers compared with those selected from inside the firm.

- Executive compensation is a highly visible and often criticized governance mechanism. Salary, bonuses, and long-term incentives are used to strengthen the alignment between managers' and shareholders' interests. A firm's board of directors is responsible for determining the effectiveness of the firm's executive compensation system. An effective system elicits managerial decisions that are in shareholders' best interests.

- In general, evidence suggests that shareholders and boards of directors have become more vigilant in their control of managerial decisions. Nonetheless, these mechanisms are insufficient to govern managerial behavior in many large companies. Therefore, the market for corporate control is an important governance mechanism. Although it, too, is imperfect, the market for corporate control has been effective in combating inefficient corporate diversification and causing managers to implement more effective strategic decisions.

- Corporate governance structures used in Germany and Japan differ from each other and from those used in the United States. Historically, the U.S. governance structure has emphasized maximizing shareholder value. In Germany, employees, as a stakeholder group, have a more prominent role in governance. By contrast, until recently, Japanese shareholders played virtually no role in the monitoring and control of top-level managers. However, all of these systems are becoming increasingly similar, as are many governance systems in developed countries, such as France and Italy, and transitional economies such as China.

▶ Effective governance mechanisms ensure that the interests of all stakeholders are served. Thus, long-term strategic success results when firms are governed in ways that foster the satisfaction of capital market stakeholders (e.g., shareholders), product market stakeholders (e.g., customers and suppliers), and organizational stakeholders (managerial and non-managerial employees). Moreover, effective governance encourages ethical behavior in the formulation and implementation of strategies.

ETHICS QUESTIONS

1. Do managers have an ethical responsibility to push aside their own values with regard to how certain stakeholders are treated (i.e., special interest groups) in order to maximize shareholder returns?
2. What are the ethical implications associated with owners assuming that managers will act in their own self-interest?
3. What ethical issues surround executive compensation? How can we determine whether top executives are paid too much?
4. Is it ethical for firms involved in the market for corporate control to target companies performing at levels exceeding the industry average? Why or why not?
5. What ethical issues, if any, do top executives face when asking their firm to provide them with a golden parachute?
6. How can governance mechanisms be designed to ensure against managerial opportunism, ineffectiveness, and unethical behaviors?

NOTES

1. M. K. Bednar, 2012, Watchdog or lapdog? A behavioral view of the media as a corporate governance mechanism, *Academy of Management Journal*, 55(1): 131–150; M. Carpenter & J. Westphal, 2001, Strategic context of external network ties: Examining the impact of director appointments on board involvement in strategic decision making, *Academy of Management Journal*, 44: 639–660.
2. A. Ignatius, 2011, CEO pay is up! Is that good? *Harvard Business Review*, 89(7/8): 14; N. Byrnes & J. Sasseen, 2007, Board of hard knocks: Activist shareholders, tougher rules and anger over CEO pay have put directors on the hot seat, *Business Week*, January 22, 37.
3. J. Shin & J. Seo, 2011, Less pay and more sensitivity? Institutional investor heterogeneity and CEO pay, *Journal of Management*, 37(6): 1719–1746; S. Werner, H. L. Tosi, & L. Gomez-Mejia, 2005, Organizational governance and employee pay: How ownership structure affects the firm's compensation strategy, *Strategic Management Journal*, 26: 377–384.
4. M. A. Chen, 2004, Executive option repricing, incentives, and retention, *Journal of Finance*, 59: 1167–1199.

5. G. Manso, 2011, Motivating innovation, *Journal of Finance*, 66(5): 1823–1860; D. Aboody, N. Johnson, & R. Kasznik, 2010, Employee stock options and future firm performance: Evidence from option repricings, *Journal of Accounting & Economics*, 50(1): 74–92.
6. T. Donaldson, 2012, The epistemic fault line in corporate governance, *Academy of Management Review*, 37(2): 256–271; R. C. Pozen, 2010, The case for professional boards, *Harvard Business Review*, 88(12): 50–58; R. K. Mitchell, B. R. Agle, & D. J. Wood, 1997, Toward a theory of stakeholder identification and salience: Defining the principle of who and what really counts, *Academy of Management Review*, 22: 853–886.
7. S. Machold, M. Huse, A. Minichilli, & M. Nordqvist, 2011, Board leadership and strategy involvement in small firms: A team production approach, *Corporate Governance: An International Review*, 19(4): 368–383; K. Bongjin, M. L. Burns, & J. E. Prescott, 2009, The strategic role of the board: The impact of board structure on top management team strategic action capability, *Corporate Governance: An International Review*, 17(6): 728–743; J. H. Davis, F. D. Schoorman, & L. Donaldson, 1997, Toward

a stewardship theory of management, *Academy of Management Review*, 22: 20–47.

8   M. Hernandez, 2012, Toward an understanding of the psychology of stewardship, *Academy of Management Review*, 37(2): 172–193; M. S. Schwartz, T. W. Dunfee, & M. J. Kline, 2005, Tone at the top: An ethics code for directors? *Journal of Business Ethics*, 58: 79–100.

9   C. S. Tuggle, D. G. Sirmon, C. R. Reutzel, & L. Bierman, 2010, Commanding board of director attention: Investigating how organizational performance and CEO duality affect board members' attention to monitoring, *Strategic Management Journal*, 31(9): 946–968; E. F. Fama & M. C. Jensen, 1983, Separation of ownership and control, *Journal of Law and Economics*, 26: 301–325.

10 T. Coville & G. Kleinman, 2012, Post-Sarbanes-Oxley changes in the composition of boards: Have they impacted spending for audit services? *International Journal of Disclosure & Governance*, 9(1): 36–51; M. Arndt, W. Zellner, & M. McNamee, 2002, Restoring trust in corporate America, *Business Week*, June 24, 30–35.

11 J. Wulf & H. Singh, 2011, How do acquirers retain successful target CEOs? The role of governance, *Management Science*, 57(12): 2101–2114; M. Carney, 2005, Corporate governance and competitive advantage in family-controlled firms, *Entrepreneurship Theory and Practice*, 29: 249–265; R. Charan, 1998, *How Corporate Boards Create Competitive Advantage*, San Francisco: Jossey-Bass.

12 P. Strebel, 2011, In touch boards: Reaching out to the value critical stakeholders, *Corporate Governance: The International Journal of Effective Board Performance*, 11(5): 603–610; G. J. Nicholson & G. C. Kiel, 2004, Breakthrough board performance: How to harness your board's intellectual capital, *Corporate Governance*, 4(1): 5–23.

13 R. Bell, C. B. Moore, & I. Filatotchev, 2012, Strategic and institutional effects on foreign IPO performance: Examining the impact of country of origin, corporate governance, and host country effects, *Journal of Business Venturing*, 27(2): 197–216; X. Wu, 2005, Corporate governance and corruption: A cross-country analysis, *Governance*, 18(2): 151–170.

14 J. Charkham, 1994, *Keeping Good Company: A Study of Corporate Governance in Five Countries*, New York: Oxford University Press, 1.

15 R. E. Hoskisson, D. Yiu, & H. Kim, 2010, Capital and labor market congruence and corporate governance: Effects on corporate innovation and global competitiveness, in D. B. Audretsch, G. B. Dagnini, R. Faraci, & R. E. Hoskisson (eds.), *New Frontiers in Entrepreneurship: Recognizing, Seizing, and Executing Opportunities*, New York: Springer, 67–93.

16 A. Mullineux, 2010, Is there an Anglo-American corporate governance model? *International Economics & Economic Policy*, 7(4): 437–448; R. Aguilera & G. Jackson, 2003, The cross-national diversity of corporate governance: Dimensions and determinants, *Academy of Management Review*, 28: 447–465.

17 M. L. Humphery-Jenner & R. G. Powell, 2011, Firm size, takeover profitability, and the effectiveness of the market for corporate control: Does the absence of anti-takeover provisions make a difference? *Journal of Corporate Finance*, 17(3): 418–437; M. A. Hitt, R. E. Hoskisson, R. A. Johnson, & D. D. Moesel, 1996, The market for corporate control and firm innovation, *Academy of Management Journal*, 39: 1084–1119.

18 Hernandez, Toward an understanding of the psychology of stewardship; P. Kakabadse, N. K. Kakabadse, & R. Knyght, 2010, The chemistry factor in the Chairman/CEO relationship, *European Management Journal*, 28(4): 285–296; B. B. Burr, 2005, Good governance rewarded, *Pensions and Investments*, 33(2): 20.

19 B. L. Connelly, L. Tihanyi, S. T. Certo, & M. A. Hitt, 2010, Marching to the beat of different drummers: The influence of institutional owners on competitive actions, *Academy of Management Journal*, 53(4): 723–742; R. E. Hoskisson, M. A. Hitt, R. A. Johnson, & W. Grossman, 2002, Conflicting voices: The effects of ownership heterogeneity and internal governance on corporate strategy, *Academy of Management Journal*, 45: 697–716.

20 G. E. Davis & T. A. Thompson, 1994, A social movement perspective on corporate control, *Administrative Science Quarterly*, 39: 141–173.

21 K. Crossan, 2011, The effects of a separation of ownership from control on UK listed firms: An empirical analysis, *Managerial & Decision Economics*, 32(5): 293–304; J. Kim & J. T. Mahoney, 2010, A strategic theory of the firm as a nexus of incomplete contracts: A property rights approach. *Journal of Management*, 36: 806–826.

22 M. Faccio, M. Marchica, & R. Mura, 2011, Large shareholder diversification and corporate risk-taking, *Review of Financial Studies*, 24(11): 3601–3641; R. M. Wiseman & L. R. Gomez-Mejia, 1999, A behavioral agency model of managerial risk taking, *Academy of Management Review*, 23: 133–153.

23 R. C. Anderson & D. M. Reeb, 2004, Board composition: Balancing family influence in S&P 500 firms, *Administrative Science Quarterly*, 49: 209–237.

24 E.-T. Chen & J. Nowland, 2010, Optimal board monitoring in family-owned companies: Evidence from Asia, *Corporate Governance: An International Review*, 18: 3–17; D. Miller & I. Le Breton-Miller, 2003, Challenge versus advantage in family business, *Strategic Organization*, 1: 127–134.

25 E. F. Fama, 1980, Agency problems and the theory of the firm, *Journal of Political Economy*, 88: 288–307.

26 L. L. Lan & L. Heracleous, 2010, Rethinking agency theory: The view from law, *Academy of Management Review*, 35: 294–314.

27 K. Vafai, 2010, Opportunism in organizations, *Journal of Law, Economics, and Organization*, 26: 158–181; O. E. Williamson, 1993, Opportunism and its critics, *Managerial and Decision Economics*, 14: 97–107.

28 F. Lumineau & D. Malhotra, 2011, Shadow of the contract: How contract structure shapes interfirm dispute resolution, *Strategic Management Journal*, 32: 532–555; R. W. Coff & P. M. Lee, 2003, Insider trading as a vehicle to appropriate rent from R&D, *Strategic Management Journal*, 24: 183–190; C. C. Chen, M. W. Peng, & P. A. Saparito, 2002, Individualism, collectivism, and opportunism: A cultural perspective on transaction cost economics, *Journal of Management*, 28: 567–583; S. Ghoshal & P. Moran, 1996, Bad for practice: A critique of the transaction cost theory, *Academy of Management Review*, 21: 13–47.

29 M. L. McDonald, P. Khanna, & J. D. Westphal, 2008, Getting them to think outside the circle: Corporate governance, CEOs' external advice networks, and firm performance, *Academy of Management Journal*, 51: 453–475.

30. P. David, J. P. O'Brien, T. Yoshikawa, & A. Delios, 2010, Do shareholders or stakeholders appropriate the rents from corporate diversification? The influence of ownership structure, *Academy of Management Journal*, 53: 636–654; R. E. Hoskisson & T. A. Turk, 1990, Corporate restructuring: Governance and control limits of the internal market, *Academy of Management Review*, 15: 459–477.

31. J. Baixauli-Soler & G. Sanchez-Marin, 2011, Organizational governance and TMT pay level adjustment, *Journal of Business Research*, 64(8): 862–870; R. Bushman, Q. Chen, E. Engel, & A. Smith, 2004, Financial accounting information, organizational complexity and corporate governance systems, *Journal of Accounting and Economics*, 7: 167–201.

32. W. Grossman, 2010, The influence of board monitoring, executive incentives, and corporate strategy on employment stability, *Employee Responsibilities & Rights Journal*, 22(1): 45–64; M. Goranova, T. M. Alessandri, P. Brandes, & R. Dharwadkar, 2007, Managerial ownership and corporate diversification: A longitudinal view, *Strategic Management Journal*, 28: 211–225.

33. O. Faleye, 2011, CEO directors, executive incentives, and corporate strategic initiatives, *Journal of Financial Research*, 34(2): 241–277.

34. M. C. Jensen, 1986, Agency costs of free cash flow, corporate finance, and takeovers, *American Economic Review*, 76: 323–329.

35. E. B. Del Brio, E. L. Maia-Ramires, & A. De Miguel, 2011, Ownership structure and diversification in a scenario of weak shareholder protection, *Applied Economics*, 43(29): 4537–4547; M. Jensen & E. Zajac, 2004, Corporate elites and corporate strategy: How demographic preferences and structural position shape the scope of the firm, *Strategic Management Journal*, 25: 507–524; T. H. Brush, P. Bromiley, & M. Hendrickx, 2000, The free cash flow hypothesis for sales growth and firm performance, *Strategic Management Journal*, 21: 455–472.

36. M. Nippa, U. Pidun, & H. Rubner, 2011, Corporate portfolio management: Appraising four decades of academic research, *Academy of Management Perspectives*, 25(4): 50–66; K. Ramaswamy, M. Li, & B. S. P. Petitt, 2004, Who drives unrelated diversification? A study of Indian manufacturing firms, *Asia Pacific Journal of Management*, 21: 403–423; K. Ramaswamy, M. Li, & R. Veliyath, 2002, Variations in ownership behavior and propensity to diversify: A study of the Indian corporate context, *Strategic Management Journal*, 23: 345–358.

37. R. I. Anderson, J. D. Stowe, & X. Xing, 2011, Does corporate diversification reduce firm risk? Evidence from diversifying acquisitions, *Review of Pacific Basin Financial Markets & Policies*, 14(3): 485–504; A. Desai, M. Kroll, & P. Wright, 2005, Outside board monitoring and the economic outcomes of acquisitions: A test of the substitution hypothesis, *Journal of Business Research*, 58: 926–934; P. Wright, M. Kroll, A. Lado, & B. Van Ness, 2002, The structure of ownership and corporate acquisition strategies, *Strategic Management Journal*, 23: 41–53.

38. R. E. Hoskisson, M. W. Castleton, & M. C. Withers, 2009, Complementarity in monitoring and bonding: More intense monitoring leads to higher executive compensation, *Academy of Management Perspectives*, 23(2): 57–74; R. Rajan, H. Servaes, & L. Zingales, 2001, The cost of diversity: The diversification discount and inefficient investment, *Journal of Finance*, 55: 35–79; A. Sharma, 1997, Professional as agent: Knowledge asymmetry in agency exchange, *Academy of Management Review*, 22: 758–798.

39. D. Hoechle, M. Schmid, I. Walter, & D. Yermack, 2012, How much of the diversification discount can be explained by poor corporate governance? *Journal of Financial Economics*, 103(1): 41–60.

40. M. Hossain, S. Mitra, Z. Rezaee, & B. Sarath, 2011, Corporate governance and earnings management in the pre- and post-Sarbanes-Oxley Act regimes: Evidence from implicated option backdating firms, *Journal of Accounting, Auditing & Finance*, 28: 279–315; V. Chhaochharia & Y. Grinstein, 2007, Corporate governance and firm value: The impact of the 2002 governance rules, *Journal of Finance*, 62: 1789–1825.

41. Z. Singer & H. You, 2011, The effect of Section 404 of the Sarbanes-Oxley Act on earnings quality, *Journal of Accounting and Finance*, 26: 556–589; D. Reilly, 2006, Checks on internal controls pay off, *Wall Street Journal*, August 10, C3.

42. 2010, The Dodd-Frank Act: Financial reform update index, Faegre & Benson, http://www.faegrecom, September 7.

43. B. Appelmaum, 2011, Dodd-Frank supporters clash with currency chief, *New York Times*, http://www.nytimes.com, July 23.

44. B. L. Connelly, R. E. Hoskisson, L. Tihanyi, & S. T. Certo, 2010, Ownership as a form of corporate governance, *Journal of Management Studies*, 47: 1561–1589; J. Coles, N. Sen, & V. McWilliams, 2001, An examination of the relationship of governance mechanisms to performance, *Journal of Management*, 27: 23–50.

45. Del Brio, Maia-Ramires, & De Miguel, Ownership structure and diversification in a scenario of weak shareholder protection; R. E. Hoskisson, R. A. Johnson, & D. D. Moesel, 1994, Corporate divestiture intensity in restructuring firms: Effects of governance, strategy, and performance, *Academy of Management Journal*, 37: 1207–1251.

46. Connelly, Hoskisson, Tihanyi, & Certo, Ownership as a form of corporate governance; M. Singh, I. Mathur, & K. C. Gleason, 2004, Governance and performance implications of diversification strategies: Evidence from large U.S. firms, *Financial Review*, 39: 489–526.

47. J. Wu, D. Xu, & P. H. Phan, 2011, The effects of ownership concentration and corporate debt on corporate divestitures in Chinese listed firms, *Asia Pacific Journal of Management*, 28: 95–114; G. Iannotta, G. Nocera, & A. Sironi, 2007, Ownership structure, risk and performance in the European banking industry, *Journal of Banking & Finance*, 31: 2127–2149.

48. M. Fackler, 2008, South Korea faces question of corporate control, *New York Times*. http://nytimes.com. April 24.

49. D. Miller, S. Le Breton-Miller, & R. H. Lester, 2011, Family and lone founder ownership and strategic behavior: Social context, identity, and institutional logics, *Journal of Management Studies*, 48: 1–25; B. Villalonga & R. Amit, 2006, How do family ownership, control and management affect firm value? *Journal of Financial Economics*, 80: 385–417.

50. A. Berle & G. Means, 1932, *The Modern Corporation and Private Property*, New York: Macmillan.

51. 2011, Urge investors to vote all their proxies, *Investment News*, http://www.investmentnews.com, May 22.

52. I. Demiralp, R. D'Mello, F. P. Schlingemann, & V. Subramaniam, 2011, Are there monitoring benefits to institutional ownership? Evidence from seasoned equity offerings, *Journal of Corporate Finance*, 17(5): 1340–1359; Hoskisson, Hitt, Johnson, & Grossman, Conflicting voices.

53. S. Morgan, 2012, Investors get say on pay—Say OK, *SmartMoney*, www.smartmoney.com, March 12.

54. Y. Ertimur, F. Ferri, & S. R. Stubben, 2010, Board of directors' responsiveness to shareholders: Evidence from shareholder proposals, *Journal of Corporate Finance*, 16: 53–72; T. W. Briggs, 2007, Corporate governance and the new hedge fund activism: An empirical analysis, *Journal of Corporation Law*, 32: 681–723.

55. J. Zweig, 2012, Will new tools help small shareholders topple giants? *Wall Street Journal*, January 7, B1, B5.

56. 2011, Largest public pension fund thrives after crisis, National Public Radio, http://www.npr.org, May 6.

57. 2010, CalPERS adopts new plan for engaging underperforming portfolio companies, CalPERS homepage, http://www.calpers.ca.gov, November 15.

58. Ibid.

59. M. Hadani, M. Goranova, & R. Khan, 2011, Institutional investors, shareholder activism, and earnings management, *Journal of Business Research*, 64(12): 1352–1360; S. M. Jacoby, 2007, Principles and agents: CalPERS and corporate governance in Japan, *Corporate Governance*, 15: 5–15; L. Tihanyi, R. A. Johnson, R. E. Hoskisson, & M. A. Hitt, 2003, Institutional ownership differences and international diversification: The effects of boards of directors and technological opportunity, *Academy of Management Journal*, 46: 195–211.

60. J. He & Z. Huang, 2011, Board informal hierarchy and firm financial performance: Exploring a tacit structure guiding boardroom interactions, *Academy of Management Journal*, 54(6): 1119–1139; J. K. Seward & J. P Walsh, 1996, The governance and control of voluntary corporate spinoffs, *Strategic Management Journal*, 17: 25–39.

61. T. Dalziel, R. J. Gentry, & M. Bowerman, 2011, An integrated agency-resource dependence view of the influence of directors' human and relational capital on firms' R&D spending, *Journal of Management Studies*, 48: 1217–1242; S. Finkelstein & A. C. Mooney, 2003, Not the usual suspects: How to use board process to make boards better, *Academy of Management Executive*, 17: 101–113.

62. B. K. Boyd, K. Haynes, & F. Zona, 2011, Dimensions of CEO-board relations, *Journal of Management Studies*, 48(8): 1892–1923; K. Haynes & A. Hillman, 2010, The effect of board capital and CEO power on strategic change, *Strategic Management Journal*, 31(11): 1145–1163; D. R. Dalton, C. M. Daily, A. E. Ellstrand, & J. L. Johnson, 1998, Meta-analytic reviews of board composition, leadership structure, and financial performance, *Strategic Management Journal*, 19: 269–290.

63. N. Chancharat, C. Krishnamurti, & G. Tian, 2012, Board structure and survival of new economy IPO firms, *Corporate Governance: An International Review*, 20(2): 144–163; B. D. Baysinger & R. E. Hoskisson, 1990, The composition of boards of directors and strategic control: Effects on corporate strategy, *Academy of Management Review*, 15: 72–87.

64. Tuggle, Sirmon, Reutzel, & Bierman, Commanding board of director attention: Investigating how organizational performance and CEO duality affect board members' attention to monitoring; Carpenter & Westphal, Strategic context of external network ties; E. J. Zajac & J. D. Westphal, 1996, Director reputation, CEO-board power, and the dynamics of board interlocks, *Administrative Science Quarterly*, 41: 507–529.

65. E. Orden, 2012, Disney governance panel assailed over Iger's dual role, *Wall Street Journal*, March 2, B3.

66. M. Huse, R. E. Hoskisson, A. Zattoni, & R. Vigano, 2011, New perspectives on board research: Changing the research agenda, *Journal of Management and Governance*, 15(1): 5–28; M. Kroll, B. A. Walters, & P. Wright, 2008, Board vigilance, director experience and corporate outcomes, *Strategic Management Journal*, 29: 363–382.

67. A. Agrawal & M. A. Chen, 2011, Boardroom brawls: An empirical analysis of disputes involving directors, http://ssrn.com/abstracts=1362143; J. Roberts, T. McNulty, & P. Stiles, 2005, Beyond agency conceptions of the work of the non-executive director: Creating accountability in the boardroom, *British Journal of Management*, 16(S1): S5–S26.

68. Dalziel, Gentry & Bowerman, An integrated agency-resource dependence view of the influence of directors' human and relational capital on firms' R&D spending; S. Lhuillery, 2011, The impact of corporate governance practices on R&D efforts: A look at shareholders' rights, cross-listing, and control pyramid, *Industrial & Corporate Change*, 20(5): 1475–1513; P. Herrmann, J. Kaufmann, & H. Van Auken, 2010, The role of corporate governance in R&D intensity of US-based international firms, *International Journal of Commerce & Management*, 20(2): 91–108; Hoskisson, Hitt, Johnson, & Grossman, Conflicting voices.

69. Hoskisson, Castleton, & Withers, Complementarity in monitoring and bonding: More intense monitoring leads to higher executive compensation; E. E. Lawler III & D. L. Finegold, 2005, The changing face of corporate boards, *MIT Sloan Management Review*, 46(2): 67–70.

70. C. Ingley, J. Mueller, & C. Cocks, 2011, The financial crisis, investor activists and corporate strategy: Will this mean shareholders in the boardroom? *Journal of Management & Governance*, 15(4): 557–587.

71. A. O'Connell, 2010, How investors react when women join boards, *Harvard Business Review*, 88(7/8): 24.

72. D. Carey, J. J. Keller, & M. Patsalos-Fox, 2010, How to choose the right nonexecutive board leader, *McKinsey Quarterly*, May; W. Shen, 2005, Improve board effectiveness: The need for incentives, *British Journal of Management*, 16(51): 581–589; D. C. Hambrick & E. M. Jackson, 2000, Outside directors with a stake: The linchpin in improving governance, *California Management Review*, 42(4): 108–127.

73. C. Shropshire, 2010, The role of the interlocking director and board receptivity in the diffusion of practices, *Academy of Management Review*, 35: 246–264.

74. D. Northcott & J. Smith, 2011, Managing performance at the top: A balanced scorecard for boards of directors, *Journal of Accounting & Organizational Change*, 7: 33–56; L. Erakovic & J. Overall, 2010, Opening the 'black box': Challenging traditional governance theorems, *Journal of Management & Organization*, 16: 250–265.

75 M. J. Conyon, J. E. Core, & W. R. Guay, 2011, Are U.S. CEOs paid more than U.K. CEOs? Inferences from risk-adjusted pay, *Review of Financial Studies*, 24: 402–438; S. N. Kaplan, 2008, Are U.S. CEOs overpaid? *Academy of Management Perspectives*, 22(2): 5–20.

76 J. A. Martin & K. J. Davis, 2010, Stacked deck: Can governance structures explain CEO compensation differences across countries? *Academy of Management Perspectives*, 24(1): 78–79; E. A. Fong, V. F. Misangyi, Jr., & H. L. Tosi, 2010, The effect of CEO pay deviations on CEO withdrawal, firm size, and firm profits, *Strategic Management Journal*, 31: 629–651; J. P. Walsh, 2009, Are U.S. CEOs overpaid? A partial response to Kaplan, *Academy of Management Perspectives*, 23(1): 73–75.

77 J. Letzing, 2012, Apple CEO's compensation, *Wall Street Journal*, www.wsj.com, January 10.

78 Y. Ertimur, F. Ferri, & V. Muslu, 2011, Shareholder activism and CEO pay, *Review of Financial Studies*, 24(2): 535–592.

79 Shin & Seo, 2011, Less pay and more sensitivity?; L. A. Bebchuk & J. M. Fried, 2004, *Pay without Performance: The Unfulfilled Promise of Executive Compensation*, Cambridge, MA: Harvard University Press.

80 J. W. Fredrickson, A. Davis-Blake, & W. G. Sanders, 2010, Sharing the wealth: Social comparisons and pay dispersion in the CEO's top team, *Strategic Management Journal*, 31(10): 1031–1053; A. Henderson & J. Fredrickson, 2001, Top management team coordination needs and the CEO pay gap: A competitive test of economic and behavioral views, *Academy of Management Journal*, 44: 96–117.

81 N. Ozkan, 2011, CEO compensation and firm performance: An empirical investigation of UK panel data, *European Financial Management*, 17(2): 260–285; D. Souder & J. M. Shaver, 2010, Constraints and incentives for making long horizon corporate investments, *Strategic Management Journal*, 31: 1316–1336.

82 I. Filatotchev & D. Allcock, 2010, Corporate governance and executive remuneration: A contingency framework, *Academy of Management Perspectives*, 24(1): 20–33.

83 C. Southam & S. Sapp, 2010, Compensation across executive labor markets: What can we learn from cross-listed firms? *Journal of International Business Studies*, 41(1): 70–87; K. Roth & S. O'Donnell, 1996, Foreign subsidiary compensation: An agency theory perspective, *Academy of Management Journal*, 39: 678–703.

84 P. Adithipyangkul, I. Alon, & T. Zhang, 2011, Executive perks: Compensation and corporate performance in China, *Asia Pacific Journal of Management*, 28(2): 401–425; K. Ramaswamy, R. Veliyath, & L. Gomes, 2000, A study of the determinants of CEO compensation in India, *Management International Review*, 40(2): 167–191.

85 M. A. Carpenter, D. C. Indro, S. R. Miller, & M. Richards, 2010, CEO stock-based pay, home-country risk, and foreign firms' capital acquisition in the US market, *Corporate Governance: An International Review*, 18(6): 496–510; J. Krug & W. Hegarty, 2001, Predicting who stays and leaves after an acquisition: A study of top managers in multinational firms, *Strategic Management Journal*, 22: 185–196.

86 A. Capezio, J. Shields, & M. O'Donnell, 2011, Too good to be true: Board structural independence as a moderator of CEO pay-for-firm-performance, *Journal of Management Studies*, 48(3): 487–513; Werner, Tosi, & Gomez-Mejia, Organizational governance and employee pay.

87 Herrmann, Kaufmann, & Van Auken, The role of corporate governance in R&D intensity of US-based international firms; R. E. Hoskisson, M. A. Hitt, & C. W. L. Hill, 1993, Managerial incentives and investment in R&D in large multiproduct firms, *Organization Science*, 4: 325–341.

88 L. K. Meulbroek, 2001, The efficiency of equity-linked compensation: Understanding the full cost of awarding executive stock options, *Financial Management*, 30(2): 5–44.

89 R. Martin, 2011, The CEO's ethical dilemma in the era of earnings management, *Strategy & Leadership*, 39(6): 43–47.

90 D. Warren, M. Zey, T. Granston, & J. Roy, 2011, Earnings fraud: board control vs CEO control and corporate performance—1992–2004, *Managerial & Decision Economics*, 32(1): 17–34.

91 A. J. Wowak & D. C. Hambrick, 2010, A model of person-pay interaction: How executives vary in their responses to compensation arrangements, *Strategic Management Journal*, 31(8): 803–821; Z. Dong, C. Wang, & F. Xie, 2010, Do executive stock options induce excessive risk taking? *Journal of Banking & Finance*, 34(10): 2518–2529.

92 Manso, Motivating innovation; J. C. Bettis, J. M. Bizjak, & M. L. Lemmon, 2005, Exercise behavior, valuation and the incentive effects of employee stock options, *Journal of Financial Economics*, 76: 445–470.

93 H. Maurer, 2007, The Feds weigh in, *Business Week*, February 26, 36.

94 M. Martynova & L. Renneboog, 2011, The performance of the European market for corporate control: Evidence from the fifth takeover wave, *European Financial Management*, 17(2): 208–259; R. Coff, 2003, Bidding wars over R&D intensive firms: Knowledge, opportunism and the market for corporate control, *Academy of Management Journal*, 46: 74–85; Hitt, Hoskisson, Johnson, & Moesel, The market for corporate control and firm innovation; J. P. Walsh & R. Kosnik, 1993, Corporate raiders and their disciplinary role in the market for corporate control, *Academy of Management Journal*, 36: 671–700.

95 G. Y. Tian & G. Twite, 2011, Corporate governance, external market discipline and firm productivity, *Journal of Corporate Finance*, 17(3): 403–417; R. Sinha, 2004, The role of hostile takeovers in corporate governance, *Applied Financial Economics*, 14: 1291–1305; D. Goldstein, 2000, Hostile takeovers as corporate governance? Evidence from the 1980s, *Review of Political Economy*, 12: 381–402.

96 M. Wright, A. Jackson, & S. Frobisher, 2010, Private equity in the U.S.: Building a new future, *Journal of Applied Corporate Finance*, 22(4): 86–95.

97 M. C. Jensen, 2010, Active investors, LBOs, and the privatization of bankruptcy, *Journal of Applied Corporate Finance*, 22(1): 77–85; O. Kini, W. Kracaw, & S. Mian, 2004, The nature of discipline by corporate takeovers, *Journal of Finance*, 59: 1511–1551.

98 Sinha, The role of hostile takeovers.

99 Walsh & Kosnik, Corporate raiders.

100 E. Thorton, F. Keenan, C. Palmeri, & L. Himelstein, 2002, It sure is getting hostile, *Business Week*, January 14, 28–30.

101 M. C. Jensen, 2010, The modern industrial revolution, exit, and the failure of internal control systems, *Journal of Applied Corporate Finance*, 22(1): 43–58; S. Chatterjee, J. S. Harrison, & D. D. Bergh, 2003, Failed takeover attempts, corporate governance and refocusing, *Strategic Management Journal*, 24: 87–96.

102 T. Sokolyk, 2011, The effects of antitakeover provisions on acquisition targets, *Journal of Corporate Finance*, 17(3): 612–627.

103 M. Ryngaert & R. Scholten, 2010, Have changing takeover defense rules and strategies entrenched management and damaged shareholders? The case of defeated takeover bids, *Journal of Corporate Finance*, 16(1): 16–37.

104 P. Jiraporn & Y. Liu, 2011, Staggered boards, accounting discretion and firm value, *Applied Financial Economics*, 21(5): 271–285; O. Faleye, 2007, Classified boards, firm value, and managerial entrenchment, *Journal of Financial Economics*, 83: 501–529.

105 D. F. Larcker, G. Ormazabal, & D. J. Taylor, 2011, The market reaction to corporate governance regulation, *Journal of Financial Economics*, 101(2): 431–448.

106 Walsh & Kosnik, Corporate raiders.

107 W. Lee, 2011, Managerial entrenchment and the value of dividends, *Review of Quantitative Finance & Accounting*, 36(2): 297–322; A. Chakraborty & R. Arnott, 2001, Takeover defenses and dilution: A welfare analysis, *Journal of Financial and Quantitative Analysis*, 36: 311–334.

108 Jiraporn & Liu, Staggered boards, accounting discretion and firm value; C. Sundaramurthy, 2000, Antitakeover provisions and shareholder value implications: A review and a contingency framework, *Journal of Management*, 26: 1005–1030.

109 A. Delios, 2011, Governance: The next frontier for research on multinational firms, *Journal of Management Studies*, 48(2): 456–459.

110 I. Filatotchev & M. Wright, 2011, Agency perspectives on corporate governance of multinational enterprises, *Journal of Management Studies*, 48(2): 471–486; A. Inkpen & K. Ramaswamy, 2006, *Global Strategy: Creating and Sustaining Advantage across Borders*, New York: Oxford University Press; Aguilera & Jackson, The cross-national diversity of corporate governance.

111 T. Yoshikawa & A. A. Rasheed, 2010, Family control and ownership monitoring in family-controlled firms in Japan, *Journal of Management Studies*, 47(2): 274–295; S. M. Jacoby, 2004, *The Embedded Corporation: Corporate Governance and Employment Relations in Japan and the United States*, Princeton, NJ: Princeton University Press; T. Yoshikawa & P. H. Phan, 2001, Alternative corporate governance systems in Japanese firms: Implications for a shift to stockholder-centered corporate governance, *Asia Pacific Journal of Management*, 18: 183–205.

112 M. Martynova & L. Renneboog, 2011, Evidence on the international evolution and convergence of corporate governance regulations, *Journal of Corporate Finance*, 17(5): 1531–1557; P. Witt, 2004, The competition of international corporate governance systems: A German perspective, *Management International Review*, 44: 309–333.

113 P. C. Fiss, 2006. Social influence effects and managerial compensation evidence from Germany, *Strategic Management Journal*, 27: 1013–1031.

114 J. T. Addison & C. Schnabel, 2011, Worker directors: A German product that did not export? *Industrial Relations: A Journal of Economy and Society*, 50: 354–374; S. Douma, 1997, The two-tier system of corporate governance, *Long Range Planning*, 30(4): 612–615.

115 M. Karnitschnig, 2005, Too many chiefs at Siemens? German consensus culture may hamper forward-looking CEO, *Wall Street Journal*, January 20, A12.

116 S. Sudarsanam & T. Broadhurst, 2012, Corporate governance convergence in Germany through shareholder activism: Impact of the Deutsche Boerse bid for London Stock Exchange, *Journal of Management & Governance*, 16(2): 235–268.

117 A. Chizema, 2010, Early and late adoption of American-style executive pay in Germany: Governance and institutions, *Journal of World Business*, 45: 9–18; W. G. Sanders & A. C. Tuschke, 2007, The adoption of the institutionally contested organizational practices: The emergence of stock option pay in Germany, *Academy of Management Journal*, 50: 33–56.

118 S. Hirota, K. Kubo, H. Miyajima, H. Paul, & P. Y. Won, 2010, Corporate mission, corporate policies and business outcomes: Evidence from Japan, *Management Decision*, 48(7): 1134–1153; T. Hoshi, A. K. Kashyap, & S. Fischer, 2001, *Corporate Financing and Governance in Japan*, Boston: MIT Press.

119 Charkham, *Keeping Good Company*, 70.

120 Inkpen & Ramaswamy, *Global Strategy*, 188.

121 A. Chizema & Y. Shinozawa, 2012, The 'company with committees': Change or continuity in Japanese corporate governance? *Journal of Management Studies*, 49(1): 77–101.

122 T. Sueyoshi, M. Goto, & Y. Omi, 2010, Corporate governance and firm performance: Evidence from Japanese manufacturing industries after the lost decade, *European Journal of Operational Research*, 203(3): 724–736.

123 X. Wu & J. Yao, 2012, Understanding the rise and decline of the Japanese main bank system: The changing effects of bank rent extraction, *Journal of Banking & Finance*, 36: 36–50; I. S. Dinc, 2006, Monitoring the monitors: The corporate governance in Japanese banks and their real estate lending in the 1980s, *Journal of Business*, 79: 3057–3081.

124 K. Kubo & T. Saito, 2012, The effect of mergers on employment and wages: Evidence from Japan, *Journal of the Japanese and International Economies*, 26(2): 263–284; N. Isagawa, 2007, A theory of unwinding of cross-shareholding under managerial entrenchment, *Journal of Financial Research*, 30: 163–179.

125 J. M. Ramseyer, M. Nakazato, & E. B. Rasmusen, 2009, Public and private firm compensation: Evidence from Japanese tax returns, *Harvard Law and Economics* Discussion Paper, No. 628, February 1.

126 N. J. Yang, J. Chi, & M. Young, 2011, A review of corporate governance in China, *Asian-Pacific Economic Literature*, 25: 15–28; N. Boubarkri, J.-C. Cosset, & O. Guedhami, 2004, Postprivatization corporate governance: The role of ownership structure and investor protection, *Journal of Financial Economics*, 76: 369–399; K. Uhlenbruck, K. E. Meyer, & M. A. Hitt, 2003, Organizational transformation in transition economies: Resource-based and organizational learning perspectives, *Journal of Management Studies*, 40: 257–282.

127 J. Chi, Q. Sun, & M. Young, 2011, Performance and characteristics of acquiring firms in the Chinese stock

markets, *Emerging Markets Review*, 12: 152–170; Y.-L. Cheung, P. Jiang, P. Limpaphayom, & T. Lu, 2010, Corporate governance in China: A step forward, *European Financial Management*, 16: 94–123; H. Zou & M. B. Adams, 2008, Corporate ownership, equity risk and returns in the People's Republic of China, *Journal of International Business Studies*, 39: 1149–1168.

[128] S. Globerman, M. W. Peng, & D. M. Shapiro, 2011, Corporate governance and Asian companies, *Asia Pacific Journal of Management*, 28: 1–14; Y. Su, D. Xu, & P. H. Phan, 2008, Principal-principal conflict in the governance of the Chinese public corporation, *Management and Organization Review*, 4: 17–38.

[129] J. S. Harrison, D. A. Bosse, & R. A. Phillips, 2010, Managing for stakeholders, stakeholder utility functions, and competitive advantage, *Strategic Management Journal*, 31(1): 58–74; S. Sharma & I. Henriques, 2005, Stakeholder influences on sustainability practices in the Canadian forest products industry, *Strategic Management Journal*, 26: 159–180.

[130] V. Ho, 2010, "Enlightened Shareholder Value": Corporate governance beyond the shareholder-stakeholder divide, *Journal of Corporation Law*, 36(1): 59–112; P. A. Argenti, R. A. Howell, & K. A. Beck, 2005, The strategic communication imperative, *MIT Sloan Management Review*, 46(3): 83–89; S. L. Hart & S. Sharma, 2004, Engaging fringe stakeholders for competitive imagination, *Academy of Management Executive*, 18(1): 7–18; P. Nutt, 2004, Expanding the search for alternatives during strategic decision-making, *Academy of Management Executive*, 18(4): 13–28.

[131] S. Muthusamy, P. A. Bobinski, & D. Jawahar, 2011, Toward a strategic role for employees in corporate governance, *Strategic Change*, 20: 127–138; F. Stinglhamber, D. De Cremer, & L. F. Mercken, 2006, Support as a mediator of the relationship between justice and trust, *Group and Organization Management*, 31: 442–468; K. A. Hegtvedt, 2005, Doing justice to the group: Examining the roles of the group in justice research, *Annual Review of Sociology*, 31: 25–45; C. C. Chen, Y.-R. Chen, & K. Xin,

2004, Guanxi practices and trust in management: A procedural justice perspective, *Organization Science*, 15: 200–209.

[132] S. Ramchander, R. G. Schwebach, & K. Staking, 2012, The informational relevance of corporate social responsibility: Evidence from DS400 index reconstitutions, *Strategic Management Journal*, 33(3): 303–314; A. Kaufman & E. Englander, 2005, A team production model of corporate governance, *Academy of Management Executive*, 19(3): 9–22.

[133] H. Jo & M. Harjoto, 2012, The causal effect of corporate governance on corporate social responsibility, *Journal of Business Ethics*, 106(1): 53–72.

[134] J. E. Hunton, R. Hoitash, & J. C. Thibodeau, 2011, The relationship between perceived tone at the top and earnings quality, *Contemporary Accounting Research*, 28(4): 1190–1224; J. R. Deckop, K. K. Merriman, & S. Gupta, 2006, The effects of CEO pay structure on corporate social performance, *Journal of Management*, 32: 329–342.

[135] I. Okhmatovskiy & R. J. David, 2012, Setting your own standards: Internal corporate governance codes as a response to institutional pressure, *Organization Science*, 23(1): 155–176; C. Caldwell & R. Karri, 2005, Organizational governance and ethical systems: A covenantal approach to building trust, *Journal of Business Ethics*, 58: 249–259; A. Felo, 2001, Ethics programs, board involvement, and potential conflicts of interest in corporate governance, *Journal of Business Ethics*, 32: 205–218.

[136] J. Pae & T. Choi, 2011, Corporate governance, commitment to business ethics, and firm valuation: Evidence from the Korean stock market, *Journal of Business Ethics*, 100(2): 323–348; J. P. O'Connor, Jr., R. L. Priem, J. E. Coombs, & K. M. Gilley, 2006, Do stock options prevent or promote fraudulent financial reporting? *Academy of Management Journal*, 49: 483–500.

[137] Hoskisson, Castleton, & Withers, Complementarity in monitoring and bonding; H. Kim & R. E. Hoskisson, 1996, Japanese governance systems: A critical review, in S. B. Prasad (ed.), *Advances in International Comparative Management*, Greenwich, CT: JAI, 165–189.

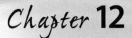

Chapter **12**

STRATEGIC ENTREPRENEURSHIP

KNOWLEDGE OBJECTIVES

Studying this chapter should provide you with the strategic management knowledge needed to:

1. Define and explain strategic entrepreneurship.

2. Explain the importance of entrepreneurial opportunities, innovation, and capabilities.

3. Discuss the importance of international entrepreneurship and describe why it is being used more frequently.

4. Describe incremental and radical innovations and the firm characteristics and actions that foster them.

5. Discuss how firms use cooperative strategies such as strategic alliances to develop innovation.

6. Explain how firms use acquisitions to increase their innovations and enrich their innovative capabilities.

7. Explain how strategic entrepreneurship can create value for customers and shareholders for all types of firms, large and small, new and established.

As we have discussed throughout this book, today's firms face a highly complex and dynamic competitive environment. Such an environment produces considerable uncertainty and generates important pressures that often constrain a firm's ability to successfully adapt to its competitive environment. A natural human tendency for inertia and resistance to change is one of those pressures.[1] In addition, the emphasis on corporate governance and control explored in Chapter 11 increases the pressure for conformity and reduces the flexibility executives have when leading their firm's efforts to respond to environmental changes. In the 21st-century competitive landscape, firm survival and success increasingly are a function of the firm's ability to continuously find new opportunities and quickly produce innovations to pursue them.[2] Consequently, those making strategic decisions must ensure that innovation is appropriately emphasized in their firms to offset forces that would otherwise damage their ability to flexibly adapt to what are often rapidly changing environmental conditions.

This chapter explores how strategic entrepreneurship facilitates a firm's efforts to effectively deal with a dynamic competitive environment.[3] **Strategic entrepreneurship** occurs as firms seek opportunities in the external environment that they can exploit through competitive advantages that are framed around innovations.[4] In the global competitive landscape, the long-term success of new ventures and established firms is a function of their ability to meld entrepreneurship with strategic management.[5] Innovative activity is essential to firms' efforts to differentiate their goods or services from competitors and create value for customers, which in turn is the foundation for developing competitive advantages.[6]

To describe how firms produce and manage innovation, we examine several topics in this chapter. To set the stage, we examine entrepreneurship and innovation in a strategic context. We then describe international entrepreneurship, a phenomenon reflecting the increased use of entrepreneurship in countries throughout the world. Next we examine the three primary means firms use to innovate. Internally, they innovate through either autonomous or induced strategic behavior; however, they may also innovate through cooperative strategies or by acquiring firms to take advantage of their innovations and innovative capabilities. This chapter focuses on **corporate entrepreneurship**, which is the application of entrepreneurship within an established firm.[7]

STRATEGIC ENTREPRENEURSHIP AND INNOVATION

Joseph Schumpeter viewed entrepreneurship as a process of "creative destruction," through which existing products or methods of production are destroyed and replaced with new ones.[8] Thus, **entrepreneurship** is the process by which individuals or groups identify and pursue entrepreneurial opportunities without the immediate constraint of the resources they currently control.[9] Entrepreneurial activity is an important mechanism for creating changes and for helping firms adapt to changes created by others.[10] Firms that encourage entrepreneurship are (1) risk takers, (2) committed to innovation, and (3) proactive—that is, they try to create opportunities rather than waiting to respond to opportunities that others create, identify, and/or exploit.[11] Some believe that today's reality is such that large companies as well as smaller ones "... will only succeed in the long-term by harnessing the ... spirit of entrepreneurship."[12]

Entrepreneurial opportunities represent conditions in which new products or services can satisfy a need in the market. These opportunities exist because of competitive imperfections in markets and among factors of production used to produce them,[13] and when information about these imperfections is distributed unevenly among individuals.[14] In other words, some people know about an opportunity to create value through satisfying an unmet need or by combining resources in a new way, whereas others are unaware of the opportunity. For example, a firm may discover an opportunity to design and sell a new product, sell an existing product in a new market, or create a product with a more efficient technology.[15] In general, thinking differently about customers' needs and how to compete against competitors are foundational to discovering opportunities.[16]

In this book, we examine the entrepreneurship of the individual firm; however, evidence suggests that entrepreneurship is the economic engine driving the economies of many nations in the global competitive landscape.[17] Entrepreneurship promotes economic growth, increases productivity, and creates jobs.[18] Thus, entrepreneurship and the innovation it spawns, is important for companies competing in the global economy and for countries seeking to stimulate economic climates with the potential to enhance the living standards of their citizens.

Innovation

Author Peter Drucker defined *innovation* as "the means by which the entrepreneur either creates new wealth-producing resources or endows existing resources with enhanced potential for creating wealth." He then argued that "innovation is the specific function of entrepreneurship, whether in an existing business, a public service institution, or a new venture started by a lone individual."[19] Thus, innovation and entrepreneurship are vital for young and old, large and small, and service and manufacturing firms, as well as for high-technology ventures. Moreover, evidence suggests that the most innovative companies are those that encourage everyone to understand that innovation as a core part of their jobs.[20] To support this conviction, innovative firms make financial slack available at all times to support employees' efforts to pursue entrepreneurial opportunities.[21]

Innovation is a key outcome firms seek through entrepreneurial activity and is often the source of competitive success especially in turbulent, highly competitive environments.[22] For example, research shows that firms competing in global industries investing more in innovation also achieve the highest returns.[23] In fact, investors often react positively to the introduction of a new product, thereby increasing the price of a firm's stock. Innovation, then, is an essential characteristic of high-performance firms.[24] Furthermore, in many global markets, innovation is increasingly becoming necessary for competitive parity much less competitive advantage. Sometimes firms restructure to enhance their ability to innovate and to earn the positive results innovation can produce. This is the case for India-based Alibaba Group, a firm that recently split its key Taobao unit into three separate companies to "foster and be more nimble for innovation."[25]

In his classic work, Schumpeter argued that firms engage in three types of innovative activity: invention, innovation, and imitation.[26] **Invention** is the act of creating or developing a new product or process. **Innovation** is the process of creating a commercial product from an invention. Innovation begins after an invention is chosen for development. Thus, an invention brings something new into *being*, and an innovation brings something new into *use*. Accordingly, technical criteria are used to determine the success of an invention, whereas commercial criteria are used to determine the success of an innovation.[27] Entrepreneurship is critical to innovative activity because it turns inventions into innovations.[28] Finally, **imitation** is the adoption of an innovation by similar firms. Imitation usually leads to product or process standardization, and products based on imitation often are offered at lower prices, but without as many features.

In the United States, innovation is the most critical of these three types of innovative activity. Many companies are able to create ideas that lead to inventions, but commercializing those inventions has at times proved difficult. This difficulty is suggested by the fact that approximately 80 percent of R&D occurs in large firms, but these same firms produce fewer than 50 percent of patents.[29] Patents are a strategic asset, and the ability to regularly produce them can be an important source of competitive advantage, especially for firms competing in knowledge-intensive industries, such as pharmaceuticals.[30]

The process of creating an innovative product or service is entrepreneurial, but individual products or services are unlikely to lead to sustainable competitive advantage because they can be imitated. Remember from Chapter 4 that resources that lead to sustainable competitive advantage must be valuable, rare, difficult to imitate, and nonsubstitutable. If a resource does not possess these characteristics, success will be only temporary. However, the ability to continuously create new innovations can be a source of sustainable competitive advantage. This ability is embedded in the entrepreneurial nature of the people in the organization, as well as in the systems and processes the firm uses to foster entrepreneurship.

Entrepreneurs

Entrepreneurs are individuals, acting independently or as part of an organization, who create a new venture or develop an innovation and take risks by introducing them into the marketplace.[31] Moreover, entrepreneurs are passionate about developing inventions with the ability to help people solves problems.[32]

Entrepreneurs are found throughout an organization—from top-level managers to those working directly to produce the company's products. For instance, entrepreneurs are found throughout W. L. Gore & Associates, where all workers are called "associates" and are given "dabble time, which is approximately 10 percent of their weekly hours." Associates are to use this time to experiment and innovate. Similarly, through "Google Time," employees spend up to 20 percent of their work time on any project that interests them with the purpose being able to innovate by pursuing projects they feel passionately about.[33] Entrepreneurs, such as those found at Gore, Google, and many other companies, as well as in start-up ventures, demonstrate several characteristics, including optimism, high motivation, willingness to take responsibility for projects, and courage.[34] They also tend to be passionate and emotional about the value and importance of their innovation-based ideas.[35]

Evidence suggests that successful entrepreneurs have an **entrepreneurial mind-set**, which values uncertainty in the marketplace and seeks to continuously identify opportunities with the potential to lead to important innovations.[36] A firm that has many individuals with an entrepreneurial mind-set can enjoy a competitive advantage because of the potential for continuous innovation. Firms need employees who think entrepreneurially. Consequently, top-level managers should try to establish an entrepreneurial culture that inspires individuals and groups to engage in corporate entrepreneurship.[37] Importantly, entrepreneurs or entrepreneurial managers must be able to identify opportunities others do not perceive.

As the CEO of Apple Inc., the late Steve was strongly committed to fostering innovation in the company and "was widely recognized as the driving force behind Apple's culture of innovation."[38] Tim Cook, Jobs's successor, intends to continue nurturing Apple's innovation-oriented culture, saying recently that "I am looking forward to the amazing opportunity of serving as CEO of the most innovative company in the world.... We are going to continue to make the best products in the world that delight our customers and make our employees incredibly proud of what they do."[39]

Having people with intellectual talent is only part of the firm's challenge to be entrepreneurial. The talent must be well-managed so that its potential can be realized. Because "innovation is an application of knowledge to produce new knowledge,"[40] effective management of knowledge within the firm is critical to strategic entrepreneurship. For instance, research has shown that firms in general as well as business units within existing firms are more innovative when they have access to new knowledge.[41] Transferring knowledge, however, can be difficult because the person receiving it must have the capacity to understand it.[42] The ability to understand new knowledge is increased if it is linked to existing knowledge. Thus, managers need to help members of the firm develop a strong knowledge base in addition to expanding that knowledge base in order to foster entrepreneurship.[43] Information systems, training programs, and cross-functional teams (described later in this chapter) can help facilitate these objectives.

International Entrepreneurship

International entrepreneurship is a process in which firms creatively discover and exploit opportunities that are outside their domestic markets in order to develop a competitive advantage.[44] Thus, entrepreneurship is a global phenomenon.[45] One reason it is so popular is that in general, internationalization leads to improved firm performance.[46] Nevertheless, decision makers should consider some of the risks associated with internationalization that are particularly relevant to entrepreneurship, such as unstable foreign currencies, inefficient markets, insufficient infrastructures to support businesses, and limitations on market size and growth.[47] Thus, the decision to engage in international entrepreneurship should be a product of careful analysis.

Because of its positive benefits, entrepreneurship is at the top of public policy agendas in many of the world's countries, including Finland, Israel, Ireland, and the members of the European Union, to name only a few. Some argue that placing entrepreneurship on these agendas may be appropriate in that regulation hindering innovation and entrepreneurship particularly in the new competitive landscape may account for some of Europe's productivity problems: "The biggest obstacle to European success in the digital economy is a lack of entrepreneurial culture."[48] While entrepreneurship in general in Europe may be underdeveloped, "... there are disproportionately even fewer women than men entrepreneurs." The European Network of Mentors for Women Entrepreneurs was launched in late 2011. This network provides "advice and support to women entrepreneurs on the start-up, running, and growth of their enterprises in the early phase of their life (from the second to the fourth year of existence of a new woman-run and owned enterprise)."[49]

In Ireland, where entrepreneurial activity is a key aspect of the national economy, evidence reported in 2012 indicated that a vibrant entrepreneurial culture was thriving in this country in spite of difficult economic conditions. The Irish Development Authority (IDA), a state agency charged with attracting and growing foreign multinational businesses in Ireland, facilitates entrepreneurial activity in this nation, as do groups such as TechBrew that are forming among those seeking to be successful entrepreneurs. TechBrew meetings, which are informal gatherings "... of software company managers and would-be entrepreneurs" who interact for the purpose of learning from each other and coalescing around product ideas, is such a group.[50] Focusing on exports, Enterprise Ireland is a second government organization that is "responsible for the development and growth of Irish enterprises in world markets." The agency's charter finds it working "in partnership with Irish enterprises to help them start, grow, innovate, and win export sales in global markets."[51]

As this information about efforts to support entrepreneurship in certain countries implies, different countries have different rates of entrepreneurship. In 2012, the 11 most entrepreneurial countries (beginning with the most entrepreneurial) were the United States, Sweden, Australia, Iceland, Denmark, Canada, Switzerland, Belgium, Norway, the Netherlands, and Taiwan (which was the first Asian country to appear in the list of the most entrepreneurial countries).[52]

National culture contributes to differences in rates of entrepreneurship across countries. For example, the tension between individualism and collectivism can affect entrepreneurship. Research has shown that entrepreneurship declines as collectivism is emphasized. However, research also suggests that exceptionally high levels of individualism can be dysfunctional for entrepreneurship—people might not combine the ideas of others with their own to create unique goods or services. These results appear to call for a balance between individual initiative and a spirit of cooperation and group ownership of innovation. For firms to be entrepreneurial, they must provide appropriate autonomy and incentives for individual initiative to surface, but they also must promote cooperation and group ownership of an innovation if it is to be implemented successfully. Thus, entrepreneurship often requires teams of people with unique skills and resources, especially in cultures where collectivism is a valued historical norm.[53]

Another important dimension of international entrepreneurship is the level of investment outside of the home country made by new ventures. In fact, with increasing globalization, a greater number of new ventures have been "born global."[54] It has been noted that "talent and ideas are flourishing everywhere— from Bangalore to Shanghai to Kiev—and no company, regardless of geography, can hesitate to go wherever those ideas are."[55] Research has shown that new ventures that enter international markets gain more new technological knowledge and thereby enhance their performance.[56] Because of these outcomes, the amount of international entrepreneurship has been increasing in recent years.[57]

The probability of entering international markets increases when the firm has top executives with international experience.[58] Furthermore, the firm has a higher likelihood of successfully competing in international markets when its top executives have such experience.[59] Because of the learning and economies of scale and scope afforded by operating in international markets, both young and established internationally diversified firms often are stronger competitors in their domestic markets as well. Additionally, research has shown that internationally diversified firms generally are more innovative.[60]

We now focus on the methods firms use to innovate: internal innovation, cooperative ventures, and purchasing innovation through acquisitions. A firm's governance mechanisms influence its choices about methods it will use to innovate. For example, research has shown that inside board members with equity positions favor internal innovation, whereas outside directors with equity positions prefer acquisitions.[61]

INTERNAL INNOVATION

In established organizations, most corporate innovation is developed through R&D. Large established firms use R&D to create the new technology and products that make the old technologies and products obsolete. Some believe that the most competitively successful firms, including large ones, learn how to reinvent their industry or develop a new one while competing with rivals.[62] *Internal corporate venturing* is the set of activities firms use to develop internal inventions and innovations.[63]

3M has an impressive record of successful internal innovations. The company developed the first cellulose tape, Scotch Tape, in 1930, and it is still popular today. Since that time, some of the company's most famous innovations include Post-It Notes, Scotchgard fabric protector, and Filtrete air-cleaning filters. Serving customers through six business segments (including consumer and office business and health care business as examples), 3M's attitude about entrepreneurship is reflected in the company's statement: "Our inspiration comes from listening to customers and creating new products and solutions for the challenges and opportunities you face."[64]

Incremental Innovations

Firms produce two types of internal innovations—incremental and radical—when using their R&D activities. Most innovations are *incremental*—that is, they build on existing knowledge bases and provide small improvements in well-defined current product lines.[65] Incremental innovations are evolutionary and linear in nature, with the underlying production technologies emphasizing efficiency. Consequently, profit margins tend to be lower and competition is often based primarily on price.[66] Adding a different kind of whitening agent to a soap detergent, Gillette's decision to add a second blade to a single-blade razor, and automobile companies' inclusion of cup holders, electric windows instead of manual windows, and several, higher-quality audio speakers instead of a single speaker are examples of incremental innovations.

Some label the process through which incremental innovations are produced *induced strategic behavior*, which is a top-down process whereby the firm's current strategy and structure foster product innovations that are closely associated with that strategy and structure. In this form of innovating, the strategy in place is filtered through the firm's existing structural hierarchy. In essence, induced strategic behavior results in internal innovations that do not alter the firm's current strategy. Often, firms that are market pioneers continue their innovation by using an induced approach, providing only incremental innovations to their existing products.[67]

Radical Innovations

In contrast to incremental innovations, *radical innovations* usually provide significant technological breakthroughs and create new knowledge.[68] These types of innovations have become increasingly important for achieving and maintaining a competitive advantage in many industries.[69] The microprocessing chip, Amazon.com's Internet-based approach to selling books, and digital photography, are examples of radical innovations. Although both incremental and radical innovations have the potential to lead to growth in revenues and profits, the potential is greater with radical innovations because they establish new functionalities for users.

Despite potential returns, radical innovations are rare because of the difficulty and risk involved in developing them. Additionally, the value of the technology and the market opportunities are highly uncertain.[70] Because radical innovation creates new knowledge and uses only some or little of a firm's current product or technological knowledge, creativity is required. However, creativity does not create something from nothing. Rather, it discovers, combines, or synthesizes current knowledge, often from diverse areas.[71] This knowledge is then integrated into the development of new products or services that a firm can use in an entrepreneurial manner to move into new markets, capture new customers, or gain access to new resources. Such innovations are often developed in separate units in a firm that start internal ventures.

Autonomous strategic behavior is a bottom-up process in which product champions pursue new ideas, often through a political process, to develop and coordinate the commercialization of a new good or service. A *product champion* is an individual with an entrepreneurial vision of a new good or service who seeks to create support in the organization for its commercialization.[72] Product champions play critical roles in moving innovations forward.[73] Commonly, product champions use their social capital to develop informal networks within the firm. As progress is made, these networks become more formalized as a means of pushing an innovation to the point of successful commercialization. Internal innovations springing from autonomous strategic behavior tend to diverge from the firm's current strategy, taking it into new markets and perhaps new ways of creating value.

Autonomous strategic behavior is based on a firm's wellsprings of knowledge and resources that are the sources of its innovation. Thus, a firm's technological capabilities and competencies are the basis for new products and processes.[74] General Electric regularly depends on autonomous strategic behavior to produce innovations.[75] Commonly, this happens when people working within a particular unit of GE try to find a new technology that will facilitate efforts to improve the unit's operations. If the new technology proves successful, the unit in which a new technology originated may try to sell that technology for use in other GE units.[76]

To be effective, an autonomous process for developing new products requires continuous diffusion of new knowledge throughout the firm. In particular, the diffusion of tacit knowledge (which is difficult to convey in writing) is important for developing effective new products.[77] Interestingly, some of the processes important for the promotion of behaviors conducive to autonomous new product development vary by the environment and country in which a firm operates. For example, the Japanese culture is high on uncertainty avoidance; thus, research has found that Japanese firms are more likely to engage in autonomous behaviors under conditions of low uncertainty.[78]

Internally developed innovations result from deliberate efforts. A larger number of radical innovations spring from autonomous strategic behavior, whereas the greatest percentage of incremental innovations comes from induced strategic behavior. Most successful firms develop both radical and incremental innovations. Although critical to long-term competitiveness, the outcomes of investments in innovative activities are uncertain and often not achieved in the short term,[79] which means that patience is required as firms evaluate the outcomes of their R&D efforts.

IMPLEMENTING INTERNAL INNOVATION

As mentioned previously, an entrepreneurial mind-set is necessary for developing successful internal innovation. This mind-set embraces uncertainty and opportunities that come from changes in the environment. Those with an entrepreneurial mind-set are able to help firms create new products and new markets. However, they also emphasize execution as they "engage the energies of everyone in their domain," both inside and outside the organization.[80] Table 12.1 shows some of the factors that encourage and discourage innovation in established firms.

Established firms that are successful at innovation encourage people to discuss new ideas and take risks. These firms tolerate failures and encourage organizational members to learn from them. Rewards systems that encourage innovation—such as pay raises, promotions, awards, perquisites, and public and private recognition— are also important.[81] The people who are the lifeblood of innovation in organizations should be rewarded adequately so that they do not feel compelled to leave the organization in order to receive the rewards they deserve.

Minimal penalties for innovation-related failures are also critical to promoting entrepreneurship in companies. According to William McKnight, the former CEO of 3M who is credited with being the catalyst for the company's unique entrepreneurial culture: "Mistakes will be made. But if a person is essentially right, the mistakes he or she makes are not as serious in the long run as the mistakes management will make if it undertakes to tell those in authority exactly how they must do their jobs. Management that is destructively critical when mistakes are made kills initiative. And, it's essential that we have many people with initiative if we are to continue to grow."[82]

TABLE 12.1 FACTORS THAT INFLUENCE INNOVATION IN ESTABLISHED FIRMS	
FACTORS THAT ENCOURAGE INNOVATION	**FACTORS THAT DISCOURAGE INNOVATION**
▶ Top management team supportive of innovation	▶ Top management team supportive of status quo
▶ Organizational idea champions	▶ Absence of idea champions
▶ Reward systems that encourage risk taking	▶ Reward systems that harshly punish failures
▶ Culture that emphasizes learning, teamwork, creativity, and accomplishment of group goals	▶ Culture that fosters individual accomplishment over team or organizational goals
▶ Decentralized decision making and innovation approval process	▶ Centralized decision making and innovation approval process
▶ Ample resources allocated to innovative processes	▶ Scarce resources allocated to innovative processes
▶ Strong communications system that records and disseminates information about innovations throughout organization	▶ Outdated communications systems, strong administrative hierarchy and "closed-door" offices throughout organization
▶ Participation with external research organizations and cooperation with other firms	▶ Strong emphasis on developing innovations "in-house"

© Cengage Learning

Effective integration of the various functions involved in innovation processes—from engineering to manufacturing and ultimately, market distribution—is required for the firm to fully benefit from its internal innovation efforts.[83] Increasingly, product development teams are being used to integrate the activities associated with different organizational functions. When used successfully, product development teams produce cross-functional integration. Such coordination involves coordinating and applying the knowledge and skills of different functional areas in order to maximize innovation.[84] Effective product development teams can also help a firm dismantle projects once they are determined to be unsuccessful.[85]

Cross-Functional Product Development Teams

Cross-functional teams facilitate efforts to integrate activities associated with different organizational functions such as design, manufacturing, and marketing.[86] In addition, new product development processes can be completed more quickly and the products more easily commercialized when cross-functional teams work effectively.[87] Using cross-functional teams, product development stages are grouped into parallel or overlapping processes so the firm can tailor its product development efforts to its core competencies and the needs of individual markets.

Horizontal organizational structures support the use of cross-functional teams in their efforts to integrate innovation-based activities across organizational functions.[88] Therefore, instead of being built around vertical hierarchical functions or departments, the organization is built around core horizontal processes that are used to produce and manage innovations. Some of the core horizontal processes that are critical to innovation efforts are formal; they may be defined and documented as procedures and practices. More commonly, however, these processes are informal routines or patterns of work that develop over time. Often invisible, informal routines are critical to successful product innovations and are supported properly through horizontal organizational structures more so than through vertical organizational structures.

Team members' independent frames of reference are a barrier that may prevent successfully using cross-functional teams as a means of integrating organizational functions.[89] Team members working within a distinct specialization (i.e., a particular organizational function) may have an independent frame of reference typically based on common backgrounds and experiences within that specialization. They are likely to use the same decision criteria to evaluate issues, such as product development efforts that they use within their functional units. Research suggests that functional departments vary along four dimensions: time orientation, interpersonal orientation, goal orientation, and formality of structure.[90] Thus, individuals from separate functional departments who have different orientations on these dimensions can be expected to emphasize unique priorities in product development activities. For example, a design engineer may consider the characteristics that make a product functional and workable to be the most important of the product's characteristics. Alternatively, a person from the marketing function may hold characteristics that satisfy customer needs most important. These different orientations can create barriers to effective communication across functions.[91]

Organizational politics is a second potential barrier to effective integration in cross-functional teams.[92] In some organizations, considerable political activity may center on allocating resources to different functions. Interunit conflict may result from aggressive competition for resources among those representing different organizational functions. This dysfunctional conflict between functions creates a barrier to their integration. Methods must be found to achieve cross-functional integration without excessive political conflict and without changing the basic structural characteristics necessary for task specialization and efficiency.

Facilitating Integration and Implementation

Shared values and effective leadership are important to achieve cross-functional integration and to effectively implement innovation.[93] Highly effective shared values are framed around the firm's mission and become the glue that promotes integration between functional units. Thus, the firm's culture promotes unity and internal innovation.[94]

Beginning with the leadership of founder Bill Gore, W. L. Gore & Associates remains a highly innovative company. It uses fluoropolymer technology as the foundation for producing a wide variety of fabrics, medical implants, industrial sealants, filters, and signal transmission and consumer products. Supporting innovation is a unique culture within the organization. Since Bill Gore founded the company in 1958, Gore has been a team-based, flat lattice organization that fosters personal initiative:

> How we work sets us apart. There are no traditional organizational charts, no chains of command, nor pre-determined channels of communication. Instead, we communicate directly with each other and are accountable to fellow members of our multi-disciplined teams. We encourage hands-on innovation, involving those closest to a project in decision making. Teams organize around opportunities and leaders emerge. This unique kind of corporate structure has proven to be a significant contributor to associate satisfaction and retention.[95]

As demonstrated by the example of Bill Gore, strategic leadership is also highly important for achieving cross-functional integration and promoting innovation. Leaders set the goals and allocate resources.[96] The goals include integrated development and commercialization of new goods and services. Effective strategic leaders continuously remind organizational members of the value of product innovations. In the most desirable situations, this value-creating potential becomes the basis for integrating and managing activities taking place in different functional departments. Effective strategic leaders also ensure a high-quality communication system to facilitate cross-functional integration. A critical benefit of effective communication is the sharing of knowledge among team members.[97] Effective communication thus helps create synergy and gains team members' commitment to an innovation. Shared values and leadership practices shape the communication systems that are formed to support the development and commercialization of new products.[98]

Creating Value from Internal Innovation

Figure 12.1 shows how the firm can create value from the internal processes it uses to develop and commercialize new goods and services. An *entrepreneurial mind-set* is necessary so that managers and employees consistently try to identify entrepreneurial opportunities the firm can pursue by developing new goods and services and new

FIGURE 12.1 CREATING VALUE THROUGH INTERNAL INNOVATION PROCESSES

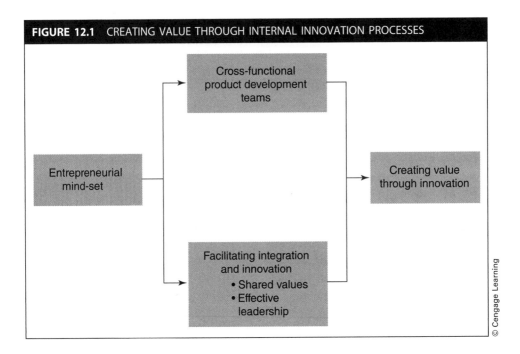

markets. *Cross-functional product development teams* are important to promote integrated new product design ideas and commitment to their implementation. *Shared values and effective leadership* promote integration and vision for innovation and commitment to it. The end result for the firm is the *creation of value* for customers and shareholders by developing and commercializing new products.

We now turn to the other ways firms innovate—by using cooperative strategies and by acquiring companies.

INNOVATION THROUGH COOPERATIVE STRATEGIES

Most firms lack the breadth and depth of internal resources and knowledge to produce the level of continuous innovation necessary to sustain competitive advantage in dynamic competitive markets.[99] With increasing frequency, alliances are used to acquire the resources needed to produce or manage innovations.[100] To innovate through a cooperative relationship, firms share their knowledge, skills, and other resources,[101] such as is the case with GE and Intel. These firms recently formed a 50/50 joint venture (called GE Care Innovations) to produce products for the telehealth care market. This market is expected to increase substantially as the population of many countries continues aging. Chronic disease management, independent living, and assistive technologies are the core areas in which the venture seeks to develop products and services for customers.[102]

Both entrepreneurial ventures and established firms use cooperative strategies, such as strategic alliances or joint ventures, to innovate. For example, an entrepreneurial venture may seek investment capital along with an established firm's distribution capabilities to successfully introduce one of its products to the market.[103]

Alternatively, more established companies may need new technological knowledge and can gain access to it through alliances with newer entrepreneurial firms.[104] Alliances between large pharmaceutical firms and biotechnology companies have become increasingly common to integrate the knowledge and resources of both to develop new products and bring them to market.[105]

Because of the importance of alliances, particularly in the development of new technology and in commercializing innovations, firms are beginning to build networks of alliances that represent a form of social capital.[106] This is the case in the global automobile manufacturing industry where multiple firms are forming networks to develop engines as the foundation for products that will be capable of meeting customers' demands for environmentally-friendly cars and trucks. Daimler, Renault, and Nissan, for example, have formed an alliance to build cars with cleaner diesel and gas engines. Similarly, BMW and PSA Peugeot-Citroen are using a network of relationships to develop the components required to successfully manufacture products based on hybrid technologies.[107]

The social capital that develops as firms collaborate, such as is happening with automobile manufacturers, helps them to obtain the knowledge and other resources they need to develop innovations.[108] Knowledge from these alliances helps firms develop new capabilities.[109] Some firms allow external firms to participate in their internal new product development processes. It is not uncommon for firms to have supplier representatives on their cross-functional innovation teams because of the importance of the suppliers' input to ensure quality materials for any new product developed. Increasingly, firms are using this collaborative approach to carry out green innovation in product development efforts.[110]

However, alliances formed for the purpose of innovation are not without risks. In addition to the conflict that is natural when firms try to work together to reach a mutual goal,[111] participants in a cooperative activity also take a risk that a partner will appropriate the firm's technology or knowledge and use it to enhance its own competitive abilities.[112] To prevent or minimize this risk, firms, particularly new ventures, need to select their partners carefully. The ideal partnership is one in which the firms have complementary skills and compatible strategic goals.[113] However, because companies are operating in a network of firms and thus may be participating in multiple alliances simultaneously, they encounter challenges in managing the alliances. Research has shown that firms can become involved in too many alliances, which can harm rather than help their innovation capabilities.[114] Thus, effectively managing the cooperative relationships to produce innovation is critical.

INNOVATION THROUGH ACQUISITIONS

Firms sometimes acquire companies to gain access to their innovations and innovative capabilities.[115] One reason for this is that the capital market values growth. Acquisitions provide a means to rapidly extend one or more product lines and increase the firm's revenues. Acquisitions pursued for this reason should have a strategic rationale though. This appears to be the case at 3M where the firm's new CEO is committed to acquiring small and mid-size companies for the purpose of supporting the firm's technological innovation skills as a key source of the firm's differentiation from its competitors.[116] Similarly, Dell Inc. seeks to innovate through acquisitions as it expands its market-leading position in "... supplying computer servers that run the Web services of clients such as Google Inc. and Baidu Inc." In describing this interest, a Dell official said that his firm wants to "... continue to bring innovation through acquisitions [and that the firm] is interested in buying everything around data centers."[117]

Similar to internal corporate venturing and strategic alliances, acquisitions are not a risk-free approach to innovating. A key risk is that a firm may substitute an ability to buy innovations for an ability to produce innovations internally. Research shows that firms engaging in acquisitions may introduce fewer new products into the market.[118] This substitution may occur because firms lose strategic control and focus instead on financial control of their original, and especially of their acquired, business units. However, firms that emphasize innovation, and carefully select companies for acquisition that also emphasize innovation, are likely to remain innovative.[119]

CREATING VALUE THROUGH STRATEGIC ENTREPRENEURSHIP

Newer entrepreneurial firms often are more effective than larger firms in identifying opportunities.[120] As a consequence, it seems that entrepreneurial ventures produce more radical innovations than do their larger, more established counterparts. The strategic flexibility and willingness of such ventures to take risks may account for their ability to spot opportunities and then develop radical innovations to pursue them.

Alternatively, larger and well-established firms often have more resources and capabilities to exploit identified opportunities.[121] Younger, entrepreneurial firms are generally opportunity seeking, while more established firms are advantage seeking. Both orientations are essential to sustaining competitive advantage in the 21st-century competitive landscape. Thus, newer entrepreneurial firms must learn how to gain a competitive advantage and older, more established firms must relearn how to identify entrepreneurial opportunities. The concept of strategic entrepreneurship suggests that firms can be simultaneously entrepreneurial and strategic regardless of their size and age.

As emphasized throughout this chapter, to be entrepreneurial, firms must develop an entrepreneurial mind-set among their managers and employees. Managers must emphasize the development of their resources, particularly human and social capital.[122] The importance of knowledge to identify and exploit opportunities, as well as to gain and sustain a competitive advantage, suggests that firms must have strong human capital.[123] Social capital is critical for access to complementary resources from partners in order to compete effectively in domestic and international markets.[124] Firms that seek knowledge from a broad group of external stakeholders can use that knowledge to sustain innovation.[125]

Many entrepreneurial opportunities continue to surface in international markets, a reality that is contributing to firms' willingness to engage in international entrepreneurship. By entering global markets that are new to them, firms can learn new technologies and management practices and diffuse this knowledge throughout the entire firm. Furthermore, the knowledge that firms gain can contribute to their innovations. As noted earlier in this chapter, firms operating in international markets tend to be more innovative.[126] Entrepreneurial ventures and large firms are now regularly moving into international markets. Both types of firms must also be innovative to compete effectively. Thus, by developing resources (human and social capital), taking advantage of opportunities in domestic and international markets, and using the resources and knowledge gained in these markets to be innovative, firms achieve competitive advantages.[127] In so doing, they create value for their customers and shareholders.

Firms that practice strategic entrepreneurship contribute to a country's economic development. In fact, as we discussed earlier, some countries, such as Ireland, are making dramatic economic progress by changing the institutional rules for businesses operating in the country and by establishing government agencies to facilitate both domestic and international entrepreneurship.[128] This could be construed as a form of institutional entrepreneurship,[129] which is the set of activities underlying the creation of new institutions or businesses. Likewise, firms that seek to establish their technology as a standard, also representing institutional entrepreneurship, are engaging in strategic entrepreneurship because creating a standard produces a sustainable competitive advantage for the firm.[130]

Research shows that because of its economic importance and individual motives, entrepreneurial activity is increasing across the globe. In particular, more women are becoming entrepreneurs because of the economic opportunity entrepreneurship provides and the individual independence it affords.[131] In the United States, for example, women, along with senior citizens, are one of the nation's fastest-growing groups of entrepreneurs.[132] In the future, entrepreneurial activity may increase the wealth of less-affluent countries and continue to contribute to the economic development of more-affluent countries. Regardless, the companies that learn how to successfully engage in strategic entrepreneurship are likely to be the winners in the 21st century.

SUMMARY

▶ Strategic entrepreneurship means taking entrepreneurial actions using a strategic perspective. More specifically, it involves seeking entrepreneurial opportunities and competitive advantage simultaneously to design and implement strategies for the purpose of creating value for customers and wealth for stakeholders.

▶ The concepts of entrepreneurial opportunity, innovation, and capabilities are important to firms. Entrepreneurial opportunities represent conditions in which new products or services can satisfy a need in the market. The essence of entrepreneurship is to identify and exploit these opportunities. Innovation is the process of commercializing the products or processes developed through invention. Entrepreneurial capabilities include building an entrepreneurial culture, having a passion for the business, and taking measured risk.

▶ Entrepreneurship is being practiced in many countries and is strongly related to a nation's economic growth. This relationship is a primary reason for the increasing incidence of entrepreneurship and corporate entrepreneurship in countries throughout the global economy.

- Three basic approaches are used to produce and manage innovation: internal innovations through corporate venturing, strategic alliances, and acquisitions. Internal innovations are either incremental or radical.
- Incremental innovations build on existing knowledge bases and provide small improvements in current product lines. Incremental innovations typically are produced through induced strategic behavior, a process whereby the firm's current strategy and structure foster product innovations that are closely associated with that strategy and structure.
- Radical innovations provide significant technological breakthroughs and create new knowledge. These types of innovations are supported by autonomous strategic behavior, a bottom-up process in which product champions pursue new ideas to develop and coordinate the commercialization of a new good or service.
- Cross-functional integration is vital to a firm's efforts to develop and implement internal corporate venturing activities and to commercialize the resulting innovation. Additionally, a firm can facilitate integration and innovation by developing shared values and practicing entrepreneurial leadership.
- It is difficult for an individual firm to possess all the knowledge needed to innovate consistently and effectively. To gain access to the kind of specialized knowledge that often is required to innovate, firms may form cooperative relationships such as strategic alliances with other firms, which may sometimes include competitors.
- Innovation can also be acquired through direct acquisition, or firms can learn new capabilities from an acquisition, thereby enriching their internal innovation processes.
- The practice of strategic entrepreneurship by all types of firms, large and small, new and more established, creates value for all stakeholders, especially for customers and shareholders. Strategic entrepreneurship also contributes to the economic development of nations. Thus, entrepreneurial activity is important to nations throughout the world and companies operating within them.

ETHICS QUESTIONS

1. Do managers have an ethical obligation to any of their stakeholders to ensure that their firms remain innovative? If so, to which stakeholders and why?
2. What types of ethical issues do firms encounter when they use internal corporate-venturing processes to produce and manage innovation?
3. Firms that are partners in a strategic alliance may legitimately seek to gain knowledge from each other. At what point does it become unethical for a firm to gain additional and competitively relevant knowledge from its partner? Is this point different when a firm partners with a domestic firm as opposed to a foreign firm? Why or why not?
4. Discuss the ethical implications associated with quickly bringing a new product to market.
5. Small firms often have innovative products. When is it appropriate for a large firm to buy a small firm for its product innovations and new product ideas?

1. T. J. Quigley & D. C. Hambrick, 2012, When the former CEO stays on as board chair: Effects on successor discretion, strategic change and performance, *Strategic Management Journal*, 33: in press; D. Ravasi & N. Phillips, 2011, Strategies of alignment: Organizational identity management and strategic change at Bang & Olufsen, *Strategic Organization*, 9: 103–135.

2. A. J. Bock, T. Opsahl, G. George, & D. M. Gann, 2012, The effects of culture and structure on strategic flexibility during business model innovation, *Journal of Management Studies*, 49: 279–305; C. A. Siren, M. Kohtamaki, & A. Kuckertz, 2012, Exploration and exploitation strategies, profit performance, and the mediating role of strategic learning: Escaping the exploitation trap, *Strategic Entrepreneurship Journal*, 6: 18–41.

3. S. W. Bradley, D. A. Shepherd, & J. Wiklund, 2011, The importance of slack for new organizations facing 'tough' environments, *Journal of Management Studies*, 48: 1071–1097; C. Navis & M. A. Glynn, 2011, Legitimate distinctiveness and the entrepreneurial identity: Influence on investor judgments of new venture plausibility, *Academy of Management Review*, 36: 479–499.

4. M. A. Hitt, R. D. Ireland, D. G. Sirmon, & C. A. Trahms, 2011, Strategic entrepreneurship: Creating value for individuals, organizations, and society, *Academy of Management Perspectives*, 25: 57–75; M. A. Hitt, R. D. Ireland, S. M. Camp, & D. L. Sexton, 2001, Strategic entrepreneurship: Entrepreneurial strategies for wealth creation, *Strategic Management Journal*, 22(special issue): 479–491; R. D. Ireland, M. A. Hitt, S. M. Camp, & D. L. Sexton, 2001, Integrating entrepreneurship and strategic management actions to create firm wealth, *Academy of Management Executive*, 15(1): 49–63.

5. J. W. Webb, D. A. Ketchen, Jr., & R. D. Ireland, 2010, Strategic entrepreneurship within family-controlled firms: Opportunities and challenges, *Journal of Family Business Strategy*, 1(2): 67–77; R. D. Ireland, M. A. Hitt, & D. G. Sirmon, 2003, A model of strategic entrepreneurship: The construct and its dimensions, *Journal of Management*, 29: 963–989.

6. A. Perez-Luno, J. Wiklund, & R. V. Cabrera, 2011, The dual nature of innovative activities: How entrepreneurial orientation influences innovation generation and adoption, *Journal of Business Venturing*, 26: 555–571; R. Amit, C. Lucier, M. A. Hitt, & R. D. Nixon, 2002, Strategies for the entrepreneurial millennium, in M. A. Hitt, R. Amit, C. Lucier, & R. Nixon (eds.), *Creating Value: Winners in the New Business Environment*, Oxford, UK: Blackwell Publishers, 1–12.

7. K. Shimizu, 2012, Risks of corporate entrepreneurship: Autonomy and agency issues, *Organization Science*, in press; B. R. Barringer & R. D. Ireland, 2011, *Entrepreneurship: Successfully Launching New Ventures*, 4th ed., Upper Saddle River, NJ: Pearson Prentice Hall.

8. J. Schumpeter, 1934, *The Theory of Economic Development*, Cambridge, MA: Harvard University Press.

9. G. T. Lumpkin, 2011, From legitimacy to impact: Moving the field forward by asking how entrepreneurship informs life, *Strategic Entrepreneurship Journal*, 5: 3–9; F. Sautet, 2012, Local and systemic entrepreneurship: Solving the puzzle of entrepreneurship and economic development, *Entrepreneurship Theory and Practice*, in press.

10. J. S. McMullen, 2011, Delineating the domain of development entrepreneurship: A market-based approach to facilitating inclusive economic growth, *Entrepreneurship Theory and Practice*, 35: 185–193; J. B. Sorensen & M. A. Fassiotto, 2011, Organizations as fonts of entrepreneurship, *Organization Science*, 22: 1322–1331.

11. E. Fauchart & M. Gruber, 2011, Darwinians, communitarians, and missionaries: The role of founder identity in entrepreneurship, *Academy of Management Journal*, 54: 935–957; R. Baron, 2006, Opportunity recognition as pattern recognition: How entrepreneurs "connect the dots" to identify new business opportunities, *Academy of Management Perspectives*, 20(1): 104–119.

12. J. S. Turley, 2010, The entrepreneurs in the cube next door, *Fast Company Online*, http://www.fastcompany.com, November 18.

13. J. C. Short, C. L. Shook, D. J. Ketchen, Jr., & R. D. Ireland, 2010, The concept of 'opportunity' in entrepreneurship research: Past accomplishments and future challenges, *Journal of Management*, 36: 40–65; S. A. Alvarez & J. B. Barney, 2005, Organizing rent generation and appropriation: Toward a theory of the entrepreneurial firm, *Journal of Business Venturing*, 19: 621–635.

14. R. Ma, Y.-C. Huang, & O. Shenkar, 2011, Social networks and opportunity recognition: A cultural comparison between Taiwan and the United States, *Strategic Management Journal*, 32: 1183–1205; M. Minnit, 2005, Entrepreneurial alertness and asymmetric information in a spin-glass model, *Journal of Business Venturing*, 19: 637–658.

15. I. Barreto, 2012, Solving the entrepreneurial puzzle: The role of entrepreneurial interpretation in opportunity formation and related processes, *Journal of Management Studies*, 49: 356–380; W. Kuemmerle, 2005, The entrepreneur's path to global expansion, *MIT Sloan Management Review*, 46(2): 42–49.

16. K. Krippendorff, 2011, What Amazon's Fire reveals about its innovation strategy, *Fast Company Online*, http://www.fastcompany.com, October 5.

17. A. Madkoh & M. Keyhani, 2011, Acquisitions as entrepreneurship: Asymmetries, opportunities, and the internationalization of multinationals from emerging economies, *Global Strategy Journal*, 2: 26–40; R. G. Holcombe, 2003, The origins of entrepreneurial opportunities, *Review of Austrian Economics*, 16: 25–54.

18. V. Govindarajan & R. Ramamurti, 2011, Reverse innovation, emerging markets, and global strategy, *Global Strategy Journal*, 1: 191–205; M. Levesque & M. Minniti, 2011, Age matters: How demographics influence aggregate entrepreneurship, *Strategic Entrepreneurship Journal*, 5: 269–284.

19. P. F. Drucker, 1998, The discipline of innovation, *Harvard Business Review*, 76(6): 149–157.

20. J. Dyer, H. Gregersen & C. M. Christensen, 2011, *The Innovator's Dilemma*, Boston: Harvard Business School Publishing.

21. M. Hirukawa & M. Ueda, 2011, Venture capital and innovation: Which is first? *Pacific Economic Review*, 16: 421–465; J. P. O'Brien, 2003, The capital

structure implications of pursuing a strategy of innovation, *Strategic Management Journal*, 24: 415–431.

[22] M. Halme, S. Lindeman, & P. Linna, 2012, Innovation for inclusive business: Intrapreneurial bricolage in multinational corporations, *Journal of Management Studies*, 49: in press; J. P. J. de Jong, 2012, The decision to exploit opportunities for innovation: A study of high-tech small-business owners, *Entrepreneurship Theory and Practice*, in press.

[23] M. K. Srivastava & D. R. Gnyawali, 2011, When do relational resources matter: Leveraging portfolio technological resources for breakthrough innovation, *Academy of Management Journal*, 54: 797–810; L. G. Franko, 1989, Global corporate competition: Who's winning, who's losing and the R&D factor as one reason why, *Strategic Management Journal*, 10: 449–474.

[24] K. Z. Zhou & F. Wu, 2010, Technological capability, strategic flexibility, and product innovation, *Strategic Management Journal*, 31: 547–561; J. W. Spencer, 2003, Firms' knowledge-sharing strategies in the global innovation system: Empirical evidence from the flat panel display industry, *Strategic Management Journal*, 24: 217–233.

[25] L. Chao, 2011, Alibaba overhauls Taobao unit, *The Wall Street Journal Online*, http://www.wsj.com, June 17.

[26] Schumpeter, *The Theory of Economic Development*.

[27] A. Kaul, 2012, Technology and corporate scope: Firm and rival innovation as antecedents of corporate transactions, *Strategic Management Journal*, 33: 347–367; R. A. Burgelman & L. R. Sayles, 1986, *Inside Corporate Innovation: Strategy, Structure, and Managerial Skills*, New York: The Free Press.

[28] M. I. Leone & T. Reichstein, 2012, Licensing-in fosters rapid invention! The effect of the grant-back clause and technological unfamiliarity, *Strategic Management Journal*, 33: in press.

[29] R. E. Hoskisson & L. W. Busenitz, 2002, Market uncertainty and learning distance in corporate entrepreneurship entry mode choice, in M. A. Hitt, R. D. Ireland, S. M. Camp, & D. L. Sexton (eds.), *Strategic Entrepreneurship: Creating a New Mindset*, Oxford, UK: Blackwell Publishers, 151–172.

[30] K. W. Artz, P. M. Norman, D. E. Hatfield, & L. B. Cardinal, 2010, A longitudinal study of the impact of R&D, patents, and product innovation on firm performance, *Journal of Product Innovation Management*, 27: 725–740; D. Somaya, 2003, Strategic determinants of decisions not to settle patent litigation, *Strategic Management Journal*, 24: 17–38.

[31] K. Burmeister-Lamp, M. Levesque, & C. Schade, 2012, Are entrepreneurs influenced by risk attitude, regulatory focus or both? An experiment on entrepreneurs' time allocation, *Journal of Business Venturing*, in press.

[32] A. Bryant, 2012, Where ideas are always on the wall, *The New York Times Online*, http://www.nytimes.com, January 8.

[33] B. Schiffer, 2012, Agile Trail, http://www.agiletrail.com, January 9.

[34] R. A. Baron, J. Tang, & K. M. Hmieleski, 2011, The downside of being 'up': Entrepreneurs' dispositional positive affect and firm performance, *Strategic Entrepreneurship Journal*, 5: 101–119; J. Brinckmann & M. Hoegl, 2011, Effects of initial team capability and initial relational capability on the development of new technology-based firms, *Strategic Entrepreneurship Journal*, 5: 37–57.

[35] C. Mitteness, R. Sudek, & M. S. Cardon, 2012, Angel investor characteristics that determine whether perceived passion leads to higher evaluations of funding potential, *Journal of Business Venturing*, in press; M.-D. Foo, 2011, Emotions and entrepreneurial opportunity evaluation, *Entrepreneurship Theory and Practice*, 35: 375–393.

[36] J. D. Hansen, G. D. Deitz, M. Tokman, L. D. Marino, & K. M. Weaver, 2011, Cross-national invariance of the entrepreneurial orientation scale, *Journal of Business Venturing*, 26: 61–78; R. G. McGrath & I. MacMillan, 2000, *The Entrepreneurial Mindset*, Boston: Harvard Business School Press.

[37] J. G. Covin & G. T. Lumpkin, 2011, Entrepreneurial orientation theory and research : Reflections on a needed construct, *Entrepreneurship Theory and Practice*, 35: 855–872; M. B. Sarkar, R. Echambadi, R. Agrawal, & B. Sen, 2006, The effect of innovative environment on exit in entrepreneurial firms, *Strategic Management Journal*, 27: 519–539.

[38] 2011, Apple faces innovation question as it moves from Steve Jobs to Tim Cook, *Forbes Online*, http://www.forbes.com, November 6.

[39] Copyright © 2011 Condé Nast. All rights reserved. Originally published on Ars Ex Technica.com. Reprinted by permission.

[40] H.-J. Cho & V. Pucik, 2005, Relationship between innovativeness, quality, growth, profitability, and market value, *Strategic Management Journal*, 26: 555–575.

[41] D. M. Sullivan & M. R. Marvel, 2011, Knowledge acquisition, network reliance, and early-stage technology venture outcomes, *Journal of Management Studies*, 48: 1169–1193; W. Tsai, 2001, Knowledge transfer in intraorganizational networks: Effects of network position and absorptive capacity on business unit innovation and performance, *Academy of Management Journal*, 44: 996–1004.

[42] M. Reinholt, T. Pedersen, & N. J. Foss, 2011, Why a central network position isn't enough: The role of motivation and ability for knowledge sharing in employee networks, *Academy of Management Journal*, 54: 1277–1297; S. A. Zahra & G. George, 2002, Absorptive capacity: A review, reconceptualization, and extension, *Academy of Management Review*, 27: 185–203.

[43] C. A. Un, 2011, The advantage of foreignness in innovation, *Strategic Management Journal*, 32: 1232–1242; M. A. Hitt, L. Bierman, K. Shimizu, & R. Kochhar, 2001, Direct and moderating effects of human capital on strategy and performance in professional service firms, *Academy of Management Journal*, 44: 13–28.

[44] A. Madhok & M. Keyhani, 2012, Acquisitions as entrepreneurship: Asymmetries, opportunities, and the internationalization of multinationals from emerging economies, *Global Strategy Journal*, 2: 26–40.

[45] J. Levie & E. Autio, 2011, Regulatory burden, rule of law, and entry of strategic entrepreneurs: An international panel study, *Journal of Management Studies*, 48: 1392–1419.

[46] S.-J. Chang & J. H. Rhee, 2011, Rapid FDI expansion and firm performance, *Journal of International Business Studies*, 42: 979–994; L. Tihanyi, R. A. Johnson, R. E. Hoskisson, & M. A. Hitt, 2003, Institutional ownership differences and international diversification: The effects of boards of directors and technological opportunity, *Academy of Management Journal*, 46: 195–211.

47 S. J. Jordan, 2012, Time-varying risk and long-term reversals: A re-examination of the international evidence, *Journal of International Business Studies*, 43: 123–142.

48 2011, Lack of entrepreneurial culture seen as Europe's biggest obstacle, *The Wall Street Journal Online*, http://www.wsj.com, June 1.

49 2011, Small and medium-sized enterprises (SMEs): Encouraging women entrepreneurs, *European Commission*, http://www.ec.europa.eu, November 11.

50 S. Lynch, 2012, Entrepreneurial spirit hasn't gone away, *The Irish Times Online*, http://www.irish times.com, February 10.

51 2012, About Us, Enterprise Ireland, http://www.enterprise-ireland.com, March 6.

52 Z. J. Acs & L. Szerb, 2012, *Global Entrepreneurship and Development Index*, London: Edward Elgar Publishing LTD.

53 K. R. Fabrizio & L. G. Thomas, 2012, The impact of local demand on innovation in a global industry, *Strategic Management Journal*, 33: 42–64; R. Ma, Y.-C. Huang, & O. Shenkar, 2011, Social networks and opportunity recognition: A cultural comparison between Taiwan and the United States, *Strategic Management Journal*, 32: 1183–1205.

54 R. Ramamurti, 2012, What is really different about emerging market multinationals? *Global Strategy Journal*, 2: 41–47; R. E. Hoskisson, J. Covin, H. W. Volberda, & R. A. Johnson, 2011, Revitalizing entrepreneurship: The search for new research opportunities, *Journal of Management Studies*, 48: 1141–1168.

55 R. Underwood, 2005, Walking the talk? *Fast Company*, March, 25–26.

56 D. M. Sullivan & M. R. Marvel, 2011, Knowledge acquisition, network reliance, and early-stage technology venture outcomes, *Journal of Management Studies*, 48: 1169–1193; S. A. Zahra, R. D. Ireland, & M. A. Hitt, 2000, International expansion by new venture firms: International diversity, mode of market entry, technological learning and performance, *Academy of Management Journal*, 43: 925–950.

57 P. D. Ellis, 2011, Social ties and international entrepreneurship: Opportunities and constraints affecting firm internationalization, *Journal of International Business Studies*, 42: 99–127; P. P. McDougall & B. M. Oviatt, 2000, International entrepreneurship: The intersection of two paths, *Academy of Management Journal*, 43: 902–908.

58 S. Nadkarni, P. Herrmann, & P. D. Perez, 2011, Domestic mindsets and early international performance: The moderating effect of global industry conditions, *Strategic Management Journal*, 32: 510–531; A. Van, G. Zhu, & D. T. Hall, 2002, International assignments for career building: A model of agency relationships and psychological contracts, *Academy of Management Review*, 27: 373–391.

59 C. B. Bingham & K. M. Eisenhardt, 2011, Rational heuristics: The 'simple rules' that strategists learn from process experience, *Strategic Management Journal*, 32: 1437–1464; H. Barkema & O. Chvyrkov, 2002, What sort of top management team is needed at the helm of internationally diversified firms? in M. A. Hitt, R. D. Ireland, S. M. Camp, & D. L. Sexton (eds.), *Strategic Entrepreneurship: Creating a New Mindset*, Oxford, UK: Blackwell Publishers, 290–305.

60 B. Cassiman & E. Golovko, 2011, Innovation and internationalization through exports, *Journal of International Business Studies*, 42: 56–70; T. S. Frost, 2001, The geographic sources of foreign subsidiaries' innovations, *Strategic Management Journal*, 22: 101–122; M. A. Hitt, R. E. Hoskisson, & H. Kim, 1997, International diversification: Effects on innovation and firm performance in product diversified firms, *Academy of Management Journal*, 40: 767–798.

61 R. E. Hoskisson, M. A. Hitt, R. A. Johnson, & W. Grossman, 2002, Conflicting voices: The effects of institutional ownership heterogeneity and internal governance on corporate innovation strategies, *Academy of Management Journal*, 45: 697–716.

62 R. Casadesus-Masanell & J. E. Ricart, 2010, Competitiveness: Business model reconfiguration for innovation and internationalization, *Management Research*, 8: 13–149.

63 M. G. Biniari, 2012, The emotional embeddedness of corporate entrepreneurship: The case of envy, *Entrepreneurship Theory and Practice*, 36: 141–170; R. A. Burgelman, 1995, *Strategic Management of Technology and Innovation*, Boston: Irwin.

64 2012, 3M Worldwide, Products and services, http://solutions.3m.com, March 9.

65 P. Sharma & C. Salvato, 2011, Exploiting and exploring new opportunities over life cycle stages of family firms, *Entrepreneurship Theory and Practice*, 35: 1199–1205.

66 J. Paartanen, S. K. Chetty, & A. Rajala, 2011, Innovation types and network relationships, *Entrepreneurship Theory and Practice*, 35: in press.

67 K. S. McElheran, 2011, Do market leaders in business process innovation? The case(s) of E-business adoption, Harvard Business School Technology & Operations Mgt. Unit Working Paper No. 10–104, http://ssrn.com/abstract=1618840; W. T. Robinson & J. Chiang, 2002, Product development strategies for established market pioneers, early followers and late entrants, *Strategic Management Journal*, 23: 855–866.

68 W. K. Smith & M. W. Lewis, 2011, Toward a theory of paradox: A dynamic equilibrium model of organizing, *Academy of Management Review*, 36: 381–403; G. Ahuja & C. M. Lampert, 2001, Entrepreneurship in the large corporation: A longitudinal study of how established firms create breakthrough inventions, *Strategic Management Journal*, 22: 521–543.

69 A. B. Goktan & G. Miles, 2011, Innovation speed and radicalness: Are they inversely related? *Management Decision*, 49: 533–547; D. G. Sirmon, M. A. Hitt, R. D. Ireland, & B. A. Gilbert, 2011, Resource orchestration to create competitive advantage Breadth, depth, and life cycle effects, *Journal of Management*, 37: 1390–1412.

70 H. Forsman, 2011, Innovation capacity and innovation development in small enterprises: A comparison between the manufacturing and service sectors, *Research Policy*, 40: 739–750; S. A. Melnyk, J. D. Hanson, & R. J. Calantone, 2010, Hitting the target … but missing the point: Resolving the paradox of strategic transition, *Long Range Planning*, 43: 555–574.

71 I. N. Dubina, E. G. Carayannis, & D. F. J. Campbell, 2011, Creativity economy and a crisis of the economy? Coevolution of knowledge, innovation, and creativity, and of the knowledge economy and knowledge society, *Journal of the Knowledge Economy*, 3: 1–24; R. I. Sutton, 2002, Weird ideas that spark innovation, *MIT Sloan Management Review*, 43(2): 83–87.

72 D. Kelley & H. Lee, 2010, Managing innovation champions: The impact of project characteristics on the direct manager role, *Journal of Product Innovation Management*, 27: 1007–1019.

73 D. Wilemon 2011, Product champions as facilitators of innovation, http://ssrn.com/abstract=1869703, June 23.

74 N. Acur, D. Kandemir, & H. Boer, 2012, Strategic alignment and new product development: Drivers and performance effects, *Journal of Product Innovation Management*, 29: 304–318; M. A. Hitt, R. D. Ireland, & H. Lee, 2000, Technological learning, knowledge management, firm growth and performance, *Journal of Engineering and Technology Management*, 17: 231–246; D. Leonard-Barton, 1995, *Wellsprings of Knowledge: Building and Sustaining the Sources of Innovation*, Cambridge, MA: Harvard Business School Press.

75 A. Taylor III, 2005, Billion-dollar bets, *Fortune*, June 27, 139–154.

76 S. S. Rao, 2000, General Electric, software vendor, *Forbes*, January 24, 144–146.

77 Z. Simsek & C. Heavey, 2011, The mediating role of knowledge-based capital for corporate entrepreneurship efforts on performance: A study of small- to medium-sized firms, *Strategic Entrepreneurship Journal*, 5: 81–100; M. Subramaniam & N. Venkatraman, 2001, Determinants of transnational new product development capability: Testing the influence of transferring and deploying tacit overseas knowledge, *Strategic Management Journal*, 22: 359–378.

78 M. Song & M. M. Montoya-Weiss, 2001, The effect of perceived technological uncertainty on Japanese new product development, *Academy of Management Journal*, 44: 61–80.

79 G. Manso, 2011, Motivating innovation, *Journal of Finance*, 66: 1823–1860.

80 McGrath & MacMillan, *The Entrepreneurial Mindset*.

81 G. Manso, 2011, Motivating innovation, *Journal of Finance*, 66: 1823–1860.

82 From William L. McKnight's Management Principles. Reprinted by permission of 3M.

83 U. Kichtenthaler, 2011, Open innovation: Past research, current debates and future directions, *Academy of Management Perspectives*, 25: 75–93.

84 M. Brettel, F. Heinemann, A. Engelen, & S. Neubauer, 2011, Cross-functional integration of R&D, marketing, and manufacturing in radical and incremental product innovations and its effects on project effectiveness and efficiency, *Journal of Product Innovation Management*, 28: 251–269; N. J. Foss, K. Laursen, & T. Pedersen, 2011, Linking customer interaction and innovation: The mediating role of new organizational practices, *Organization Science*, 22: 980–999.

85 G. Castellion, 2011, The innovation manual: Integrated strategies and practical tools for bringing value innovation to market, *Journal of Product Innovation Management*, 28: 611–613.

86 S. Ghobadi & J. D'Ambra, 2012, Knowledge sharing in cross-functional teams: A competitive model, *Journal of Knowledge Management*, 16: in press; M.-S. Cheung, M. B. Myers, & J. T. Mentzer, 2011, The value of relational learning in global buyer-supplier exchanges: A dyadic perspective and test of the pie-sharing premise, *Strategic Management Journal*, 32: 1061–1082.

87 A. Majchrzak & P. H. B. More, 2012, Transcending knowledge differences in cross-functional teams, *Organization Science*, in press.

88 G. von Krogh, 2012, Leadership in organizational knowledge creation: A review and framework, *Journal of Management Studies*, 49: 240–277.

89 R. Santa, P. Bretherton, M. Ferrer, C. Soosay, & P. Hyland, 2011, The role of cross-functional teams on the alignment between technology innovation effectiveness and operational effectiveness, *International Journal of Technology Management*, 55: 122–137.

90 A. C. Amason, 1996, Distinguishing the effects of functional and dysfunctional conflict on strategic decision making: Resolving a paradox for top management teams, *Academy of Management Journal*, 39: 123–148; P. R. Lawrence & J. W. Lorsch, 1969, *Organization and Environment*, Homewood, IL: Irwin.

91 D. Dougherty, L. Borrelli, K. Munir, & A. O'Sullivan, 2000, Systems of organizational sensemaking for sustained product innovation, *Journal of Engineering and Technology Management*, 17: 321–355; D. Dougherty, 1992, Interpretive barriers to successful product innovation in large firms, *Organization Science*, 3: 179–202.

92 A. Moses, 2011, Cross-functional make or buy decision process ownership, *Management Research Review*, 34: 1042–1060.

93 D. E. Hughes, J. Le Bon, & A. Malshe, 2012, The marketing-sales interface at the interface: Creating market-based capabilities through organizational synergy, *Journal of Personal Selling and Sales Management*, 32: 57–72.

94 L. Garicano, 2012, Knowledge, communication, and organizational capabilities, *Organization Science*, in press.

95 2012, W. L. Gore & Associates, Corporate culture, http://www.gore.com, March 8.

96 J. C. Sarros, B. K. Cooper, & J. C. Santora, 2011, Leadership vision, organizational culture, and support for innovation in not-for-profit and for-profit organizations, *Leadership & Organization Development Journal*, 32: 291–309.

97 M. B. O'Leary, M. Mortensen, & A. W. Woolley, 2011, Multiple team membership: A theoretical model of its effects on productivity and learning for individuals and teams, *Academy of Management Review*, 36: 461–478.

98 Q. M. Roberson & J. A. Colquitt, 2005, Shared and configural justice: A social network model of justice in teams, *Academy of Management Review*, 30: 595–607.

99 L. Kester, A. Griffin, E. J. Hultink, & K. Lauche, 2011, Exploring portfolio decision-making processes, *Journal of Product Innovation Management*, 28: 641–661; B.-S. Teng, 2007, Corporate entrepreneurship activities through strategic alliances: A resource-based approach toward competitive advantage, *Journal of Management Studies*, 44: 119–130.

100 A. G. Karamanos, 2012, Leveraging micro- and macro-structures of embeddedness in alliance networks for exploratory innovation in biotechnology, *R&D Management*, 42: 71–89.

101 E. Fang, 2011, The effect of strategic alliance knowledge complementarity on new product innovativeness in China, *Organization Science*, 22: 158–172.

102 A. Schwartz, 2011, GE, Intel team up on joint health care initiative for the elderly, *Fast Company Online*, http://www.fastcompany.com, January 3.

103 Y. Zhao, Y. Li, S. H. Lee, & L. B. Chen, 2011, Entrepreneurial orientation, organizational learning, and performance: Evidence from China, *Entrepreneurship Theory and Practice*, 35: 293–317.

104 M. Bianchi, A. Cavaliere, D. Chiaroni, & F. Frattini, 2011, Organizational modes for open innovation in the bio-pharmaceutical industry: An exploratory analysis, *Technovation*, 31: 22–33; S. A. Alvarez & J. B. Barney, 2001, How entrepreneurial firms can benefit from alliances with large partners, *Academy of Management Executive*, 15(1): 139–148; F. T. Rothaermel, 2001, Incumbent's advantage through exploiting complementary assets via interfirm cooperation, *Strategic Management Journal*, 22(special issue): 687–699.

105 H. Ernst, U. Lichtenthaler, & C. Vogt, 2011, The impact of accumulating and reactivating technological experience on R&D alliance performance, *Journal of Management Studies*, 48: 1194–1216.

106 A. M. Hess & F. T. Rothaermel, 2011, When are assets complementary? Star scientists, strategic alliances, and innovation in the pharmaceutical industry, *Strategic Management Journal*, 32: 895–909.

107 P. Hockenos, 2012, At risk the core of a car's identity, *The New York Times Online*, http://www.nytimes.com, January 8.

108 H. Yli-Renko, E. Autio, & H. J. Sapienza, 2001, Social capital, knowledge acquisition and knowledge exploitation in young technology-based firms, *Strategic Management Journal*, 22(special issue): 587–613.

109 J. Yu, B. A. Gilbert, & B. M. Oviatt, 2011, Effects of alliances, time, and network cohesion on the initiation of foreign sales by new ventures, *Strategic Management Journal*, 32: 424–446.

110 K.-H. Lee & J.-W. Kim, 2011, Integrating suppliers into green product innovation development: An empirical case study in the semiconductor industry, *Business Strategy and the Environment*, 20: 527–538.

111 F. Lumineau & D. Malhotra, 2011, Shadow of the contract: How contract structure shapes interfirm dispute resolution, *Strategic Management Journal*, 32: 532–555.

112 D. Li, L. Eden, M. A. Hitt, R. D. Ireland, & R. P. Garrett, 2012, Governance in multilateral R&D alliances, *Organization Science*, in press; R. D. Ireland, M. A. Hitt, & D. Vaidyanath, 2002, Strategic alliances as a pathway to competitive success, *Journal of Management*, 28: 413–446.

113 M. Meier, 2011, Knowledge management in strategic alliances: A review of empirical evidence, *International Journal of Management Reviews*, 13: 1–23; M. A. Hitt, M. T. Dacin, E. Levitas, J. L. Arregle, & A. Borza, 2000, Partner selection in emerging and developed market contexts: Resource-based and organizational learning perspectives, *Academy of Management Journal*, 43: 449–467.

114 C. Lin, Y.-J. Wu, C. Chang, W. Wang, & C.-Y. Lee, 2012, The alliance innovation performance of R&D alliances—the absorptive capacity perspective, *Technovation*, in press.

115 A. Madhok & M. Keyhani, 2012, Acquisitions as entrepreneurship: Asymmetries, opportunities, and the internationalization of multinationals from emerging economies, *Global Strategy Journal*, 2: 26–40.

116 J. Hagerty 2012, 3M picks veteran as new chief, *The Wall Street Journal Online*, http://www.wsj.com, February 9.

117 M. Lee, 2011, Dell explores acquisitions to widen lead in Internet servers, *Bloomberg News Online*, http://www.bloomberg.com, May 31.

118 G. Valentini, 2012, Measuring the effect of M&A on patenting quantity and quality, *Strategic Management Journal*, 33: 336–346; M. A. Hitt, R. E. Hoskisson, R. A. Johnson, & D. D. Moesel, 1996, The market for corporate control and firm innovation, *Academy of Management Journal*, 39: 1084–1119.

119 M. Wagner, 2011, To explore or to exploit? An empirical investigation of acquisitions by large incumbents, *Research Policy*, 40: 1217–1225.

120 Hitt, Ireland, Sirmon, & Trahms, Strategic entrepreneurship.

121 F. Delmar, K. Wennberg, & K. Hellerstedt, 2011, Endogenous growth through knowledge spillovers in entrepreneurship: An empirical test, *Strategic Entrepreneurship Journal*, 5: 199–226.

122 D. G. Sirmon, M. A. Hitt, & R. D. Ireland, 2007, Managing firm resources in dynamic environments to create value: Looking inside the black box, *Academy of Management Review*, 32: 273–292.

123 K. Laursen & A. Prencipe, 2012, Regions matter: How localized social capital affects innovation and external knowledge acquisition, *Organization Science*, in press.

124 M. A. Hitt, H. Lee, & E. Yucel, 2002, The importance of social capital to the management of multinational enterprises: Relational networks among Asian and Western firms, *Asia Pacific Journal of Management*, 19: 353–372.

125 A. Leiponen, 2011, Location, decentralization, and knowledge sources for innovation, *Organization Science*, 22: 641–658.

126 M. J. Nieto & A. Rodirguez, 2011, Offshoring of R&D: Looking abroad to improve innovation performance, *Journal of International Business Studies*, 42: 345–361.

127 E. Golovko & G. Valentini, 2011, Exploring the complementarity between innovation and export for SMEs' growth, *Journal of International Business Studies*, 42: 362–380.

128 2012, InterTradeIreland, Entrepreneurial businesses spearhead Northern Irish economic recovery, http://www.intertradeireland.com, February 2.

129 P. Tracey, N. Phillips, & O. Jarvis, 2011, Bridging institutional entrepreneurship and the creation of new organizational forms: A multilevel model, *Organization Science*, 22: 60–80.

130 T. Lawrence, R. Suddaby, & B. Leca, 2011, Institutional work: Refocusing institutional studies of organization, *Journal of Management Inquiry*, 20: 52–58; R. Garud, S. Jain, & A. Kumaraswamy, 2002, Institutional entrepreneurship in the sponsorship of common technological standards: The case of Sun Microsystems and JAVA, *Academy of Management Journal*, 45: 196–214.

131 S. Marlow & M. McAdam, 2012, Analyzing the influence of gender upon high-technology venturing within the context of business incubation, *Entrepreneurship Theory and Practice*, in press.

132 D. Sweeney, 2011, Women entrepreneurs are taking over, thanks to the recession, *Business Insider*, http://www.businessinsider.com, April 8.

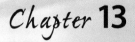

Chapter **13**

STRATEGIC FLEXIBILITY AND REAL OPTIONS ANALYSIS

KNOWLEDGE OBJECTIVES

Studying this chapter should provide you with the strategic management knowledge needed to:

1. Define real options and contrast them with other types of strategic investments by firms.

2. Describe the different types of real options that exist and in what strategic circumstances they are important.

3. Explain the purposes and importance of real options analysis.

4. Describe the value drivers underlying real options.

5. Value simple real options using two techniques: (1) the Black–Scholes and the Black–Scholes approximation method; and (2) the binomial lattices and risk-neutral method.

6. Explain some of the most important assumptions underlying real options valuation methods.

One of the key points that the preceding chapters have underscored is that strategic decisions are complex and ambiguous. They often touch upon multiple functional areas of the firm, involve sizable resource commitments that may or may not prompt reactions by rivals, and are difficult to analyze because they include many qualitative inputs that can be difficult to integrate. Strategic decisions also tend to be made in the context of considerable uncertainty, which further complicates analyses of investment choices and strategic courses of action for organizations.[1] All indications are that such uncertainties—whether due to economic risks, technological developments, industry convergence and creative destruction, geopolitical crises, the global integration of industries, and so forth—are becoming increasingly important for many organizations and are likely to continue to be so.[2]

In response to uncertainty, firms seek to craft strategies that enhance their strategic flexibility.[3] A strategy is flexible when it allows a firm to react to changing uncertainties by quickly changing course or, better still, allows the firm to position itself to take advantage of the resolution of uncertainty.[4] The concept of strategic flexibility was introduced in Chapter 1 and has been applied in various contexts throughout this book. Specifically, Chapter 5 examined use of a flexible structure to implement an integrated cost leadership/differentiation strategy. Chapter 7 explained that cooperative strategies often increase strategic flexibility because they tend to be temporary arrangements that require fewer resource commitments. Chapter 8 demonstrated that an M-form structure in unrelated firms increases flexibility by allowing corporate headquarters to allocate resources to the most promising areas. Chapter 9 mentioned that firms sometimes make acquisitions to diversify into product lines they may wish to emphasize in the future, thus enhancing their strategic flexibility.

Entrepreneurial activities, described in Chapter 12, also enhance strategic flexibility. As firms make decisions to invest in new ventures, they are also opening a number of future opportunities. For instance, a firm that decides to open a small hotel on a large property could, at a later date, decide to enlarge the hotel, add a restaurant, or convert the hotel to condominiums. Consequently, firms that are entrepreneurial tend to have greater strategic flexibility.[5] The common dimension among all these applications is that the firm is in a better position to adapt to changes and opportunities as they present themselves.

Caterpillar was mentioned previously as a firm that was able to adapt well to the "great recession" that began in late 2007 or early 2008 (depending on source of information). A closer look at Caterpillar reveals why a company that depends so much on the highly cyclical construction industry had record profits at the bottom of the economic cycle. The company dramatically increased its ability to deal with hostile economic conditions by training its managers to deal with adversity. Doug Oberhelman, CEO, described it this way: "Let's say you're running mining, and sales drop 80% in two years. How are you going to make money? Well, you can imagine how popular that was in 2005. Nobody wanted to talk about it. But we forced them through the exercise."[6] Caterpillar also increased its flexibility through decisions to expand into areas that were growing fast, with highly profitable customers, and where the company could capitalize on its dealer network or existing businesses. The result was investments in mining, eco-friendly engines, and railroad equipment. Through these wise strategic actions the company was able to prosper in spite of the downturn. They are also well positioned to continue to grow during good economic times.

Strategic flexibility is influenced by organizational structures, systems, or other internal resources that augment the responsiveness of an organization.[7] Strategic flexibility might also be advanced through the particular design of investments and operations. Investment design and operation can be enhanced in several ways: by incorporating staging opportunities (i.e., investing sequentially in a project as milestones are reached), by switching opportunities (i.e., shifting inputs or outputs across machines, geographic markets), and by articulating the follow-on opportunities embedded in strategic choices (i.e., other prospective investments opened up by initial resource commitments).[8]

The preceding chapters have also introduced several tools used for dealing with uncertainty when making strategic decisions. For example, environmental analysis (see Chapter 3) can be used as an input to scenario planning, which aims to collapse the many uncertainties confronting a firm into a small number of internally consistent scenarios of the future.[9] Also, the analysis of competitive rivalry and competitive dynamics (see Chapter 6) helps firms understand how the effectiveness of their strategies can hinge upon the simultaneous decisions or subsequent reactions of rivals. A firm does not need to accept rivals' actions and their consequences passively. In fact, it can shape them through its own investments and strategies, which in turn figure into rivals' own decisions.[10]

Real options analysis is also a tool that helps firms deal with uncertainty and increase strategic flexibility. In the past few years, real options analysis has received increased attention as a tool for strategic decision making.[11] It has attracted interest because it offers a means of quantitatively evaluating the role of uncertainty in firms' investment decisions; it changes the ways in which strategists think about particular investments and the ways in which they can deliver value to firms; and it offers the promise of beginning to reconcile strategic and financial analyses in organizations. Real options analysis does this by simultaneously injecting strategic reality into traditional financial valuation models while rigorously bringing the discipline of financial markets into strategic analyses.[12]

This chapter begins with a description of various types of real options and explains some of the primary purposes of real options analysis. It also contains a brief introduction to some of the ways that real options can be valued, both for firms as a whole and for individual strategic investments. An appendix provides detailed instructions for two of the most common valuation approaches. Even if individual investments are not valued using some of the formal techniques of real options analysis, an understanding of the value drivers underlying real options and their implications can be useful in the design and implementation of strategic investments (e.g., acquisitions, supply contracts, alliances, foreign direct investment) and working constructively with uncertainty in strategic decision making.

REAL OPTIONS ANALYSIS

A definition of **real options** must explain both why the options are real and why they are options. For the analysis of real options to offer something that is distinctive to executives, consultants, and analysts, precision is needed to distinguish the term *option* from related concepts. For example, it is true that options provide strategic alternatives, yet alternatives are not necessarily options per se as the latter have a particular structure as well as a set of additional criteria that must be met for firms to actually obtain option value. Real options are real because unlike financial options the immediate underlying asset is a real asset rather than a financial security.

An analogy with financial options helps us to clarify the definition of real options. Suppose an individual purchases a financial call and pays $5 per share to obtain the right, but not the obligation, to purchase 10 shares of a company's stock for $100 per share in the future. If the firm's share price collapses, the individual does nothing and has lost only the original option purchase price of $50 (i.e., $5 per share times 10 shares). He or she is not compelled to make the second stage investment. However, if the individual discovers through monitoring the company's stock price that the price surges above $100 to $120 because of a change in demand for the company's products, technological improvement, or some other development, the individual can exercise his or her option to purchase the shares at $100 each, and in the process makes $20 per share (or $200 total) on the terminal purchase.

This example yields the five criteria necessary for an option to exist. An option provides a firm (1) with the right, (2) but not the obligation, (3) to take some future specified action, (4) enabling the firm to reduce its downside risk (5) while accessing upside opportunities. Each of these criteria deserves attention when considering whether options are embedded in a firm's investments or its operational practices. To say that an option provides a right and that it confers access to upside opportunities means that it gives the firm some preferential claim to a follow-on investment opportunity.[13] In the case of financial options, this right is to claim the shares for $100 each, and this right costs $50 total at the outset. In the case of real options, this means that other firms cannot obtain the same investment on the same terms in the second stage, and the potential second-stage investment is conditional upon the first. In the case of the financial call, this right accounts for the difference between the $100 purchase price and the $120 market price, as the former is set contractually and the latter is set by the stock market. It is equally important that the firm *not* have an *obligation* to make the second-stage investment. If the firm is compelled to make a follow-on investment, there is no flexibility and an option does not exist because a commitment has already been made.

The asymmetry between having the *right but not the obligation* gives rise to a parallel asymmetry in outcomes: options help firms *reduce downside risk while accessing upside opportunities*.[14] In the case of the financial option, the individual's initial $50 investment is entirely sunk, and he or she purchases the shares only if it makes economic sense to do so; if not, the individual obtains a terminal payoff of zero. In the case of a firm that is diversifying, a small investment in a new business area reduces downside risk in the event that the venture is not successful; and although it is not compelled to expand, it is able to do so if conditions in the business area turn out to be favorable.

Types of Real Options

Just as strategic commitments come in many varieties (e.g., acquisitions to achieve market power, staking out competitive positions, etc.), a wide range of real options can be seen in firms' investments and their operations. Table 13.1 shows examples of different types of options and the contexts in which they are often relevant.

Growth Options. Growth options represent investments that enable the firm to expand the investment in the future, if that action turns out to be valuable. For example, Mumbai-based Reliance Industries Ltd, a firm with interests in oil, retail and telecommunications, formed a joint venture with the global investment firm D. E. Shaw to establish a financial services business in India. The decision was made as a result of slowing growth prospects in its existing businesses. According to analysts, the venture provides Reliance the option to invest its abundant revenue stream in a new area, if the venture proves successful.[15]

Another example of a growth option is an *equity joint venture,* which involves firms establishing a business with joint ownership, such as a 50/50 ownership split.[16] A pharmaceutical firm can invest in a biotechnology joint venture rather than simply acquiring the firm to obtain its technology. By doing so, the pharmaceutical firm potentially reduces its downside risk by limiting its initial outlay relative

TABLE 13.1 TYPES OF REAL OPTIONS

OPTION	DESCRIPTION	TYPICAL CONTEXTS
Growth	An early investment opens future expansion opportunities.	▶ Infrastructure investments ▶ Investments in products with multiple generations
Abandonment	The presence of resale markets allows the firm to realize value from exiting markets with deteriorating conditions.	▶ New product introductions ▶ Capital-intensive industries
Switching	Product flexibility allows shifts in output mix; process flexibility permits shifts in inputs.	▶ Consumer goods susceptible to volatile demand ▶ Tapered vertical integration
Defer	A lease or option to buy land allows the firm to wait to see whether output prices justify investment.	▶ Natural-resource extraction industries ▶ Real estate development
Compound	Investments conferring multiple options of the types listed above.	▶ Any of the above

SOURCE: Based on Lenos Trigeorgis, *Real Options: Managerial Flexibility and Strategy in Resource Allocation*, © 1996 Lenos Trigeorgis, published by The MIT Press.

to what would be required if it purchased the biotechnology firm outright. If the technology proves to be unattractive or the market for the biotech firm's products doesn't materialize, the pharmaceutical firm is not compelled to expand; but if the technology or products prove to be favorable, the pharmaceutical firm can expand by buying out the biotech firm from the venture.[17] Of course, the question is at what price this acquisition of additional equity occurs for this strategy to make sense. Although only a limited number of firms take the time to negotiate an option clause directly into joint venture contracts, it is an important part of the agreement.[18]

Abandonment Options. If growth options are akin to financial calls, then **abandonment options** are akin to financial puts. Abandonment options provide firms flexibility by allowing them to reverse course and exit deteriorating competitive situations.[19] For instance, in high-tech start-ups, it might be possible for firms to sell technologies, capital equipment, or other assets through a resale market. Such options might also be negotiated in individual contracts between firms. In a highly publicized and contentious collaborative relationship between Fiat and General Motors, Fiat had negotiated the ability to sell its shares to GM at an agreed-upon price that ultimately became quite unattractive to GM with the worsening of Fiat's financial condition and other problems.[20]

Switching Options. Switching options combine the features of the options just discussed by allowing firms to change the mix of outputs or inputs.[21] For instance, flexible manufacturing systems allow firms to shift output across two or more products at a relatively low switching cost. For firms producing different products that have highly variable demands, this option can be attractive because it enables firms to alter production decisions on the basis of the conditions of the market for the firm's products. A second example of a switching option is the network of generating units in the electric utility industry.[22] Within a given day, the profitability of a given unit is based on its "spark gap," or the price it can charge less the cost of production, which can vary on the basis of environmental and operational contingencies. To meet demand at a given time, a utility seeks to bring online the units with the highest spark gap. By contrast, units with the lowest spark gaps are brought off-line first. A final example of switching options is provided by firms' foreign direct investment, or ownership of assets in multiple countries.[23] As currency rates or other environmental conditions change over time, firms can reallocate production or other activities throughout their network of operations to reduce their cost structure relative to rivals that have operations in only one country and are therefore subject to the currency and other risks associated with that particular country.[24]

Option to Defer. The **option to defer** is present when there is value in waiting.[25] Some students might find graduate school valuable not only because of the knowledge they obtain, but also because of an option to defer other commitments, such as marriage or full-time work. For executives, the option to defer comes into existence because uncertainty surrounds a strategic investment, and the commitment to that investment is irreversible. The combination of irreversibility and uncertainty makes such options valuable because of the gains from waiting. For this reason, executives judging investment projects may require the net present value (NPV) to be significantly greater than zero to compensate for the value of deferral options that are lost when the firm makes a strategic commitment. Options to defer can be found in natural resource-based industries and in decisions such as whether to harvest timber or extract natural resources such as copper or oil. Deferral options can also figure into real estate development decisions.

Compound Options. In formal analyses that value real options, analysts, consultants, or others will often simplify an investment decision to capture a single option. In most real-life investment projects or operations, however, multiple options are often present. **Compound options** refer to investments that confer multiple options that are built upon one another. Another way to understand compound options is to consider that the underlying asset is not a real asset, but another option. For instance, in R&D activities, a number of stages proceed from basic research to applied research, and then development work, prototyping, and commercialization, which together amount to a series of options on options. Treating such compound options as simple options will understate the flexibility available to the firm holding such options and therefore their value, yet such treatment can yield important insights concerning an investment decision. Moreover, simply understanding the direction of this bias can be sufficient for making a strategic investment decision.

Purpose and Importance of Real Options Analysis

We now turn to the purpose of real options analysis and the question of how important real options are in strategic management.[26] Real options and the analyses of these investments are important because they have recast motives for a variety of strategic decisions, have opened new opportunities to bridge strategic and financial analyses, and have shown how managers need to alter their investment thresholds.

They are also important because they are practically relevant, as they can represent an important source and share of firm value.

Challenging Received Wisdom on Motives for Strategic Investments. Real options analysis changes the way managers think about strategic investments and the benefits that accrue from them.[27] Consider the example above of switching options offered by foreign direct investment and contrast this view of multinational strategy with the traditional perspective. Before the advent of real options theory, the received view was that multinational firms largely make foreign direct investments involving the ownership of foreign affiliates in order to maintain control over their intangible assets such as brands or technologies.[28] Not only are such assets difficult to value for potential licensees, but they are difficult to monitor and control appropriately without the parent firm's ownership and control. In contrast to this perspective emphasizing the efficiencies associated with ownership, the real options perspective instead focuses attention on the dynamic gains that firms can obtain by shifting their value chain activities across country borders in response to changes in environmental conditions (e.g., currencies, wages, demand, etc.). The central focus is operational *flexibility* rather than operational *control*. For example, during recessions or other hardships, firms may reallocate production flexibly to locations with relatively lower production costs to reduce their global cost structure.[29]

A second example demonstrates how a real options perspective directly challenges a conventional perspective on strategic investment and the benefits it provides a company. Traditionally, joint ventures were routinely compared to marriages or interpersonal relationships, and the objectives of the investing firm were therefore thought to be making such collaborations as long-lasting and harmonious as possible.[30] Under the real options lens, however, termination no longer has the negative connotations of "divorce." With the development of real options theory, joint ventures and minority investments have come to be seen as transitional investments providing companies with flexibility rather than as marriages or investments meant to last forever.[31]

Reconciling Strategic Analysis and Financial Analysis. The power of real options analysis can be further illustrated with a very simple question: Would you invest in a project with a negative NPV? Presented with this question, some managers and students respond that strategic considerations need to be taken into proper account. Presumably, negative-NPV projects might be acceptable, provided that they are "strategic." But what does this really mean? On the basis of finance theory, others respond that such decisions are not in the interest of shareholders and therefore should definitely be rejected. As a variant on this answer, someone who is uncomfortable with qualitative analyses might suggest that if strategic considerations do matter, they should be reflected in firms' cash flow forecasts such that the NPV should be positive for the firm to proceed.

Resolution of this dilemma comes in part from an understanding of the histories of strategic analysis and capital budgeting.[32] It can be argued that both blossomed in parallel after World War II and that both are inherently interested in the allocation of a firm's resources to achieve value for shareholders. The key strength of capital budgeting lies in its ability to handle tangible cash flows as well as its explicit decision criterion for corporate investment (i.e., NPV > 0). Its chief weakness is that the tools are designed to value passive investments without flexibility. On the side of strategic analysis, it is intrinsically interested in active management and follow-on opportunities, yet it lacks the type of tight decision criterion to make resource allocation decisions. Ideally, a tool could bridge corporate finance and strategy by injecting strategic reality (e.g., uncertainty, follow-on opportunities, active management) into financial models of investment while also incorporating the discipline of financial markets and mathematical rigor into strategic analyses. At the broadest level, this is the promise and potential contribution of real options analysis.

To see the importance of real options analysis, consider why traditional valuation techniques are flawed for many strategic investments as well as how the presence of embedded options moves firms' investment thresholds away from the NPV > 0 standard. Suppose a firm is investing in a high-tech project that has two equally likely outcomes, yielding a payoff of $V^+ = \$180$ million under "good" market conditions and $V^- = \$60$ million under "poor" market conditions one year hence.[33] Assume that the risk-adjusted discount rate is 20 percent and the risk-free rate is 8 percent. The present value (PV) of the project is the expected value of the payoff, discounted to time zero at the risk-adjusted rate. Thus, $PV = (1 + 0.20)^{-1}$ $[0.5(180) + 0.5(60)] = \$100$ million.

Now suppose the firm is able to write a contract with another company, which is able to take over the technology in one year's time and is willing to commit to paying $180 million at that time. What should the firm be willing to pay for such a contract? Using the above formula and subtracting the $100 million value yields $(1.2)^{-1}$ $[0.5(180) + 0.5(180)] - 100 = \$50$ million. However, given that the firm obtains $180 million under all conditions, it is inappropriate to use the same discount rate for a 100 percent chance of getting $180 million as for a 50/50 chance of getting $180 million versus $60 million. Since the former payoff is riskless, it should be discounted by the risk-free rate of 8 percent. This means that the correct value for this abandonment option is $(1.08)^{-1}$ $[0.5(180) + 0.5(180)] - 100 = \$67$ million, which is 34 percent higher than the value previously calculated. Of course, this simple example works because the risk-free rate can be used since the future payouts are made certain. In real-life situations, it is necessary to use option valuation methods since this discount rate cannot be obtained so easily. An important lesson of this example is that traditional financial valuation methods will undervalue projects with flexibility and overvalue commitment-intensive projects, which means that firms are likely to underinvest in projects with embedded options and overinvest in inflexible projects.

Shifting Investment Thresholds. Another implication of the example above is that the presence of real options changes firms' investment thresholds. For instance, suppose a potential start-up (e.g., Wellington Synthetics) is considering offering synthetic mats for construction sites, and these mats are superior to wooden mats, as the latter suffer from drawbacks such as lack of durability, cumbersome transportation and storage, and risks of damage to heavy equipment.[34] Previous efforts to develop synthetic mats ran into difficulties, such as excessive "memory" from prior loads and electrostatic properties that are problematic for usage in industries such as oil and gas exploration. Initial analyses estimated the initial investment to proceed with commercialization of the new patent to be $6.5 million for a plant and working capital for a post-test start-up period, and the estimated NPV was −$1.1 million.

Traditional valuation approaches would suggest that the new venture not be launched because the expected cash flows are inadequate in relation to the investment required (i.e., NPV < 0). However, the entrepreneur was convinced that if the project was successful, it would pave the way for additional applications for the synthetic technology. Algebraically stated, it is economically sensible for the entrepreneur to launch the business if the "package" of the value attached to any such growth options and the value attached to the first-stage investment is greater than zero, or $NPV_1 + C_2 > 0$, where NPV_1 is the NPV just described (−$1.1 million) and C_2 is the call option value of the growth options obtained from the first-stage investment. In other words, the value of the call option (C_2) must be worth at least $1.1 million for the firm to proceed with the launch (i.e., for −$1.1 million + $C_2 > 0$). If not, the business should not be started, unless other valuable options can be identified.

Whereas the previous example illustrates the point that a firm might invest in a project even if its NPV is negative, if embedded growth options are sufficiently valuable, the reverse side of the coin also holds: it can make sense for a firm *not* to sell assets or exit a business even if an NPV of doing so is *positive*. Consider Eli Lilly or other firms in pharmaceuticals or high-tech fields as an example. Such firms hold a wide range of patents and need to decide how best to manage the intellectual property they possess. For any given patent, the firm might proceed with commercialization, license the technology out to another firm, donate the patent to a university to obtain a tax write-off, or hold onto the technology. At first, it might appear irrational that these firms are holding on to many patents that are seemingly unrelated to their current businesses. Such investment choices might make sense rather than commercialization, but why not simply donate the patent to obtain tax benefits (or license it for royalties)? Suppose that $NPV_{d,p}$ is the NPV from donating patent p, and $NPV_{d,p} < 0$. Given uncertainty surrounding the value of the technology and other circumstances, this patent can have a call option value (i.e., C_p) because the firm has the right but not the obligation to commercialize the underlying technology in the future. Donating (or licensing) the patent today implies giving up the value of these embedded options. Thus, while $NPV_{d,p} < 0$, it might be the case that $NPV_{d,p} - C_p < 0$. It makes sense to donate if the package value, $NPV_{d,p} - C_p$, is greater than zero or, in other words, if the NPV obtained from donating is greater than the call value from holding onto the patent (i.e., $NPV_{d,p} > C_p$).[35] Thus, it is important that managers account for embedded options whether they are on the buy side (e.g., expanding, acquiring, or launching businesses) or on the sell side (e.g., selling or exiting businesses) of strategic investment decisions. The presence of real options suggests that it might make economic sense for firms to take on negative-NPV investments or to avoid positive-NPV investments not simply because these investments are "strategic," but because valuable options are embedded in such investments.

Driving Actual Firm Value. From a conceptual standpoint, real options are therefore important in providing a bridge between strategic analyses and capital budgeting, and they are important when a firm makes important strategic investment decisions because they can alter the firm's investment thresholds as opposed to using the standard criterion of NPV > 0.

The importance of options to the projects firms pursue and the overall value of companies can be demonstrated with actual data from actual firms. A simple way to do this is to consider that the value of a firm can be expressed in terms of the value of its assets in place, or the value derived from assets in their present use, plus the value of the firm's growth opportunities. The present value of a firm's growth opportunities has been defined as its *value of growth options* because growth in economic profits reflects discretionary future investments by the firm.[36] This leads to the formula $V = V_{AIP} + V_{GO}$, where V is the value of the firm, V_{AIP} is the value of assets in place, and V_{GO} is the value of the firm's growth options. If we divide V_{GO} by the value of the firm, this yields an expression that can be labeled "growth option value," or GOV, which represents the proportion of firm value attributable to growth options (i.e., GOV $= V_{GO}/V$).[37]

The technical details of how to estimate these values are beyond the scope of this chapter, but a few illustrations using data patterns can illustrate the importance of growth options across industries as well as across firms within industries. Data on firms' economic profits, discount rates, and capital invested were obtained from Stern Stewart & Co. to arrive at estimates of GOV.[38] Figure 13.1 illustrates how

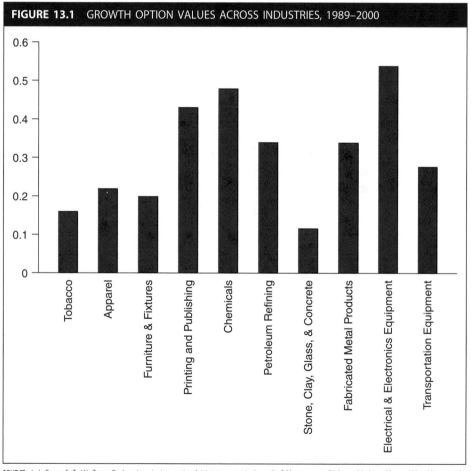

FIGURE 13.1 GROWTH OPTION VALUES ACROSS INDUSTRIES, 1989–2000

SOURCE: J. J. Reuer & T. W. Tong, Real options in international joint ventures in Journal of Management (Volume 31, Issue 3) pp. 403–423, copyright © 2005 by Journal of Management. Reprinted by Permission of SAGE Publications.

the proportion of firm value attributable to growth options varies across industries. For example, in the electrical and electronics equipment industry, on average 54 percent of firm value is due to growth options. In the chemicals industry, this proportion is also high at 48 percent. At the opposite end of the spectrum, firms in industries such as stone, clay, glass, and concrete derive little of their value from growth options (i.e., 12 percent), and similar patterns exist in industries such as furniture and fixtures (i.e., 20 percent).[39]

Despite these general tendencies across industries, the degree to which growth options matter within industries varies greatly. For example, within the electrical and electronics equipment industry (see Figure 13.2), the average growth option value is 0.54. Yet some firms obtain most of their value from growth options, and others, such as Rockwell, have more modest value attributable to growth options (18 percent). Likewise, even in industries such as stone, clay, glass, and concrete, in which firms tend to derive very little of their value from growth options, firms exist that obtain more than a quarter (i.e., 26 percent) of their value from growth options. The value of a firm's growth options will therefore be driven not only by its industry, but by its own strategic investments and capabilities. When investing in a new industry or when benchmarking a firm vis-à-vis rivals, it can be useful to

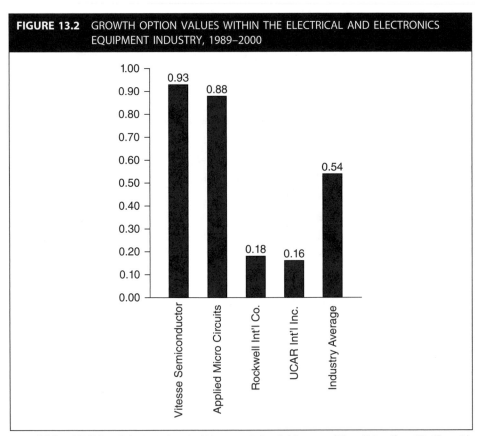

FIGURE 13.2 GROWTH OPTION VALUES WITHIN THE ELECTRICAL AND ELECTRONICS EQUIPMENT INDUSTRY, 1989–2000

SOURCE: J. J. Reuer & T. W. Tong, Real options in international joint ventures in *Journal of Management* (Volume 31, Issue 3) pp. 403–423, copyright © 2005 by Journal of Management. Reprinted by Permission of SAGE Publications.

determine when value is due to growth options or to reliance on assets in their present uses. Such a determination contributes to understanding firms' competitive positions and future prospects.[40]

These patterns indicate that real options analysis is important not only as a tool that can begin to reconcile strategic considerations and capital budgeting, and as a method for evaluating "go–no go" decisions for individual strategic investments, but also because real options are an important source of value for many firms. As such, companies need to obtain, exercise, and manage options appropriately. The objective of the firm is not to maximize option value per se, but to obtain the option value from the investments they undertake specifically for their flexibility benefits. Managers therefore need to understand what drives option value and how specific options can be valued.

Value Drivers for Real Options

Once a particular type of option has been identified as being embedded in a strategic investment decision, the next task for decision makers is to determine how particular aspects of the investment correspond to the value drivers for real options. The value of real options is driven by five factors, as shown in Table 13.2.[41] For simplicity, we will focus on call options, though the value of put options can also be described in terms of the same five variables. Furthermore, each of these factors is analogous to the individual value drivers for financial calls.

TABLE 13.2 DRIVERS OF CALL OPTION VALUE

PARAMETER	DEFINITION	EFFECT OF INCREASE IN PARAMETER	LOGIC
S	Value of the underlying asset	↑ Value of option	The higher the value is today, the better the chance the option has to finish in the money, or be worth more than its exercise price.
X	Cost of exercise	↓ Value of option	Increasing the cost to exercise decreases the opportunity for a positive payout.
r_f	Risk-free rate	↑ Value of option	The exercise price is discounted at the risk-free rate. Increases in the risk-free rate therefore decrease the cost of investment (X).
t	Time to investment	↑ Value of option	Additional time increases the likelihood for the option to finish in the money.
σ	Volatility	↑ Value of option	Volatility creates both additional upside and downside potential. Since options allow firms to access upside opportunities while limiting downside risk, higher volatility increases option value.

First, the current value of the underlying asset (S) is akin to the current price of a stock. For real options, the current value of the underlying asset is equivalent to the present value of the estimated cash flows associated with the underlying asset, or second-stage investment. This value sets the starting point for potential variations in the value of the second-stage investment in the future. For example, if a firm builds a scalable plant in Stage I, the value of the underlying asset is equal to the present value of the cash flow attributable to expansion of the plant in Stage II, say, three years in the future. The higher this present value, the greater the likelihood that it will ultimately finish higher than the cost of exercising the option, X. The exercise price is therefore equal to the amount that must be paid three years in the future to expand the plant. In this particular example, X amounts to capital expenditures that the firm must make to expand the facility. As such, option value increases in S and decreases in X, just as the NPV of any investment increases in the cash flows generated in the future and decreases in the initial investment required.

However, in the case of an option, the commitment is made in the future rather than at time zero. This future commitment, or exercise price, is therefore discounted at the risk-free rate of return (r_f) because it is assumed to be fixed and known with certainty at the time the option is purchased. Increases in the risk-free rate therefore discount the exercise price more substantially, which implies that the option value increases. It is also the case that the ability to delay this decision for a longer period of time enhances the firm's discretion and flexibility, so with everything else held constant, the value of the option also increases in the time to investment (t). In the simple example just discussed, the option value of building a second-stage plant after four years will be greater than for a similar project after three years, with everything else held constant.

Finally, whereas uncertainty is considered a liability for typical investment projects, in the case of call options, uncertainty relates *positively* to option value. This is because of the inherent properties of options: the firm has the right but not the obligation to take some future specified action. In the presence of uncertainty, this means that the firm is able to limit its downside risk and access upside opportunities. Given these two asymmetries between right versus obligation and upside opportunities versus downside risk, this implies that increases in uncertainty enhance, rather than detract from, option value. In the worst-case scenario, the firm is compelled to do nothing, but if uncertainty leads to very favorable outcomes, the firm is positioned to act on them. In other words, with options the firm is more exposed to positive developments and not exposed to negative developments.[42] The uncertainty dimension is represented by the parameter *volatility* (σ) in Table 13.2.

The five parameters can be summarized by two values that fully capture the value of real options.[43] First, the value of the underlying asset (S) can be divided by the present value (PV) of the exercise price [$PV(X) = X/(1 + r_f)^t$] to yield $NPV_q = S/PV(X)$. This expression is called NPV_q because the value attached to the future cash flows relative to the exercise price is stated in quotient form. It provides an indication of how far the value of the underlying asset is above or below the present value of the exercise price of the option. When $NPV_q > 1$, the option is "in the money," in that the value of the underlying asset is worth more than the present value of the cost of obtaining it. Conversely, when $NPV_q < 1$, the option is "out of the money," or the value of the underlying asset falls short of the present value of the cost to acquire it. The greater the value of NPV_q, the greater the value of the option, as depicted in Figure 13.3.

Second, the volatility and time to investment parameters can similarly be combined into a single variable driving option value. In this case, the variable is referred

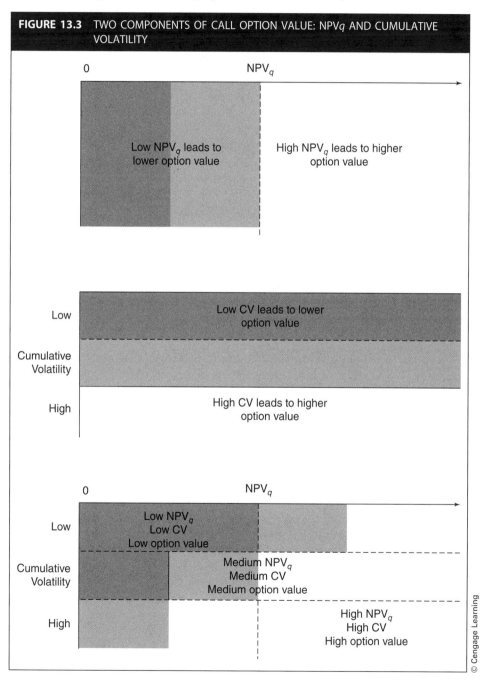

FIGURE 13.3 TWO COMPONENTS OF CALL OPTION VALUE: NPV*q* AND CUMULATIVE VOLATILITY

0   NPV_q

Low NPV_q leads to lower option value

High NPV_q leads to higher option value

Low

Cumulative Volatility

High

Low CV leads to lower option value

High CV leads to higher option value

0   NPV_q

Low

Cumulative Volatility

High

Low NPV_q
Low CV
Low option value

Medium NPV_q
Medium CV
Medium option value

High NPV_q
High CV
High option value

© Cengage Learning

to as *cumulative volatility* and is defined as: Cumulative Volatility (CV) $\sigma\sqrt{t}$. Sigma, σ, is equal to the standard deviation in annual returns to the underlying asset, and t is equal to the number of years until exercise. This expression indicates that it is the combination of volatility per period and the time until exercise that drives option value. As Figure 13.3 indicates, holding NPV_q constant, the higher the value of cumulative volatility, the higher the value of the call option. As will be discussed in the next section, once NPV_q and $\sigma\sqrt{t}$ are determined, it is possible to use a table to look up the value of an option.

VALUATION OF REAL OPTIONS

Many different techniques are used to value real options, and it is not the purpose of this chapter to present these approaches in an exhaustive manner or to delve into the technical complexities of valuing real options in practice. Rather, the objective is to illustrate the application of two different approaches commonly used in the valuation of real options and to offer a brief introduction to real option valuation. We recommend that readers refer to the appendix for an overview of real options valuation techniques as well as application guidelines. In large-scale projects for which real option valuation is appropriate, financial experts and others may be engaged in developing very sophisticated and customized valuation models. However, even relatively straightforward models such as those presented in the appendix can yield important insights, and such insights can assist managers in reconciling strategic analyses and capital budgeting processes.

IMPLEMENTATION REQUIREMENTS OF REAL OPTIONS

While current thinking on real options has focused primarily on identifying the options that firms obtain from various investments and operational practices, considerably less has been considered or written on the side of organization and the implementation requirements presented by real options. At the broadest level, it seems intuitive to suggest that firms seeking value from real options require organizations and systems that enable them to implement flexible strategies effectively; however, details on how real options or strategic flexibility ought to be implemented best require more development.

When implementation requirements are being considered, it is important as a first broad-brush distinction to differentiate the *analysis* of real options from real option investments *per se*. Regarding the former, the above discussion of how real options analyses might be used in strategic decision-making processes suggests a variety of approaches, ranging from the qualitative to the very formal.[44] For some firms, real options can be as much a way of thinking or an organizational process in itself as a formal analytical tool. However, critics of real options analysis sometimes suggest that it is overly technical and beyond the mathematical competence of many managers. It is true that many of the firms that have adopted real options analysis, often without appropriate procedures to evaluate options,[45] have abandoned this technique, and many express concerns about its complexity.[46] Although these concerns are often well-placed and tend to deal with violation of assumptions and difficulties associated with valuation models, sometimes they are merely a result of communication problems rather than more substantive ones.[47] The fact that this technique became popular during the time when Internet stocks became highly overvalued (and subsequently lost most of their value) didn't help its cause.[48] The cause was further damaged when Enron and other companies that were early adopters were caught up in scandals.

Nevertheless, as the illustrations found in this chapter and appendix suggest, considerable insights can be gained from relatively simple extensions of existing techniques such as discounted cash flow models and decision tree analysis. Firms will also likely benefit from establishing ground rules for the use of this technique and targeting its application to large projects for which the NPV is uncertain. The adoption of real options analysis in some ways might resemble the replacement of other valuation methods (e.g., payback criteria, valuation multiples, etc.) by currently used financial valuation approaches. Suggestions for beginning this transition in firms include conducting one or more experimental pilot projects, getting support from top managers and those involved in the project, codifying the real options technique through an expert group and training materials, and institutionalizing real options analysis as a way of thinking as well as an analytical tool.[49]

Turning attention to the real options themselves, the question of implementation requirements in essence boils down to whether and how executives of business units that depend on real options should be managed any differently from other units. If much of the value that such managers add to, or detract from, the firm is due to their option formation and exercise decisions, the use of financial metrics geared to assessing current operational performance can be problematic. As one example, if managers are punished for "failures" that arise on the basis of the state of the world that is actually realized, this approach to performance assessment misses the more important point that the manager might have faced a wide range of possible outcomes at the time of investment and appropriately structured an investment to minimize downside risk while positioning the firm to capture upside opportunities had external conditions turned out differently. Such problems might be avoided by examining a portfolio of projects under the control of management, distinguishing uncertainties that are partially under the control and beyond the control of managers, and relying on additional information to judge management performance and provide incentives for appropriate behavior.

One additional problem with implementation has to do with the mentality of employees who see that investing their human capital in projects that might be terminated will create less asset-specific investment in the firm. There is a tendency to invest in projects that are more certain and in developing skills that are transferable to other projects or companies.[50] Thus, implementation of a real options approach needs to consider this ramification.

SUMMARY

▶ A real option provides a firm with the right, but not the obligation, to take some future specified action. This enables the firm to reduce its downside risk while accessing upside opportunities. Types of real options include growth, abandonment, switching, deferral, and compound options. Each of these types is relevant in different strategic contexts.

- Real options challenge received wisdom on firms' motives and payoffs from strategic investments. For example, joint ventures are seen as stepping stones rather than marriages. The benefits of foreign direct investment include not only operational control, but also operational flexibility.

- Real options help reconcile strategic analysis and financial analysis. Real options inject strategic reality (active management and follow-on opportunities) into traditional financial theory (discounted cash flow analyses and net present value), while bringing the discipline of the financial markets and the rigor of quantitative investment criteria into strategic analyses.

- Real options shift firms' investment thresholds. Firms might economically invest in projects that have negative net present values if the value of embedded options is sufficiently high such that the value of the first-stage investment plus the value of embedded options is greater than zero. Conversely, firms might avoid investment decisions with positive net present values if such decisions require them to give up valuable options. In such cases, the net present value of the investment has to not only be greater than zero, but also greater than the value of options that are sacrificed. Managers intuitively incorporate the value of foregone deferral options into their investment decisions by requiring net present values to be substantially positive.

- Options can represent a substantial portion of firm value. The economic importance of real options differs across industries as well as across firms within industries.

- The value of an option is driven by five parameters: the underlying asset, the exercise price, the risk-free rate of return, the time to exercise, and uncertainty (volatility). These can be collapsed into two summary parameters: NPV_q and cumulative volatility. Quantitative assessment of options can be conducted, and options can be compared, using these parameters.

- Real options have unique implementation requirements, so businesses that depend on real options must use appropriate monitoring, control, and incentive systems to address potential biases in managers' option purchases and exercise decisions. Firms using real options analyses as a part of their strategic resource allocation process must also institute appropriate systems for this tool to evaluate investment projects.

- Adoption of real options analysis might be facilitated by pilot projects, endorsement by top managers, codification efforts, and institutionalizing both the strategic thinking and more formal aspects of real options analysis.

- The appendix shows that option values can be calculated using the Black-Scholes approach, the Black-Scholes approximation technique, and binomial lattices. Each of these methods requires different input data and assumptions. In instances in which assumptions are violated, more sophisticated option valuation models can be used, or simple valuation models can be implemented based on knowledge of the expected direction of bias.

- In Black-Scholes valuation models, the uncertainty parameter is often the one that is most difficult to obtain. Sigma can be estimated from historical returns data and from benchmark, pure-play companies, yet sensitivity analyses that calculate option value for a range of uncertainty values are useful.

1. What are the ethical implications of making an investment that appears to be a money loser in the short term on the basis that there will be options to make money from the opportunities that the investment provides in the longer term? For instance, as a shareholder, would you be comfortable with a management team that routinely makes these types of decisions?
2. How can a firm include human issues (such as the well-being of employees, or human risk factors) in a real options analysis?
3. Can real options analysis be used to justify poor decisions? If so, what are the agency implications (e.g., the risks that managers might use the technique to their advantage)? What are the legal implications?
4. How can a board of directors ensure that real options analysis does not result in management decisions that hurt shareholders and other important stakeholders?

APPENDIX: DETAILED VALUATION GUIDELINES

Here we provide detailed guidelines for using the Black-Scholes valuation method, as well as an alternative to the Black-Scholes method called *binomial lattices*. We conclude with a discussion of several practical application issues.

Black-Scholes Valuation

The **Black-Scholes option pricing formula** for a European financial call option is often used to value real options. A European option can be exercised only on the date of the option's maturity. Finance textbooks present the details of this technique, and we will only summarize the essentials for application to real option valuation. The Black-Scholes formula is:

$$\text{Call Option Value} = [S \times N(d_1)] - [PV(X) \times N(d_2)],$$

where S = current value of the underlying asset, $PV(X)$ = present value of the exercise price, N = standard normal cumulative distribution function, $d_1 = [\log(S/X) + (r_f + 0.5\sigma^2)t]/[\sigma\sqrt{t}]$, $d_2 = d_1 - \sigma\sqrt{t}$, σ = standard deviation of returns, and t = years to maturity.

Notice that in addition to a table for the normal distribution, the five parameters just discussed are sufficient to calculate option values using the Black-Scholes formula. There are four steps to calculating a call option's value using this approach:

1. Calculate the value of the underlying asset and the present value of the exercise price, $PV(X)$.
2. Determine d_1 and d_2 using these two values as well as σ and t.
3. Use the normal distribution table to find $N(d_1)$ and $N(d_2)$.
4. Use the Black-Scholes formula to compute the option value.

An example will help to clarify this approach. Upon graduation, an MBA student takes a position as the vice president of purchasing for a small firm in Wisconsin, an airline called Dairy Air. She is trying to complete negotiations with a

French aircraft manufacturer for a new plane. Given her firm's current financial condition, she does not seek to acquire a new plane for operations today. In fact, the French firm is demanding a price of $100 million, but she determines that it would only be worth $90 million given the current industry environment. However, for planning purposes she would like to be able to lock in a price and potentially add a new aircraft to the firm's fleet in the next few years if demand for travel improves. She assumes that $\sigma = 0.50$ and the risk-free rate of return is 5 percent. The French company is requesting a payment of $25 million for an option to purchase the plane for $100 million in three years, and the question is whether Dairy Air should secure this option at a price of $25 million.

Step 1: Calculate the value of the underlying asset and the present value of the exercise price, PV(X). The student has already estimated the value of the underlying asset to be $90 million. The present value of the exercise price, PV(X), is given by $100e^{-0.05(3)} = \$86.07$ million. This latter expression reflects continuous compounding at 5 percent for three years. (If annual compounding were used as a simplification, the present value of the exercise price would be $86.38 million.)

Step 2: Determine d_1 and d_2 using these two values as well as σ and t.

$$d_1 = [\log(S/X) + (r_f + 0.5\sigma^2)t]/[\sigma\sqrt{t}]$$
$$= [\log(90/100) + (0.05 + 0.5(0.5)^2)3]/[0.5\sqrt{3}] = 0.4846;$$
$$d_2 = d_1 - \sigma\sqrt{t} = 0.4846 - 0.5\sqrt{3} = -0.3815.$$

Step 3: Use the normal distribution table to find $N(d_1)$ and $N(d_2)$. Using a table for the standard normal cumulative distribution function yields $N(d_1) = N(0.4846) = 0.6860$ and $N(d_2) = N(-0.3815) = 0.3514$.

Step 4: Use the Black-Scholes formula to compute the option value. By this formula, the call option value $= [S \times N(d_1)] - [PV(X) \times N(d_2)] = 90(0.6860) - 86.07(0.3514) = \$31.49$ million.

Given that this value exceeds the price the aircraft manufacturer is asking for the option on the plane, $25 million, Dairy Air should proceed with the option purchase.

This example simplified the calculation in a number of ways. First, the value of the underlying asset was given. When this value is not available, it can be estimated by pro forma statements of cash flows and by addressing two complications. These cash flows include both the cost of exercising the option and the cash flows enjoyed by the firm after it exercises the option. Hence, the costs associated with the commitment to the project (e.g., the capital expenditure) need to be separated from the cash flows and counted as part of X. Other cash flows, including routine capital expenditures, become part of the cash flows used to calculate S. The cash flows attached to S will be discounted by the risk-adjusted discount rate to reflect the riskiness of these cash flows. By contrast, cash flows making up X are discounted at the risk-free rate to reflect the fact that the cost of exercise is assumed by the Black-Scholes approach to be fixed and known with certainty at time zero.

Second, the volatility parameter was also given. Obtaining a measure of the investment's volatility can also be a challenging task. Obtaining an estimate for this parameter can be accomplished by gathering historical data, using industry

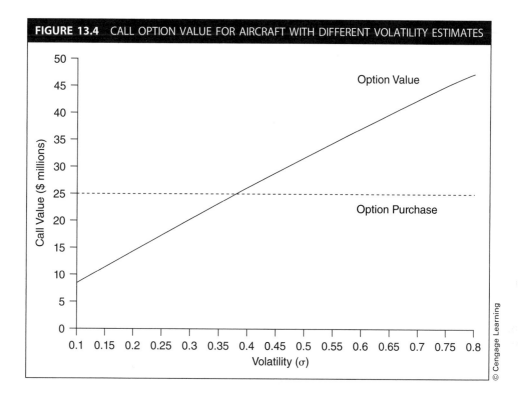

FIGURE 13.4 CALL OPTION VALUE FOR AIRCRAFT WITH DIFFERENT VOLATILITY ESTIMATES

standards as a benchmark, or taking an educated guess based on similar projects or experience. Sensitivity analysis therefore becomes important when estimating volatility, and it is recommended that a range of volatilities and their corresponding option values be computed. For example, if call option values are calculated for a range of sigmas (σ), a chart like Figure 13.4 can be constructed to determine the break-even value for the volatility parameter for the firm to go forward with the purchase of the option. The horizontal dashed line represents the payment of $25 million for the option, and the graph indicates that as long as the volatility parameter is clearly greater than 0.40, it makes sense for Dairy Air to purchase the option. If uncertainty is lower than this value, the value of the option drops below its purchase price, and the firm should not go forward with the contract with its present terms.

Black-Scholes Approximation

As noted earlier in the chapter, the five parameters making up the value drivers for options can be reduced to two summary parameters: (1) NPV_q, and (2) cumulative volatility. Once these two values are known, the value of an option can be approximated by looking up a value in a table instead of using the Black-Scholes formula above. Even when values can readily be obtained by the Black-Scholes approach, this approximation technique is useful because it is intuitively appealing, requires less mathematical background, and is easier to communicate to others involved in evaluating a project. This method involves the following four steps:

1. Calculate NPV_q.
2. Calculate cumulative volatility.
3. Look up the table value expressing the value of the option as a percentage of the value of the underlying asset (see Table 13.3).
4. Multiply the table value by the value of the underlying asset in order to calculate the option value.

This approach can be applied to the option contract for the aircraft just discussed:

Step 1: Calculate NPV_q. $NPV_q = S/PV(X)$, and for simplicity we will use annual compounding to discount the exercise price. Hence, $NPV_q = S/[X/(1 + r_f{}^t)] = 90/[100/(1.05)^3] = 1.04$.

Step 2: Calculate cumulative volatility. Cumulative volatility $= \sigma\sqrt{t} = 0.5\sqrt{3} = 0.87$.

Step 3: Look up the table value expressing the value of the option as a percentage of the value of the underlying asset. On Table 13.3, NPV_q is found moving from top to bottom along the left side of the chart, and cumulative volatility is found moving from left to right along the top of the chart. $NPV_q = 1.04$ is found along the left side and the closest cumulative volatility of 0.85 is found on the other axis; the table value equals 34.2 percent for this pair. Interpolation yields 34.92 percent for the cumulative volatility of 0.87.

Step 4: Multiply the table value by the value of the underlying asset to calculate the option value. The value of the call option equals 34.92 percent of the value of the underlying asset, and the value of the underlying asset is $90 million. Therefore, the value of the option is (34.92 percent)($90 million) = $31.42 million.

The result of $31.42 million compares favorably with the $31.49 million calculated earlier.

Binomial Lattices

An alternative to the Black-Scholes methods described above that is also intuitively appealing and mathematically straightforward relies upon the construction of lattices, also known as *decision trees*.[51] These lattices are referred to as *binomial lattices* because the value of an asset can assume two values based on an "up" or "down" movement in value each period; and following a succession of such up and down movements, the possible values for the underlying asset follow a binomial distribution. In the Black-Scholes example above, this stochastic process was reflected in the uncertainty parameter sigma instead, but as the number of nodes in a lattice increases, the distributions approach one another, as do the valuations obtained from the two methods.

These up and down movements are represented by two parameters, u and d, respectively. For instance, suppose that $u = 1.1$ and $d = 0.9091$. If these parameters are known, along with the value of the underlying asset at time zero, then the entire stochastic process for the asset over time can be modeled by constructing an event tree. For example, if the value of the underlying asset begins at $V_0 = \$100$, then

TABLE 13.3 BLACK-SCHOLES EUROPEAN CALL OPTION PRICING TABLE (% OF UNDERLYING ASSET VALUE)

NPV_q	CUMULATIVE VOLATILITY																			
	0.05	0.10	0.15	0.20	0.25	0.30	0.35	0.40	0.45	0.50	0.55	0.60	0.65	0.70	0.75	0.80	0.85	0.90	0.95	1.00
0.50	0.0	0.0	0.0	0.0	0.0	0.2	0.4	0.9	1.7	2.6	3.8	5.1	6.5	8.1	9.8	11.5	13.3	15.2	17.1	19.1
0.60	0.0	0.0	0.0	0.0	0.2	0.7	1.4	2.4	3.7	5.1	6.6	8.3	10.0	11.9	13.7	15.7	17.6	19.6	21.6	23.6
0.70	0.0	0.0	0.1	0.4	1.0	2.0	3.3	4.8	6.5	8.2	10.0	11.9	13.8	15.8	17.8	19.8	21.8	23.8	25.8	27.7
0.75	0.0	0.0	0.2	0.8	1.8	3.1	4.6	6.3	8.1	10.0	11.9	13.8	15.8	17.8	19.8	21.8	23.8	25.8	27.7	29.7
0.80	0.0	0.1	0.5	1.5	2.8	4.4	6.2	8.0	9.9	11.8	13.8	15.8	17.8	19.8	21.8	23.7	25.7	27.7	29.6	31.6
0.82	0.0	0.1	0.7	1.9	3.3	5.0	6.8	8.7	10.6	12.6	14.6	16.6	18.6	20.6	22.5	24.5	26.5	28.4	30.4	32.3
0.84	0.0	0.2	1.0	2.3	3.9	5.7	7.5	9.4	11.4	13.4	15.4	17.4	19.4	21.3	23.3	25.3	27.2	29.2	31.1	33.0
0.86	0.0	0.3	1.3	2.8	4.5	6.3	8.2	10.2	12.2	14.2	16.1	18.1	20.1	22.1	24.1	26.0	28.0	29.9	31.8	33.7
0.88	0.0	0.5	1.8	3.4	5.2	7.1	9.0	11.0	13.0	14.9	16.9	18.9	20.9	22.9	24.8	26.8	28.7	30.6	32.5	34.4
0.90	0.0	0.8	2.3	4.0	5.9	7.8	9.8	11.8	13.7	15.7	17.7	19.7	21.7	23.6	25.6	27.5	29.4	31.3	33.2	35.1
0.92	0.1	1.2	2.8	4.7	6.6	8.6	10.6	12.6	14.5	16.5	18.5	20.5	22.5	24.4	26.3	28.3	30.2	32.0	33.9	35.8
0.94	0.3	1.7	3.5	5.4	7.4	9.4	11.4	13.4	15.4	17.3	19.3	21.3	23.2	25.2	27.1	29.0	30.9	32.7	34.6	36.4
0.96	0.6	2.3	4.2	6.2	8.2	10.2	12.2	14.2	16.2	18.1	20.1	22.0	24.0	25.9	27.8	29.7	31.6	33.4	35.2	37.0
0.98	1.2	3.1	5.1	7.1	9.1	11.1	13.0	15.0	17.0	18.9	20.9	22.8	24.7	26.6	28.5	30.4	32.2	34.1	35.9	37.7
1.00	2.0	4.0	6.0	8.0	10.0	11.9	13.9	15.9	17.8	19.7	21.7	23.6	25.5	27.4	29.2	31.1	32.9	34.7	36.5	38.3
1.02	3.1	5.0	7.0	8.9	10.9	12.8	14.8	16.7	18.6	20.5	22.5	24.3	26.2	28.1	29.9	31.8	33.6	35.4	37.2	38.9
1.04	4.5	6.1	8.0	9.9	11.8	13.7	15.6	17.5	19.5	21.3	23.2	25.1	27.0	28.8	30.6	32.4	34.2	36.0	37.8	39.6
1.06	6.0	7.3	9.1	10.9	12.8	14.6	16.5	18.4	20.3	22.1	24.0	25.9	27.7	29.5	31.3	33.1	34.9	36.6	38.4	40.1
1.08	7.5	8.6	10.2	11.9	13.7	15.6	17.4	19.3	21.1	22.9	24.8	26.6	28.4	30.2	32.0	33.8	35.5	37.3	39.0	40.7
1.10	9.1	10.0	11.4	13.0	14.7	16.5	18.3	20.1	21.9	23.7	25.5	27.3	29.1	30.9	32.7	34.4	36.2	37.9	39.6	41.3
1.12	10.7	11.3	12.6	14.1	15.7	17.4	19.2	21.0	22.7	24.5	26.3	28.1	29.8	31.6	33.3	35.1	36.8	38.5	40.2	41.8
1.14	12.3	12.7	13.8	15.2	16.7	18.4	20.1	21.9	23.5	25.3	27.0	28.8	30.5	32.3	34.0	35.7	37.4	39.1	40.7	42.4
1.16	13.8	14.1	15.0	16.3	17.7	19.3	21.0	22.6	24.4	26.1	27.8	29.5	31.2	32.9	34.6	36.3	38.0	39.6	41.3	42.9
1.18	15.3	15.4	16.2	17.4	18.7	20.3	21.9	23.5	25.2	26.8	28.5	30.2	31.9	33.6	35.3	36.9	38.6	40.2	41.8	43.4
1.20	16.7	16.8	17.4	18.5	19.8	21.2	22.7	24.3	26.0	27.6	29.3	30.9	32.6	34.2	35.9	37.5	39.2	40.8	42.4	44.0
1.25	20.0	20.0	20.4	21.2	22.3	23.5	24.9	26.4	27.9	29.5	31.0	32.6	34.2	35.8	37.4	39.0	40.6	42.1	43.7	45.2

(Continued)

TABLE 13.3 (CONTINUED)

CUMULATIVE VOLATILITY

NPV$_q$	0.05	0.10	0.15	0.20	0.25	0.30	0.35	0.40	0.45	0.50	0.55	0.60	0.65	0.70	0.75	0.80	0.85	0.90	0.95	1.00
1.30	23.1	23.1	23.3	23.9	24.7	25.8	27.1	28.4	29.8	31.3	32.8	34.3	35.8	37.4	38.9	40.4	41.9	43.5	45.0	46.5
1.35	25.9	25.9	26.0	26.4	27.1	28.1	29.2	30.4	31.7	33.1	34.5	35.9	37.4	38.8	40.3	41.8	43.3	44.7	46.2	47.7
1.40	28.6	28.6	28.6	28.9	29.9	30.2	31.2	32.3	33.5	34.8	36.1	37.5	38.9	40.3	41.7	43.1	44.5	46.0	47.4	48.8
1.45	31.0	31.0	31.1	31.2	31.7	32.3	33.2	34.2	35.3	36.5	37.7	39.0	40.3	41.7	43.0	44.4	45.8	47.1	48.5	49.9
1.50	33.3	33.3	33.4	33.5	33.8	34.3	35.1	36.0	37.0	38.1	39.2	40.4	41.7	43.0	44.3	45.6	46.9	48.3	49.6	50.9
1.75	42.9	42.9	42.9	42.9	42.9	43.1	43.5	44.0	44.6	45.3	46.1	47.0	48.0	49.0	50.1	51.1	52.2	53.3	54.5	55.6
2.00	50.0	50.0	50.0	50.0	50.0	50.1	50.2	50.5	50.8	51.3	51.9	55.5	53.3	54.0	54.9	55.8	56.7	57.6	58.6	59.5
2.50	60.0	60.0	60.0	60.0	60.0	60.0	60.0	60.1	60.2	60.4	60.7	61.0	61.4	61.9	62.4	63.0	63.6	64.3	65.0	65.7

SOURCE: Adapted from BARNEY, JAY B., *Gaining and Sustaining Competitive Advantage*, 2nd Edition, © 2002. Reprinted by permission of Pearson Education, Inc., Upper Saddle River, NJ.

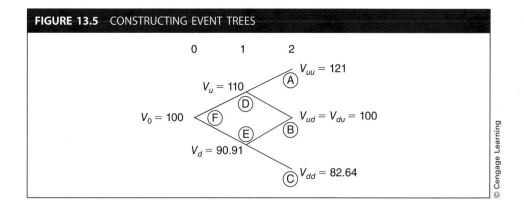

FIGURE 13.5 CONSTRUCTING EVENT TREES

0   1   2

$V_u = 110$

$V_{uu} = 121$ (A)

(D)

$V_0 = 100$ (F)

(E) (B) $V_{ud} = V_{du} = 100$

$V_d = 90.91$

(C) $V_{dd} = 82.64$

© Cengage Learning

after one period, the value of the asset will be either $V_u = 1.1(100) = 110$ or $V_d = 0.9091(100) = 90.91$. Suppose that these values occur with equal probability. In the second period, the asset will be worth $V_{uu} = (1.1)^2(100) = 121$ if an up movement was followed by another up movement. At the opposite extreme, following two down movements, the asset will be valued at $V_{dd} = (0.9091)^2(100) = 82.64$. If the asset experiences an up movement followed by a down movement in the lattice, it will take on a value of $V_{ud} = (1.1)(0.9091)(100) = 100$, which is equivalent to $V_{du} = (0.9091)(1.1)(100) = 100$. Note that these values equal the initial value of the asset, $V_0 = 100$, because $u = 1/d$. Figure 13.5 gives the event tree for this asset. The first step in valuing options using binomial lattices is to construct such an event tree.

The next step is to convert the event tree to a decision tree. While an event tree portrays how the value of the underlying asset moves over time, a decision tree depicts how managers make decisions within this tree in order to maximize the value of the option. For illustration, suppose that a manager has the right to acquire the above asset initially worth $100 for an exercise price of $115. The question is how much such an option is worth. If we define C_0 to be the value of this option at time zero, we can similarly define the value of the option at various nodes in the lattice. For example, after a single up movement, the value of the call option is C_u, the value of the call option after an up and down movement is C_{ud}, and so forth. The nodes on the event tree in Figure 13.5 have been labeled A–F to describe particular positions in the lattice.

The key to constructing the decision tree is to work backwards in the event tree to calculate the value of the option at each node. Starting at node A (see Figure 13.6), the manager has the decision to do nothing and earn zero, or to exercise the call option and obtain the value of the asset, V_{uu}, less the exercise price of $115. The value of the option at this node can therefore be written as $C_{uu} = \max(V_{uu} - 115, 0)$. Since $V_{uu} = 121$, this formula can be rewritten as $\max(121 - 115, 0)$. The manager therefore chooses to exercise the option to get $6, rather than do nothing and get zero. C_{uu} therefore equals 6. At node B, the same calculation is made. Here, $C_{ud} = \max(V_{ud} - 115, 0) = \max(100 - 115, 0)$. Here, exercising the option would lead the firm to obtain -$5, while the manager could do nothing and obtain zero; so the option is not exercised. Thus,

$C_{ud} = 0$. Similarly at node C, the value of the underlying asset falls short of the exercise price; the option would not be exercised, and $C_{dd} = 0$.

At this time, the last column in the tree is complete, and the intermediate nodes that occur at the end of one year, nodes D and E, can be analyzed. At node D, the manager's choice is to exercise the option and claim the value of the underlying asset or to leave the option open for potential exercise in the future. In order to calculate this latter value, we need to be able to determine a present value for C_{uu} and C_{ud} by discounting these values for one period of time. The problem noted earlier is that we cannot simply use the risk-adjusted rate to calculate present values for option payouts.

The solution to this problem lies in using a technique called the *risk-neutral method*. Under typical applications of using discounted cash flow analysis to calculate present values, estimated cash flows are discounted at a risk-adjusted rate. For instance, in our particular illustration, given that there is an equal probability (0.5) of an up or down movement in the lattice, these objective probabilities can be used to calculate an expected payout in a successive period. This approach incorporates risk into the present value calculation by "punishing" the cash flows through a higher denominator, which incorporates the risk-adjusted discount rate. An alternative, less-known technique is to adjust the cash flows in the numerator in such a way that these cash flows can simply be discounted at the risk-free rate instead. In the valuation of real options, this approach is particularly helpful because the risk of the project changes throughout the lattice, yet a single, simple discount rate can be employed by using the risk-neutral method (i.e., the risk-free rate). The technical details of the risk-free method are beyond the scope of this chapter, but for our purposes it is sufficient to introduce a single formula to permit such calculations of present values in decision trees.

The solution is to convert the objective probabilities ($q = 0.50$ and $1 - q = 0.50$ in our case) to "risk-neutral" probabilities that can be used to weight payouts from different nodes in the lattice. The formula for the risk-neutral probability for the up movement is simply $P_u = [(1 + r_f) - d] \div (u - d)$ and $P_d = 1 - P_u$. If the risk-free rate of return is 5 percent, then $P_u = (1.05 - 0.9091) \div (1.1 - 0.9091) = 0.74$, and $P_d = 1 - 0.74 = 0.26$. We can now calculate the value of holding the option open at node D (see Figure 13.6) by weighting the option payouts at the two successive

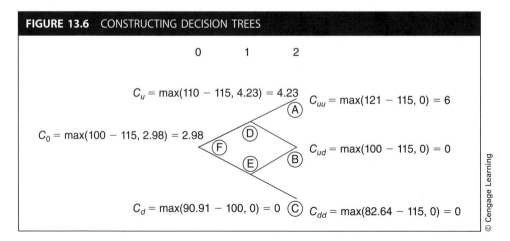

FIGURE 13.6   CONSTRUCTING DECISION TREES

0   1   2

$C_u = \max(110 - 115, 4.23) = 4.23$

$C_{uu} = \max(121 - 115, 0) = 6$ Ⓐ

$C_0 = \max(100 - 115, 2.98) = 2.98$

Ⓓ

Ⓕ

Ⓔ

Ⓑ

$C_{ud} = \max(100 - 115, 0) = 0$

$C_d = \max(90.91 - 100, 0) = 0$ Ⓒ

$C_{dd} = \max(82.64 - 115, 0) = 0$

© Cengage Learning

nodes in this "nest" by the risk-neutral probabilities and by discounting one period at the risk-free rate. Specifically, this value is $(P_u C_{uu} + P_d C_{ud}) \div (1 + r_f) = [0.74(6) + 0.26(0)] \div (1.05) = 4.23$. Thus, at node D, the value of the option is $C_u = \max(110 - 115, 4.23)$. In this case, the firm would obtain $110 - 115 = -5$ from exercising the option, and this option is worth 4.23 if a manager continues to hold it; so it is optimal to hold it rather than exercise it.

Moving to node E, the above calculations become considerably easier. We noted earlier that managers will not exercise the option at successive nodes B and C because the value of the underlying asset is less than the exercise price in both cases. Since there is certainty that the option will not be exercised regardless of the state of nature, the value of holding the option open at node E is also zero. Thus, the value of the option at node E can be written as $C_d = \max(90.91 - 115, 0)$. Even though the value of holding the option open at this node has no value, the manager will not exercise it because doing so yields a value of $90.91 - 115 = -24.09$. This suggests that the manager will simply allow the option to expire and ultimately obtain a value of zero.

Since we now know the value of the option at nodes D and E, we can fold back the calculations a final time to obtain the value of the option at time zero, C_0, which is the objective of the exercise. The firm can exercise the option at time zero, but it will not do so because the value of the asset (i.e., 100) is less than the exercise price (i.e., 115). The value of holding the option open is 4.23 at node D and 0 at node E. The value of holding the option open at time zero can be obtained by weighting these two values by the appropriate risk-neutral probabilities and discounting one period at the risk-free rate. That is, $C_0 = (P_u C_u + P_d C_d) \div (1 + r_f) = [0.74(4.23) + 0.26(0)] \div (1.05) = 2.98$.

The completed decision tree of Figure 13.6 can be used to draw several conclusions from this problem. First, as long as it costs no more than 2.98 to purchase this option, it is valuable for the firm to do so. Second, the option will not be exercised after one year because it is more valuable to hold the option rather than obtain the underlying asset at a price of $115. Third, in the final year, the option will be exercised only at node A, which means that the best-case scenario of two up movements in the asset's value has transpired.

This example illustrates that the risk-neutral method consists of five steps: (1) estimate the value of the underlying asset at time zero as well as the up and down parameters, u and d; (2) construct an event tree that depicts how the value of the underlying asset increases or decreases over time; (3) calculate the value of the risk-neutral probabilities used in weighting values in the lattice for discounting purposes; (4) construct a decision tree that shows how the decision maker chooses to hold open or exercise the option at various nodes in the event tree; (5) work backwards in the lattice to value the option at all of the nodes. During this final step, the value of holding the option will be obtained by weighting the value of the option in the two successive nodes in the corresponding "nest" in the lattice and discounting at the risk-free rate. This technique can also be applied to put options, using a real-life example that was briefly mentioned above.

An entrepreneur (e.g., Wellington Synthetics) is considering starting up a firm to commercialize a new technology for producing synthetic mats to be used at construction sites to enable the transportation of heavy equipment around sites that often have poor soil conditions.[52] Most firms use wooden mats to create temporary roads, staging areas, and support around the site, but such mats are quite heavy and bulky and therefore difficult to store and move. Firms had previously tried to produce mats of synthetic materials, but these initial products had serious drawbacks: they often maintained a "memory" of prior traffic of equipment and vehicles, and, even more problematic for use around hazardous materials, they exhibited electrostatic properties that created sparking conditions. The entrepreneur believes that the new technology solves these problems and represents a potential breakthrough product for construction sites.

Initial analysis indicated that $6.5 million would be needed in capital expenditures and working capital to start up this business, yet discounted cash flow analysis placed the NPV at −$1.112 million. This initial calculation suggests that the business idea should not be pursued, but the entrepreneur also believes that the initial plant could be sold for $4 million in three years and converted for the production of molded synthetics products if the initial business does not develop favorably. The entrepreneur wonders whether this embedded put option is sufficiently valuable to make the launch of the business sensible despite the negative NPV.

Step 1: Estimate the value of the underlying asset at time zero as well as the up and down parameters, u and d. To value the put option and draw a conclusion on this question, a number of inputs are needed. First, assume that the value of the underlying asset can increase by 64.9 percent or decrease by 39.3 percent each year, which corresponds to up and down parameters of 1.649 and 0.607, respectively. Also assume that the risk-free rate stands at 5.5 percent. We also need to obtain the starting value of the underlying asset in order to develop an event tree. This value can be inferred from the $6.5 million initial expenditure and the −$1.112 million NPV, which together indicate that the present value of the business's cash flows stands at $5.388 million.

Step 2: Construct an event tree that depicts how the value of the underlying asset increases or decreases over time. Based on the information provided, $V_0 =$ $5.388, and in this case we have a three-year problem, so we need to calculate $V_{uuu} = (1.649)^3(5.388) = 24.157$, $V_{uud} = (1.649)^2(0.607)(5.388) = 8.884$, $V_{udd} = 1.649(0.607)^2(5.388) = 3.270$, $V_{ddd} = (0.607)^3(5.388) = 1.205$, and the values in all intermediate years. Figure 13.7 shows the event tree for this problem.

Step 3: Calculate the value of the risk-neutral probabilities used in weighting values in the lattice for discounting purposes. The formula for the risk-neutral probability for the up movement is simply $P_u = [(1 + r_f) − d] ÷ (u − d)$, and $P_d = 1 − P_u$. For this particular problem, the inputs are as follows: the risk-free rate, r_f, is 5.5 percent; $u = 1.649$; and $d = 0.607$. Thus, $P_u = (1.055 − 0.607) ÷ (1.649 − 0.607) = 0.43$, and $P_d = 1 − P_u = 1 − 0.43 = 0.57$.

Steps 4 and 5: (4) Construct a decision tree that shows how the decision maker chooses to hold open or exercise the option at various nodes in the event tree; and (5) work backwards in the lattice to value the option at all of the nodes.

In this problem, the decision maker has the right but not the obligation to sell the underlying asset for $4 million. Examining nodes A and B, the value of the underlying asset is considerably greater than $4 million, so the put option is not exercised and is allowed to expire, yielding a payout of zero. These facts, combined

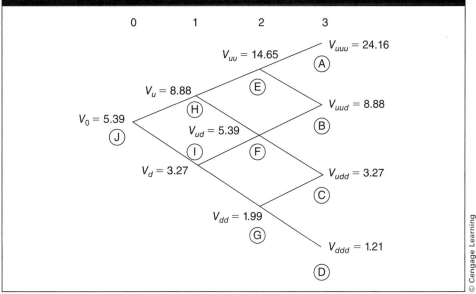

FIGURE 13.7 EVENT TREE FOR ENTREPRENEURIAL START-UP

0   1   2   3

$V_{uuu} = 24.16$ (A)

$V_{uu} = 14.65$ (E)

$V_u = 8.88$ (H)

$V_{uud} = 8.88$ (B)

$V_0 = 5.39$ (J)

$V_{ud} = 5.39$ (I) (F)

$V_{udd} = 3.27$ (C)

$V_d = 3.27$

$V_{dd} = 1.99$ (G)

$V_{ddd} = 1.21$

(D)

© Cengage Learning

with the observation that the value of the underlying asset is worth more than 4 at node E, also imply that the option is worth zero at this node as well.

The firm will exercise the abandonment, or put, option at nodes C and D. At node C we have $C_{udd} = \max(4 - 3.27, 0) = 0.73$. Notice for this problem that the value of the underlying asset is subtracted from the exercise price of the option in this case because the firm is *selling* the underlying asset because this is a put option. Similarly, at node D, $C_{ddd} = \max(4 - 1.21, 0) = 2.79$. Using this information from nodes C and D, we can work back to determine the value of the option at node G. The value to holding the option at node G is obtained by using the risk-neutral probabilities to weight the option values at nodes C and D, and then discounting this weighted value back one year at the risk-free rate. Thus, $C_{dd} = (P_u C_{udd} + P_d C_{ddd}) \div (1 + r_f) = [0.43(0.73) + 0.57(2.79)] \div (1.055) = 1.81$. The problem was set up such that the entrepreneur could only sell the equipment after three years, making the put option a European option, or one that could be exercised only at maturity. However, note in this case that if the entrepreneur could sell the equipment early, or an American option was involved, the entrepreneur would sell the equipment at this node and obtain $4 - 1.99 = 2.01$, which is greater than the value of holding onto the option (i.e., 1.81).

A similar approach is used to calculate the value of the option at node F. Here, $C_{ud} = (P_u C_{uud} + P_d C_{udd}) \div (1 + r_f) = [0.43(0) + 0.57(0.73)] \div (1.055) = 0.39$. Likewise, now that the value of the option at nodes E (i.e., 0), F (i.e., 0.39), and G (i.e., 1.81) are known, the values at H and I can be quickly obtained. At node H, $C_u = (P_u C_{uu} + P_d C_{ud}) \div (1 + r_f) = [0.43(0) + 0.57(0.39)] \div (1.055) = 0.21$. At node I, $C_d = (P_u C_{ud} + P_d C_{dd}) = (1 + r_f) = [0.43(0.39) + 0.57(1.81)] \div (1.055) = 1.14$. Finally, now that the values at nodes H and I are determined, the value at node J, C_0, can be calculated. Specifically, $C_0 = (P_uC_u + P_dC_d) \div (1 + r_f) = [0.43(0.21) + 0.57(1.14)] \div (1.055) = 0.70$.

Note that because the problem constrains the decision maker to exercise the option, if at all, only after three years, the initial value of the option could have been obtained directly from the option values present at nodes A–D in the rightmost column of the tree. Specifically, $C_0 = (P_u{}^3C_{uuu} + 3P_u{}^2P_dC_{uud} + 3P_uP_d{}^2C_{udd} + P_d{}^3C_{ddd}) \div (1 + r_f) = [(0.43)^3(0) + 3(0.43)^2(0.57)(0) + 3(0.43)(0.57)^2(0.73) + (0.57)^3(2.79)] \div (1.055)^3 = 0.70$. The discounting is for three periods in this case, and the more complicated weighting scheme reflects the fact that there are eight potential paths to the final four nodes—one path for node A, three for node B, three for node C, and one for node D. The probability weight for each node reflects the multiplication of risk-neutral probabilities to reach that node over three time periods (i.e., $P_u{}^3 + 3P_u{}^2P_d + 3P_uP_d{}^2 + P_d{}^3 = 1$). In other words, $P_u{}^3$ is used because node A is reached after three up movements; $3P_u{}^2P_d$ is used because node B is reached after two up movements and one down movement, and there are three such paths; $3P_uP_d{}^2$ is used because node C is reached after one up movement and two down movements, and there are three such paths; and $P_d{}^3$ is used because node D is reached after three down movements.

So what decision should the entrepreneur make concerning the launch of this business? The base case NPV is $-\$1.112$. Incorporation of the abandonment option to sell the plant and equipment in three years brings $0.70 million in additional value, but this value is not sufficient to go forward (i.e., $-1.112 + 0.70 = -0.412 < 0$). Absent some other embedded option and source of flexibility, the business should not be started.

Application Issues and Guidelines

We conclude with a few practical application issues concerning option valuation models, emphasizing the Black-Scholes approach because it rests on several important assumptions, all of which have the potential to create problems for analysts and decision makers and which deserve sensitivity analysis when the approaches discussed above are used.

European versus American Options. As mentioned previously, Black-Scholes assumes that all options are European, meaning that the option can be exercised only on the date of the option's maturity. In reality, real options are often more like American options, which can be exercised early. The main reason to exercise a financial option early would be to realize a dividend payment, which Black-Scholes assumes to be zero. Since dividend payments go to those who hold the underlying asset, one holding open an option does not benefit from these payments. In the case of real options, there might not be dividend payments as such, but analysts might be able to identify dividend-like features to the options they hold, including competitor preemption, loss of required skills, and so forth, that may lead the firm to want to exercise the option early rather than wait.

Known and Fixed Exercise Price. Black-Scholes also assumes that the exercise price is known and constant, just as it would be in a financial option contract. For many projects, this assumption is not valid because of the changing nature of the external environment. In many instances, the same economic factors that influence the value of the underlying asset also affect the cost of investment. Assuming that the cost of investment is fixed, especially when a contract is not in place, can be overly simplistic and may cause a disconnect between the calculated value and the actual value of the option. When the exercise price is not fixed, the decision maker ideally needs to account for the joint distribution of the exercise price and value of the underlying asset, which requires modeling approaches more technical than those described here.

Single Source of Uncertainty. Many real-world investment decisions are affected by several different sources of uncertainty. The Black-Scholes method assumes that there is a single source of uncertainty that simplifies a complex set of factors into one measure. The complex nature of estimating multiple sources of risk, and the relationship between these sources of uncertainty, is beyond the scope of this chapter. For example, Monte Carlo simulation techniques can be used to deal with multiple sources of uncertainty affecting option value.

Simple versus Compound Options. Besides having multiple sources of risk, many real options are compound options, which means that the value of the original real option is affected by follow-on options. For instance, option A's value may be affected by subsequent options B and C. A simple way to obtain a conservative estimate of option A's value is to treat all follow-on options as commitments made at the time of A's exercise. The valuation exercise is then amenable to the Black-Scholes and NPV q techniques presented above because a compound option is converted to a simple option. By neglecting flexibility in future estimates, however, the value of option A is understated.

Distribution of the Underlying Asset's Value. For the Black-Scholes and approximation approaches, one assumes that the underlying asset's value follows a lognormal distribution with a constant level of volatility. The returns to the underlying asset are assumed to be normally distributed. For some applications, the distribution of the underlying asset's value does not become wider over time as depicted by the lognormal distribution. Other option pricing models have been developed for projects requiring different distributional assumptions.

Value of the Underlying Asset. Using Black-Scholes to compute real option values means that the user has to estimate the components required by the formula. Although the market sets the current price for a financial asset (S), there is often no such market estimation for the value of underlying assets in a real option calculation. Real option theory adds significantly to the valuation of uncertain investments, but it does not address management concerns about the accuracy of cash flow projections or the appropriate discount rate. Practitioners have accepted the imperfections of discounted cash flow analysis as it relates to cash flow projections, and the estimation of the value of the underlying asset using this methodology will therefore not be a significant obstacle.

Different Values of t. The specification of the years to maturity, *t*, would appear to be straightforward. In some projects, however, the cost of investment can occur at a point after the resolution of the uncertainty associated with the project. For this reason, different values of *t* may need to be used for discounting the exercise price and calculating cumulative volatility. For example, consider an option to purchase a piece of property three years from today. The value of this property is highly uncertain because of the possibility of a new highway system being built near the land. Public disclosure of the coordinates of the new highway will be made in one year, resolving the uncertainty of the land value. Although the option contract to buy the property is three years out, the uncertainty surrounding the property value will be known in one year. In this case, the exercise price is discounted *t* = 3 years, but *t* = 1 is used in estimating cumulative volatility.

NOTES

1. A. J. Bock, T. Opsahl, G. George, & D. M. Gann, 2012, The effects of culture and structure on strategic flexibility during business model innovation, *Journal of Management Studies*, 49(2): 279–305.

2. A. Borlson & G. Hamm, 2010, Prediction markets: A new tool for strategic decision making, *California Management Review*, 52(4), 125–141.

3. V. Arnold, T. Benford, J. Canada, & S. G. Sutton, 2011, The role of strategic enterprise risk management and organizational flexibility in easing new regulatory compliance, *International Journal of Accounting Information Systems*, 12(3), 171–188; K. R. Harrigan, 2001, Strategic flexibility in old and new economies, in M. A. Hitt, R. E. Freeman, & J. R. Harrison (eds.), *Handbook of Strategic Management*, Oxford, UK: Blackwell Publishers, 97–123.

4. P. Ussahawanitchakit & P. Sriboonlue, 2011, Transformational leadership, strategic flexibility, learning capability, continuous improvement, and firm performance: Evidence from Thailand, *International Journal of Business Strategy*, 11, 162–172; R. D'Aveni, 1994, *Hypercompetition*, New York: The Free Press.

5. M. Augusto, J. Lisboa, & M. Yasin, 2011, The impact of innovation on the relationship between manufacturing flexibility and performance: A structural modeling approach, *International Journal of Business Research*, 11, 65–72; K. Eisenhardt, N. R. Furr, & C. B. Bingham, 2010, Microfoundations of performance: Balancing efficiency and flexibility in dynamic environments, *Organization Science*, 21, 1263–1273.

6. G. Colvin, 2011, Caterpillar is absolutely crushing it, *Fortune*, May 23, 141.

7. E. Maitland & A. Sammartino, 2012, Flexible footprints: Reconfiguring MNCs for new value opportunities, *California Management Review*, 54(2): 92–117; M. Vilkas, 2011, Overstandardization of organizational processes, *Economics & Management*, 16: 992–999.

8. R. Qin & D. A. Nembhard, 2010, Workforce agility for stochastically diffused conditions—A real options perspective, *International Journal of Production Economics*, 125: 324–334.

9. O. L. Kuye & B. A. Oghojafor, 2011, Scenario planning as a recipe for corporate performance: The Nigerian manufacturing sector experience, *International Journal of Business & Management*, 6(12), 170–179; D. A. J. Axson, 2011, Scenario planning: Navigating through today's uncertain world, *Journal of Accountancy*, 211(3), 22–27.

10. J. J. Marcel, P. S. Barr, & I. M. Duhaime, 2011, The influence of executive cognition on competitive dynamics, *Strategic Management Journal*, 32, 115–138; R. S. Livengood & R. K. Reger, 2010, That's our turf! Identity domains and competitive dynamics, *Academy of Management Review*, 35, 48–66.

11. C. Krychowski & B. V. Quélin, 2010, Real options and strategic investment decisions: Can they be of use to scholars? *Academy of Management Perspectives*, 24(2), 65–78; A. Cuervo-Cazurra & C. Annique Un, 2010, Why some firms never invest in formal R&D, *Strategic Management Journal*, 31, 759–779.

12. H. T. J. Smit & L. Trigeorgis, 2010, Flexibility and games in strategic investment, *Multinational Finance Journal*, 14, 1–27.

13. K. D. Brouthers, L. E. Brouthers, & S. Werner, 2008, Real options, international entry mode choice and performance, *Journal of Management Studies*, 45, 936–960; J. J. Reuer & M. J. Leiblein, 2001, Real options: Let the buyer beware, in J. Pickford (ed.), *Financial Times Mastering Risk*, Vol. 1, London: FT Prentice Hall, 79–85.

14. J. J. Reuer & M. J. Leiblein, 2000, Downside risk implications of multinationality and international joint ventures, *Academy of Management Journal*, 43: 203–214.

15 2011, Reliance forays into financial services business, *Wall Street Journal Online*, March 28.

16 C. C. Chung & P. W. Beamish, 2010, The trap of continual ownership change in international equity joint ventures, *Organization Science*, 21: 995–1015; B. Kogut, 1991, Joint ventures and the option to expand and acquire, *Management Science*, 37: 19–33.

17 T. B. Folta & K. D. Miller, 2002, Real options and equity partnerships, *Strategic Management Journal*, 23: 77–88.

18 J. J. Reuer, J. J. Tong, & T. Tong, 2005, Real options in international joint ventures, *Journal of Management*, 31: 403–423.

19 R. Smith, R. Pedace, & V. Sathe, 2011, VC fund financial performance: The relative importance of IPO and M&A exits and exercise of abandonment options, *Financial Management*, 40, 1029–1065.

20 2005, Valentine's day divorce, *Economist*, February 19, 59.

21 L. A. Johnson, 2010, Switching options and the impact on business strategy and risk management, *Academy of Accounting & Financial Studies Journal*, 14, 75–83.

22 2002, Real Options at Polaris Energy Corporation (A): The Spectrum Alliance, European Case Clearing House 302-093-1, http://www.ecch.com/casesearch/.

23 M. A. R. Malik, C. A. Rehman, M. Ashraf, & R. Z. Abbas, 2012, Exploring the link between foreign direct investment, multinational enterprises and spillover effects in developing economies, *International Journal of Business & Management*, 7: 230–240; J. E. Wahl & U. Broll, 2010, Mitigation of foreign direct investment risk and hedging, *Frontiers in Finance & Economics*, 7, 21–33.

24 Y. Sanjo, 2012, Country risk, country size, and tax competition for foreign direct investment, *International Review of Economics & Finance*, 21, 292–301.

25 H. K. Baker, S. Dutta, & S. Saadi, 2011, Management views on real options in capital budgeting, *Journal of Applied Finance*, 21, 18–29.

26 Krychowski & Quélin, Real options and strategic investment decisions; T. Malik, 2011, Real option as strategic technology uncertainty reduction mechanism: Inter-firm investment strategy by pharmaceuticals, *Technology Analysis & Strategic Management*, 23, 489–507.

27 Ibid.

28 R. E. Caves, 1996, *Multinational Enterprise and Economic Analysis*, 2nd ed., New York: Cambridge University Press.

29 B. Auguste, S. Lund, & J. Manyika, 2011, The changing shape of US recessions, *McKinsey Quarterly*, Issue 4, 100–101.

30 M. W. McCarter, J. T. Mahoney, & G. B. Northcraft, 2011, Testing the waters: Using collective real options to manage the social dilemma of strategic alliances, *Academy of Management Review*, 36(4): 621–640; G. Hamel, 1991, Competition for competence and interpartner learning within international strategic alliances, *Strategic Management Journal*, 12: 83–103.

31 A. S. Cui, R. J. Calantone, & D. A. Griffith, 2011, Strategic change and termination of interfirm partnerships, *Strategic Management Journal*, 32: 402–423; J. H. Dyer, P. Kale, & H. Singh, 2004, When to ally and when to acquire, *Harvard Business Review*, 82: 109–115.

32 S. C. Myers, 1984, Finance theory and financial strategy, *Interfaces*, 14: 126–137.

33 T. Copeland & V. Antikarov, 2001, *Real Options*, New York: Texere.

34 2004, Wellington Synthetics, European Case Clearing House 804-014-1, http://www.ecch.com/casesearch/.

35 2004, Innovis Technology: Capturing the Value of Intellectual Property, INSEAD Case Series, http://www.insead.edu/facultyresearch/research/details_cases.cfm?id=13359.

36 T. W. Tong, J. J. Reuer, & M. W. Peng, 2008, International joint ventures and the value of growth options, *Academy of Management Journal*, 51(5): 1014–1029; S. C. Myers, 1977, Determinants of corporate borrowing, *Journal of Financial Economics*, 5: 147–175.

37 W. C. Kester, 1984, Today's options for tomorrow's growth, *Harvard Business Review*, 62: 153–160.

38 G. B. Stewart, 1991, *The Quest for Value: A Guide for Senior Managers*, New York: Harper; S. D. Young & S. F. O'Byrne, 2001, *EVA and Value-Based Management*, New York: McGraw-Hill.

39 J. J. Reuer & T. W. Tong, 2007, Corporate investments and growth options, *Managerial and Decision Economics*, 28: 863–877.

40 P. J. Strebel, 1983, The stock market and competitive analysis, *Strategic Management Journal*, 4: 279–291.

41 R. Black & M. Scholes, 1973, The pricing of options and corporate liabilities, *Journal of Political Economy*, 81: 637–659.

42 J. H. Fisch, 2011, Real call options to enlarge foreign subsidiaries—The moderating effect of irreversibility on the influence of economic volatility and political instability on subsequent FDI, *Journal of World Business*, 46(4): 517–526; K. D. Miller & J. J. Reuer, 1998, Asymmetric corporate exposures to foreign exchange rate changes, *Strategic Management Journal*, 19: 1183–1191.

43 T. Luehrman, 1998, Investment opportunities as real options: Getting started on the numbers, *Harvard Business Review*, 26: 51–67.

44 T. Driouchi & D. J. Bennett, 2012, Real options in management and organizational strategy: A review of decision-making and performance implications, *International Journal of Management Reviews*, 14(1): 39–62; R. G. McGrath, W. J. Ferrier, & A. L. Mendelow, 2004, Real options as engines of choice and heterogeneity, *Academy of Management Review*, 29: 86–101.

45 M. L. Barnett, 2008, An attention-based view of real options reasoning, *Academy of Management Review*, 33(3): 606–628; J. S. Busby & C. G. C. Pitts, 1997, Real options in practice: An exploratory survey of how finance officers deal with flexibility in capital appraisal, *Management Accounting Research*, 8: 169–186.

46 R. Adner & D. A. Levinthal, 2004, What is not a real option: Considering boundaries for the application of real options to business strategy, *Academy of Management Review*, 29(1): 74–85; 1999, Keeping all options open, *Economist*, August 14, 62.

47 A. B. Bukhvalov, 2011, The principal role of the board of directors: The duty to say "no", *Corporate Governance: The International Journal of Effective Board Performance*, 11(5): 629–640; E. H. Bowman & G. T. Moskowitz, 2001, Real options analysis and strategic decision making, *Organization Science*, 12: 772–777.

48 X. Huang, T. F. Gattiker, & R. G. Schroeder, 2010, Do competitive priorities drive adoption of electronic commerce applications? Testing the contingency and institutional views, *Journal of Supply Chain Management*, 46(3): 57–69; E. S. Schwartz & M. Moon, 2000, Rational pricing of internet companies, *Financial Analysts Journal*, 56: 62–75.

49 H. Chengru, H. Biqing, & M. Foley, 2011, Do investors apply real option thinking in valuating corporate assets? Evidence from new product development projects, *Journal of International Finance & Economics*, 11(2): 52–68; A. Triantis & A. Borison, 2001, Real options: State of the practice, *Journal of Applied Corporate Finance*, 14: 8–24.

50 H. C. Wang, J. He, & J. T. Mahoney, 2009, Firm-specific knowledge resources and competitive advantage: The roles of economic- and relationship-based employee governance mechanisms, *Strategic Management Journal*, 30(12): 1265–1285; H. Wang & S. Lim, 2008, Real options and real value: The role of employee incentives to make specific knowledge investments, *Strategic Management Journal*, 29(7): 701–721.

51 T. Copeland & P. Tufano, 2004, A real-world way to manage real options, *Harvard Business Review*, 82: 90–99; Copeland & Antikarov, *Real Options*.

52 Wellington Synthetics.

GLOSSARY

Abandonment options—Provide firms flexibility by allowing them to reverse course and exit deteriorating competitive situations.

Acquisition—A strategy through which one firm buys a controlling, 100 percent interest in another firm with the intent of making the acquired firm a subsidiary business within its portfolio or melding with another division.

Agency costs—Sum of incentive costs, monitoring costs, enforcement costs, and individual financial losses incurred by principals, because governance mechanisms cannot guarantee total compliance by the agent.

Agency relationship—It exists when one or more people (the principal or principals) hire another person or people (the agent or agents) as decision-making specialists to perform a service.

Agency theory—Agency problems exist when managers take actions that are in their own best interests rather than those of the shareholders.

Assessing—To determine the timing and significance of the effects of environmental changes and trends on the strategic management of the firm.

Balanced scorecard—A framework that strategic leaders can use to verify that they have established both financial controls and strategic controls to assess their firm's performance.

Black-Scholes option pricing formula—European financial call option is often used to value real options. The Black-Scholes formula is: Call Option Value $[S \times N(d_1)]$ − $[PV(X) \times N(d_2)]$.

Board of directors—A group of shareholder-elected individuals whose primary responsibility is to act in the owners' interests by formally monitoring and controlling the corporation's top-level executives.

Business-level strategy—An integrated and coordinated set of commitments and actions the firm uses to gain a competitive advantage by exploiting core competencies in specific product markets.

Capabilities—A firm's capacity to deploy resources that have been purposely integrated to achieve a desired end state.

Capability—Resources that allow a firm to perform a task or an activity in an integrative manner.

CEO duality—When the CEO serves as chair of the board in addition to the CEO responsibilities. It enhances the CEO's power.

Competitive action—A strategic or tactical action the firm takes to build or defend its competitive advantages or improve its market position.

Competitive advantage—Formulation and execution of strategies that are different from and create more value than the strategies of competitors.

Competitive behavior—Set of competitive actions and competitive responses the firm takes to build or defend its competitive advantages and to improve its market position.

Competitive dynamics—The total set of actions and responses all firms competing within a market take.

Competitive form—A structure in which the firm's divisions are completely independent.

Competitive response—A strategic or tactical action the firm takes to counter the effects of a rival's competitive action.

Competitive rivalry—The ongoing set of competitive actions and competitive responses occurring between competitors as they contend with each other for an advantageous market position.

Competitor environment—Complements the insights provided by studying the general and industry environments.

Competitor intelligence—Set of data and information the firm gathers to better understand and better anticipate competitors' objectives, strategies, assumptions, and capabilities.

Competitors—Firms operating in the same market, offering similar products, and targeting similar customers.

Complementary strategic alliance—Business-level alliances in which firms share some of their resources and capabilities in complementary ways to develop competitive advantages.

Complementors—Companies that sell complementary goods or services that are compatible with the focal firm's own products or services.

Compound option—Investments that confer multiple options that are built upon one another. Another way to understand compound options is to consider that the underlying asset is not a real asset, but another option.

Cooperative form—A structure in which horizontal integration is used to bring about interdivisional cooperation.

Cooperative strategy—A strategy in which firms work together to achieve a shared objective.

Co-opetition—Cooperative strategies are formed by firms who also compete against one another.

Core competencies—Resources and capabilities that serve as a source of competitive advantage for a firm over its rivals.

Corporate entrepreneurship—The application of entrepreneurship within an established firm.

Corporate governance—Set of mechanisms used to manage the relationships among stakeholders and to determine and control the strategic direction and performance of organizations.

Corporate-level core competencies—Complex sets of resources and capabilities that link different businesses, primarily through managerial and technological knowledge, experience, and expertise.

Corporate-level strategy—Actions a firm takes to gain a competitive advantage by selecting and managing a portfolio of businesses that compete in different product markets or industries.

Cost leadership strategy—An integrated set of actions designed to produce or deliver goods or services with features that are acceptable to customers at the lowest cost, relative to that of competitors.

Costly-to-imitate capabilities—Capabilities that are difficult for competitors to imitate.

Cross-border strategic alliance—An international cooperative strategy in which firms with headquarters in different nations combine some of their resources and capabilities to create a competitive advantage.

Demographic segment—A population's size, age structure, geographic distribution, ethnic mix, and income distribution.

Deterministic perspective—Strategy formulation argues that firms should adapt to their environments because characteristics of the environment determine which strategies will succeed.

Differentiation strategy—An integrated set of actions designed by a firm to produce or deliver goods or services (at an acceptable cost) that customers perceive as being different in ways that are important to them.

Diversifying strategic alliance—A cooperative strategy in which firms share some of their resources and capabilities to diversify into new product or market areas.

Economic environment—Nature and direction of the economy in which a firm competes or may compete.

Economic power—Ability to provide or withhold economic support from a firm.

Economies of scope—Cost savings that the firm creates by successfully transferring some of its capabilities and competencies that were developed in one of its businesses to another of its businesses.

Enactment—Firms do not have to entirely submit to environmental forces because they can, in part, create their own environments through strategic actions.

Entrepreneurial mind-set—Values uncertainty in the marketplace and seeks to continuously identify opportunities with the potential to lead to important innovations.

Entrepreneurial opportunities—Represent conditions in which new products or services can satisfy a need in the market.

Entrepreneurs—Individuals, acting independently or as part of an organization, who create a new venture or develop an innovation and take risks by introducing them into the marketplace.

Entrepreneurship—The process by which individuals or groups identify and pursue entrepreneurial opportunities without the immediate constraint of the resources they currently control.

Equity strategic alliance—An alliance in which two or more firms own a portion of the equity in the venture they have created.

Executive compensation—A governance mechanism that seeks to align the interests of top managers and owners through salaries, bonuses, and long-term incentive compensation, such as restricted stock awards and stock options.

Fast-cycle markets—Markets in which the firm's capabilities that contribute to competitive advantages are not shielded from imitation and where imitation is often rapid and inexpensive.

Financial controls—Financial controls are used to evaluate the performance of business units in unrelated diversified firms.

Financial economies—Cost savings realized through improved allocations of financial resources based on investments inside or outside the firm.

First mover—A firm that takes an initial competitive action to build or defend its competitive advantages or to improve its market position.

Focus strategy—An integrated set of actions designed to produce and deliver goods or services that serve the needs of a particular competitive segment.

Forecasting—Analysts develop feasible projections of potential events, and how quickly they may occur, as a result of the changes and trends detected through scanning and monitoring.

Formal power—Laws or regulations that specify the legal relationship that exists between a firm and a particular stakeholder group.

Franchise—A contractual agreement between two legally independent companies whereby the franchisor grants the right to the franchisee to sell the franchisor's product or do business under its trademarks in a given location for a specified period of time.

Franchising—A cooperative strategy in which a firm (the franchisor) uses a franchise as a contractual relationship to describe and control the sharing of its resources and capabilities with partners (the franchisees).

Functional structure—It consists of a chief executive officer and a limited corporate staff, with functional line managers in dominant organizational areas such as production, accounting, marketing, R&D, engineering, and human resources.

General environment—It is composed of dimensions in the broader society that influence an industry and the firms within it.

Global mind-set—Ability to study conditions inside a firm in ways that do not depend on the assumptions of a single country, culture, or context.

Global segment—The segment of the general environment that includes relevant new global markets, existing markets that are changing, important political events, and critical cultural and institutional market characteristics.

Global strategy—An international strategy through which the firm offers standardized products across country markets, with the competitive strategy being dictated by the home office.

Globalization—Increasing economic interdependence among countries as reflected in the flow of goods and services, financial capital, and knowledge across country borders.

Growth options—Investments that enable the firm to expand the investment in the future, if that action turns out to be valuable.

Heterogeneous top management team—A team composed of individuals with different functional backgrounds, experience, and education.

Hostile takeover—An acquisition by an external party that is not only unexpected, but undesired by the target firm's managers.

Hubris—Excessive pride, leading to a feeling of invincibility; can magnify the effects of multiple biases.

Hypercompetition—Dynamics of strategic maneuvering among global and innovative combatants in a volatile economy.

Imitation—The adoption of an innovation by similar firms. Imitation usually leads to product or process standardization; products based on imitation often are offered at lower prices, but without as many features.

Independent board leadership structure—Different people hold the positions of CEO and board chair; it is believed to enhance a board's ability to monitor top-level managers' decisions and actions, particularly in terms of the firm's financial performance.

Industry—A group of firms producing products that are close substitutes.

Industry environment—Set of factors that directly influence a firm and its competitive actions and competitive responses: the threat of new entrants, the power of suppliers, the power of buyers, the threat of product substitutes, and the intensity or rivalry among competitors.

Innovation—The process of creating a commercial product from an invention.

Institutional owners—Financial institutions such as stock mutual funds and pension funds that control large-block shareholder positions.

Intangible resources—Assets that typically are rooted deeply in the firm's history and have accumulated over time.

Integrated cost leadership/differentiation strategy—A strategy to provide customers with relatively low-cost products that have some valued differentiated features.

International corporate-level strategy—It focuses on the scope of a firm's operations through both product and geographic diversification.

International diversification—A strategy through which a firm expands the sales of its goods or services across the borders of global regions and countries into different geographic locations or markets.

International entrepreneurship—A process in which firms creatively discover and exploit opportunities that are outside their domestic markets in order to develop a competitive advantage.

International strategy—A strategy through which the firm sells its goods or services outside its domestic market.

Invention—The act of creating or developing a new product or process.

Joint venture—A strategic alliance in which two or more firms create a legally independent company to share resources and capabilities to develop a competitive advantage.

Large-block shareholders—Typically own at least 5 percent of a corporation's issued shares.

Late mover—A firm that responds to a competitive action, but only after considerable time has elapsed after the first mover's action and the second mover's response.

Managerial opportunism—The seeking of self-interest with guile (i.e., cunning or deceit).

Market commonality—Concerned with the number of markets with which the firm and a competitor are jointly involved and the degree of importance of the individual markets to each.

Market for corporate control—An external governance mechanism that becomes active when a firm's internal controls fail.

Market power—It exists when a firm is able to sell its products above the existing competitive level, or to reduce the costs of its primary and support activities below the competitive level, or both.

Market segmentation—Clusters people with similar needs into individual and identifiable groups.

Matrix organization—An organizational structure in which a dual structure combines both functional specialization and business product or project specialization.

Merger—A strategy through which two firms agree to integrate their operations on a relatively co-equal basis.

Monitoring—Analysts observe environmental changes to identify important emerging trends from among those spotted by scanning.

Multidivisional structure—It consists of operating divisions, each representing a separate business or profit center in which the top corporate officer delegates responsibilities for day-to-day operations and business-unit strategy to division managers.

Multidomestic strategy—An international strategy in which strategic and operating decisions are decentralized to the strategic business unit in each country to allow that unit to tailor products to the local market.

Multimarket competition—Firms competing against each other in several product or geographic markets.

Multipoint competition—It exists when two or more diversified firms simultaneously compete in the same product or geographic markets.

Network cooperative strategy—A cooperative strategy in which multiple firms agree to form partnerships to achieve shared objectives.

Nonequity strategic alliance—An alliance in which two or more firms develop a contractual relationship to share some of their unique resources and capabilities to create a competitive advantage.

Nonsubstitutable capabilities—These capabilities lack strategic equivalents. This criterion for a capability to be a source of competitive advantage "is that there must be no strategically equivalent valuable resources that are themselves either not rare or imitable."

Opportunity—A condition in the external environment that, if exploited, helps a company create value.

Option to defer—It is present when there is value in waiting.

Organizational controls—An important aspect of the M-form. They guide the use of strategy, indicate how to compare actual results with expected results, and suggest corrective actions to take when the difference between actual and expected results is unacceptable.

Organizational culture—It consists of a complex set of ideologies, symbols, and core values that is shared throughout the firm and influences the way business is conducted.

Organizational structure—It specifies the firm's formal reporting relationships, procedures, controls, and authority and decision-making processes.

Outsourcing—Purchase of a value-creating activity from an external supplier.

Ownership concentration—Defined by both the number of large-block shareholders and the total percentage of shares they own (typically owning at least five percent for the equity).

Physical environment segment—Dimensions of the physical environment.

Political power—Ability to influence others to withhold economic support or to change the rules of the game.

Political/legal segment—The arena in which organizations and interest groups compete for attention, resources, and a voice in overseeing the body of laws and regulations guiding the interactions among nations.

Quality—It exists when the firm's goods or services meet or exceed customers' expectations.

Rare capabilities—Possessed by few, if any, current or potential competitors.

Real option—An investment that allows the owner to use an alternative in the future (e.g., buy a piece of land on which to potentially build in the future).

Relational advantage—It exists when a firm's relationships with other firms put it at an advantage relative to rival firms.

Resource similarity—Extent to which the firm's tangible and intangible resources are comparable to a competitor's in terms of type and amount.

Resources—Capital equipment, the skills of individual employees, patents, finances, and talented managers resources are inputs into a firm's production process.

Restructuring—A strategy through which a firm changes its set of businesses or its financial structure.

Risk—An investor's uncertainty about the economic gains or losses that will result from a particular investment.

Scanning—Entails the study of all segments in the general environment, industry environment and/or the competitor environment.

Scope—The breadth of a firm's activities across products, markets, geographic regions, core technologies, and value creation stages.

Second mover—A firm that responds to the first mover's competitive action, typically through imitation.

Slow-cycle markets—Markets in which the firm's competitive advantages are shielded from imitation for what are commonly long periods of time and where imitation is costly.

Sociocultural segment—It is concerned with a society's attitudes and cultural values.

Stakeholders—Individuals and groups who can affect, and are affected by, the strategic outcomes a firm achieves and who have enforceable claims on a firm's performance.

Standard-cycle markets—Markets in which the firm's competitive advantages are moderately shielded from imitation and where imitation is moderately costly.

Stewardship theory—A theory suggesting that top managers want to do the right thing for the firm's shareholders and that reducing the amount of interference with their actions will increase the profit potential of the firm.

Strategic alliance—A cooperative strategy in which firms combine resources and capabilities to create a competitive advantage.

Strategic business-unit—A profit center that is controlled and evaluated by the headquarters office.

Strategic controls—Largely subjective criteria intended to verify that the firm is using appropriate strategies for the conditions in the external environment and the company's competitive advantages.

Strategic direction—This defines a firm's image and character over time, framed within the context of the conditions in which it operates.

Strategic entrepreneurship—It occurs as firms seek opportunities in the external environment that they can exploit through competitive advantages that are framed around innovations.

Strategic flexibility—A set of capabilities used to respond to various demands and opportunities existing in a dynamic and uncertain competitive environment.

Strategic group—A set of firms emphasizing similar strategic dimensions to use a similar strategy.

Strategic intelligence—The information firms collect from their network of stakeholders; can be used to help a firm deal with diverse competitive situations and can also stimulate innovation.

Strategic leadership—An ability to anticipate, envision, maintain flexibility, and empower others to create strategic change as necessary.

Strategic management process—The full set of commitments, decisions, and actions required for a firm to create value and earn returns that are higher than those of competitors. In its simplest form, the process involves analyzing the firm and its environment, and then using the information to formulate and implement strategies that lead to competitive advantage.

Strategic thinking competency—The knowledge, skills, and abilities needed to detect market opportunities, formulate a vision to capitalize on these opportunities, and engineer feasible strategies to realize organizational and stakeholder value.

Support functions—Activities or tasks the firm completes in order to support the work being done to produce, sell, distribute, and service the products the firm is producing.

Sustainable competitive advantage—The speed with which competitors are able to acquire the skills needed to duplicate the benefits of a firm's value-creating strategy determines how long the competitive advantage will last.

Sustainable development—Business growth that does not deplete the natural environment or damage society; results from firms' commitment to sustainability.

Switching options—Combine the features of various options by allowing firms to change the mix of outputs or inputs.

Synergy—It exists when the value created by business units working together exceeds the value those same units create working independently.

Tacit knowledge—Knowledge that is complex and hard to codify.

Tactical action or a tactical response—A market-based move that is taken to fine-tune a strategy; it involves fewer resources than a competitive action or response and is relatively easy to implement and reverse.

Takeover—A special type of acquisition strategy wherein the target firm did not solicit the acquiring firm's bid.

Tangible resources—Assets that can be observed and quantified, such as production equipment.

Taper integration—Arises when a firm sources inputs externally from independent suppliers as well as internally within the boundaries of the firm, or disposes of its outputs through independent outlets in addition to company-owned distribution channels.

Technological segment—The institutions and activities involved with creating new knowledge and translating that knowledge into new outputs, products, processes, and materials.

Threat—A condition in the general environment that may hinder a company's efforts to achieve a competitive advantage and create value.

Top management team—It is composed of the CEO and other key managers who are responsible for setting the direction of the firm and formulating and implementing its strategies.

Transaction cost economics—Firms are better off purchasing required resources through a market transaction unless particular conditions exist that make creating them internally more efficient.

Transnational strategy—An international strategy through which the firm seeks to achieve both global efficiency and local responsiveness.

Valuable capabilities—Allow the firm to exploit opportunities or neutralize threats in its external environment.

Value—It is measured by a product's performance characteristics and attributes for which customers are willing to pay.

Value chain activities—Activities or tasks the firm completes in order to produce products and then sell, distribute, and service those products in ways that create value for customers.

Vertical integration—It exists when a company produces its own inputs (backward integration) or owns its own source of distribution of outputs (forward integration).

Worldwide combination structure—It draws characteristics and mechanisms from both the worldwide geographic area structure and the worldwide product divisional structure.

Worldwide geographic area structure—It emphasizes national interests and facilitates the firm's efforts to satisfy local or cultural differences and is used to implement the multidomestic strategy.

Worldwide product divisional structure—Decision-making authority is centralized in the worldwide division headquarters to coordinate and integrate decisions and actions among divisional business units.

NAME INDEX

Aaker, D. A., 169nn29
Aarstad, J., 224nn125
Abbas, R. Z., 403nn23
Abbott, A., 314nn67
Abebe, M. A., 65nn68
Abele, J., 67nn127
Abell, D. F., 66nn107
Abrahamson, E., 63nn19, 196nn27
Acedo, F. J., 30nn109
Ackermann, F., 31nn134, 139nn108
Ackoff, R., 28nn70
Acs, Z. J., 369nn52
Acur, N., 370nn74
Adams, R. B., 29nn79, 135nn10, 139nn106
Adams, S, 68nn159
Adams. M. B., 350nn127
Addison, J., 318nn163
Addison, J. T., 349nn114
Adegbesan, J. M., 140nn128
Adithipyangkul, P., 348nn84
Adler, P. S., 68nn160
Adner, R., 403nn46
Adobor, H., 220nn8
Adolph, A., 280nn67
Adolph, G., 281nn106
Afuah, A., 103nn72, 104nn125
Afza, T., 255nn122
Agarwal, R., 223nn106
Agarwal, S., 254nn108
Aggarwal, R., 253nn89
Agle, B. R., 139nn113, 344nn6
Agrawal, A., 347nn67
Agrawal, R., 368nn37
Aguilera, R., 345nn16, 349nn110
Ahlstrom, D., 103nn87, 315nn97
Ahmed, M., 26nn4, 135nn21
Ahmed, R., 197nn54
Ahn, M. J., 104nn101
Ahuja, G., 136nn33, 195nn10, 279nn43, 280nn65, 369nn68
Aiello, R. J., 281nn103
Arikan, A. T., 104nn123

Ajinomoto, Masatoshi Ito, 213
Akbar, M., 254nn97
Akkermans, H., 104nn116
Albanese, R., 65nn73
Alcacer, J., 313nn28
Aldrich, H., 102nn46
Alessandri, T. M., 256nn138, 346nn32
Alexander, M., 250nn5
Alexiev, A. S., 64nn51
Allcock, D., 256nn137, 348nn82
Allen, J., 29nn77, 136nn35
Allred, C. R., 220nn5
Alon, I., 348nn84
Alred, B. B., 314nn51
Altaay, A., 27nn20
Alton, R., 278nn5
Alvarez, S. A., 137nn56, 367nn13, 371nn104
Amason, A. C., 370nn90
Ambos, B., 317nn139
Ambrosini, V., 136nn29, 137nn62
Ames, C., 137nn64
Amit, R., 135nn21, 138nn78, 138nn84, 254nn95, 346nn49, 367nn6
Anand, J., 136nn30, 138nn79, 221nn47, 224nn111, 278nn1
Anand, V., 28nn51, 66nn93, 68nn162
Andal-Ancion, A., 103nn74
Anderson, B. S., 136nn42, 170nn73, 198nn63
Anderson, R. C., 256nn144, 345nn23
Anderson, R. I., 346nn36
Andersson, U., 317nn133
Andrews, K. R., 28nn67
Andrews, Kenneth, 9
Andrews, T. G., 318nn148
Angriawan, A., 65nn68
Anokhin, S., 221nn56
Anquan, W., 32nn172
Ansari, S., 139nn120
Ansoff, H. I., 28nn66

Ansoff, Igor, 9
Ante, S. E., 64nn61
Anthony, C., 26nn7, 279nn56
Antikarov, V., 403nn33
Apaydin, M., 170nn70
Appelmaum, B., 346nn43
Ardeniz, M. B., 317nn126
Areddy, J., 223nn95
Arend, R. J., 137nn62
Argenti, P. A., 31nn150, 350nn130
Argote, L., 134nn4, 135nn18, 137nn56
Argyres, N., 29nn91, 66nn116, 103nn96, 137nn51
Arikan, A. M., 29nn104, 30nn109
Ariño, A., 27nn24, 224nn121, 316nn105
Arino, M. A., 135nn10
Arkan, A. T., 221nn48
Armstrong, R. W., 171nn103
Arndt, M., 345nn10
Arnold, V., 28nn59, 402nn3
Arnott, R., 349nn107
Arora, A., 135nn6, 170nn86, 315nn91
Arregle, J.-L., 26nn5, 30nn115, 101nn10, 104nn97, 314nn39, 318nn153, 371nn113
Arslan, B., 30nn128
Artz, K. W., 105nn137, 368nn30
Arvids, A., 63nn37
Ashford, S. J., 67nn139
Ashforth, B. E., 68nn162
Ashkanasy, N. A., 66nn94
Ashkenas, R, 280nn76
Ashraf, M., 403nn23
Aslan, H., 282nn133
Audet, J., 136nn40
Audretsch, D. B., 65nn86, 223nn106, 345nn15
Auguste, B., 403nn29
Augusto, M., 402nn5
Aulakh, P. S., 316nn114

Autio, E., 101nn25, 221nn56, 315nn82, 368nn45, 371nn108
Awazu, Y., 220nn8, 224nn112
Axson, D. A. J., 402nn9
Aybar, B., 316nn108
Aydin, S., 30nn122

Babakus, E., 315nn88
Bach, S. B., 67nn128, 196nn19
Backmann, J. W., 29nn97
Baden-Fuller, C., 221nn40
Badham R., 69nn170
Baik, Y.-S., 196nn19
Baiman, S., 170nn58
Bain, J. S., 29nn93
Baixauli-Soler, J., 346nn31
Bakay, A., 30nn121, 251nn20
Baker, H. K., 403nn25
Baldauf, A., 32nn159
Baldwin, T. T., 137nn58
Balfour, F., 103nn79, 315nn92
Ballantyne, D., 138nn83
Ballmer, Steve, 41
Banerji, K., 314nn67
Banker, R. D., 254nn94
Bannert, V., 279nn41
Bansal, P., 30nn115, 68nn168, 136nn27
Bantel, K. A., 63nn18, 64nn55
Bardley, S. W., 102nn46
Barefield, R. M., 254nn105
Barham, B., 251nn39
Barkema, H. G., 103nn77, 103nn82, 254nn102, 280nn63, 369nn59
Barnard, C. I., 28nn70, 220nn11
Barner-Rasmussen, W., 318nn159
Barnes, B.R., 281nn90
Barnes, R., 62nn2
Barnes, R. R., 69nn180
Barnett, M. L., 403nn45
Barney, J. B., 26nn8, 29nn104, 30nn109, 30nn119, 32nn153, 156, 67nn131, 69nn171, 113, 135nn5, 135nn7, 135nn8, 137nn65, 138nn70, 138nn71, 138nn72, 138nn77, 170nn60, 224nn120, 250nn8, 280nn77, 367nn13, 371nn104
Barnir, A., 66nn120

Baron, R. A., 367nn11, 368nn34
Barr, A. J., 402nn10
Barr, P. S., 195nn6, 318nn162
Barreto, I., 367nn15
Barrett, P. M., 68nn165
Barringer, B. R., 31nn152, 69nn172, 220nn9, 367nn7
Barron, J. M., 66nn94
Barroso, C., 30nn109
Barth, H., 169nn39
Bartlett, C. A., 67nn126, 102nn66, 314nn55, 314nn65, 315nn94
Bartunek, J. M., 135nn17
Basuil, D., 101nn2
Bateman, C. R., 26nn14
Bates, K. A., 136nn39, 252nn41
Bates, T. W., 256nn144
Bates, Tony, 41
Batjargal, B., 318nn153
Baucus, M. S., 223nn90
Bauerschmidt, A., 169nn41
Baum, J. A. C., 196nn31, 223nn102
Baum, J. R., 68nn148
Baumgartner, P., 104nn110
Baysinger, B. D., 347nn63
Bayus, B. L., 222nn61, 222nn72
Bazerman, M. H., 63nn24
Beal, B. B., 198nn67
Beal, B. D., 315nn75
Beamish, P. W., 68nn147, 103nn78, 223nn97, 224nn113, 224nn124, 279nn39, 313nn24, 313nn33, 314nn39, 315nn98, 317nn129, 317nn131, 317nn140, 403nn16
Bebchuk, L. A., 348nn79
Becerra, M., 64nn53
Beck, B., 102nn64
Beck, K. A., 31nn150, 350nn130
Bednar, M. K., 344nn1
Beer, M., 64nn45
Begley, T. M., 312nn5
Belau, L., 64nn47
Belderbos, R., 26nn17, 197nn47, 316nn119
Bell, G. G., 221nn54
Bell, R. G., 314nn45, 345nn13
Bell, S. T., 64nn47, 68nn146
Bendoly, E., 171nn98

Bener, M., 316nn100
Benford, T., 28nn59, 402nn3
Benner, K., 27nn28
Bennett, D. J., 278nn23, 403nn44
Benson, G., 65nn79
Berfield, S., 66nn103
Berger, A. N., 254nn97
Bergh, D.D., 101nn5, 250nn7, 252nn47, 254nn102, 255nn115, 279nn52, 281nn104, 281nn110, 282nn122, 349nn101
Bergman, S. L., 31nn148
Bergmann, H., 318nn158
Berle, A., 346nn49
Berman, S. L., 136nn34, 221nn34
Bernardo, A. E., 255nn125
Bernstein, J., 313nn28
Berry, H., 318nn154
Berry, L. L., 169nn20
Berument, H., 102nn45
Best, A., 281nn101
Bettis, J. C., 348nn92
Bettis, R. A., 27nn42, 32nn167, 66nn99
Beugelskijk, S., 318nn154
Bhambri, A., 66nn91
Bhattacharyya, S., 278nn27
Bhaumik, S. K., 316nn115
Bianchi, M., 313nn14, 371nn104
Bierman, L., 65nn74, 137nn51, 345nn9, 347nn64, 368nn43
Bingham, C. B., 29nn77, 369nn59, 402nn5
Biniari, M. G., 369nn63
Biqing, H., 404nn49
Birger, J., 30nn117
Birkinshaw, J. M., 254nn109, 314nn50, 315nn70, 315nn72, 316nn111
Bizjak, J. M., 256nn144, 348nn92
Bjorkman, I., 102nn67, 318nn159
Black, R., 403nn41
Blankfeld, K., 278nn26, 279nn35, 280nn84
Blankson, C., 313nn17
Blettenr, D., 32nn167
Blyler, M., 30nn118, 140nn128
Bobinski, P. A., 350nn131
Bock, A. J., 67nn132, 138nn74, 367nn2, 402nn1

Bode, C., 104nn117
Boeh, K., 279nn38
Boeker, W., 64nn53
Boer, H., 370nn74
Boisot, M., 103nn79
Bolivar-Ramos, M. T., 29nn105
Bolton, L. E., 169nn26
Bonardi, J. P., 102nn50
Bongjin, K., 64nn52, 344nn7
Bonn, I., 32nn173, 103nn92
Boone, C., 64nn62
Borgatti, S. P., 223nn99
Borison, A., 404nn49
Borlson, A., 402nn2
Borrelli, L., 370nn91
Borza, A., 371nn113
Bosse, D. A., 31nn136, 66nn101, 220nn12, 350nn129
Bostan, I., 251nn37
Botosan, C., 253nn89
Boubarkri, K., 349nn126
Boulding, W., 198nn66
Bouquet, C., 316nn117
Bourgeois, Jay, 11
Bourgeois, L. J., III, 29nn86, 198nn61
Bowen, H. P., 137nn59, 254nn106, 313nn35, 317nn129
Bower, J. L., 254nn110
Bowerman, M., 347nn61, 347nn68
Bowman, C., 136nn29, 137nn62, 137nn63
Bowman, E. H., 29nn92, 255nn123, 403nn47
Bowonder, B., 220nn25
Boyd, B. K., 65nn70, 65nn80, 101nn5, 347nn62
Boyd, D. P., 312nn5
Boyd, J. L., 28nn55
Boyd, N. G., 30nn119, 220nn11
Bozionelos, N., 283nn137
Bradley, F., 317nn139
Bradley, S. W., 137nn67, 198nn62, 367nn3
Brady, D., 26nn16
Brandenburger, A., 104nn125
Brandes, P., 256nn138, 346nn32
Brandic, I., 28nn49
Brant, J., 65nn83
Brass, D. J., 68nn162
Brauer, M., 282nn115
Bresman, H., 316nn111
Bresser, R. K. F., 28nn55
Bretherton, P., 370nn89

Brettel, M., 370nn84
Brickley, P., 135nn20
Bridoux, F., 196nn20
Briggs, A. L., 64nn47
Briggs, T. W., 347nn54
Brigham, K. H., 140nn129
Brinckmann, J., 136nn24, 368nn34
Broadhurst, T., 349nn116
Brodsky, N., 146, 169nn23
Broll, U., 403nn23
Bromiley, P., 32nn156, 102nn46, 139nn110, 139nn115, 169nn49, 250nn6, 346nn35
Brooks, Rebekah, 56
Brousseau, K. R., 315nn96
Brouthers, K. D., 104nn126, 402nn13
Brouthers, L. E., 104nn126, 169nn19, 403nn13
Brown, S. L., 66nn110
Browning, J., 68nn165
Brown-Philpot, S., 103nn68
Brroks, G. R., 104nn104
Bruce, A., 170nn92
Bruneel, J., 136nn31
Brush, C. G., 29nn98
Brush, T. H., 250nn6, 252nn46, 346nn35
Bruton, G. D., 69nn176
Bryan, C., 102nn36
Bryant, A., 368nn32
Bryce, D. J., 255nn135
Buchanan, R., 278nn10
Buchholtz, A. K., 169nn41
Buckley, M. R., 67nn125
Buil, I., 68nn161
Bukhvalov, A. B., 403nn47
Bunderson, J., 64nn51
Burgelman, R. A., 67nn138, 250nn3, 368nn27, 369nn63
Burke, D., 65nn67, 252nn59
Burke, L. M., 64nn59
Burkitt, L., 197nn45
Burmeister-Lamp, K., 368nn31
Burns, M. L., 64nn52, 344nn7
Burns, N., 315nn92
Burns, T., 169nn36
Burns, Ursala, 46
Burr, B. B., 345nn18
Busby, J. S., 403nn45
Busch, T., 139nn111
Busenitz, L. W., 135nn22, 251nn26, 282nn114,

282nn116, 283nn135, 283nn141, 368nn29
Bushman, R., 346nn31
Butler, F. C., 62nn8
Butterfield, D. A., 66nn95, 68nn162
Buyl, T., 64nn62
Buysse, K., 101nn24
Buyya, R., 28nn49
Byrnes, N., 344nn2

Cabrera, R. V., 197nn55, 367nn6
Cairo, R., 221nn42
Calantone, R. J., 26nn7, 101nn8, 199nn108, 279nn56, 370nn70, 403nn31
Caldwell, C., 350nn135
Cambra-Fierro, J., 137nn56
Camerer, C. F., 139nn115, 280nn71, 281nn95
Cameron, David, 57
Camillus, J. C., 134nn2
Camison, C., 170nn69, 312nn7
Camp, S. M., 101nn14, 103nn80, 135nn22, 168nn3, 251nn26, 367nn4, 368nn29, 369nn59
Campa, J. M., 253nn92, 278nn12
Campbell, A., 250nn5
Campbell, D. F. J., 337, 370nn71
Campbell, J. D., 32nn166
Campbell, K., 66nn96
Campbell, R., 337
Campbell J. T., 26nn5, 30nn115, 101nn10
Canada, J., 28nn59, 402nn3
Canela, M. A., 135nn10
Canina, L., 104nn123, 197nn36, 221nn48
Cannella, A. A., Jr., 65nn87, 66nn99, 222nn71, 253nn68
Cantes, A., 101nn20
Cantwell, J., 315nn69
Capaldo, A., 222nn62
Capaldo, A., 222nn62
Capezio, A., 253nn90, 348nn86
Capozucca, P., 140nn125
Cappelli, P., 312nn11
Caprar, C. V., 135nn16
Capron, L., 252nn55, 252nn56, 255nn134, 278nn27, 278nn30, 279nn52

Carayannis, E. G., 370nn71
Cardinal, L. B., 135nn21, 251nn17, 368nn30
Cardon, M. S., 368nn35
Carey, D., 347nn72
Carey, D. C., 65nn89
Carini, G., 104nn113
Carmeli, A., 64nn43, 64nn57, 67nn122, 135nn13
Carney, M., 198nn84
Carpenter, M. A., 62nn12, 65nn65, 65nn75, 65nn81, 255nn136, 318nn164, 344nn1, 347nn64, 348nn85
Carroll, G. R., 198nn70
Carson, M., 102nn54
Carter, R., 253nn74
Carton, A. M., 68nn152
Cartwright, P. A., 103nn74
Casadesus-Masanell, R., 369nn62
Casey, A., 32nn158
Casey, J., 112
Cash, James I., 41
Cashen, L. H., 198nn61, 256nn137
Casio, W. F., 283nn137
Cassiman, B., 317nn142, 369nn60
Castañer, X., 221nn44
Castanias, R., 64nn44
Castellion, G., 370nn85
Castleton, M. W., 346nn38, 347nn69, 350nn137
Castrogiovanni, G. J., 195nn1
Catan, T., 279nn36
Cavaliere, A., 371nn104
Caves, R. E., 195nn8, 403nn27
Cavusgil, S. T., 104nn116, 312nn3, 317nn126
Ceccagnoli, M., 253nn66
Certo, S. T., 345nn19, 346nn44, 346nn46
Cetin, A. T., 30nn122
Ceylan, N. B., 102nn45
Chacar, A. S., 137nn55, 170nn84, 196nn23, 221nn34, 223nn99, 313nn26
Chakraborty, A., 349nn107
Chakravarthy, B., 251nn26
Champlin, D. P., 254nn112
Chan, C. M., 314nn43
Chan, D. S. K., 138nn81

Chancharat, N., 347nn63
Chandler, A. D., 9, 28nn65, 169nn46, 231
Chang, C., 371nn114
Chang, H.-C., 251nn36
Chang, K., 316nn110
Chang, R. M., 222nn63
Chang, S. J., 26nn19, 140nn129, 197nn49, 220nn29, 254nn97, 313nn19, 316nn121, 317nn127, 369nn46
Chang, S.-C., 317nn130
Chang, Y., 255nn122
Chao, L., 368nn25
Chao, Y., 220nn7
Chappuis, B. E., 278nn6
Charan, R., 65nn85, 345nn11
Chari, M. D. R., 134nn1, 250nn3, 316nn110
Charkham, J., 345nn13, 345nn14, 349nn119
Charns, M. P., 221nn53
Chatain, O., 66nn99, 136nn28, 169nn31, 221nn46
Chatterjee, L., 138nn90
Chatterjee, S. J., 251nn18, 252nn48, 255nn115, 255nn132, 279nn31, 349nn101
Chatterji, D., 171nn100
Chattopadhyay, J., 101nn2
Chattopadhyay, S., 138nn81
Chaudhuri, S., 28nn51
Chavas, J.-P., 251nn39
Chen, C. C., 32nn154, 345nn28, 350nn131
Chen, C. J. P., 317nn144
Chen, E. L., 29nn90, 32nn175
Chen, E.-T., 345nn24
Chen, J., 32nn172
Chen, L. B., 371nn103
Chen, M. A., 344nn4, 347nn67
Chen, M.-J., 27nn23, 64nn52, 101nn10, 103nn88, 135nn9, 174, 175, 178, 195nn5, 195nn7, 196nn12, 196nn25, 197nn38, 197nn46, 198nn71, 198nn72, 198nn84, 199nn85, 199nn86, 318nn160

Chen, Q., 346nn31
Chen, S, 136nn26
Chen, S. S. M., 313nn17
Chen, S.-F., 29nn81
Chen, Y. Y., 316nn112
Chen, Y.-L., 253nn92
Chen, Y.-R., 32nn154
Chen, Z., 139nn104
Chen Y.-R., 350nn131
Cheng, J., 368nn39
Cheng, J. L., 314nn45
Cheng, J. L. C., 197nn57
Cheng, J. M.-S., 313nn17
Chengru, H., 404nn49
Chen-Jui, H, 281nn107
Chernatony, L., 68nn161
Chetty, S. K., 369nn66
Cheung, M.-S., 104nn112, 370nn86
Cheung, Y.-L., 350nn127
Chhaochharia, V., 346nn40
Chi, J., 349nn126, 349nn127
Chi, P. S. K., 104nn104
Chi, T., 137nn62, 170nn68
Chiang, J., 197nn55, 369nn67
Chiaroni, D., 371nn104
Child, J., 315nn67, 318nn155
Chinta, R., 67nn138
Chirico, F., 136nn33, 168nn2
Chittoor, R., 316nn114
Chiu, I.-M., 254nn108
Chiu, Y.-C., 252nn54
Chiu, Y.-H., 318nn156
Chizema, A., 349nn117, 349nn121
Cho, H.-J., 368nn40
Cho, T. S., 64nn52
Choi, J., 31nn148
Choi, T. Y., 138nn96, 220nn15, 350nn136
Chompusri, N., 318nn148
Chon, G., 102nn48, 278nn11
Chowdhry, B., 255nn125
Chozick, A., 102nn48
Chreim, S., 280nn73
Chrisman, J. J., 169nn41
Christen, M., 198nn66
Christensen, C. M., 27nn45, 64nn45, 112, 136nn32, 278nn5, 367nn20
Christensen, C. R., 9, 28nn67
Christophe, S. E.,, 317nn130
Chronopoulos, D. K., 251nn21
Chu, R., 220nn33

Chu, W., 198nn80, 220nn13
Chua, R., 278nn29
Chuang, C.-M., 315nn96
Chui, Y., 315nn85
Chulkov, D. V., 66nn94
Chun, R., 169nn35
Chung, C., 254nn97, 278nn28
Chung, C. C., 224nn113, 403nn16
Chung, L., 318nn155
Chung, Mong Koo, 185
Chung, S., 222nn58
Chung, W., 199nn99, 313nn28, 314nn44
Chvyrkov, O., 369nn59
Cimilluca, D., 278nn11
Cinatti, F., 26nn18
Citrin, J. M., 65nn84
Clark, K. D., 101nn6
Clarke, C., 139nn115
Clarysse, B., 136nn31
Clifford, P. G., 136nn31
Clinton, E., 104nn99, 136nn24
Clougherty, J. A., 195nn6, 278nn16
Cochran, P. L., 68nn155, 68nn168, 139nn107
Cocks, C., 347nn70
Coelho, D. A., 198nn74
Coff, R. W., 30nn113, 30nn118, 137nn52, 140nn128, 254nn104, 279nn44, 281nn105, 345nn28, 348nn94
Coffee, J. C., 255nn120
Cohen, J. R., 68nn168
Cohen, S. S., 221nn48
Colak, G., 251nn22
Coles, J., 65nn70, 346nn44
Collier, P. A., 69nn174
Collingwood, H., 67nn130
Collins, C. J., 101nn6
Collins, J., 27nn39, 35, 62nn7, 63nn41
Collins, J. C., 68nn151
Collis, D., 250nn6
Colquitt, J. A., 137nn56, 370nn98
Colvin, G., 27nn40, 31nn141, 278nn18, 402nn6
Combs, J. G., 65nn76, 135nn8, 197nn60, 222nn83, 223nn92
Conger, J., 65nn79
Connell, J., 223nn107

Connelly, B. L., 29nn106, 135nn6, 312nn4, 313nn25, 317nn128, 317nn141, 345nn19, 346nn44, 346nn46
Connors, W., 197nn42
Contractor, F. J., 316nn101
Conyon, M. J., 348nn75
Cook, Timothy, 333
Cool, K., 196nn17
Coombs, J. E., 350nn136
Coombs, J. G., 31nn129
Cooper, A. C., 255nn128
Cooper, B. K., 370nn96
Cooper, R. W., 221nn43
Copeland, T., 403nn33, 404nn51
Core, J. E., 256nn137, 348nn75
Cornell, B., 32nn155
Cornett, M., 278nn20
Corzine, Jon, 56, 68nn159
Cosset, J.-C., 349nn126
Costa, J., 104nn103
Costea, C., 26nn18
Cotteleer, M., 171nn98
Coulson, Andrew, 56–57
Coutu, D. L., 67nn130
Coville, T., 345nn10
Covin, J. G., 282nn134, 368nn37, 369nn54
Cowan, A. P., 136nn45
Coyne, K. P., 69nn183, 136nn31
Coyne, S. T., 69nn183
Cramer, R. D., 102nn53
Crane, A., 105nn139
Cravens, D. W., 32nn159
Credeur, M., 278nn23
Crook, T. R., 31nn129
Crosby, L. B., 198nn74, 198nn77
Cross, R., 67nn127
Crossan, K., 345nn21
Crossan, M. M., 65nn71, 68nn168, 136nn27, 170nn70
Crossland, C., 63nn19
Cuervo-Cazurra, A., 168nn8, 402nn11
Cui, A. S., 403nn31
Cullinan, G., 278nn18, 280nn80
Cummings, J. L., 30nn112
Cummings, L. L., 63nn19
Cummings, T., 66nn91

Cunningham, S.W., 103nn71
Cyr, L. A., 67nn128

Dabal, A., 220nn25
Dabrowski, R. V., 314nn56
Dacin, M. T., 26nn17, 63nn15, 65nn73, 103nn86, 103nn87, 222nn75, 315nn97, 316nn104, 371nn113
Daft, R. L., 252nn53
Dagnini, G. B., 65nn86
Dagnino, G.B., 101nn3, 197nn40, 251nn38, 317nn135, 345nn15
Dahlsten, F., 101nn23
Daigler, R. T., 251nn18
Daily, C. M., 65nn71, 168nn11, 282nn134, 347nn62
Daley, J., 222nn85
Dalpiaz, E., 136nn39
Dalsace, F., 138nn94
Dalton, D. R., 65nn71, 168nn11, 282nn134, 347nn62
Dalziel, T., 347nn61, 347nn68
D'Ambra, J., 370nn86
Danese, P., 255nn130
Danielson, C. C., 137nn58
Danneels, E., 27nn45, 30nn118, 135nn15, 138nn92, 168nn10
Darner, E., 198nn69
Das, A., 66nn112, 255nn133, 278nn11
Das, K., 28nn56
Das, S., 138nn79, 221nn36
Das, S. S., 255nn133
Das, T. K., 63nn21, 63nn25, 223nn104, 223nn107
Datta, D.K., 101nn2, 280nn71, 283nn136
Daus, C. S., 66nn94
D'Aveni, R. A., 26nn3, 27nn42, 27nn43, 101nn3, 197nn40, 251nn38, 317nn135, 402nn4
Davenport, T. H., 26nn19, 136nn41
David, P., 134nn1, 250nn3, 253nn80, 346nn30
David, R. J., 350nn135
Davidovitch, L., 253nn81, 253nn83
Davidson, J. M., 171nn100
Davies, G., 169nn35

Davies, H., 318nn155
Davis, G. E., 345nn20
Davis, J. H., 65nn73, 68nn167, 224nn127, 344nn7
Davis, K., 281nn93
Davis, K. J., 348nn76
Davis-Blake, A., 348nn80
Davis-Sramk, B., 223nn90
Dawson, C., 27nn36, 104nn115
Day, G. S., 197nn51
Dayal, U., 28nn51
daCosta, R. C., 317nn131
de Colle, S., 31nn149, 220nn11, 224nn127
de Jong, J. P. J., 368nn22
de la Fuente Sabate, J. M., 105nn134
de la Torre, J., 316nn105
de Luque, A. S., 313nn32
de Luque, M., 62nn14
de Oliveira Matias, J. C., 198nn74
de Vilhers, C., 103nn93
De Benedetto, C. A., 279nn42
De Carolis, D. M., 30nn119, 67nn126, 101nn8
De Cremer, D., 32nn154, 350nn131
De Kluyver, C., 171nn104
De La Torre, J. R., 170nn84, 196nn23
De Miguel, A., 346nn35
De Zoyza, N., 30nn123
Dean, J. W., Jr., 184
Dean, T. J., 67nn128
Deans, G. K., 278nn6
Debaise, C., 102nn63
DeCecco, Dave, 99
Deckop, J. R., 350nn134
Deeds, D. L., 67nn126
Deephouse, D. L., 104nn121, 136nn44
DeFillippi, R., 138nn76
Degravel, D., 313nn36
Deitz, G. D., 368nn36
Dekimpe, M.G., 27nn38
Del Brio, E. B., 346nn35, 346nn45
Deleersnyder, B., 27nn38
Deligonul, S. Z., 317nn126
Delingonul, S., 312nn3
Delios, A., 253nn80, 282nn111, 316nn117, 317nn143, 346nn30, 349nn109
Delmar, F., 371nn121
Delmas, M., 103nn91

Delong, G., 252nn46
DeMarie, S. M., 27nn42
Deming, W. E., 198nn75
Demiralp, I., 347nn52
Deng, F. J., 69nn175
Denis, D. J., 254nn95
Denis, D. K., 254nn95
DeNisi, A. S., 28nn50, 137nn56
Denning, K. C., 223nn103
Desai, A., 346nn36
Desarbo, W. S., 198nn71
Dess, G. G., 67nn134, 67nn136, 137nn57, 138nn81, 139nn101, 168nn9, 169nn18, 170nn86, 170nn88
Dessler, G., 102nn40
Desyllas, P., 280nn65
Deutsch, Y., 65nn70, 139nn114
Devan, J., 63nn29
Devaraj, S., 250nn3
Devers, C., 27nn22
Devinney, T. M., 26nn19
DeVito, R., 198nn77
Dewitt, R. L., 254nn102
Dey, A., 65nn69, 65nn72
Dezember, R., 197nn52
Dhanaraj, C., 223nn95
Dhanda, K. K., 222nn77
Dharwadkar, R., 256nn138, 346nn32
Di Benedetto, C. A., 251nn25
Di Minin, A., 313nn14
Dial, J., 283nn141
Diamantopoulos, A., 255nn131
DiBemardino, F., 66nn120
Diestre, L., 253nn73, 282nn113
DiMicco, Dan, 48
Ding, Y., 317nn144
Dino, R. H., 64nn57
Disney, Roy, 189
Disney, Walt, 189
Distefano, J. J., 64nn56
D'Mello, R., 347nn52
Dobbs, R., 102nn37, 102nn43
Dobni, C. B., 168nn6
Dobrev, S. D., 198nn70
Doh, J. P., 317nn134
Dokko, G., 224nn125
Dollinger, M., 280nn75
Domoto, H., 252nn55
Donaldson, L. G., 31nn133, 65nn73, 344nn7
Donaldson, T., 31nn149, 344nn6
Dong, Z., 348nn91
Donkin, R., 101nn18

Dooms, E., 252nn49
Dorner, N., 171nn105
Doswell, G. W. S., 27nn39
Doucet, T. A., 254nn105
Dougherty, D., 370nn91
Douglas, T.J., 26nn3
Doukas, J. A., 254nn110
Douma, S., 349nn114
Dous, M., 26nn19
Doving, E., 252nn51
Dowell, G., 198nn64
Dowell, K., 222nn66, 222nn81
Dowling, G. R., 199nn89
Down, J., 136nn34, 221nn34
Doz, Y. L., 28nn56, 67nn138, 250nn3
Dragoni, L., 26nn10, 32nn161
Dranikoff, L., 282nn123
Driouchi, T., 403nn44
Driver, M. J., 315nn96
Drnevich, P. L., 30nn114, 195nn1
Droge, C., 101nn8, 199nn108
Druck S., 28nn57
Drucker, P. F., 367nn19
Dubina, I. N., 370nn71
Duhaime, I. M., 195nn6, 402nn10
Dumaine, B., 27nn29
Dunfee,, T. W., 345nn8
Dunlap-Hinkler, D., 170nn68, 313nn15
Durand, R., 63nn35
Duso, T., 278nn16
Dussauge, P., 137nn49, 221nn44, 221nn45, 221nn57, 252nn55
Dutra, A., 169nn27
Dutta, S., 104nn120, 403nn25
Dutton, J. E., 67nn139
Dyer, J. H., 137nn52, 198nn80, 220nn13, 221nn50, 222nn79, 224nn110, 224nn111, 224nn122, 367nn20, 403nn31
Dykes, B. J., 196nn16
Dyson R. G., 69nn177
Dysters, G., 317nn126

Eban, K., 29nn94
Ebbers, H., 278nn9
Echambadi, R., 368nn37
Echols A., 222nn58
Edelman, L. F., 254nn99
Eden, C., 31nn134, 139nn108

Eden, L. E., 313nn31, 314nn45, 316nn106, 371nn112
Edgar, W. B., 30nn120
Edmondson, A. C. A., 64nn43, 67nn122, 135nn13
Edwards, C., 198nn68
Eesley C., 31nn134
Efrati, A., 66nn112
Ehrenfeld, J. R., 32nn180
Eiche, J., 318nn152
Eisenhardt, K. M., 29nn77, 29nn90, 32nn175, 66nn110, 102nn41, 224nn117, 253nn80, 279nn48, 279nn53, 369nn59, 402nn5
Eisenmann, T. R., 254nn95, 254nn110
Eisenstat, R., 64nn45, 253nn91
Elango, D., 316nn118
Elbashir, M. Z., 69nn174
Elenkov, D. S., 67nn134, 318nn164
Elfenbein, H. A., 104nn124, 196nn30
Elgar, Edward, 28nn69
Elkassabgi, A., 30nn121, 251nn20
Elkind, P., 65nn67
Ellis, K. M., 279nn55
Ellis, P. D., 369nn57
Ellonen, H. K., 279nn42
Ellram, L. M., 104nn117
Ellstrand, A. E., 168nn11, 347nn62
Elmuti, D., 171nn97
Engel, E., 65nn69, 65nn72, 346nn31
Engelen, A., 370nn84
Englander, E., 350nn132
Ensign, P. C., 315nn72
Enz, A., 221nn48
Enz. C. A., 104nn123, 197nn36
Ephron, D., 68nn164
Epstein, M. J., 26nn11
Erakovic, L., 347nn74
Eriksson, M., 198nn75
Ernst, H., 138nn78, 138nn91, 371nn105
Ertimur, Y., 347nn54, 348nn78
Escrihuela-Villar, M., 222nn68
Eshima, Y., 136nn42
Estrin, S., 316nn115

Ethiraj, S. K., 28nn51
Evan, W. M., 67nn142
Evans, P., 32nn176
Evans, R. W., 62nn8
Ezrati, M., 102nn58

Fabrizio, K. R., 369nn53
Faccio, M., 345nn22
Fackler, M., 346nn48
Fahey, L., 101nn9, 101nn21, 101nn27, 101nn29, 102nn44, 103nn96
Fairclough, G., 315nn99
Fairlie, R. W., 102nn65
Faleye, O., 346nn33, 349nn104
Fama, E. F., 256nn141, 345nn9, 345nn25
Fanelli, A., 30nn124
Fang, E., 30nn122, 250nn11, 370nn101
Fang, Y., 313nn24
Faraci, R., 65nn86, 345nn15
Faria, A., 170nn92
Farjoun, M., 278nn3
Farrell, D., 317nn134
Farzad, R., 68nn165
Fassiotto, M. A., 367nn10
Fast, N. J., 63nn38
Fauchart, E., 367nn11
Fawcett, S. E., 220nn5
Fee, C. E., 278nn28
Fehr, E., 31nn137
Feils, D. J., 138nn94
Feldman, E., 68nn158
Feldman, L. F., 29nn98
Feldman, W. S., 136nn36
Felo, A., 350nn135
Feng-Jyh, L., 29nn103, 31nn129
Fenn, P., 170nn92
Fenwick, L., 221nn86
Ferdnandez-Araoz, C., 136nn41
Ferguson, G., 27nn48
Fern, M. J., 135nn21
Fernandez, N., 197nn33
Fernandez-Araoz, C., 66nn117
Ferrer, M., 370nn89
Ferri, F., 347nn54, 348nn78
Ferrier, J., 27nn23
Ferrier, W. J., 196nn14, 196nn21, 196nn22, 197nn50, 197nn51, 198nn70, 199nn84, 199nn88, 199nn93, 199nn97, 279nn58, 403nn44
Field, J. M., 29nn82

Fields, G., 221nn48
Fields, P., 313nn31
Fiet, J. O., 139nn109
Filatotchev, I., 65nn70, 220nn24, 256nn137, 312nn4, 314nn45, 345nn13, 348nn82, 349nn110
Finegold, D. L., 65nn79, 347nn69
Finkelstein, S., 63nn19, 64nn58, 66nn102, 102nn40, 318nn164, 347nn61
Fiol, C. M., 67nn131
Firsch, J. H., 403nn42
Fischer, S., 349nn118
Fishburn, D., 102nn30
Fisher, J., 103nn92
Fisher, J. D., 250nn9
Fiss, P. C., 349nn113
Fitza, M. A., 251nn26
Fitzgerald, D., 26nn12
Fladmoe-Lindquist, K., 28nn57, 313nn36, 316nn103
Fleisher, C. S., 105nn138
Fleming, T., 103nn69
Florin, F., 137nn56
Florou, G., 171nn96
Flynn, B., 103nn89, 170nn54
Foer, A. A., 255nn118
Foley, M., 404nn49
Folta, T. B., 255nn131, 403nn17
Foltz, J., 251nn39
Fombrun C. J., 67nn143, 135nn23, 168nn4, 196nn27
Fong, E. A., 348nn76
Fong, M., 103nn83
Fontaine, A., 161
Fontevecchia, A., 278nn24, 282nn124
Foo, M.-D., 368nn35
Foote, N., 253nn91
Forbes, S. J., 253nn73
Ford, R. C., 68nn147
Forest, S. A., 68nn157, 255nn116
Fornahl, D., 252nn64, 252nn65
Forsgren, M., 317nn133
Forsyth, M., 282nn125
Fortado, L., 68nn165
Fortune, A., 136nn36
Fosfuri, A., 315nn91
Fosman, H., 370nn70

Foss, N. J., 134nn3, 136nn43, 317nn142, 368nn42, 370nn84
Fouskas, K. G., 197nn48
Fowler, G. A., 315nn99
Fowler, S. W., 314nn66
Fox, C. R., 197nn41
Fracassi, C., 64nn64
Francis, S., 280nn76
Franko, L. G., 368nn23
Frary, J., 169nn27
Frattini, F., 371nn104
Frazier, G., 220nn16
Frecet, M., 224nn109
Frederickson, J. W., 48, 49, 62nn12, 63nn31, 63nn32, 64nn43, 65nn81, 66nn105, 168nn6, 250nn2, 250nn10, 318nn164, 348nn80
Freeman, Edward, 17
Freeman, J., 139nn102
Freeman, R. E., 26nn9, 26nn10, 28nn59, 31nn130, 31nn135, 31nn142, 31nn143, 31nn144, 31nn149, 32nn155, 32nn156, 32nn162, 32nn180, 66nn101, 67nn142, 67nn143, 69nn170, 102nn50, 139nn108, 139nn112, 139nn115, 169nn38, 196nn14, 220nn10, 220nn11, 222nn74, 224nn127, 250nn7, 252nn63, 254nn102, 312nn7, 402nn3
Fremeth, A. R., 222nn77
French, S., 32nn158
Frick, K. A., 278nn6
Fried, J. M., 348nn79
Frisch, B., 64nn45
Frobisher, S., 348nn96
Frooman, J., 139nn111
Frost, T. S., 315nn72, 369nn60
Frow, P., 138nn83, 139nn105
Frynas, J. G., 317nn146
Fuchs, P. H., 67nn138
Fuda, P., 69nn170
Fuentelsaz, L., 196nn14, 196nn31

Fuerbringer, J., 103nn84
Fuhrmans, V., 26nn12
Fulmer, I. S., 255nn136
Furr, N. R., 402nn5

Gachter, S., 31nn137
Gadiesh, O., 314nn54
Gaetson, A., 223nn88
Gaimon, C., 67nn126, 67nn129
Galagan, P., 282nn118
Galan, J. I., 251nn33
Galan, J. L., 30nn109
Galbraith, J. G., 253nn84
Galbraith, J. R., 169nn38, 169nn42
Galinsky, A. D., 63nn38
Galunic, D. C., 253nn80
Galvin, B. M., 62nn5
Gander, J. P., 64nn44
Ganesan S., 169nn20
Gann, D. M., 67nn132, 138nn74, 367nn2, 402nn1
Gannon, M. J., 199nn94, 317nn139
Gantumur, T., 198nn62
Garbuio, M., 219nn3
García, D., 63nn37
Garcia-Castro, R., 135nn10
Garcia-Morales, V. J., 29nn105
Gardberg, N. A., 32nn155
Gardner, T., 199nn87
Garg, V. K., 101nn17
Garicano, L., 370nn94
Garnham, P., 102nn49
Garrett, R. P., 371nn112
Garrette, B., 221nn44, 221nn45, 221nn57
Garriga, E., 220nn10
Garten, J. E., 317nn127
Garund, R., 371nn130
Garvin, D., 184
Gary, M. S., 63nn23
Gaspar, J.-G., 254nn106
Gaspar, J.-M., 253nn86
Gates, Bill, 41
Gattiker, T. F., 404nn48
Gavetti, G., 135nn15, 168nn1
Gedajivoic, E. R., 198nn84
Geiger, S. W., 198nn61, 256nn137
Gentry, R. J., 347nn61, 347nn68
Gentry, W. A., 63nn15
George, B. A., 67nn134

George, G., 67nn132, 138nn74, 315nn82, 367nn2, 368nn42, 402nn1
George, R., 250nn11
Gerchak, Y., 252nn42
Gerhart, B., 255nn136
Geringer, J. M., 313nn34, 317nn131
Germain, R. N., 223nn90
Gerstenhaber, M., 223nn89
Gertner, J., 169nn21
Geyskens, I, 253nn70
Ghauri, P. N., 278nn4
Ghemawat, P., 314nn47
Ghobadi, S., 370nn86
Ghobadian, A., 104nn97
Ghosh, C., 337
Ghoshal, S., 67nn126, 314nn55, 314nn65, 315nn94, 345nn28
Giaglis, G. M., 197nn48
Giardone, C., 251nn21
Giarrantana, M. S., 104nn107, 223nn108
Gibb, J., 32nn171
Gibbert, M., 28nn55
Gibbons, P. T., 318nn158
Gibson, C., 314nn61
Giglio, M., 68nn164
Gilbert, B. A., 30nn116, 63nn20, 66nn100, 104nn120, 135nn5, 138nn91, 150, 169nn50, 170nn66, 195nn7, 223nn95, 251nn25, 313nn16, 370nn69, 371nn109
Gilbert A., 145
Gile, C., 138nn82
Gillette, F., 68nn165
Gilley, K. M., 68nn155, 350nn136
Gil-Pechuán, I., 30nn127
Gilson, R., 255nn120
Gimeno, J., 196nn14, 196nn31, 197nn33, 197nn35, 198nn67, 222nn72, 253nn67, 315nn75
Gittell, J. H., 69nn174
Glaister, K. W., 316nn100
Gleason, K. C., 346nn46
Glick, W.H., 28nn51, 64nn59, 66nn93, 101nn2
Globerman, S., 350nn128

Glunk, U., 67nn139, 199nn85
Gluskie, Angus, 245
Glynn, M. A., 318nn162, 367nn3
Gnyawali, D. R., 134nn3, 170nn71, 196nn18
Goerzen, A., 223nn100
Goffee, R., 68nn153
Goktan, A. B., 370nn69
Golden, B. R., 64nn64, 65nn64
Goldman, E. F., 32nn158
Goldstein, D., 348nn95
Golovko, E., 317nn142, 318nn165, 369nn60, 371nn127
Gomes, G. Z., 313nn13
Gomes, L., 348nn84
Gomez, J., 196nn14, 196nn31
Gomez-Mejia, L., 344nn3, 345nn22, 348nn86
Gonenc, H., 280nn86
Gong, Y., 316nn103
Gooderham, P. N., 252nn51
Goold, M., 250nn5, 250nn6
Goranova, M., 256nn138, 346nn32, 347nn59
Gordon, R. A., 28nn62, 29nn106
Gorsky, Alex, 187
Goshal, S., 102nn66
Gospel, H., 254nn103
Gotto, M., 349nn122
Gottschalg, O., 102nn60
Govindarajan, V., 26nn18, 27nn45, 63nn16, 63nn17, 67nn131, 312nn5, 312nn9, 367nn18
Gozalez, I. S., 105nn134
Graebner, M., 281nn100
Graffin, S. D., 63nn39
Graham, P., 251nn13
Grahovac, J., 27nn44
Granston, T., 348nn90
Grant, R. M., 113, 114
Gratton, L., 67nn122
Graves, S. B., 32nn156
Gray, B., 223nn94
Gray, D., 171nn97
Greco, J., 62nn4, 251nn28
Greening, D. W., 137nn53
Greensberg J., 170nn57
Gregersen, H., 367nn20
Gregg, T., 139nn120
Greiner, L., 66nn91
Gresko, J., 170nn64

Greve, A., 224nn125
Greve, H. R., 32nn164, 105nn130, 105nn134, 196nn31, 198nn69, 221nn49, 223nn102, 253nn68, 281nn98
Grewal, R., 30nn122, 198nn71, 250nn11
Griffin, A., 370nn99
Griffith, D. A., 102nn66, 314nn36, 403nn31
Griffith, W., 315nn99
Grimm, C. M., 101nn3, 195nn3, 195nn9, 196nn12, 196nn16, 196nn20, 196nn29, 196nn32, 197nn50, 198nn73, 199nn85, 199nn93, 199nn94
Grinstein, Y., 346nn40
Grinyer, P., 135nn17
Groen, A. J., 26nn8
Grohmann, B., 222nn80
Gröne, F., 253nn78
Grosse, R., 318nn148, 318nn162
Grossman, W., 345nn19, 346nn32, 347nn52, 347nn68, 369nn61
Grove, L., 68nn164
Grove, S., 255nn132
Groysberg, B., 66nn117, 136nn41
Gruber, M., 367nn11
Grundei, J., 199nn107
Guay, W. R., 256nn137, 348nn75
Gubbi, S. R., 316nn114
Gudergan, S. P., 221nn37
Gudridge, K., 255nn116
Guedhami, O., 102nn61, 349nn126
Guedri, Z., 105nn133, 196nn13
Guillen, M. F., 318nn154
Gul, F. A., 66nn96
Gulati, R., 224nn119, 253nn70
Gunkel, J. D., 69nn181
Guo, R., 251nn19, 251nn24
Guo, S., 282nn131
Guo, Z.-F., 250nn17
Gupta, A. K., 26nn18, 63nn16, 67nn131, 138nn81, 170nn88, 312nn5
Gupta, D., 252nn42
Gupta, S., 350nn134

Guth, W. D., 9, 28nn67, 135nn17
Guthrie, J. P., 101nn2, 283nn136
Gwynne, P., 281nn104
Gynawali, D. R., 199nn115, 220nn17, 368nn23

Haahti, A., 315nn88
Haanaes, K., 68nn150
Haar, J. M., 32nn171
Habisch, A., 139nn107
Hadani, M., 347nn59
Hadjimarcou, J., 169nn19
Haeussler, C., 32nn176
Hafeez, K., 137nn61, 138nn92
Hagedoorn, J., 317nn126
Hagerty, J., 371nn116
Hair, J. F., Jr., 169nn27
Haleblian, J., 62nn10, 196nn16, 281nn91, 281nn107
Halikas, J., 169nn32
Hall, D. T., 67nn123, 369nn58
Hall, R., 114
Hall, R. H., 170nn58, 170nn59
Hallaq, J. H., 105nn142
Hallikas, J., 136nn29
Halme, M., 368nn22
Hambrick, D. C., 48, 49, 63nn19, 63nn38, 64nn52, 64nn58, 66nn99, 66nn102, 66nn105, 102nn40, 168nn6, 198nn71, 223nn102, 250nn2, 250nn10, 256nn140, 279nn57, 281nn93, 316nn104, 318nn164, 347nn72, 348nn91, 367nn1
Hamel, G, 32nn163, 32nn169, 66nn104, 137nn61, 138nn92, 403nn30
Hamm, G., 402nn2
Hamza, T., 281nn103
Han, K., 222nn63
Han, S., 252nn41
Handerson, A., 348nn80
Handfield, R. B., 313nn21
Hanlon, S. C., 220nn11
Hannan, M., 139nn102
Hansen, J. D., 368nn36
Hansen, M. H., 32nn153, 224nn120
Hansen, M. T., 27nn39
Hanson, J. D., 370nn70
Hanvanich, S., 101nn8, 199nn108

Harder, J., 139nn97
Harjoto, M., 350nn133
Harlan, C., 105nn140
Harrigan, K. R., 28nn59, 402nn3
Harris, D., 66nn97
Harris, I. C., 65nn73
Harris, J., 103nn90
Harris, J. D., 32nn180, 136nn41
Harris, M., 253nn89
Harris, R., 282nn133
Harrison, D. A., 68nn155, 139nn107
Harrison, J. R., 26nn9, 26nn10, 28nn59
Harrison, J. S., 28nn69, 29nn83, 29nn88, 29nn89, 31nn135, 31nn136, 31nn137, 31nn138, 31nn140, 31nn142, 31nn147, 31nn149, 31nn150, 31nn152, 32nn155, 32nn156, 32nn162, 66nn101, 67nn143, 69nn170, 69nn172, 102nn50, 104nn123, 137nn66, 139nn108, 139nn109, 139nn115, 169nn38, 171nn104, 196nn14, 197nn36, 220nn9, 220nn11, 220nn12, 220nn14, 221nn39, 221nn48, 222nn74, 224nn127, 250nn7, 251nn35, 252nn43, 252nn63, 254nn102, 255nn115, 278nn5, 279nn38, 279nn42, 279nn47, 279nn54, 280nn86, 281nn99, 281nn100, 281nn101, 312nn7, 316nn108, 337, 349nn101, 350nn129, 359, 402nn3
Hart, S. L., 31nn150, 350nn130
Hartel, C. E. J., 66nn94
Harvey, M. G., 67nn125, 314nn36
Harzing, A.-W., 220nn29, 250nn9
Hasan, I., 134nn1, 135nn9, 252nn41, 254nn97, 312nn1

Hatch, N. W., 137nn52, 221nn50, 224nn111
Hatfield, D. E., 368nn30
Hathaiveseawong, N., 224nn114
Haughland, S. A., 224nn125
Haunschild, P., 220nn21
Haveman, H. A., 196nn13
Hawawini, G., 31nn129
Hayes, E., 67nn139
Haynes, K., 347nn62
Haynes, K. T., 26nn1, 68nn145, 101nn5, 102nn48
Hayward, M. L. A., 63nn40, 280nn64, 281nn93, 281nn95, 281nn96
He, J., 347nn60, 404nn50
He, X., 66nn106, 196nn18
Healey, M. P., 135nn13
Heavey, C., 370nn77
Hegarty, W., 348nn85
Hegtvedt, K. A., 32nn154, 350nn131
Heijlties, M. G., 67nn139
Heimeriks, K. H., 224nn115
Heinemann, F., 370nn84
Heinick, R., 280nn76
Helfat, C. E., 29nn92, 64nn44, 66nn97, 137nn50, 279nn53
Hellerstedt, K., 371nn121
Helm, S., 67nn143
Hempel, J., 32nn160
Hemphill, T. A., 220nn4
Henard, D. H., 137nn63
Henderson, A. D., 26nn4, 135nn21
Hendricks W., 64nn62
Hendrickx, M., 250nn6, 346nn35
Henisz, W. J., 223nn98, 317nn143
Hennart, J.-F., 138nn81, 170nn88, 315nn83
Henneberg, S. C., 219nn3
Henriques, I., 31nn133, 350nn129
Henry, N., 197nn41
Heracleous, L., 256nn138, 345nn26
Herbert, L., 316nn117
Hermelo, F. D., 27nn22
Hernandez, M., 345nn8, 345nn18

Herper, M., 279nn34, 279nn45
Herrmann, P., 27nn27, 30nn107, 347nn68, 348nn87, 369nn58
Hess, A. M., 170nn72, 224nn118, 371nn106
Hesterly, W. S., 65nn70, 223nn99
Heugens, P. M. A. R., 198nn84
Higgins, M. J., 140nn128
Hijitjes, M. G., 199nn85
Hill, C. W. L., 31nn143, 63nn28, 103nn72, 136nn34, 138nn81, 170nn88, 220nn10, 221nn34, 253nn85, 254nn107, 281nn88, 282nn133, 348nn87
Hiller, N. J., 63nn38
Hillman, A. J., 31nn148, 102nn50, 102nn53, 347nn62
Hilman, H., 196nn11
Himelstein, L., 348nn100
Hirai, Kazuo, 24
Hirota, S., 349nn118
Hirukawa, M., 367nn21
Hitt, M. A., 26nn1, 26nn2, 26nn4, 26nn8, 26nn9, 26nn10, 27nn42, 28nn59, 28nn60, 28nn63, 28nn64, 28nn69, 29nn91, 29nn105, 30nn110, 30nn115, 30nn116, 30nn123, 32nn156, 32nn174, 63nn15, 63nn20, 63nn28, 64nn63, 65nn78, 66nn99, 66nn100, 67nn134, 67nn143, 68nn145, 68nn149, 69nn170, 69nn183, 100nn1, 101nn5, 101nn10, 101nn14, 102nn48, 102nn50, 102nn53, 103nn72, 103nn74, 103nn76, 103nn78, 103nn80, 103nn86, 103nn87, 104nn97, 104nn103, 104nn120, 105nn137, 114, 123, 124, 135nn5, 135nn22, 136nn31, 136nn43, 137nn48, 137nn51, 137nn56, 137nn59, 139nn108, 139nn115, 145, 150, 156,

168nn3, 168nn8, 169nn22, 169nn38, 169nn50, 170nn66, 170nn87, 195nn7, 196nn14, 198nn79, 220nn7, 221nn39, 221nn42, 223nn104, 248, 250nn7, 251nn25, 251nn26, 252nn63, 253nn71, 254nn102, 254nn106, 254nn107, 255nn125, 255nn132, 278nn5, 279nn38, 279nn42, 279nn43, 279nn46, 279nn47, 279nn54, 279nn60, 280nn64, 280nn66, 280nn78, 280nn85, 280nn86, 281nn89, 281nn90, 281nn92, 281nn99, 281nn100, 281nn101, 282nn114, 282nn117, 282nn120, 282nn126, 283nn140, 293, 297, 300, 312nn4, 312nn5, 312nn7, 313nn16, 313nn25, 314nn39, 314nn45, 315nn90, 315nn97, 316nn104, 316nn106, 316nn108, 316nn110, 317nn128, 317nn132, 317nn133, 317nn137, 317nn141, 318nn150, 318nn153, 318nn159, 318nn165, 345nn17, 345nn19, 346nn45, 347nn52, 347nn59, 347nn68, 348nn87, 348nn94, 349nn126, 367nn4, 367nn5, 367nn6, 368nn29, 368nn43, 369nn46, 369nn56, 369nn59, 369nn60, 369nn61, 370nn69, 370nn74, 371nn112, 371nn113, 371nn118, 371nn120, 371nn122, 371nn124, 402nn3

Hmieleski, K. M., 368nn34
Ho, V., 350nn130
Hoang, H., 221nn35
Hoberg, G., 252nn40, 280nn75
Hochwarter, W. A., 68nn152
Hockenos, P., 371nn107
Hodgetts, R., 314nn49

Hodgkinson, G. P., 135nn13
Hodgson, G. M., 253nn74
Hodgson, J., 278nn15
Hoechle, D., 346nn39
Hoegl, M., 136nn24, 368nn34
Hoetker, G., 170nn90
Hofer, C. W., 10, 28nn61, 29nn84, 29nn100, 169nn41
Hofmann, V. H., 103nn91
Hogarth R. M., 63nn24
Hoitash, R., 350nn134
Hoiweg, M., 198nn71
Holburn, G. L. F., 317nn146
Holcomb, T. R., 29nn106, 282nn114, 317nn132, 317nn133
Holcombe, R. G., 367nn17
Holm, U., 317nn133
Holmes, R. M., Jr., 29nn106, 103nn76, 318nn150, 318nn159
Homqvist, M., 315nn96
Hong, J., 169nn37, 254nn97, 317nn127
Hope, O.-K., 256nn139, 278nn8
Hopkins, H. D., 196nn10, 314nn58
Hoppner, J. J., 317nn126
Hornsby, J. S., 28nn52, 101nn16
Hoskisson, R. E., 28nn64, 29nn91, 30nn109, 32nn153, 63nn28, 64nn63, 65nn78, 65nn86, 69nn176, 69nn183, 103nn78, 114, 123, 124, 135nn22, 145, 150, 156, 169nn37, 198nn67, 220nn24, 221nn39, 222nn59, 224nn120, 248, 250nn3, 251nn23, 251nn26, 251nn32, 254nn96, 254nn99, 254nn102, 254nn106, 254nn107, 255nn132, 256nn142, 278nn1, 279nn43, 279nn46, 279nn47, 279nn60, 280nn66, 281nn88, 281nn89, 281nn90, 281nn92, 282nn126, 282nn128, 283nn135, 283nn141, 293, 297, 300, 312nn4,

313nn34, 315nn75, 317nn127, 317nn137, 318nn157, 318nn165, 345nn15, 345nn17, 345nn19, 346nn30, 346nn38, 346nn44, 346nn46, 347nn52, 347nn59, 347nn63, 347nn66, 347nn68, 347nn69, 348nn87, 348nn94, 350nn137, 368nn29, 369nn46, 369nn54, 369nn60, 369nn61, 371nn118
Hossain, M., 346nn40
Hotchkiss, E. S., 282nn131
Hough, J. R., 101nn17
House, R. J., 62nn14, 65nn83, 313nn32
Howard, E., 282nn111
Howell, J. E., 28nn62, 29nn106
Howell, R. A., 31nn150, 350nn130
Hrebiniak, L. G., 29nn85, 69nn170
Hsieh, Y.-J., 223nn98
Hsieh-Lung, L., 281nn107
Hsu, C.-W., 250nn1
Hsu, I.-C., 252nn55
Hsu, L.-C., 251nn36
Hsuan, J., 138nn95
Hu, S., 32nn167
Huan, C.-J., 251nn19
Huang, C.-H., 223nn88
Huang, L.-Y., 223nn98
Huang, X., 404nn48
Huang, Y.-C., 367nn14, 369nn53
Huang, Z., 347nn60
Huber, G. P., 101nn2
Huey, J., 138nn73
Huff, A. S., 105nn131
Huff, L., 316nn105
Hughes, A., 280nn65
Hughes, D. E., 370nn93
Hulland, J., 255nn134
Hult, G. T. M., 29nn103, 104nn100, 312nn3, 317nn126
Hultink, E. J., 370nn99
Humphery-Jenner, M. L., 281nn97, 345nn16
Hung, J.-H., 255nn128, 256nn138, 279nn58
Hung, S.-W., 253nn78

Hunt, M. S., 104nn128
Hunton, J. E., 350nn134
Huse, M., 64nn63, 344nn7, 347nn66
Huselid, M. A., 69nn178
Hussey, D., 169nn37
Hutzschenreuter, T., 32nn174, 253nn78
Huyghebaert, N., 199nn87
Hyland, P., 370nn89

Iannotta, G., 346nn47
Iaquito, A. L., 64nn43
Ignatius, A., 344nn2
Im, K. S., 222nn63
Immelt, Jeff, 49, 66nn90
Inagaki, K., 279nn40
Indro, D. C., 348nn85
Ingeelsson, P., 198nn75
Ingley, C., 347nn70
Ingram, P., 137nn56
Inkpen, A. C., 28nn50, 313nn24, 314nn53, 314nn64, 315nn68, 315nn70, 315nn73, 318nn149, 349nn110, 349nn120
Insinga, R. C., 139nn98
Ireland, R. D., 26nn2, 28nn52, 29nn90, 29nn105, 30nn116, 30nn123, 32nn174, 63nn20, 66nn99, 66nn100, 67nn134, 68nn149, 100nn1, 101nn14, 101nn16, 103nn72, 103nn74, 103nn80, 104nn120, 105nn137, 114, 123, 124, 135nn5, 135nn8, 135nn22, 136nn43, 137nn51, 137nn59, 145, 150, 156, 168nn3, 168nn9, 169nn22, 169nn50, 170nn66, 195nn7, 197nn60, 198nn79, 220nn7, 221nn39, 221nn87, 223nn104, 251nn25, 251nn26, 255nn125, 278nn5, 279nn38, 279nn42, 279nn46, 279nn47, 279nn54, 280nn66, 280nn86, 281nn90, 281nn92, 281nn99, 281nn100,

281nn101, 293, 297, 300, 315nn90, 316nn106, 316nn108, 317nn132, 367nn4, 367nn5, 367nn7, 367nn13, 368nn29, 369nn56, 369nn59, 370nn69, 370nn74, 371nn112, 371nn120, 371nn122
Irwin, Richard D., 169nn36
Isaak, R., 315nn84
Isobe, T., 314nn43
Ito, K., 317nn128
Itoh, H., 251nn29
Ivancevich, J. M., 252nn65
Iverson, R., 282nn121
Iyer, B., 27nn21, 196nn33

Jackson, A., 348nn96, 349nn110
Jackson, E. M., 347nn72
Jackson, G., 345nn16
Jackson, S. E., 63nn18, 137nn56
Jacobides, M. G., 253nn77
Jacobson, K. J. L., 62nn5
Jacoby, S. M., 102nn52, 347nn59, 349nn111
Jacque, L. L., 318nn147
Jagersma, P. K., 316nn104
Jain, S., 147, 371nn130
Jakobsen, J., 102nn56
Jan-Benedict, E. M., 27nn38
Janney, J. J., 168nn9, 256nn142
Jansen, J. P., 64nn51
Jantunen, A., 279nn42
Jargon, J., 26nn12, 140nn122
Jarrar, N., 69nn178
Jarvis, O., 371nn129
Jarzemsky, M., 26nn12
Javidan, M., 312nn5
Jawahar, D., 350nn131
Jawahar, M., 101nn24
Jayachandran, S., 222nn72
Jayanti, R. K., 26nn15
Jayanti, S.V., 26nn15
Jean, R.-J., 104nn116
Jenkins, M., 197nn41
Jensen, M., 346nn35
Jensen, M. C., 31nn131, 139nn119, 254nn107, 255nn119, 278nn20, 280nn83, 345nn9, 346nn34, 348nn97, 349nn101

Jensen, Michael, 10, 29nn78
Jenster, P., 169nn37
Jeong, E., 282nn117
Jia, H., 171nn97
Jiang, C., 278nn29
Jiang, G.-L. F., 313nn24
Jiang, M. S., 220nn33
Jiang, P., 350nn127
Jiang, R. J., 220nn6, 224nn118
Jin, B., 313nn25
Jin, K., 136nn44
Jiraporn, P., 349nn104, 349nn108
Jo, H., 350nn133
Jobe, L. A., 253nn71
Jobs, Steve, 36, 68nn159, 333
Johannesson, J., 31nn151
Johhnson, Ronald, 53
Johnson,, J. L., 222nn80, 224nn122, 347nn62
Johnson, L. A., 403nn19, 403nn21
Johnson, M. W., 27nn45
Johnson, R. A., 64nn63, 65nn78, 69nn183, 103nn78, 254nn102, 279nn43, 279nn46, 281nn89, 281nn90, 282nn114, 282nn116, 282nn126, 282nn128, 317nn137, 345nn17, 345nn19, 346nn45, 347nn52, 347nn59, 347nn68, 348nn94, 369nn46, 369nn54, 369nn61, 371nn118
Johnson, S. G., 65nn77
Johnson N., 344nn5
Jones, C., 223nn99
Jones, G., 68nn153
Jones, T. M., 31nn132, 31nn143, 31nn148, 31nn149, 220nn10
Jordan, C., 199nn95
Jordan, S. J., 369nn47
Joshi, A. M., 221nn53
Joshi, A. W., 169nn29
Joshi, M., 68nn162
Joyce, W. F., 29nn85, 69nn170
Judge, W. Q., 64nn63, 67nn128, 67nn134, 318nn164
Junttila, M. A., 136nn39, 252nn41
Jwu-Rong, J., 281nn107

Kabir, R., 250nn11
Kabst, R., 318nn152
Kahan, M., 256nn142,
    256nn143
Kahn, R. L., 28nn73
Kahneman, D., 63nn22,
    63nn34, 64nn42
Kaipa, P., 30nn124
Kakabadse, A. P., 65nn82,
    65nn84
Kakabadse, N. K., 65nn82,
    65nn84, 345nn18
Kakabadse, P., 345nn18
Kale, P., 28nn51, 222nn79,
    224nn110, 224nn116,
    279nn48, 403nn31
Kallendar, P., 170nn75
Kalnins, A., 199nn99
Kamins, M. A., 169nn35
Kammel, B., 103nn94
Kan, O. B., 254nn110
Kandemir, D., 370nn74
Kang, W., 222nn72
Kanter, R. M., 69nn172,
    101nn6
Kaplan, N. S., 348nn75
Kaplan, R. S., 69nn177,
    69nn179, 69nn180,
    69nn182, 168nn2,
    196nn27, 198nn76
Karakaya, F., 199nn93
Karamanos, A. G., 370nn100
Karim, S., 251nn30
Kark, R., 68nn167
Karnani, A., 199nn96
Karnitschnig, M., 349nn115
Karreman, D., 138nn74
Karri, R., 350nn135
Kashyap, A. K., 349nn118
Kassinis, G., 64nn64, 68nn150,
    140nn121
Kasznik, R., 344nn5
Katila, R., 29nn90, 32nn175,
    136nn33, 279nn43
Kato, Y., 69nn175
Katz, D., 28nn73
Katz, M., 139nn99
Kaufman, A., 350nn132
Kaufmann, J., 347nn68,
    348nn87
Kaul, A., 29nn88, 279nn44,
    368nn27
Kay, N. M., 255nn131
Kayworth, T. K., 28nn52
Kazanjian, R. K., 253nn84
Keasler, T. R., 223nn103

Keats, B. W., 27nn42, 169nn38,
    169nn43, 252nn63
Kedia, S., 253nn92, 278nn31
Keen, C., 67nn124
Keenan, F., 348nn100
Keil, T., 65nn70, 139nn114
Keim, G. D., 31nn148,
    102nn50
Keller, J. J., 347nn72
Keller, S. B., 170nn52
Kelley, D., 370nn72
Kelley, L., 316nn105
Kelly, J., 282nn132
Kendall, B., 279nn36
Kenney, M., 281nn109
Kenny, G., 135nn11, 252nn49
Kerr, S., 68nn152
Kesmodel, D., 66nn113
Kesner, I. F., 197nn57
Kester, L., 370nn99
Kester, W. C., 403nn37
Ketchen, D. J., Jr., 29nn103,
    30nn109, 31nn129,
    32nn175, 101nn5,
    104nn100, 135nn5,
    135nn6, 135nn8,
    168nn2, 168nn3,
    197nn60, 222nn82,
    367nn5, 367nn13
Keuslin, W., 255nn133
Keyhani, M., 367nn17,
    368nn44, 371nn115
Khan, R., 347nn59
Khanna, P., 220nn21, 346nn29
Khanna, T., 27nn20, 254nn96,
    254nn100, 254nn101
Khavul, S., 314nn56
Kho, J., 140nn124
Khorana, A., 281nn89,
    282nn127, 282nn128
Kichtenthaler, U., 370nn83
Kiel, G. C., 345nn12
Kiessling, T., 67nn125
Kilbourne, L., 67nn138
Kilduff, G. J., 104nn124,
    196nn30
Kim, C., 317nn144
Kim, E. N., 255nn133
Kim, H., 65nn86, 169nn37,
    222nn58, 222nn59,
    223nn94, 254nn106,
    317nn127, 318nn157,
    318nn165, 345nn15,
    350nn137, 369nn60
Kim, J., 197nn59, 315nn87,
    345nn21

Kim, J.-J., 281nn91, 281nn107
Kim, J.-W., 371nn110
Kim, K., 251nn39
Kim, K.-H., 196nn22
Kim, Y. J., 315nn93
Kimble, C., 170nn55
Kimes, M., 220nn22
King, A. W., 138nn76, 219nn3
King, R., 101nn29
Kini, O., 348nn97
Kinicki, A. J., 62nn5
Kirca, A. H., 312nn3,
    317nn126
Kirkpatrick, S. A., 68nn148
Kiron, D., 68nn150
Kirsch, D. A., 169nn37
Kirsch, L. J., 69nn174
Kishinev, U., 26nn18
Kistruck, G. M., 198nn79,
    221nn87
Klein, A., 67nn131
Kleindienst, I., 32nn174
Kleinman, G., 345nn10
Klijn, E., 221nn36, 224nn115
Kline, D., 315nn90
Kline, J. P., 255nn116
Kline, M. J., 345nn8
Knight, D., 62nn13, 64nn50
Knight, G. A., 316nn107
Knoedler, J. T., 254nn112
Knolt, A. M., 255nn135
Knyght, R., 65nn82, 345nn18
Kobeissi, N., 135nn9
Kochhar, R., 137nn51,
    368nn43
Kock, A., 64nn46
Kogut, B., 403nn16
Kohtamaki, M., 139nn104,
    198nn61, 367nn2
Koissa, N., 312nn1
Kolev, K., 196nn16
Koller, T., 282nn123
Kono, T., 252nn49
Konopaske, R., 252nn65
Kopalle, P., 27nn45
Korza, M. P., 27nn20
Kosnik, R., 348nn94, 348nn99,
    349nn106
Kostopoulos, K., 283nn137
Kotabe, M., 138nn88,
    139nn99, 170nn68,
    252nn55, 278nn29,
    313nn15
Kotha, S., 26nn7, 31nn148
Kotter, J., 67nn132
Kowitt, B., 65nn85

Kraaijenbrink, J., 26nn8
Kraatz, M. S., 135nn18, 283nn136
Kracaw, W., 348nn97
Kramer, M. R., 139nn120
Kramer, R. J., 315nn71
Kretschmer, T., 197nn43
Kriaucinus, A. P., 30nn114, 195nn1
Kriauciunas, A. P., 314nn45
Kriger, M., 30nn124
Krippendorff, K., 367nn16
Krishna, A., 199nn95
Krishnamurti, C., 347nn63
Krishnan, H. A., 282nn120, 283nn136
Krishnan, R., 224nn126
Krishnan, S., 28nn51
Kroeger, F., 278nn6
Kroll, M., 30nn119, 346nn36, 347nn66
Krug, J. A., 280nn72, 348nn85
Kruger, M. W., 199nn95
Krühler, M., 282nn125
Kruschwitz, N., 68nn150
Kruse, T. A., 282nn116
Krychowski, C., 32nn178, 402nn11, 403nn26
Kubo, K., 349nn118, 349nn124
Kuckertz, A., 139nn104, 198nn61, 367nn2
Kuemmerle, W., 104nn126, 313nn13, 367nn15
Kukalis, S., 104nn122
Kumar, M. V. S., 220nn31, 255nn135
Kumar, N., 134nn4, 253nn70
Kumar, P., 282nn133
Kumar, S., 220nn25
Kumaraswamy, A., 371nn130
Kunc, M. H., 30nn112, 197nn35
Kune, M. H., 199nn108
Kuo, Y.-C., 255nn128, 256nn138, 279nn58
Kuratko, D. F., 28nn52, 101nn16
Kusisto, L., 255nn129
Kuss, M., 103nn91
Kuye, O. L., 402nn9
Kwak, M., 197nn49
Kwan, M., 278nn2
Kwok, C. C. Y., 102nn61
Kwon, S.-W., 68nn160

Kyaw, N. A., 253nn89

Laamanen, T., 65nn70, 139nn114
Lado, A., 346nn36
Lado, A. A., 30nn119, 220nn11
Lafley, A. G., 62nn1, 65nn83
Lafontaine, F., 222nn84
Lages, C. R., 315nn84
Lages, L. F., 315nn84
Lai, H.-C., 252nn54
Laitnen, L., 199nn114
Lakshman, C. C., 280nn71
Lakshman, N., 254nn98
Lamb, C. W., Jr, 169nn27
Lamey, L., 27nn38
Lamont, B. T., 279nn55, 316nn113
Lamper, C. M., 370nn68
Lampert, C., 280nn65
Lan, L. L., 256nn138, 345nn26
Landauer, S., 68nn152
Landstrom, H., 315nn90
Lane, P. J., 103nn81, 170nn87, 221nn42, 224nn109, 280nn78
Langer, E. J., 63nn35
Lango, B., 314nn37
Larcker, D. F., 170nn58, 349nn105
Larimo, L., 313nn29
Larsson, R., 315nn96
Lauche, K., 370nn99
Laursen, K., 134nn3, 370nn84, 371nn123
Laux, J. A., 28nn54
Laverty, K. J., 69nn176
Lavie, D., 32nn157, 68nn146, 220nn21, 221nn47, 221nn52, 224nn119
Lawler, E. E., III, 65nn79, 347nn69
Lawless, M. W., 68nn152
Lawrence, P. R., 169nn36, 169nn44, 253nn70, 370nn90
Lawrence, T. B., 314nn66, 371nn130
Lay, Kenneth, 56
Le Bon, J., 370nn93
Le Breton-Miller, I., 345nn24, 346nn49
Le Roux, J.-M., 278nn18, 280nn80

Leahy, D., 222nn69
Learned, E. P., 28nn67
Learned, Edmund, 9
Leca, B., 371nn130
Lederman, M., 253nn73
Lee, C., 30nn113
Lee, C.-H., 27nn21, 196nn33
Lee, C.-Y., 197nn59, 371nn114
Lee, D., 253nn85, 281nn110
Lee, G. K., 279nn41
Lee, H., 101nn3, 103nn74, 137nn48, 137nn51, 195nn3, 195nn9, 197nn51, 197nn60, 254nn101, 314nn58, 317nn130, 370nn71, 370nn74, 371nn124
Lee, H.-U., 282nn117
Lee, K., 30nn113, 250nn4
Lee, K-H., 371nn110
Lee, M., 67nn138, 371nn116, 371nn117
Lee, P. M., 136nn44, 283nn136, 345nn28
Lee, R. P., 224nn122
Lee, R. P.-W., 222nn80
Lee, S., 254nn109
Lee, S. H., 27nn39, 196nn19, 371nn103
Lee, T.-Y., 252nn54
Lee, W., 349nn107
Lee, Y., 101nn19
Lei, D., 26nn3, 66nn99
Leiblein, M. J., 30nn119, 32nn179, 138nn94, 403nn13, 403nn14
Leidtka, J. M., 32nn162
Leiponen, A., 371nn125
Leiponen, A. E., 222nn62
Leleux, B., 196nn17
Lemmon, M. L., 256nn144, 348nn92
Lengnick-Hall, C. A., 66nn118
Lenox, M.J., 31nn134
Lentz, P., 104nn118
Lenway, S. A., 314nn45
Leonard-Barton, D., 139nn103, 370nn74
Leone, M. I., 368nn28
Leonel, J. N., 313nn13
Lerner, J., 283nn135, 283nn141
Lertwongsatien, C, 30nn121
Leslie, T. W. K., 223nn91
Lester, R. H., 346nn49
Letzing, J., 348nn77

Levesque, M., 137nn62, 367nn18, 368nn31
Levie, J., 368nn45
Levin, D. Z., 136nn48
Levin, I. M., 68nn151
Levinson, D., 198nn67
Levinthal, D. A., 135nn15, 168nn1, 255nn123, 403nn46
Levitas, E., 103nn87, 170nn68, 315nn97, 316nn104, 371nn113
Lev-Ram, M., 222nn64
Lewellen, W., 250nn8
Lewin, A. Y., 137nn55, 314nn58
Lewis, M. W., 369nn68
Ley, B., 68nn168
Lhuillery, S., 347nn68
Li, D., 171nn95, 316nn106, 371nn112
Li, H., 313nn27
Li, J., 223nn102, 316nn104, 318nn157
Li, J. J., 224nn123
Li, L., 314nn51, 314nn56, 318nn155, 318nn159
Li, M., 346nn36
Li, S., 102nn59, 316nn123, 317nn131
Li, X., 281nn111, 282nn126
Li, Y., 104nn97, 278nn18, 313nn27, 318nn155, 371nn103
Liang, Y., 250nn9
Liaw, Y.-C., 252nn54
Licht, A. N., 29nn79, 135nn10, 139nn106
Lichtenthaler, U., 138nn78, 91, 371nn105
Lictschert, R. J., 63nn15
Lieberman, M. B., 198nn63, 279nn41
Liebeskind, J. P., 282nn131
Liedtka, J. M., 26nn10
Liesch, P. W., 316nn107
Liker, J. K., 220nn15
Lilja, J., 198nn75
Lim, E. N.-K., 281nn110, 282nn122
Lim, S., 404nn50
Limpaphayom, P., 350nn127
Lin, C. A., 313nn18, 371nn114
Lin, H., 67nn133

Lin, H.-C., 27nn23, 101nn10
Lin, J.-R., 251nn19
Lin, X., 220nn33
Lin, Y., 220nn4
Lin, Z., 220nn4, 280nn62, 281nn102
Lindeman, S., 368nn22
Linderman, K., 171nn102
Ling, Y., 32nn168
Linna, P., 368nn22
Lioukas, S., 103nn96
Lisboa, J., 402nn5
Liu, C., 169nn33
Liu, F. H., 252nn56
Liu, H.-Y., 250nn1, 252nn56
Liu, R., 138nn94
Liu, X., 65nn69, 65nn72
Liu, Y., 65nn68, 252nn41, 349nn104
Livengood, R. S., 402nn10
Livnat, J., 254nn95
Lo, H.-P., 31nn128
Locke, E. A., 68nn148
Lockett, A., 221nn40
Lockwood, C. A., 30nn120
Lohr, S., 196nn24
Lopes, E. J., 255nn117
Lopez-Duarte, C., 222nn65
Lord, M. D., 102nn53
Lorsch, J. W., 31nn133, 65nn72, 169nn36, 169nn44, 256nn142, 370nn90
Lovallo, D., 63nn34, 64nn42, 139nn115, 197nn41, 219nn3
Love, E. G., 282nn119, 283nn136
Lowe, J., 253nn91
Lowe, R. A., 63nn37
Lowenstein, L., 255nn120
Lu, J. W., 103nn78, 223nn97, 279nn39, 315nn98, 317nn129
Lu, Qi, 41
Lu, W.-M., 253nn78
Lu, Y., 27nn48, 222nn69
Lubatkin, M. H., 32nn168, 64nn57, 252nn48, 254nn111, 255nn115
Lubit, R., 136nn37
Lublin, J. S., 64nn61, 66nn112, 199nn91
Lucier, C., 367nn6
Ludema, R. D., 314nn40

Luehrman, T., 403nn43
Luffman, G., 168nn7
Lukasik, M. A., 64nn47
Lumineau, F., 345nn28, 371nn111
Lumpkin, G. T., 67nn134, 67nn136, 140nn129, 169nn18, 170nn86, 367nn9, 368nn37
Lund, S., 403nn29
Lundquist, G., 32nn168
Lunimeau, F., 224nn109
Luo, Y., 101nn23, 103nn86, 170nn62, 170nn74, 224nn123, 314nn52, 315nn86, 316nn103, 316nn123, 318nn156
Lupton, N. C., 224nn124
Lursinap, C., 220nn23
Lusch, R. F., 169nn26
Lyles, M. A., 103nn81, 223nn95, 224nn109
Lynch, D. F., 170nn52
Lynch, S., 369nn50

Ma, R., 367nn14, 369nn53
McAdam, M., 371nn131
McAfee, A., 28nn53, 171nn96
McCabe, K., 138nn79
McCann, B. T., 104nn108
McCardle K. F., 279nn48
McCarter, M. W., 403nn30
McCarthy, D. J., 318nn151
McCarthy, M. J., 103nn70, 103nn79
McClellan, J., 29nn79
Maccoby, M., 31nn151
McCrea, E. A., 222nn85
McDaniel, C., 169nn27
McDonald, M. L., 345nn29
McDonald, R., 29nn90, 32nn175
McDonnell, J., 221nn88
McDonough, E. F., III, 67nn133
McDougall, P.P., 104nn105, 282nn134, 369nn57
McDowell, M., 222nn73
McElheran, K. S., 369nn67
McEvily, B., 224nn123
McEvily, S. K., 138nn79, 251nn26
MacFadyen, K., 279nn33
McFadyen, M. A., 137nn63
McFarland, L., 255nn124

McGahan, A. M., 26nn5, 26nn7, 29nn91, 29nn103, 103nn96

McGee, J. E., 169nn18, 170nn86, 196nn21

McGrath, R. G., 195nn2, 314nn57, 368nn36, 370nn80, 403nn44

McGuire, J., 105nn133, 196nn13

Machold, S., 64nn63, 344nn7

Mackelprang, A. W., 170nn94

McKendrick, D. G., 314nn60

McKenna, T. M., 101nn16

MacKenzi, W. J., 66nn115

Mackey, A., 30nn107, 32nn156

Mackey, T. B., 32nn156

McKinley, W., 104nn98, 282nn118

McKinnon, R., 102nn47

McKnight, W. L., 370nn82

McLaughlin, G. L., 101nn24

McMahan, G. C., 66nn121, 137nn53, 169nn18

MacMillian, I. C., 9, 28nn71, 28nn74, 184, 198nn84, 314nn57, 368nn36, 370nn80

McMullen, J. S., 367nn10

McNamara, G., 27nn22, 196nn16

McNamee, M., 345nn10

McNeill, L. S., 223nn91

McNulty, T., 347nn67

McVea, J., 26nn9, 139nn108

McWilliams, A., 136nn27, 139nn106, 312nn6

McWilliams, V., 346nn44

Madhavan, R., 196nn18, 199nn100, 253nn85, 281nn110

Madhok, A., 223nn104, 367nn17, 368nn44, 371nn115

Madsen, T. L., 104nn113

Madupu, V., 315nn88

Magnan, G. M., 220nn5

Magretta, J., 64nn54

Mahlich, J. C., 104nn106, 315nn81

Mahmood, I. P., 136nn34, 221nn51

Mahnke, V., 138nn95

Mahoney, J. T., 345nn21, 404nn50

Maia-Ramires, E. L., 346nn35, 346nn45

Mainardi, C., 280nn67, 281nn106

Mair, J., 281nn92, 283nn140

Maitland, E., 402nn7

Maitlis, S., 139nn118

Majchrzak, A., 370nn87

Makadok, R., 104nn109, 197nn50

Makhija, M., 27nn39

Makino, S., 313nn24, 314nn43, 317nn140

Makri, M., 170nn87, 221nn42, 280nn66, 280nn78

Malak, N., 137nn61, 138nn92

Malburg, C., 170nn51

Malhotra, D., 67nn144, 139nn118, 345nn28, 371nn111

Malhotra, M. K., 170nn94

Malik, M. A. R., 403nn23

Malik, T., 403nn26

Malnight, T. W., 314nn63

Malshe, A., 370nn93

Malter, A. J., 169nn20

Manev, I. M., 318nn161

Manigart, S., 221nn40

Manikutty, S., 254nn98

Mankins, M. C., 26nn11

Manolova, T. S., 29nn98, 254nn99

Mansfield, I, 136nn46

Manso, G., 344nn5, 348nn92, 370nn79, 370nn81

Manyika, J., 102nn37, 102nn43, 403nn30

Manz, C. C., 28nn51, 66nn93

Marcel, J. J., 136nn45, 195nn6, 250nn10, 402nn10

March, J. G., 28nn70, 63nn25, 63nn27, 63nn31, 253nn84

Marchica, M., 345nn22

Marcus, A. A., 222nn77

Marin, P. L., 197nn33

Marino, L. D., 368nn36

Markham, G. D., 196nn14

Markides, C. C., 30nn113, 250nn4, 281nn89, 282nn129

Markle, A. B., 139nn117

Markóczy, L., 62nn13, 281nn107

Marks, M. L., 252nn44, 278nn2, 281nn104, 281nn105

Marlow, S., 371nn131

Marmenout, K., 280nn73

Marshall, V., 283nn139

Martens, R., 224nn110

Martin, J. A., 69nn171, 281nn93, 348nn76

Martin, R., 348nn89

Martin, X., 224nn126, 252nn55

Martynova, M., 348nn94, 349nn112

Marvel, M. R., 103nn75, 368nn41, 369nn56

Mas-Ruiz, F., 105nn129, 196nn17, 198nn83

Massa, M., 253nn86, 254nn106

Massey, P., 222nn73

Massini, S., 137nn55, 314nn58

Mathis, J., 318nn148

Mathur, I., 346nn46

Mathur, S., 27nn48

Mathys, N. J., 68nn152

Matlack, C., 197nn44

Matsusake, J. G., 255nn132

Matthyssens, P., 64nn62, 138nn95, 224nn110

Mattila, A. S., 197nn37

Mattioli, D., 135nn19, 135nn20

Matusik, S. F., 251nn26

Maurer, C. C., 68nn168, 136nn27

Maurer, H., 348nn93

Mauri, A. J., 313nn21

Mayer, D., 281nn109

Mayer, N. D., 63nn38

Mayer, R. C., 68nn167, 224nn127

Maznevski, M. L., 32nn157, 64nn56

Mazure, T. C., 68nn155

Mazzola P., 136nn33, 168nn2

Meadows, M. M., 69nn177

Means, G., 346nn49

Mecham, R. L., III, 312nn6

Meckling, W. H., 31nn131, 254nn107

Meckling, William, 10, 29nn78

Meek, W. R., 223nn90

Mehdudia, S., 199nn105

Meier, M., 371nn113

Mellahi, K., 317nn146

Melnikas, B., 251nn40

Melnyk, S. A., 370nn70

Mena, J. A., 317nn126

Mendelow, A. L., 403nn44
Mention, A.-L., 220nn18
Mentzer, J. T., 104nn112, 370nn86
Merchant, H., 254nn111, 255nn115
Mercken, L. F., 32nn154, 350nn131
Merriman, K. K., 350nn134
Meulbroek, L. K., 348nn88
Meuleman, M., 221nn40, 223nn97
Meyer, K. E., 28nn60, 101nn4, 316nn115, 316nn120, 349nn126
Meyer, M. W., 101nn11
Mezias, J. M., 135nn17, 168nn4, 223nn100
Mian, S., 348nn97
Michael, S. C., 223nn88, 223nn91
Michaels, D., 66nn113
Michel, J. G., 27nn23, 101nn10
Mickeviciene, M., 219nn2
Mifflin, K. E., 67nn138
Miguel, 346nn45
Mihi-Ramirez, A., 29nn105
Miles, G., 370nn69
Millan, K., 63nn29
Miller, C. C., 29nn90, 64nn59, 68nn152, 168nn9, 251nn17
Miller, D., 103nn88, 253nn91, 318nn160, 345nn24, 346nn49
Miller, D. J., 27nn44, 66nn92, 67nn138, 196nn12, 198nn72, 199nn86, 252nn57, 313nn25, 317nn128, 317nn141, 318nn159
Miller, J. C., 317nn126
Miller, K. D., 32nn156, 139nn115, 403nn17, 403nn42
Miller, S. R., 313nn31, 314nn45, 348nn85
Miller, T., 103nn76, 312nn4, 314nn39, 318nn150, 318nn153
Milliot, J., 26nn12
Mills, S., 26nn13, 220nn19
Min, J., 197nn34
Minichilli, A., 64nn63, 344nn7
Minniti, M., 367nn14, 367nn18
Mintzberg, Henry, 10, 28nn74, 29nn75, 29nn76

Miron-Spektor, E., 135nn18
Mirvis, P. H., 252nn44, 278nn2, 281nn105
Misangyi, V. F., Jr., 30nn124, 348nn76
Mische, M. A., 69nn182
Mishra, A., 254nn97
Mitchell, J. R., 199nn107
Mitchell, R. K., 344nn6
Mitchell, W., 28nn60, 100nn1, 136nn36, 195nn10, 221nn45, 221nn47, 221nn57, 252nn55, 278nn30, 279nn52
Mitra, S., 280nn61, 346nn40
Mitsuhashi, H., 169nn37, 196nn31, 197nn34, 221nn49, 223nn102
Mitteness, C., 368nn35
Miyajima, H., 349nn118
Mo, J. P. T., 138nn81
Moeller, M., 67nn125
Moesel, D. D., 279nn43, 279nn46, 345nn17, 346nn45, 348nn94, 371nn118
Moffett, S., 102nn35
Mohama, O., 224nn114
Mohamed, Z. A., 196nn11
Mohammed, S., 66nn110, 67nn139
Mohanty, R. P., 136nn30
Mohr, A. T., 316nn101
Mohr, J. J., 170nn53
Mok, V., 198nn80, 312nn6
Mol, M. J., 137nn49, 138nn88, 138nn95, 139nn99
Molin, A., 26nn12
Monczka, R. M., 27nn20
Monga, V., 66nn112
Monteiro, P. R. R., 313nn13
Montgomery, C. A., 29nn97
Montogermery, D. B., 198nn63
Montoya-Weiss, M. M., 370nn78
Moody, A., 101nn12
Moon, C. W., 252nn43, 280nn78
Moon, M., 404nn48
Mooney, A. C., 347nn61
Moore, C. B., 345nn13
Moore, J. H., 135nn18
Moqbel, M., 30nn121, 251nn20
Mor, M. L., 171nn105

Moran, P., 345nn28
More, P. H. B., 370nn87
Morecroft, J. D. W., 30nn112, 197nn35, 199nn108
Moreton, B., 62nn3
Morgan, A., 198nn78
Morgan, S., 347nn53
Morita, Akio, 34, 35, 62nn4
Morrison, A. J., 315nn70
Morrow, J. L., Jr., 282nn114, 282nn116
Morse, E. A., 314nn66
Mortensen, M., 370nn97
Mortimer, T., 28nn57
Moschieri, C., 278nn12, 281nn92, 282nn127, 283nn140
Moses, A., 370nn92
Mosey, S., 137nn60
Moskowitz, G. T., 403nn47
Moss, M., 105nn141
Mossholder, K., 139nn117
Mountford, A., 102nn42
Mowday, R. T., 68nn169
Mowery, D. C., 220nn28
Mudambi, R., 101nn4, 170nn68, 313nn15, 315nn69
Mudambi, S. M., 221nn40
Mudd, S., 318nn148
Muehlfeld, K., 135nn14, 135nn22
Mueller, J., 347nn70
Muhanna, W. A., 137nn65
Mulcahy, Anne, 46
Mullineux, A., 345nn16
Munir, K., 139nn120, 370nn91
Muñoz-Bullon, F., 282nn117
Mura, R., 345nn22
Murnighan, J. K., 136nn48
Murphy, K. J., 139nn119
Murphy, P. J., 222nn77
Murpy, P. E., 68nn169
Murray, J., 278nn29
Murtha, T. P., 314nn45
Muslu, V., 348nn78
Muthusamy, S., 350nn131
Myer, K. E., 316nn122
Myers, M. B., 104nn112, 370nn86
Myers, R., 281nn108
Myers, S. C., 403nn31, 403nn32, 403nn36
Mykolaityte, V., 219nn1

Nachum, L., 135nn16, 220nn9, 313nn22, 314nn47, 315nn81
Nadkarni, S., 27nn27, 30nn107, 66nn110, 369nn58
Nagurney, A., 255nn130
Naiker, V., 103nn93
Nain, A., 278nn27
Nair, A., 26nn7, 138nn69
Nakazato, M., 349nn125
Nalebuff, B., 104nn125
Nambisan, S., 254nn105
Nandkumar, A., 135nn6, 170nn86
Nankervis, J. C., 251nn21
Napoleon, K., 67nn126, 67nn129
Naraasayya, V., 28nn51
Narasimhan, O., 104nn120
Narayanan, V. K., 101nn29, 102nn44, 103nn96
Narula, R., 101nn4
Nason, R. S., 104nn99, 136nn24
Naudé, P., 219nn3
Navarro, P., 102nn46
Navickas, V., 219nn1
Navis, C., 367nn3
Nazir, M. S., 255nn122
Ndofor, H., 64nn59, 66nn106, 135nn23, 196nn14, 196nn18, 196nn22, 198nn70, 199nn84, 199nn88, 199nn97
Neal, W. D., 169nn27
Neely, J., 281nn106
Neff, J., 199nn92
Nelly, J., 280nn67
Nembhard, D. A., 402nn8
Nerer, A., 197nn60
Nerkar, A., 28nn51, 101nn15, 221nn53
Neville, B., 68nn146
Newman, K. L., 103nn84
Ng, E., 62nn11
Nguyen, D. K., 103nn92
Nguyen, H. N., 67nn139
Nguyen, H. V., 316nn120
Nicholson, G. J., 345nn12
Nickel, N., 255nn123
Nielson, A. P., 280nn76
Nieto, M. J., 371nn126
Nijssen, E. J., 104nn118
Nippa, M., 279nn52, 282nn125, 346nn36

Nisar, T. M., 223nn89
Nixon, R. D., 104nn103, 136nn31, 282nn117, 367nn6
Nobeissi, N., 134nn1
Nobel, R., 316nn111
Nobre, F. S., 30nn120
Nocera, G., 346nn47
Noe, R. A., 137nn56
Nohria, N., 66nn117, 136nn41, 282nn119
Nonnemaker, L., 196nn13
Noorderhaven, N. G., 224nn126
Nord, W. R., 63nn30
Nordqvist, M., 64nn63, 344nn7
Norman, P. M., 105nn137, 223nn106, 368nn30
Northcott, D., 347nn74
Northcraft, G. B., 403nn30
Norton, D. P., 69nn177, 69nn179, 69nn180, 69nn182, 168nn2, 198nn76
Novak, S., 253nn75
Nowland, J., 345nn24
Nozawa, K., 27nn35
Numagami, T., 314nn58
Nutt, P. C., 135nn12
Nyaw, M.-K., 316nn103
Nyberg, A. J., 255nn136, 282nn121

Öberg, C., 278nn3
O'Brien, J. P., 253nn80, 255nn131, 346nn30, 368nn21
O'Bryne, F., 403nn38
O'Connell, A., 347nn71
O'Connor, J. P., Jr., 350nn136
O'Donnell, E., 169nn19
O'Donnell, M., 253nn90, 348nn86
O'Donnell, S., 348nn83
Oetzel, J., 27nn33
Ogden, D., 65nn89
Oghojafor, B. A., 402nn9
O'Grady, M. A., 103nn85
Oh, C. H., 27nn33
Oh, H., 222nn63
Oh, I.-S., 26nn10, 32nn161
Oh, W., 222nn63
Okhmatovskiy, I., 350nn135
O'Leary, M. B., 370nn97
Olexa, R., 170nn93

Olgun, H., 102nn45
Olian, J. D., 62nn13, 64nn50
Oliver, C., 222nn75
Olsen, J. M., 313nn34
Omi, Y., 349nn122
O'Neill, H. M., 135nn21, 169nn38, 169nn41, 169nn43, 252nn63
O'Neill, J. W., 197nn37
O'Neill, R. M., 67nn139
Onwumere, R., 27nn38
Opsahl, T., 67nn132, 138nn74, 367nn2, 402nn1
Ordanini, A., 102nn66
Orden, E., 347nn65
O'Reilly, C. A., III, 169nn34
Ormazabal, G., 349nn105
Ormiston, M. E., 64nn58, 139nn121
Ortqvist, D., 221nn56
Osawa, J., 138nn85, 138nn86, 279nn40
Osborne, J. D., 105nn134
O'Sullivan, A., 370nn91
Ouyang, H., 220nn24
Overall, J., 347nn74
Oviatt, B. M., 138nn91, 223nn95, 369nn57, 371nn109
Ovide, S., 138nn85
Oxley, J., 220nn9, 220nn28
Oxman, J. A., 66nn115
Ozcan, P., 224nn117
Ozer, G., 30nn122
Ozkan, G. F., 67nn126, 67nn129
Ozkan, N., 348nn81
Ozment, J., 170nn52
Ozturan, M., 30nn128

Paartanen, J., 369nn66
Pae, J., 350nn136
Paez, B. L., 255nn116
Paik, Y., 317nn143
Palacios-Marqués, D., 30nn127
Palank, J., 26nn12
Palazzo, G., 102nn51, 139nn113
Palepu, K. G., 27nn20, 254nn96, 254nn100, 254nn101
Palia, K. A., 137nn59
Palich, L. E., 251nn17
Palmatier, R. W., 30nn122, 250nn11

Palmer, T. B., 29nn103, 104nn100
Palmeri, C., 348nn100
Palmisano, Samuel, 21, 42, 45
Palona, I., 31nn151
Pan, Y., 104nn104, 220nn33, 313nn33, 316nn106
Pandey, A., 101nn2
Pant, L. W., 68nn168
Pantzalis, C., 314nn37, 314nn38
Parent, J. D., 66nn95
Park, B. I., 224nn114, 278nn4
Park, B.-J., 199nn115, 220nn17, 254nn101
Park, C., 252nn46, 255nn122, 279nn53
Park, D., 63nn15, 67nn138, 103nn86, 282nn120, 283nn136
Park, J. W., 199nn100
Park, K., 254nn109
Park, N., 168nn4
Park, S. H., 26nn19, 63nn40, 101nn23, 103nn86, 197nn43
Park, W., 279nn46, 279nn47
Parmar, B. L., 31nn149, 220nn11, 224nn127
Parmigini, A., 28nn60
Parush, A., 253nn83
Passeriello, C., 138nn68
Patel, P. C., 171nn95
Patelli, L., 139nn107
Patsalos-Fox, M., 347nn72
Patton, K. M., 101nn16
Patzelt, H., 32nn176
Paul, H., 349nn118
Pauwels, P., 138nn95
Pavelin, S., 222nn69
Payne, A., 138nn83, 139nn105
Pearce, C. L., 62nn13, 64nn50
Pearce, J. A., II, 337
Pearson, J. M., 198nn77
Pedace, R., 403nn19
Pedersen, T., 101nn4, 134nn3, 136nn43, 368nn42, 370nn84
Pedrini, M., 139nn107
Pe'er, A., 102nn60
Peeters, C., 137nn55
Pegels, C., 64nn46, 138nn87
Pehrsson, A., 252nn42, 253nn66
Pelled, L. H., 64nn56, 102nn41
Peloza, J., 67nn142, 139nn105

Peng, M. W., 105nn131, 250nn4, 280nn62, 281nn102, 312nn4, 314nn58, 315nn97, 316nn102, 316nn115, 345nn28, 350nn128, 403nn36
Penner-Hahn, J., 317nn136, 317nn138
Pennings, J. M., 30nn113
Penny, T., 68nn165
Penrose, E. T., 14
Penrose, Edith, 30nn108
Perersen, T., 317nn142
Perez, L., 137nn56
Perez, P. D., 27nn27, 369nn58
Perez-Luno, A., 197nn55, 367nn6
Perez-Nordtvedt, L., 314nn56
Perrone, V., 224nn123
Perryman, A. A., 223nn91, 223nn92
Perryy, M. Z., 312nn3, 317nn126
Peteraf, M., 105nn132, 135nn23
Petersen, B., 315nn95
Petersen, K. J., 104nn117, 313nn21
Peterson, S. J., 62nn6
Petitt, B. S. P., 346nn36
Petkova, A. P., 31nn152
Petrick, J. A., 68nn167
Petrova, M., 337
Petruzzelli, A. M., 222nn62
Pettigrew, A., 66nn99, 314nn58
Pettit, J., 198nn69
Pfarrer, M. D., 199nn89
Pfeffer, J., 66nn118, 66nn121, 169nn34, 171nn101, 281nn94
Pfeffer, Jeffrey, 9–10, 28nn72
Phan, P. H., 196nn14, 282nn133, 346nn47, 349nn111, 350nn128
Phatak, A. V., 313nn21
Phelps, C. C., 198nn63, 221nn50, 224nn127
Phelps C., 28nn50
Philip, M., 281nn104
Phillips, G., 252nn40, 280nn75
Phillips, N., 367nn1, 371nn129
Phillips, R. A., 26nn9, 28nn69, 31nn135, 31nn136, 31nn139, 31nn142, 66nn101, 220nn12, 350nn129

Pick, K., 256nn142
Picken, J. C., 64nn59, 137nn57, 139nn101
Pickford, J., 403nn13
Pidun, U., 279nn52, 282nn125, 346nn36
Piepenbrink, A., 316nn101
Piercy, N. F., 32nn159
Pigman, G. A., 317nn146
Pil, F. K., 198nn71
Pinch S., 197nn41
Pine, B. J., II, 104nn110
Pinsonneault, A., 32nn165, 222nn63
Pirson, M., 67nn144, 139nn118
Pisano, G., 26nn4, 279nn38
Pisano, V., 280nn69, 316nn108, 316nn110
Pistre, N., 252nn56
Pitts, C. G. C., 403nn45
Plambeck, J., 279nn59
Plambeck, N., 198nn76
Plehn-Dujowich, J. M., 254nn94
Ployhart, R. E., 66nn115
Poliodoro, F., 195nn2, 195nn10
Pollitte, W. A., 317nn126
Pollock, T. G., 63nn39, 63nn40, 136nn44, 199nn89
Pons, V., 278nn31
Poppo, L., 224nn123
Porac, J. F., 63nn39
Porath, C., 32nn170
Porras, J. I., 68nn151
Porrini, P, 281nn102
Porter, A. L., 103nn71
Porter, M. E., 26nn5, 26nn7, 29nn92, 29nn99, 29nn101, 29nn102, 29nn103, 104nn127, 105nn136, 110, 136nn25, 138nn80, 138nn84, 139nn120, 145, 150, 156, 168nn5, 168nn12, 169nn13, 169nn14, 169nn15, 169nn16, 169nn17, 169nn24, 169nn47, 170nn63, 170nn65, 170nn76, 170nn77, 170nn79, 171nn106, 196nn19, 196nn21, 221nn38, 250nn2, 251nn39, 253nn87, 293–294, 315nn76
Porter, Michael, 12–13

Pose, H. E., 255nn135
Post, J. E., 63nn30
Pouder, R. W., 169nn41
Powell, G. N., 66nn95
Powell, R. G., 281nn97,
345nn17
Powell, T. C., 139nn100,
197nn41
Pozen, R. C., 344nn6
Praet, A., 282nn115
Prahalad, C. K., 32nn163,
66nn104, 137nn61,
138nn92
Prakhya, S., 314nn56
Prasad, S. B., 350nn137
Prasso, S., 279nn32
Prencipe, A., 371nn123
Prescott, J. E., 64nn52,
221nn39, 344nn7
Preston, L. E., 31nn148,
31nn149, 63nn30
Priem, R. L., 64nn59, 101nn17,
350nn136
Prince, J. T., 222nn70
Prior, V., 101nn13
Probst, G., 69nn181
Prusak, L., 67nn127
Pucik, V., 368nn40
Puck, J. F., 316nn101
Puffer, S. M., 103nn79,
318nn151
Puranam, P., 65nn83, 135nn4,
253nn70, 279nn48,
280nn61
Purda, L. D., 280nn85
Purkayastha, S., 254nn99
Purnell, L., 31nn149, 224nn127
Puthod, D., 224nn109
Pynnonen, M., 136nn29,
169nn32

Qiaozhuan, L., 64nn53
Qin, R., 402nn8
Qu, Z., 199nn99
Quah, P., 316nn113
Quélin, B. V., 32nn178,
402nn11, 403nn26
Qui, L. D., 223nn94
Quigley, T. J., 367nn1
Quinlan, J. P., 313nn12
Quinn, J. F., 68nn167
Quintens, L., 138nn95

Raes, A. M. L., 67nn139,
199nn85
Raffety, A. E., 281nn105

Ragatz, G. L., 313nn21
Ragozzino, R., 222nn65,
316nn120
Rahman, N., 223nn104
Raithel, S., 198nn77
Rajagopalan, N., 62nn10,
65nn88, 65nn89, 253nn73,
281nn91, 281nn107,
282nn113
Rajala, A., 369nn66
Rajan, M. V., 170nn58
Rajan, P., 222nn72
Rajan, R., 253nn92, 346nn38
Rajand, M., 282nn125
Rajiv, S., 104nn120
Ramamurthi, R., 312nn9
Ramamurthy, K., 27nn48
Ramamurti, R., 367nn18,
369nn54
Raman, A. P., 278nn18,
280nn68
Ramaprasad, A., 105nn134
Ramaswamy, K., 63nn15,
196nn17, 278nn29,
313nn24, 314nn53,
314nn64, 315nn68,
315nn70, 315nn73,
318nn149, 346nn36,
348nn84, 349nn110,
349nn120
Ramayah, T., 224nn114
Ramchander, S., 350nn132
Ramirez, G. G., 65nn83
Ramsey, J. R., 313nn13
Ramseyer, J. M., 349nn125
Ranft, A. L., 279nn55
Rangan, S., 222nn76, 315nn94
Ransbotham, S., 280nn61
Rao, S. S., 370nn76
Rapoport, H., 102nn42
Rapp, Ed, 6
Rapp, N., 27nn28
Rappaport, A., 278nn21,
280nn81
Rasheed, A. A., 314nn45,
349nn111
Rasmussen, E., 137nn60,
349nn125
Rau, D., 32nn156, 139nn115
Raubitschek, R. S., 137nn50
Rauwald, C., 220nn30
Ravasi, D, 136nn39, 367nn1
Ravenscraft, D. J., 255nn115
Ravichandran, T., 252nn41
Ravid, S. A., 278nn31
Ravinchandran, T., 30nn121

Rawley, E., 253nn76, 281nn88
Ray, G., 137nn65
Ray, S., 316nn114
Raymond, M. A., 315nn87
Raynor, M. E., 26nn4, 135nn21,
250nn2
Reddy, S., 101nn22, 102nn38
Reeb, D. M., 345nn23
Reed, A., II, 169nn26
Reed, R., 138nn76, 197nn47
Reger, R. K., 105nn131,
402nn10
Rehbein, K., 102nn53
Rehman, C. A., 403nn23
Reibstein, D. J., 197nn51
Reichestein, T., 368nn28
Reinert, U., 318nn147
Reingold, J., 65nn67
Reinhardt, A., 104nn114
Reinholt, M., 136nn43, 368nn42
Reitzig, M., 170nn61
Remes, J., 102nn37, 102nn43
Ren, H., 223nn94
Renneboog, L., 348nn94,
349nn112
Renzi, A., 252nn52
Restrepo, A., 102nn37, 102nn43
Reuer, J. J., 32nn179,
138nn94, 221nn36,
222nn65, 224nn115,
224nn121, 278nn19,
315nn95, 316nn107,
316nn120, 381, 403nn13,
403nn14, 403nn18,
403nn36, 403nn39,
403nn42
Reus, T. H., 279nn55, 316nn113
Reutzel, C. R., 65nn74, 345nn9,
347nn64
Revilla, E., 138nn96
Rezaee, Z., 346nn40
Rhee, J. H., 197nn49, 313nn19,
369nn46
Ribeiro-Soriano, D., 30nn127
Ricart, I., 104nn103
Ricart, J. E., 369nn62
Richards, M., 348nn85
Richardson, H. A., 139nn117
Rigby, D. K., 27nn45, 313nn26
Rindova, V. P., 31nn152,
63nn40, 135nn23, 136nn39,
168nn4, 199nn89
Ring, P. S., 316nn105
Rising, C., 278nn5
Ritala, P., 136nn29, 169nn32
Ritholz, B., 102nn33

Ritzman, L. P., 29nn82
Rivkin, J. W., 168nn1, 254nn100
Roberson, Q. M., 370nn98
Roberts, A., 197nn44
Roberts, H. V., 184
Roberts, J., 65nn69, 347nn67
Roberts, P. W., 197nn60,
 199nn89
Robertson, C. J., 68nn155
Robie, C., 252nn65
Robinosn, W. T., 197nn55
Robins, J. A., 28nn57, 252nn52,
 316nn103
Robinson, K. C., 104nn105
Robinson, R. B., Jr., 337
Robinson, W. T., 369nn67
Roche, P. J., 278nn6
Rock, E. B., 256nn143
Rockoff, J. D., 199nn91
Rodlophe, D., 26nn2
Rodriguez, A., 371nn126
Rodriguez, M. C., 255nn123
Roe, R. A., 67nn139, 199nn85
Rogers, J. E., 68nn147
Roller, L. H., 196nn17
Romano, P., 255nn130
Rometty, Virginia, 42, 45
Rose, E. L., 317nn128
Rose-Ackerman, S., 255nn120
Rosenkopf, L., 28nn51,
 101nn15, 224nn125
Rosenthal, P., 104nn119
Rosenzweig, P. M., 220nn29,
 316nn121
Ross, D., 255nn113
Ross, T. W., 221nn43
Rossetti, C., 138nn96
Rost, K., 64nn50
Roth, K., 317nn126, 348nn83
Rothaermel, F. T., 103nn72,
 170nn72, 221nn35,
 222nn60, 224nn118,
 253nn71, 371nn104,
 371nn106
Rouse, T., 318nn147
Rowe, W. G., 65nn71
Rowley, T. J., 196nn31,
 223nn102
Roxburgh C., 102nn37,
 102nn43
Roy, J.-P., 222nn75, 316nn120,
 316nn122, 348nn90
Rubach, M. J., 196nn21
Rubera, G., 102nn66
Rubner, H., 279nn52,
 282nn125, 346nn36

Rueutzel, C. R., 224nn126
Rugman, A., 314nn37, 314nn49
Ruiz-Mallorqui, M., 337
Ruiz-Moreno, F., 105nn129,
 196nn17, 198nn83, 337
Rumelt, R. P., 26nn6, 68nn160,
 169nn15, 221nn38,
 251nn12, 251nn31,
 251nn34, 252nn50,
 253nn85, 255nn114
Rust, K. G., 282nn118
Ryman, J. A., 26nn3
Ryngaert, M., 337, 349nn103

Saadi, S., 403nn25
Sadarasanam, S., 349nn116
Sadri, G., 63nn15
Safizadeh, M. H., 29nn82
Sagiv, L., 29nn79, 135nn10,
 139nn106
Sahib, P. R., 135nn14, 135nn22
Saini, A., 222nn80
St. John, C. H., 29nn88,
 32nn155, 137nn66,
 171nn104, 220nn12,
 220nn14, 251nn35,
 252nn43
Saito, T., 349nn124
Sajid, K. M., 283nn138
Salancik, Gerald, 9–10, 28nn72
Salge, T. O., 135nn14
Salk, J. E., 103nn81, 224nn109
Salmador, M.P., 103nn76,
 318nn150, 318nn159
Salomo, S., 64nn46, 64nn50
Salomon, R., 313nn25
Salter, C., 196nn28
Salvato, C., 369nn65
Samhi, R., 222nn76
Sammartino, A., 402nn7
Sammer, J., 224nn110
Sampson, R. C., 224nn111
Sanchez, R., 170nn91,
 199nn111
Sanchez-Bueno, M. J., 251nn33,
 282nn117
Sanchez-Marin, G., 346nn31
Sanders, L., 255nn116
Sanders, W. G., 348nn80,
 349nn117
Sandstrom, C., 27nn47
Sangiorgi, F., 63nn37
Sanjo, Y., 403nn24
Santa, R., 370nn89
Santana-Martin, D. J., 337
Santora, J. C., 370nn96

Santoro M. D., 220nn6,
 224nn118
Santos, J., 28nn56
Sanzhar, S., 281nn89, 282nn128
Saparito, P. A., 345nn28
Sapienza, H. J., 31nn148,
 101nn26, 315nn82,
 371nn108
Sapp, S., 348nn83
Sarala, R., 102nn67
Sarath, B., 346nn40
Sargut, G., 195nn2
Sarin, A., 254nn95
Sarkar, M. B., 138nn88,
 223nn106, 316nn114,
 368nn37
Sarni, W., 140nn125
Sarros, J. C., 370nn96
Sarstedt, M., 198nn77
Sasseen, J., 344nn2
Sathe, T., 403nn19
Sauter-Sachs, S., 63nn30
Sautet, F., 367nn9
Savetpanuvong, P., 220nn23
Savitz, E., 282nn130
Savsar, M., 171nn95
Saxton, T., 280nn75
Sayles, L. R., 368nn27
Schachter, K., 279nn50,
 279nn51
Schade, C., 368nn31
Scharf, S., 198nn77
Schatz, A., 279nn36
Schaubroeck, J., 64nn57
Schendel, D. E., 26nn6, 28nn61,
 29nn83, 29nn84, 29nn100,
 169nn15, 221nn38,
 251nn31, 251nn34,
 253nn85, 255nn114
Schendel, Dan, 10
Scherer, A. G., 102nn51,
 139nn113
Scherer, R. M., 255nn113,
 255nn115
Schiffer, B., 368nn33
Schijven, M., 254nn102
Schilling, M. A., 104nn123,
 221nn48
Schlingemann, F. P., 347nn52
Schmid, M., 346nn39
Schmidt, J. A., 280nn68
Schmitt, P., 136nn28
Schnabel, C., 349nn114
Schneider, A., 282nn123
Schneider, M., 65nn82,
 282nn129

Schoemaker, P. J. H., 138nn78
Schoenberg, R., 136nn29, 253nn81
Scholes, M., 255nn120, 403nn41
Scholnick, B., 138nn94
Scholten, R., 337, 349nn103
Schomaker, S., 135nn16
Schoorman, F. D., 65nn73, 68nn167, 224nn127, 344nn7
Schreyoegg, G., 136nn37
Schroeder, R. G., 136nn39, 171nn102, 252nn41, 404nn48
Schuler, D. A., 102nn53
Schultz, Howard, 145, 146
Schumpeter, J. A., 7, 27nn46, 197nn56, 198nn83, 199nn112, 367nn8, 368nn26
Schwaiger, M., 198nn77
Schwartz, A., 370nn102
Schwartz, C., 139nn107
Schwartz, E. S., 404nn48
Schwartz, M. S., 345nn8
Schwebach, R. G., 350nn132
Schweitzer, J., 221nn37
Schwenk, C. R., 63nn21, 63nn26
Schwens, C., 318nn152
Sciascia, S., 136nn33, 168nn2
Scott, P., 318nn158
Scott, W. R., 222nn75
Scott-Jackson, W., 28nn57
Scudder, T., 31nn151
Sears, G., 62nn11
Sechler, B., 197nn53
See, K. E., 68nn152
Seifert, B., 280nn86
Selden, L., 278nn18
Selover, D. D., 138nn69
Semadeni, M., 170nn73, 198nn63, 280nn64, 281nn100
Sen, B., 368nn37
Sen, N., 346nn44
Sen, P.K., 221nn36
Sengul, M., 169nn40
Sengupta, S., 170nn53, 221nn36
Seo, J., 344nn3, 348nn79
Serpa, R., 26nn1, 68nn145, 102nn48
Servaes, H., 253nn92, 346nn38
Seth, A., 29nn93

Settoon, R. P., 139nn117
Sever, J. M., 31nn152
Seward, J. K., 256nn144, 347nn60
Sexton, D. L., 101nn14, 103nn80, 135nn22, 168nn3, 251nn26, 315nn90, 367nn4, 368nn29, 369nn59
Shackell, M. B., 27nn39
Shah, B., 27nn48
Shah, M. H., 32nn177
Shaikh, F. M., 32nn177
Shamsie, J., 29nn96, 104nn105, 136nn45, 199nn89
Shan, W., 313nn18
Shane, S., 101nn4
Shanely, M., 105nn132
Shaner, J., 32nn157
Shang, J., 67nn142, 139nn105
Shankar, V., 222nn61
Shao, A. T., 315nn87
Shao, L., 102nn61
Shapira, Z., 63nn25, 63nn27, 63nn31, 63nn33, 63nn36
Shapiro, A. C., 32nn155
Shapiro, C., 280nn79
Shapiro, D. M., 350nn128
Shapiro, J., 136nn41
Sharda, K., 138nn90
Sharfman, M. P., 199nn107
Sharma, A., 346nn38
Sharma, P., 369nn65
Sharma, S., 31nn133, 31nn150, 350nn129, 350nn130
Sharp, D. J., 68nn168
Sharpe, W. F., 139nn116
Shaver, J. M., 101nn4, 280nn74, 315nn87, 317nn136, 317nn138, 348nn81
Shen, W., 65nn87, 347nn72
Sheng, T., 169nn33
Shenkar, O., 313nn32, 314nn44, 316nn102, 316nn103, 316nn120, 369nn53, 367nn14
Shepard, S. B., 66nn90
Shepherd, D. A., 102nn46, 137nn67, 198nn62, 199nn107, 367nn3
Sherr, I., 136nn47
Sheth, J., 31nn148
Shi, H., 29nn93

Shi, W., 221nn39
Shields, J., 253nn90, 348nn86
Shields, M. D., 69nn175
Shill, W., 280nn72
Shimizu, K., 26nn4, 137nn51, 168nn8, 283nn140, 367nn7, 368nn43
Shimoni, B., 318nn158
Shin, H. H., 254nn101, 109
Shin, J., 344nn3, 348nn79
Shinkle, G. A., 314nn45
Shinozawa, Y., 349nn121
Shipilov, A. V., 221nn52
Shirke, P., 63nn29
Shirodkar, A., 220nn25
Shivdasani, A., 281nn89, 282nn128
Shleifer, A., 255nn114
Shoemaker, P. J. H., 135nn21
Shook, C. L., 222nn82, 367nn13
Short, J. C., 29nn103, 30nn109, 104nn100, 222nn82, 250nn3, 251nn23, 255nn132, 278nn1, 367nn13
Shortell, S. M., 221nn53
Shrivastava, P., 139nn114
Shropshire, C., 347nn73
Shtub, A., 253nn83
Shuen, A., 26nn4
Shyu, J., 253nn92
Sibony, O., 64nn42
Sidhu, J. S., 67nn123, 138nn87
Siegel, D. S., 136nn27, 139nn106, 278nn6, 282nn116, 282nn133
Sieger, P., 104nn99, 136nn24
Silverman, B. S., 251nn23
Silverman, S., 220nn28
Simans, C. C., 337
Simmering, M. J., 137nn56
Simon, D., 195nn9, 196nn16, 196nn21, 196nn29, 196nn32
Simon, D. H., 222nn70
Simon, H., 28nn70
Simone, C., 252nn52
Simons, K. L., 278nn6, 282nn116
Simons, R., 69nn175
Simons, T., 64nn56
Sims, H. P., 62nn13, 64nn50
Simsek, Z., 32nn168, 64nn57, 65nn77, 370nn77

Sinatra, A., 281nn92
Sine, W. D., 169nn37
Singer, Z., 346nn41
Singh, H., 222nn79, 224nn110,
    224nn116, 224nn119,
    280nn61, 280nn69,
    281nn92, 282nn129,
    313nn11, 345nn11,
    403nn31
Singh, J. V., 28nn51,
    104nn118, 251nn18,
    313nn11
Singh, M., 346nn46
Sinha, I., 251nn25, 254nn100
Sinha, J., 27nn20
Sinha, R., 348nn95, 348nn98
Sinkovics, R. R., 104nn116
Sinofsky, Steven, 41
Siren, C. A., 139nn104,
    198nn61, 367nn2
Sirmans, C. C., 337
Sirmon, D. G., 26nn2, 26nn5,
    26nn8, 30nn110, 30nn115,
    30nn116, 63nn20, 65nn74,
    66nn100, 66nn106,
    67nn134, 100nn1, 103nn72,
    104nn97, 104nn120,
    135nn5, 135nn23, 136nn33,
    145, 150, 156, 168nn2,
    169nn22, 169nn50,
    170nn66, 195nn7, 196nn18,
    251nn25, 255nn125,
    255nn132, 282nn114,
    313nn16, 345nn9, 347nn64,
    367nn4, 367nn5, 370nn69,
    371nn120, 371nn122
Sironi A., 346nn47
Sirower, M., 278nn21, 280nn81
Sisodia, R., 31nn148
Sitkin, S. B., 68nn152
Sitlington, H., 283nn139
Sivanathan, N., 63nn38
Skaggs, B. E., 68nn162
Skiera, B., 136nn28
Skill, M. S., 65nn76
Slahudin, C., 255nn122
Slangen, A. H. L., 316nn115,
    318nn154
Slater, S. F., 62nn12, 63nn15,
    103nn92, 135nn6,
    170nn53
Sleuwaegen, L., 26nn17, 197nn47
Sloan, Alfred, P., Jr., 251nn28
Slocum, J.W., 26nn3
Slovic, P., 63nn22

Sluyts, K., 224nn110
Smart, D. L., 169nn18, 280nn85
Smirchich, L., 29nn87
Smiske, J., 26nn14
Smit, H. T. J., 402nn12
Smit, S., 102nn37
Smith, A., 346nn31
Smith, C. G., 255nn128
Smith, G., 313nn20
Smith, J., 347nn74
Smith, K. A., 62nn13, 64nn50,
    64nn56
Smith, K. G., 62nn13, 64nn50,
    101nn3, 101nn6, 102nn43,
    195nn3, 195nn9, 196nn12,
    196nn14, 196nn16,
    196nn20, 196nn22,
    196nn29, 196nn32,
    197nn40, 197nn50,
    198nn70, 198nn73,
    199nn84, 199nn85,
    199nn88, 199nn93,
    199nn94, 199nn97,
    251nn38, 317nn135
Smith, M., 69nn178
Smith, R., 403nn19
Smith, R. D., 255nn135
Smith, W.K., 369nn68
Snell, S. A., 66nn119
Snow, C. C., 32nn175, 168nn3
Soda, G., 222nn61
Soh, P.-H., 221nn57
Sokolyk, T., 349nn102
Solvell, O., 317nn136
Somaya, D., 368nn30
Sonenshein, S., 279nn47
Song, J., 101nn1, 168nn4,
    313nn18, 314nn44
Song, M., 26nn7, 101nn8,
    199nn108, 251nn25,
    279nn42, 370nn78
Song, P., 199nn99
Song, S., 220nn9
Song, W., 282nn131
Song, Y., 64nn46, 138nn87
Soosay, C., 370nn89
Sorcher, M., 65nn83
Sorensen, J. B., 367nn10
Sorensen, M., 283nn135,
    283nn141
Sottile, P., 102nn46
Souder, D., 65nn77, 139nn110,
    348nn81
Soupata, L., 138nn75
Souphom, V., 254nn108

Southam, C., 348nn83
Spanos, Y. E., 103nn96
Spector, M., 26nn12, 135nn20
Spencer, J. W., 252nn58,
    314nn45, 368nn24
Spender, J.-C., 26nn8
Spiegel, Y., 251nn27, 251nn34
Spreitzer, G., 32nn170
Sprengel, D. C., 139nn111
Sriboonlue, P., 28nn58, 402nn4
Srinidhi, B., 66nn96
Srinivasan, N., 255nn115
Srivastava, M. K., 134nn3,
    170nn71, 197nn60,
    368nn23
Srivnivasan, M., 254nn111
Srodes, J., 27nn28
Stadter, G., 137nn59
Stahl, G. K., 102nn67
Staking, K., 350nn132
Stalk, G., Jr., 252nn64
Stalker, G. M., 169nn36
Stallen, P. J., 63nn36
Stanford, D., 103nn95
Staw, B. M., 63nn19, 104nn124,
    196nn30
Steele, R., 26nn11
Steenkamp, J.-B. E. M.,
    253nn70
Steensma, H. K., 28nn50,
    68nn155, 139nn107,
    223nn95
Steers, R. M., 312nn5
Steindel, C., 255nn121
Steinhorst, K., 105nn142
Stendevad, C., 281nn89,
    282nn128
Stephan A., 198nn62
Stern, I., 63nn40
Stern, S., 253nn75
Stevens, J. M., 68nn155,
    139nn107
Stevenson, R. W., 103nn84
Stevenson, W. B., 318nn161
Stewart, G. B., 403nn38
Stewart, R., 27nn38
Stewart, T. A., 68nn161
Stewart, W. H., 66nn120
Stiles, P., 65nn69, 347nn67
Stimper, J. L., 28nn54
Stinglhamber, F., 32nn154,
    350nn131
Stipp, D., 102nn34
Stone, F., 32nn171
Storz, C., 315nn79

Stourred-Barnes, S. F., 197nn47
Stowe, J. D., 346nn36
St.-Pierre, J., 136nn40
Strebel, P. J., 345nn12,
    403nn40
Street V. L., 32nn175, 168nn3
Streukens, S., 224nn110
Strömberg, P., 283nn135,
    283nn141
Stuart, N. V., 27nn39
Stubbart, C. I., 29nn87,
    105nn134
Stubben, S. R., 347nn54
Stumpf, D., 102nn57
Su, K.-H., 135nn9, 195nn7
Su, Y., 350nn128
Subramaniam, M., 28nn57,
    103nn80, 103nn81,
    222nn71, 253nn68,
    370nn77
Subramanian, V., 31nn129,
    347nn52
Suddaby, R., 371nn130
Sudek, R., 368nn35
Sueyoshi, T., 349nn122
Suh, Y. G., 282nn111
Sullivan, D. M., 103nn75,
    368nn41, 369nn56
Sun, J., 170nn62, 170nn74
Sun, Q., 349nn127
Sun, S. L., 254nn100,
    280nn62
Sundaramurthy, C., 349nn108
Surroca, J., 252nn52
Sutcliffe, K. M., 101nn28,
    198nn79
Sutter, C. J., 221nn87
Sutton, R. I., 370nn71
Sutton S. G., 28nn59, 69nn174,
    402nn3
Svejnar, J., 281nn111, 282nn126
Svobodina, L., 103nn87,
    315nn97
Swaminathan, A., 198nn64,
    278nn30, 279nn52
Swan, K. S., 314nn51
Sydow, J., 136nn37
Szerb, L., 369nn52

Tafaghod, M., 280nn73
Tahir, R., 313nn29
Takeishi, A., 138nn90,
    316nn124
Talaulicar, T., 199nn107
Talke, K., 64nn46, 64nn50

Talley, K., 67nn141
Tallman, S., 27nn20, 28nn57,
    102nn59, 137nn55,
    197nn41, 221nn34,
    221nn40, 223nn99,
    223nn104, 312nn7,
    313nn26, 313nn34,
    313nn36, 316nn103,
    317nn131, 318nn157
Tallon, P. P., 32nn165
Tan, H. H., 224nn127
Tan, J. J., 105nn131,
    314nn58
Tang, J., 65nn71, 368nn34
Tanlamai, U., 220nn23
Tanriverdi, H., 27nn21,
    196nn33, 251nn38
Tanyeri, B., 278nn20
Tao, Q. T., 220nn6, 224nn118
Tapinos, E. E., 69nn177
Tate, G., 64nn64
Taylor, A., III, 370nn75
Taylor, D. J., 349nn105
Taylor, P., 253nn91, 278nn22
Teece, D. J., 26nn4, 26nn6,
    66nn116, 169nn15,
    221nn38, 251nn31,
    251nn34, 253nn85,
    255nn114
Teerikangas, S., 280nn69
Tehranian, H., 278nn20
Teng, B.-S., 30nn112, 63nn21,
    63nn25
Terjesen, S., 171nn95
Terlep, S., 26nn12
Terziovski, M., 32nn169
Tesluk, P. E., 26nn10, 32nn161
Tetlock P. E., 64nn58,
    139nn121
Theordorou, P., 171nn96
Thibodeau, J. C., 350nn134
Thomas, A. S., 63nn15, 140nn123
Thomas, Andrea, 132
Thomas, D. E., 313nn31,
    318nn162
Thomas, Evans, 274
Thomas, H., 29nn93, 255nn122
Thomas, L. G., 369nn53
Thomas, P., 102nn64
Thomas, S., 278nn28
Thomas, W. B., 256nn139,
    278nn8
Thome, W. H., 196nn15
Thompson, K. R., 68nn152
Thompson, T. A., 345nn20

Thornton, E., 278nn14
Thorton, E., 348nn100
Thronton, E., 278nn25
Thurm, S., 282nn112
Tian, G. Y., 347nn63,
    348nn95
Tian, J., 62nn10
Tichy, N. M., 62nn1,
    65nn83
Tienari, J., 134nn2
Tihanyi, L., 64nn63, 69nn183,
    103nn78, 168nn11,
    169nn37, 198nn79,
    220nn24, 223nn95,
    282nn128, 312nn4,
    313nn25, 317nn127,
    317nn128, 317nn137,
    317nn141, 345nn19,
    346nn44, 346nn46,
    347nn59, 369nn46
Timmons, H., 68nn157
Tishler, A., 64nn43, 64nn57,
    67nn122, 135nn13
Todd, S. Y., 31nn129
Toffler, D. G., 68nn168
Toh, P. K., 195nn2
Tokman, M., 368nn36
Tomson, B., 140nn122
Tong, C. H., 62nn3
Tong, J. J., 403nn18
Tong, L.-I., 62nn3
Tong, T. W., 105nn131,
    222nn65, 278nn18,
    315nn95, 381,
    403nn18, 403nn36,
    403nn39
Torres-Baumgarten, G.,
    222nn85
Torrisi, S., 104nn107,
    223nn108
Tosi, H. L., 30nn124, 344nn3,
    348nn76, 348nn86
Tostão, E., 278nn28
Tracey, P., 371nn129
Trahms, C. A., 67nn134,
    103nn72, 169nn22,
    371nn120
Trent, R. J., 27nn20
Treviño, L. K., 32nn180,
    68nn168
Trevor, C. O., 282nn121
Triantis, A., 404nn49
Tribo, J. A., 252nn52
Trigeorgis, L., 402nn12
Trigeorgis, Lenos, 376

Tsai, W. H., 135nn9, 195nn7, 196nn22, 222nn58, 255nn128, 279nn58, 368nn41
Tsai, W.-H., 256nn138
Tsang, E. W. K., 28nn50, 29nn81
Tschirky, H., 279nn41
Tse, D. K., 316nn106
Tsui, A. S., 62nn14, 223nn102, 316nn104, 318nn153
Tsui, J., 66nn96
Tufano, P., 404nn51
Tuggle, C. S., 65nn74, 345nn9, 347nn63, 347nn64
Tully, S., 27nn31
Turban, D. B., 137nn53
Turk, T. A., 256nn142, 346nn30
Turley, J. S., 367nn12
Turner, J., 67nn138
Turner, M., 279nn37
Tuschke, A. C., 349nn117
Tversky, A., 63nn22
Twite, G., 348nn95
Tyler, B. B., 63nn15, 103nn86

Ucbasaran, D., 315nn89
Ueda, M., 367nn21
Uhlenbruck, K., 28nn60, 220nn24, 280nn64, 281nn100, 349nn126
Ulrich, D., 66nn120, 69nn178
Un, C. A., 168nn8, 368nn43, 402nn11
Underhill, W., 68nn164
Underwood, R., 369nn56
Untiedt, R., 282nn125
Uroševi, B., 63nn37
Useem, M., 139nn97, 313nn11
Ussahawanitchakit, P., 28nn58, 402nn4

Vaaler, P. M., 27nn22, 318nn147
Vaara, E., 26nn2, 102nn67, 134nn2
Vafai, K., 345nn27
Vafeas, N., 64nn64, 68nn150, 140nn121
Vagadia, B., 139nn98
Vaidyanath, D., 30nn123, 136nn43, 220nn7, 223nn104, 279nn38, 316nn108, 371nn112
Valenti, A., 282nn129
Valenti, G., 318nn165

Valentini, G., 371nn118, 371nn127
Valikangas, L., 28nn55
Van, A., 316nn102, 369nn58
Van, Y., 315nn67
Van Arnum, P., 222nn67
Van Auken, H., 347nn68, 348nn87
Van den Bosch, F. J., 64nn51
Van den Bulte, C., 136nn28
Van Fleet, D. D., 312nn6
Van Idderkinge, C. H., 66nn115
Van Ness, B., 346nn36
Van Oijen, A. A., 252nn49
Van Witteloostuijn, A., 135nn14, 135nn22
Vance, A., 64nn48, 66nn111
Vankatwyk, P, 26nn10, 32nn161
Varey, R. J., 138nn83
Varga, A., 26nn18
Vassolo, R., 27nn22
Vasudeva, G., 136nn30, 138nn79, 224nn111
Veiga, J. F., 64nn57
Veliyath, R., 346nn36, 348nn84
Venkatraman, N., 27nn21, 28nn57, 103nn81, 196nn33, 251nn38, 370nn77
Vera, A. M., 66nn96, 135nn14
Verbeke, A., 101nn24, 314nn37
Verdin, P., 31nn129
Verma, A., 136nn30
Vermeulen, F., 103nn77, 103nn82, 280nn63, 280nn64
Verstring, T., 318nn147
Véry, P, 280nn69
Vicente-lorente, J. D., 101nn2
Vidal-Suarez, M., 222nn65
Viega, J. F., 32nn168
Vigano, R., 347nn66
Vilkas, M., 402nn7
Villado, A. J., 64nn47
Villalonga, B., 346nn49
Villar-Lopez, A., 170nn69, 312nn7
Villena, V. H., 138nn96
Viney, J., 28nn57
Vishny, R. W., 255nn114
Viswanathan, S., 279nn48
Vitols, S., 254nn103
Vlek, C., 63nn36
Voelpel, S. C., 26nn19
Vogt, C., 371nn105
Volberda, H. W., 64nn51, 67nn123, 138nn87, 369nn54

Voola, R., 223nn107
Vorhies, D. W., 198nn78
Vos, B., 104nn116
Vroom, G., 104nn108
van Dallen, R., 197nn53
van den Bosch, A. J., 221nn36
van De Gucht, L. M., 199nn87
van De Vijver, M., 104nn116
van Essen, M., 198nn84
van Oosteerhout, 198nn84
van Putten, A. B., 314nn57
van Staden, C. J., 103nn93
von Krogh, G., 281nn92, 370nn87, 370nn88
von Streng Velken, I., 68nn150
Vyas, D., 278nn8

Wada, T., 220nn9, 220nn28
Waddell, G. R., 66nn94
Waddock, S. A., 32nn156, 252nn52
Wade, J. B., 63nn39
Wagner, M., 280nn63, 371nn119
Wagner, S. M., 104nn117, 170nn61
Wahl, J. E., 403nn23
Waldeck, A., 278nn5
Waldman, D. A., 62nn14, 65nn83, 313nn32
Walker, D. S., 30nn120
Walker, G., 104nn113
Walker, R., 104nn111
Wallace, E., 68nn161
Wallace, W., 68nn163
Wallin, C., 220nn5
Wally, S., 64nn53, 196nn20
Walsh, I. J., 135nn17
Walsh, J. P., 26nn9, 63nn30, 256nn144, 347nn60, 348nn76, 348nn94, 348nn99, 349nn106
Walter, I., 346nn39
Walter, J., 136nn48
Walters, B. A., 101nn17, 347nn66
Walton, Sam, 34–35
Wan, W. P., 27nn39, 28nn64, 29nn91, 30nn109, 103nn76, 198nn67, 222nn59, 250nn3, 251nn23, 254nn96, 254nn99, 254nn102, 255nn132, 278nn1, 282nn128, 312nn3, 313nn34, 315nn75, 318nn157
Wang, C., 348nn91
Wang, C. L., 220nn33

Wang, C.-F., 317nn130
Wang, F., 197nn58
Wang, H. C., 31nn148, 62nn14,
   134nn1, 135nn9, 170nn55,
   170nn74, 250nn8, 312nn1,
   404nn50
Wang, L., 318nn155
Wang, S. I., 170nn62
Wang, W., 371nn114
Wang, Y.-S., 252nn55
Warren, D., 348nn90
Wasden, M., 68nn149
Washburn, M., 169nn49
Washburn, N. T., 62nn14,
   313nn32
Wassmer, U., 137nn49,
   224nn116
Waters, R., 278nn22, 279nn50
Watkins, M. D., 281nn103
Watson, W., 66nn120
Wattal, S., 254nn94
Waychal, P., 136nn30
Weaver, G. R., 32nn180,
   68nn168
Weaver, K. M., 368nn36
Webb, J. W., 135nn8, 138nn82,
   197nn60, 198nn79,
   221nn87, 318nn153,
   367nn5
Webber, A. M., 136nn38
Weber, J., 278nn13
Weber, K., 101nn28
Weber, R. A., 280nn71, 281nn95
Weber, T. J., 63nn15
Webster, F. E., Jr., 169nn20
Weddigen, R.-M., 278nn18,
   280nn80
Wei, C., 101nn19
Weick, K. E., 198nn79
Weigelt, C., 138nn88, 221nn37
Weinstein, D., 313nn28
Welbourne, T. M., 67nn128
Welch, D. E., 315nn95
Welch, Jack, 34, 45, 62nn2,
   66nn90
Welch, L. S., 315nn95
Wen, S. H., 315nn96
Wennberg, K., 371nn121
Werder, A. V., 199nn107
Werle, M. J., 139nn98
Werner, S., 104nn126, 344nn3,
   348nn86, 403nn13
Wernerfelt, B., 29nn97,
   30nn111, 199nn96,
   255nn132

Westbrook, R. A., 26nn11
Westeny, D. E., 27nn32
Westhead, P., 315nn89
Westphal, A. D., 26nn14, 42,
   65nn65, 65nn66, 256nn144
Westphal, J. D., 63nn40,
   65nn75, 344nn1, 346nn29,
   347nn64
Wexner, Leslie, 126
Whiford, D., 252nn59
White, M. A., 101nn17
White, R. C., 317nn126,
   317nn127
White, R. E., 69nn176,
   69nn183, 282nn128
Whitelock, J., 137nn56
Whitman, Meg, 46
Whitney, J. O., 67nn138
Whittington, R., 63nn20
Whitwell, G., 68nn146
Wickramasinghe, V., 30nn123
Wicks, A. C., 31nn132, 31nn135,
   31nn142, 31nn143,
   31nn148, 31nn149,
   220nn11, 224nn127
Wierba, E. E., 67nn139
Wiersema, M. F., 30nn107,
   63nn18, 64nn55,
   137nn59, 222nn80,
   252nn52, 254nn106,
   282nn131, 313nn35,
   317nn129
Wiklund, J., 102nn46, 137nn67,
   197nn55, 198nn62,
   367nn3, 367nn6
Wilemon, D., 370nn73
Wiliamson, P., 28nn56
Wilke, P., 254nn103
Williams, C., 100nn1
Williams, J. R., 199nn99,
   199nn100, 199nn101,
   199nn109, 199nn113,
   220nn20, 255nn116
Williams, M., 170nn75
Williams, P., 283nn138
Williamson, I. O., 31nn152
Williamson, O. E., 29nn80,
   169nn45, 251nn31,
   253nn74, 253nn88,
   280nn68, 280nn79,
   345nn27
Williamson, Oliver, 10
Williamson, P. J., 250nn4,
   278nn18
Wilson, D., 199nn104

Wilstrom, P., 279nn42
Wincent, J., 221nn56
Wind, J., 198nn71
Wingfield, N., 103nn73
Winter, S. G., 30nn118,
   137nn50
Wise, R., 104nn110, 169nn27
Wiseman, R. M., 345nn22
Withers, M. C., 346nn38,
   347nn69, 350nn137
Witt, P., 349nn112
Wkjnberg, N. M., 137nn49
Wolf, B., 32nn176
Wolfe, D. B., 31nn148
Wolff, J. A., 66nn118
Wolfson, M., 255nn120
Wolfson, P. J., 66nn97
Wolterman, D. J, 30nn125,
   30nn126
Wolterman, Daniel, 16
Won, P. Y., 349nn118
Wong, E. M., 64nn58, 139nn121
Woo, C. Y., 196nn31, 197nn35,
   253nn67
Wood, D. J., 139nn113,
   344nn6
Wood, E., 314nn56
Wood, R. E., 63nn23
Woodford, Michael, 56
Woodley, J. A., 316nn101
Woodward, J., 169nn36
Woolley, A. W., 370nn97
Woolley, J., 101nn7
Workman, M., 63nn21
Worthington, J. D., 224nn126
Wowak, A. J., 256nn140,
   348nn91
Wright, J., 222nn69
Wright, M., 30nn109, 65nn70,
   136nn31, 220nn24,
   221nn40, 223nn97,
   282nn133, 283nn135,
   283nn141, 312nn4,
   315nn89, 318nn164,
   348nn96, 349nn110
Wright, P. M., 30nn119,
   66nn121, 67nn134,
   135nn5, 137nn53,
   137nn60, 169nn18,
   312nn6, 346nn36,
   347nn66
Wu, B., 255nn123
Wu, F., 169nn33, 368nn24
Wu, J., 346nn47
Wu, P. C. S., 313nn17

Wu, X., 345nn13, 349nn123
Wu, Y., 67nn124
Wu, Y.-J., 371nn114
Wu, Z., 282nn111
Wujin, C., 224nn122
Wulf, J., 345nn11
Wurdoch, Rupert, 56–57
Wurst, J., 169nn27

Xia, J., 314nn66
Xiao, Q., 197nn37
Xie, F., 198nn67, 348nn91
Xin, K., 32nn154, 223nn102, 316nn104, 350nn131
Xin, K. R., 62nn14, 102nn41
Xin, L., 64nn59
Xing, X., 346nn36
Xiyao, L., 69nn180, 281nn90
Xu, D., 313nn33, 314nn44, 346nn47, 350nn128
Xu, X., 198nn66
Xu, Y., 253nn67

Yaffee, T., 68nn167
Yago, G., 280nn82
Yamashiro, G. M., 254nn108
Yan, A., 67nn123
Yang, B., 64nn46, 138nn87
Yang, H., 28nn50, 220nn4, 254nn100, 280nn62, 281nn102
Yang, N. J., 349nn126
Yang, Y., 31nn128
Yannopoulos, P., 199nn93
Yao, J., 349nn123
Yaprak, A., 314nn60
Yarbrough, L., 198nn78
Yasin, M., 402nn5
Yavas, U., 315nn88
Yermack, D., 346nn39
Yeung, G., 198nn80, 312nn6
Yeung, V. W. S., 171nn103
Yi, L., 69nn180, 281nn90
Yi-Min, C., 29nn103, 31nn129
Yip, G. S., 103nn74
Yiu, D., 345nn15
Yiu, D. W., 27nn39, 28nn64, 29nn91, 30nn109, 65nn86, 69nn176, 250nn3, 251nn23, 254nn102, 255nn132, 278nn1, 282nn128
Yli-Renko, H., 101nn25, 371nn108
Yoffie, D. B., 197nn49

Yong, W., 64nn53
York, A. S., 104nn101
Yoshikawa, T., 253nn80, 279nn48, 346nn30, 349nn111
You, H., 346nn41
You, L., 251nn18
Youndt, M. A., 66nn119
Young, D., 250nn6
Young, G., 195nn9, 196nn12, 196nn16, 196nn20, 196nn29, 196nn32, 198nn73
Young, G. J., 221nn53
Young, M. N., 316nn112, 349nn126, 349nn127
Young, S. D., 316nn113, 403nn38
Young-Ybarra, C., 222nn80
Yu, J., 138nn91, 223nn95, 371nn109
Yu, S., 27nn38
Yu, T., 222nn71, 253nn68
Yuan, L., 69nn180, 281nn90
Yucel, E., 137nn48, 371nn124

Zack, M. H., 101nn25
Zaefarian, G., 219nn3
Zaheer, A., 104nn102, 224nn123
Zaheer, S., 104nn102, 135nn16, 313nn22
Zahra, S. A., 32nn176, 280nn76, 315nn82, 317nn132, 368nn42, 369nn56
Zajac, E. J., 42, 64nn64, 65nn64, 65nn66, 65nn75, 136nn34, 221nn51, 346nn35, 347nn64
Zalewski, D. A., 255nn116
Zander, C., 26nn12
Zander, I., 317nn136
Zattoni, A., 347nn66
Zatzick, C., 282nn121
Zeisel, S., 278nn6
Zeithaml, C. P., 64nn63, 138nn76
Zelleke, A., 65nn72
Zelleke, A. S., 256nn142
Zellmer-Bruhn, M., 314nn61
Zellner, C., 252nn64, 252nn65
Zellner, W., 68nn157, 345nn10
Zellwegar, T., 136nn24

Zellweger, T., 104nn99
Zelner, B. A., 223nn98, 317nn146
Zelong, W., 64nn53
Zemsky, P., 221nn46
Zey, M., 348nn90
Zhang, C., 199nn99
Zhang, D., 171nn102
Zhang, H., 252nn46
Zhang, J., 199nn95, 220nn16, 221nn40, 278nn9
Zhang, T., 348nn84
Zhang, Y., 30nn107, 65nn88, 65nn89, 137nn61, 313nn27
Zhang, Y. B., 138nn92
Zhao, J., 282nn118
Zhao, N. B., 317nn140
Zhao, Y., 371nn103
Zhao, Z., 221nn47
Zhen, Z., 62nn6
Zheng, C., 314nn56
Zhoa, X., 254nn100
Zhou, C., 278nn9
Zhou, D., 197nn43
Zhou, H., 251nn29
Zhou, K. Z., 169nn32, 169nn33, 224nn123, 252nn44, 252nn51, 368nn24
Zhou, L.-A., 313nn27
Zhou, M., 254nn97
Zhou, N., 318nn154
Zhou, Y. M., 280nn74, 281nn111, 282nn126
Zhou, Z., 32nn172, 139nn104
Zhu, G., 67nn123, 369nn58
Zhu, H., 136nn34, 221nn51, 313nn31
Zhu, W., 198nn66
Zingales, L., 253nn92, 346nn38
Ziobro, P., 195nn4
Zitkus, L, 219nn2
Zmuda, N., 67nn140
Zollo, M., 280nn61, 280nn69, 280nn71
Zona, F., 347nn62
Zook, C., 29nn77, 136nn35, 313nn26
Zott, C., 137nn60, 138nn84
Zou, H., 350nn127
Zucchini, L., 197nn43
Zuniga-Vincente, J. A., 101nn2, 105nn134
Zweig, J., 347nn55
Zweig, P. L., 255nn116

COMPANY INDEX

Note: Italic page numbers indicate material in tables or figures.

3M, 357, 359, 363–364

Aaon, 162, 166
Abbott Laboratories, 179, 187
Accor, 177
Acer, 187
Acura, 147
Adidas, 159
Advanced Micro Devices, 191
Aeroflot, 202
Air China, 4
Air France, 202
Airbus, 94, 97, 299
Ajinomoto Company, 213
Alcatel-Lucent, 75
Alcon, 55
Alibaba Group, 179
Amazon.com, 76, 146, 147,
    176, 358
American Airlines, 4, 73, 202
Andersen Windows, 164
Apax Partners, 274
Apple Computer, 36, 50, 53,
    76, 114, 117, 147, 187,
    333, 354
Arizona, 53
Arkansas Best, 177
Arthur Andersen, 56
AT&T, 214, 261
Aviall, 164
Aviation and Transportation,
    236

Bacyrus International, 301
Baidu Inc., 364
Baker Hughes, 179
BankRate, 274
BASF, 298
Bausch & Lomb, 297
Baxter International, 187
BGC Partners Inc., 245
Big Lots Inc., 151
Big-Dog Motorcycles, 161
BMW, 147, 204, 363
Boeing, 50, 94, 97, 173
Bolsa Electronica de Chile
    (BEC), 212

Bombardier, 174
Borders, 3
Bose, 155
Boston Consulting Group,
    9, 115
Bristol-Myers Squibb, 179,
    261, 263
British Airways, 202
Burger King, 132, 177

Cadillac, 147
Callaway Golf Company, 159
Cambria Suites, 49
Campbell Soup, 173, 228
Capital, 236
Cargill, 211
Carrefour, 179
Caterpillar, 6, 155, 301
Catholic Health Initiatives, 235
CBRE Group, 245
China National Tobacco
    Corporation (CNTC), 301
Chipotle Mexican Grill, 132
Choice Hotels, 49
CIGNA, 177
Circuit City, 3
Cisco Systems, 207, 214, 271
Citibank, 268
Citigroup, 271
Clarion, 49
Coca-Cola Company, 89,
    98–99, 114, 121,
    192, 204
Comfort Inn, 49
Commerzbank, 339
Compaq, 187
ConocoPhillips, 273
Consolidated International, 151
Continental, 260
Con-way Inc., 177
Cooper Tire & Rubber
    Co., 188
Courtyard (Marriot), 237
Credit Suisse, 268
CreditCards.com, 274
CSX, 202
Cummins, 301

D. E. Shaw, 375
DAC. *See* Davies Arnold Cooper
    (DAC) LLP
Daimler, 363
Danone, 206
Davies Arnold Cooper (DAC)
    LLP, 209, 211
Dell Inc., 50, 76, 187, 207,
    238, 364
Delta Airlines, 4, 202
Deutsche Bank, 339
Deutsche Post DHL Worldwide
    Express, 288–289
Dimension Films, 239
Disney, 211
Dresdner Bank, 339
Dunkin' Donuts, 181
DuPont, 231

EADS. *See* European Aeronautic
    Defence And Space Com-
    pany N. V. (EADS)
Econolodge, 49
Eddie Bauer, 162
eBay, 45
Egyptair, 4
Eli Lilly, 380
Embraer, 174
EMC, 207
Energy Future Holdings
    (EFH), 274
Energy Transer Equity
    LP, 259
Enron Corporation, 56, 327
Ericsson, 213, 271
Ethernet Alliance, 214
Ethiopian Airlines, 4
European Aeronautic Defence
    And Space Company N. V.
    (EADS), 173

Facebook, 176
Fairfield Inn, 237
FedEx, 173, 178
Fiat, 376
First Boston, 268
Flextronics, 238

Flint Energy Services Ltd., 181
Ford, 238, 288
Frito-Lay, 85, 245
Frontier Airlines, 48
Fundación Chile, 211

Gateway, 187
GE. *See* General Electric
GE Healthcare, 148
General Electric, 34, 44, 45, 48, 49, 51–52, 228, 236, 264, 358, 362
General Motors (GM), 231, 238, 288, 309, 376
Gilead Sciences, 261, 263
Gillette, 357
Goldman Sachs, 56
Google Inc., 114, 115, 117, 176, 259, 263, 354, 364
Grubb & Ellis Co., 245
Gruma, 287
Gucci, 119

Halliburton, 179
Hampton Inn, 237
Hanwha-SolarOne, 237
Harley-Davidson, 91, 160
Harris Poll, 187
Healthcare, 236
Heinz, 173
Hewlett Packard, 45, 50, 76, 147, 187
Hilton, 177, 178, 237
Hilton Worldwide, 212
Hitachi, 94
Hoeschst, 298
Hollywood Pictures, 239
Home and Business Solutions, 236
Home Depot, 162
Honda, 6, 91, 147, 288, 304
Hostess, 3, 21
Hotel de Glace, 179
Hulu, 179
Hyundai, 186

IBM, 7, 21, 42, 45, 159, 187, 191, 202
iRobot, 263
IKEA, 160
IKEA International, 293–294
Infosys Technologies Ltd., 85
Inhibitex, 261
Intel, 183, 191, 207, 214, 238, 362

Intercontinental, 177
International Harvester, 301
Izod, 53

J. D. Power, 186
Jaguar, 185
Japan Airlines, 202
JBS Company, 258, 260, 261, 268
JCPenney, 53
Johnson & Johnson, 179, 186, 187, 228
Jubilant FoodWorks, 181

Kellogg, 213
Kentucky Fried Chicken, 245
Keystone Foods, 258
Kmart, 151
Kodak, 3, 73, 109
KKR, *See* Kohlberg Kravis Roberts & Co., 245, 274
Komatsu, 301.

Lenova Group, 76, 159, 187
Lexus, 147, 155
Li & Fung LTD, 264
Li Ning Company, 159
Limited Brands Inc, 126
Lincoln Electric, 120, 187
Liz Claiborne, 53
Lockheed Martin Cyber Security Alliance, 207
L'Oréal, 211
Louis Vuitton SA, 119. *See also* LVMH
Lucent, 271
Lufthansa, 4
LVMH, 119

Mabel, 245
McAfee, 207
McDonald's, 48, 49, 85, 114, 132, 177, 212, 258, 302
McKinsey & Co., 117, 120, 155, 157
Mainstay Suites, 49
Marfrig, 258
Marriott, 49, 177, 178, 237
Matsushita, 94
Medifast, 227
Mercedes, 147
Merck & Co., 228
Metro, 291
MF Global, 56
Michael Graves, 162

Microsoft, 41, 50, 81, 91, 97, 114, 176, 207, 209
Middle East Airlines, 202
Mitsubishi, 94
Moet Hennessy, 119. *See also* LVMH
Moody's, 268
Mossimo, 162
Motion, 76
Motorola Mobility, 259, 263
Murray Goulbrum Co-operative (MGC), 206

Nasdaq OMX, 212
National Beef Packing, 261
NEC, 94
Nekton Research, 263
NetApp, 115
NetFlix, 179
NetQuote, 274
Newmark Knight Frank, 245
News Corp., 56–57
NexGen Cyber Innovation And Technology Center, 207
Nextag, 176
Nike, 112, 155, 159
Nissan, 6, 92, 304, 363
Nokia, 85, 209
Nortel, 271
Novartis, *54*, 54–55, 58
Novo Nordisk, 132
Nucor, 48
Nycomed, 262

Olympus, 56
Oneworld Alliance, 202
Oracle, 214, 261
Outsourcing Institute, 125

Peace River Coal, 204
PepsiCo, 45, 85, 89, 98–99, 121, 192, 204, 245
Pfizer, 43, 187, 189
Pharmasset, 261, 263
Philip Morris International (PMI), 301, 304
Phillips 66, 312
Pilgrim's Pride, 258, 260, 268
Pinault-Printemps-Redoute *See* PPR SA
Pizza Hut, 245
Polaroid, 75–76
Porsche, 147
PPR SA, 119
PriceWaterhouseCoopers, 42
Procter & Gamble, 187, 228

Prudential, 177
PSA Peugeot-Citroen, 363

Quaker Oats, 245
Quality Inn, 49

Ralph Lauren, 155
Ranbaxy Laboratories, 189–190
RaynAir, 4
Renault, 363
Research in Motion (RIM), 147, 209
Ritz-Carlton, 237
Rodeway Inn, 49
Rolls-Royce, 147
Royal Bank of Canada, 148
Ryanair Holdings, 148

Saab, 3
Saks Fifth, 147
Samsung Electronics, 201, 228
Sandoz, 55
Sanofi, 179
SAP, 211
SAS, 115–116, 202
SAS Institute, 148
Schlumberger, 179
Sears, 151
Seguros Lex, 209, 211
Seven Group Holdings, 245
Seven Network Ltd., 245
SGL Carbon SE, 204
Shanghai Airlines, 202
Shanghai Automotive Industry Corp. (SAIC), 288, 302
Siemens AG, 27, 48, 85
Singapore Airlines, 4, 177, 202
Sinopec, 302
SkyTeam Alliance, 202
Sleep Inn, 49

Smithfield Beef, 260, 268
Snow Village, 179
Sonia Kushauk, 162
Sony Corporation, 34, 35, 48, 94, 201
South Africa, 202
Southern Union, 259
Southwest Airlines, 4, 49, 114, 120, 177
Spanair, 4
Standard & Poor's, 268
Star Alliance, 4, 202
Starbucks, 49, 146, 181
Studio Entertainment, 239
Suburban Extended Stay, 49
Subway, 258
Samsung, 94
Sun Microsystems, 97, 261
Sustainability Consortium, 211
Swift, 260, 268
Symantec, 207

Taco Bell, 245
Takeda, 262
Target Corporation, 162, 166
Tata Consultancy Services Ltd., 85
Tata Global Beverages Ltd., 181
Texas Instruments (TI), 183
Textron, 228
TGP, 274
Tingyi-Asahi Beverages Holding, 204
T-Mobile, 261
TNT Express NV, 181
Touchstone Pictures, 239
Toyota, 6, 92, 147, 155, 201, 304, 304–305, 309
Transparency International, 307
Tropicana, 245

TXU, 274

Unilever, 5, 211
United Airlines, 4, 187–188, 202, 260
United Parcel Service (UPS), 120, 173, 178, 181, 212, 227
United Technologies, 228
UPS. *See* United Parcel Service (UPS)
URS Corp., 181

Volkswagen, 288
Vudu, 179

W. L. Gore & Associates, 354, 361
Waldorf Astoria, 237
Walmart, 16, 34, 35, 79, 117–118, 132, 147, 151, 154, 162, 179, 180, 291, 303–304
Walt Disney Co., 188, 239
Walter Energy, 204
Watson Pharmaceuticals, 189
Wegmans Food Markets, 115
WesTrac, 245
White Funds Management, 245
Whole Foods Market, 18–19
Whole Planet Foundation, 19
Williams Company, 258
Wisconsin Toy, 151
WorldCom, 327
Wrigley Company, 187

Xerox, 45

Yahoo! Inc., 50
Yellow Freight System, 177
Yihaodian, 179

SUBJECT INDEX

Note: Italic page numbers indicate material in tables or figures.

Abandonment options, 376
Ability (of firm), 180
Above-average returns
    and 5 elements of strategy, 49
    and competitive dynamics, 121
    and industry environment,
        72–73, 86–87
    and international strategies, 23.
        See also International
        strategy
    I/O model, 11–14, *13*
    and organziational culture, 52
    resource based model, 14–17, *15*
    and value creation, 110–111
Acquisition strategy
    and cost and risk reduction,
        262–263
    as different from takeovers,
        259–260
    and diversification and
        growth, 263–264
    and increased market power,
        260–261
    and innovation, 363–364
    as international entry
        modes, 303
    and new capabilities, 264
    overcoming entry barriers, 262
    popularity of, 257–258
    and restructuring, 272–276
    and speed to market, 263
    successful acquisitions, 270
Acquisition strategy, problems with
    and debt, 267–268
    and integration difficulties,
        266–267
    and manager focus, 269
    and overdiversification,
        268–269
    reasons for, *265*, 265–266
    and size of firm, 269–270
    and target evaluation, 267
Acquisitions, effective, 270–272
Actions, competitive, 179–181,
    186, 187–188
Actor's reputation, 175, 181,
    186–187

Advantage, competitive
    overview of, 2–3
    sustainable, 106–107
Age structure, 78, 79
Agency costs, 326–328, 334
Agency relationship
    costs and governance, 326–328
    definition of, 324, 324–325
    and diversification, 325–326
Agency theory, 10
Alliance network, 207
Alliance portfolio, 216
Alliances
    global, 4
    and innovation, 362–363
    and international strategies, *285*
    and joint ventures, 11
    strategic alliances, 124–125,
        302–304
Analysis
    of competitor, 73, 176–179,
        178. See also Competitor
        analysis
    denial and internal analysis,
        108–109
    of direct competitors, 96–97
    of industry environment.
        See Industry environment
        analysis
    internal, 108–110, *111*
    likelihood of attack, 182–184
    organizational, 106–107
    organizational size, 107
    real option. *See* Real option
        analysis
    value chain, *12*, 121–124
Analysis, internal, 106–110,
    107, 111
Antitrust Modernization Act of
    2002, 244
Antitrust regulation, 243–244
Arenas, 48, 143
Assessing (environmental
    changes), 77–78
Attacks, by rivals, 173–174
Automobile industry
    and cooperative strategy, 363

    and determining customers,
        146–147
    and economic volatility, 6–7
    and international
        diversification, 306
    rivalry in, 199
    and suppliers, 91–92
    and transnational
        strategy, 296
Autonomous strategic
    behavior, 358
Autonomy, 52

Backdating, 335
Backward integration, 237
Balanced scorecard, 59–60
Bargaining power, 91–92
Barriers, exit, 94–95
Biases and discretion, 37–40
Binomial lattices, 392–400.
    See also Decision trees
Black-Scholes approximation,
    391–392
Black-Scholes Valuation
    (option pricing formula)
    application of, 400–402
    overview of, 389–391, *391*
Board of Directors
    effectiveness of, 332–333
    and ethics codes, 342
    members of, 331
    overview of, 330–332
Business policy, 10
Business-level strategy
    five strategies, 145
    and integrated cost leadership/
        differentiation, 165
    as internal strategy, *285*
    overview of, 142–144
    serving customers, 145–148
    and structure, 148–149
    types of, 144–145
    and value creation, 289
        See also Cost leadership
        strategy
        See also Differentiation
        strategy

Buyers, 91–92
  and cost leadership strategy, 152
  and differentiation strategy, 157

CAFTA, 290
CalPERS, 330
Capabilities
  and acquisitions, 264
  as core competencies, 16, 50
  costly to imitate capabilities,
    119–120
  definition of, 115–116
  evolution of, 15–16
  of firms, *117*
  nonsubstitutable capabilities,
    120–121
  rare capabilities, 119
  valuable capabilities, 119
  and value creation, 14
Capital
  allocation of, 230, 240, 242
  budgeting of, 378–379,
    383, 386
  and globalization, 4, 9
  human, 50–52, 115–116, 120,
    124, 266, 275
  and resources, 14
  social, *56*, 115–116, 358,
    363–364
  and stakeholder objectives,
    17, 18
Capital expenditures, 384
Capital Market Allocation,
  240–241
Capital market stakehholders,
  17, *18*, 128–129, 131.
  See also Shareholders
Capital requirements and
  barriers to entry, 89–90
Capital structure change, 337
Captial requirements, 89–90
Casually ambiguous
  capabilities, 120
Celler-Kefauver Act, 244
Central American Free Trade
  Agreement, 290
Centralization, 234
CEO duality, 331
CEOs
  and code of ethics, 56–57, 342
  and corporate governance,
    320–321
  and executive compensation,
    333–334, 339
  and executive sucession
    processes, 44–46

and functional structure,
  148–149
and hostile takeovers, 336–338
and hubris, 39–40
and hypercompetitive
  influences, 7
and large block shareholders,
  329
and portofolio responsibilities,
  226
and R&D investment
  curtailment, 127
and strategic leadership, 46–47
succession of, 44–46, *46*
as tone setter for decision
  making, 36–37
and top management teams,
  40–44, 61
Change and success, 3–4, 6–7,
  36–37
Chief executive officers. *See* CEOs
Chief learning officer (CLO), 116
Chief operation officer
  (COO), 40
Code of ethics, 56–57, 342
Competition model, 87–88
Competitive, 186
Competitive actions,
  179–181, 186
Competitive advantage,
  sustainable
  4 criteria of, 118–119, *119*
  and acquisitions, 260, 266, *270*
  and Black-Scholes, *393*
  and corporate governance,
    321–322
  an corporate level strategies,
    225–226, 235, 239
  costly to imitate capabilities,
    119–120
  definition of, 2–3
  developing and managing
    resources, 12–15
  erosion of, 190
  and firm environment, 73
  and innovation, 353–354, 362
  and intangible resources,
    113–114
  and international entre-
    preneurship, 355, 364–365
  and international strategies,
    286, 289, 297, 299, 306
  nonsubstitutable capabilities,
    120–121
  overview of, 2–3, 106–107
  rare capabilities, 119

resource based model, 15
  and resources, 112–115
  and rivalry, 93–95
  and technology, 83–84
  and temporary advantages, 192
  valuable capabilities, 119
Competitive aggressiveness, 52
Competitive behavior, 173–174
Competitive dynamics
  and competitors, 174
  overview of, 188
  slow-cycle markets, 188–190
Competitive landscape, 3–8, *5*
Competitive response, 181
Competitive risks
  and cost leadership
    strategy, 154
  of differentiation strategy, 159
  of focus strategy, 161–162
  of integrated cost leadership/
    differentiation strategy,
    165–166
Competitive rivalry
  and competitive dynamics,
    188–193
  and cooperative strategy,
    214–216
  definition of, 173–174
  fast-cycle markets, 190–191
  framework for, 178
  likelihood of attack, 181–185
  likelihood of response,
    184–188
  model of, 175–176
  overview of, 180–181
  standard-cycle markets,
    192–193
  strategic and tactical actions
    of, 181
Competitive scope, 263–264
Competitor analysis, 73, 176–179
Competitor environment, 73–75
Competitor intelligence, 97–99
Competitors, 97–99, *98*, 173,
  174
Competitve dynamics, 173–174
Complementary strategic
  alliances, 206
Complementors, 95
Compound options, 377
Conditions affecting managerial
  decisions, 109–110
Conglomerates, 229
Controls, 231–232
COO. *See* Chief operation officer
  (COO)

"Cookies", 76–77
Cooperative form, 233–235
Cooperative strategy
  competitive risks of, 214–216
  and cost reduction, 205–209
  and diversification and
    growth, 211–214
  in fast-cycle markets, 203
  implementing and managing,
    216–217
  importance of, 201–203
  in slow-cycle markets, 203
  in standard-cycle markets, 204
  types of alliances, 204–205
Co-opetititon, 201–202
Core competencies
  analysis of, 108
  as competitive advantages, 112
  and cross-functional product
    development teams, 360
  definition of, 16
  determining, 118
  and downscoping, 273
  and dynamic modes of
    entry, 305
  formulation of, 109
  and horizontal acquisitions, 261
  and international diversifica-
    tion, 284–285, 288
  and the I/O model, 48–50
  outsourcing, 125–126
  and private synergy, 266
  and related diversification,
    232–235, 235
  and restructuring, 272
  and strategic alliances,
    302–303
  as strategic assets, 116–118
  as strategic capability, 119
  tools for building, 118–124.
    See also Sustainable
    competitive advantage;
    Value chain analysis
  and value loss, 126
  and worldwide combination
    structure, 295
Core rigidity, 126
Corporate charter
  amendment, 337
Corporate governance
  and boards of directors,
    330–333
  and executive compensation,
    332–335
  global, 341

internal, 338–341
market for control,
  335–336
mechanisms for, 322
overview of, 320–323
and ownership concentration,
  328–330
and separation of ownership
  and managerial control,
  323–328
Corporate-level strategy
  acquisition strategy,
    260–272
  corporate relatedness,
    235–239
  definition of, 23, 225
  diversification strategy,
    226–228
  diversification and
    performance, 228
  and market power, 237
  and the multidivisional
    structure, 231–232,
    242–243
  and reasons for
    diversification, 229,
    243–247
  related diversification, 232
  restructuring, 241
  and synergy, 232–233
  unrelated diversification,
    239–241
  and value creation, 230
  vertical integration,
    237–238
Corporate relatedness, 230,
  238–239
Corporate social responsibility
  (CSR), 18
Cost advantages, 90
Cost leadership strategy
  as business-level strategy,
    144–145
  competitive risks of, 154
  successful execution of,
    149–152
  using functional structure to
    implement, 152–154
  value creation, 150
Cost minimization, 216
Costly to imitate capabilities,
  119–120
Costs
  high, 93–94
Creating value, 110–112

Creation of value, 362
Cross-border acquisitions,
  262
Cross-border strategic alliance,
  212–213
Cross-functional product
  development teams,
  360–361, 362
Cross-shareholding, 340
CSR. See Corporate social
  responsibility (CSR)
Customer relationship
  management (CRM), 164
Customers and business-level
  strategy, 145–148
  and competitive risks, 165

Debt
  and acquisitions, 303
  and captial allocation, 240
  costs, 275
  debt to equity, 129
  extraordinary, 267–268, 270
  and finance, 150
  low or moderate level, 271
  restructuring, 85, 274
  and risk taking, 52
Decision trees, 392–400,
  393–396, 399
Demographic segment
  (of general environment),
  79–80
Denial and internal analysis,
  108–109
Deterministic perspective,
  10–11
Development, sustainable,
  131–133
Differentiation strategy
  as business-level strategy,
    144–145
  competitive risks of, 159
  and cost reduction,
    205–209
  overview of, 154–155
  successful execution of,
    155–157
  using functional structure to
    implement, 157–158
  and value creation,
    156, 158
Differentiators, 49, 143
Direct competitors, analysis
  of, 96–97
Disruptive technologies, 7

Distributed alliance networks,
213
Distribution channels, access
to, 90
Diversification
and acquisitions, 263–264,
268–269
international. *See* International
diversification
product, 289, 325–326, 328
and shareholders,
326–327
too much of, 268–269
Diversification, international,
284–286, 305–307
Diversification, related
and cooperative form, 233–235
and core competencies,
232–235
and marketing power, 237–238
operational readiness, 233
overview of, 232–233
simultaneous operational
relatedness, 238–239
and strategic business-unit
form, 235–237
Diversification, unrelated
and capital market allocation,
240–241
and M-form, 242–243
overview of, 228, 239–241
and resources, 246
restructuring, 241
Diversification, value-neutral,
243–246
Diversification, value-reducing,
246–248
Diversification and acquisition,
268–269
Diversification strategy
and acquisitions, 265, 265
and competitive scope, 263
as an example of agency
problem, 325–326
and firm performance, 248
and horizontal acquisitions, 260
levels of, 227
low levels of, 226–227
and M-form structure, 230–231
moderate and high levels of,
227–229
and performance, 228
reasons for, 229, 229–231
and shareholder risk, 327
and value creation, 230

Diversifying strategic
alliances, 212
Dodd-Frank Wall Street Reform
and Consumer Protection
Act, 18, 327–328, 330
Dominant business diversification
strategy, 227
Downscoping, 273–274
Downsizing, 272–273
Drivers, of competive actions,
179–180
Due diligence, 267, 271
Dynamic alliance networks, 208

Economic environment, 80–81
Economic logic, 50, 143–149
Economic power, 127
Economic segment (of general
environment), 80–81
Economic volatility, 5–6
Economies of scale, 89
Economies of scope, 232
Elements of strategy, 48–50, 49
Embedded options, 379–380
Enactment, 11
Enterprise relationship manage-
ment (ERM), 164
Enterprise resource planning
system (ERP), 164–165
Entrants, potential
and cost leadership
strategy, 152
and differentiation strategy, 157
Entrepreneurial mind-set,
361–362
Entrepreneurs, 354–355
Entrepreneurship, strategic. *See*
Strategic entrepreneurship
Environmental, external. *See*
External environment
Environmental determinism, 11
Environmental segments
demographic segment, 78–80
economic segment, 80–81
global segment, 84–86
physical environment
segment, 86
political/legal segment, 81–82
sociocultural segment, 82–83
technological segment, 83–84
Equity growth venture, 375
Equity strategic alliance, 204
Ethical practices, 56–57, 341–342
Ethics, code of, 56–57, 342
Ethnic mix, 79–80

European Union (EU), 290
Event trees, 396, 399
Executive succession processes,
44–46
Executive compensation,
333–335
Exporting, 299–301
External environment
assessing, 75, 77–78
and cooperative strategy,
209–211
definition and overview of,
72–76
forecasting, 77
monitoring, 77
scanning, 76–77
segments and elements of, 74
External managerial labor
market, 44

Fast-cycle markets, 190–191, 203
Financial Accounting Standards
Board (FASB), 335
Financial controls, 60, 232
Financial diversification, 239–240
Financial slack, 271
Firm performance
and balancing stakeholder
performance, 131
and capabilities, 15
and capital market perspective,
129
and cooperative strategy. *See*
Cooperative strategy
and diversification, 227, 248
and downscoping, 273–274
and executive compensation,
333
and internal entrepreneurship,
355
and international strategies,
285–286
and the I/O model, 11–14
measures of, 128–131
and organziational structure,
148
overview of, 126–127
and ownership concentration,
328–329
and restructuring, 275
stakeholder model of,
17–20
and stakeholder objectives,
127–128
and strategic controls, 232

and sustainable development, 131–133

and the top management team, 41, 47

First mover, 182

First-mover incentives, 182–183

Flexibility, strategic, 8, 163, 372–374

Flexible manufacturing systems (FMS), 163–164

Focus strategy
  competitive risks of, 161–162
  overview of, 159–161
  using functional structure to implement, 161

Focused cost leadership strategy
  as business-level strategy, 144–145
  definition of, 160

Focused differentiation strategy
  as business-level strategy, 144–145
  definition of, 160–161

Forecasting (environmental changes), 77

Foreignness, liability of, 290

Formal power, 127

Formalization, 235

Fortune magazine, 18, 115

Forward integration, 238

Franchising, 212

Free cash flows, 326

Friendly acquisitions, 271

Fukushima Dai-ichi power plant, 6

Functional structure
  characteristics, 152–153

GDP (gross domestic product), 5–6

General environment, 73, 74

Geographic distribution, 79

"Global competency", 51

Global corporate governance, 341
  mechanisms for, 341–342

Global mandate, 295

Global mind-set, 108

Global segment (of general environment), 84–86

Global strategy, 293–295, 294

Globalization, 4–5

Golden parachute, 337, 338

Government policy, 90–91

"Great Recession", 5

Greenfield venture, 303–304

Greenmail, 337, 338

Growth options, 375

Growth vehicles, 48–49, 143

Guanxi, 85

Heterogeneous top management team, 40–42

Heuristics, 37–39

High strategic stakes, 94

Horizontal acquisitions, 233, 260–261
  and core competencies, 261

Hostile takeovers, 260, 336–337, 337

Hubris, 39–40

Human capital, 50–52, 115–116, 120, 124, 266, 275

Hypercompetition, 4–5, 7–8, 172

Imitation, 253

Income distribution, 80

Incremental innovations, 357

Induced strategic behavior, 357

Industrial organization (I/O) model
  and core competencies, 48–50
  overview of, 11–14
  and strategic leadership, 46–47, 47

Industry, 86, 86–87

Industry environment, 73

Industry environment analysis
  bargaining power of buyers and suppliers, 91–92
  complementors, 95
  interpreting, 95–96
  overview of, 86–88
  rivalry among competitors, 93–95
  threat of new entrants, 88–91
  threat of substitute products, 92–93
  understanding competitors, 97–99

Industry growth, 93

Information networks, 164–165

Information technology, 7

Inhwa, 85

Innovation
  and acquisitions, 363–364
  creating value from, 362
  creating value from internal, 362
  facilitating integration of internal, 361

factors affecting, 359

and internal incremental innovations, 357

overview of internal, 359–360

radical, 357–359

Schumpeterian, 7

through cooperative strategies, 362–363

Innovativeness, 52

"Inpatriation", 51

Institutional owners, 329

Intangible resources, 113–115, 114

Integrated cost leadership/ differentiation strategy
  as business-level strategy, 144–145, 165
  competitive risks of, 165–166
  overview of, 162
  successful execution of, 162–163
  using a flexible structure to implement, 163–165

Integration, types of, 237–238

Internal analysis, 108–110, 111

Internal corporate governance
  in Germany, 339–340
  in Japan, 340–341

Internal managerial labor market, 44

International business level strategy, 296–299

International cooperative strategy, 212–214

International corporate-level strategy, 289–292

International diversification
  complexity of, 309–310
  and corporate level strategy, 289
  and dynamic modes of entry, 305
  and innovation, 306–307
  overview of, 284–287, 285
  and returns, 305–306
  and risks, 307–309

International entrepreneurship, 355–357

International entry modes
  and acquisitions, 303
  dynamics of, 304–305
  exporting, 299–301
  licensing, 301–302
  overview of, 300
  strategic alliances, 302–303
  and wholly owned subsidiaries, 303–304

International experience, importance of, 51
International strategy
  and complexity of management, 309–310
  and economies of scale, scope and learning, 287–288
  global strategy, 293–295
  and international diversification, 305–307
  and investment return, 287
  location advantages of, 288–289
  and market size, 286–287
  multidomestic strategy, 292
  outcomes of, 285
  risks in, 307–309
  transnational, 295–296
Internet (and business), 7
Invention, 253
I/O economics. *See* Industrial organization (I/O) model
Irish Development Authority (IDA), 355–356

Joint venture, 204
Junk bonds, 267–268

Keiretsu, 207, 340
Knowledge, as resorce, 7

Landscape, competitive, 3–8
Large-block shareholders, 328
Late mover, 183
Leadership, strategic
  discretion and decision biases of, 37–40
  as a key resource, 35–36
  leaders and leadership style, 35–40
  management models, 47
  overview of, 34–35
  style of, 36–37
  top management teams, 40–46
Leadership responsibilities, strategic
  determining strategic direction, 54–57
  developing and managing resources, 50–53
  and economic position, 48–50
  establishing controls, 58–60, 60
  formulation and implementation of strategies, 57–58
  overview of, 46–48

and relationships with stakeholders, 53–54
Legislation, business
  1986 Tax Reform Act, 244–245
  Antitrust Modernization Act of 2002, 244
  Celler-Kefauver Act, 86
  Dodd-Frank Wall Street Reform and Consumer Protection Act, 18, 327–328, 330
  Financial Accounting Standards Board (FASB), 335
  Sarbanes-Oxley Act (SOX), 327–328, 332
  U. S. Securities and Exchange Commission (SEC), 84, 330, 332
  U.S. Energy Policy Act of 2005, 86
Leveraged buyouts, 274–275
Licensing, 301–302
Likelihood of attack
  first-mover incentives, 182–183
  organizational size, 183–184
  overview of, 181
  quality, 184–185
Likelihood of response, 186–187
  dependence on market, 187–188
  overview of, 185–186
Local implementation, 296
Low switching costs, 94

Management, strategic
  beginnings of, 8–9
  discretion and decision biases of, 37–40
  early influences of, 9–10
  models of, 47
  modern, 10–11
  process of, 3, 22–24
Management teams, top
  and the CEO, 42–44
  and executive sucession processes, 44–46
  and heterogeneity, 40–42
Managerial control and ownership. *See* Ownership and managerial control, separation of
Managerial discretion, 37–40, 38
Managerial opportunism, 325
Market commonality, 176–177

Market dependence, 187–188
Market for corporate control
  and managerial defense, 337–338
  overview of, 335–336
Market microstructure, 88
Market power, 237–238, 260
Markets
  capital market allocation, 240–241
  and cooperative form, 233–235
  and diversification, 225–226, 230, 263–264
  and entry barriers, 262–263
  global, 286–287, 290–296
  globalization of, 4–6
  and merger and acquisition strategies, 258–259
  and M-form structure, 235–237
  and restructuring, 272
  and vertical acquistions, 261
Matrix organization, 239
Merger strategy, 3
Mergers, 259–260
M-form (multi-divisional structure), 149
Mission statement, 54–57
Modes of entry
  acqisitions, 303
  dynamics of, 304–305
  exporting, 299–301
  licensing, 301–302
  new wholly owned subsidiary, 303–304
  overview of, 300
  strategic alliances, 302–303
Monitoring, 77
Motivation (of firm), 179
Multidivisional structure (M-form), 149, 231–232, 234, 236, 242–243
Multidomestic strategy, 292, 293
Multimarket competition, 173, 237
Multinational firms, management of, 309–310
Multi-point competition, 237
Mutual forebearance, 237

NAFTA, 82, 290, 301
National advantage, 297, 299
Network cooperative strategy, 207–209

New Entrants, threats of
and barriers to entry, 88–90
and retaliation, 91
1986 Tax Reform Act, 244–245
Nonequity strategic alliance,
204–205
Nonsubstitutable capabilities,
120–121
North American Free Trade
Agreement, 290

"Occupy Wall Street", 18
Off-shoring, 306
Operational relatedness,
230–231, 233
and core competencies,
238–239
Opportunity, 75
Opportunity maximization, 217
Option to defer, 377
Organization of American States
(OAS), 290
Organizational analysis,
106–107, 107
Organizational controls,
231–232
Organizational culture,
52–53
Organizational size (competitive
rivalry), 183–184
Outsourcing, 125–126
Over-diversification, 268–269
Ownership and managerial
control, separation of
and agency costs, 326–328
agency relationships,
324–325
and diversification, 325–326
overview of, 323–324
Ownership concentration
definition of, 328–329
influence of institutional
owners, 329–330

Physical environment
segment, 86
Poison pill, 337
Political power, 127
Political/legal segment (of general
environment), 81
Portfolios of business, 216,
225–226, 323, 325
Power, of stakeholders,
127–128
Private synergy, 266
Proactiveness, 52

Product champion, 358
Product differentiation, 89
Product diversification, 226
Product substitutes
and cost leadership
strategy, 152
and differentiation
strategy, 157
Products
quality of, 184–185
and standardization, 12–13

Quality, 184–185

Radical innovations, 357–359
Rare capabilities, 119
Real option analysis
growth option values,
381, 382
implementation requirements
of, 386–387
and organizational culture, 52
purpose and importance of,
377–378
and strategic flexibility,
372–374
and strategic leadership, 10,
22, 24, 40
valuation of, 386
value drivers for, 383–385
Real options
definition of, 374
types of, 375–377, 376
Regionalization, 290
Related acquisitions, 261
Related constrained diversification
strategy. See Diversification,
related
Related diversification strategy.
See Diversification, related
Repricing, 335
Reputation, 56, 85, 113, 114,
175, 181
Resource based model, 3,
14–17, 15
Resource dissimilarity, 180
Resource similarity, 177–179
Resources, 14–15
definition of, 112–113
intangible, 113–115
tangible, 113
Resources and diversificaiton,
246
Restructuring strategy
definition of, 272–273
and downscoping, 273–274

and downsizing, 272–273
and leveraged buyouts,
274–275
outcomes of, 275–276
use of, 241
Retaliation, 88
Risk taking, 52
Risks, competitive. See
Competitive risks
Risks, of international
environment, 307–309
Rivalry
among competitors, intensity
of, 93–95
competitive. See Competitive
rivalry
and cost leadership
strategy, 151
on international scope,
298–299
"Rules of Thumb", 37–39

Sarbanes-Oxley Act (SOX),
327–328, 332
SBU form. See Strategic
business units (SBU
form)
Scandals, 56–57
Scanning, 76–77
Schumpeterian innovation, 7
Second mover, 183
Shareholders. See also
Stakeholders
and corporate governance,
320–323
and diversification,
325–326, 327
large-block, 328, 330
Shareholders rights, 338
Simultaneous operational
relatedness, 238–239
Single business strategy,
226–227
Slow-cycle markets, 188–190,
203
Social capital, 56, 115–116,
358, 363–364
Social complexity, 120
Sociocultural segment (of
general environment),
82–83
Specialized contribution, 296
Stable alliance network,
207–208
Staging, 50, 143
Stakeholder model, 17–20

Stakeholders
  and above-average returns, 24
  balancing for optimal firm
    performance, 131
  and cooperative strategy, 201
  definition of, 17
  management of, 341–342
  model of responsible firm
    behavior, *20*
  objectives and power of,
    127–128
  relationships with leadership,
    53–54
  three groups, 18
Standard-cycle markets, 204
Standardization, 235
Standstill agreement, 337
Stategic flexibility. *See* Flexibility,
  strategic
Strageties, implementation of,
  57–58
Strategic alliances, 124–125,
  285, 302–303
Strategic assets, 116
Strategic business units (SBU
  form), 235–237, 239
Strategic center firm, 207
Strategic controls, 232
Strategic dimensions, 96
strategic direction
  overview of, 54–55
  and sustainable
    development, 55
Strategic elements, 48–50, *49*
Strategic entrepreneurship
  and entrepreneurs, 354–355
  implementing internal
    innovation, 359–362
  and innovation, 352–354
  and internal innovation,
    357–358
  and international entre-
    preneurship, 355–357
  radical innovations, *357–359*
  and value creation, 364–365
Strategic groups, 96–97
Strategic leadership. *See*
  Leadership, strategic
Strategic Management. *See*
  Management, strategic
Strategic management process,
  22, 22–24
Strategic thinking, 3, 20–22

Strategic thinking competency, 21
Strategic value of resources, 115
Strategy, business-level. *See*
  Business-level strategy
Subsidiaries, wholly owned,
  303–304
Substitute products, 92–93
Suppliers, 92
  and cost leadership strategy,
    152
  and differentiation strategy, 157
Support functions, 122
Sustainable competitive
  advantage. *See* Competitive
  advantage, sustainable
Sustainable development, *55*,
  131–133
Switching costs, 90, 93, 94
Switching options, 376–377
Synergy, 232, 245–246,
  266–267

Tacit knowledge, 204
Tactical actions, 181, 186,
  187–188
Tactical responses, 181
Takeovers, 259–260
Tangible resources, 113
Taper integration, 238
Tax laws, 244–245
Technological advances,
  6–7
Technological segment
  (of general environment),
  83–84
"Ten-step talent", 44
Threat, 75–76
Threat of new entrants,
  88–91
Top management teams, 40
  and the CEO, 42–44
  and executive succession
    processes, 44–46
  and heterogeneity, 40–42
Total quality management
  systems (TQM), 110, 165
TQM. *See* Total quality
  management systems
  (TQM)
Transaction cost economics,
  10, 268
Transnational strategy,
  295–296

U. S. Securities and Exchange
  Commission (SEC), 84,
  330, 332
Unrelated diversification
  strategy. *See* Diversification,
  unrelated

Valuable capabilities, 119
Value, definition of, 110
Value chain analysis,
  121–124
Value creation
  and above-average returns,
    110–111
  and cost leadership strategy,
    150
  and differentiation strategy,
    156, 158
  and entrepreneurship,
    364–365
  and internal analysis,
    110–112
  and the I/O model, 11–14
  and the resource based model,
    3, 14–17
  and the stakeholder model,
    17–20
  and strategic entrepreneurship,
    364–365
Value-creating diversification,
  229–230
Value-neutral diversification,
  230
Value-reducing diversification,
  230
Vertical complementary strategic
  alliances, 206
Vertical integration, 237–238
Vorstand, 339

Wa, 85
Wi-Fi (wireless fidelity), 84
Women
  as BOD members, 332
  as CEOs, 46
  as entrepreneurs, 355
  in the workforce, 74,
    82–83
World Trade Organization, 85
Worldwide combinations
  structure, 295–296
Worldwide geographic area
  structure, 292